CAMBRIDGE

Official Cambridge Exam Preparation

CB126818

OPEN WORLD

B2

FIRST

STUDENT'S BOOK WITH ANSWERS

with Online Practice

Anthony Cosgrove and Deborah Hobbs

Cambridge University Press
www.cambridge.org/elt

Cambridge Assessment English
www.cambridgeenglish.org

Information on this title: www.cambridge.org/9781108759052

First published 2019

20 19 18 17 16 15 14 13

Printed in Dubai by Oriental Press

A catalogue record for this publication is available from the British Library

ISBN 978-1-108-75905-2 Student's Book with answers with Online Practice

CONTENTS

SPEAKING	GRAMMAR	VOCABULARY	REAL WORLD
Getting to know your classmates	Present perfect review Comparatives and Superlatives	Adjectives to describe emotions	
Part 2 Describing a pair of photographs	Gerunds and Infinitives Comparing and contrasting ideas with linkers C1 Understanding health	Health and fitness Idioms for health and fitness weak forms	Being active in Zurich
Speculating	The passive *Used to, be used to, get used to* C1 Hedging	Describing your family Phrasal verbs for describing friends and family Stress in phrasal verbs	Making friends in Seoul
Parts 3 and 4 A collaborative task and discussion	First and second conditionals Giving advice C1 Other conditional structures	Education and study Idioms and phrasal verbs for education and study Consonant groups at the beginning of words	Educating yourself in Toronto
Part 1 Talking about yourself	Countable and uncountable nouns Articles C1 Nouns that are both countable and uncountable	Holidays and travel Compound adjectives	Travelling around Buenos Aires
Reaching agreement	Past simple, past perfect simple and past perfect continuous	Books and reading Positive and negative adjectives C1 Building your vocabulary Connected speech	Making arrangements in Bristol
Part 2 Describing a pair of photographs	Prepositions Relative clauses C1 Complex prepositions	The natural world Commonly confused words Stress in compound nouns	Going into the wild in Florida
Describing a restaurant experience	Wish clauses Third and mixed conditionals	Describing food Prefixes	Dining out in Athens
Part 1 Talking about yourself Short and long vowels	Direct and indirect objects Modals of speculation and deduction C1 Other ways of expressing speculation and deduction	Technology Idioms for science and technology	Getting to grips with technology in Singapore
Parts 3 and 4 A collaborative task and discussion Adding emphasis	Future forms Future perfect and future continuous C1 Talking about the future	The weather Phrases with *far*	Broadening your horizons in Los Angeles
Part 1 Talking about yourself	Causatives *–ed* and *–ing* adjectives	Cohesive devices Sport and leisure Stress in word families 1	Going on an adventure in the Brecon Beacons
Part 2 Describing a pair of photographs	Reported speech Reporting verbs	The media Phrases to talk about the media Intonation when giving an opinion	Having fun in Copenhagen
Short responses with *so, neither, either* and *too*	Expressing obligation and permission Expressing ability C1 Expressing obligation and permission in different tenses	Festivals and celebrations Suffixes Stress in word families 2	Having a great time in Essaouira
Parts 3 and 4 A collaborative task and discussion Main stress in questions C1 Disagreeing politely	Like vs. as Past modals: *shouldn't have, didn't have to, needn't have, didn't need to*	Going, Going, Gone! The business of shopping	Going shopping in Milan
Evaluating the advantages and disadvantages of an idea	Adding emphasis and sentence fronting	Phrasal verbs with business Jobs and careers C1 Compound words with *work* Auxiliary verb stress	Going for a job in Frankfurt

HOW TO USE THIS BOOK

WELCOME TO OPEN WORLD

THE COURSE THAT TAKES YOU FURTHER

Learn about the features in your new Student's Book

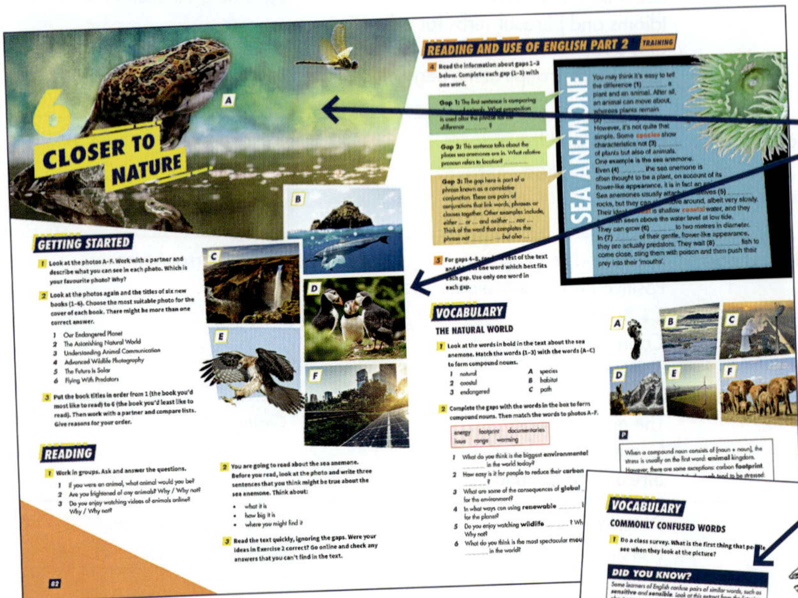

Large images at the start of each unit introduce the topic and get you talking

DID YOU KNOW?

Useful tips about the English language

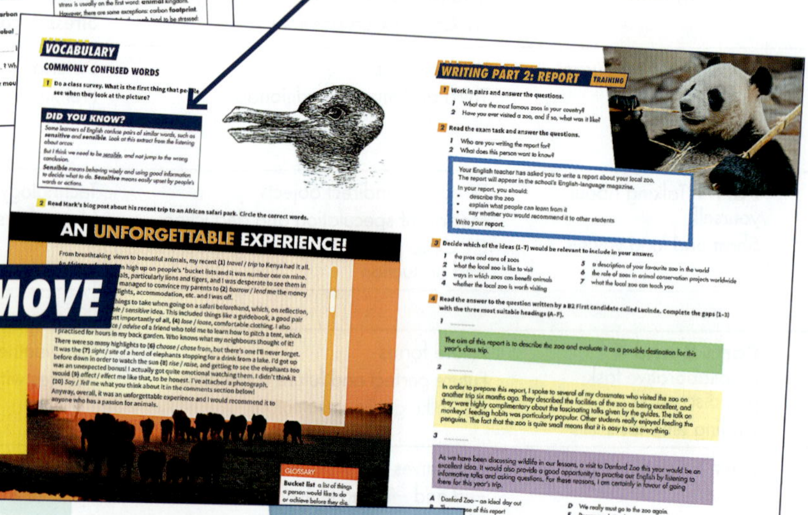

GRAMMAR ON THE MOVE

Scan the QR codes to watch grammar animations in your free time to learn about each grammar point

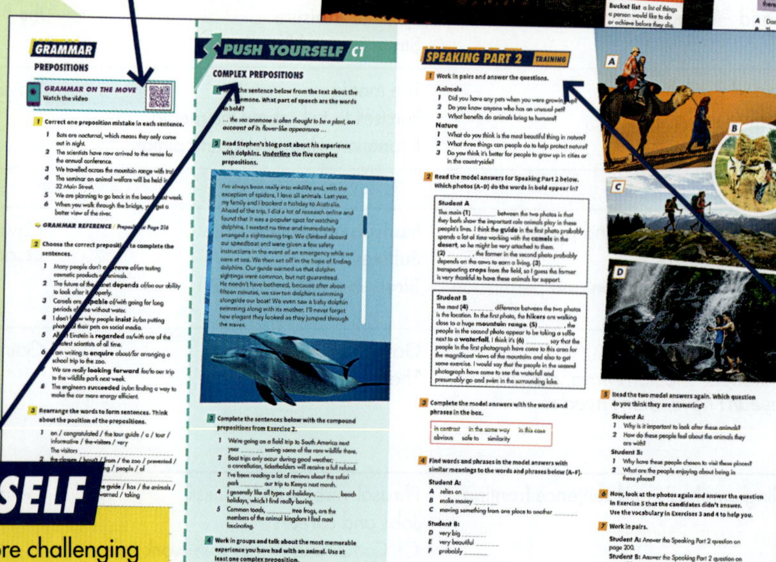

'Training' exam tasks provide guidance and tips on each part of the exam

PUSH YOURSELF

Learn and practise more challenging language and skills that take you to the next level

EXAM FOCUS

after every unit.
Read exam tips and facts and do three complete practice exam tasks

EXAM CHECKS

test what you remember about the exam

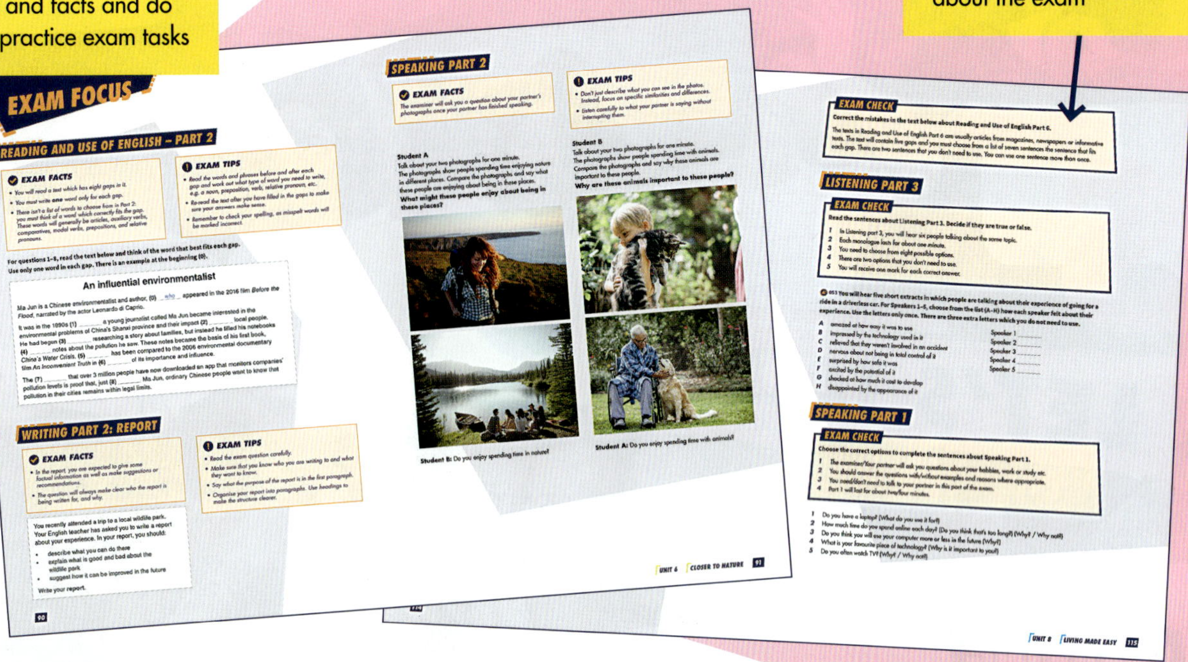

REAL WORLD

pages take you outside the classroom and into the real world

PHRASES YOU MIGHT USE AND HEAR

Learn and practise phrases you might use and hear when you are using English in the real world

Scan the QR codes to watch videos of different locations around the world on your mobile phone or tablet

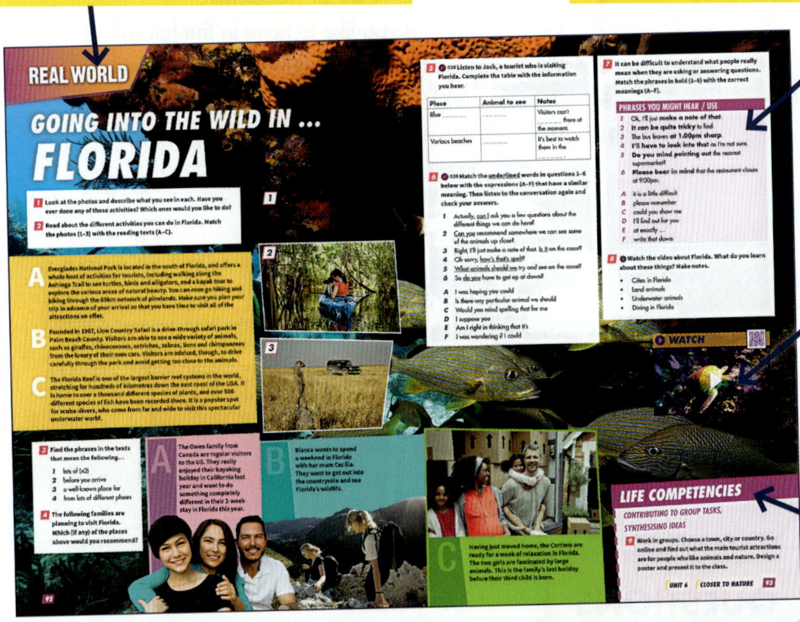

LIFE COMPETENCIES

Develop important skills, knowledge and attitudes that you can use in your daily life

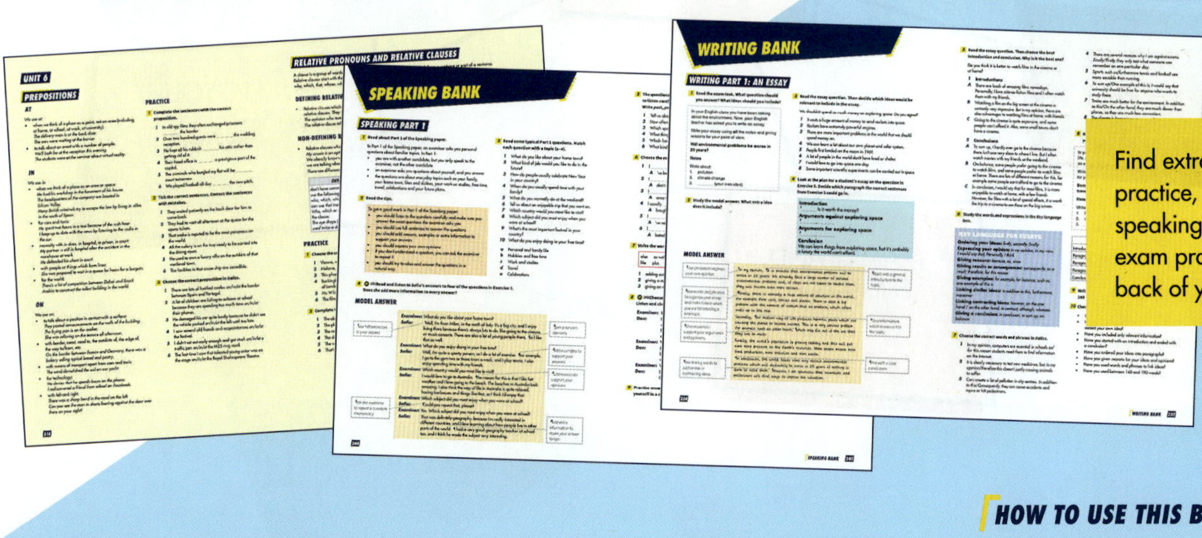

Find extra grammar practice, and extra speaking and writing exam practice at the back of your book

S LET'S TALK

SPEAKING

GETTING TO KNOW YOUR CLASSMATES

1 **Write the questions under the correct topics. The first one has been done for you.**

1. Where are you from?
2. What's your favourite subject?
3. What's your favourite hobby?
4. How many brothers and sisters do you have?
5. What's your favourite part of the day?
6. What do you like to do at weekends?
7. What job would you like to have in the future?
8. What do you like most about your hometown?
9. What's your favourite kind of food?
10. Who are the most important people in your life?

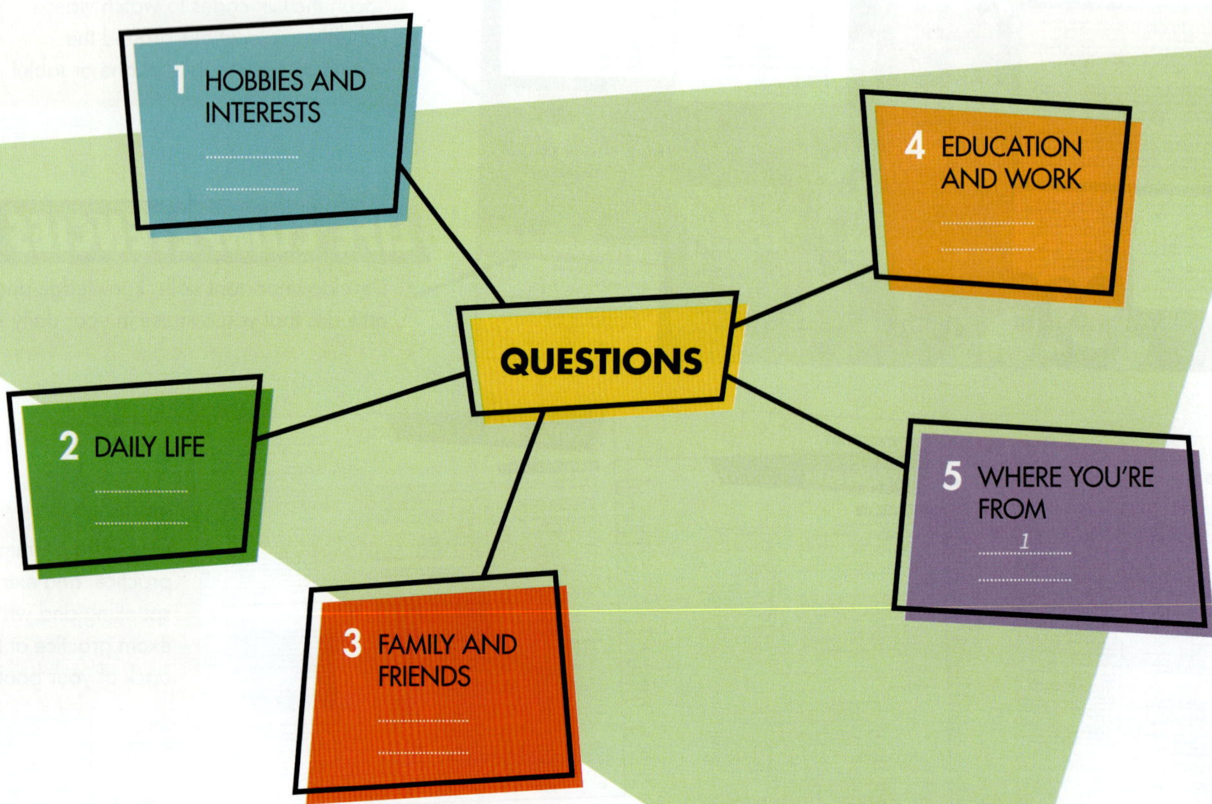

2 **Look at the phrases below. Which questions in Exercise 1 are they answering?**

1. I come from … which is in … ....
2. I have one … and two … ....
3. One of my favourite subjects is … because … ....
4. One of the best times of the day is … because … ....
5. In my city, there is a … which I love because … ....
6. I would really like to be a … in the future because … ....
7. On Saturdays, I usually … ....
8. I'm really interested in … ....
9. My … is an important person in my life because … ....
10. One thing I love eating is … ....

3 **Add one question of your own to each topic. Then talk to your classmates and ask and answer at least one question from each category. Use the phrases in Exercise 2 to help you.**

VOCABULARY

ADJECTIVES TO DESCRIBE EMOTIONS

1 **Work in pairs and answer the questions.**

1. How often do you use emojis? Do you have a favourite emoji?
2. What are the benefits of using emojis?

DID YOU KNOW?

The word *emoji* comes from the Japanese *e* (meaning "picture") and *moji* (meaning "character").

2 **Match the emojis (1–6) in the picture with the adjectives (A–F).**

- **A** annoyed ....
- **B** delighted ....
- **C** disappointed ....
- **D** shocked ....
- **E** upset ....
- **F** worried ....

3 **Work with a partner. When was the last time you felt the emotions in Exercise 2? Explain what happened.**

> The last time I was annoyed was when I missed the bus. I arrived one hour late for my English lesson!

READING

EMOJIS

1 **Look at five text messages (A–E) that Miranda sent in reply to her friends' questions (1–5). Match the questions with the text messages.**

1. What have you been up to?
2. What did you do last night?
3. Is everything ok?
4. Have you been shopping?
5. It's Mum and Dad's wedding anniversary this weekend.

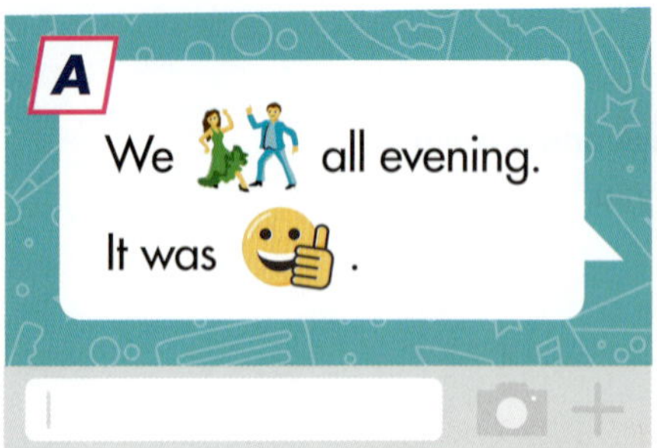

2 **Look at the emojis (A–E) in Exercise 1 again. Replace the emojis in the answers with words.**

3 **Read Miranda's blog post about using emojis and choose the best summary.**

1. Using emojis has had a negative impact on our written communication.
2. There are a lot of benefits to using emojis.
3. It's better to express yourself with emojis than with words.

Home
About
Reviews
Search

A NEW WAY OF COMMUNICATING

OK, I admit it. I'm a big fan of emojis. You can't stop me! There's hardly a text I send out or a comment I post on social media which doesn't have a big smiley face, a stylish flamenco dancer or a cute little puppy!

Initially, I was a bit sceptical. When emojis appeared a few years ago, my best friend used them all the time. My first impression was that they were a bit, well, childish. Why was she putting pictures all over her messages to me instead of expressing herself in words like the rest of us? But then whenever I was looking through social media, I realised I was always looking at her posts first! These bright red broken love-hearts and freshly sliced cucumbers, or whatever emoji she used, were working because I was looking at them!

These days, I can't stop using emojis! *Why?* I hear you ask. *Can't you express yourself in words?* Of course I can! But when you're writing messages or responding to comments on social media, emojis help you to get your message across much quicker than writing out full sentences. What's more, they're universal, meaning that people who speak different languages to me can still understand how I'm feeling. They also make your message seem friendlier. That's true even when you're giving bad news, like refusing an invitation to see friends. Somehow people don't seem to mind when you cancel plans with an emoji of a bunch of flowers! It doesn't mean that every word can be replaced by an emoji, though, so it's important to find a balance between the two forms of communication.

4 **Read the text again. Decide if the statements are true or false.**

1. At first, Miranda loved emojis and used them all the time.
2. Miranda didn't understand why her friend used emojis instead of words.
3. Miranda noticed her best friend's social media posts because she used emojis.
4. Miranda thinks it's harder for people who speak different languages to understand emojis.
5. Miranda believes that emojis can make a message less unfriendly.
6. Miranda thinks that people should always use emojis instead of words.

5 **Work in pairs and answer the questions.**

1. Do you agree with Miranda that emojis 'help to get your message across much quicker than writing out full sentences'?
2. Do you think emojis have a negative impact on written communication? Why? / Why not?

6 **Work in groups and complete the task.**

- Think of a message in English, then decide how you could say this using emojis.
- Write the message for one of the other groups.
- Exchange your messages with other groups. Decide what the other group's message means.

GRAMMAR

PRESENT PERFECT REVIEW

GRAMMAR ON THE MOVE
Watch the video

1 **Look at Miranda's text messages (A–E) in Reading Exercise 1 on page 10 again. Match the rules with the correct text messages.**

1. We use the past simple for completed actions in the past.
2. We use the present perfect simple to focus on the result of a recent event.
3. We use the simple form (not continuous) with stative verbs.
4. We use the present perfect continuous to emphasise the action rather than the result.
5. We use the present perfect with the phrases *just*, *already* and *yet* (UK English).

➡ **GRAMMAR REFERENCE** / *Present perfect: Page 204*

2 **Find and correct the mistakes in the verbs in the following sentences.**

1. I've been knowing Richard for about ten years.
2. I've sent him a message yesterday.
3. **A** You look really tired.
   B Yes, I am. I've painted the flat all afternoon.
4. I've got my first phone when I was eighteen years old.
5. I didn't see the new film yet.
6. Have you watched the documentary on TV last night?
7. I lived in London for the past five months.
8. I've already been drinking three cups of coffee this morning.

3 **Change the second sentence so that it has a similar meaning to the first, using the word given.**

1. I moved here six months ago.
   LIVING
   I .... for six months.
2. What have you been up to recently?
   DOING
   What .... recently?
3. I'm eating sushi for the first time.
   EATEN
   I .... sushi before.
4. It's been two years since I saw Robert.
   EACH
   Robert and I haven't ....
   two years.
5. Paulo and Antonia are married. They got married in 2016.
   BEEN
   Paulo and Antonia ....
   since 2016.

4 **Make questions using the present perfect simple or present perfect continuous.**

1. best film / ever / see
   What's the best film you've ever seen?
2. how long / learn / English
3. ever / visit / another continent
4. how long / live / present home
5. blogs / read / recently
6. most exciting thing / ever / do
7. ever / meet / a famous person

5 **Work with a partner. Ask and answer the questions in Exercise 4.**

LISTENING

A BREAKDOWN IN COMMUNICATION

1 **Read the information about Poland. How similar or different is Poland to your country?**

NAME: Poland
CAPITAL CITY: Warsaw
POPULATION: approx. 38 million
LAND SIZE: approx. 312,679 km^2
AVERAGE TEMPERATURE IN WINTER (WARSAW): -2 °C
HIGHEST PEAK IN POLAND: approx. 2,500 m (Rysy Mountain)
BORDER COUNTRIES: Russia, Lithuania, Belarus, Slovakia, Ukraine, Czech Republic and Germany
NATIONAL SYMBOL: White eagle
NATIONAL SPORT: Football (other popular sports include basketball, volleyball, ice hockey and cross-country skiing)
FUN FACT: 30% of Poland is covered by forest.

2 **002 Listen to Andrew talking about buying a tram ticket in Poland. Answer the questions.**

1. When Andrew was in Poland, he was
   - **A** living alone.
   - **B** living with other people.
2. Why didn't he ask for help to buy a tram ticket?
   - **A** His flatmates were busy.
   - **B** He didn't need any help.
3. Andrew thought the woman at the kiosk couldn't understand him because
   - **A** she couldn't hear very well.
   - **B** he wasn't saying the words correctly.
4. How many items did the woman give to Andrew?
   - **A** Two
   - **B** Three
5. Why did Andrew laugh?
   - **A** because the woman gave him the wrong items
   - **B** because the woman finally understood what he was saying

3 **Work with a partner. Ask and answer the questions.**

1. Have you ever been in a similar situation to Andrew? What happened?
2. How would you communicate with someone if you couldn't speak each other's language?

GRAMMAR

COMPARATIVES AND SUPERLATIVES

GRAMMAR ON THE MOVE
Watch the video

1 **Read about Alice's experience of taking the train in Germany. Have you ever been in a similar situation to Alice?**

The funniest thing happened to me and my friend on a recent trip to Germany. We went to Berlin, which is the biggest city in Germany. Actually, it's as big as my home city in terms of land area, but it has a smaller population.

After a few days of exploring the city, we wanted to take the train to Hannover, which is about an hour and a half away from Berlin. My friend is much more confident than me and actually speaks better German, so she went to the ticket office to buy two train tickets. We decided to take the express train as it was faster than the regional train. It was nicer and more relaxing, too. We sat down in our seats and the train departed. We chatted the whole way and admired the beautiful view from the train window.

After an hour and a half, we arrived at our final destination. Hamburg! We realised then that we had somehow got on the wrong train. I couldn't believe it! We ended up having a great time, even though we had originally planned to visit Hannover.

GRAMMAR REFERENCE / *Comparatives and superlatives: Page 205*

2 **Read the text again. Underline the comparative and superlative adjectives.**

3 **Match the comparative and superlative adjectives you underlined in Exercise 2 with the rules (1–7) below.**

1. For one-syllable adjectives, add *-er* to form the comparative and *-est* to form the superlative. For example: .... and ....
2. For one-syllable adjectives that end in the letter *e*, add *-r* to form the comparative and *-st* to form the superlative. For example: ....
3. For two-syllable adjectives that end in the letter *y*, remove *-y*, and add *-ier* to form the comparative and *-iest* to form the superlative. For example: ....
4. For adjectives that have two or more syllables (that don't end in *-y*), add the word *more* before the adjective to form the comparative and add the words *the most* before the adjective to form the superlative. For example: .... and ....
5. For one-syllable adjectives that end in a vowel (*a, e, i, o* and *u*) and one of the consonants *-b, -d, -g, -n, -p* or *-t*, repeat the last consonant and add *-er* to form the comparative and *-est* to form the superlative. For example: ....
6. Some adjectives have irregular comparative and superlative forms. For example:
   bad → worse → the worst
   good → .... → the best
7. We use *as* + adjective + *as* to compare two things that are the same. For example: ....

4 **Correct the mistakes in each of the questions.**

1. What is the better film you have ever seen?
2. What is the difficultest thing about learning English?
3. Would you prefer to live in the coldest or hotest place on earth?
4. Is it easyer to learn a musical instrument or learn a new language?
5. Do you think that nurses should be paid as much money than footballers?
6. What's the more expensive thing you have ever bought?

5 **Work in pairs. Ask and answer the questions in Exercise 4.**

WRITING

A STORY

1 **You are going to read Sarah's story about a lost suitcase. Before you read, look at the four pictures. Put them in order and predict what you think happens in the story.**

2 **Read the story and check your predictions. Then find and correct the <u>eight</u> spelling mistakes.**

THE LOST SUITCASE

While I was walking back home, I came across a brite blue suitcase just behind a café next to my house. It was quite large and had a pink ribbon on the side of it. I looked for a label to see who it belonged to but it didn't have one. As I only lived next door, I desided to take it home, open it up and see if there was a name or adress, anything that would help me to find the owner. The first thing I noticed when I opened it was a gorgous green dress. It was beautiful. So beautiful, in fact, that I tried it on!

I went back out, still wearing the dress. I was just turning the corner when I bumped into an old frend, who I hadn't seen for a while. She was in town visiting her sister.

"Hey, nice dress!" she said. "I have one just like that. Well, actualy, I had one just like that."

"What do you mean?" I asked.

"I left my suitcase here about 15 minutes ago. I walked off and just completly forgot about it. I don't know where it is!"

"I think I know where it might be." I said, feeling extremely embarassed.

3 **Study how Sarah uses the highlighted words *while* and *when*. Complete the sentences below with the correct form of the verbs in brackets.**

1. While I .... (watch) TV, the phone .... (ring).
2. I .... (sit) on the sofa when suddenly there .... (be) a knock at the door.
3. When I .... (walk) into the shop, the sales assistant .... (talk) to a customer.
4. I .... (break) a plate while I .... (prepare) dinner.

4 **Write a story using 140–190 words. It must begin with the sentence below.**

While I was walking down the street, I found a small, gold ring on the pavement.

1 FIGHTING FIT

GETTING STARTED

1 **Look at the headlines of the magazine articles. What do you think the articles are about? Which would you be most interested in reading?**

2 **003 Listen to two people talking about health and fitness. Which headline are they discussing?**

3 **003 Listen again. Complete the sentences with one or two words from the recording.**

1 … sit down and enjoy our lunch. We've got ______ time.

2 I get a bit of heartburn if I eat too much ______ .

3 Well, research suggests there's a link between ______ and eating quickly.

4 Therefore, the quicker you eat, the more ______ you'll ______

4 **Work with a group and answer the questions.**

1 Is there a problem with unhealthy eating in your country? Why / Why not?

2 Should there be a ban on junk food for people under 14 years old? Why / Why not?

3 Do you think about the calories in your food before you eat? Why / Why not?

P WEAK FORMS: THE SCHWA /ə/

One of the most common vowel sounds in English is the schwa /ə/. It is an unstressed (weak) sound that can typically be found in connected speech when pronouncing articles, prepositions, conjunctions and auxiliaries. For example:
*We've got plenty **of** time.*
*I get a bit **of** heartburn.*

5 004 **Look at the sentences and underline the schwa sounds. Then listen and check your answers.**

1. It's time for dinner.
2. It's a health and fitness book.
3. How long has she worked there?
4. I can play tennis on Saturday.
5. We've got quite a lot of work to do.

VOCABULARY

HEALTH AND FITNESS

1 Read an extract of Mauro's blog. Does he lead a healthy or unhealthy lifestyle?

I love eating junk food and for years I **overdid** it. I mean, I used to eat junk food every week and was about five kilos **overweight**. Not quite obese, but I was getting there. Anyway, I went hiking with some friends, and I just couldn't **keep up**. My legs were **aching** after the first day and it was a bit embarrassing to be honest! So, when I got back, I decided to start **keeping track** of what I ate by recording it in a food diary. I realised I needed to **cut down** on processed food, like all those burgers I was eating! I monitored the amount of salt I was consuming too – just to make sure I kept it within a reasonable limit. And, I started exercising: walking to work instead of taking the bus, that type of thing, and then, after about 12 months, I decided I'd like to run a marathon. Yeah, I know! It was hard work, all that training, but I was really pleased with my **rate** of progress and, well, I ran my first one last month in under four hours!

2 Match the words in bold in the blog with the definitions (1–7).

1. reduce the amount of something you consume ....
2. stay level or equal with someone ....
3. recording something over a period of time ....
4. too heavy ....
5. did or used too much of something ....
6. the speed at which something happens ....
7. having a continuous pain that is unpleasant but not strong ....

3 Decide what type of word is needed for each gap (1–7). Then complete the sentences using the words in bold in Exercise 2. You may need to change the tense or word form.

1. You're training too hard at the gym. If you keep .... it, you may get injured.
2. He decided to go on a low-fat diet as he was a little ....
3. I went jogging with my brother yesterday. He ran too fast and I couldn't ....
4. After a few hours of playing basketball, your muscles can really start to ....
5. After .... on the amount of coffee I was drinking, I started to sleep much better.
6. I use an app to .... of how many calories I consume each day.
7. The .... at which he recovered from his illness was quite remarkable.

4 Imagine you are going to interview someone who has recently made a healthy lifestyle change. Using the health and fitness vocabulary to help you, write five questions to find out about this change.

Why did you decide to make a healthy lifestyle change?

5 Work with a partner. Student A is the interviewer and asks Student B their questions from Exercise 4. Student B, imagine you have recently made a healthy lifestyle change. Answer Student A's questions. Then swap roles.

READING AND USE OF ENGLISH PART 7 TRAINING

1

2

3

1 **Work with a partner and answer the questions.**

1. Look at the photos. In what ways are the photos similar or different? How would you describe the people's lifestyles?
2. Do you know anyone who has a similar lifestyle to the people in the photos?

2 **Read the short texts quickly. Match the photos (1–3) with the texts (A–D). Which person isn't shown in the photos?**

3 **Read the texts again. For questions 1–5 on page 17, choose from the texts (A–D). The texts may be chosen more than once.**

4 **In what ways do you admire the people in the texts?**

5 **Choose a person from the texts. Research them online and note down a few interesting facts. Tell your group. As a group, decide who you most admire and why.**

NO AGE, NO LIMIT

A Dr Peggy Styles

At 86, Peggy Styles has become the oldest ever person to graduate from Bristol University. To say it was an uphill struggle at times is an understatement. Midway through her program, Peggy needed to take a few years out to rest after suffering severe kidney failure. At one stage, it was **touch and go** whether she'd make it. Although Peggy's physical health suffered and she even had to learn to walk again, it appears her brain continued to function effectively. The title of her dissertation for her doctorate was, "Changing perceptions: higher education amongst elderly populations" and, although it took eight years to complete, Peggy has confessed that she's now hooked on writing and research.

B Dr Allan Stewart

Australian born Allan broke his own age record when he successfully completed his degree at the advanced age of 97. Alan, who has now completed his fourth degree, returned to education in his 80s after retiring from work in order to **keep his brain sharp** and stay mentally active. While he's more famous for his mental rather than physical agility, Allan keeps himself in shape by walking, fishing and swimming. Allan says this will be his last degree as he's getting bored with studying, although he has said that at least once before so who knows – perhaps he's obsessed!

C Doreen Pechey

Doreen, who had to rethink her diet and fitness plan when she took up ballet at 61, became the oldest ballerina in Britain to pass the Royal Academy Grade 6 dance exam just ten years later. The semi-retired electrical engineer, who despite recently having knee replacement surgery, **is now back on her feet** and claims to have more agility than ever. In fact, she believes without ballet she'd have been out of action for some time. Not only that, Doreen has dropped two dress sizes too. Although in her 70s, Doreen has chosen to train with teenagers who don't appear to mind the age difference at all. And, why should they?

D Lou Batori

Although he's never taken an exam, Hungarian born Lou Batori, 106, has been skiing for over 96 years. He puts his good health down to a healthy diet, a love of good food and drink and a healthy marriage. Nevertheless, the risk-taking grandfather, who can be seen speeding down the slopes in the USA, clearly **keeps in shape** by doing tough physical exercise. Although he still skis regularly, Lou has slowed down to **recharge his batteries** and enjoys reading to relax. After all, he doesn't want to get injured, does he?

Who

takes time out to relax?	1
tries to keep their brain and body in good health?	2
is the most senior person to have graduated from university?	3
has become addicted to what they are doing?	4
recovered more rapidly because of what they're doing?	5

VOCABULARY

IDIOMS

1 **Match the expressions in red in the texts with the correct definitions.**

A to be well again after an illness ....
B to stay physically healthy ....
C an uncertain situation ....
D to rest for a period of time ....
E to stay mentally active ....

2 **Complete the second sentence with a phrase from Exercise 1 so that it has a similar meaning to the first sentence. Use between two and five words for each sentence, including the word in bold. The first one has been done for you.**

1 He's now well again after his recent operation.
BACK
He's now *back on his feet* after his recent operation.

2 I've been doing a lot of puzzles to stay mentally active.
SHARP
I've been .... by doing a lot of puzzles.

3 She feels much better after resting for two weeks in Italy.
RECHARGE
After .... for two weeks in Italy, she feels much better.

4 I stayed physically active by running in the local park.
SHAPE
I ran in the local park ....

SPEAKING PART 2 TRAINING

1 **Work with a partner and answer the questions.**

1 What's the difference between mental and physical health?
2 What are two ways someone might stay mentally active and two ways they might stay physically active?
3 Why is it important to stay in good physical and mental shape?

A

B

2 005 **Listen and decide which question Maria is answering.**

1 What do you think these people like about these types of food?
2 Why have these people chosen to eat these types of food?
3 What are the advantages and disadvantages of eating in these different ways?

3 005 **Look at the words and phrases in the box. Listen again and tick the words and phrases Maria uses.**

both	looks as though	the same as	even though
looks like	though	instead of	neither
unlike	looks as if	rather than	while

4 **Read the responses from candidates completing Part 2 of the Speaking exam. Correct the mistake in each response.**

1 At the first photograph, you can see a picture of two people eating in a restaurant.
2 The second photo appears to show a woman eat on a bus.
3 It looks as two people are enjoying a meal together in the first photo.
4 I think the woman eats a burger or a sandwich in the second photo.
5 A lot of people tend being quite busy at work, so they don't have much time to eat.

5 **Work in pairs.**

Student A: Answer the Speaking Part 2 question on page 199.
Student B: Answer the Speaking Part 2 question on page 198.

LISTENING

UNDERSTANDING DISTRACTORS

1 **Look at the photos of health and fitness apps and answer the questions.**

1. What information does each app give you? Which have you tried?
2. What do you think are the advantages and disadvantages of these apps?

2 006 **Listen to Chloe talking to her friend Ali about health and fitness apps. Which app (A–D) is she trying out?**

3 006 **Read the information in the box. Then listen again and answer the questions.**

> *When answering questions, listening only for key words may distract you from choosing the correct answer. Notice too that the speakers may correct themselves or each other. Always listen to the whole conversation to understand the whole idea.*

1. What is Chloe's opinion of smartwatches according to Ali?
2. Which app does Ali suggest is unnecessary for Chloe?
3. Which app does Chloe think is too difficult to use?
4. Which app does Chloe think she'll quickly lose interest in?
5. Why is Ali surprised by the app Chloe has chosen to use?

4 007 **Look at the phrases in the box below and check you know what they mean. Now listen to a later conversation between Ali and Chloe. Which phrase describes why Chloe has given up?**

an injury	extremely hungry	didn't lose weight
sore muscles	too tired	

A

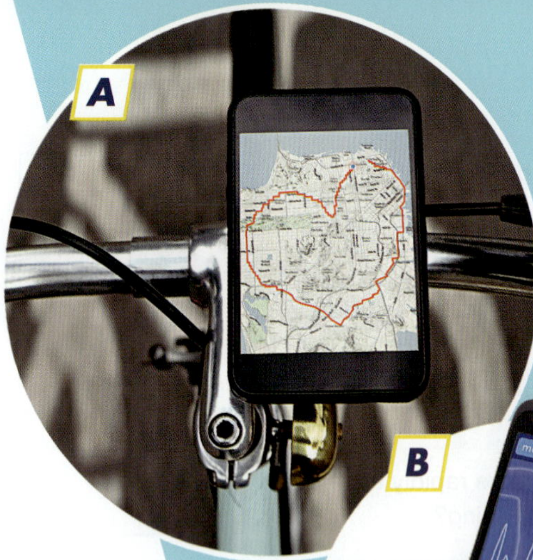

B

C

D

5 007 **Listen again. Make notes about what Ali and Chloe say about the other phrases in the box. Why are they distractors?**

6 **Work with a partner and answer the questions.**

1. To what extent can apps like these help with weight loss or to get adequate sleep? How beneficial is an app which measures your heart rate?
2. Some people believe that technology has had a negative impact on our health in recent years. Do you agree? Why? / Why not?
3. Do you believe it's possible to become too focused on healthy eating? Why / Why not?
4. What do you think about smartwatches? Would you ever buy one? Why / Why not?

GRAMMAR

GERUNDS AND INFINITIVES

GRAMMAR ON THE MOVE
Watch the video

1 **Look at the sentences from the conversation between Ali and Chloe.**

1. *I've **wanted** to buy a smartwatch for ages.*
2. *My legs didn't **stop** aching for days after that.*

What is the form of the words after the verbs in bold?

GRAMMAR REFERENCE / *Gerunds and infinitives: Page 206*

2 **Complete the sentences with the correct form of the verb in brackets.**

1. Having a high protein diet is supposed ______ good for you, but I'm not convinced. (be)
2. I tend ______ breakfast during the week but I know that isn't good for me. (skip)
3. A lot of people use apps to keep track of their food intake, but I can't stand ______ them. (use)
4. If you don't have a balanced diet, you may risk ______ yourself in the future. (harm)
5. Many people, myself included, refuse ______ energy drinks because of their high sugar level. (drink)
6. If you want to train to run a marathon, you should avoid ______ foods that are high in fat. (eat)
7. I would never give up ______ a sport I love just to concentrate more on my studies. (play)

3 **Work with a partner and discuss the sentences in Exercise 2. Do you agree with the speaker?**

4 008 **Listen to an extract of a conversation between two friends, Matilde and Franco. Complete the gaps with words you hear.**

Matilde: Well, when I saw the poster at the food market, I [1] ______ a look. I wanted to get more information. You'd said more and more people have [2] ______ meat these days.

Franco: Yes, I [3] ______ you about the benefits of vegetarianism when we met in the café last week. Although, I didn't [4] ______ you the address of the food market, so I'm glad you found it.

Matilde: No problem. It was really interesting and I loved the variety of fruit and vegetables on offer. A friend of mine also told me that I should [5] ______ meat and fish from my diet. I wanted to speak to a professional, so I [6] ______ a meeting with a nutritionist but sadly no-one was available.

Franco: That's a shame.

5 **Read the extract in Exercise 4 again and look at your answers. What is the difference in meaning between each pair of verb forms?**

6 **Circle the correct option.**

1. I've stopped *to consume/consuming* foods which are high in fat as I want to lose weight.
2. I'm trying *to cut out/cutting out* sugar from my diet, but I'm finding it really difficult.
3. I was starving, so I stopped *to grab/grabbing* a quick bite to eat on my way to class.
4. When I'm really busy, I find it hard to remember *to eat/eating* regular meals.
5. I lived in Thailand for a while and remember *to try/trying* some of the local dishes. They were delicious!
6. A friend of mine told me that I should try *putting/to put* honey and lemon in my tea to help with my sore throat.

7 **Write one sentence for each of the points below. Then work in groups and compare your answers.**

Think of something that you …

- can't stand doing
- refuse to eat
- have given up doing recently
- stopped to do before coming to class today
- tend to do before going to sleep
- remember doing when you were very young

DID YOU KNOW?

We can use the expression *high in* to say that certain foods contain a large amount of something. For example: *I avoid eating food which is high in sugar.*

WRITING PART 1 TRAINING

1 **Complete the questionnaire.**

IS YOUR LIFESTYLE HELPING OR HINDERING YOUR HEALTH?

1 How many hours do you typically sleep at night?
  - **a** 6 or less
  - **b** 7 to 9
  - **c** 10 or more

2 How much water do you drink each day?
  - **a** 0 to 2 glasses
  - **b** 3 to 5 glasses
  - **c** 6 to 8 glasses

3 How much physical exercise do you do?
  - **a** Once a week or less
  - **b** 2 to 3 times per week on average
  - **c** On a daily basis

4 What is your preferred after-dinner activity?
  - **a** Eating dessert
  - **b** Lying on the sofa and watching TV
  - **c** A walk and chat with a friend

5 What do you consider first when choosing meals?
  - **a** The taste
  - **b** The calorie count
  - **c** Whether it's balanced

6 You're really tired at school or work. Do you …
  - **a** take a nap in your lunch break?
  - **b** grab a coffee or an energy drink?
  - **c** go for a quick walk in the fresh air?

7 You wake up an hour before the alarm goes off in the morning. Do you …
  - **a** close your eyes and go back to sleep?
  - **b** stay in bed and check social media?
  - **c** get up and get active?

2 **Work with a partner. Who has the healthiest lifestyle? Why? Turn to page 198 and see how healthy your lifestyle is.**

3 **Work with a partner. How have people's lifestyles changed in recent years? Think about:**

Diet Exercise Work

4 **Read the essay question and model answer. Which, if any, of your ideas in Exercise 3 have been included?**

In your English class you have been talking about health and fitness.
Now, your English teacher has asked you to write an essay.
Some people say modern lifestyles are ruining our health. Do you agree?

Notes

Write about:
1 diet
2 exercise
3 .... (your own idea)

Although not impossible, it is arguably more challenging to stay in shape these days because of the changes in our diet, a lack of physical activity and increased levels of stress.
Even though foods high in vitamins and minerals are available in most shops, people tend to be busier now and often prefer eating junk food rather than a balanced meal. Despite its convenience, junk food is very unhealthy and consuming too much can lead to serious health issues.
Nowadays, people tend to use their cars instead of walking, even for short journeys. As a result of this change, people are getting less and less exercise. Therefore, they have less opportunity to build their muscles and burn calories.
Finally, due to our fast-paced lifestyles, people are under more pressure to work longer hours than ever before. Working parents, for example, have little time to relax, which means they risk suffering from illnesses such as stress.
To sum up, I agree that it is more difficult to be fit and healthy in modern society. However, with the right attitude to eating, exercise and work, it is possible to protect our physical and mental well-being.

Focus on structure

1 Does the writer cover the two compulsory points in the notes?
2 What is the writer's own idea?
3 In which paragraph does the writer give his/her own opinion?
4 What phrase does the writer use to conclude the essay?

GRAMMAR

COMPARING AND CONTRASTING IDEAS WITH LINKERS

GRAMMAR ON THE MOVE
Watch the video

1 **Study how the writer uses the highlighted linkers in the model essay. Complete the sentences below with these linkers. There may be more than one correct option.**

1 .... the rates of obesity have increased, many people still lead healthy lifestyles.
2 People should be encouraged to do more physical exercise .... taking the car or bus to work.
3 .... being cheap, processed foods do not generally make up a healthy and nutritious diet.
4 Eating a balanced diet which includes plenty of fruit and vegetables, ... consuming foods high in sugar and fats, helps maintain healthy blood pressure.
5 Many people are aware of the benefits of doing physical exercise. .... , it's important not to overdo it.
6 With the amount of processed food found in supermarkets these days, people should consider nutritional content more ....

2 **Correct the mistake in each of the sentences. One sentence is correct.**

1 Despite hate carrots, he tried to eat one or two portions with his dinner each week.
2 The government is encouraging kids to walk to school, however it might take them half an hour or more.
3 It's important to eat organic food on a daily basis. However, this can be quite expensive.
4 Tatiana prefers to run in her local park, rather pay money to go to the gym.
5 Despite writing down her weekly food intake on paper, Martina used an app.

3 **Write your answer for the essay question below.**

In your English class, you have been talking about health and fitness. Now your English teacher has asked you to write an essay.
Young people these days tend to be less interested in their health. Do you agree?
Notes
Write about:
1 Technology
2 Food
3 .... (your own idea)

PUSH YOURSELF C1

UNDERSTANDING HEALTH

1 **Look at the pictures below. What do you think happens at a fitness boot camp?**

2 **009 Listen to Gavin, a boot camp instructor, welcoming the new students to the boot camp. Complete the itinerary with the words in the box.**

digestion	nutrition	posture	stamina	well-being

FIRST FIT BOOT CAMP
Date: 20th August–25th August
Instructor: Gavin
Location: Green Meadows
List of activities
Day 1: ....
Day 2: ....
Day 3: ....
Day 4: ....
Day 5: ....

3 **009 Listen again. Make notes about the types of activities they will do each day.**

4 **Which day would you most and least prefer and why? Go online and research other activities that are provided by boot camps. What should someone consider when choosing a boot camp?**

EXAM FOCUS

READING AND USE OF ENGLISH PART 7

EXAM FACTS

- *You will read one long text divided into sections or four to five shorter texts.*
- *You must answer ten questions.*

EXAM TIPS

- *Read the questions carefully and underline the key words.*
- *The information in the questions may not be written in exactly the same words as the information in the texts so look for synonyms and paraphrases.*

You are going to read an article in which four people discuss health and fitness. For questions 1–10, chose from the people, (A–D). The people may be chosen more than once.

A Oleg
I'd never been one to worry about what I ate or how active I was, and in my 20s and 30s it didn't seem to matter. I was slim, and I looked fit, even if I drank too much coffee and never actually exercised. Then suddenly, my clothes were tight, and I got out of breath walking up the shortest of hills – it was only when I turned 40 the reality of my poor physical condition started to hit home. I'm trying to do something about it now but it's a struggle to get motivated. I've joined a gym, but I've only been once over the past few months as I've got such a busy schedule. It's regrettable that I didn't do more when I had the chance, but I think I've left it too late now.

B Bruno
Everyone assumed I could do it, although I was a little uncertain, and it wasn't easy changing my diet and how active I was. At first, I underestimated how critical it is to get into a routine and how easy it would be to make excuses. I'd started to slip into old unhealthy habits when someone I'm close to suggested I sleep in my running gear, so I didn't have any excuses when I woke up in the morning and as crazy as it sounds, it worked. Anyway, my hard work paid off in the end and I'm in better condition now than I was thirty years ago. Who says retired people like me can't get in shape!

C Anthony
I've always loved food and even as a child I was never a fussy eater, so I think it's definitely possible to eat what you want and be a professional athlete. Of course, I don't eat all the junk food I used to have as a kid, but I'm not going to stop myself having a treat if I really want it. I just don't get the obsession athletes have these days with protein shakes and energy drinks as I think our bodies are designed to get everything they need from real food. I tend to watch what I eat in the lead up to a big competition but other than that I listen to my body. I train for six hours a day and on my days off when I need to rest, you'll find me baking in the kitchen, which, unsurprisingly, my family really appreciate.

D Marcus
Friends and acquaintances say that as a personal trainer and cyclist I must be on a strict diet but that's just not the case. I try to avoid processed food and cook everything from fresh. In fact, I do most of the cooking when I'm at home, although I don't always have a lot of time these days. At school, I avoided anything which involved any sort of physical activity and was quite overweight. But I really got into cycling when I was watching the Olympic Games one year, and thought I'd give it a go. The training was almost impossible initially, as I was so out of shape, but I was determined to make positive changes and I'm glad I stuck with it.

Which person

1 believes it's possible to be unhealthy without being overweight?
2 says that people are unaware of what he eats?
3 was surprised by how unfit he had become?
4 is healthier now than when he was a child?
5 does not agree with the changes to the diets of sportspeople?
6 did not allow challenges to stop him from improving his health?
7 believes a friend helped him succeed?
8 wishes he had taken more care of his health when he was younger?
9 had not realised the importance of planning when he trained?
10 uses cooking to help them relax?

WRITING PART 1

EXAM FACTS

- You need to write between 140–190 words.
- You must write about the two points in the notes as well as your own idea.

EXAM TIPS

- Read the essay question and notes carefully in order to understand what you need to write about.
- Make sure that your ideas are relevant to the essay question.
- Allow time at the start to plan your essay.
- Make sure that you include your own personal opinion to the question.

In your English class you have been talking about health and fitness. Now your English teacher has asked you to write an essay.

Write an essay using **all** the notes and giving reasons for your point of view.

There are lots of ways that technology can help us to maintain a healthy lifestyle. Do you agree?

Notes

Write about:

1 diet

2 exercise

3 … (your own idea)

Write your **essay**. You must use grammatically correct sentences with accurate spelling and punctuation in a style appropriate for the situation.

➡ **WRITING BANK** / Pages 234–235

EXAM FOCUS

SPEAKING PART 2

EXAM FACTS

- *In this part of the exam, you have to compare two photographs and answer a question about them.*
- *You also have to answer a question about your partner's photo.*

EXAM TIPS

- *Candidates often describe the photographs instead of comparing them. Remember that you are comparing and contrasting two photographs not describing one.*
- *Candidates sometimes run out of things to say and stop before the time is up. Practise comparing two photos of a similar theme for one minute. You can easily find photos online.*

In this part of the test, you are given two photographs.

Student A

Talk about your two photographs for one minute. The photographs show people eating food in different situations. Compare the photographs and say what you think these people like about eating food in these situations.

Student B

Do you prefer eating at home or at a restaurant?

SPEAKING PART 2

Student B

Talk about your two photographs for one minute. The photographs show people using technology while exercising. Compare the photographs and say how these things might help these people while exercising.

Student A

Which sports do you enjoy doing?

➡ **SPEAKING BANK** / *Pages 246–249*

REAL WORLD

BEING ACTIVE IN ... ZURICH

FACT FILE: Zurich

+ Zurich isn't actually the capital of Switzerland, despite the fact that a lot of people think it is. The capital of Switzerland is Bern.
+ Zurich is Switzerland's largest city. It has a population of just over 400,000.
+ There are over 1,200 drinking fountains in Zurich.
+ Lake Zurich, which is approximately 40 km long, has frozen over twice in the last one hundred years. The most recent was in 1962/63 and the residents organised a festival on the ice.
+ Zurich is home to a large number of banks and financial centres. It is considered to be one of the world's biggest financial capitals.

1 **Read the travel advice about how to prepare for a trip abroad. Complete the advice with the correct verbs in the box.**

find   make sure   need   pack   read   refer to   subscribe   take out

1 ________ health insurance before you travel to avoid high medical costs.
2 ________ your policy if you need to make a claim against the insurance.
3 ________ the label carefully if you are prescribed medication by a local doctor.
4 ________ that your passport and visa are up to date.
5 ________ to news alerts in case of any flight cancellations or delays.
6 Check if you ________ any vaccinations for the country before travelling.
7 ________ out how much you'll be charged for using your phone abroad to avoid high roaming charges.
8 ________ an extra set of clothes in your carry-on luggage in case your checked luggage gets lost.

2 **Find the words and phrases in the sentences in Exercise 1 which mean the following.**

1. a treatment, usually an injection, to prevent a disease ....
2. a document showing an agreement you have made with an insurance company ....
3. the amount of money you pay for using your phone in another country ....
4. luggage that you are allowed to take on an aeroplane ....
5. a document or card that allows you to enter or leave a country ....
6. notifications or warnings often sent to your phone or email ....

3 **010 Listen to two university friends, Gina and Pierre, discussing their trip to Zurich. Which pieces of advice in Exercise 1 do they talk about?**

4 **011 While they're away, Gina starts to feel ill. Listen and replace the phrases in italics with the phrases they use in the recording.**

PHRASES YOU MIGHT HEAR / USE

1. I've eaten something which *made me feel unwell.* (Gina)
   ....
2. Well, I've got a bit of *pain in my stomach.* (Gina)
   ....
3. Oh dear. You do look a little *ill.* Do you have any other symptoms? (Pierre)
   ....
4. I've got a slight temperature and I'm feeling *dizzy and slightly faint* when I stand up. (Gina)
   ....
5. I'm sure it's nothing serious but maybe you're *beginning to suffer from an illness.* (Pierre)
   ....
6. It's probably just a cold but it might *be helpful if you got* some sleep. (Pierre)
   ....

5 **If you are prescribed medication, it's important that you can understand the label. Read the label on the bottle and match the phrases with the correct meanings.**

1. It might make you feel sleepy.
   ....
2. Take two tablets a day.
   ....
3. Speak to a doctor if you don't feel better.
   ....
4. Don't take more or less than you are told to.
   ....
5. You may feel sick as a result of taking the medicine.
   ....

6 **Work in groups and answer the questions.**

1. Have you ever eaten something which didn't agree with you? What?
2. When was the last time you felt under the weather? What were your symptoms?
3. What advice would you give someone who is coming down with a cold?

7 **Watch the video about Zurich. What do you learn about these things? Make notes.**

- The city of Zurich
- Things to see and do
- The fondue tram
- Sports and recreation in and around Zurich

WATCH

LIFE COMPETENCIES

CREATING NEW CONTENT, SYNTHESISING INFORMATION

8 **Work in groups and choose a city. Go online and research health and fitness information for travellers. Make notes and share what you've learnt with the class.**

2 KEEPING IN TOUCH

GETTING STARTED

1 Complete the sentences to make true statements about yourself. Then compare your answers with a partner.

1. One great advantage of having friends online is that …
2. The last thing I 'liked' on social media was …
3. When I 'like' a post or 'follow' someone, it's usually because …
4. A difference between how I socialise face to face and how I socialise online is …
5. If I had to choose between chatting online or hanging out with someone in person, I would …
6. If my parents followed me on social media, I would ...

READING AND USE OF ENGLISH PART 6 TRAINING

1 You are going to read an article about social media and friendship. Look at the highlighted words from the article and choose the correct definitions.

1 After all, what can be wrong with having a wider group of people to **hang out with**?
A socialise with **B** become closer friends with

2 Is it feasible to maintain **meaningful** relationships with so many people, in particular those you may never actually meet in person?
A pleasant **B** important and worthwhile

3 Now, I see her pop up in my **feed** every now and again and I 'like' her photos …
A public messages on social media **B** private messages

4 My most important relationships haven't grown out of a few **trivial** online exchanges.
A funny; entertaining **B** unimportant; with no value

5 It's taken years of shared experiences to develop strong and lasting **bonds**.
A ways of getting in touch **B** close relationships

6 This has led some people to question just how **sincere** the friendship is.
A enjoyable **B** honest

DID YOU KNOW?

The phrase *pop up* can be used as a verb or noun.

pop up (verb) – to appear suddenly

pop-up (noun) – a new window that opens on a computer screen

2 Read the statements about social media and friendship. Which ones do you agree with and which ones do you disagree with?

A The only reason that people want to have lots of online friends is to boost their confidence and feel better about themselves.

B I enjoy having friends on social media, but I sometimes wonder whether it's all a bit unnecessary.

C Using electronic devices to communicate instead of spending time with real people might actually do more harm than good.

D Social media allows us to develop and strengthen relationships with the people we know and see.

3 **Quickly read the article below, ignoring the gaps. Which statement in Exercise 2 most closely reflects the writer's view?**

SOCIAL MEDIA AND FRIENDSHIP

Lucy Forrester explores the effect social media is having on friendships.

Having too many friends doesn't sound like the kind of thing anyone should really be too concerned about. After all, what can be wrong with having a wider group of people to **hang out with**?

According to the latest figures, the average number of friends people have on social media is somewhere between 200 and 300. **(1)** ________ But is this a realistic amount? Is it feasible to maintain **meaningful** relationships with so many people, in particular those you may never actually meet in person?

Nowadays, we are just one click away from making new friends on social media. **(2)** ________ For instance, when I see that a friend has updated their profile with snaps from their latest holiday, I'd typically reply with a comment like "Wow, looks great!" even though in actual fact, it doesn't. The unwritten agreement is that the next time I post, that friend will respond with a similarly appreciative comment, so I'll feel better about myself.

Not long ago, I got chatting to someone at a concert, who told me that she loved going to gigs. We got along pretty well that evening, despite the fact that the music was so loud! We even swapped numbers and added each other on social media. Now, I see her pop up in my **feed** every now and again and I 'like' her photos from various gigs she's been to, but I'm pretty certain that we'll never arrange to meet up in real life.

(3) ________ That being said, we're living in a time where we expect things to happen instantly, so is it really all that surprising that the way we form friendships has adapted to this trend? Perhaps it shows how social media has made friendships less sincere, reducing them to a series of meaningless 'adds' and 'likes'.

Real friendships, on the other hand, take time to build. My most important relationships haven't grown out of a few **trivial** online exchanges. **(4)** ________ And these for me – and I believe for most other people too – are much more valuable and meaningful. It's something that cannot be replicated on social media, no matter how many times you have 'liked' a person's posts.

It has been suggested that technology is ruining our relationships with other people. **(5)** ________ However, it seems undeniable that it has now altered people's priorities, and transformed the way that we manage our friendships in the most fundamental ways. Ultimately, though, it's up to us to decide how real and meaningful those friendships truly are.

A Personally I wouldn't go so far as to say that.
B Research suggests that this figure is actually higher for teenagers.
C Social media has made this kind of problem increasingly more common.
D It's taken years of shared experiences to develop strong and lasting **bonds**.
E This has led some people to question just how **sincere** the friendship is.
F It could be argued that this is just another example of how life has changed in recent years.

4 012 **Listen to two students, Jan and Anna, talking about the text and the exam task for Reading and Use of English Part 6. What strategy do they use for finding the answer to the first gap?**

5 **Now read the sentences A–F. Using the same strategy as Jan and Anna, work with a partner to decide which sentence best fits the first gap.**

6 **Look at the second gap in the article and answer the questions below.**

1. What do you think the main idea of the third paragraph is?
2. Which sentence (A–F) talks about the effect of this on friendship?

7 **Using the strategies in Exercises 4, 5 and 6, choose from the remaining sentences (A–F) the one which fits each gap (3–5). There is one extra sentence which you do not need to use.**

GRAMMAR

THE PASSIVE

GRAMMAR ON THE MOVE
Watch the video

THIS WEEK'S BLOG POST

by Lorenzo Garcia
Social Media Guru, Presenter, Entrepreneur

We all want our posts on social media **to be seen**. Whether your social media account **is being used** as part of your business or just for socialising, you really want your voice **to be heard**, and encourage people to engage with the post. Tons of research **has been done** on what makes a good social media post. But here's the key thing to remember – people are much more likely to notice your content if it contains an image. Posts with photos have a much greater chance of being liked and shared. And if a video **is included** in your post, that's even better. Remember, though, that quality is more important than quantity – your post **might not be liked** if it's just got a couple of dark and blurry photos that **haven't been taken** with any attention to the background or lighting.

1 **Work in groups and identify two things which you think can make a post on social media successful or unsuccessful.**

2 **Quickly read the extract from a blog about using social media. Does Lorenzo mention any of your ideas from Exercise 1?**

3 **Read the blog again. Match the passive structures in bold with the correct tenses (1–5).**

1 Present simple passive:
2 Present continuous passive:
3 Present perfect passive:
4 Modal verb + passive:
5 Passive infinitive (with to): *to be seen*

➔ **GRAMMAR REFERENCE** / *The passive: Page 208*

4 **Complete the sentences using the correct passive form of the verbs in brackets.**

1 It's my birthday today and I'm really looking forward to *being taken out* (take out) for dinner by my parents.
2 The joke I posted online this morning ________ already ________ (share) over a hundred times!
3 Our cat ________ (look after) by a family friend at the moment.
4 Over ten thousand copies of the book ________ (sold) since it ________ (publish) last month.
5 The website ________ (update) every day.
6 All mobile devices must ________ (switch off) during the flight.
7 The restaurant ________ (own) by my cousin, who lives nearby.
8 The kitchen was supposed ________ (clean) by my little brother but he hasn't done it yet.

5 **Work in groups to create a story of what happened in one of the cartoons. Use at least five passive verbs, in a variety of verb forms. Then tell your story to the other groups.**

PUSH YOURSELF C1

HEDGING

Hedging (or cautious language) is a form of language used in written English. It is often used when you want to make a point politely or to protect yourself from being wrong. Hedging language sometimes uses the passive. For example:
It could be said that social media is having a negative effect on our communication skills.

1 **Read the article about social media and friendship on page 29 again. Find two examples of hedging language using the passive (one in the final paragraph and one in the answer options A–F).**

2 **Put the words in the correct order to form statements using hedging language. The first word has been done for you.**

1 important / argued / than family / are / ~~it~~ / that / more / be / could / friends
It ....

2 suggested / than / are / ~~it~~ / has / friendships nowadays / in the past / less / been / sincere / has / that
It ....

3 social media / made / said / lonely / has / feel / ~~it~~ / that / more / is / people
It ....

3 **Work with a partner. Which statements in Exercise 2 do you agree or disagree with?**

VOCABULARY

DESCRIBING YOUR FAMILY

1 **Work in pairs.**

Student A: Describe your family to your partner.
Student B: Make notes about the information you hear. Then repeat it back to your partner.

2 **Describe the words and phrases to a partner. Can they guess which word you are describing?**

sibling widow niece/nephew daughter-in-law
stepson fiancé(e) cousin godmother
half-brother extended family

3 **Look at the picture of the Dumont family. Read the sentences (1–7) below and decide the names of each family member.**

1 Leonard is the oldest male in the family and has two sons, Desmond and Anthony.
2 Faye has an older sibling called Tiffany.
3 Anthony has two nieces, one of whom is called Faye.
4 Leonard is a widow. Chantelle is his daughter-in-law.
5 Desmond has two daughters. He also has a nephew called Jackson.
6 Chantelle is married to Desmond. Her daughter Tiffany is sitting on her lap.
7 Anthony is divorced but remarried Sandra. Jackson is Sandra's stepson.

The males shown in the picture are:
Anthony Desmond Leonard Jackson

The females shown in the picture are:
Chantelle Faye Sandra Tiffany

SPEAKING

SPECULATING

1 **Think of yourself with your best friend. Which of the photos (A–D) are you most like? Why?**

2 **Put the words into the correct order to form sentences.**

These are also useful phrases to use in the B2 First Speaking Part 2 exam.

1. they / be / fancy-dress / party / must / a / at

   ....

2. though / the women / are / looks / as / it / at / a spa

   ....

3. could / home / be / at / someone's / this / party / a

   ....

4. are / looks / music / they / it / dancing / like / some / to

   ....

5. have / with / the girl / had / might / an argument / someone

   ....

3 **Match the descriptions in Exercise 2 with the photos (A–D).**

4 **Put the phrases in bold in the correct category. The first one has been done for you.**

1. **It's obvious that** the man with the sunglasses is the host of the party.
2. **It looks as though** the woman is helping her friend.
3. **I guess that** the woman's just had some bad news.
4. The people are **likely to be** at a party.
5. **I can tell that** both of the women are enjoying themselves.
6. The guy **must be** singing something.
7. The couple in the garden **might be** brother and sister.
8. **There's a chance that** they are about to have a massage.

ALMOST CERTAINLY TRUE	LIKELY	POSSIBLE
It's obvious that		

5 **Look at the photos below. Using the phrases in Exercise 4, speculate about who the people in the pictures are, what their relationships are and what might be happening.**

GRAMMAR

USED TO, BE USED TO, GET USED TO

GRAMMAR ON THE MOVE
Watch the video

1 Have you ever visited or lived in another country? What were the similarities and differences with your home country?

2 013 Listen to Maribel comparing her life in Mexico and Spain. Look at the activities and decide if Maribel did them in Mexico (M) or Spain (S).

1. travel around the city ....
2. cycling ....
3. listen to the local music ....
4. go shopping with friends ....
5. spend time at the beach ....

3 013 Listen again. Complete the extracts from the recording.

1. I remember during my early childhood, my family and I .... a lot around the city.
2. We never had bikes, so I .... at all back then in Mexico.
3. And during my teenage years, I .... with my friends in the local shopping mall.
4. My life in Spain is different, but just as fun, although it took me a while to .... the different types of food!
5. I spend a lot of time at the beach with my friends, which is something I .... in Mexico.
6. I .... my new life in Spain and I'm very lucky to have lived in two beautiful countries. .... any of the same things as me?

➔ **GRAMMAR REFERENCE** / *Used to and Would: Page 209*

4 Circle the correct option. Sometimes both answers are possible.

1. I *used to/would* be an actor when I was in my twenties.
2. When I was a kid, my grandfather *used to/would* tell me these amazing stories.
3. My parents *used to/would* take my sister and me to France on holiday each year when we were kids.
4. My grandparents *used to/would* be very happy whenever we visited them in the holidays.
5. When I was a teenager, my friends and I *used to/would* spend hours in the shopping centre.
6. When they were both kids, my mum and dad *used to/would* live on the same street, but they didn't know each other!

5 Look at the sentences below from the extract. What is the difference between *be used to* and *get used to*? How are they different to *used to*?

... it took me a while ***to get used to eating*** *the different types of food!*
I'm used to *my new life in Spain now and I'm very lucky to have lived in two beautiful countries.*

➔ **GRAMMAR REFERENCE** / *Be used to / get used to: page 209*

6 Read about the people in sentences 1–5. Complete the sentences with the correct form of *be/get used to*.

1. Julia is eighteen and has just started university. She's slowly .... all the lectures and seminars.
2. David and Matilda have just had their first baby. It's hard for them .... waking up in the middle of the night.
3. Sergei is very tired this morning. He .... going out so late with his friends.
4. Sarah has a new job as a nurse. It's taken her a while .... the long working hours.
5. Because she's lived abroad for 20 years, Patricia .... the different language and culture.

7 Complete the second sentence so that it has a similar meaning to the first sentence, using the word given. Do not change the word given. You must use between two and five words, including the word given.

1. Previously, Darren was a security guard at his cousin's company.
   EMPLOYED
   Darren used .... a security guard at his cousin's company.
2. Janine is adapting to living on her own.
   GETTING
   Janine's .... by herself.
3. Working by myself at home seems strange to me.
   NOT
   I'm .... by myself at home.
4. In those days, Sue and Harriet spent a lot of time together.
   HANG
   Sue and Harriet used .... each other a lot in those days.

8 Imagine you have just moved to a new country. Write a letter home to your family describing your experiences. Say

- what you used to do but no longer do now
- what you are used to / not used to
- what you are getting used to

LISTENING PART 4 TRAINING

1 Work with a partner and answer the questions.

1. Who are you close to in your family?
2. Is there anyone who you don't get on so well with? Why not?

2 You will hear an interview between Maya and Aidan. Read question 1. Match the options (A–C) with the phrases from the interview (i–iii) which have a similar meaning.

1. Aidan says that throughout his childhood, his grandad was someone that he
   - **A** always respected.
   - **B** saw a great deal of.
   - **C** learnt a lot from.

   - **i** *had a lot of face-to-face contact with*
   - **ii** *looked to for answers*
   - **iii** *looked up to*

3 014 Now listen to the first part of the interview. Choose the correct answer from Exercise 1, A, B or C.

4 Look at questions 2–5 and the words and phrases in bold. Think of different ways of expressing each one.

2. What does Aidan particularly admire about his fiancée?
   - **A** her **optimism**
   - **B** her **sense of humour**
   - **C** her **intelligence**
3. Who does Aidan feel he **is most similar to**?
   - **A** his mum
   - **B** his dad
   - **C** his fiancée
4. Why is Aidan not as close to his dad as he was five years ago?
   - **A** They **fell out** with each other.
   - **B** His dad **moved away** from the area.
   - **C** They **stopped seeing each other** so regularly.
5. How has social media **influenced** Aidan's relationship with his family?
   - **A** It has caused more arguments with his parents.
   - **B** It has brought him closer to his extended family.
   - **C** It has strengthened his relationship with Dilys.

5 015 Listen to the rest of the interview. For questions 2–5, choose the correct answer A, B or C. Were any of your suggested words and phrases in Exercise 4 used?

VOCABULARY

PHRASAL VERBS

1 Work with a partner and answer the questions about phrasal verbs.

1. Do you find it easy or difficult to learn phrasal verbs?
2. Do you use many phrasal verbs in your speaking and writing?
3. What do you do to help study and remember phrasal verbs?

2 Match the phrasal verbs (1–7) with the definitions (A–G).

1. hang out (with someone) ____
2. fall out (with someone) ____
3. get on (with someone) ____
4. take after (someone) ____
5. look up to (someone) ____
6. grow apart (from someone) ____
7. split up (with/from someone) ____

- **A** to have a good relationship
- **B** to admire or respect someone
- **C** to be similar to someone, e.g. a family member
- **D** to spend time with a person or people
- **E** to argue with someone and stop speaking to them
- **F** to separate when a romantic relationship ends
- **G** to become less close

3 Complete the sentences with the correct phrasal verb from Exercise 2. You may need to change the form of the phrasal verb.

1. Thulani and I used to be best friends when we were at school. But over time, we gradually ____, and we eventually lost contact.
2. My brother and I are ____ much better now that we don't live together.
3. He ____ his father as they are both brilliant at mathematics.
4. I ____ with my best friend last year after a silly argument at a party, and we haven't spoken since.
5. My aunt and uncle ____ in 2010 and got divorced the following year.
6. My grandmother was a big inspiration to me while she was alive. I really ____ her.
7. I used to really enjoy ____ with my friends at the local shopping mall after school.

P STRESS IN PHRASAL VERBS

The second word in a phrasal verb is usually stressed, e.g.
*After school, my friends and I usually just hang **out**.*
*After school, I usually hang **out** with my friends in the park.*
*I always looked **up** to my teachers at school.*
*I picked **up** a few words of Ukrainian when I visited Kiev.*

4 **Read the pronunciation tip. Then read the sentences again in Exercise 3 with the correct pronunciation.**

5 **Work in groups and invent a story about the people in the picture. Use as many of the phrasal verbs from this section as possible. Then tell your story to the other groups.**

WRITING PART 1: ESSAY TRAINING

1 **Look at the essay question from Part 1 of a B2 First writing exam. Work in groups and think of an idea to add as the third point.**

In your English class, you have been talking about friendship and social media. Now, your English teacher has asked you to write an essay.
Write an essay using all the notes and giving your reasons for your point of view.

> 'Some people say that rather than having lots of friends on social media, it's more important to have a couple of really close friends.'
>
> Do you agree?
>
> **Notes**
>
> Write about:
>
> 1 advantages or disadvantages of having friends on social media
>
> 2 the types of friends people have on social media
>
> 3 .... (your own idea)
>
> Write your answer in **140–190** words in an appropriate style.

2 **To begin effectively, which of the following should your opening paragraph do? You can choose more than one option.**

A grab the reader's attention
B tell the reader your opinion
C include four or five sentences
D use the same wording as the question
E make clear what the essay is going to be about

3 **Quickly read the following opening paragraphs for the essay question in Exercise 1, written by four different students. Which one do you think is the strongest one? Why?**

1 There are both advantages and disadvantages of having friends on social media. A lot of people have various types of friends on social media, for example ones who are interested in the same sports.

2 Out of all the social networks available, the one I find most enjoyable to use is called meetupandhangout.com. Not only is it a great way to meet new friends, but it's also really user-friendly, as I will explain in this essay.

3 These days, it's not unusual for a person to have 500 friends on social media, which can be great for their self-confidence. However, there's also a danger that socialising online could replace socialising in real life and therefore make people lonely.

4 It's sometimes said that instead of having lots of mates on social networks, it's more important to have a smaller number of really close friends.

4 **Now match the following comments from B2 First examiners (A–D) with the opening paragraphs (1–4) from Exercise 3.**

A The opening sentence is almost identical to the statement which candidates are asked to discuss. This makes it less interesting to read.
B The paragraph introduces a new topic, which isn't relevant to the question. It suggests that the rest of the essay will discuss this, instead of the question which was asked.
C The wording is copied almost word for word from the first two numbered points. The candidate has not shown what they are capable of writing for themselves.
D The writer successfully presents pros and cons of social media use.

5 **Now write your own answer to the question in 140–190 words.**

EXAM FOCUS

READING AND USE OF ENGLISH PART 6

EXAM FACTS

- *In this part of the exam, you will read a text with six gaps in it.*
- *You must choose from a list of seven sentences, the one that best fits each gap. There is one extra sentence that you don't need to use.*

EXAM TIPS

- *Read the text quickly to get a better understanding of what it is about.*
- *Underline the key words before and after each gap. Look for reference words such as it, they, this, etc.*
- *When you have selected a sentence for each gap, read the paragraph again to check that it makes sense with the sentence you've chosen.*

You are going to read an article about friendships at work. Six sentences have been removed from the article. Choose from the sentences A–G the one which fits each gap (1–6). There is one extra sentence which you do not need to use.

Why we all need 'frolleagues'

Being friends with your colleagues is important – and beneficial, argues part-time journalist and part-time office worker **Amy McDuffit**.

We're told that people are working longer hours than ever before, and that we now encounter more people during our lifetimes than has been the case at any time in human history. Put the two together, and perhaps it's no surprise that so many of us enjoy close friendships with the people we work with. Instead of having one group of friends and another group of colleagues, we increasingly have what have become known as 'frolleagues'.

It can certainly be argued that this is a 'win-win' situation for both the employee and the employer. Research has shown that having really close friendships in the workplace can boost employee satisfaction by as much as 50%. **(1)** .... Workers who consider themselves to have 'many' workplace friends are three times more likely to say that they 'love' being at work.

It's common for people to enjoy going out with friends at the end of a hard day's work. **(2)** .... Well, according to a study by workplace researchers Peldon Rose, 83% of people consider their colleagues to be their friends, with the vast majority of them saying that they value the friendships. The benefits are well documented.

I should know. For the last year or so I've sat next to Sally in the office, and she's certainly helped the time go more quickly. We've been spending at least 40 hours a week in close proximity. More if you include our evenings out. That's more time than I spend with my friends, my flatmates and my boyfriend. **(3)** .... In fact I sometimes even call them by her name!

Sally and I were halfway through our lunch the other day when she came out with it. 'Anyway, I've got some news' she said. 'I've got another job, so I'm leaving.' **(4)** .... It's that strange feeling, when someone who's been an important part of your life just goes away, and there's nothing you can do about it.

And when I think about it, my experience with Sally seems to confirm much of the current research into workplace friendships, at least anecdotally. OK, I admit, she and I probably spent rather longer than we should have done on tea breaks. **(5)** .... But the thing is that coming to work, I always had a smile on my face, because I knew that Sally would make the next few hours fun.

And this is what study after study has found. When employees are surrounded by colleagues they are friendly with, in other words 'frolleagues', they tend to be in a positive frame of mind. **(6)** .... Their interactions with other people, such as customers, tend to be viewed by both parties as successful, which it goes without saying is good for business. Those who enjoy positive workplace relationships tend to be more committed and work harder. They are also less likely to quit, and the advantages of high employee retention are well documented.

So, as I said, frolleagues are 'win-win' all the way, both for employer and employee. But I'll still miss Sally!

A Perhaps unsurprisingly, this has several benefits.

B This explains why I consider Sally to be a 'frolleague'.

C When I told my friends, it was a bit like announcing a break-up.

D Having said that, I don't think there was anyone in our office who didn't.

E And the quantity as well as the quality of these relationships plays a part too.

F And if those companions happen to be workmates too, well, that's no bad thing surely?

G Most of them have never met her, but I mention her so often that they all feel as though they do.

LISTENING PART 4

EXAM FACTS

- *You'll have a short time to read the questions before the recording starts.*
- *You'll hear the recording twice.*

EXAM TIPS

- *Don't expect to hear all the same words as you read in the questions.*
- *Instead, listen out for synonyms, e.g. 'colleagues' instead of 'people she works with'.*
- *Use the second listening as an opportunity to check all your answers.*

016 **You will hear part of a radio interview with Dr Leonora Stockley, an expert in communication, talking about her research. For questions 1–7, choose the best answer (A, B or C).**

1 Who did Dr Stockley get her research data from?
A friends and family
B people she works with
C her connections on the internet

2 Dr Stockley believes that a problem of online technology is that
A it stops people from concentrating on those around them.
B not everybody has a reliable internet connection.
C false information can spread very quickly.

3 What did Fred find difficult when communicating online?
A expressing his emotions
B building strong bonds with people
C knowing how someone actually feels

4 When talking about online humour, Dr Stockley says that it is not clear whether
A a joke seems funnier when it is shared with other people.
B looking at amusing content online has any health benefits.
C people are telling the truth when they say online material is funny.

5 Dr Stockley's opinion was that Josephine
A was addicted to social media.
B spent too much time with other social media users.
C became lonely because of her use of social media.

6 What advice does Dr Stockley have for people who have relationship problems?
A search online for advice
B resolve them face to face
C talk to older people

7 What does Dr Stockley feel that online communication is best for?
A asking people to do things
B making arrangements
C keeping in touch

WRITING PART 1

EXAM FACTS

- *Writing Part 1 is a compulsory question. You must answer it.*
- *You must write your essay using grammatically correct English in an appropriate style.*
- *The question may take the form of a direct question or statement.*

EXAM INFORMATION

- *Remember to cover both points in the notes as well as your own idea.*
- *Look at the situation and write in a style that is appropriate to the question.*
- *Include an introduction and a conclusion. Your introduction should outline the main ideas of your essay and the conclusion should summarise these ideas.*

Write your answer in 140–190 words in an appropriate style.

In your English class, you have been talking about the role of the family. Now, your English teacher has asked you to write an essay.

Write an essay using all the notes and giving your reasons for your point of view.

Some people say that bringing up a child should be the responsibility not just of the child's parents, but also of the child's grandparents and other relatives.

Do you agree?

Notes

Write about:

1 the role of the extended family
2 effects of children spending time with relatives
3 .... (your own idea)

Write your **essay**. You must use grammatically correct sentences with accurate spelling and punctuation in a style appropriate for the situation.

WRITING BANK / Pages 234–235

REAL WORLD

MAKING FRIENDS IN ... SEOUL

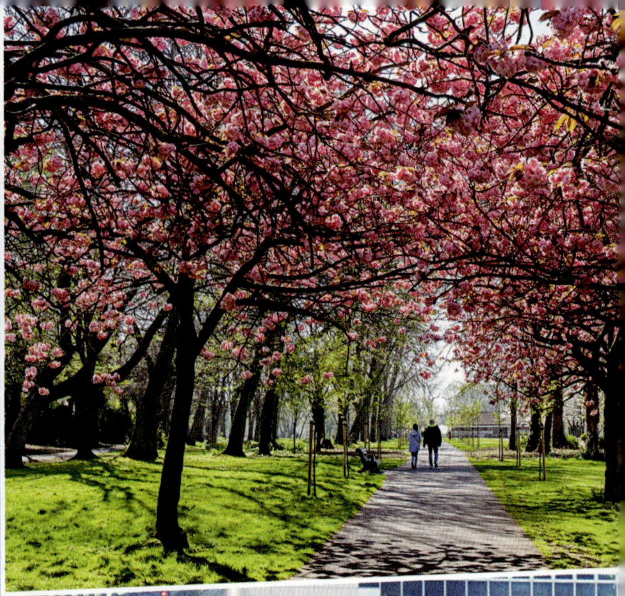

1 Look at the three photos of Seoul, the capital of South Korea. Work with a partner and describe what you can see in each photo. How similar or different is Seoul to your town or city?

2 Read about three ways of making friends in Seoul. Which have you tried? Describe your experiences with a partner. What other ways can you make friends in a new city?

A LANGUAGE EXCHANGES

Whether you're looking to improve your language skills or just meet people from another country, language exchanges are a great way to make new friends. By meeting native speakers of the language you're learning, you'll have the chance to pick up colloquial expressions that you wouldn't typically come across in a language course. What's more, they're free! They're usually held in cafés and restaurants so it's also a great way to try new food as well as practise your language.

B SOCIAL EVENTS

One of the best ways to meet new people is to join local clubs and events. What's great about this is the fact that you are doing something you enjoy, with the added benefit of meeting new people who you already have something in common with. Whether it's going hiking or playing football in the local park, you're bound to find something you like. There are tons of companies who set up events all over the city, and send weekly updates of what's on, so you can pick and choose the events you want to attend.

C CITY TOURS

If you're new to a city, then going on a city tour is the ideal way of exploring your new environment. Your tour guide will lead you through the city, sharing their expert knowledge and even showing you the hidden secrets and hotspots of the city that even the locals don't know about. The tours are usually free and most guides will ask for a tip at the end of the tour, so you can give as much or as little as you like – although it's always nice to give a little bit extra, especially for a really good tour.

3 **Find the words and phrases in the text which mean the following.**

1 learn something new (Text A) ....
2 find / see (Text A) ....
3 take place in (Text A) ....
4 advantage (Text B) ....
5 certain to (Text B) ....
6 a lot of (Text B) ....
7 perfect (Text C) ....
8 popular or exciting places (Text C) ....
9 a small amount of money (Text C) ....

4 **017 Listen to Eun-ju, who is meeting her language exchange partner, Simon, for the first time. Put the topics in the order they discuss them.**

Family
Hobbies and interests
Hometown

5 **017 Listen again. What phrases does Simon use to say the following things?**

PHRASES YOU MIGHT USE

1 Nice to meet you, too.
2 Really?
3 What other sports do you enjoy?
4 You're welcome!
5 I'll contact you.

6 **What does Simon mean by the phrase 'what a small world'?**

7 **Read the informal phrases (1–5) that people sometimes use when socialising. Match the phrases with the correct meanings (A–E).**

1 Long time, no see
2 What's up?
3 Ciao for now
4 I've gotta run
5 Catch you later

A I'm leaving
B Bye for now
C I haven't seen you for a while
D See you soon
E How's it going?

8 **018 Read the conversation below between two friends, George and William, who are native British English speakers. Match the underlined words (1–7) with the expressions (A–G) that have a similar meaning. Then listen and check your answers.**

PHRASES YOU MIGHT HEAR

George: Hey, how's it going?
William: Good thanks! **(1)** I haven't seen you for a long time!
George: **(2)** You're right. What have you been up to?
William: This and that. I'm doing a bit of volunteering at the moment.
George: No way! **(3)** Where are you doing that?
William: At the local animal shelter. It's been really enjoyable so far.
George: **(4)** I'm sure it has. Do you know if they're looking for any more volunteers?
William: **(5)** Actually, they are. Shall I **(6)** give them your contact details?
George: That would be great, **(7)** thanks!

A whereabouts
B pass your name on
C I bet
D tell me about it
E cheers
F as a matter of fact
G it's been a while

9 **Watch the video about Seoul. What do you learn about these things? Make notes.**

- The city of Seoul
- Famous districts and landmarks
- Places to socialise

WATCH

LIFE COMPETENCIES

MAKING DECISIONS, MANAGING CONVERSATIONS

10 **Plan a language exchange. Write down four activities that you can do together at the language exchange. Then work in groups and decide who has created the best plan.**

PROGRESS CHECK 1

PRESENT PERFECT REVIEW

1 Complete the sentences with the past simple, present perfect simple or present perfect continuous form of the verbs in the box.

be	buy	graduate	go
know	meet	reply	run

1. I ______ to a fantastic fish restaurant by the river last night.
2. It ______ five years since I last went to see a film at the cinema.
3. I sent him a text message the other day but he ______ yet.
4. You look exhausted! ______ ?
5. I ______ my first car when I was 19 years old.
6. She ______ Lucy for about ten years. They met in secondary school.
7. I ______ from university earlier this year but I haven't found a job yet.
8. I ______ a famous person before but I'd like to one day.

COMPARATIVES AND SUPERLATIVES

2 Complete the sentences with either the comparative or superlative form of the adjective in brackets.

1. During the summer, the weather in Spain is usually ______ (hot) than in the UK.
2. Personally, I don't think the film version is as ______ (good) as the book.
3. I find it ______ (easy) to write an email in English than to speak it on the phone.
4. One of ______ (bad) things about air travel is the turbulence.
5. Learning to speak a language is ______ (difficult) than learning to play a musical instrument.
6. I usually go to bed ______ (late) than my brother.
7. I think he's ______ (funny) person I've ever met!
8. I'd probably say that this one is ______ (good) option out of the three.

COMMUNICATION

3 Replace the underlined words and phrases with the correct word from the box.

delighted	disappointed	
shocked	upset	worried

1. They will be very surprised to hear that the fitness centre is closing down.
2. She was unhappy to hear that her flight had been cancelled.
3. They don't seem to be too nervous about the test tomorrow.
4. I was really happy when I found out I passed my English exam.
5. Sarah was really sad about missing her best friend's birthday party.

HEALTH AND FITNESS

4 Replace the underlined words and phrases with the correct word or phrase from the box.

ache	cut down on	keep in shape
keep track of	stamina	touch and go

1. I am trying to reduce the amount of sugar I consume.
2. My friend uses an app to monitor his heart rate before and after running.
3. I stay healthy by running twice a week and eating a balanced diet.
4. I can only run for about 20 minutes before my feet start to hurt.
5. It was uncertain for a while whether or not she would make a full recovery.
6. My nephew is so active, I just don't have the energy to keep up.

GERUNDS AND INFINITIVES

5 Complete the sentences with the infinitive or gerund form of the verbs in brackets.

1. I really want ______ (run) in the city marathon next month.
2. You should avoid ______ (eat) junk food if you're serious about losing weight.
3. I had to give up ______ (play) football after I suffered a serious injury to my leg.
4. I was thirsty so I stopped ______ (buy) a drink on my way home.

5 The fitness centre was supposed ________ (open) at 7 am but it was closed when I arrived.
6 If you don't eat a balanced diet, you may risk ________ (develop) health issues later in life.
7 My friend is refusing ________ (see) a doctor about the rash on her leg.
8 I always remember ________ (take) sun cream with me whenever I go on holiday.

COMPARING AND CONTRASTING IDEAS WITH LINKERS

6 Choose the correct option to complete the sentences.

1 I decided to go by car, *instead of/rather than* walk, because it was raining.
2 I really enjoy my job as a fitness instructor, *despite/instead of* the low salary.
3 *Even though/However* I'd trained really hard, I wasn't able to finish the marathon.
4 The fitness centre has a great swimming pool. *Even though/However*, it's currently closed.
5 *Despite/Instead of* going to the gym every day, why don't you save money and run around the park?

AN ESSAY

7 Read the essay and think of a word that best fits each gap.

Technology is having a negative impact on our health. Do you agree?

With the help of modern technology, such **(1)** ________ apps, it's never been easier to **(2)** ________ track of what you are eating and how much exercise you are doing. **(3)** ________ , levels of obesity in young people are higher than ever **(4)** ________ .

Firstly, a lot of young people are using their phones to play games, chat with friends and even go shopping. In the past, children **(5)** ________ to do these activities outside but nowadays, they can be done from the sofa. This can result in higher levels of stress and bad health due **(6)** ________ the lack of inactivity.

In **(7)** ________ , studies have shown that **(8)** ________ and more young people are becoming addicted to technology, especially computer games. This can lead to serious mental and physical health issues, not **(9)** ________ for the young person affected, but also the family. Therefore, it is vital to spot the symptoms early to avoid serious problems in the future.

(10) ________ though technology has improved our lives in many ways, I believe that it's important that we don't become too dependent on it for the sake of our health.

PASSIVE

8 Rewrite the sentences in the passive form.

1 James Richardson wrote the book "Best of Friends" in 2009.
The book "Best of Friends" was written in 2009 (by James Richardson) .
2 I haven't cleaned the car yet.
____
3 My dad is fixing my bike.
____
4 Peter might have broken the window.
____
5 The company offered her a job in New York.
____
6 Despite the good weather, the organisers cancelled the concert.
____
7 A friend of mine gave me your contact information.
____
8 The consultant is supposed to give the training tomorrow.
____

USED TO / WOULD / BE USED TO / GET USED TO

9 Correct the mistakes in the sentences.

1 I used go with my family to the park every weekend.
2 My friends and I would to meet in the shopping centre close to my house.
3 I'm not used to live in a big city as I grew up in a small village.
4 I didn't used to like mushrooms, but now I love them.
5 Did use to you have a pet when you were younger?
6 We would live in New York when I was a kid.
7 I am slowly get used to my new life in Spain.

FRIENDS AND FAMILY

10 Match the words in the box with the correct meanings.

extended family	father-in-law/mother-in-law
half-sister/half-brother	niece/nephew
stepdaughter/stepson	widow

1 the child of your husband or wife from a previous marriage
2 a person whose husband or wife has died and who hasn't remarried
3 the sibling who is the child of only one of your parents
4 your grandparents, aunts, uncles and cousins, for example
5 the parents of your wife or husband
6 the child of your brother or sister

3 BEYOND THE CLASSROOM

Virtual reality learning

GETTING STARTED

1 Look at the photographs and answer the questions.

1. Which of these ways of learning have you experienced?
2. What are the advantages and disadvantages of each of these learning experiences?
3. How can virtual reality be used in the following industries:
   Healthcare Tourism Automotive

READING AND USE OF ENGLISH PART 5 TRAINING

1 Read the text on page 43 quickly. Which ways of learning are mentioned?

2 Read question 1 and the four options (A–D). It mentions a specific name, Ted Milmorrow. Find the paragraph that first introduces him. Then consider each option and answer the question. Which option, A–D, is correct?

1 How does Ted Milmorrow feel about the new technology?

- **A** concerned that it isn't realistic enough
- **B** frustrated that it's taken so long to develop
- **C** worried that surgeons won't want to use it
- **D** unsure that it will work in practice

Option A: What is Ted doing when he says *'Oh don't worry, it only looks realistic'*? Is this showing *concern*?
Option B: When Ted talks about the latest technology, what word is used to describe how it started? Is this similar to the word *frustrated*?
Option C: What phrase does Ted use to talk about the surgeons attitude to using the new technology? Is this the same as *worried*?
Option D: What adjective does Ted use to describe the potential of the new technology in the final sentence of the paragraph? Is this similar to being *unsure*?

Collaborative learning

Blended learning

Distance learning

Traditional classroom education

On the job training

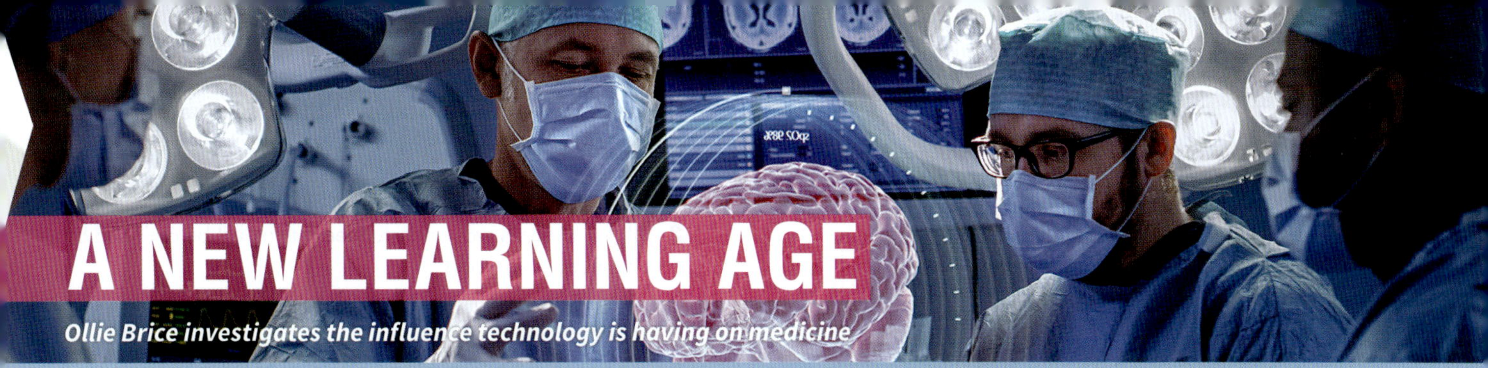

A NEW LEARNING AGE

Ollie Brice investigates the influence technology is having on medicine

When Ted Milmorrow, chief medical trainer at the prestigious Queen's College of Surgeons, asked if I wanted to witness open heart surgery, I was less than enthusiastic. The sight of blood has always made me nauseous. Ted chuckled when I expressed my concerns. 'Oh, don't worry', he smiled, 'it only looks realistic'. He then stopped smiling and explained that, following an irritatingly slow start, the health industry is testing the latest in technological devices to transform training for medical staff, a much needed development, he says. 'Surgeons need practical as well as theoretical training and are passionate about using the technology, which has the potential to provide invaluable hands-on experience, without the need to practise on patients.'

One of the devices Queen's College of Surgeons is hoping to take advantage of is mixed reality headsets. These show three-dimensional images which surround the user so that they are completely involved in the experience. Providing all goes as planned, the aim of this immersive technology is for the headset to create holograms, which are so realistic that students are able to practise surgical procedures in real time. If holograms can be used, then there wouldn't be any further need for cadavers – the dead bodies typically used for this area of medical training. The learning experience will be further boosted by the development of devices which let the wearers experience other senses, such as touch.

After a tour of this stunning institution, I was introduced to a headset-wearing trainee who was clearly enjoying the experience. 'It's incredible and far more realistic than I'd ever imagined.' It's obvious the student looks up to Ted, whose commitment to the project is inspiring. Ted and I take a seat, and he reminds me that this really is quite momentous. 'It's huge, if you stop and think about it.' Having seen it in action, I can't help but agree with him.

I'm then introduced to Tony Reed, head of the public relations team, whose main responsibility is to promote the new technology. 'The hardest thing for us at the moment is convincing people that using immersive technology in the development of medical training is a worthwhile cause', he explains. I can easily see how ***this*** might prove challenging, given the fact that there is *line 36* considerable nervousness when it comes to change, especially when the change in question has the potential to affect people's lives. But then again, why shouldn't healthcare take advantage of the latest in technological breakthroughs, much like the financial and automotive industries have done?

I then discover that it isn't all as new as I'd originally thought. Carol Brigsea, a leading surgeon and forward thinker in medical training techniques, has already taught her trainees by live-streaming an operation using a similar technological device. More recently, her undergraduates witnessed the first 360-degree online video of an operation. Her vision has, for some time, been to shake up surgical training and substitute traditional approaches, where students in the operating theatre can barely see surgical procedures, with these new types of learning methods.

It remains to be seen whether teachers teaching lessons in traditional classrooms will be completely replaced or not. However, attitudes towards conventional teaching methods appear to be changing. I come away with the feeling that immersive technologies, like the 3D headset, will undoubtedly enhance learning beyond anything being experienced currently. It was tentatively suggested they might even be able to explore entire brains in the not-too-distant future, which would support research into things like dementia. The educational possibilities do seem endless, however, and not solely in the field of medicine.

3 Now read the rest of the article and answer questions 2–6.

2 What is the purpose of using mixed reality headsets?
- ***A*** to increase the number of procedures that students observe
- ***B*** to improve the speed of operations
- ***C*** to replace a traditional teaching tool
- ***D*** to allow learners to touch objects

3 In the third paragraph, the writer admires
- ***A*** the range of facilities in the college.
- ***B*** the student's enthusiasm towards the headset.
- ***C*** the willingness of the college to undertake a big project.
- ***D*** Ted's strong belief in the work he's doing.

4 What does *this* refer to in line 36?
- ***A*** convincing people
- ***B*** immersive technology
- ***C*** the development of medical training
- ***D*** a worthwhile cause

5 Carol Brigsea's idea of the future is that
- ***A*** operations will regularly be shown online.
- ***B*** medical education will be completely reorganised.
- ***C*** traditional teaching methods will be replaced.
- ***D*** students will see medical operations on bodies.

6 What is the main idea of the last paragraph?
- ***A*** Teachers will be encouraged to use more technology.
- ***B*** Medical students may no longer need face-to-face lessons.
- ***C*** Doctors could discover more about a major organ.
- ***D*** New technologies will change learning environments.

4 Work in groups and answer the questions.

1 Would you feel confident being operated on by a surgeon trained using a 3D headset?
2 In which other areas could this type of technology be used to improve learning?
3 Is virtual reality a useful way of learning or just a form of entertainment?
4 Do you agree there'll soon be no need for face-to-face teaching?

GRAMMAR

1ST AND 2ND CONDITIONAL

GRAMMAR ON THE MOVE
Watch the video

1 **Read the sentences (A–D) and answer the questions.**

A If you go to university, it'll help you get a job.
B I'd help you if I could, but it's just not my area of expertise.
C If I were you, I'd spend less time out with your friends and more time studying.
D If I come up with an effective study plan, I'll get the grades I need.

1 Which refer to something that is possible?
2 Which refer to something that is unlikely or impossible?

GRAMMAR REFERENCE / *Zero, 1st and 2nd conditionals: Page 210*

2 **Complete the first and second conditional sentences with a verb from the box in the correct form.**

lose	graduate	teach
retake	support	drop out

1 If I don't pass my exam, I ________ my scholarship.
2 Even if things were tough, I ________ of university.
3 I ________ you guitar if I were good enough.
4 If all goes to plan, I ________ from university next year.
5 I ________ my exam next year if I fail.
6 If you were stressed about the test, I ___ you.

3 **Find and correct the mistakes in the first or second conditional sentences.**

1 If I listen to music, it would distract me from my studies.
2 If the research was underfunded, I think it'll be criticised by the academic world.
3 If no formal training is given, I'll tried and get on an apprenticeship scheme.
4 I'll become a fully qualified electrical engineer if I could pass the final exam.
5 I'll become rich and famous if I will manage to start selling my artwork.
6 If the lessons were more interesting, I'd studying a bit harder.

4 **Match the sentence halves (1–5) with the most suitable endings (A–E).**

1 Unless I can find some online tuition,
2 As long as I can afford the university fees,
3 As soon as I've retaken my driving test and passed,
4 Provided I graduate with a good degree,
5 Assuming I can find a workplace apprenticeship,

A I'll be able to find a job in my chosen field.
B I won't go on to tertiary education after secondary school.
C I won't be able to learn the basics at home.
D I won't need to apply for a scholarship.
E I'll hold a licence and won't need an instructor.

5 **Work with a partner and answer the questions.**

1 If you could study anywhere in the world, where would you go and why?
2 If you could be taught by anyone famous, who would it be and what would they teach you?
3 If you pass the B2 First exam, how will you celebrate?
4 If you won 10 million euros, how would you spend it?

PUSH YOURSELF C1

OTHER CONDITIONAL STRUCTURES

1 **Complete the second sentence so that it means the same as the first. Use a maximum of five words, including the word in brackets.**

1 If you decide to go to university, I believe your opportunities will improve.
________ to go to university, I believe your opportunities will improve. (SHOULD)
2 Were the government to reduce education spending, fewer students would be able to attend university.
________ education spending, fewer students would be able to attend university. (IF)
3 Should you fail to get 70% or over in maths and science, you won't be accepted on that course.
You won't be accepted on that course ________ 70% or over in maths and science. (UNLESS)
4 If you got that scholarship, you could do your PhD next year.
________ that scholarship, you could do your PhD next year. (WERE)
5 If she passes the first round, she'll move on to a second interview.
________ the first round, she'll move on to a second interview. (SHOULD)

VOCABULARY

EDUCATION AND STUDY

1 Read the sentences and match the words and phrases in bold with the correct definitions (A–H).

1. I don't think I'll attend my **graduation ceremony** – they can just send me my diploma by post.
2. I can't believe I've **won a scholarship**! I don't think I would be able to afford the fees otherwise.
3. The class is taking place in the **lecture theatre** behind the sports field.
4. I've only got five hundred words of my **dissertation** left to write.
5. We've had a look around the university **campus**. The facilities are really impressive.
6. My professor has carried out a **study** on the benefits of experiential learning.
7. I'm going to have to **cram** for my final exam. It's in two days and I haven't even started revising yet.
8. If I don't pass this exam, I will have to **resit** it next year.

A to study a lot in a short period of time
B a celebration for when you finish your studies
C a long piece of writing on a particular subject
D to receive money from a university to pay for your fees
E a room or hall at university where you listen to someone speak
F the buildings and land of a university
G to take an exam again
H a piece of academic research

2 Work with a partner and answer the questions. Ask follow-up questions.

Have you ever …

- had to resit an exam?
- had to cram for an exam?
- attended a graduation ceremony?
- read or written a study or a dissertation on a particular subject?

P CONSONANT GROUPS AT THE BEGINNING OF WORDS

Sometimes learners add a sound before a consonant group or in the middle of it, which can create a different word.

3 019 Listen and choose the correct sentence you hear.

1. Where's the dress? / Where's the address?
2. That's a slow car. / That's a low car.
3. I liked the sport. / I liked the support.
4. I had an ice cream. / I had a nicer cream.
5. There's a spot over there. / There's a pot over there.

DID YOU KNOW?

In the UK, the place where people study for an undergraduate degree is called a *university*. In the USA, it is known as a *college*.

WRITING

UNDERSTANDING HOW YOU'RE ASSESSED IN THE B2 FIRST WRITING EXAM

1 Decide if the following statements are true or false.

1. My writing is assessed only on how accurate my grammar and vocabulary are.
2. It doesn't matter if I haven't answered all the points in the question, as long as I write the correct number of words.
3. How I organise my answer is important and I will lose marks if there are not clear links between the sentences and paragraphs.
4. It doesn't matter if I write in a formal or informal style as long as the language is correct and I answer the question.

2 Match the four assessment criteria (1–4) with the descriptions (A–D).

1. Content ....
2. Communicative achievement ....
3. Organisation ....
4. Language ....

A how accurate and appropriate the language is, for example, correct use of tenses, complex sentence structures, correct choice of vocabulary and correct spelling

B how logically the writing is presented and structured, for example, the correct use of paragraphs and having an appropriate beginning, middle and end

C how effective the writing style is for the task, for example if it is formal or informal

D how fully the question has been answered, for example, the correct number of words and writing about what the question has asked

3 Look at the following Part 2 task and the candidate's answer. For each of the four criteria in exercise 2, find at least one example in the candidate's writing which could be improved.

You have received an email from your friend, Annie Jones:

> I want to improve my English skills but I don't know how. I remember you said you'd been studying English so could you give me some advice? What if I watched more TV? And, how about practice? I'm not sure I'm doing enough of that. It'll be great to hear your ideas and don't forget to let me know how your studies are going.

Write your email. You should write 140–190 words.

Candidate's answer

Dear Mrs Jones,

If you don't like watching television, I would certainly recommend it to help improve your English. Moreover, you can watch shows with English subtitles which will also help you with difficult words and phrases. My mum actually bought a new television last week, which is great.

With reference to practice, I would definitely suggest sign up to language learning websites. They give you the chance to practice your listening skills through webiners and check your written work with native speakers and practise your reading skills with daily articles. A friend of mine has been doing this for the past two months and she loves it!

Let me know how you get on. It's great to hear from you and I'd be more than happy to give you some advise.

Yours sincerely,

Marcello Pinotti

4 What areas does Marcello need to work on? Work in pairs and rewrite the letter, making the improvements you've identified.

5 Now individually, answer the following question.

You have received an email from your English-speaking friend, Adele.

> Hi!
>
> I've recently started an English course and we're doing a project about learning a foreign language. I know you said you've been studying English and so could you help me? What's the most difficult thing about learning English and what's the easiest? What's the best way to improve your speaking skills? Anyway, it'll be great to hear your experiences and don't forget to let me know how your studies are going.

Write your email. You should write 140–190 words.

6 Assess your writing and then assess your partner's writing. Give them some advice on two things they could improve.

LISTENING PART 1 TRAINING

1 **Answer the questions.**

1. What complaints might a student have about a classmate or a teacher?
2. What's the difference between complaining *to* someone and complaining *about* someone?

2 **Read the extract and choose the correct option, A, B or C. Why are the other two options incorrect? Underline the words and phrases that helped you decide.**

You will hear two friends talking about university life.
Who is Adira complaining about?

A a classmate **B** a lecturer **C** a tutor

Veronica: Hey Adira, how did it go?
Adira: Not good. I just couldn't follow her ideas.
Veronica: Why not?
Adira: Well, it's not just me; the other students on the course didn't understand her either. I know she's supposed to be an expert in her field, and she's carried out loads of research, but nevertheless…
Veronica: Have you spoken to your tutor about her?
Adira: Yes, I told her I wasn't happy, and she was helpful. She gave me some useful websites, where I could look the subject up online, and suggested that might help me understand more clearly. I'm going to try it.

3 **Now listen. For questions 1–3, choose the best answer (A, B or C).**

1. 020 You will hear two colleagues talking at work. What does Frank recommend?
   A a course that is partly online and partly in the classroom
   B a traditional course in a classroom
   C a course that is completely online
2. 021 You will hear two students talking about a university that they are thinking of going to. What do they both say about it?
   A The accommodation isn't in a convenient location.
   B The university buildings are outdated.
   C The courses are too expensive.
3. 022 You will hear a man talking to his friend on the phone. Why is he phoning?
   A to describe a problem
   B to get some advice
   C to confirm an arrangement

VOCABULARY

IDIOMS AND PHRASAL VERBS

1 **Read what two students have said about their studies. Are you similar to Phil or Ingrid? Why?**

Phil

So, I took my final English exam last week and I **passed with flying colours**. As you can imagine, I'm **over the moon**! It wasn't easy though. I did have to **pull a few all-nighters**, especially the week before the exam. I spent that week reading a book on English grammar and trying to **learn** all the tenses **by heart**. It's a bit of an **old-school** method, I know, but I found it really useful.

Ingrid

I loved my time at school. My friends would say that I was a **bookworm** because I'd spend all my free time reading. That didn't stop them from stealing my answers in class, though. They were such **copycats**! The teacher said some of my project work really **stood out** from the others. I wouldn't say I was the **teacher's pet** or anything, but I loved all of my lessons and often **went the extra mile** on homework assignments.

2 **In pairs, choose either Ingrid or Phil and, using the context to help you, write down what you think the phrases in bold mean. Then, change partners and see if you agree.**

3 **Complete the questions with the idioms in Exercise 1, using the correct form. There may be more than one possible answer.**

1. Have you ever had to .... before an important exam or deadline?
2. Would you ever send out paper invitations for a party or is that a bit .... ?
3. When was the last time you went .... for someone?
4. Have you ever passed an exam .... ?
5. Would you describe yourself or anyone you know as a .... ?
6. Have you or anyone you know completed a piece of work that .... from all the rest?

4 **Work in pairs and answer the questions in Exercise 3.**

5 **Write a paragraph to describe your experiences of studying. Use at least five of the idioms. Then, share your paragraph with your partner. How similar or different are they?**

GRAMMAR

GIVING ADVICE

GRAMMAR ON THE MOVE
Watch the video

1 Complete the sentences with the words and phrases in the box.

might want/like	make sure	ought to
recommend	would	could try

1 You _______ find someone in the same field. They'll be able to give you lots of advice.
2 _______ you take notes during the lecture. You'll need them after to write your essay.
3 I _______ suggest talking to a number of people who've already taken the exam.
4 You _______ to check with your tutor before submitting the completed coursework online.
5 I'd _______ using a monolingual dictionary when studying English.
6 You _______ enrolling on a blended-learning course which combines classroom and online study.

➡ **GRAMMAR REFERENCE** / *Giving advice: Page 211*

2 Rewrite the sentences using the phrases in bold so that they have the same meaning.

1 How about using a spell checker on your report?
might want to
____

2 I'd recommend specialising in a particular field of education.
ought to
____

3 It's important that you check with your lecturer first.
had better
____

4 You really shouldn't miss the cut-off date for your coursework submission.
whatever you do
____

5 We might want to highlight the effect of using virtual reality in the classroom.
What if
____

➡ **GRAMMAR REFERENCE** / *Giving advice: common mistakes: Page 211*

3 Find and correct the five mistakes in the conversation between two lecturers.

Isabella: I'm trying to organise an overseas trip for our final year students but I've run into a few problems. Would you mind helping me out?
Martin: Not at all.
Isabella: Well, first, I can't decide where the best place to go is.
Martin: Why not to create a poll and list 10 places for people to vote for and choose the most popular?
Isabella: Good idea! Provided I can work out the technology, I could easily set that up. Do you have any ideas about finding the best accommodation?
Martin: You ought look at a few comparison websites. They'll have lots of reviews as well as offers for large groups. Although on second thoughts, made sure you don't book the hotel before asking the students first. Furthermore, you better ask the students about how much they want to spend, otherwise they might not be able to afford it!
Isabella: Thanks Martin! Should you thinking about a career as a travel agent.

4 Work in pairs. Read the issues that some students are having and then role play giving advice.

Josh
I'm a student at university and I don't have enough money to go out with my friends at the weekend.

Tiffany
I'm in my final year at school and I'm really struggling to revise for my English language exam. I just don't know how to study effectively when I'm outside of the class.

Erin
I've left home to study abroad and I'm finding it hard to adapt to the new culture. Everything's just so different. I know it's a great opportunity but I'm terribly homesick.

Kim
I've got to hand my assignment in next week and I just don't know how I'm going to get it finished on time. I can't afford to miss the deadline as it'll affect my grades which are already on the low side.

SPEAKING PART 3 TRAINING

1 **Read the following three case studies and give advice on the most suitable type of course or training from the options in the box.**

Volunteering	On-the-job training
Distance learning	Traditional education
Apprenticeship	

1 **MANUELA** works full-time for an accountancy company as an administrative assistant. She wants to study to become a qualified accountant. Although she can't afford to give up work and study full-time, her employer is really supportive.

2 **BELLA** is passionate about learning. She has just graduated from university and passed all her exams with flying colours. She's been trying to get a job in the education sector, but fears her lack of experience is holding her back. She's working part-time in a café and shares a flat with two others. She recently spent six months in Africa helping to build a new school for the local children.

3 **IAN** is retired. He is bored at home and is in need of a challenge. He didn't like school much but realises things have changed since he was there. He loves technology and enjoys developing new skills. He wants to learn to play the guitar.

2 **Read the short dialogue between Faye and Ryan. Which one of the five options in the box in Exercise 1 are they discussing?**

Faye: Shall we start with this one? I think it would be suitable for someone who's quite self-motivated and who doesn't need much face-to-face interaction. Perhaps they've finished tertiary education. What do you think?

Ryan: Yes, that's a good point and I'd add that it would probably benefit someone who needs some flexibility; perhaps they have to look after their children and would prefer to study from home. Ok, I think we've covered that one. Shall we move onto the next one?

3 **Underline the two phrases in Exercise 2 used to say an option is about to be discussed and circle the phrase Ryan uses to agree with Faye.**

4 **023 Listen to the rest of the conversation and put the four remaining options in the order they are discussed.**

5 **023 Listen again and decide who says each of the phrases to agree and disagree (1–6). Write F (Faye) or R (Ryan) next to each phrase.**

1. I'm not sure I'm in complete agreement.
2. Yes, I take your point.
3. I couldn't agree more.
4. I think you're absolutely right about that.
5. I agree up to a point.
6. I'd go along with that.

6 **024 Now Faye and Ryan must decide which they think is the best way for a mature student to learn. Listen and answer the questions.**

1. What phrase is used to indicate they're making a decision?
2. What phrase is used to refer to what's already been said?
3. How do they agree or disagree?

7 **Work with a partner and answer the question. Use the options and decide which is the most important.**

Is it important for people to learn a foreign language?

travel	**work**	**making new friends**
culture	**studying abroad**	

SPEAKING PART 4 TRAINING

8 **Work in pairs and talk about the sentences (1–5). Student A must argue in favour and Student B must argue against.**

1. Learning a second language is unnecessary in today's world.
2. The only way to learn a language effectively is in the classroom with a teacher.
3. It's impossible to get a good job if you don't go to university.
4. It should be compulsory for all students to wear a school uniform.
5. It doesn't matter if some languages are allowed to die out.

9 **Change partners. Take it in turns to ask and answer the Speaking Part 4 questions (1–5).**

1. Some people believe that it isn't necessary to learn a second language in today's world. What do you think?
2. Is it true that the best way to learn a language is in a class with a teacher? Why? / Why not?
3. Do you think it's possible to get a good job if you don't go to university? Why? / Why not?
4. Do you agree that all students should wear a school uniform? Why? / Why not?
5. Some people argue that it doesn't matter if some languages are allowed to die out. What's your view?

EXAM FOCUS

READING AND USE OF ENGLISH PART 5

You are going to read an article about becoming a teacher. For questions 1–6 choose the answer (A, B, C or D) which you think best fits according to the text.

Teaching young learners

Reporter Lauren Hobbs reveals the barriers to training Early Years Teachers

Before becoming a journalist, I was a nursery school teacher. My decision to quit wasn't to do with the actual teaching itself, rather the poor pay and working conditions. It came as no surprise to my editor then, that after reading the worrying findings from a detailed study undertaken by children's charity *Education for Children*, in collaboration with *Young Learners*, a fortnightly publication specialising in education for the under 5s, I was keen to find out more about the barriers to taking on and becoming a qualified Early Years Teacher, or EYT for short.

For the majority of employers who responded to the study, the main issue when employing an Early Years Teacher for the under 5s is the high cost of their salaries. I don't want to make them sound profit driven. They weren't. From their responses, it was obvious that they felt disappointed at being unable to offer wages which were comparable to those who had a graduate qualification. As one institution pointed out, 'the government wants to raise standards of pre-school education with graduate level staff, which is admirable, but I simply don't have the funds to pay the salaries they expect. It's very frustrating.' For the candidates who responded, there was a lack of interest in completing several years of training to obtain a qualification in an area which was poorly paid and with limited career progression, even though they understood the need to improve teaching standards. All of which I could relate to from my own pre-journalism experiences.

I interviewed Charlotte Raymond, policy advisor at *Educate the Children*, and posed the question, 'why does the government bother to encourage graduate entry when the pay simply isn't available?' She was **at a loss**. 'When children attend a nursery led by an EYT, they are 10 percent more likely to reach expected levels of development at age 5. Yet, there is a continued reduction in the numbers completing the training. I simply don't get why graduate teachers aren't paid what they are worth. It goes against everything we are all trying to achieve.'

One senior teacher explained that, although the qualification is not recognised by all elementary schools, they were not dissatisfied with the training, as they felt they were more fully prepared to enter the world of teaching. It gave those with the qualification the specialised knowledge to pass on the skills they had learnt, to help both children and teachers in the classroom, which might not have been possible if they hadn't attended.

Even with these benefits, however, many elementary schools felt they were prevented from giving jobs to those holding a qualification because they couldn't afford the cost. The majority of school managers without qualified teachers did, though, give their support to members of staff who wanted to pay for the training themselves, whereby **they** would allow time off to be taken for work placements in which teachers could develop their skills further. Of managers who did employ fully trained teachers, more than half employed a graduate because of their specialist knowledge in the field of early years development.

In excess of 350 people in the field of education shared their experiences of the barriers to university graduates entering the workforce. Clearly pre-schools and teaching staff, whether qualified or not, want to offer the best education possible. However, although it's been over ten years since I was where these teachers are now, the challenges are not dissimilar from those I faced, which sadly drove me from a career I had truly wanted to succeed in. While the sector is passionate about having teachers with the necessary qualifications and university education, it appears to be struggling to overcome the issues caused by lack of funding and status. And unfortunately, I can't see this changing any time soon.

EXAM FACTS

- *For this task, you read a long text and choose the correct answer (A, B, C or D) for six questions.*
- *The questions are presented in the same order as the information in the text.*

EXAM TIPS

- *Read the text quickly to get a better idea of what it's about.*
- *Underline the words, phrases or sentences that you think contain the answer to each question.*
- *The reference question may refer to a word or phrase before or after the pronoun, so check the information either side of it.*

1 According to the first paragraph, research was carried out by

A a charitable organisation.
B organisations working together.
C a magazine published twice a month.
D a group of Early Years Teachers.

2 What is the writer's attitude towards the employers in the second paragraph?

A annoyed that employers don't pay pre-school teachers higher wages
B regretful that employers don't offer teachers development opportunities
C sympathetic to employers and the reasons they underpay qualified teachers
D respectful towards employees who want to provide higher quality lessons

3 What is the purpose of the phrase *at a loss* in line 20?

A to indicate that Charlotte doesn't believe nursery schools are paying teachers enough
B to highlight that Charlotte doesn't understand why graduate numbers are going down
C to emphasise that Charlotte doesn't know how to answer the question
D to show that Charlotte doesn't think the question needs to be answered

4 When discussing training to become an EYT, one senior teacher suggests

A teachers can support colleagues following training.
B teachers are not happy with the training.
C more schools should accept the certification.
D the course is not suitable for all teachers.

5 Who does *they* refer to in line 32?

A government officials
B the majority of school managers
C qualified teachers
D members of staff

6 What is the main idea of the last paragraph?

A The writer interviewed a significant number of teachers and institutions.
B Nursery schools want to employ qualified teachers.
C The writer regrets giving up the job she loved.
D Nursery schools are unable to resolve the problems of poor pay.

EXAM FOCUS

LISTENING PART 1

EXAM FACTS

- *You will listen to eight short recordings of one or two people speaking.*
- *You must choose the correct answer (A, B, or C) for each of the eight questions.*

EXAM TIPS

- *Each question is formed of two parts. The first part tells you who is talking and what they are talking about. The second part asks a question that you must answer or starts a sentence which you have to complete. Read the question carefully before listening and underline the key words.*
- *You will hear each recording twice. Try to answer the question after the first listening and then check your answer during the second listening.*

025 **You will hear people talking in eight different situations. For questions 1–8, choose the best answer (A, B or C).**

1 You overhear two friends talking in a corridor. What did the man find difficult when he was studying Arabic?

A the grammar
B the writing
C the pronunciation

2 You hear a student talking about his future plans. What is he going to do when he leaves university?

A get a job as a teacher
B do voluntary work
C study to become a psychologist

3 You hear a man and a woman discussing the qualities of a traditional education. What does the woman think?

A Learning doesn't stop once children have left school.
B Children learn from a traditional education how to become good citizens.
C A traditional education provides more career opportunities.

4 You hear two students talking about one of their university courses. What do they agree about?

A how boring it is
B how difficult it is
C how relevant it is

5 You hear two friends talking at a graduation ceremony. Why didn't the woman want to attend?

A She didn't enjoy her time at university.
B Her family aren't there.
C She doesn't enjoy parties.

6 You hear a woman talking on the phone to her son. What does she suggest?

A he works harder at school
B he spends time with his friends
C he starts his next assignment

7 You hear a man talking on the radio about his job. What disappoints him about being a lecturer?

A the marking
B the salary
C the long hours

8 You hear a teacher talking about a colleague at work. What does she admire most about her colleague?

A His lessons are interesting.
B He gets enjoyment from teaching.
C He treats students equally.

SPEAKING PART 3 AND 4

EXAM FACTS

- *In Part 3, you are given a discussion question with five prompts. You must talk to your partner (the other candidate) and answer the question, using the prompts. After you've discussed your ideas, the examiner will then ask you both a question with the aim of reaching a decision.*
- *In Part 4, the examiner will ask you both more general questions about the topic presented in Part 3. The questions will focus more on giving an opinion than on giving personal information.*

EXAM TIPS

- *In Part 3, it's not necessary to cover all five prompts. The main focus is to discuss the question with the other candidate and keep the conversation going. Make sure to listen and respond to what they say – don't just wait to give your own ideas.*
- *You will not be penalised if you fail to reach an agreement with the other candidate at the end of Part 3.*
- *In Part 4, try to give full answers to the questions the examiner asks you. You are assessed on the language you use and not on your opinions or ideas. You may be asked questions individually or be asked to discuss questions with your partner.*

PART 3

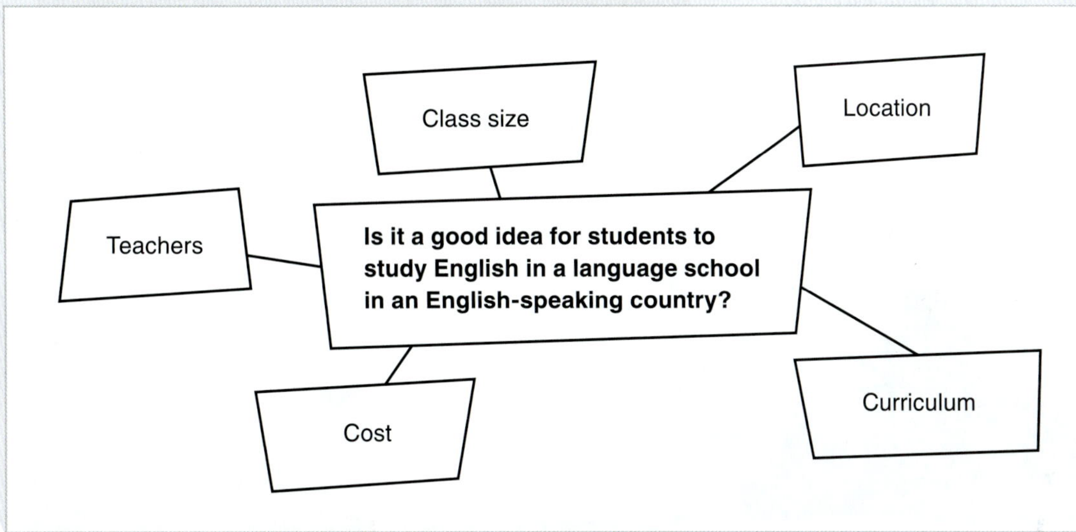

➡ **SPEAKING BANK** / *Pages 250–251*

PART 4

1. Would you like to study a language in another country? (Why? / Why not?)
2. Some people think that everyone should learn at least two languages. What do you think?
3. Is it better to speak one language really well or to be able to say a few things in several languages? Why?
4. Do you think school uniforms are a good idea? (Why / Why not?)

➡ **SPEAKING BANK** / *Pages 252–253*

EDUCATING YOURSELF IN … TORONTO

1 **What's the most interesting course you've ever taken? What did you learn?**

2 **Read about four courses (A–D) that you can take in Toronto. Rank them in order from 1 (the class you'd most like to take) to 4 (the class you'd least like to take). Then compare your ideas with a partner.**

A

Have you got what it takes to fly a commercial jet? Then sign up to our flight simulator course. Experience what it's like to be a pilot without any of the danger that comes with it. You will master the take-off and landing as well as learn how to deal with difficult situations such as turbulence and poor weather conditions.

B

Ever wanted to know how to prepare one of the most famous dishes in the world? Learn to make your own sushi with our highly-trained, vastly-experienced sushi chefs, who will teach you everything you need to know about this delicate dish. From choosing the perfect flavours to making dishes look authentic, you are sure to impress your friends with your new culinary skills.

C

Using a cross between a ski boot and a mini trampoline, Kangoo jumping is sure to give you a great workout. Originally developed for athletes, runners and joggers, it ensures a safer, easier way of exercising, giving you a unique feeling of walking on air while getting in shape at the same time.

3 **Find the words and phrases in the texts which mean the following.**

1. to join (a new course) (Text A)
2. to learn something really well (Text A)
3. real / not fake (Text B)
4. to make someone admire or respect you (Text B)
5. a period of physical exercise (Text C)
6. like no other (Text C)
7. to take a picture of something (Text D)
8. appropriate for (Text D)

4 **026 Listen to a student talking to a teacher about a course. Correct the information in the brochure below.**

CODING FOR BEGINNERS

Start date: March 15th (4-week intensive programme)

Course details

- Introduction to coding
- Learning to build a basic app
- Introduction to Python (compulsory)

Location: Room 40A

Price: $315 (price includes lunch)

Exam: Yes

Accredited by the school

5 **026 Listen again and complete the gaps with the words the student uses. You can use these questions to ask about a course.**

PHRASES YOU MIGHT USE

1. What is the ________ of the course?
2. What ________ are included in the course?
3. Where are the classes ________ ?
4. How much does it cost to ________ ?
5. Is there an ________ exam?
6. Will I receive a ________ at the end of the course?

6 **Some people believe that coding is the most important subject at school. Do you agree? Why? / Why not?**

D

Whether it's a delicious meal you've just prepared, a beautiful view you've come across or a family gathering you're enjoying, we'll teach you the skills you need to capture these perfect moments. We'll start with the basics, teaching you the importance of light when taking photos and what to look for when buying a camera, before moving on to taking more dynamic, professional looking photos. Suitable for all ages and levels.

7 **Sometimes people use colloquial expressions when talking about school and education. Match the phrases people might hear (1–6) with the phrases (A–F) which have a similar meaning.**

PHRASES YOU MIGHT HEAR

1. The course is fully booked now, I'm afraid.
2. You'll still be charged the full amount if you drop out at any point.
3. If you're into cooking, this course is for you.
4. Just pop your name down on this list.
5. Bear with me one moment, I'll check.
6. Would you mind giving me a hand?

A. You still need to pay in full if you decide to leave the course early.
B. Please wait a minute while I find out.
C. Could you help me?
D. This course is ideal for people who enjoy cooking.
E. Write your name here.
F. There aren't any places left on the course.

8 **Watch the video about Toronto. What do you learn about these things? Make notes.**

- The city of Toronto
- Famous landmarks
- Education

WATCH

LIFE COMPETENCIES

EVALUATING IDEAS, TAKING AN ACTIVE ROLE

9 **Read the descriptions of the two people below. Go online and find a course you think they would be interested in. Make notes about why the course you have chosen is suitable for them. Then work in groups and share your ideas.**

1. Davide wants to learn how to code. He doesn't have much money and would prefer a self-study course.
2. Julia has just won the lottery. She has left her job and now wants to learn how to cook from a famous chef. She is happy to travel anywhere in the world.

4 A TRIP TO REMEMBER

GETTING STARTED

1 Work with a partner. Look at photos A–F and answer the questions.

1. Which scene would you most (or least) like to be in yourself? Why?
2. Why have these people chosen to travel in these ways?

VOCABULARY

HOLIDAYS AND TRAVEL

1 Which of the photos show the following?

- steering wheel
- departure lounge
- commuters
- runway
- handlebars
- cockpit
- motorist
- backpackers
- rush hour

2 In groups, think of at least three ideas to add to each group below.

Flying vehicles: *jet*
Environmentally-friendly ways to travel: *driving an electric car*
Vehicles with four wheels: *van*
Parts of a car: *engine*

3 What kind of vehicle(s) might you be using if you were …

1. being welcomed on board?
2. filling up with diesel?
3. stuck in a traffic jam?
4. being overtaken?
5. pedalling?
6. getting jet lag?
7. in a carriage full of commuters?
8. taxiing on the runway?
9. listening to an announcement from the cockpit?
10. wearing a helmet?

4 **Complete the sentences with the words and phrases in the box. You don't need to change the form of the words and phrases.**

cockpit	motorists	overtaking	runway
commuter	diesel	jet lag	departure lounge

1. The ______ at Qamdo Bamda Airport in Tibet is 5.5 kilometres long; it needs to be this length to allow planes to accelerate enough to take off at high altitude.
2. A ______ is the area of a plane where the pilot and co-pilot sit, and is also known as the flight deck.
3. It is estimated that there will be about 2 billion ______ in the world by 2035.
4. Research shows the average American ______ spends 142 hours every year stuck in traffic.
5. Vehicles running on ______ are believed to be more harmful to the environment and members of the public than petrol vehicles.
6. Dangerous ______ is the most common cause of car accidents worldwide.
7. ______ feels worse if you are travelling by plane from east to west.
8. The first ever beach ______ has been planned in Barbados, where passengers can check in, pick up their boarding passes and relax until their flight.

5 **Four of the sentences in Exercise 4 are factually incorrect. Work in pairs and decide which four sentences you think these are.**

6 **Work with a partner and answer the questions about the sentences in Exercise 4.**

1. Have you ever been in a cockpit? Why?
2. Do you think there are too many motorists and too much traffic where you live?
3. What do you think are the most common causes of traffic accidents?
4. Have you ever had jet lag? Why did you have it? How did it make you feel?

LISTENING

LISTENING FOR DETAIL

1 **Work with a partner and answer the questions.**

1. Have you ever been to a theme park? What did you think of it?
2. What do you think makes a really good theme park?

2 **Look at three experiences available at the Velocity Valley Adventure Park. What do you think happens in each experience?**

3 **027 You will hear an employee at Velocity Valley Adventure Park talking about the three experiences (A–C). What is each experience called? Write the names in the brochure below.**

4 **027 Listen again and complete the notes (1–7) with a word, phrase or number from the recording.**

ATTRACTIONS

GETTING THERE

Leave the motorway and go along **(1)** ______ Valley Road. Velocity Valley can provide transport if necessary.

A THE ______

A professionally trained **(2)** ______ takes you at 100kmph. The course has some sharp bends.

B ______

Riders are raised **(3)** ______ metres in a harness.
Riders swing at speeds of up to **(4)** ______ km/hour.

C ______

This wind tunnel experience is described as a **(5)** '______'.
There is a **(6)** ______ to stop people from getting blown away.
Age and **(7)** ______ restrictions apply.

5 **Put the attractions in order from the most interesting (1) to the least interesting (3). Then compare your answers in groups.**

P

Some two-syllable words which have the same verb and noun form (e.g. *transport*) have a different word stress depending on the word form. When the word is a noun, the stress is on the first syllable. When the word is a verb, the stress is on the second syllable.

6 028 **Listen to the extract from the listening. Circle the stressed syllable in each of the underlined words. Which word is a noun and which one is a verb?**

If you don't have your own transport, we can pick you up, as we have a complimentary shuttle service which transports you between Rotorua CBD and Velocity Valley.

7 029 **Decide if the underlined words are verbs or nouns. Circle the stressed syllable. Then listen and check your answers.**

1. The travel agency has recently increased their prices. Because of this increase, many people have decided to book their holidays themselves.
2. Usain Bolt recorded a time of 9.58 seconds in the 100 metres sprint in 2009. This is still the world record today.
3. The airport transfer costs 10€. It takes about an hour to transfer you from the airport to the city centre.

8 Work in groups. You are going to design a ride for a theme park. Each group will design one attraction. Make notes as you plan your design then present your ideas to the class. Think about:

- The name of the attraction
- How it works
- Statistics (size, maximum speed, etc.)
- What it feels like

DID YOU KNOW?

When reading the numbers after a decimal point out loud, such as 9.58 in Exercise 7 above, we say each number individually. For example:

9.58 seconds *"nine point five eight seconds"*

14.253 *"fourteen point two five three"*

GRAMMAR

COUNTABLE AND UNCOUNTABLE NOUNS

GRAMMAR ON THE MOVE
Watch the video

1 Find and correct the mistake in each sentence.

1. My advice to travellers have always been to take out comprehensive travel insurance.
2. The last time we went away, we left it too late to find a self-catering accommodation.
3. We tried to find some subway station.
4. The latest news are that the travel company has gone bankrupt.
5. I couldn't believe it when the airline told us that they had lost our luggages.
6. Our tour guide gave us an advice about the best places to visit.
7. The travel has always been a passion for me.
8. There's often some traffic jam in my neighbourhood.

GRAMMAR REFERENCE / *Countable and uncountable nouns: Page 212*

2 Find the nouns in each sentence in Exercise 1. Decide if they are countable or uncountable and write them in the correct column. The first sentence has been done for you.

UNCOUNTABLE	COUNTABLE
advice *travel insurance*	*travellers*

3 Match the words with similar meanings. Which is countable and which is uncountable?

advice	backpack	congestion
dollars	luggage	money
scenery	suggestions	traffic jam
transport	vehicle	view

4 **Use the pairs of words in Exercise 3 to complete the following sentences. Think about**

- **the words' meanings (general or specific meaning).**
- **the words' grammar (countable or uncountable).**

1 I've always said that Wales has really spectacular .... In fact, I don't think there's a better .... anywhere in the UK than the panorama you get from the top of Mount Snowdon.
2 When I go travelling, I always take a few extra .... with me just in case because I'm always worried that I might run out of ....
3 Severe .... affects many cities; in 2010, Beijing experienced a .... that lasted for 12 days and covered a 100-kilometre stretch of road.
4 I usually hire a .... when I go on holiday as I don't like to use local ....
5 One piece of .... I would give to first-time travellers is to read travel blogs. They often have a lot of really good .... for things to do and see.
6 I've always been a believer in taking as little .... as possible when going away. I only ever take what I can fit into a small ....

5 **Complete the sentences with a word from the box. Sometimes more than one word is possible. You will need to change the form of one of the words.**

few	many	much	several	less

1 Even though I don't have .... money at the moment, I still enjoy booking trips away.
2 The hotel's in a great location and there are .... restaurants nearby.
3 I've noted that there are .... and .... hotels offering all-inclusive holiday packages these days.
4 Ever since they opened the new tram system, there is .... congestion on the roads.
5 There don't seem to be .... cafés around here.

6 **Think of a town or city you have visited. Write five suggestions or pieces of advice and tell these to your partner. Use one word from Exercise 3 in each sentence.**

You can avoid getting stuck in traffic jams by taking the underground.

PUSH YOURSELF C1

NOUNS THAT ARE BOTH COUNTABLE AND UNCOUNTABLE

1 **Complete the sentences with the words in the box. Add *a / an* if necessary. You may need to change the form of the words.**

business	competition	noise
paper	room	time

1 **A** I am going to Berlin on .... next week.
B I am planning to start .... with my friend.
2 **A** We still have .... available at the hotel.
B Unfortunately, there isn't much .... left at the hotel.
3 **A** It's difficult to sleep when there is so much ....
B I can hear .... coming from the street. I think it's a car alarm.
4 **A** Due to the increased .... , lots of hotels are offering more deals
B I won two round-the-world tickets in .... last week.
5 **A** He's just written .... on the importance of green tourism.
B I don't have any .... with me at the moment. Can I borrow some?
6 **A** Unfortunately, I don't have any .... to meet you this week.
B I've been to Croatia three .... already this year. I love it there.

2 **Decide which word is countable and which word is uncountable in each pair of sentences in Exercise 1.**

READING

1 **Look at the object in the picture. How would you describe it? What do you think it is used for?**

2 **Quickly read the text *Shweeb*, ignoring the gaps. Check your ideas in Exercise 1.**

Shweeb

To celebrate Google's 10th birthday in 2008, Google launched a competition which it called 10^{100}. **(0)** ________ of the public were asked to take part and **(1)** ________ suggestions for projects which they wanted to bring to life in order to make the world a better place. One of the winning **(2)** ________ was from a company in New Zealand called Shweeb. Their aim was to **(3)** ________ elements of the monorail together with those of the bicycle, and to produce a clean and fast vehicle, which could reduce congestion. In the end, Google **(4)** ________ $1 million in Shweeb's research and development.

The world's first Shweeb was built at the Velocity Valley Adventure Park in New Zealand. Riders sit in a capsule suspended from a rail, and pedal as fast as they can for three laps around a 200-metre **(5)** ________ . In the past, prizes were awarded to anyone who broke a speed **(6)** ________ , such as being the fastest rider from their country. However, the adventure park has recently stopped these records after upgrading the capsules to have electric assistance.

Shweeb has become a very popular visitor **(7)** ________ and time will tell if it may also be the **(8)** ________ of the future for commuters, business travellers and tourists.

3 **Would you enjoy riding Shweeb? Why? / Why not?**

READING AND USE OF ENGLISH PART 1 TRAINING

4 **Read the first two sentences of the text more carefully and look at the example (0). Then look at sentences 1–8 in Exercise 4 on page 57 again. Find the word from the list (A–D) below which is used with the phrase *of the public*.**

0	**A** Members	**B** Aspects	**C** Representatives	**D** Elements

5 **Match the sentence halves below. Then look at gap 1. Which word below has a similar meaning to the word *suggestions*? Which verb is used before this word?**

1 They've asked people to submit
2 I am going to apply
3 We want to encourage
4 I would like to approach

A more people to cycle to work.
B the company to ask for more money.
C ideas for a new amusement park.
D for a new job as a travel agent.

1	**A** submit	**B** apply	**C** encourage	**D** approach

6 **Read the rest of the text. Choose the answer (A, B, C or D) which best fits gaps 2–8.**

2	**A** offers	**B** statements	**C** proposals	**D** products
3	**A** associate	**B** improve	**C** attach	**D** combine
4	**A** spent	**B** awarded	**C** invested	**D** provided
5	**A** lane	**B** track	**C** court	**D** distance
6	**A** record	**B** list	**C** accomplishment	**D** statistic
7	**A** appeal	**B** recreation	**C** enjoyment	**D** attraction
8	**A** movement	**B** transport	**C** carriage	**D** motor

030 **Now, listen and check your answers.**

GRAMMAR

ARTICLES

GRAMMAR ON THE MOVE
Watch the video

1 **Look at the underlined examples (1–7) from the Reading and Use of English Part 1 extracts. Match the sentences with the correct rules (A–G).**

1 … such as being the fastest rider from their country.
2 … Google launched a competition which it called 10^{100}.
3 … in order to make the world a better place.
4 … after upgrading the capsules to have electric assistance.
5 … to produce a clean and fast vehicle …
6 … which could reduce congestion.
7 … In the past, prizes were awarded …

A *The* is used when we know who or what we are referring to.
B *a* / *an* is used with singular nouns mentioned for the first time.
C No article is used when using singular, uncountable nouns.
D *the* is used when there is only one of something.
E No article is used when talking in general and in the plural.
F *the* is used with superlative adjectives and adverbs.
G *a* / *an* is used to say what kind of thing something is.

GRAMMAR REFERENCE / *Articles: Page 213*

2 **Underline the correct options to complete the text.**

Home About Search

BEST HOLIDAY EVER!

When I was 14 years old, my family and I went to Cappadocia, which is **(1)** *a/the/(–)* historic region in central Turkey. Even though it doesn't have **(2)** *a/the/(–)* coastline, it is one of **(3)** *a/the/(–)* most popular tourist destinations in **(4)** *a/the/(–)* country due to its world-famous geological and cultural features. On our first night there, we decided to go to **(5)** *a/the/(–)* local restaurant close to our hotel. **(6)** *A/The/(–)* region is famous for Manti, a kind of ravioli, which was delicious. They were also showing **(7)** *a/the/(–)* football match, which was great as we love **(8)** *a/the/(–)* football.

The next day, we embarked upon **(9)** *a/the/(–)* trip that I will never forget – a hot air balloon ride! I'm a little afraid of **(10)** *a/the/(–)* heights, but my parents convinced me to go, and I'm so happy they did. The views were stunning, as you can see from **(11)** *a/the/(–)* enclosed photo. Our guide was extremely friendly, always saying **(12)** *a/the/(–)* right thing to keep us feeling safe. I would recommend it to anyone who loves **(13)** *a/the/(–)* adventure holidays!

3 **Would you like to visit Cappadocia? Why / Why not?**

4 **Complete the questions with *a*, *an*, *the* or no article (–).**

1 What is ______ best holiday you have ever been on?
2 If you could go on a trip around ______ world, which countries would you like to visit and why?
3 How much ______ luggage do you usually take with you on holiday? What are your three essential items that you always take?
4 Would you ever like to go on ______ cruise?
5 Do you prefer ______ active or relaxing holidays?
6 Where did you use to go on holiday when you were ______ child?
7 Some people think tourism is bad for ______ environment. Do you agree?
8 Is ______ pollution an issue where you live?

5 **Work with a partner. Ask and answer the questions in Exercise 4.**

VOCABULARY

COMPOUND ADJECTIVES

1 **Find the word(s) in the *Best Holiday Ever!* text on page 61 that completes the following extract.**

… due to its ________ geological and cultural features.

Compound adjectives

A compound adjective is a single adjective made up of more than one word. For example:

The tour guide was very friendly and ***easy-going****.*

Compound adjectives are usually written with a hyphen (-).

2 **Combine a word from column A with a word from column B to form compound adjectives.**

COLUMN A	COLUMN B
air	minute
cut	price
duty	time
last	conditioned
long	distance
part	free

3 **Now complete the sentences with the correct compound adjective from Exercise 2.**

1. Our hotel room wasn't ________ so we were really warm during the night.
2. I love going ________ shopping when I have free time at an airport.
3. My parents booked a ________ holiday to Greece.
4. I work as a ________ waiter during the summer holidays.
5. I don't enjoy ________ travel as I always suffer from jet lag.
6. My friend offered us ________ tickets for the trip. They were really cheap!

4 **Write five questions using the compound adjectives in Exercise 2. Then ask and answer your questions with a partner.**

SPEAKING PART 1 TRAINING

1 **031 Listen to an extract of Olek and Anna doing this part of the test. Which statements (A–D) describe Olek? Which describe Anna?**

Olek
Anna

A speaks English accurately
B uses a wide variety of vocabulary
C answers the examiner's questions, but doesn't develop the answers
D answers the examiner's questions, and develops the answers with explanations and extra details

2 **031 Listen again and write down the examiner's questions.**

1. Where are ________ you from ________?
2. What's the best ________?
3. What sort of ________?
4. Did you ________?

3 **Work with a partner. Ask and answer the questions in Exercise 2.**

4 **Write three questions for each of the categories below. Work in groups and take turns to ask and answer the questions. The first question for each category has been done for you. Look at the previous units to help you.**

SPEAKING PART 1

HOLIDAYS AND TRAVEL
1 *What's the most interesting place you have ever visited?*
2 ________
3 ________

HOME / DAILY LIFE
1 *What do you most enjoy doing at home?*
2 ________
3 ________

FRIENDS AND FAMILY
1 *Can you tell me about your family?*
2 ________
3 ________

EDUCATION AND STUDY
1 *How long have you been learning English?*
2 ________
3 ________

WRITING PART 2: ARTICLE TRAINING

1 Work in pairs. Read the following statements about writing an article in the B2 First exam. Decide which statements you think are true.

1 The article must be interesting for the reader to read.
2 The information you provide in your article must be true.
3 You lose marks for each mistake you make in your article.
4 Your article will need to contain opinion as well as facts.
5 It is worth memorising some articles by heart, as you will be able to use one of them in the exam.
6 You should try to demonstrate that you can use a wide range of grammar and vocabulary.

2 Read the exam task below. Underline the questions you must answer.

You see this notice on an English language website.

Articles wanted!

Terrible holidays

Have you had a holiday where something went wrong?

What happened?

How can people avoid having a problem like this when they go on holiday?

We will publish the best articles on our website.

3 Think of a time when something went wrong on holiday. Make notes, using the questions you underlined to help you. Then work with a partner and talk about your ideas.

4 Two students have written a plan for the exam question in Exercise 2. Which student has made the best plan? Why? How could the other one be improved?

Alex's plan

- my best ever holiday – trip to Spain last year with four friends
- my worst ever holiday – boring family holiday when I was 11
- different kinds of holiday – beach, backpacking, city breaks
- conclusion

Georgina's plan

- examples of holiday problems I've experienced (horrible noisy hotel, badly selected destination)
- my main point – careful planning should stop many problems from occurring
- conclusion – say how important it is for holidays to be successful (rest from work, family time together)

5 Match the beginnings of the sentences (1–4) with the endings of the sentences (A–D) which could be used in the article.

1 All sorts of things can go wrong
2 It's always worth doing thorough research before
3 Some of my holidays have been fantastic; others
4 It's vital that you have the chance

A you book a holiday.
B have been a disaster.
C to take a break from your work or studies.
D when you're on holiday.

6 Which sentence from Exercise 5 could go at the start of a paragraph which will …

1 introduce problems that can happen on holiday?
2 summarise the writer's experience of good and bad holidays?
3 recommend what people should do before deciding where to go?
4 explain why it's important that holidays are a success?

7 Write your own article for the exam question in Exercise 2. Use your ideas in Exercise 3 to help you.

EXAM FOCUS

READING AND USE OF ENGLISH PART 1

EXAM FACTS

- *In Reading and Use of English Part 1, you read a text with eight gaps.*
- *You must choose the correct word (A, B, C or D) which best fits each gap.*

EXAM TIPS

- *Read the whole text, including the title, first to help you get a better idea of what the text is about.*
- *Look at the words before and after each gap. The areas you will be tested on include collocations, fixed expressions and commonly confused words.*

Staycations

A staycation is a word sometimes used to refer to a **(0)** *period* of time when people stay in their own country, instead of travelling abroad on holiday, and take part in leisure activities close to their homes. The word is formed by **(1)** ________ the word *stay* with *vacation*, forming the neologism *staycation*. It **(2)** ________ a popular choice for people wanting to spend their time away from work or education, giving them the same **(3)** ________ of rest and relaxation without the need to spend large amounts of money on flights and hotels overseas. It also gives them a welcome opportunity to go and spend time at some of the tourist **(4)** ________ close to their home, something which they might not otherwise ever do.

That being said, a staycation isn't necessarily the most **(5)** ________ choice of holiday for everyone. For many people, the whole **(6)** ________ of a holiday is to visit towns and cities in other countries. Critics also argue that people find it difficult to **(7)** ________ themselves from their daily lives, particularly when they're staying in their own homes. For example, it can be **(8)** ________ to check work emails or even do the housework, things they wouldn't necessarily do while on holiday.

0	**A** period	**B** duration	**C** part	**D** point
1	**A** mixing	**B** securing	**C** combining	**D** attaching
2	**A** continues	**B** lasts	**C** remains	**D** endures
3	**A** impression	**B** mood	**C** emotion	**D** feeling
4	**A** pleasures	**B** attractions	**C** delights	**D** interests
5	**A** appropriate	**B** capable	**C** effective	**D** acceptable
6	**A** worth	**B** point	**C** profit	**D** aim
7	**A** distinguish	**B** split	**C** separate	**D** divide
8	**A** tempting	**B** desirable	**C** attractive	**D** compulsory

SPEAKING PART 1

EXAM FACTS

- *In this section of the exam, the examiner asks you questions about yourself.*
- *The questions are usually about your friends and family, interests, future plans, etc.*

EXAM TIPS

- *Answer in complete sentences. Don't give one or two word answers. Ask yourself why you think something or do something, and use the reason to extend your answer.*
- *You can ask the examiner to repeat a question if you don't understand something.*

Work in pairs. Take turn asking and answering questions from Part 1 of the B2 First speaking exam.

Hometown

Where are you from?
What do you like about living there? (Why?)
What changes have taken place in your town recently? (Are these changes good or bad? Why?)

Travel and holidays

How often do you travel? (Is that a good way to travel? Why?)
Is there a lot of traffic in your town? (Is it ever a problem for you?)
Where would you really like to go on holiday in the future? (Why would you like to go there?)

Free time

What's your favourite way to spend your free time? (How often do you do this?)
Did you do anything interesting last weekend? (What did you do?)
What are the sports facilities like in your hometown? (How often do you use them?)

➔ **SPEAKING BANK** / *Pages 244–245*

WRITING PART 2: ARTICLE

EXAM FACTS

- *You may be asked to write an article in Part 2 of the Writing exam at B2 First.*
- *You have to write between 140–190 words in the appropriate style.*
- *The Writing exam lasts 1 hour and 15 minutes.*

EXAM TIPS

- *Create a plan for your article before you start writing.*
- *Think of ways to make your article interesting to the reader. One way to achieve this is to use descriptive adjectives and adverbs.*
- *Allow a few minutes to check your work before the exam ends.*

Write an answer to the question below. Write your answer in 140–190 words in an appropriate style.

Articles wanted!

Your best holiday

We're looking for articles about the best holidays.

Write an article telling us about your best holiday.

Where did you go?

What did you do and why was it was such a good holiday?

We will publish the best articles in our magazine.

Write your article.

➔ **WRITING BANK** / *Pages 240–241*

A Palacio Barolo

TRAVELLING AROUND … BUENOS AIRES

B Caminito Street

C Casa Rosada

1 **Work with a partner. Compare the photos, saying what people might enjoy about visiting these places.**

2 **Read Maddie's blog post about her and a friend's visit to these three places. Which of the places, A, B or C**

1. seemed like a unique experience?
2. was difficult to find?
3. was quieter than expected?
4. provided a good opportunity to meet the locals?
5. is based on a piece of literature?
6. is close to a popular sports venue?

BUENOS AIRES, DAY ONE …

I can't believe we're finally here! Today was our first day in Buenos Aires, and I've got to say that it was AWESOME! Chantelle had read in her guidebook about this street called Caminito, close to where we're staying, with all these multi-coloured buildings. We did have a little trouble getting there, though, but that's only because we jumped on the wrong bus! It's also near the world-famous Boca Juniors football stadium. We managed to get tickets to a game and the atmosphere was incredible. Caminito is well worth a visit and it's popular with both tourists and locals.

Next on the list was Palacio Barolo. It's something of a local landmark and when it was completed in 1923 it was the tallest building, not just in Argentina, but in the whole of South America. So arriving by bus, it was hard to miss! We were prepared to queue for a long time behind hundreds of other visitors but there were only a handful of people there. The architect who built it was inspired by Dante's poem 'The Divine Comedy', and so different sections of the building are supposed to represent heaven and hell. It was amazing!

We then took the metro, and four stops on an eastbound train got us to Plaza de Mayo to see Casa Rosada, which is the president's mansion. I'd never been into a building where a head of state works or lives. In fact, there can't be many other places anywhere in the world where you can do this, so this was an opportunity we didn't want to miss. We joined a tour – it was in Spanish, so we couldn't understand much, but we got chatting to a group of Buenos Aires residents who translated the main things the guide said. I'm really glad we bumped into them, as we got to hear about some other places to visit in the city, including several that weren't in our guidebook.

3 **Which of the places would you like to visit? Why?**

4 **Replace the words in italics with the words Maddie uses in her blog.**

1. We did have a little *difficulty* getting there …
2. … we *got* on the wrong bus!
3. So arriving by bus, it was *easy to see*.
4. … but there were only *a few* people there.
5. … but we *started talking* to a group of Buenos Aires residents …
6. I'm really glad we *met* them …

5 **032 Maddie has arrived at Buenos Aires International airport and is about to fly to her next destination. Look at Maddie's boarding pass and listen to four announcements. Decide if the announcements are for Maddie or someone else. If they're for Maddie, what does she need to do?**

FLY AiR — BOARDING PASS

Passenger Name: MADDIE JONES

From: BUENOS AIRES, EZE

To: SANTIAGO SCL

Flight: FA 6509

Date: 10/03/2019

Time: 09:45

Gate: 14 Seat: 13B

ECONOMY CLASS

BOARDING PASS

Passenger Name: MADDIE JONES

From: BUENOS AIRES, EZE

To: SANTIAGO

Flight: FA 6509 Date: 10/03/2019

Gate: 14 Seat: 13B

Announcement	Maddie / someone else	Maddie needs to …
1		
2		
3		
4		

6 **032 Listen to the announcements again. Replace the words in *italics* with the words used in the announcements.**

1. We regret to *say* that this flight has now been cancelled. Please *go* to the check-in desk for further information.
2. This is an announcement for all *people* on flight …
3. Could passengers *sitting* in rows …
4. This is a *particular* announcement for passenger …

7 **Sometimes people use colloquial expressions at the airport. Match the phrases people might use (1–6) with the phrases (A–F) which have a similar meaning.**

PHRASES YOU MIGHT HEAR / USE

1. I have a stopover in …
2. Are you travelling with any hold luggage?
3. Have you left your bags unattended at any point?
4. Please step aside.
5. Please place all electronical devices in a separate …
6. Where can I pay for excess baggage?

A Could you just stand here?
B I have too much luggage. Who do I need to speak to?
C I have to wait for my connecting flight in …
D Did you leave your luggage somewhere you couldn't see it?
E Are you taking any bags onto the flight?
F Please put mobile phones, tablet and laptops in a different …

8 **Watch the video about Buenos Aires. What do you learn about these things? Make notes.**

- The city of Buenos Aires
- 9 de Julio Avenue
- Teatro Colón
- Palacio del Congreso
- La Boca

WATCH

LIFE COMPETENCIES

UNDERSTANDING CULTURES, PARTICIPATING WITH CONFIDENCE

9 **Go online and research other things to do in Buenos Aires. Organise a three-day visit and present it to your classmates. Decide who has arranged the most interesting trip.**

5 GRAB SOME CULTURE

GETTING STARTED

1 Walk around the class. Find someone who …

- plays a musical instrument
- has been to a music festival
- likes the same artist / music as you
- enjoys singing karaoke
- listens to classical music
- enjoys listening to the same music as their parents

2 Look at the photos. Why do you think these people have chosen to listen to music in these ways? Which do you enjoy?

3 Read the statements about music below. Do you agree or disagree with the statements? Discuss your ideas with a partner and give reasons for your answers.

1. It is good to listen to music while studying or working.
2. Listening to music can increase your intelligence.
3. The lyrics are more important than the beat of the music.
4. A musician is just as important to society as a doctor or teacher.
5. Music is a form of medicine.

LISTENING PART 3 TRAINING

1 You are going to complete a shorter version of a Listening Part 3 task. First, answer the questions (1–3) about the exam task in Exercise 3.

1. What is the topic of the listening?
2. What will each speaker talk about?
3. How many letters (A–E) do you need to use?

2 Before you listen, <u>underline</u> the key words in each option (A–E). The first one has been done for you. Then, look at the words you have underlined and decide what synonyms you might hear.

3 033 You will hear three short extracts in which people are talking about the benefits of listening to music. For questions 1–3, choose from the list (A–E) the benefit each speaker has experienced. Use the letters only once. There are two extra letters you do not need to use.

Speaker 1 ....
Speaker 2 ....
Speaker 3 ....

A It has <u>increased</u> my <u>creativity.</u>
B It has improved my concentration.
C It has made me more content with my life.
D It has helped me to make more friends.
E It has reduced my stress levels.

READING

GOING TO THE MOVIES

1 Work with a partner and answer the questions.

1 What was the last film you saw at the cinema? What was it about?
2 What type of film do you most enjoy?
3 Do you enjoy watching films from other countries?
4 How popular is going to the cinema in your country?
5 How would you feel about acting in a film or play?

2 Read the first paragraph of the article about a cinematic experience. What type of cinema do you think the writer is going to?

3 Look at the words in bold in the article. Work in pairs and decide the meaning of these words from the context.

4 Read the rest of the article and check your answers to Exercise 2. Then answer the questions below.

1 Why wasn't the writer optimistic about this type of cinema experience in the second paragraph?
   A because she had to dress up
   B because she felt she was spending too much money
   C because she was new to acting
2 What does the writer mean by 'think twice' in the third paragraph?
   A choose not to do something
   B consider something carefully before making a decision
   C think that something is a good idea
3 Who does the writer say would particularly enjoy this type of cinema in the final paragraph?
   A people who really like films
   B people who have been to acting classes
   C people who live in towns or cities

5 Work in pairs and answer the questions.

1 Would you enjoy going to this type of cinema experience? Why / Why not?
2 Which type of films would work well in this format?
3 Do you think this type of immersive experience will become more and more popular in the future? Why? / Why not?

CINEMA, but not as we know it

A friend recently asked me if I fancied going to the cinema. Being a huge fan of **the big screen**, I said yes straightaway. I usually go to the cinema once or twice a week, so it's normal for me to spend a lot of money on going to see the latest **blockbuster**. But when she'd asked me for £105 for one ticket, I was shocked. What's more, she said I'd be sent my personalised character by email. Character? Was I going to be in the **cast**? I prefer watching films to performing in them. And since when did it cost more than a hundred pounds to go to the cinema? That being said, my friend was really enthusiastic about it, so, reluctantly, I handed the money over.

After I'd carried out some online research into what I was spending my cash on, I realised that I'd signed up for an immersive cinema experience. This is a type of cinema where both actors and the audience participate in a **remake** of a classic film. Prior to the event, you receive information about your character and you need to spend time getting to know your new self. I was a little pessimistic at first, given that I had never acted before. I also found out that not only do you need to act like your character, you need to dress like them, too. That means, going out and buying a costume. But I was committed – if only because my ticket was **non-refundable**.

When I arrived, I was amazed at how professional everything looked. The **set**, music and lighting were all outstanding. I felt like I was actually in the film, which, of course, is the whole point of this experience. It was a remake of an old horror film, so everyone was dressed in scary-looking **outfits**. I'd thought mine was pretty good, but when I saw how much effort others had made, I felt self-conscious. If you don't enjoy dressing up, you may want to think twice about going. There was a mix of professional actors who played the main characters and members of the public, like me, who were given minor **roles** to play. The professionals were fantastic and really supportive. They offered lots of encouragement to all of us who were pretending to act.

If you ever see an experience like this advertised in your town or city, I'd highly recommend it, especially if you are a big fan of movies. Was it worth the ticket price? I'd say so, yes. Would I go again? Absolutely! But I probably need to go to a few acting classes first.

READING AND USE OF ENGLISH PART 4 TRAINING

6 **Complete the second sentence so that it has a similar meaning to the first sentence, using the word given. Write between two and five words.**

1 A friend recently asked me if I fancied going to the cinema.
BY
I ________ friend if I fancied going to the cinema.
Tip: What grammar structure is often used with *by* + subject?

2 It's normal for me to spend a lot of money on going to see the latest blockbusters.
USED
I ________ a lot of money on going to see the latest blockbusters.
Tip: Think about the correct form of *used to*

3 I prefer watching films to performing in them.
RATHER
I ________ perform in them.
Tip: Which verb + gerund/infinitive could be used that includes *rather*.

7 **For questions 1–5, complete the second sentence so that it has a similar meaning to the first sentence, using the word given. Do not change the word given. You must use between two and five words, including the word given.**

1 We went to the open-air concert despite the cold weather.
EVEN
We went to the open-air concert ________ cold.

2 The director had the respect of everyone in the play.
UP
Everyone in the play ________ the director.

3 Luke had not expected the film to be so good.
BETTER
The film ________ Luke had expected.

4 We didn't go to the cinema because of the train cancellation.
PREVENTED
The train cancellation ________ to the cinema.

5 There were very few people at the book club last night.
CAME
Hardly ________ the book club last night.

VOCABULARY

BOOKS AND READING

1 **Work with a partner and answer the questions.**

1 How often do you read books?
2 Do you prefer paper books or e-books?
3 What is the best book you've ever read?

2 **Read Lucy's description about a book she has read. Find phrases in the description which mean the following:**

1 I couldn't stop reading it: *I couldn't put it down*
2 from beginning to end: ________
3 extremely popular, having sold lots of copies: ________
4 a book that's very exciting: ________
5 made me laugh a lot: ________
6 difficult or boring to read: ________
7 to quickly read: ________
8 enjoying something so much you can't stop reading it; addicted: ________
9 a book or magazine you read before sleeping: ________

READER REVIEWS

I'd wanted to read some of the author's best-selling work for a while, so when I came across a little bookshop on holiday, which had a reasonably priced signed copy, I bought it immediately. I hadn't thought it'd make great bedtime reading – my friend said it was heavy-going when she'd read her copy on holiday recently, but not for me. I found it to be such a thrilling page-turner, I couldn't put it down. I remember I'd gone to bed at 10 pm, intending to flick through a magazine for 30 minutes, but once I'd picked it up, I was hooked. I read it from cover to cover, turning the last page at 3 am! I couldn't believe it! I had no idea I'd been reading for so long and it was so late – or early! The book has it all. It's not only exciting, it's sensitively written and funny too: the humour had me in stitches at times. Having said that, make sure you have plenty of tissues handy: the ending is a real tearjerker.

3 **Complete the sentences below with the words and phrases from Exercise 2.**

1. While I was waiting for the show to start, I decided ________ the programme to find out who was playing the lead role.
2. The comedian was hilarious. He ________ the moment he stepped on stage.
3. I found the book quite ________ as it was written in an old style of English.
4. I've just finished reading the ________ novel by Jane Smith. It was fantastic. I can see why it was top of the book charts for so long.
5. I read the whole book ________ in about a week. I plan to read it again next week!
6. The latest crime thriller by Thomas Moore is a real ________ . I can't wait to find out who solves the mystery at the end.
7. As soon as I read the first chapter, I was ________ by the author. I intend to buy all her work.
8. This book will make excellent ________ . The subject matter isn't heavy, and the chapters are short.
9. I hadn't intended to read all afternoon but once I'd started ________ .

P **CONNECTED SPEECH**

Often in spoken English, we connect sounds which are written separately. This linking typically happens when a word ending with a consonant sound is followed by one starting with a vowel sound. For example:

My friend said it was heavy-going…

It's not only exciting, it's sensitively written …

Practising this linking helps improve your speaking and listening skills.

4 **Read Lucy's description in Exercise 2 again. Underline the words that can be connected. Then practise reading the description, focusing on the connected speech.**

5 **Write a description of your favourite book and read it to your classmates. Include**

- who the author is.
- where the story is set.
- who the main characters are.
- what happens (a short summary).
- why you liked it.

GRAMMAR

PAST SIMPLE, PAST PERFECT SIMPLE AND PAST PERFECT CONTINUOUS

GRAMMAR ON THE MOVE
Watch the video

1 Read the extract from Lucy's review on page 71 and answer the questions.

I'd wanted to read some of the author's best-selling work for a while, so when I came across a little bookshop on holiday, which had a reasonably priced signed copy, I bought it immediately.

1 Underline the main verbs. What tenses are used?
2 Which order of events, A or B, is correct?
  A 1 wanted to read some of the author's work
   2 came across a little bookshop
   3 bought book
  B 1 came across a little bookshop
   2 wanted to read some of the author's work
   3 bought book

➡ **GRAMMAR REFERENCE** / *Past perfect simple and past perfect continuous: Page 214*

2 Look at the extract below and identify the events. Put the events in the order they happened.

I was bored yesterday afternoon. I had already been to the supermarket, cleaned the house and cooked lunch, so I decided to go for a walk around the park.

3 Complete the sentences with the correct form of the past simple, past perfect simple or past perfect continuous.

1 I ________ (never / be) to a music festival until last year, when I ________ (go) to one in England.
2 I ________ (think) about buying a new guitar for ages when, to my surprise, my parents ________ (buy) me one for my birthday last month.
3 When I ________ (arrive) for rehearsals, the band ________ (already / start) playing.
4 The audience were shocked when they ________ (discover) that Sam was guilty. Up until then, they ________ (think) that he was innocent.
5 The audience ________ (wait) for over two hours by the time the concert ________ (start).
6 A friend of mine ________ (recommend) the new John Smith thriller but I ________ (already / read) it the week before.
7 I was tired and hungry when I ________ (get) home because I ________ (cycle) around the city all afternoon.

4 Read about Micha's night at the theatre. Complete the gaps with the past simple, past perfect simple or past perfect continuous form of the verbs in the box.

be	book	manage	read	sell out	start

I was gripped by the classic novel and couldn't wait to see the play. It's a tragic tale of forbidden love, set in a small town in southern Italy. I couldn't believe that I managed to get tickets as I thought it **(1)** ________ months ago. On the night, the taxi that I **(2)** ________ the day before turned up an hour late but fortunately we still **(3)** ________ to arrive on time. We were allocated seats near the front of the stage. I **(4)** ________ through the programme for a few minutes when, all of a sudden, the show **(5)** ________ . During the interval, I grabbed a coffee and a small snack. I **(6)** ________ on my feet all day so it was good to sit down and relax a little. I then went back in for the second half. It was such a wonderful adaptation – the set design and the costumes in particular were stunning.

5 Have you ever seen a film or play based on a book you have read? Did you enjoy it? Why / Why not?

6 Read the start of two short stories. Choose one of them and finish writing the story.

1 I'd just been to dinner with a friend, but it was getting late and I had to get up early. While I was walking home, I saw a clown standing in a dark doorway. I'd never been afraid of clowns, but this one looked suspicious. He started hurrying toward me and…

2 I'd never been to see a live band so I was really excited when my friend managed to get tickets. We'd left early because we wanted to grab a bite to eat on the way. Just as we were leaving the restaurant we noticed a bag full of money. No-one was looking, so we…

The Legend of the Wild

'The Legend of the Wild' is one of the best games that I have ever played. This game is perfect for anybody who enjoys action adventure games. The graphics are spectacular and the storyline is first-rate. When I first got the game I wasn't able to put it down. In fact, even now I don't want to write anymore, so I can go back to playing it. A truly marvellous game!

◉◉◉◉◉

I was really looking forward to playing 'Legend of the Wild', and when I first started playing I was really impressed by the graphics. However, as a whole, the game is pretty monotonous and the overall experience is disappointing to say the least. I was left feeling frustrated by the storyline and the absurd missions that you needed to complete the game. I won't be buying another game in this series again, that's for sure!

◉○○○○

1 Read the short reviews. Work with a partner and answer the questions.

1. Why do you think the people wrote these reviews?
2. What do we typically write reviews about?
3. How often do you read reviews? Do you trust them?

2 Look at the reviews again and find the following:

1. five adjectives in the first review that mean *very good*
2. an adjective in the second review which means *it is boring because it doesn't change*
3. an adjective in the second review which means *when you feel annoyed because you can't do what you want to*
4. an adjective in the second review which means *stupid*

Reviews wanted!

The most interesting book I have ever read!

Have you read an interesting book recently which you couldn't put down?

Write us a review of the book. You should include information on:

- why it is interesting
- what it is about
- who you would recommend it to

Write between 140–190 words

3 Read the B2 First review of a book. Match the parts of the review (A–D) with the descriptions below (1–4).

1. This part of the review gives an opinion of the book and answers who you would recommend it to.
2. This is the heading. You should choose an interesting heading for your review.
3. This part of the review provides an overview and says why the book is interesting.
4. This part of the review offers a description of the book.

4 A positive review often ends with a recommendation. Tick the recommendation below which is grammatically correct. Correct the other sentences.

1. I suggest you to go out and see the film.
2. I would high recommend this book to anyone who enjoys thrillers.
3. I would urge you to buy a ticket for the film as soon as possible.
4. I advise yourself to go and watch the play.

5 Write your own answer for the Writing Part 2 exam task. Write between 140–190 words.

A ***Open Heart* – A must-read!**

B One of the most absorbing books I've ever read was *Open Heart* by Natalie Windows. It's a work of contemporary fiction, set in modern-day Peru. It deals with the concept of friendship and is also a tale of mystery and murder. What makes this book so fascinating is the vivid descriptions of both the characters and the places.

C The plot centres on two main characters who were adopted at birth. They meet and become friends. One day, tragedy strikes on an abandoned train when someone is killed and our heroes must find out who did it before they can return home.

D Overall, I thought this was a very well-written book. It is a must-read for anyone who likes a good thriller. It would make perfect bedtime reading as it's not too long nor too heavy. The only downside is there are lots of twists which made the storyline a little complicated to follow at times.

◉◉◉◉○

VOCABULARY

POSITIVE AND NEGATIVE ADJECTIVES

1 Decide if the following adjectives are positive or negative and complete the table.

appealing average confusing delightful
dense entertaining gripping hilarious
impressive informative predictable stunning

POSITIVE	***NEGATIVE***

DID YOU KNOW?

We use the word *sequel* to talk about a book or film that continues the story of a previous book or film. We use the word *prequel* to talk about a book or film that is set at an earlier stage of the original story but was made or written after the original story.

2 Complete the following sentences with the adjectives in the box.

~~appealing~~ average confusing
dense gripping hilarious
impressive informative predictable

1. The characters in the book were really *appealing* to me, as you felt a lot of sympathy for them and by the end of the book they almost felt like old friends.
2. The explanations in the book were too long, at 700 pages it was too ________ and could have been shortened by about 200 pages!
3. The film was totally ________ – you could tell how the plot was going to develop after only 15 minutes.
4. Overall, I'd say that the film was pretty ________ . I mean it was OK, but nothing special.
5. The book was so ________ that I couldn't put it down. I spent the whole night reading it.
6. The documentary was really ________ – there was a lot of information about the wildlife in Iceland that I would not have got from elsewhere.
7. We didn't stop laughing through the whole of the film – it was ________ .
8. The story was very ________ – I wasn't able to understand what was happening.
9. The graphics in the game are very ________ and they really helped you to feel that you were actually there.

PUSH YOURSELF C1

BUILDING YOUR VOCABULARY

1 Choose the correct collocation with the word in bold.

1. It was an **absorbing** *song/film*.
2. Although written 100 years ago, the poem has a **contemporary** *feel/sense* to it.
3. As an artist, he was known for his **vivid** *thought/imagination*.
4. The *novel/painting* **centres around** her journey of self-discovery.
5. The musician's life was touched by *personal/sympathetic* **tragedy**.
6. The film has an unexpected **twist** *at the end/at the beginning*.
7. The *article/theatre* is a **must-read** for anyone interested in drama.
8. The film has a *complicated/difficult* **plot**.

2 Match the words in bold in Exercise 1 with the correct meanings.

1. a very sad situation or event
2. the story
3. is the main subject of interest
4. something everyone should read
5. a surprising change
6. happening now
7. very interesting
8. producing a very clear picture in your mind

3 Work in groups and create the storyline for a film or book. You should

- say what the story centres around.
- say what the plot is.
- create an interesting twist in the story.
- say why you think your story would be a must-read or must-watch.

SPEAKING

REACHING AGREEMENT

1 **Look at images A–D. Which one do you prefer and why? Would you describe all these images as art?**

2 034 **Listen to two friends reaching an agreement before they leave an art gallery. Which image (A–D) do they choose?**

3 034 **Listen again and complete the sentences.**

1 We need to .... about which one to buy.
2 I thought I'd .... but I'm no longer sure.
3 You've .... several times.
4 I'm .... these two.
5 I .... I think the landscape is quite complex …
6 I'm not .... that one because the colours …
7 I'm .... on the price.
8 So should we forget .... then?
9 So, we're .... ?

> *Remember to use these phrases in Speaking Part 3, when you and a partner must try and decide on an answer to the question.*

4 **Match the phrases (1–8) with the phrases (A–H) which have a similar meaning.**

1 I've made up my mind. ....
2 I've changed my mind. ....
3 I'm stuck (between) … ....
4 I see what you're saying. ....
5 I don't follow you. ....
6 I'm in favour of … ....
7 I'd like to eliminate it. ....
8 Have we come to an agreement? ....

A I have formed a new opinion.
B I'm not sure I'm with you.
C I see what you mean.
D Have we made up our minds?
E I want to remove that one.
F I can't decide.
G I've reached a decision.
H My preference would be …

5 **Look at the words the two friends used to describe the photos. Match the words (1–6) with the definitions (A–F).**

1 vibrant
2 creative
3 distinctive
4 complex
5 contemporary
6 unique

A using new or unusual ideas
B existing or happening now
C using strong or bright colours
D unlike anything else
E easy to recognise
F involving a lot of different but related parts

6 **Work in groups. Look at the pieces of art (A–F). Describe each one and decide which one you think would be best for your classroom. Use the language in Exercises 3–5 to help you.**

EXAM FOCUS

READING AND USE OF ENGLISH PART 4

EXAM FACTS

- *In this part of the exam, there are six sentences, each with one word in capital letters.*
- *You need to complete the second sentence so that it has a similar meaning to the first sentence, using the key word in capital letters. You mustn't change the form of the key word.*

EXAM TIPS

- *It's a good idea to underline the words in the first sentence which correspond to the gap in the second sentence.*
- *Think carefully about how the key word is commonly used.*
- *Remember, you must write between two to five words, so make sure you count the number of words you have used. Contractions such as* ***don't*** *count as two words.*
- *Check your answers to make sure they fit grammatically.*
- *Check that you have covered all the meaning from the first sentence.*

For questions 1–6, complete the second sentence so that it has a similar meaning to the first sentence, using the word given. Do not change the word given. You must use between two and five words, including the word given.

1 He sings in the musical and dances in it as well.
ONLY
Not ________ in the musical, he also dances in it.

2 The author doesn't write as well as he did in the past.
USED
The author ________ he does now.

3 Our very friendly tourist guide showed us around.
SHOWN
We ________ our very friendly tourist guide.

4 Everyone apart from Steven thought it was an excellent performance.
PERSON
Steven was ________ not think it was an excellent performance.

5 The singer said it was harder to sing rock than most other kinds of music.
ONE
The singer said rock was ________ kinds of music to sing.

6 "Don't forget to pick up the tickets on the way home, Maria", said her husband.
REMINDED
Maria's husband ________ the tickets on the way home.

WRITING PART 2: REVIEW

EXAM FACTS

- *The main purpose of the review is to describe and express an opinion about something you have experienced.*
- *You must write between 140–190 words in an appropriate style.*

EXAM TIPS

Content

- *Make sure that you cover all the points in the question.*
- *Include both factual information and an opinion.*

Communicative achievement

- *Think about who is reading the review and adapt your writing style accordingly.*
- *Make sure your writing style is consistent throughout your review.*

Organisation

- *Make sure you divide your review into paragraphs.*
- *Use linking words to make your review easier to follow.*

Language

- *Use a variety of past tenses and descriptive adjectives and adverbs.*

Write an answer to the question below. Write your answer in 140–190 words in an appropriate style.

Reviews wanted!

A music event

Have you been to a concert or other musical event recently?

Write a review of the event explaining where it was, why you liked it and who you would recommend it to.

The best review will be posted on our website.

Write your review.

➡ **WRITING BANK** / *Pages 238–239*

LISTENING PART 3

EXAM FACTS

- *In Listening Part 3, you hear five short extracts, each with a different speaker. You need to match one option (A–H) to each speaker.*
- *You will hear each recording twice.*

EXAM TIPS

- *Use the time you are given at the beginning to read through the questions to understand what you are listening for.*
- *Underline key words and listen for how the same thing is said using different words.*

035 **You will hear five short extracts in which actors are talking about how to be successful in the film industry. For questions 1–5, choose from the list (A–H) what advice each actor gives. Use the letters only once. There are three extra letters you don't need to use.**

Speaker 1 ....

Speaker 2 ....

Speaker 3 ....

Speaker 4 ....

Speaker 5 ....

A Find out how other actors became successful.

B Invest money in acting classes.

C Get in touch with other actors.

D Be prepared for rejection.

E Don't be afraid to ask questions.

F Always be professional.

G Consider the roles you want to play.

H Find an agent you can trust.

MAKING ARRANGEMENTS IN...

BRISTOL

1 **Look at the images and the information about Bristol. How similar or different is Bristol to your own town or city?**

BRISTOL

Bristol's population is just over 450,000. It is the 8th largest city in the UK.

There are two universities in Bristol.

Bristol was voted the best city to live in Britain by a national newspaper.

2 **Read about the different things to do in Bristol. Which activity would you most like to do and why?**

BALLOON FIESTA

A must-see for anyone wanting to visit Bristol, this annual event attracts hundreds of thousands of people from around the globe, who flock to Bristol to see this spectacular hot air balloon display. Sit back and enjoy as over 130 hot air balloons, which come in all shapes and sizes, fill the skies around Bristol. Don't forget to stay for the magnificent nightglow display, when balloons are inflated and glow in the dark.

CLIFTON SUSPENSION BRIDGE

For those who are into architecture and engineering, don't miss out on visiting the world-famous Clifton Suspension Bridge. It was originally designed by Isambard Kingdom Brunel, who's considered to be one of the greatest engineers of all time, and first opened to the public in 1864. Standing at a height of 101 metres, visitors are treated to some of the most picturesque views of Bristol. It's a good idea to join one of the many guided tours on offer to get the most out of your visit, and don't forget to bring your camera along with you.

THE HARBOURSIDE

Once a busy spot for sailors and tradesmen, the Harbourside in Bristol is now home to a wide variety of galleries, restaurants, shops and hotels. The area comes alive in the summer months when visitors can take advantage of the numerous water activities on offer, including paddle boarding, rowing and yachting. There are even guided boat tours available on which you can enjoy an afternoon tea and take in the sights of the city from the water. It is also home to the Bristol Harbour Festival, a lively celebration of music, food and fireworks.

3 **Find the words in the texts that mean the following:**

1. a place considered to be essential to visit (Text A)
2. happening once every year (Text A)
3. known about by many people from different countries (Text B)
4. attractive in appearance (Text B)
5. a place or location (Text C)
6. many, great in number (Text C)
7. full of energy and enthusiasm (Text C)

4 036 **Two friends, who are studying in Bristol, are making arrangements for the weekend. Listen and complete the conversation to form questions for making arrangements.**

Joe: Hey Olivia, What are you **(1)** *up to* this weekend? I thought we might do something.

Olivia: Yes, that would be great – though I'm tied up on Friday night. It's my sister's birthday remember?

Joe: Ah that's right. Have you got any **(2)** .... Saturday? I thought we might go to the balloon fiesta. I've always wanted to see it.

Olivia: I've got a few things planned but I'm sure I could make time for it. What did you have **(3)** .... ?

Joe: I wanted to see the nightglow.

Olivia: What's a nightglow?

Joe: It's where a lot of the hot air balloons turn on their flames at night. It's supposed to be quite spectacular, with a really vivid display of colour. It starts at 9 pm.

Olivia: It sounds amazing, especially against the night sky, but I'm afraid I've got something on between 8 and 8:30 pm. I don't think I can make it for 9 pm.

Joe: Ah, that's a shame. I guess I could go with Tom. **(4)** .... you can't get out of it?

Olivia: Well, if I can, I'll let you know. Otherwise, I can meet you there a bit later, **(5)** .... 9:30?

Joe: Ok. That would be great. I'm sure you won't have missed much by then.

5 **Look at the underlined phrase Olivia used to talk about her availability on Friday night.**

Yes, that would be great – though I'm tied up on Friday night.

Sometimes people use informal or idiomatic expressions when making arrangements. Match the expressions from the conversation (1–6) with the correct meanings (A–F).

PHRASES YOU MIGHT HEAR / USE

1. I'm tied up on ...
2. I've got something on ...
3. I can meet you a bit later, say ...
4. I don't think I can make it ...
5. Are you sure you can't get out of it ...
6. I'm sure I could make time for it ...

- **A** How about meeting at ...
- **B** I don't think I can come ...
- **C** I'm certain I can find time for it ...
- **D** Do you think you can avoid it ...
- **E** I'm not available on ...
- **F** I already have plans ...

6 **Watch the video about Bristol. What do you learn about these things? Make notes.**

- The city of Bristol
- Famous ships
- The Clifton Suspension Bridge
- Festivals
- Music and art in Bristol

WATCH

LIFE COMPETENCIES

CREATING NEW CONTENT, RESPONDING CONSTRUCTIVELY

7 **Go online and make of list of things to do in Bristol. Then talk to as many of your classmates as possible and make arrangements for the weekend. Write your plans. Remember, you can rearrange your plans if you like.**

PROGRESS CHECK 2

CONDITIONALS

1 Complete the sentences with the first or second conditional and a verb in the box.

be able to | come | go | graduate | have | join

1 If I fail the exam next week, I ________ until next semester.
2 She would definitely study abroad if she ________ the opportunity.
3 If I didn't have to work in the evenings, I ________ a gym.
4 If you go to the concert tonight, let me know and I ________ with you.
5 Assuming he can finish his homework on time, he ________ to meet his friends.
6 Unless we can find a babysitter, we ________ go out tonight.

GIVING ADVICE

2 Correct the mistake in each sentence below.

1 You ought ask your teacher for advice.
2 You could to try doing an online class for extra practice.
3 He has better arrive soon or we'll be late for the seminar.
4 Whichever you do, don't cheat in your exam.
5 You might want try using a spellchecker to check your spelling.
6 I wouldn't to ask him if I were you. He's in a bad mood.

AN EMAIL

3 Complete Lisa's email with the words and phrases in the box.

campus | dissertation | graduation ceremony | lecture theatre | over the moon | pull a few all-nighters | tutor | volunteering

From: Lisa
To: Anna
Reply Forward

Hi Anna,

How are you? I finally got the results back from my end-of-year exams. I got 95%! I'm **(1)** ________ with the result. As you know, I wrote my **(2)** ________ on the effects of social media on communication. Well, my **(3)** ________ told me that it was one of the best he'd seen, which is great. I had to **(4)** ________ in the final week before the deadline but I'm so glad I did.

Anyway, the **(5)** ________ will be next Tuesday. I'm allowed to bring four guests. Would you like to come? It's being held in the **(6)** ________ behind the main reception, in the northwest of the **(7)** ________ . It would be great if you can make it and we can catch up on all your news, too. How is the **(8)** ________ going at the local hospital? Are you learning a lot?

Looking forward to your reply!

Lisa

ARTICLES

4 Find and correct the mistakes in each sentence. Two of the sentences are correct.

1 We had really great trip to Prague last month.
2 Dubrovnik is a beautiful city, located in a south of Croatia.
3 Overall, I was really impressed with the service at the restaurant.
4 An advice the tourist guide gave us was really useful.
5 My city has a big problem with the congestion.
6 Venice is one of the most beautiful cities I've ever been to.
7 I've been thinking about starting ice cream business.
8 Spanish is one of most widely spoken languages in the world.

COUNTABLE AND UNCOUNTABLE NOUNS

5 Put the words in the box in the correct categories.

advice | backpack | business | competition | congestion | luggage | money | noise | paper | scenery | traffic jam | vehicle | view

COUNTABLE
UNCOUNTABLE
BOTH

HOLIDAYS AND TRAVEL

6 Complete the crossword with the correct answers to the clues below.

Across

1 a line of cars close together moving very slowly or not at all: *traffic* ________

7 The thing you wear while cycling to protect your head

8 the place where you wait before boarding an aeroplane: ________ *lounge*

9 The busy part of the day when people are travelling to and from work

10 The part of an aeroplane where the pilots sit

Down

2 someone who drives a car or van

3 information you hear at a train station or at an airport

4 someone who regularly travels between home and work

5 the object in a car that you use to turn left and right: ________ *wheel*

6 the feeling of tiredness after a long plane journey

PAST SIMPLE, PAST PERFECT SIMPLE AND PAST PERFECT CONTINUOUS

7 Complete the sentences with the correct form of the past simple, past perfect simple or past perfect continuous.

1 By the time he ________ (arrive) at the cinema, the film ________ (already / start).

2 Julia ________ (never / be) to the theatre before, so she ________ (be) thrilled when her parents ________ (buy) her tickets for her birthday.

3 We ________ (sleep) for four hours when she suddenly ________ (wake) us up.

4 That evening, the children ________ (tell) their father which animals they ________ (see) at the zoo.

5 We ________ (be) disappointed to hear that the show ________ (cancel) because the singer was unwell.

6 They ________ (be) very tired in the evening because they ________ (help out) in the shop all day.

7 We ________ (visit) the exhibition that our friend ________ (tell) us about the week before.

8 Before she ________ (become) an actor, Melissa ________ (work) as a waitress for four years.

THE ARTS

8 Choose the correct word or phrase to complete the sentences.

1 It had sold 20 million copies, making it the *best-selling/best-seller* book of the year.

2 The film was *gripping/hilarious*. My friends and I couldn't stop laughing.

3 Personally, I found the ending really *confusing/entertaining* but everyone else seemed to get it.

4 From the lighting to the stage design, the whole *cast/set* was incredible.

5 The book was so *compelling/dull* that I just couldn't put it down.

6 The play was so *absorbing/awful* that everyone walked out halfway through.

7 It's a work of *contemporary/historical* fiction, set in modern-day China.

8 The film had an unexpected *storyline/twist* at the end that nobody had seen coming.

A POSTER

9 Find and replace the words in the poster which have a similar meaning to the words in the box.

cast	costumes	critics	entertaining	lead

6 CLOSER TO NATURE

GETTING STARTED

1 **Look at the photos A–F. Work with a partner and describe what you can see in each photo. Which is your favourite photo? Why?**

2 **Look at the photos again and the titles of six new books (1–6). Choose the most suitable photo for the cover of each book. There might be more than one correct answer.**

1. Our Endangered Planet
2. The Astonishing Natural World
3. Understanding Animal Communication
4. Advanced Wildlife Photography
5. The Future Is Solar
6. Flying With Predators

3 **Put the book titles in order from 1 (the book you'd most like to read) to 6 (the book you'd least like to read). Then work with a partner and compare lists. Give reasons for your order.**

READING

1 **Work in groups. Ask and answer the questions.**

1. If you were an animal, what animal would you be?
2. Are you frightened of any animals? Why / Why not?
3. Do you enjoy watching videos of animals online? Why / Why not?

2 **You are going to read about the sea anemone. Before you read, look at the photo and write three sentences that you think might be true about the sea anemone. Think about:**

- what it is
- how big it is
- where you might find it

3 **Read the text quickly, ignoring the gaps. Were your ideas in Exercise 2 correct? Go online and check any answers that you can't find in the text.**

4 **Read the information about gaps 1–3 below. Complete each gap (1–3) with one word.**

Gap 1: The first sentence is comparing plants and animals. What preposition is used after the phrase *tell the difference* ________ ?

Gap 2: This sentence talks about the places sea anemones are in. What relative pronoun refers to location? ________

Gap 3: The gap here is part of a phrase known as a *correlative conjunction*. These are pairs of conjunctions that link words, phrases or clauses together. Other examples include, *either … or …* and *neither … nor …* Think of the word that completes the phrase *not* ________ *… but also …*

5 **For gaps 4–8, read the rest of the text and think of one word which best fits each gap. Use only one word in each gap.**

SEA ANEMONE

You may think it's easy to tell the difference **(1)** ________ a plant and an animal. After all, an animal can move about, whereas plants remain **(2)** ________ they are. However, it's not quite that simple. Some **species** show characteristics not **(3)** ________ of plants but also of animals. One example is the sea anemone. Even **(4)** ________ the sea anemone is often thought to be a plant, on account of its flower-like appearance, it is in fact an animal. Sea anemones usually attach themselves **(5)** ________ rocks, but they can also move around, albeit very slowly. Their ideal **habitat** is shallow **coastal** water, and they are often seen above the water level at low tide. They can grow **(6)** ________ to two metres in diameter. In **(7)** ________ of their gentle, flower-like appearance, they are actually predators. They wait **(8)** ________ fish to come close, sting them with poison and then push their prey into their 'mouths'.

VOCABULARY

THE NATURAL WORLD

1 **Look at the words in bold in the text about the sea anemone. Match the words (1–3) with the words (A–C) to form compound nouns.**

1	natural	**A**	species
2	coastal	**B**	habitat
3	endangered	**C**	path

2 **Complete the gaps with the words in the box to form compound nouns. Then match the words to photos A–F.**

energy	footprint	documentaries
issue	range	warming

1 What do you think is the biggest **environmental** ________ in the world today?

2 How easy is it for people to reduce their **carbon** ________ ?

3 What are some of the consequences of **global** ________ for the environment?

4 In what ways can using **renewable** ________ be good for the planet?

5 Do you enjoy watching **wildlife** ________ ? Why?/ Why not?

6 What do you think is the most spectacular **mountain** ________ in the world?

A

B

C

D

E

F

P

When a compound noun consists of [noun + noun], the stress is usually on the first word: **animal** kingdom. However, there are some exceptions: carbon **footprint**. With [adjective + noun], both words tend to be stressed: **coastal scenery**; **endangered species**.

3 **Work with a partner. Ask and answer the questions in Exercise 2, paying attention to the stress of the compound nouns.**

GRAMMAR

PREPOSITIONS

GRAMMAR ON THE MOVE
Watch the video

1 **Correct one preposition mistake in each sentence.**

1. Bats are nocturnal, which means they only come out in night.
2. The scientists have now arrived to the venue for the annual conference.
3. We travelled across the mountain range with train.
4. The seminar on animal welfare will be held in 32 Main Street.
5. We are planning to go back in the beach next week.
6. When you walk through the bridge, you get a better view of the river.

➔ **GRAMMAR REFERENCE** / *Prepositions: Page 216*

2 **Choose the correct preposition to complete the sentences.**

1. Many people don't **approve** *of/on* testing cosmetic products on animals.
2. The future of the planet **depends** *of/on* our ability to look after it properly.
3. Camels are **capable** *of/with* going for long periods of time without water.
4. I don't know why people **insist** *in/on* putting photos of their pets on social media.
5. Albert Einstein is **regarded** *as/with* one of the greatest scientists of all time.
6. I am writing to **enquire** *about/for* arranging a school trip to the zoo.
7. We are really **looking forward** *for/to* our trip to the wildlife park next week.
8. The engineers **succeeded** *in/on* finding a way to make the car more energy efficient.

3 **Rearrange the words to form sentences. Think about the position of the prepositions.**

1. on / congratulated / the tour guide / a / tour / informative / ~~the visitors~~ / very
   The visitors ________
2. ~~the closure~~ / hasn't / from / the zoo / prevented / the lion exhibit / visiting / people / of
   The closure ________
3. against / visitors / ~~the guide~~ / has / the animals / photographs / of / warned / taking
   The guide ________
4. stopped / the museum / from / everyone / entering / ~~the security guard~~
   The security guard ________
5. was / money / the office / of / from / ~~the researcher~~ / accused / stealing
   The researcher ________

PUSH YOURSELF C1

COMPLEX PREPOSITIONS

1 **Read the sentence below from the text about the sea anemone. What part of speech are the words in bold?**

... the sea anemone is often thought to be a plant, ***on account of*** *its flower-like appearance ...*

2 **Read Stephen's blog post about his experience with dolphins. Underline the five complex prepositions.**

I've always been really into wildlife and, with the exception of spiders, I love all animals. Last year, my family and I booked a holiday to Australia. Ahead of the trip, I did a lot of research online and found that it was a popular spot for watching dolphins. I wasted no time and immediately arranged a sightseeing trip. We climbed aboard our speedboat and were given a few safety instructions in the event of an emergency while we were at sea. We then set off in the hope of finding dolphins. Our guide warned us that dolphin sightings were common, but not guaranteed. He needn't have bothered, because after about fifteen minutes, we saw ten dolphins swimming alongside our boat! We even saw a baby dolphin swimming along with its mother. I'll never forget how elegant they looked as they jumped through the waves.

3 **Complete the sentences below with the compound prepositions from Exercise 2.**

1. We're going on a field trip to South America next year ________ seeing some of the rare wildlife there.
2. Boat trips only occur during good weather; ________ a cancellation, ticketholders will receive a full refund.
3. I've been reading a lot of reviews about the safari park ________ our trip to Kenya next month.
4. I generally like all types of holidays, ________ beach holidays, which I find really boring.
5. Common toads, ________ tree frogs, are the members of the animal kingdom I find most fascinating.

4 **Work in groups and talk about the most memorable experience you have had with an animal. Use at least one complex preposition.**

SPEAKING PART 2 TRAINING

1 **Work in pairs and answer the questions.**

Animals

1 Did you have any pets when you were growing up?
2 Do you know anyone who has an unusual pet?
3 What benefits do animals bring to humans?

Nature

1 What do you think is the most beautiful thing in nature?
2 What three things can people do to help protect nature?
3 Do you think it's better for people to grow up in cities or in the countryside?

2 **Read the model answers for Speaking Part 2 below. Which photos (A–D) do the words in bold appear in?**

Student A
The main **(1)** .... between the two photos is that they both show the important role animals play in these people's lives. I think the **guide** in the first photo probably spends a lot of time working with the **camels** in the **desert**, so he might be very attached to them. **(2)** .... , the farmer in the second photo probably depends on the cows to earn a living, **(3)** .... transporting **crops** from the field, so I guess the farmer is very thankful to have these animals for support.

Student B
The most **(4)** .... difference between the two photos is the location. In the first photo, the **hikers** are walking close to a huge **mountain range**. **(5)** .... , the people in the second photo appear to be taking a selfie next to a **waterfall**. I think it's **(6)** .... say that the people in the first photograph have come to this area for the magnificent views of the mountains and also to get some exercise. I would say that the people in the second photograph have come to see the waterfall and presumably go and swim in the surrounding lake.

3 **Complete the model answers with the words and phrases in the box.**

in contrast	in the same way	in this case
obvious	safe to	similarity

4 **Find words and phrases in the model answers with similar meanings to the words and phrases below (A–F).**

Student A:
A relies on ....
B make money ....
C moving something from one place to another ....

Student B:
D very big ....
E very beautiful ....
F probably ....

5 **Read the two model answers again. Which question do you think they are answering?**

Student A:
1 Why is it important to look after these animals?
2 How do these people feel about the animals they are with?

Student B:
1 Why have these people chosen to visit these places?
2 What are the people enjoying about being in these places?

6 **Now, look at the photos again and answer the question in Exercise 5 that the candidates didn't answer. Use the vocabulary in Exercises 3 and 4 to help you.**

7 **Work in pairs.**

Student A: Answer the Speaking Part 2 question on page 200.
Student B: Answer the Speaking Part 2 question on page 199.

LISTENING

LISTENING FOR ATTITUDES AND OPINIONS

1 **Work in pairs. Say which way of life you think is better for the animals in the photos and why.**

Living in a zoo

Living in the wild

2 **Read the first line from an online article. Which of the following responses in the comments section do you most agree with?**

HOME
ABOUT
NEWS
CONTACT

SEARCH

THE WORLD'S FIRST
TALKING ORCA

Researchers at a marine park in France have taught an orca called Wikie to copy their speech. Wikie was heard to repeat the words 'hello' and 'bye bye' by pressing air through the blow-hole on top of her head.

COMMENTS

1 Sounds like a waste of time to me! — 1 · 13 · 2

2 This proves that orcas can speak too! — 2 · 7 · 0

3 I have concerns about the ethics of projects like this … . — 5 · 3 · 4

3 037 **Listen to part of a radio discussion programme in which three people discuss a news story about an orca (also known as a killer whale). Which opinions are expressed by which people?**

	JOEY	LIZ	ISAAC
1 People are too quick to believe that animals have special abilities.			
2 The orca is trying to communicate a message to the people.			
3 The noises made by the orca cannot be considered as communication.			
4 More research needs to be done on how animals communicate.			
5 The orca probably doesn't understand the words she is hearing.			

4 **Look at the audioscript and underline the phrases where the speakers ask for or express opinions.**

Which of the speakers …

1 makes positive statements about something they disagree with?

2 asks and then answers a question?

5 **Plan and write your own response to the news article in Exercise 2.**

GRAMMAR

RELATIVE CLAUSES

GRAMMAR ON THE MOVE
Watch the video

1 Look at these examples from the radio discussion programme.

A) Apparently, the orca can say several words, which is just unbelievable!
B) I bet people will be able to interpret most of the sounds that animals make.

Which sentence (A or B) contains:
a defining relative clause?
a non-defining relative clause?

GRAMMAR REFERENCE / *Relative pronouns and relative clauses: Page 217*

The words in boxes above are relative clauses. **Defining relative clauses** give essential information to make the sentence clear. **Non-defining relative clauses** give additional information.

2 Decide if the rules apply to defining or non-defining relative clauses. Write D (defining) or ND (non-defining) next to each sentence.

1 We use the relative pronouns *who* for people, *which* for things, and *that* for both people and things.
2 We use the relative pronouns *who* for people and *which* for things, but **not** *that* for people and things.
3 The relative pronoun can be omitted when it is the object of the relative clause.
4 The relative pronoun cannot be omitted from the relative clause.
5 We use commas to separate the relative clause.
6 We don't use commas to separate the relative clause.

3 Complete the sentences with the correct relative pronoun. Decide which sentences are defining relative clauses (D) and which are non-defining relative clauses (ND) and add commas where necessary.

1 Giraffes ______ are the tallest mammals on earth are able to run up to 55 kilometres per hour.
2 Edmund Hillary and Tenzing Norgay were the two explorers ______ first climbed Mount Everest back in 1953.
3 The scientist Stephen Hawking ______ work greatly enhanced our understanding of the universe died aged 76.
4 The North Pole is the one place ______ you can go 1km south, 1km east and 1km north, and be back at your starting position.
5 That's the book ______ I was telling you about last week.
6 1752 was the year ______ the world's first zoo opened in Vienna.
7 There's a river in Peru ______ the water is so hot that any animals ______ fall in are quickly killed.

4 Complete the sentences with correct relative pronouns and prepositions.

1 The recycling project *which* I received funding *for* is due to begin next month.
2 The man ______ Jenny bought her mountain bike ______ suggested some routes for her to try.
3 What was the name of the radio programme ______ we were listening ______ last night?
4 The national park, ______ I was reading ______ last week, has just won a conservation award.
5 Andy, ______ I shared a flat ______ at university, has just come back from Antarctica.
6 The presentation, ______ I worked so hard ______ , was cancelled at the last minute.

Non-defining relative clauses can begin with a pronoun, number or determiner, such as *all, most, some, none, neither, one,* followed by *of which* and *of whom.*

5 Choose a phrase from the box and an appropriate relative pronoun (*which* or *whom*) to complete the sentences.

all of	most of	both of	one of	neither of

1 The five pandas, *all of which* are female, have been transferred to a wildlife park in America.
2 There used to be two scientists working on the project, ______ were from universities in the Netherlands.
3 My friend wrote two books on butterflies, ______ sold very well unfortunately.
4 The zoo has three giraffes, ______ are female.
5 The late English actor Richard Attenborough had two brothers, ______ , David, presented the popular *Blue Planet* TV series.
6 Scientists estimate that our planet is home to 8.7 million species, ______ have still not been identified.

6 Go online and find five facts about animals. Rewrite these facts as sentences using relative clauses. Take turns telling them to your partner. Which facts do you find most interesting?

VOCABULARY

COMMONLY CONFUSED WORDS

1 **Do a class survey. What is the first thing that people see when they look at the picture?**

> **DID YOU KNOW?**
>
> *Some learners of English confuse pairs of similar words, such as **sensitive** and **sensible**. Look at this extract from the listening about orcas:*
>
> *But I think we need to be <u>sensible</u>, and not jump to the wrong conclusion.*
>
> ***Sensible** means behaving wisely and using good information to decide what to do. **Sensitive** means easily upset by people's words or actions.*

2 **Read Mark's blog post about his recent trip to an African safari park. Circle the correct words.**

AN UNFORGETTABLE EXPERIENCE!

From breathtaking views to beautiful animals, my recent **(1)** *travel / trip* to Kenya had it all. An African safari is often high up on people's *bucket lists and it was number one on mine. I've always loved animals, particularly lions and tigers, and I was desperate to see them in their natural habitat. I managed to convince my parents to **(2)** *borrow / lend* me the money I needed to book the flights, accommodation, etc. and I was off.

I read a list of useful things to take when going on a safari beforehand, which, on reflection, was a really **(3)** *sensible / sensitive* idea. This included things like a guidebook, a good pair of binoculars and most importantly of all, **(4)** *lose / loose*, comfortable clothing. I also followed the **(5)** *advice / advise* of a friend who told me to learn how to pitch a tent, which I practised for hours in my back garden. Who knows what my neighbours thought of it!

There were so many highlights to **(6)** *choose / chose* from, but there's one I'll never forget. It was the **(7)** *sight / site* of a herd of elephants stopping for a drink from a lake. I'd got up before dawn in order to watch the sun **(8)** *rise / raise*, and getting to see the elephants too was an unexpected bonus! I actually got quite emotional watching them. I didn't think it would **(9)** *affect / effect* me like that, to be honest. I've attached a photograph. **(10)** *Say / Tell* me what you think about it in the comments section below!

Anyway, overall, it was an unforgettable experience and I would recommend it to anyone who has a passion for animals.

> GLOSSARY
>
> **Bucket list** a list of things a person would like to do or achieve before they die.

3 **Work in groups and answer the questions.**

1 Would you like to go on a safari? Why / Why not?

2 What would be on your bucket list? Make a list of four things and then compare them with a partner.

WRITING PART 2: REPORT TRAINING

1 Work in pairs and answer the questions.

1 What are the most famous zoos in your country?
2 Have you ever visited a zoo, and if so, what was it like?

2 Read the exam task and answer the questions.

1 Who are you writing the report for?
2 What does this person want to know?

> Your English teacher has asked you to write a report about your local zoo.
> The report will appear in the school's English-language magazine.
>
> In your report, you should:
> - describe the zoo
> - explain what people can learn from it
> - say whether you would recommend it to other students
>
> Write your **report**.

3 Decide which of the ideas (1–7) would be relevant to include in your answer.

1 the pros and cons of zoos
2 what the local zoo is like to visit
3 ways in which zoos can benefit animals
4 whether the local zoo is worth visiting
5 a description of your favourite zoo in the world
6 the role of zoos in animal conservation projects worldwide
7 what the local zoo can teach you

4 Read the answer to the question written by a B2 First candidate called Lucinda. Complete the gaps (1–3) with the three most suitable headings (A–F).

1 ....

The aim of this report is to describe the zoo and evaluate it as a possible destination for this year's class trip.

2 ....

In order to prepare this report, I spoke to several of my classmates who visited the zoo on another trip six months ago. They described the facilities of the zoo as being excellent, and they were highly complimentary about the fascinating talks given by the guides. The talk on monkeys' feeding habits was particularly popular. Other students really enjoyed feeding the penguins. The fact that the zoo is quite small means that it is easy to see everything.

3 ....

As we have been discussing wildlife in our lessons, a visit to Danford Zoo this year would be an excellent idea. It would also provide a good opportunity to practise our English by listening to informative talks and asking questions. For these reasons, I am certainly in favour of going there for this year's trip.

A Danford Zoo – an ideal day out
B The purpose of this report
C Summary of my main findings
D We really must go to the zoo again.
E Recommendation for visiting the zoo
F What I learnt about penguins when I visited Danford Zoo

5 Look at the report again and find phrases that Lucinda has used to ...

A explain why she's writing the report.
B describe what she did to write the report.
C report what other students told her about the zoo.
D explain why she would like there to be another trip to the zoo.

6 Using some of the ideas and phrases in Lucinda's report, write your own answer to the exam question in Exercise 2.

EXAM FOCUS

READING AND USE OF ENGLISH – PART 2

EXAM FACTS

- *You will read a text which has eight gaps in it.*
- *You must write* ***one*** *word only for each gap.*
- *There isn't a list of words to choose from in Part 2: you must think of a word which correctly fits the gap. These words will generally be articles, auxiliary verbs, comparatives, modal verbs, prepositions, and relative pronouns.*

EXAM TIPS

- *Read the words and phrases before and after each gap and work out what type of word you need to write, e.g. a noun, preposition, verb, relative pronoun, etc.*
- *Re-read the text after you have filled in the gaps to make sure your answers make sense.*
- *Remember to check your spelling, as misspelt words will be marked incorrect.*

For questions 1–8, read the text below and think of the word that best fits each gap. Use only one word in each gap. There is an example at the beginning (0).

An influential environmentalist

Ma Jun is a Chinese environmentalist and author, **(0)** *who* appeared in the 2016 film *Before the Flood*, narrated by the actor Leonardo di Caprio.

It was in the 1990s **(1)** ________ a young journalist called Ma Jun became interested in the environmental problems of China's Shanxi province and their impact **(2)** ________ local people. He had begun **(3)** ________ researching a story about families, but instead he filled his notebooks **(4)** ________ notes about the pollution he saw. These notes became the basis of his first book, *China's Water Crisis*, **(5)** ________ has been compared to the 2006 environmental documentary film *An Inconvenient Truth* in **(6)** ________ of its importance and influence.

The **(7)** ________ that over 3 million people have now downloaded an app that monitors companies' pollution levels is proof that, just **(8)** ________ Ma Jun, ordinary Chinese people want to know that pollution in their cities remains within legal limits.

WRITING PART 2: REPORT

EXAM FACTS

- *In the report, you are expected to give some factual information as well as make suggestions or recommendations.*
- *The question will always make clear who the report is being written for, and why.*

You recently attended a trip to a local wildlife park. Your English teacher has asked you to write a report about your experience. In your report, you should:

- describe what you can do there
- explain what is good and bad about the wildlife park
- suggest how it can be improved in the future

Write your **report**.

EXAM TIPS

- *Read the exam question carefully.*
- *Make sure that you know who you are writing to and what they want to know.*
- *Say what the purpose of the report is in the first paragraph.*
- *Organise your report into paragraphs. Use headings to make the structure clearer.*

➡ **WRITING BANK** / **Pages 242–243**

SPEAKING PART 2

EXAM FACTS

The examiner will ask you a question about your partner's photographs once your partner has finished speaking.

EXAM TIPS

- *Don't just describe what you can see in the photos. Instead, focus on specific similarities and differences.*
- *Listen carefully to what your partner is saying without interrupting them.*

Student A

Talk about your two photographs for one minute.
The photographs show people spending time enjoying nature in different places. Compare the photographs and say what these people are enjoying about being in these places.

What might these people enjoy about being in these places?

Student B: Do you enjoy spending time in nature?

➡ ***SPEAKING BANK*** / *Pages 246–249*

Student B

Talk about your two photographs for one minute.
The photographs show people spending time with animals. Compare the photographs and say why these animals are important to these people.

Why are these animals important to these people?

Student A: Do you enjoy spending time with animals?

REAL WORLD

GOING INTO THE WILD IN … FLORIDA

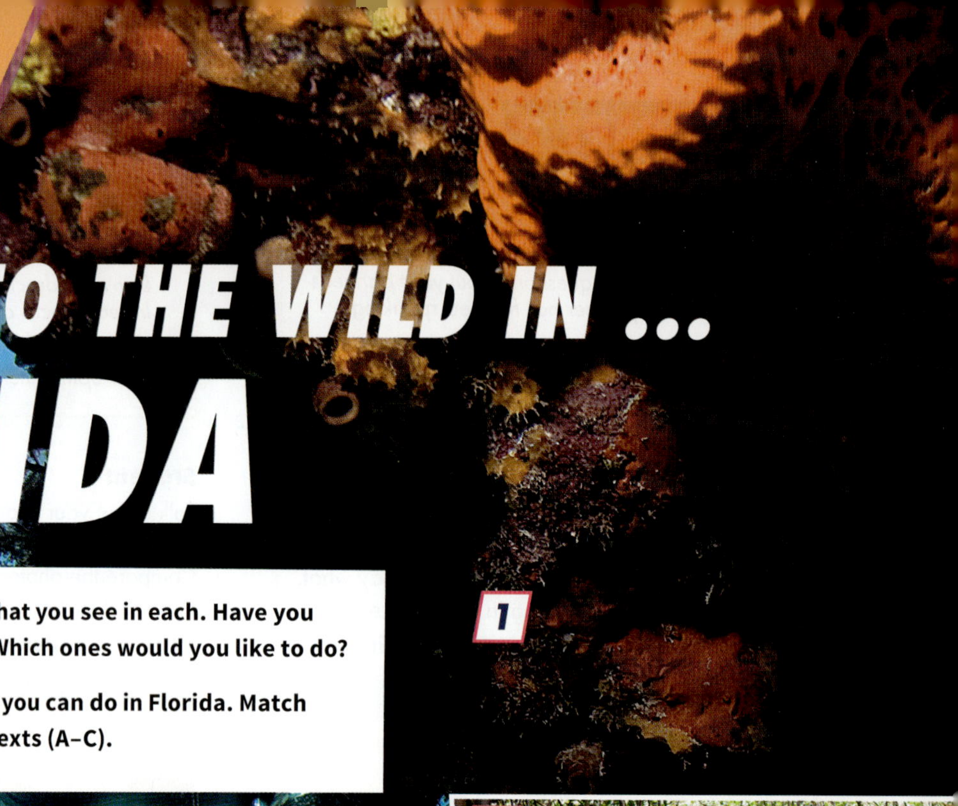

1

1 **Look at the photos and describe what you see in each. Have you ever done any of these activities? Which ones would you like to do?**

2 **Read about the different activities you can do in Florida. Match the photos (1–3) with the reading texts (A–C).**

A Everglades National Park is located in the south of Florida, and offers a whole host of activities for tourists, including walking along the Anhinga Trail to see turtles, birds and alligators, and a kayak tour to explore the various areas of natural beauty. You can even go hiking and biking through the 69km network of pinelands. Make sure you plan your trip in advance of your arrival so that you have time to visit all of the attractions on offer.

B Founded in 1967, Lion Country Safari is a drive-through safari park in Palm Beach County. Visitors are able to see a wide variety of animals, such as giraffes, rhinoceroses, ostriches, zebras, lions and chimpanzees from the luxury of their own cars. Visitors are advised, though, to drive carefully through the park and avoid getting too close to the animals.

C The Florida Reef is one of the largest barrier reef systems in the world, stretching for hundreds of kilometres down the east coast of the USA. It is home to over a thousand different species of plants, and over 500 different species of fish have been recorded there. It is a popular spot for scuba-divers, who come from far and wide to visit this spectacular underwater world.

2

3

3 **Find the phrases in the texts that mean the following…**

1. lots of (x2)
2. before you arrive
3. a well-known place for
4. from lots of different places

4 **The following families are planning to visit Florida. Which (if any) of the places above would you recommend?**

A The Owen family from Canada are regular visitors to the US. They really enjoyed their kayaking holiday in California last year and want to do something completely different in their 2-week stay in Florida this year.

B Bianca wants to spend a weekend in Florida with her mum Cecilia. They want to get out into the countryside and see Florida's wildlife.

5 038 **Listen to Jack, a tourist who is visiting Florida. Complete the table with the information you hear.**

Place	Animal to see	Notes
Blue	....	Visitors can't .... there at the moment.
Various beaches	....	It's best to watch them in the ....

6 039 **Match the underlined words in questions 1–6 below with the expressions (A–F) that have a similar meaning. Then listen to the conversation again and check your answers.**

1. Actually, <u>can I</u> ask you a few questions about the different things we can do here?
2. <u>Can you</u> recommend somewhere we can see some of the animals up close?
3. Right, I'll just make a note of that. <u>Is it</u> on the coast?
4. Oh sorry, <u>how's that's spelt</u>?
5. <u>What animals should we</u> try and see on the coast?
6. So <u>do you</u> have to get up at dawn?

A I was hoping you could
B Is there any particular animal we should
C Would you mind spelling that for me
D I suppose you
E Am I right in thinking that it's
F I was wondering if I could

7 **It can be difficult to understand what people really mean when they are asking or answering questions. Match the phrases in bold (1–6) with the correct meanings (A–F).**

PHRASES YOU MIGHT HEAR / USE

1. Ok, I'll just **make a note of that**.
2. **It can be quite tricky** to find.
3. The bus leaves **at 1.00pm sharp**.
4. **I'll have to look into that** as I'm not sure.
5. **Do you mind pointing out** the nearest supermarket?
6. **Please bear in mind** that the restaurant closes at 9.00pm.

A it is a little difficult
B please remember
C could you show me
D I'll find out for you
E at exactly ...
F write that down

8 **Watch the video about Florida. What do you learn about these things? Make notes.**

- Cities in Florida
- Land animals
- Underwater animals
- Diving in Florida

WATCH

C **Having just moved home, the Cortinis are ready for a week of relaxation in Florida. The two girls are fascinated by large animals. This is the family's last holiday before their third child is born.**

LIFE COMPETENCIES

CONTRIBUTING TO GROUP TASKS, SYNTHESISING IDEAS

9 **Work in groups. Choose a town, city or country. Go online and find out what the main tourist attractions are for people who like animals and nature. Design a poster and present it to the class.**

7 WHAT'S IN YOUR FOOD?

GETTING STARTED

1 Work in pairs. Look at the photos and answer the questions.

1. What do you think these people are enjoying about these eating experiences?
2. Which would you most and least enjoy? Why?

2 Complete the quiz. Then check your answers on page 200. Which answers most surprised you?

1 On average, McDonald's sells 75 hamburgers every …
A second. **B** 20 seconds. **C** 60 seconds.

2 In 1800, what was used as a medicine for stomach pain?
A chocolate **B** tea **C** tomato ketchup

3 In the UK, what % of fruit sold in supermarkets is imported?
A 50% **B** 75% **C** 95%

4 Arachibutyrophobia is a fear of …
A peas rolling across your plate.
B peanut butter sticking to the top of your mouth.
C finding a spider in your food.

5 Which food has an eternal shelf life?
A honey **B** lentils **C** dried pasta

6 Which of these have been used as currency?
A chocolate **B** coffee beans **C** tea leaves

3 040 Listen to speaker one talking about food. Which topic from the quiz does the speaker talk about?

4 041 **Now listen to all five speakers. Choose from the list (A–H) what each speaker says. There are three letters that you don't need to use.**

Which speaker …

A thinks restaurant food is overpriced.
B stops eating before they've had enough.
C has given up eating desserts which are high in sugar.
D likes eating food made with butter, oil or other fats.
E eats less than other people.
F tends to eat locally grown produce.
G needs to eat a lot of food.
H used to take vitamin supplements.

5 Look at the options (A–H) in Exercise 4. Which statements are true for you or someone you know?

VOCABULARY

DESCRIBING FOOD

1 Match the words and phrases in the box with the correct definitions (1–8).

appetite	full	gone off	in season
portions	savoury	stick to	vitamins

1 salty and/or spicy food, not sweet in taste: ....
2 not being able to eat any more food: ....
3 available and ready to eat: ....
4 natural substances that help to keep the body healthy: ....
5 the feeling that you want to eat food: ....
6 describing food or drink that is not good to consume: ....
7 continue to do something: ....
8 the amounts of a particular food: ....

2 Complete the advice below using words and phrases from the box in Exercise 1.

✓ Avoid eating food which has **(1)** .... Always check the best-before date on the packaging.
✓ It's important to eat a lot of food rich in **(2)** .... and minerals.
✓ Try not to eat lots of **(3)** .... snacks, such as crisps and chips.
✓ One of the effects of stress is a loss of **(4)** .... , so make sure you always find time to eat.
✓ As you get older, it's important that you **(5)** .... a healthy, balanced diet.
✓ If you want to lose weight, try eating smaller **(6)** .... of food.
✓ You should avoid doing exercise on a **(7)** .... stomach.
✓ If you want your diet to be more organic, try only eating fruit and vegetables when they're **(8)** ....

3 Work with a partner. Add three more points to the pamphlet in Exercise 2.

DID YOU KNOW?

In British English, the food in the picture is known as ***crisps****. In American English, it is known as* ***chips****.* ***Chips*** *in British English are* ***fries*** *in American English.*

4 Work in pairs and discuss the questions.

1 Do you tend to eat large or small portions?
2 Do you prefer eating sweet or savoury food?
3 Would you say you have a large or small appetite?
4 Have you ever given up eating or drinking anything? Why?
5 Do you have any food allergies?
6 Do you think people should rely on food supplements?

GRAMMAR

WISH AND IF ONLY

GRAMMAR ON THE MOVE
Watch the video

1 **Match the sentences (1–3) with the pictures (A–C).**

1 I wish I could go to the restaurant tonight.
2 I wish I didn't have so much washing-up to do.
3 I wish I hadn't eaten all that chocolate.

2 **Look at the sentences in Exercise 1 and underline the tense in each. Then match the sentences to the correct functions (A–C).**

1 We use ________ to talk about wishes for the past.
2 We use ________ to talk about wishes for the present.
3 We use ________ to talk about wishes for the future.

A something we would like to do but can't.
B a regret about something that has either happened or didn't happen.
C something we would like to be different now but is unlikely or impossible.

➡ **GRAMMAR REFERENCE** / *Wish, If only and hope:* *Page 218*

3 **Read the information in the boxes. Then match the example sentences (A–D) with the correct boxes.**

(1) Sometimes, when talking about yourself, we use ***were*** not *was*.	**(2)** ***Wish*** **+ person + *would* + infinitive** is used when someone is doing something we do not like and wish it could change.
(3) Regret + verb *-ing* can also be used to talk about past regrets. For negative regrets use **Regret + *not* + verb *-ing***	**(4)** If you think something might happen or want something to happen in the future, use ***hope*** not *wish*.

A I wish you would stop borrowing my clothes.
B I hope the food will be good tonight.
C I wish I were a famous chef.
D I regret not going to the restaurant last night.

4 **Correct the sentences. The first one has been done for you.**

1 I wish Martin ~~came~~ *had come* to the restaurant with us last night.
2 It was great seeing you yesterday and I wish to see you again soon.
3 I not regret choosing the pasta dish. It looks delicious.
4 I wish I would come to dinner with you tomorrow but I already have other plans.
5 I really wish that person at the other table talking more quietly. It's driving me up the wall.
6 I was in Venice last week and had trouble ordering in a restaurant. If only I would speak Italian.
7 I wish I pay more attention to the teacher yesterday. I don't understand any of this.

5 **Complete the second sentence so that it has a similar meaning to the first sentence, using the word given.**

1 I regret not doing more to help my mum prepare dinner.
WISH
I ________ more to help my mum prepare dinner.
2 I regret not applying for that job as a chef last week.
APPLIED
If only ________ that job as a chef last week.
3 I wish I had learnt to bake when I was younger.
REGRET
I ________ to bake when I was younger.
4 Luke told Diane that he wished he were a first-class chef.
IF
Luke said to Diane "________ a first-class chef."
5 They regretted trying the overpriced restaurant.
HAD
They ________ the overpriced restaurant.
6 I regret eating so much chocolate before dinner
LESS
I wish ________ chocolate before dinner.

6 **Jake and Kristi are friends, but recently they've been having problems. Student A, read Jake's story on page 200. Student B, read Kristi's story on page 202. Highlight 3–5 issues or regrets which need to be discussed. Make notes, then have a conversation as Jake and Kristi using *wish*, *if only*, and *regret +ing*.**

READING

1 **Work in pairs and answer the questions.**

1. Look at the pictures. What are they? What do you think they all have in common?
2. What's the strangest thing you've ever eaten?
3. Would you ever eat or drink something which you know might harm you?

2 **Read the first paragraph of the article, ignoring the gaps. How does the writer feel about eating puffer fish?**

READING AND USE OF ENGLISH PART 3 TRAINING

3 **Read the first part of the article again and use the word given in capitals at the end of some of the lines to form words that fit in gaps 1–3. Use the tips to help you.**

4 **Now look at gaps 4–8. Decide what type of word is needed for each gap (noun, adjective, adverb etc.). Then complete gaps 4–8.**

TIPS

(1) The form of the word needed in this gap is an adverb. What suffix do you use at the end of the word *recent* to form an adverb?

(2) What type of word is used with the phrase as … as?

(3) What suffix is used with the word harm to say that it isn't dangerous?

YOU'RE DYING TO EAT ME!

I've always enjoyed eating new things, **(0)** *particularly* dishes from other cultures different to my own. **(1)** ________ , on a trip to Japan with friends, we came across a restaurant and our Japanese guide suggested that we go for a delicate dish of 'fugu', or pufferfish, which, he told us, contains enough poison to kill 30 people and is known to be one of the most dangerous animals in the world. Admittedly, I wasn't as **(2)** ________ as my friends, who were really keen to try it. The guide reassured me though and said that as long as the preparation is carried out carefully, fugu is quite delicious and **(3)** ________ .

The pufferfish gets its name from its **(4)** ________ to increase its size to look like a large spikey ball when it senses danger, making it difficult for predators to eat. It can grow to more than sixty centimetres in **(5)** ________ depending on the species and it has brilliant eyesight so it can spot danger easily. In fact, the pufferfish can move its eyes independently, meaning that it can look in two directions at the same time. It can also be found in a variety of different colours.

Although pufferfish taste revolting to other fish, humans have been consuming them for many years and, therefore, the dangers are **(6)** ________ known; chefs must undergo extensive training for several years. Even though I knew fugu chefs were fully trained, I was **(7)** ________ of the fact that poisonings still happen every year. My guide pointed out, with a casual smile, that a local supermarket had to recall several packs of this poisonous meat after it was discovered that the liver, which is highly toxic, hadn't been removed. This, unsurprisingly, didn't make me feel at **(8)** ________ before going into the restaurant.

PARTICULAR
RECENT
ENTHUSIASM
HARM
ABLE
LONG
WIDE
AWARE
EASY

5 **Work with a partner and answer the questions.**

1. What would you have done if you'd been in the writer's position?
2. Why does the guide appear not to take the writer's fears seriously?
3. Why might tourists want to try this dish?

PUSH YOURSELF C1

USING ADVERBS AS MODIFIERS

1 Read the sentence below about the pufferfish. Choose the correct option (1–3).

Undoubtedly, I'd be rushed to hospital but, given we'd already established there was no antidote, what could the doctors possibly do for me?

By using *undoubtedly*, the writer wants to emphasise that

1 something is true.
2 something is false.
3 they are not sure if something is true or false.

2 Read the sentences. Then match the underlined adverbs to the correct meanings (A–E).

1 Apparently, he's giving up his job as a chef to go and travel around the world.
2 Due to the health risks, the food industry will inevitably have to reduce the amount of sugar in food.
3 Remarkably, the restaurant has closed down. It had only been open for two weeks.
4 Carrots can supposedly help you to see in the dark, but I'm not convinced they can.
5 Ultimately, it will be the government's responsibility to tackle obesity in young children.

A ________ is used to emphasise that something cannot be avoided.
B ________ is used to emphasise you are not certain that something is true.
C ________ is used to emphasise the most important fact in a situation.
D ________ is used to emphasise how surprised you are by the information.
E ________ is used to emphasise you do not believe that something you've been told is true.

3 Choose the correct option to complete the sentences.

1 *Ultimately/Supposedly*, it's the food industry who have the money and who will therefore drive the development of genetically modified food.
2 *Apparently/Inevitably*, the colour of your plate influences the amount of food you put on it and therefore eat. While I can see this might be the case, I won't be convinced until I see more evidence.
3 *Inevitably/Remarkably*, I actually lost weight when I started eating dessert from a spoon made with zinc. I'd been doubtful at first but realised after a while, I'd cut down on sugar consumption.
4 *Ultimately/Supposedly*, the new chef is a scientific genius, but I can't see how combining sweet ice cream with a savoury meat pie is ever going to work!
5 *Apparently/Inevitably* the government will have to tackle growing concerns over the link between processed food and obesity. Rising rates of related illnesses simply cannot be ignored.

P STRESS IN ADVERBS

Notice that the stress on these adverbs is placed on the second syllable.

a**ppa**rently	re**mar**kably
inevitably	su**ppo**sedly

The exception to this pattern is the word ***ul****timately*, which has the stress on the first syllable.

4 042 Read the information in the box. Then practise saying the sentences in Exercise 3, focusing on the correct pronunciation of the adverbs. Listen and check.

LISTENING PART 2 TRAINING

1 What do you think a food scientist does?

2 You will hear a food scientist called Lucy Johnson talking about her job. Read the transcript of the first part of her talk quickly. Were any of your ideas in Exercise 1 correct?

Hi, my name's Lucy and I'm here to talk about my life as a food scientist. I've always been interested in food. I suppose it runs in the family. My father works as a chef at a top restaurant in London and my mother is a food critic for a national newspaper. I had several part-time jobs to earn some money while I was studying for my degree, including working as a waitress, which was good money but hard work. After graduating from university with a degree in food science, I got my first job as an analyst for a global chocolate company, where I studied the effect different cocoa beans had on the overall taste of the chocolate.

3 **Read the information in the box. Then look at three candidates' answers for question 1. Why are they incorrect?**

In Listening Part 2, each answer will be no longer than three words. You need to complete each gap with the word, number or short phrase you hear in the recording without changing the form in any way.

1 Lucy started working as an ________ after finishing her studies.

1 waitress

2 analyst for a global chocolate company

3 analyser

4 **Now complete question 1 with one word from the text.**

5 **Look at questions 2–7 below. What key information will you need to listen for?**

2 Lucy must deal with a variety of problems connected to ________ on a daily basis.

3 Lucy believes the best thing about being a food scientist is the ________ .

4 In September, Lucy is going on a trip to speak to ________ .

5 Lucy thinks some people find information given on food packaging slightly ________ to understand.

6 In most situations, Lucy tries to ________ having processed foods.

7 Not long ago, a workmate of Lucy's discovered a problem with the ________ due to a chemical used by a farmer.

6 **043 Listen to the rest of the talk. For questions 2–7, complete the sentences with a word or short phrase.**

7 **Work with a partner and answer the questions.**

1 Based on what you've heard, would you like to be a food scientist? Why / Why not?

2 What do you think are the benefits of working in the food and drink industry?

3 Is there anything about food production that you would rather not know?

VOCABULARY

PREFIXES

1 **Would it be impolite not to try something offered to you by a host, even if you didn't like the look of it?**

2 **Read the sentences. Match the words in bold with the correct meanings (A–F).**

1 My dad always gets annoyed at slow service in restaurants. He's so **impatient**.

2 The restaurant owner has a reputation for being **dishonest**, so make sure you check the bill carefully at the end of the meal.

3 The café is planning to **reapply** for a licence to sell food and drink.

4 It seems a bit **illogical** to buy food and drink at the event when we can just take it with us.

5 I was **unaware** that the bistro had actually closed down.

6 I quit my job as a waiter because I had to work **irregular** hours.

A not making sense

B make another request or application

C easily irritated by having to wait for something

D not normal

E not telling the truth

F not knowing something

3 **Complete the questions below with the correct prefix from the box.**

dis-	il-	im-	ir-	re-	un-

1 Is there a food or drink item that you really ________like?

2 Do you think food will be ________placed by a small tablet one day?

3 Do you think it's ________responsible of people to throw leftover food away?

4 Would you post a negative review online if the service in a restaurant was ________acceptable?

5 Some people think it should be ________legal to sell energy drinks to people under 16 years old. Do you agree?

6 Is it ________polite to use your mobile phone at the dinner table?

4 **Work with a partner. Ask and answer the questions in Exercise 3.**

SPEAKING

DESCRIBING A RESTAURANT EXPERIENCE

1 **Read sentences (1–7) and match them with the criteria in the box. The first one has been done for you.**

location	ambience	value for money
service	cuisine	hygiene	decor

1 The restaurant specialises in Mediterranean food. *cuisine*
2 The restaurant is reasonably priced.
3 The staff at the restaurant are well-informed and efficient.
4 The restaurant is situated just off the main square.
5 The interior is quite traditional-looking.
6 The restaurant has a great atmosphere and can seat up to 100 people.
7 The restaurant scores highly in terms of cleanliness.

2 **Put the criteria in Exercise 1 in order of importance from 1 (the most important) to 7 (the least important) when choosing a restaurant.**

3 **Find the words and phrases in sentences 1–7 in Exercise 1 which mean the following.**

1 the inside
2 not too expensive
3 focuses on one particular type of food
4 fast / in an organised way
5 located

4 **Work in pairs. Answer the questions.**

1 What's your favourite restaurant? Where is it situated and what does it specialise in?
2 Would you ever consider 'dark dining' where the restaurant's interior is completely dark and you can't see what you're eating?

5 **Think about a restaurant experience you've had recently. Use the criteria in Exercise 1 and give the restaurant a score out of three. Then describe your experience to your classmates.**

I would like to talk about … which is situated …
In terms of service, I would give it a score of … because …

GRAMMAR

THIRD AND MIXED CONDITIONALS

GRAMMAR ON THE MOVE
Watch the video

1 **Read the sentences below. Then read the statements (A–C) and decide if they are true or false.**

1 *If I'd known the food was going to be that bad, I wouldn't have let Liz talk me into going to the restaurant.*
2 *If I hadn't stayed up late last night, I wouldn't be so tired now!*

Sentence 1
A The speaker knew the food was going to be bad.
B Liz talked her into going to the restaurant.
C The speaker is talking about two events in the past.

Sentence 2
A The speaker stayed up late.
B The speaker isn't tired now.
C The speaker is talking about two events in the past.

➔ **GRAMMAR REFERENCE** / *Third and mixed conditionals: Page 219*

2 **Rewrite the sentences using the third or mixed conditional.**

1 Tonya didn't attempt to make a dessert, because she's a terrible cook.
If …
2 Rebecca tried the pufferfish while she was in Japan.
If …
3 Peter has an allergy, so he didn't eat the nut cake.
If …
4 Kim didn't realise the meat was off, so she used it to cook with.
If …
5 Leonardo feels sick now because he ate too much ice cream.
If …

3 **Make a list of three decisions you have made in your life, or which were made for you. Use the following topics or another idea of your own to help you:**

- things you have eaten or drunk
- subjects you studied in school or university
- places you visited or lived
- a decision you are happy with or regret

Now, using third and mixed conditional structures, work with your partner and decide what might have happened if a different decision had been made.

Student A: *'My mum made me go to a big family celebration last weekend which was really dull.'*
If I hadn't gone there, I would have seen my mates.
Student B: *Yeah, but if you'd seen your friends instead, your mum would probably still be angry with you now!*

WRITING PART 2: LETTER/EMAIL TRAINING

1 **Work in pairs and answer the questions.**

1 What occasions do you think are being celebrated in the photos?

2 On which other occasions might someone dine in, or out, with friends or family?

3 Do you typically prefer dining in or out? Do you think this is influenced by your culture?

2 **Look at the exam style question below. Underline the points you need to include in your answer.**

You have received this email from your English-speaking friend, Sarah.

> Hi!
>
> It's my mum's birthday next week and I'd like to organise a birthday meal for her at a restaurant. I remember you telling me that you recently organised a birthday meal for your dad. I'd love to know more about it. What kind of restaurant did you go to? What was the food like? Who did you invite and how did it go?
>
> Thanks, Sarah

3 **Read the model answer to the question in Exercise 2. For gaps 1–10, choose the correct word or phrase (A–C).**

> Hi Sarah,
>
> **(1)** ________ for your email. It's great **(2)** ________ from you.
>
> We had a wonderful time **(3)** ________ my dad's birthday. The new French restaurant in the city centre was fully **(4)** ________ , so we ended up going to the Korean place near the river.
>
> It was a good choice. The food was superb, and what's more, there was a wide **(5)** ________ of mild and spicy dishes to keep everyone happy. We invited loads of my dad's cousins, plus his sister, and most were able to **(6)** ________ it. My aunt had **(7)** ________ said that she wouldn't be able to come but managed to turn up at the end, which was a lovely surprise for dad.
>
> Everyone had a fantastic time. The waiters were really friendly and the restaurant had a great **(8)** ________ .
>
> Good luck with **(9)** ________ your mum's birthday.
>
> **(10)** ________ ,
>
> Paula

1	**A** Thanks	**B** With thanks	**C** Thanking you
2	**A** to have heard	**B** to hear	**C** to hearing
3	**A** to celebrate	**B** celebrating	**C** celebrate
4	**A** reserved	**B** unavailable	**C** booked
5	**A** option	**B** variety	**C** choose
6	**A** make	**B** do	**C** have
7	**A** originally	**B** always	**C** before
8	**A** value for money	**B** hygiene	**C** ambience
9	**A** organise	**B** organising	**C** to organise
10	**A** Yours faithfully	**B** Truly	**C** Bye for now

4 **Match the formal phrases (1–7) with their informal equivalent (A–G). Then decide if they are used at the beginning or end of a letter/email.**

1 I look forward to hearing from you
2 With reference to your email
3 Kind regards
4 I regret to inform you
5 I would be grateful if you could
6 Do not hesitate to contact me should you require further assistance
7 I'm writing to inform you

A Cheers
B I'm sorry to say
C Can you
D Let me know if you need anything
E Regarding your email
F Just a quick line to let you know
G I can't wait to hear back from you

5 **Turn to page 201. Write an answer for the question. Write your answer in 140–190 words in an appropriate style.**

EXAM FOCUS

READING AND USE OF ENGLISH PART 3

EXAM FACTS

- *In this part of the exam, you will read a text with eight gaps.*
- *You must use the word in capital letters at the end of some of the sentences to form a word that fits the gap.*

EXAM TIPS

- *Look at the words before and after each gap and think about the type of word you need, e.g. a noun, verb, adjective, adverb etc.*
- *Decide if the context before and/or after the gap is positive or negative and use the correct prefix or suffix.*

For questions 1–8, read the text below. Use the word given in capitals at the end of some of the lines to form a word that fits in the gap in the same line. There is an example at the beginning (0).

Write your answers IN CAPITAL LETTERS.

Example: **(0)** *actually*

The history of ketchup

Loved by millions, ketchup, that bottled tomato sauce enjoyed with all sorts of dishes,
(0) *actually* dates back over 500 years to China where it was used **ACTUAL**
(1) ________ south-east Asia to enhance the taste of savoury dishes. It might be hard to **THROUGH**
believe, but **(2)** ________ , ketchup was tomato-free. In the 1500s, many considered the **ORIGIN**
tomato to be **(3)** ________ and refused to eat it. **POISON**

The first known published sauce recipe including tomato was in 1812 although,
(4) ________ the ketchup of today, it didn't include vinegar. The addition of tomatoes **LIKE**
meant ketchup included vitamins and, in 1834, ketchup was made into pills by Dr John
Cooke Bennet and sold as medicine to treat a variety of **(5)** ________ , such as indigestion **ILL**
and muscle pain.

The popularity of these pills spread **(6)** ________ , and they were soon copied. However, **RAPID**
some **(7)** ________ businessmen replaced tomatoes with other ingredients and made **HONEST**
false claims that their new sauce could cure anything from vitamin deficiency to broken
bones. While the ketchup medicine industry collapsed soon after, the rapid **(8)** ________ **GROW**
of ketchup as a food item continued and it still remains high on people's shopping
lists today.

WRITING PART 2: LETTER/EMAIL

EXAM FACTS

- *You must write between 140–190 words in the appropriate style.*
- *You can expect to be asked to write an email or letter to a friend, a college principal, a magazine editor or a potential employer.*

EXAM TIPS

- *Read the exam question carefully and check whether you need to write in a formal or informal style.*
- *After you have written your answer, check that you have covered all the points in the question.*
- *Remember to use words and phrases that you would typically find in an email or letter.*

Write your answer in 140–190 words in an appropriate style.

You have received the following email from your English-speaking friend, Sonya:

> My mum told me that you're going to organise a surprise meal to celebrate your sister's graduation. I'd love to know more about it. What kind of restaurant are you going to? Why did you choose that restaurant? Is there anything about the surprise that you are worried about?
>
> See you soon,
>
> Sonya

Write your **email**.

➜ **WRITING BANK** / *Pages 236–237*

LISTENING PART 2

EXAM FACTS

- *In this part of the exam, you will listen to one person speaking.*
- *There are ten sentences and each sentence has some information missing. You must complete the sentences with the words you hear in the recording.*

EXAM TIPS

- *Before the listening begins, read the instructions, title and sentences quickly and think about the type of information you need to listen for.*
- *The sentences will follow the same order as the information in the recording.*

044 You will hear a chef called Tobias Stewart talking about his career and new book. For questions 1–10, complete the sentences with a word or short phrase.

Becoming a successful chef

Tobias studied **1** ______ at university.

After he left university, Tobias volunteered to work for a **2** ______ .

Based on his observations of the **3** ______ where he was working, Tobias decided on a different career.

Tobias ran his first restaurant when the owner **4** ______ .

When his restaurant was reviewed, Tobias' dishes were described as **5** ______ by the reviewer.

Tobias explains that as his wife works as a **6** ______ , she understands the pressures of his job.

Tobias finished writing his cookery book in **7** ______ .

Tobias is concerned about the effects of **8** ______ .

Tobias has decided to call his book **9** ______ .

By signing up to Tobias' blogpost, listeners can win a prize and discover new **10** ______ .

REAL WORLD

DINING OUT IN ... ATHENS

Street food specialities

Fine dining delights

Casual comfort

1 Look at the photos below. In what ways would you expect the food, price and overall experience to be different? Which dining option would you prefer when travelling?

2 Read the article about three different dining experiences in Athens. Work in pairs and talk about which experiences you would most / least like to try.

A GREAT FOR GATHERINGS

Immerse yourself in the traditional flavours of Greece while you relax over three courses of mouth-watering cuisine. Expect to eat generous portions of typical dishes, like Tzatziki – a garlic cucumber and yoghurt dip, or Dolmades – stuffed vine leaves which are filled with mincemeat and rice. You might not get a menu, so if you're not sure, asking the waiter for a recommendation is always a good idea. Rather than a formal dining experience, you can expect the atmosphere to be lively and fun with lots of music and Greek dancing. Bring your dancing shoes and be prepared to join in.

B HANDS-ON FUN

Discover how to make classic Greek dishes with an experienced local chef before heading up to the rooftop terrace to enjoy your home-made three-course dinner amid breathtaking views. Dishes vary but typically include favourites like Keftedes – meatballs cooked with herbs and onions, or Kolokithokeftedes – courgette fritters which are often served with Tzatziki. Your evening starts with a visit to the food market where you will be given tips on buying the best local ingredients and ends when you and your fellow foodies have finished eating their meal.

C AUTHENTIC AND INFORMATIVE

Real Athenians, famed for being incredibly hospitable, introduce you to the secrets of local food as they welcome you into their homes. Not only can you expect a creative twist on well-known Greek dishes, like Moussaka – an aubergine dish with spiced meat and béchamel, but also a lesson on the social side of dining which includes tips on fine dining, restaurant recommendations and local food culture. With an appetiser, main course and dessert, you are guaranteed one of the most genuine dining experiences the city has to offer.

3 **Find words or phrases in the text which mean the following:**

1. food which looks and smells delicious (Text A)
2. a large amount of food (Text A)
3. beautiful scenery (Text B)
4. people who love food (Text B)
5. when people are friendly and welcoming to visitors (Text C)
6. real and authentic ways to eat dinner (Text C)

4 **Marianne, a tourist, has gone to a restaurant in Athens and is talking to the waiter. Read four extracts (1–4) from the conversation and match them with the correct functions (A–D).**

1. Could we pay separately?
2. I'm sorry, but my cutlery is a little dirty.
3. I wanted to know if it's suitable for vegetarians?
4. I was wondering if you could squeeze us in?

A asking for a table
B checking dietary requirements
C asking about the bill
D complaining

5 **Listen to the conversation and complete the sentences. Write 2 or 3 words.**

1 045

ASKING FOR A TABLE

Waiter: How many of you are there?
Marianne: There's four **(1)** ________ ________ .

2

TALKING ABOUT A DISH

Waiter: Are you ready to order?
Marianne: Almost. I like **(2)** ________ ________ ________ the Moussaka. ________
Waiter: It's an oven baked dish of mixed vegetables which I highly recommend.
Marianne: Is that a speciality **(3)** ________ ________ ________ ? ________
Waiter: Do you have any allergies?
Marianne: No, I'm **(4)** ________ ________ anything but my friend is gluten intolerant. He can't eat wheat.

3

MAKING A COMPLAINT

Marianne: Excuse me. I think this might be someone else's. It's not what **(5)** ________ ________ .

MAKING A REQUEST

Waiter: Yes of course. Is there anything else? Would you like any more drinks?
Marianne: Yes. The **(6)** ________ ________ for me please. Plus a jug of tap water.

4

ASKING ABOUT PAYMENT

Waiter: Of course. I can bring you separate bills if you like? How do you wish to pay?
Marianne: Is it possible to pay by **(7)** ________ ________ ?
Waiter: Here you go, madam.
Marianne: Thank you. Is the **(8)** ________ ________ ?

6 **Work in pairs. One of you is a customer in a restaurant and the other is a waiter / waitress. Use the menu below and role play a conversation. Use the phrases in Exercise 5. Then change roles.**

MENU	**€**
Appetisers	
Greek style roasted olives	**2**
Tzatziki	**3**
Red pepper dip with feta cheese and yoghurt	**3**
Main	
Moussaka	**9**
Dolmades	**7.50**
Keftedes	**8**
Dessert	
Baklava	**5**
Orange cake	**4**

7 **Watch the video. Watch the video about Athens. What do you learn about these things? Make notes.**

- The landmarks of Athens
- Shopping
- Food markets
- Restaurants
- The Athens Street Food Festival

WATCH

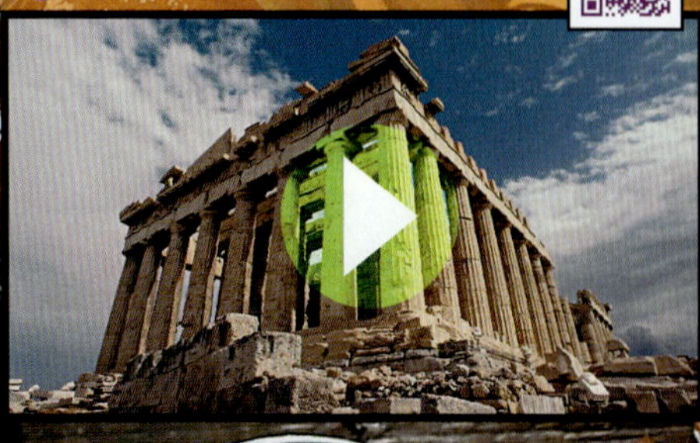

LIFE COMPETENCIES

TAKING PART IN CREATIVE ACTIVITIES

8 **Work in pairs. Go online and research food experiences in a city of your choice. Then in small groups, decide which experiences you would most enjoy and why.**

8 LIVING MADE EASY

Air travel

GETTING STARTED

1 **Work with a partner. Look at the photos and decide which three scientific or technological breakthroughs you think are the most important. Can you think of any others?**

2 **Read the statements. Which do you agree or disagree with? Give reasons for your answers.**

1. There will be a music festival one day where all the performers are robots.
2. Every car on the road will be driverless by 2050.
3. People will stop using social media sites because of data and privacy issues.
4. More and more food will be grown in laboratories to cope with the increase in the world's population.
5. People will use online doctors rather than visiting them face to face.
6. There will be no need for students to go to a university building in the future as all lessons will be available online.

3D printing

Artificial intelligence

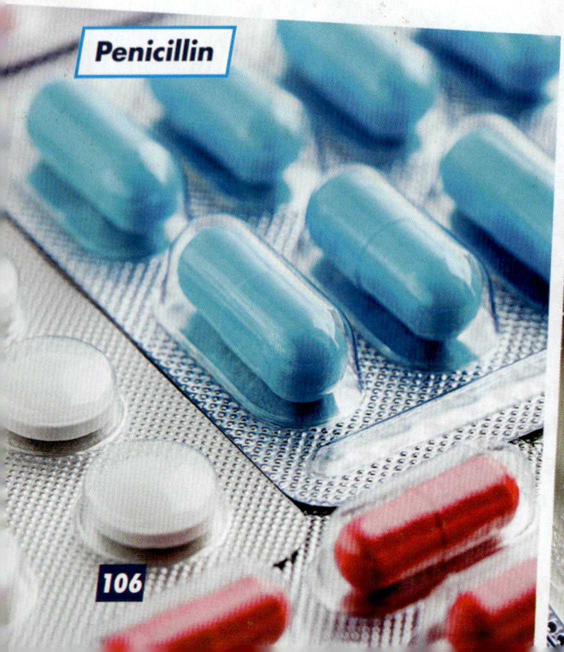
Penicillin

Washing machine

Food preservation

LISTENING PART 3 TRAINING

1 **Do you think it's possible to become fluent in a language that has been taught completely online?**

2 **Look at the list of experiences people have had with learning a language online in Exercise 3 (A–H). Find the words and phrases in the list which mean the following.**

1 cheap; affordable
2 a list of planned activities
3 personal requirements
4 support; help
5 improved x2

3 **046 Now listen to five short extracts in which people are talking about their experience of learning a language online. For Speakers 1–5, choose from the list (A–H) what each speaker says about their experience. Use the letters only once. There are three extra letters which you do not need to use.**

Speaker 1 ....
Speaker 2 ....
Speaker 3 ....
Speaker 4 ....
Speaker 5 ....

A It helped me to improve my speaking skills.
B I could organise the lessons around my work schedule.
C It boosted my vocabulary in particular.
D There were a variety of teachers to choose from.
E I received a lot of extra assistance from my online teacher.
F I developed my computer skills as well as my language skills.
G The lessons were designed to meet my individual needs.
H It was more economical than going to a school.

4 **Work in pairs. Decide if these things can be successfully learnt online without a teacher.**

driving a car	playing an instrument
delivering effective presentations	
photography	fixing your bike

GRAMMAR

DIRECT AND INDIRECT OBJECTS

GRAMMAR ON THE MOVE
Watch the video

1 **In one minute, think of as many different verbs as possible that could complete the gap.**

My dad .... me a tablet.

How many objects are there in this sentence?
Can the order of the objects be changed?

GRAMMAR REFERENCE / *Direct and Indirect Objects: Page 220*

2a **Match the verbs with the indirect object (someone) and a direct object to make phrases.**

VERB	INDIRECT OBJECT	DIRECT OBJECT
1 forward		a present
2 lend		a meal
3 buy		a favour
4 cook	someone	a song
5 tell		an email
6 sing		a story
7 do		some money

2b **Now, express each phrase you wrote in a different way by changing the word order and using *for* or *to*.**

e.g. *buy a meal* ***for*** *someone; tell a story* ***to*** *someone*

3 **Complete the sentences with the correct form of the verbs in the box and either *to* or *for*.**

pre-order	buy	lend	forward

1 I .... a new laptop .... my mum last week and she loves it.
2 My friend dropped my phone and cracked the screen after I .... it .... him yesterday.
3 She .... the new tablet .... her husband ahead of its official release next month.
4 I've just .... a copy of the document .... you.

4 **Correct the preposition mistakes in four of the sentences below.**

1 The technicians are constantly being asked to do favours for their customers.
2 Is there any chance you could lend your mobile phone for me?
3 I can't believe you cooked that meal to me using only a microwave – it was really good!
4 My artist friend painted a portrait of me using only digital tools.
5 I downloaded the instruction manual my grandfather.
6 On the day the famous physicist retired, his colleagues sang him a song.
7 When was the last time you actually wrote someone a letter by hand?
8 My phone tells to me the temperature inside and outside my home.

5 **Work in groups. Find out the interests of three or four of your classmates. Think of something unforgettable that you could do for them.**

I know that Ella's really into classical music. I know, I'm going to order her a piano, so she can play it! It will be custom-made for her.

Well, I'm actually going to write a symphony for her!

What?! That's nothing, I'm planning to design her a concert hall!

VOCABULARY

TECHNOLOGY

1 047 **Listen to Aziz talking about his first job. How do you think his boss felt about him?**

2 047 **Match the syllables to make the compound words which Aziz uses. Then listen again and check your answers.**

back	grade
break	sheet
file	shot
screen	through
spread	up
up	name

3 Complete the sentences with the compound words from Exercise 2.

1 Whenever I ________ to the latest software my phone's performance always gets worse.
2 I'm currently doing an internship at an accountancy firm where I record what has been spent onto a ________ .
3 The IT Helpdesk said that if I could email them a ________ of the error message, they'll try and fix the problem.
4 I'd say the invention of the internet is probably the greatest technological ________ of all time.
5 A friend of mine had to rewrite his university dissertation from scratch after his computer died and he hadn't made a ________ of his work.
6 Never save a document as something vague like 'homework'; instead, use a specific ________ such as 'Enrico_environment_essay_23 June'.

DID YOU KNOW?

Many old words have taken on new meanings to describe aspects of technology. For example:

Follow (*verb*)

1 to move behind someone or something
2 to subscribe to a person's social media updates

It's useful to know both meanings of these kinds of words.

4 Match the words in the box with the definitions (1–7).

bookmark	bug	crash	run	network	icon	browse

1 an illness / a very small insect / a problem in a computer program
2 a small picture or symbol on a computer screen / a very famous person or thing
3 to look through a book or magazine / to look at information on the internet
4 to manage a business / to start a computer program
5 an object used in a book so that you can find a page again / to save a website address on your computer or browser / a saved website
6 a group of friends or people you know / a group of computers that are connected together so that they can share information
7 to be in an accident involving vehicles / to stop working (computer)

5 Complete each sentence using a word from Exercise 4. Decide if you are using the old or the new meaning of each word.

1 The Taj Mahal has long been an ________ of India.
2 It's a good idea to ________ interesting webpages so that you can find them easily again later.
3 I can't believe it – my computer has ________ , and the essay I was writing is lost!
4 She has a great ________ of friends and colleagues that she can rely on for support.
5 Just click on the envelope ________ , and it'll show your email inbox.
6 I thought I'd just have a quick look at my phone – and then the next thing I knew, I'd spent a whole hour ________ the web!
7 I caught a stomach ________ and had to spend two whole days in bed.
8 Arthur knew at an early age that he wanted to ________ his own business, and now he is.
9 The ________ I was using slipped out and onto the floor, so now I can't remember what page I was on.
10 Users have reported finding a ________ in the software, which the software engineers are trying to fix.

6 Choose three of the words in the box in Exercise 4 and make questions using either meaning. Then work in pairs and ask and answer the questions.

Which building do you think has become an icon of your country?

How much time on average do you spend browsing the web each day?

WRITING

FORMAL AND INFORMAL WRITING

1a Would you be more likely to use formal or informal language when writing …

1 to ask a former lecturer or teacher for a reference when you apply for a job?
2 a response to a photo posted by someone you follow on social media?
3 a report for the company department you work for?
4 to answer an email from a friend who is asking for advice?
5 to invite a friend to visit you next weekend?
6 to request a refund on a faulty product you recently bought?

1b Tell a partner about any of the messages in 1a you have written.

2 Look at sentences 1–10 and complete the table. Decide the function of each sentence and if it is formal or informal. The first one has been done for you.

	FORMAL	INFORMAL
Beginning		
Requesting		
Suggesting		
Apologising	*sentence 1*	
Complaining		

1 I regret the inconvenience caused and can assure you that it will not happen again.
2 Do you reckon you could put me up for a few days?
3 To whom it may concern, I am writing to apply for the internship position at your company.
4 The receptionist was very rude, which I consider unacceptable behaviour.
5 Hi Yutian, hope all's well with you!
6 I would be most grateful if you could provide further details.
7 I know I messed you around, and I'm really sorry.
8 It may be worth holding the event at the college.
9 How about inviting a few friends round for a barbecue?
10 I can't believe they served the food cold – what a letdown!

3 Quickly read the email and decide whether the language used is …

A consistently formal.
B mostly formal, but with a few phrases that are too informal.
C mostly informal, but with a few phrases that are too formal.
D consistently informal.

Dear Sir or Madam,

Having recently purchased your 'Photo Editing Magic' software, I am writing to express my disappointment with it. First of all, your advertisement described the software as 'fully meeting the needs of a professional photographer'. **(1)** This isn't true. Not only **(2)** are there lots of things that it can't do properly, it also freezes for long periods of time. **(3)** I really need the software for my work as an architectural photographer.

(4) Another thing is that the software can only cope with small file sizes. Customers wishing to edit larger files are invited to upgrade to the premium package **(5)** for more money. I feel that this is **(6)** not good at all, and it should have been made clear when I bought it that there was a size limit.

(7) That's why **(8)** I want my money back, and I look forward to being reimbursed within the next 14 days.

(9) Bye for now,

Maria Postani

4 Replace the underlined phrases (1–9) with the more formal phrases (A–I).

A totally unacceptable
B in addition
C this is clearly not the case
D is it unable to perform many functions
E I am requesting a full refund
F the software is essential
G for the reasons above
H at an additional cost
I yours faithfully

5 Imagine that you have paid for a product or a service which you are disappointed with. Write an email or letter to the company you purchased it from, explaining why you are disappointed. Include the following points:

- what the product is
- what is wrong with it
- what you want the company to do

READING AND USE OF ENGLISH PART 6 TRAINING

1 **Look at the pictures below. Work in pairs and talk about ways in which these things could become smarter.**

doorbell

fridge

lock

temperature control

2 **You are going to read a newspaper article about living in a smart home. Read the article quickly, ignoring the gaps. Does the writer talk about any of the ideas you discussed in Exercise 1?**

3 **Read the text around the five highlighted pronouns carefully. Identify what each one refers to.**

A	it	*i)*	the video feed	*ii)*	the door
B	This	*i)*	floorplan	*ii)*	controlling energy use
C	it	*i)*	tablet device	*ii)*	household budget
D	it	*i)*	the kitchen	*ii)*	the fridge
E	it	*i)*	smart technology	*ii)*	the home

WELCOME TO YOUR SMART HOME OF TOMORROW

Journalist Sam Wood spent a day in a smart home to find out what the homes of tomorrow might look like.

Nowadays, it's difficult to think of an area of life that isn't partly or fully automated. We have all seen the evolution of the car industry, where manufacturers are pumping billions of pounds into research and development of driverless technology. Even surgeons are being assisted by automated robotics on the cutting edge of technology to perform real-time operations. But what about our homes? Is this area of life next in line for the so-called digital takeover? I visited a smart home in London to find out.

Let's start with the front door. When I arrived at the smart home, I was asked to ring the doorbell. **(1)** .... This activates as soon as the doorbell is pressed and sends a live video feed to the resident, showing them who's there before they electronically open the door. Interestingly, you do not even need to be at home to view [A]it. This can all be done remotely – handy for letting in delivery men when you are not at home, I am told.

The other thing I couldn't see on the door was a lock. 'There must be one, I mean, where does my door key go?' I thought to myself. **(2)** .... All you need to do is place it up against the door and after a few seconds, it opens, working on a principle much like when you use contactless payment. Furthermore, it's personalised to your phone so that nobody else can access it or enter your home, and it's compatible with any of your smart devices connected to the home's Wi-Fi network. Admittedly, I'm not the sharpest tool in the box but even I found it incredibly easy to use!

Upon entering the smart home, I walked into the living room and saw a tablet device on the coffee table, which showed a floorplan of the whole home.

(3) .... The guide who was showing me around informed me that one of the additional benefits of this was that you could have better control of how much energy you're using and therefore how much money you're spending. [B]This could become a really important feature in the future, especially when it comes to managing your household budget. I did find myself wondering how much people would actually use [C]it though.

One of the rooms where you would expect to see a lot of automation is the kitchen. As I walked in, and to my great surprise, I was greeted by the fridge! It informed me that I was running low on eggs and that my milk was nearly out of date, which [D]it's able to detect via a small camera placed on the inside of the door. **(4)** .... When you are not at home, the camera can be accessed through a smartphone or similar device, making it possible to check on your grocery needs wherever you are – something which could occasionally prove quite handy when you are in the supermarket.

As I left the smart home, I reflected on what I had just seen. Experts often argue that these products are being developed to enhance and support our lifestyles. **(5)** .... It felt to me like the technology in the smart home was unnecessary, and may end up making us lazier, even over-reliant on technology. It remains to be seen though just how much of this technology will stand the test of time, but there is no doubt that [E]it will become more of a feature in the homes of tomorrow.

4 **Read the article again. Five sentences have been removed from the article. Choose from sentences A–G the one which fits each gap (1–5). There are two extra sentences which you do not need to use.**

A I'm not sure I am entirely convinced this is actually the case.
B Apparently, it has been installed to make people's lives easier.
C What I had not noticed was the tiny camera that had been installed just above it.
D However, they might be considered a luxury more than a necessity.
E I realised that using this, you could control the majority of the appliances in the house, such as the lights and radiators.
F I was amazed that it could recognise this.
G As it turns out, it was on my smartphone.

5 **Work in groups and answer the questions.**

1 Would you like to live in a home like the one you have just read about? Why / Why not?
2 What other gadgets or devices can make a home smarter?
3 Do you agree with the journalist's opinion at the end of the article that more technology in the home might make us lazier?

VOCABULARY

IDIOMS FOR SCIENCE AND TECHNOLOGY

1a **Re-read the first paragraph from the reading text. Find an idiom which means 'the latest and the most advanced'.**

1b **Re-read the text quickly and underline two other idioms (one in the third paragraph and one in the final paragraph). What do you think they mean?**

1

2

3

4

5

6

2 **Find the items in the box below in the pictures (1–6).**

fuse	light bulb	plug	rocket	steam	wires

3 **Look at the pictures. Using the words in Exercise 2, can you think of the idiom that each picture represents?**

4 **048 Listen to two people talking about the six pictures. Write down the idioms they mention. Then match the idioms (1–6) with the definitions (A–F).**

1 ______ ______ ______ steam
2 ______ ______ plug on something
3 not ______ rocket ______
4 ______ your wires ______
5 have ______ ______ fuse
6 ______ light-bulb ______

A stop something from continuing
B be mistaken about what someone else means
C become easily angry or upset
D lose energy or interest in something
E suddenly have a good idea
F not difficult to do or understand

5 **Complete the sentences with one of the idioms in Exercise 4. You may need to change the form.**

1 Sorry, I ______ . I thought you were talking about something else there.
2 My friend ______ ; she loses her temper so easily.
3 Programming the timer on your phone ______ .
4 We were about to start a big new project with an IT company, but then they ______ on it, so we aren't as busy as we thought.
5 I couldn't work out how to get the software to work. But then I had ______ , and worked out a solution.
6 Jim started an online course to learn how to code, but he ______ and gave up after only two weeks.

GRAMMAR

MODALS OF SPECULATION AND DEDUCTION

GRAMMAR ON THE MOVE
Watch the video

1 **It's 9:05 am and Joao hasn't turned up for his 9:00 am meeting. His colleagues are wondering where he is. Decide if the statements refer to something which is ...**

A certainly true.
B certainly not true.
C possibly true.

1 He must be stuck in traffic.
2 He may have gone to the bathroom prior to the meeting.
3 He can't have gone to another room.
4 He must have been delayed.
5 He can't be making a phone call.
6 He could be in the wrong meeting room.

→ **GRAMMAR REFERENCE** / *Modals of speculation and deduction: Page 221*

2 **Look at the statements in Exercise 1 again. Which statements are in the present? Which are in the past? Complete the table with the correct statements. The first one has been done for you.**

	PRESENT	PAST
CERTAINLY TRUE	*Sentence 1*	
CERTAINLY NOT TRUE		
POSSIBLY TRUE		

3 **Complete the sentences with a modal verb and the correct form of the verb in brackets.**

1 She ________ (see) the film because it hasn't been released yet.
2 He ________ (forget) his password because he's been locked out of his computer.
3 They ________ (be) at the cinema because they were talking about going this morning, but I'm not entirely sure.
4 I sent them an invitation two weeks ago – they ________ (receive) it by now.
5 The answer ________ (possibly / be) wrong. I've checked it three times!
6 Paul ________ (hold up) in traffic because he isn't usually late.

4 **Complete the second sentence so that it has a similar meaning to the first, using the word given.**

1 I'm certain he's held up in traffic.
STUCK
He ________ in traffic
2 It is possible that your charger wasn't connected properly.
BEEN
I think your charger ________ connected properly.
3 It's highly unlikely that we've used up all the toner for the printer already.
RUN
We can't ________ toner for the printer already
4 It is possible that they cancelled the project due to lack of interest.
PLUG
They ________ on the project due to lack of interest.

5 **Read the crime report below. In pairs, decide who had the opportunity to steal the computer equipment. Use *must have*, *can't have*, *could/might/may have* to complete the sentences.**

Paula ________ the computer equipment because ________
Tony ________ the computer equipment because ________
Richard ________ the computer equipment because ________
Martina ________ the computer equipment because ________
Matt ________ the computer equipment because ________

Crime: Computer equipment worth over £3,000 has been stolen from the office.
Where: Third floor of office building.
When: Between 5 and 6.30pm on Tuesday evening.

Paula (manager)

Paula has been working at the company for 30 years. She is due to retire at the end of the month. She says she left the office as usual at 6pm but nobody saw her leave. She has a set of keys to the office.

Tony (cleaner)

Tony had been cleaning the second-floor offices between 5–6pm and then took a break and was chatting with another colleague before going up to clean the third floor at 6.30pm. He says he saw Richard leave at 6.30pm looking worried.

Richard (office worker)

Richard had been working late in the office. He left at 6.30pm but then failed to show up to work on Wednesday, telling his boss, Paula, that he was ill. He used to have a key to the office in his desk, but says he noticed on Tuesday that it was missing.

Martina (office administrator)

Martina joined the company two weeks ago. She used to work at a security company who specialised in installing security cameras. She left the office at just after 6pm when she bumped into Tony for a chat. She lives less than one minute's walk from the office building.

Matt (consultant)

Matt had been hired on a temporary contract to update the computer software. He had been working on the third floor on Tuesday morning but left early in the afternoon. Martina told the police that she saw Matt leaving the office carrying a small bag.

SPEAKING PART 1 TRAINING

1 Read the Speaking Part 1 questions (A–D) then answer the questions (1–3).

A Do you listen to music on your mobile phone?
B What do you use your mobile phone for?
C Do you like to have the latest mobile phone?
D How easily do you think you could get by without a mobile phone?

1 Do the questions ask you to talk about a more personal or a more abstract topic?
2 Do the questions require you to work with a partner or to look at any material?
3 Are the questions Yes/No, *Wh-* questions, or both?

2 049 **Listen to people answering the questions (A–D). Put the questions in the order they are answered.**

P SHORT AND LONG VOWELS

In English, there are similar but distinct long and short vowel sounds. Consider the following examples:

Short vowel sound (ɪ)	long vowel sound (iː)
bit	*beat*
live	*leave*
fit	*feet*

Pronouncing these vowel sounds correctly will help you sound more fluent.

3 050 **Listen to Extract 1 again. Complete the gaps with the words you hear. Then practise reading the extract out loud, focusing on your pronunciation of long and short vowels.**

Extract 1:
Well, I'm a student, so I find that my phone is really handy for making **(1)** ________ or taking photographs of **(2)** ________ during lectures. I suppose the other main thing I do with **(3)** ________ is **(4)** ________ the latest news or catch up with my friends on social **(5)** ________ , especially before going to bed.

P LINKING WORDS IN CONNECTED SPEECH

When a word ends in a consonant and the next word begins with a vowel, the consonant is often connected to the vowel. For example:
I went out with my friends last week.
In spoken English, the *t* in went and the *o* in out are often connected, so the phrase *went out* is often pronounced as *wen tout.*

PUSH YOURSELF C1

OTHER WAYS OF EXPRESSING SPECULATION AND DEDUCTION

1 Put the words in the correct order. Use the punctuation and capital letters to help you.

1 the / software / It / though / have / failed. / installation / might / looks / as
____

2 fully / My / laptop / be / charged / yet. / can't / possibly
____

3 the / that / drug / might / effective. / Research / be / suggests
____

4 possibility / that / the / Is / device / might / update? / need / an / there / a
____

5 machinery / all / the / damaged / in transit. / likelihood / must / In / been / have
____

6 breakthrough. / Scientists / may / well / believe / they / have / made / a / major
____

4 051 **Read and listen to Extract 2. Notice how the underlined words are linked. Work with a partner and take turns to read the extract out loud.**

Extract 2
I'm not sure I could, to be honest. I'm so reliant on my mobile phone, whether it's keeping in touch with my friends or using the latest apps to help me with learning French, that I can't really imagine my life without it.

5 052 **Now look at Extract 3. Underline the words you think the speaker will link. Then listen and check your answers.**

Extract 3
Yes, I do. I travel abroad a lot and having all my favourite tracks with me on the go is a lifesaver. The only issue I have is that I'm always running out of storage space, so I can't store all of my albums on my phone.

6 Write your own answers to the questions in Exercise 1. Underline the words you should link. Then work in pairs and take turns to answer the questions.

EXAM FOCUS

READING AND USE OF ENGLISH PART 6

You are going to read an article about unsuccessful inventions of the 19th century. Six sentences have been removed from the article. Choose from the sentences A–G which one fits each gap (1–6). There is one extra sentence which you do not need to use.

Unusual inventions from the Victorian age

Inventions and inventors were at their peak during the Victorian era in the UK. Sewing machines, underground railways, lifebuoys, hydroelectric power stations and many more innovations that are still in use today date from the latter two thirds of the nineteenth century. But what about the other more bizarre inventions like a pair of glasses for horses or flying chairs? A new book tells the story of some of the more unusual creations dreamt up by Victorian inventors.

These have been brought back to life in a new book by Caroline Rochford. Caroline came across a collection of rare magazines from the 1880's, many of which enthusiastically advertised what were seen as the next big technological breakthroughs. **(1)** .... Before long, Caroline had details of a substantial number of remarkable contraptions. One of her favourites was an office chair 'railway' system which used steam to move a chair around the office, so that the person working there wouldn't need to keep getting up from their seat all day. There were hundreds more.

Caroline was hooked on the illustrations of the inventions as soon as she saw them. She loved their charm and the unique ideas, as well as the diversity of the technology. **(2)** ....Perhaps unsurprisingly, neither of these took off.

One of several striking inventions depicted in Caroline's book is the steam-powered man, which was invented in about 1893 by a Canadian professor, George Moore. Moore dreamt that one day, all work would be carried out by robots, and so he set about building a mechanical man powered by steam, which would pull a small train filled with commuters through city streets. **(3)** .... Looking like a robot, the body contained the furnace, boiler and engine, and inside the legs were the mechanisms for walking.

Sadly, it is not known what became of the steam man, and Professor Moore's invention appears to have been a one-off. **(4)** .... After seeing the success of the railway network, an unnamed American inventor from New Jersey came up with the idea of a bicycle railway, which enjoyed some success both in Britain and in the US for a while. There was no danger of falling off, and no need to steer. This meant that commuters could look about and enjoy the nature and scenery. It also combined exercise with travel. Plans were made for double tracks, to allow travellers to go both ways, and to provide stations at intervals where they could get on and off. Although similar railways existed for a time in a number of English coastal towns, this unusual mode of transportation fell out of favour, and the New Jersey railway was demolished.

Another variation on the bicycle was the road and river cycle, which was introduced in America. It was essentially a boat with wheels, meaning that a person could travel over roads and rivers in a single vehicle. **(5)** .... As a result, they would have more time for leisure activities.

Caroline believes that people often see the Victorians as boring and conservative. **(6)** .... As she argues very persuasively, in our modern technology-obsessed world we should be grateful to our 19th century ancestors for the innovations they left.

A This chance discovery led to further research.
B Probably for this reason, the design never really became popular.
C The idea was that this would make journeys significantly quicker.
D In actual fact, many of them were full of wonderfully creative ideas.
E The futuristic figure could move at a pace of eight kilometres an hour.
F However, other Victorian inventors came closer to reaching the mass market.
G Designs ranged from an automatic egg-boiling machine to a steamship made out of paper.

EXAM CHECK

Correct the mistakes in the text below about Reading and Use of English Part 6.

The texts in Reading and Use of English Part 6 are usually articles from magazines, newspapers or informative texts. The text will contain five gaps and you must choose from a list of seven sentences the sentence that fits each gap. There are two sentences that you don't need to use. You can use one sentence more than once.

LISTENING PART 3

EXAM CHECK

Read the sentences about Listening Part 3. Decide if they are true or false.

1 In Listening part 3, you will hear six people talking about the same topic.
2 Each monologue lasts for about one minute.
3 You need to choose from eight possible options.
4 There are two options that you don't need to use.
5 You will receive one mark for each correct answer.

053 You will hear five short extracts in which people are talking about their experience of going for a ride in a driverless car. For Speakers 1–5, choose from the list (A–H) how each speaker felt about their experience. Use the letters only once. There are three extra letters which you do not need to use.

A amazed at how easy it was to use
B impressed by the technology used in it
C relieved that they weren't involved in an accident
D nervous about not being in total control of it
E surprised by how safe it was
F excited by the potential of it
G shocked at how much it cost to develop
H disappointed by the appearance of it

Speaker 1 ....
Speaker 2 ....
Speaker 3 ....
Speaker 4 ....
Speaker 5 ....

SPEAKING PART 1

EXAM CHECK

Choose the correct options to complete the sentences about Speaking Part 1.

1 *The examiner/Your partner* will ask you questions about your hobbies, work or study etc.
2 You should answer the questions *with/without* examples and reasons where appropriate.
3 You *need/don't need* to talk to your partner in this part of the exam.
4 Part 1 will last for about *two/four* minutes.

1 Do you have a laptop? (What do you use it for?)
2 How much time do you spend online each day? (Do you think that's too long?) (Why? / Why not?)
3 Do you think you will use your computer more or less in the future (Why?)
4 What is your favourite piece of technology? (Why is it important to you?)
5 Do you often watch TV? (Why? / Why not?)

➡ **SPEAKING BANK** / *Pages 244–245*

GETTING TO GRIPS WITH TECHNOLOGY IN ... SINGAPORE

1 **What kind of apps and websites would you find useful if you were visiting a country like Singapore for the first time? Think about:**

- Planning your trip
- Deciding what to see
- Finding your way around
- Placing an order in a restaurant

2 **Read the texts about useful apps for visitors in Singapore. Put the apps in order of 1 (the most useful) to 5 (the least useful). Then compare your answers with a partner. What other apps do you know that offer a similar service?**

LIMSIMI

Want a coffee, but don't know your *Kop-C* from your *Kopi Gah Dai*? Then fear not – help is at hand with the LimiSimi app. *LimSimi* means '*What are you drinking*?' and the app shows you how to order your perfect coffee, just the way you like it.

IRIS

Iris is an acronym for Intelligent Route Information System. It tracks the arrival and departure times throughout Singapore's public transport network. It enables you to find the best way to get from A to B, which is particularly useful if you have a choice of two or more buses, as you can check which one will get you to your destination first.

TAXI BOOKING

It's never hard to call or flag down a taxi in Singapore, but this app can be a real time-saver. All you do is enter your mobile number and pick-up point. And if you've lost your bearings, don't worry, as you can enable the location detection function, and the app will do the rest. You'll get a notification with the licence plate number and arrival time and, once your cab is on its way, you can track its progress.

HUNGRYGOWHERE

This app allows you to search by neighbourhood or type of cuisine to find the best places to eat. Star ratings are based on feedback from diners and you can book a table or order a takeaway via the app.

HERE GOT SALE

If you love shopping, then this app is a must-have for your trip to Singapore. The app notifies you with the latest sales and promotions in shops all over the country, meaning that you'll never miss out on the biggest and best deals during your stay. Users can also inform other shoppers of sales they have found themselves via the discussion feature of the app.

3 **Complete the questions with phrases from the text. Use the definitions to help you.**

1. What are the ………… apps for people your age at the moment?
   Definition: an essential item
2. In rush hour, what's the best way to ………… in your town or city?
   Definition: go from one place to another
3. What would you do if you ………… in a city that you didn't know well?
   Definition: did not know where you were
4. Apart from looking at the ………… , how else can you choose good shops and restaurants?
   Definition: a score based on quality

4 **Work in pairs and ask and answer the questions in Exercise 3.**

5 054 **Listen to a conversation between a customer (Ethan) and a shop assistant (Jasmine). Answer the questions.**

1. What problem does Ethan have?
2. What's the first thing that Jasmine suggests Ethan tries?
3. What suggestion does Jasmine make that Ethan agrees to try?

6 **Sometimes people use colloquial expressions when talking about problems with technology. Match the sentences from the conversation between Ethan and Jasmine (1–6) with the correct meanings (A–F).**

PHRASES YOU MIGHT HEAR / USE

1	I thought you might be able to take a look at it	A	I'm having difficulty
2	I can't get it to	B	find a solution
3	I checked out	C	I'll try that to see if it works
4	get to the bottom of	D	achieve the desired result
5	do the trick	E	I hoped you could tell me what the problem is
6	I'll give that a go	F	I had a look at

7 **Work in pairs. One of you is a customer who has a problem with a technological device. The other is a shop assistant. Role play a conversation. Use the language in Exercise 6. Then swap roles.**

8 **Watch the video about Singapore. What do you learn about these things? Make notes.**

- The history of Singapore
- Places to visit
- The Smart Nation initiative

WATCH

LIFE COMPETENCIES

EVALUATING OPTIONS, WORKING TOWARDS A RESOLUTION

9 **Work in groups. Choose three items you might need if you visit Singapore. Then go online and find the best retail store(s) from which to buy them at the lowest price. See who can get the best deals.**

PROGRESS CHECK 3

PREPOSITIONS

1 **Circle the correct preposition to complete the sentences.**

1. The performance will be held *at/in/on* 147 King Street, just off the main square.
2. The headline act travelled to the venue *by/in/with* private helicopter which was paid for by the event organisers.
3. I'm not sure why they've insisted *in/of/on* holding the event outside as there's a good chance it will pour down with rain.
4. She will always be regarded *as/at/for* one of the best actors of all time.
5. Even the rain didn't prevent people *by/from/with* coming to watch the outdoor concert.
6. With the exception *from/of/to* one reviewer, everyone loved the band's new album.
7. The cast took part in the Q&A session, along *about/to/with* the director.
8. The organisers pointed out the exits in the event *for/from/of* an emergency.

RELATIVE CLAUSES

2 **Combine the sentences using the relative clause. Make sure you use the correct punctuation.**

1. Charles Dickens died in 1870. He wrote the book "Great Expectations".

   ....

2. There used to be two lions in the zoo. Both of the lions were male.

   ....

3. The concert starts at 7 pm. I have tickets for it.

   ....

4. John Forrest is an award-winning actor. I met him last year.

   ....

5. The dishes use ingredients grown on the local farm. They are all suitable for vegetarians.

   ....

6. Unfortunately, the market has closed down. I buy my food from there.

   ....

ANIMALS AND NATURE

3 **Find and correct the spelling mistake in each of the sentences below.**

1. The polar bear is now considered to be an indangered species.
2. Global warming is one of the biggest enviromental challenges in the world today.
3. Solar and geothermal are two examples of reneweble energy.
4. The views from the top of the mountain were astonershing.
5. The coastle path was closed due to the severe weather conditions.
6. We went on a siteseeing trip last year to Rome. It was incredible.

PREFIXES

4 **Use the word given in capitals at the end of the sentence to form a word that best fits each gap.**

1. I really .... eating blueberries. I can't stand the texture of them. (LIKE)
2. I was .... that the tomato was a fruit – I'd always thought it was a vegetable. (AWARE)
3. My restaurant application was rejected so I'm going to .... next month. (APPLY)
4. Personally, I think it's .... of supermarkets to throw away food that's still edible. They should give it to a local charity instead. (RESPONSIBLE)
5. I thought the waiter was very .... so I didn't leave him a tip at the end of the meal. (POLITE)
6. The government has passed a law making it .... to sell energy drinks to people under 16 years old. (LEGAL)

THIRD AND MIXED CONDITIONALS / *WISH*

5 **Find and correct the mistakes in the sentences below.**

1. If I had known that you were hungry, I would had prepared dinner.
2. I wish I hadn't ate all that ice cream. I feel really sick now.
3. I really regret not to go to the restaurant with my friends last night. Apparently they met Ed Sheeran!
4. I would love to go on a road trip around Europe. Only if I could drive!
5. If I hadn't gone to the concert last night, I wouldn't have been so tired now.
6. I wish the meal will be good tonight.
7. I wish the man would stopping smoking. It's so annoying.
8. I can't understand anything on the menu, sadly. If only I would speak French.

FOOD AND DRINK

6 **Complete the sentences with the words and phrases in the box in the correct form.**

appetite	cuisine	go off	hygiene	in season
portion	savoury	split the bill	stick to	vitamin

1 The new restaurant serves really big .... of food and it's really cheap too.
2 The milk we have smells terrible. I think it might have ....
3 Avocados are a great source of .... and minerals. I try to eat one a day.
4 In Germany, asparagus is typically .... from April to June.
5 I usually prefer eating .... dishes rather than sweet ones in restaurants.
6 I usually suffer from a loss of .... before big exams due to stress.
7 My personal trainer suggested .... a low-fat diet while I prepare for the marathon.
8 The restaurant is really clean. In fact, it has the highest .... rating out of all the restaurants in the town.
9 The restaurant specialises in Japanese .... and the chef comes from Tokyo.
10 At the end of the meal, we decided to .... between the three of us and pay 20€ each.

DIRECT AND INDIRECT OBJECTS

7 **Rearrange the words to make sentences. The first two words have been written for you.**

1 their / a new car / have / son / ~~must~~ / ~~they~~ / bought
They must ....
2 it's / birthday / ~~Stephanie~~ / cooking / his / a meal / be / him / because / ~~might~~ / for
Stephanie might ....
3 any / her / have / musical instruments / play / ~~he~~ / a song / he / written / because / can't / ~~couldn't~~
He couldn't ....
4 lent / have / some money / ~~can't~~ / she / any / because / her friend / doesn't / herself / ~~Mary~~ / have
Mary can't ....
5 forgotten / me / have / ~~Simon~~ / to / the email / ~~must~~ / send
Simon must ....

MODALS OF SPECULATION AND DEDUCTION

8 **Complete the second sentence so that it has a similar meaning to the first sentence, using the word given.**

1 I'm sure Luis forgot about the meeting today.
MUST
Luis .... about the meeting today.
2 There is a possibility that the files were backed up online.
MIGHT
The files .... online.
3 There's a chance that you can fix the computer yourself.
ABLE
You .... the computer yourself.
4 It's possible that Martina is making a phone call.
BE
Martina .... a phone call.

SCIENCE AND TECHNOLOGY

9 **Choose the correct word or phrase to complete each sentence.**

1 I always make sure that I back *down/up* my files on an external hard drive.
2 The message has bounced *back/down* so I must have typed the email address incorrectly.
3 The developers are currently fixing the *bugs/crashes* which were reported during the app's testing stage.
4 My dad gets really annoyed when his computer crashes. He has a really *short/small* fuse when it comes to technology.
5 Due to financial issues, they decided to *pull the plug/run out of steam* on the project.
6 I bought a new graphics card but unfortunately the one I bought isn't *compatible/functional* with my laptop.
7 My internet connection is really slow and websites usually take ages to *charge/load*.
8 For me, the invention of the 3D printer is a huge technological *breakaway/breakthrough*.

9 THE GREAT OUTDOORS

GETTING STARTED

1 **Do the world knowledge quiz. Then compare your answers with a partner.**

WORLD KNOWLEDGE QUIZ

1 What are the top three most spoken languages in the world?
1 ....
2 ....
3 ....

2 What are the top three largest countries by population?
1 ....
2 ....
3 ....

3 What is the highest temperature ever recorded in the world? Where and when?

4 What is the heaviest land animal in the world?

5 How old was the oldest human being in the world?

READING

1 **Match the newspaper headlines with the photos (A–G).**

SELFIE-TAKERS FLEE AS VOLCANO ERUPTS

DOUBLE RAINBOW DELIGHTS IN DAYLIGHT

Coastal darkness lit up by breathtaking night sky

SINKING SOIL AS EARTHQUAKE STRIKES

Falling amphibians cause confusion

Tornado rips through rural farmland

STORMY TROPICS CUT OFF TRAVELLERS

2 **Which of the stories would you be most and least interested in reading about?**

3 **Quickly read the first sentence of the newspaper article. Which headline in Exercise 1 does it refer to?**

> We've all heard of the saying *raining cats and dogs*, but residents of a small suburb in Auckland were left puzzled when their vehicles were hit by frozen frogs instead of ice.

4 **What do you think caused this strange weather phenomenon? Read the rest of the article, ignoring the gaps for now, and see if you were correct.**

> New Zealand is no stranger to heavy downpours, but residents of a small town (0) *in* Auckland were confused (1) ________ what appeared to be small green frogs falling to earth during a violent storm. Strange as it seems, sightings of frogs and toads which seem to be raining down to earth (2) ________ surprisingly common. According to scientists in Australasia, some of (3) ________ have been studying these meteorological events for several years, unusual weather events like these are a result (4) ________ small, localised tornadoes, known as waterspouts. These waterspouts suck up water along (5) ________ small creatures as they pass over the sea or a lake. Another possible scientific explanation for raining animals relates (6) ________ birds carrying small creatures before dropping (7) ________ as they fly overhead. In one incident in Japan, a flock of migrating birds was found to (8) ________ dropped clouds of dead tadpoles – the small, black creatures which later develop into frogs or toads – on the heads of local villagers.

READING AND USE OF ENGLISH PART 2 TRAINING

5 **Read the article again. For questions 1–8, think of the word which best fits the gap. Use only one word in each gap. Remember to think about what type of word goes in each gap.**

VOCABULARY

THE WEATHER

1 **055 Listen to a weather forecast. Find and correct the seven mistakes in the weather report.**

2 **055 Match the words to form collocations about the weather. Then listen again and check your answers.**

persistent	storms
mild	visibility
violent	fog
gale-force	rain
dense	winds
poor	temperatures

3 **Choose the correct particle for statements 1–7.**

1. By January, the lake had frozen *through/over.*
2. It started to cloud *over/up* so we went inside.
3. After a heavy downpour, it brightened *out/up.*
4. The winds are picking *over/up* in the south.
5. The tornado ripped *out/through* the city.
6. The strong winds will die *down/off* by the afternoon.
7. The sun came *on/up* at around six in the morning.

TODAY
Early morning: windy / 40 km/h
Late morning / afternoon: sunshine
Temperature: below average

TOMORROW
Morning: rain moving south
Lunchtime: bright skies
Afternoon: winds up to 75 km/h
Evening: less wind

THE DAY AFTER TOMORROW
Morning: fog
Afternoon: heavy rain
Night: dry and clear

4 **Use the illustrations and the weather vocabulary to write a weather report. Then present the weather report to your classmates.**

SPEAKING PARTS 3 AND 4 TRAINING

A

B

C

D

E

F

G

H

1 **Match the words and phrases in the box with the photos (A–H). Then choose three of the issues and discuss the causes and effects these have on the environment.**

coastal erosion	rising sea levels	deforestation	greenhouse gas emissions
littering	urban sprawl	toxic waste	oil spills

2 **Complete the sentences with the words and phrases in Exercise 1.**

1. By switching to a renewable energy only policy, we could reduce the number of ________ and the devastating effect these have on the sea and marine wildlife.
2. One of the main causes of ________ is the high cost of living in cities.
3. Not only does ________ mean indigenous people lose their homes, but also that less oxygen is released into the atmosphere.
4. Increased ________ could lead to the destruction of a number of homes by the sea.
5. If we disposed of waste more carefully, perhaps by recycling, ________ wouldn't be such an issue.
6. Melting ice and warming of the oceans are the two major causes of ________ .
7. Irresponsible disposal of ________ can contaminate both the soil and groundwater.
8. The main human sources of ________ are deforestation, burning fossil fuels and intensive farming.

3 **Work with a group and answer the questions.**

1. Of the above issues, which, in your opinion, are the most and least serious?
2. For the most serious issue, what steps can people take to tackle it?

DID YOU KNOW?

effect (noun) affect (verb)

SPEAKING PART 3

1 **056 Listen to two students, Harry and Emma, doing Part 3 of the B2 First Speaking exam. Match the environmental issues (1–5) with the effects (A–E) they talk about. Which issue and which effect do they <u>not</u> talk about?**

1	Coastal erosion	A	wildlife is endangered
2	Deforestation	B	increase in pollution levels
3	Littering	C	greater dependence on cars
4	Urban sprawl	D	reduction in the amount of green areas
5	Oil spills	E	higher risk of disease

2 **056 Listen again and answer the questions.**

1. Which question does Harry ask to offer to begin the conversation?
   Which phrase does Emma use to answer Harry's question?
2. Which phrase does Emma use to move on to the next topic of littering?
3. Which phrase does Emma use to agree with Harry's comment about littering?
4. Which question does Harry ask Emma to introduce the topic of urban sprawl?
5. Which phrase does Harry use to refer back to a point Emma made about transportation?

P WORD STRESS: ADDING EMPHASIS

Sometimes we pronounce certain words differently when we speak, depending on the words we want to emphasise.

3 057 **Listen to the final part of the conversation between Harry and Emma. Which of the highlighted words below does Harry stress?**

It's the same in my city. The traffic is terrible and it often takes me over an hour to reach the city centre. I would love to use public transport but, as you say, it isn't always available, so I use my car instead.

4 058 **The examiner has now given Emma and Harry one minute to decide which two issues they think are the most serious. Listen and answer the questions.**

1. Which phrase does Emma use to express her opinion about deforestation and oil spills?
2. Which phrase does Harry use to suggest another option, urban sprawl?
3. Which phrase does Emma use to politely disagree about urban sprawl?
4. Which phrase does Harry use to resolve the disagreement?
5. Do Emma and Harry reach an agreement?

5 **Work with a partner and answer the Speaking Part 3 exam question below. Talk for about two minutes.**

SPEAKING PART 4

1 **Say these 'time to think' phrases as naturally as possible. Which words should be stressed?**

1. I've never really thought about that, but if I had to express an opinion, I'd say …
2. Actually, I've thought about this before and I think ….
3. It's quite difficult to say, but I guess …
4. That's an interesting question to answer. I reckon …
5. That's a difficult question. Let me consider that for a moment. Ok, I think …
6. That's an interesting question and something I have strong views about. I firmly believe …

2 059 **Listen to Harry and Emma using the 'time to think' phrases. Which words do they stress?**

3 **Work in pairs and answer the questions. Start each answer with a 'time to think' phrase.**

1. Is littering a problem where you live?
2. Do you think the amount of pollution in cities has increased in recent years?
3. Some people think that cars should be banned from city centres? Do you agree?
4. Do older people care more about the environment than younger people?
5. Do you think people should do more to help protect the environment?

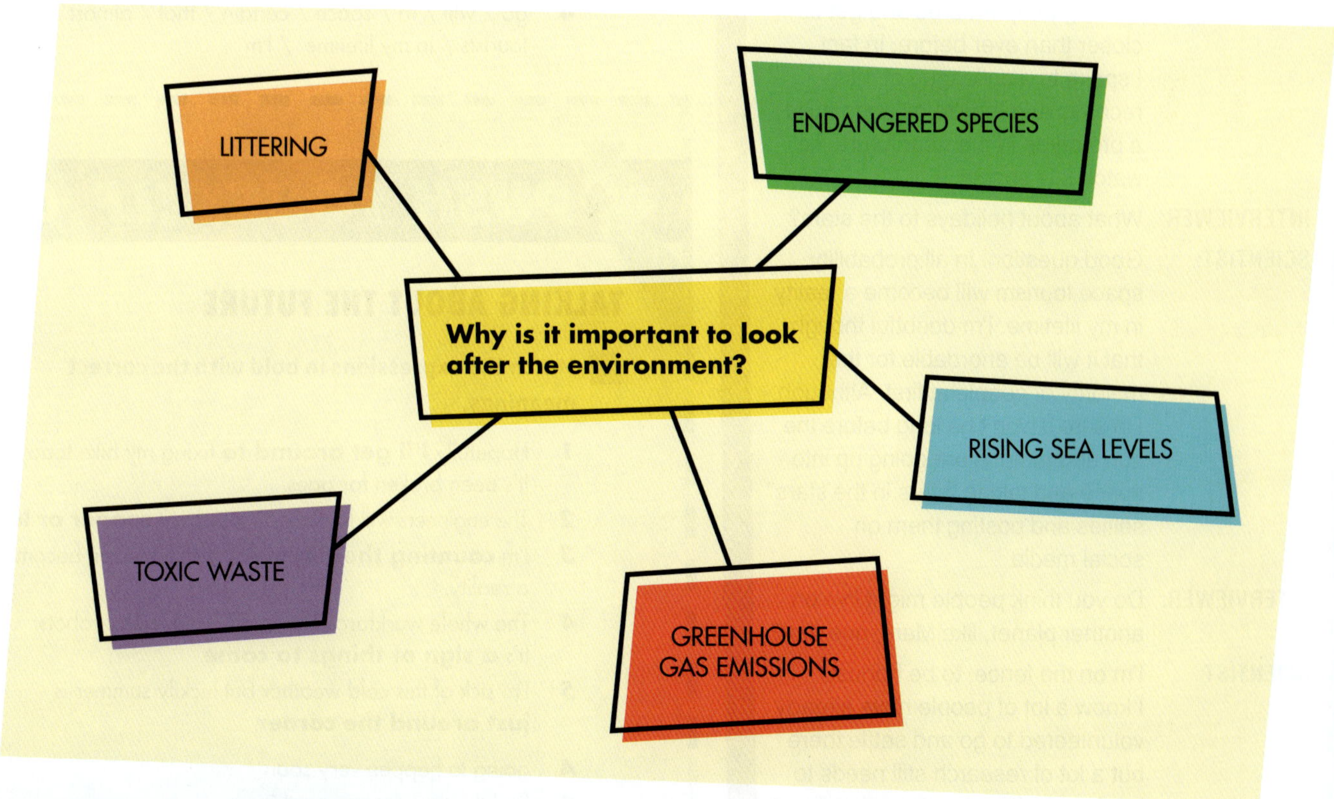

6 **Now spend one minute answering the question below. Try to reach a decision.**

Which of these issues is the most important to think about when considering how to protect the environment?

GRAMMAR

FUTURE FORMS

GRAMMAR ON THE MOVE
Watch the video

1 **Look at the pictures and describe what you see. What do you think each picture represents?**

2 **You are going to read an extract from a short interview about space exploration. Before you read, predict what you think the interviewee will say about:**

1. the future of space exploration
2. space tourism
3. living on another planet

3 **Quickly read the text and see if your predictions were correct.**

INTERVIEWER: What do you think the future holds for space exploration?

SCIENTIST: I think it's more than likely that we will try and get nearer the sun. Scientists are keen to learn more about it and, as technology improves, engineers are bound to develop a probe that can resist the soaring temperatures and get us closer than ever before. In fact, I spoke to a colleague of mine recently and they're going to build a prototype in the near future, so watch this space!

INTERVIEWER: What about holidays to the stars?

SCIENTIST: Good question. In all probability, space tourism will become a reality in my lifetime. I'm doubtful though that it will be affordable for the majority of people at first. Although, I'm sure it won't be long before the rich and famous are going up into space and taking "stars in the stars" selfies and posting them on social media.

INTERVIEWER: Do you think people might live on another planet, like Mars, one day?

SCIENTIST: I'm on the fence, to be honest. I know a lot of people have already volunteered to go and settle there but a lot of research still needs to be done before we can safely send people to live there forever. We'll have to wait and see if it becomes a reality. Time will tell I guess.

4 **Read the interview again and find the following.**

1. four examples of using *will* to make predictions about the future
2. one example of using *be going to* to talk about future plans which have already been decided
3. one example of using *bound to* to talk about something we are almost certain will happen in the future
4. one example of a future modal
5. two phrases that mean *soon*
6. an idiom that means the person is undecided

➡ **GRAMMAR REFERENCE** / *Future forms: Page 222*

5 **Rearrange the words to form statements. Then work in pairs and say whether you agree or disagree with the statements.**

1. to spend / space exploration / continue / on / In all probability / vast amounts / of money / we'll
2. settle / people / more / likely / that / It's / than / Mars / will / on
3. finding / There's / life / on / prospect / of / little / another planet
4. go / will / to / space / certain / that / almost / tourists / in my lifetime. / I'm

PUSH YOURSELF C1

TALKING ABOUT THE FUTURE

1 **Match the expressions in bold with the correct meanings.**

1. Hopefully **I'll get around to** fixing my bike today. It's been broken for ages.
2. The engineers will find a way to solve it **sooner or later**.
3. I'm **counting the days** until space tourism becomes a reality.
4. The whole workforce has been replaced by robots. It's **a sign of things to come**.
5. I'm sick of this cold weather but luckily summer is **just around the corner**.

A going to happen very soon
B find the time to do something
C a change now that will become normal in the future
D definitely happening in the future but you do not know exactly when
E waiting excitedly for something to happen.

LISTENING

1 **Look at the photos of great explorations. Which, in your opinion, was the most ground-breaking?**

2 **Work in pairs and do the quiz. Then match the questions (1–4) with the photos (A–D).**

1 Edmund Hillary and Tenzing Norgay were the first to reach the summit of Mount Everest. What is its height?

A 8,848 metres
B 10,630 metres
C 15,375 metres

2 Not only did Charles Lindbergh help invent the first artificial heart in 1935, but he also became famous for

A the first nonstop solo flight across the Atlantic Ocean.
B being the first stunt pilot to star in a film.
C the first nonstop solo flight around the world.

3 Although Naomi James didn't know how to swim until the age of 23, in 1977 she was the first woman to sail single-handed around the world. It took her

A 158 days.
B 205 days.
C 272 days.

4 With a depth of around 10,900 metres, *Challenger Deep* is the deepest known point of Earth's seabed. To date, how much of the ocean floor has been explored?

A less than 5%
B around 25%
C more than 55%

3 **060 Listen to two students, Abeer and Omera. Which exploration are they discussing?**

4 **060 Listen again and correct the phrases in *italics* in the extracts below.**

1 As far as I know, a trip costs on average eight million dollars. *Do you think* the expense is outweighed by the scientific benefits though?
2 To be honest, *I'm convinced it is.* I can't see the point of exploring somewhere where the probability of finding anything living is pretty much zero.
3 So, you think it's a *completely waste of time*?
4 Well, I wouldn't go *as far that*, but, I think there are better things to spend our money on.
5 *What's the matter with that*, I don't. I think the costs are relatively cheap.
6 Really? *How is that?*
7 Well, *you need to take account that* …
8 So, *by far as* I'm concerned, the money is well-spent.

5 **Who do you agree with more? Why?**

6 **Look back at the photos in Exercise 1. Do you think we will ever have more great explorations like these? What great explorations might be yet to come?**

VOCABULARY

SET PHRASES WITH *FAR*

1 **Match the phrases (1–6) with their meanings (A–F).**

1	as far as I know	**A**	in my opinion
2	by far	**B**	it's certainly not true
3	I wouldn't go as far as that / that far	**C**	I think it's true
4	as far as I'm concerned	**D**	I don't agree to that extent
5	far more/too	**E**	much more
6	far from it	**F**	by a great amount

2 **Choose the correct option to complete the sentences.**

1 Putting a man on the moon is *by far/far more* our greatest ever achievement.
2 "So, you know the country well then?" "*I wouldn't go that far/As far as I'm concerned* – I've only visited twice."
3 There are *by far/far too* many chemicals being dumped in our seas.
4 *As far as I'm concerned,/I wouldn't go as far as,* global warming is being influenced by too many human-driven actions.
5 Exploring the ocean floor will not solve all our environmental problems. *By far/Far from it.*
6 *As far as I'm concerned/As far as I know,* NASA aren't sending another spacecraft to the moon any time soon.

GRAMMAR

FUTURE PERFECT AND FUTURE CONTINUOUS

GRAMMAR ON THE MOVE
Watch the video

1 **Imagine you are on a desert island and can only select three items from the list below to help you survive. Choose three items that you think would be most helpful in this situation.**

toilet paper guitar tent matches medicine
rope compass torch whistle hammock
mirror tin can

2 **Compare your choices with a partner and give reasons why you chose each item.**

3 **061 Listen to Angeline and Josh talking about their trip. Choose how Josh is feeling.**

A capable
B uncertain
C cautious
D enthusiastic

4 **061 Listen again and complete the sentences.**

1. By this time next week, we'll .... our own lunch!
2. This time tomorrow, we'll .... about how to keep warm in the wild.
3. By the end of the day we'll .... how to build a fire from scratch.
4. I'm not sure those are skills I'll .... advantage of once I get home.
5. I'll .... myself before the week's out.
6. The group leaders will .... everything into account when they put the trip together.
7. By the time we get back we're .... on nothing but what we trapped and cooked ourselves for a whole week.

➡ **GRAMMAR REFERENCE** / *Future Perfect and Future Continuous: Page 223*

5 **Complete the sentences using the future perfect or future continuous form of the verbs in brackets. Then discuss which statements you agree with in pairs.**

1. Within the next fifty years, some countries .... (vanish) due to rising sea levels.
2. By 2030, engineers .... (develop) a system capable of transporting people at more than 1000 km/h.
3. In five years' time, people .... (use) instant translation apps, making language learning pointless.
4. By the end of the century, all non-renewable energy .... (replace) by more renewable sources such as wind and solar.
5. Some people believe that we .... (fly) in planes that are entirely see-through at some point in the future.

6 **Correct the mistakes in each sentence.**

1. By the end of today, I'll have defeating my fear of heights.
2. This time tomorrow, I'll be decided how to cross a river without a bridge.
3. A week from now, I'll probably suffering from exhaustion.
4. By this time next week, I'll completed the first aid course and know how to give CPR.
5. By the time I get home, I'll be learning how to make a shelter with sticks.
6. Within the next hour, I'll hope I'll have gathered enough firewood to keep the fire going all night.
7. Sooner or later, I expect I'll be managing to get this fire started.

7 **Imagine your life when you are 65 years old. Write three things that you will have done by this time and three things you will be doing. Then walk around the class and compare answers. Decide who in the class you will be most similar to in the future.**

WRITING PART 1: ESSAY TRAINING

EXPRESSING AND SUPPORTING IDEAS AND OPINIONS

1 **Would you like the opportunity to explore extreme environments like the ones shown in the pictures? Why / Why not?**

2 **Work in pairs. Read the essay question and decide whether you agree or disagree.**

In your English class you have been talking about exploration. Now your English teacher has asked you to write an essay.

Write an essay using all the notes and give reasons for your point of view. Write 140–190 words

'Tourism to remote parts of the world is damaging to the environment and should be discouraged at all costs.' Do you agree?

Notes

Write about:

1. personal safety
2. environmental damage
3. .... (your own idea)

3 **Match the ideas (1–4) with the notes above. What is the writer's own idea?**

1. Tourists must ensure that they respect the environment and dispose of rubbish responsibly.
2. The increasing popularity of adventure tourism ruins previously unexplored areas.
3. If people are adequately prepared and follow the guidance, they should not be at risk of getting injured or injuring others.
4. It must be remembered that tourism provides more jobs in areas which may otherwise have high unemployment.

Paragraph development

State your main idea clearly at the beginning of each paragraph by using a topic sentence. Then support it with reasons, examples and results. Use linking language to show the relationship between your main idea and your supporting sentences.

4 **Match the topic sentences (1–4) in Exercise 3 with the supporting sentences (A–D) below.**

A However, unlike other forms of tourism, there is more of an emphasis on preserving what is there rather than developing new hotels and facilities.

B This will help keep the area clean for locals and tourists alike and safe for wildlife.

C Consequently, the local population can be in favour of increased tourism if it means they are getting economic benefits from it.

D However, being unprepared could result in hospitalisation or a fatal accident.

5 **Read the writing prompt and the candidate's answer, ignoring the gaps for now. Underline the topic sentence in each paragraph.**

In your English class you have been discussing the importance of exploration. Now your teacher has asked you to write an essay. Write an essay using all the notes and give reasons for your point of view. Write 140–190 words.

Some people think we should stop exploring space. Do you agree?

Notes

Write about:

1. Research
2. Cost
3. .... (your own idea)

Humans have always been fascinated by the stars. Over the years, we have explored more and more of the universe and I don't believe this should end.

One area that has greatly benefited from space exploration is meteorology. Research into space has improved our ability to both understand and predict weather patterns, (1) .... we can warn people of extreme weather conditions much quicker.

It has been suggested that space exploration is too expensive. (2) .... , the fact that we now have global communication via mobile devices, a much better understanding of the human body, (3) .... a wider knowledge of the universe, is worth the investment, in my opinion.

Finally, I think that air travel is now much safer thanks to what we have learnt from exploring space. (4) .... have the materials used to build aeroplanes improved, but also the communication system is much more sophisticated, making it easier to communicate with air traffic control.

Overall, I believe that space exploration has had a huge benefit on our lives and I truly hope that we will continue to explore space in the future.

6 **Read the model answer again and complete the supporting sentences with the linking words and phrases in the box. Does the writer agree or disagree with the statement in the question?**

however	meaning that	not only	not to mention

7 **Think of two other reasons why exploring space is a good or bad idea. Work with a partner and write a topic sentence and one or two supporting sentences for each.**

8 **Write your answer to the question in Exercise 5 in an appropriate style. Use all the notes and give reasons for your point of view.**

EXAM FOCUS

READING AND USE OF ENGLISH PART 2

EXAM CHECK

Complete the information about Reading and Use of English Part 2 with the words in the box.

eight	example	prepositions	sport	topics	160

In Reading and Use of English Part 2, you must complete a text which contains **(1)** .... missing words. The missing words can be **(2)** .... , verb forms, relative pronouns, linkers and articles. The first sentence of the text contains a gap with an **(3)** .... and the text you have to read will be no longer than **(4)** .... words. Part 2 texts can be about a variety of **(5)** .... , including education, work, **(6)** .... , the environment, and daily life, but they will not contain vocabulary which is too technical.

For questions 1–8, read the text below and think of the word that best fits each gap. Use only one word in each gap. There is an example at the beginning (0).

Communication in plants

Research **(0)** *has* shown that although plants do not have the same senses as humans and animals, **(1)** .... are able to understand what is going **(2)** .... around them and can communicate with other plants and animals. Both seeds and roots can tell the difference **(3)** .... what is above and what is below: the former to grow upward, the **(4)** .... downward.

Plants can also sense when they are **(5)** .... attack from insects and are able to communicate with each other via their roots and other underground systems. This ability enables them to release chemicals through their leaves which can prevent the hungry insects **(6)** .... attacking the plant.

Not only does this work for the plant **(7)** .... is being threatened, but it also works for neighbouring plants. These plants know that an attack is close and can react quickly enough **(8)** .... the danger to avoid being harmed.

WRITING PART 1: ESSAY

EXAM CHECK

➡ ***WRITING BANK*** / *Pages 234–235*

Work with a partner. Write down five things to remember about Writing Part 1. Then look back at Unit 1 and Unit 2 and check your answers.

You must answer this question. Write your answer in **140–190** words in an appropriate style on the separate answer sheet.

In your English class you have been talking about the environment. Now, your English teacher has asked you to write an essay.

Write an essay using all the notes and give reasons for your point of view.

'Every country in the world must do more to protect the planet.' Do you agree?

Notes

Write about:

1. drinking water
2. wild animals
3. .... (your own idea)

SPEAKING PART 3

EXAM CHECK

Read the sentences about Speaking Parts 3 and 4. Decide if the sentences are true or false.

Part 3

1 In Speaking Part 3, you will have a conversation with the examiner only.
2 You will be given written prompts and a question for you to answer.
3 You must talk about all of the prompts on the exam card.

Part 4

4 In Speaking Part 4, your partner will ask you questions.
5 These questions are related to the topic in Speaking Part 3.
6 You are not allowed to disagree with the other candidate.

➡ **SPEAKING BANK** / *Pages 250–251*

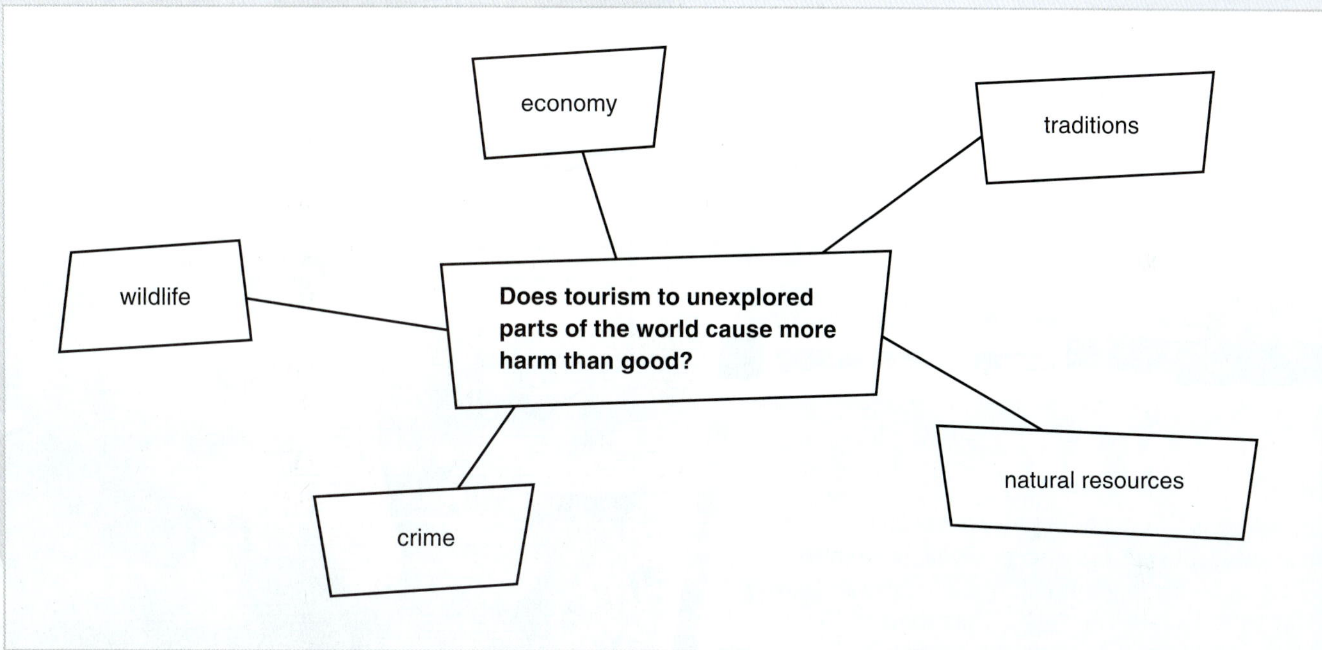

SPEAKING PART 4

Do you think it would be a good idea to stop people visiting places of great natural beauty in the world?
Do you think tourism in remote places will ever replace more traditional holiday destinations?
Do you think local communities in remote areas benefit from an increase in tourism?
How important is it to go on holiday every year?
Do you think investing in space tourism is a waste of money?
Some people say it's necessary to explore the world we live in so that we learn how to protect it. What do you think?

➡ **SPEAKING BANK** / *Pages 252–253*

REAL WORLD

BROADENING YOUR HORIZONS IN ... LOS ANGELES

1 In one minute, write down everything you know about Los Angeles. Then compare your notes with a partner.

2 Look at the pictures and then read the short article about things to see in Los Angeles. Which of the three options would you prefer to see and why?

URBAN ART

Street art is gaining popularity in LA. It is incredibly diverse and offers free expression to artists. Celebrating this cultural diversity and with over 1500 murals, Los Angeles has some of the best urban art in the USA. From ground-breaking exhibitions which include immersive environments and underground sensations, to transport projects commissioned by the Metro's Art Department, Los Angeles is at the forefront of the street art movement and a must-see for all visitors.

THEATRE AND DANCE

Boasting more theatres than any other city in the USA, Los Angeles will not disappoint those wishing to experience the theatre scene. Home to a wealth of talent, Los Angeles puts on an average of 1500 performances a year. From classical ballet to avant-garde productions, Los Angeles has it all. Where the best of the best come to write, direct and perform and in a city which lives and breathes 'performance', audiences can be guaranteed not only a lively atmosphere, but also an incredible choice.

3 <u>Underline</u> **the words and phrases in the texts which mean ...**

Urban Art

1. becoming more well-known
2. public displays of art which are new and interesting
3. in a leading position

Theatre and Dance

4. a lot of natural ability
5. organises
6. an exciting environment

Hollywood Walk of Fame

7. very well-known or important
8. theatre and film

4 062 **Listen to a man called Martin phoning a theatre office to book tickets for a play. Answer the questions.**

1. What show does Martin choose to see?
2. What day and time would Martin like to book? What day and time does he end up booking?
3. How much are the tickets and how does Martin choose to pay?

5 062 **Listen again. Complete the sentences you hear with the words from the recording to form phrases that you might use when booking tickets.**

PHRASES YOU MIGHT HEAR / USE

1. I'm visiting Los Angeles with my family in August and I wanted to ask you about ....
2. It does come with an ...., though. Attendees must be aged 16 years or over.
3. Great. Due to the school holidays, we do have .... in August.
4. Unfortunately, the performance on Saturday is ....
5. Please also note that these tickets are ....
6. As you're booking over the phone, you can collect the tickets ....
7. Ok, so for two adults and two children, ... a grand total of $150 dollars.

HOLLYWOOD WALK OF FAME

With more than 2,600 stars fixed to the sidewalks along Hollywood Boulevard, the Hollywood Walk of Fame is perhaps one of the most prominent sights in Los Angeles. As you walk down the 2.1 km stretch of road, you will come across some of the biggest names, both past and present, from stage and screen. Make sure you leave enough time, though, as it can take up to three hours to take in all of the names.

6 **Match the phrases in Exercise 5 with the correct meanings below.**

1. the age at which you are allowed or not allowed to attend somewhere
2. your money won't be returned
3. no more tickets available
4. that costs
5. at the venue
6. not many tickets on offer
7. what performances are showing

7 **Watch the video about Los Angeles. What do you learn about these things? Make notes.**

- The city of Los Angeles
- The entertainment industry
- Museums
- The Hollywood Walk of Fame
- The Arts District
- Beaches

WATCH

LIFE COMPETENCIES

USING APPROPRIATE REGISTER, PARTICIPATING WITH CLARITY

8 **Go online and find out about a film, musical or play that's on in your town next weekend. Write information about the points below. Then work in groups and compare what you've found and choose one that you'd all like to go and see.**

venue	time	price	reviews	cast

9 **Work in pairs. Choose one of the shows that you found in Exercise 8. One of you is a customer who is phoning to book tickets for it. The other person works as a ticket officer. Role play a conversation. Use the phrases in Exercise 5. Then swap roles.**

10 TO THE LIMIT

GETTING STARTED

1 Work with a partner and answer the questions.

1. Are you interested in sport? Do you do any of the sports in the photos?
2. Is there a sport you'd really like to try?
3. Why do you think the people in the pictures have decided to do these sports?
4. Do you think competitive sports are always a good thing?

LISTENING

LISTENING FOR GIST AND DETAIL

1 Work in pairs and answer the questions.

1. Would you ever go skydiving?
2. Why do you think people go skydiving?

2 You will hear a man called Kevin talking about his life as a skydiving instructor. Before you listen, write down what you already know about skydiving.

3 Now work in groups. Write five questions that you would like to ask Kevin about skydiving.

4 063 **Listen to Kevin. Write the answers to your questions that Kevin talked about.**

5 063 **Listen to Kevin again. What do these numbers refer to?**

18 and 50 | 360 | 4,000
800 | 60 | 750

6 **Think about your answer to the first question in Exercise 1. After listening to Kevin, are you more or less likely to go skydiving?**

7 **Work in pairs and do the role-play.**

Student A

You really want to go skydiving. Convince your friend that you should both go at the weekend.

Student B

You are really nervous about going skydiving. Listen to your friend and ask lots of questions.

GRAMMAR

CAUSATIVES

GRAMMAR ON THE MOVE
Watch the video

1 064 **Read Kevin's final piece of advice to people wanting to go skydiving. Complete the sentence with the correct verb forms. Then listen and check. Who do you think took the photograph?**

And finally, don't forget to smile when you're ________ your photo ________ in mid-air!

➔ **GRAMMAR REFERENCE** / *Causatives: Page 224*

2 **Complete the sentences with the correct form of *have* or *get* and the verbs in the box.**

clean	correct	dye	make	renew	repair

1 My laptop developed a problem so I took it to an IT specialist and ________ it ________ .
2 I found a really useful website where you can ________ your English homework ________ by an expert.
3 Make sure you ________ your passport ________ before flying off to Mexico next month.
4 I was surprised to hear that my friend ________ his car professionally ________ . I always do it myself.
5 I'm ________ my hair ________ next week. I just booked an appointment with the hairdresser.
6 After winning the championship, the parents ________ trophies ________ for all the kids on the team.

As well as *have*, we can also use the following verbs to express the idea of somebody or something causing something to happen. These are known as causative verbs.

A *let – Our teacher let us have the afternoon off.*
B *made – My friend made me watch every minute of the football match.*
C *help – Yoga is really helping me (to) feel more relaxed.*
D *get – I can never get my housemate to come jogging with me.*

3 **Read the information in the box. Match the meanings (1–4) with the example sentences (A–D) in the box.**

1 force someone to do something
2 allow something to happen
3 support someone in doing something
4 encourage or convince someone to do something

4 **Correct the mistakes in these sentences.**

1 Our boss made us all to stay at work late today.
2 I got my friend check my homework assignment.
3 My parents let me stayed up late last night to watch the match.
4 My coach really helped me improving my tennis serve.
5 Apparently the owner of the team is trying to get the trainer to sacked.
6 I've just had my application for a day off turn down by my boss.

5 **Complete the second sentence so that it has a similar meaning to the first, using the word given.**

1 Convincing children that they should play outside can be hard.
GET
It can be hard ________ outside.
2 The organisers cancelled Simon's match.
CALLED
Simon had ________ the organisers.
3 "You can finish your dinner in front of the TV" said their mum.
LET
Their mum ________ in front of the TV.
4 My friend forced me to watch his holiday video three times.
MADE
My ________ his holiday video three times.
5 Someone stole my suitcase at the airport last week.
HAD
I ________ at the airport last week.

6 **Work in groups. Plan a day of leisure where you treat yourselves to different services and luxuries. Describe your day using causatives.**

READING

1 **Match the extreme sports in the questionnaire with the pictures (1–7). Then complete the questionnaire. Compare your answers with a partner and give reasons why you would or wouldn't like to do these activities.**

WOULD YOU EVER GO	not in a million years	possibly	where do I sign?
bungee jumping	☐	☐	☐
wingsuit flying	☐	☐	☐
kitesurfing	☐	☐	☐
hang gliding	☐	☐	☐
zorbing	☐	☐	☐
ice diving	☐	☐	☐
white water rafting	☐	☐	☐

1

2

3

4

5

6

7

2 **Work with a partner. Make a list of reasons why people might take part in extreme sports likes the ones in Exercise 1. Then read the text on the next page quickly. Does it mention any of your ideas?**

READING AND USE OF ENGLISH PART 5 TRAINING

3 **Read question 1 and the four options (A–D). It mentions a specific name, Alan Eustace. Find the sections of the text that mention him. Now consider each option and answer the questions.**

1 Why does the writer mention Alan Eustace and his skydive?

A to argue that extreme sports are becoming riskier
B to describe a typical fan of extreme sports
C to provide an example of an extreme sport
D to show that people of all ages can enjoy extreme sports

Option A: *Is the writer arguing that extreme sports are risky? Does she say anything in particular about the risks taken by Alan Eustace?*
Option B: *Does the writer suggest that Alan Eustace is a fan of extreme sports?*
Option C: *Is skydiving just the first of several extreme sports referred to in the article? Is Eustace discussed throughout the article or just mentioned at the beginning?*
Option D: *Does the writer mention how old Alan Eustace is? Is this point developed in the article?*

4 **Read question 2 and the four options (A–D). Underline the sentence(s) in the second paragraph of the article in which the writer asks a question. Then read the four options and decide which one is the most similar to the question the writer has asked.**

2 In the second paragraph, the writer asks

A how people minimise the level of risk in extreme sports.
B how old people who do extreme sports typically are.
C why people choose to take part in extreme sports.
D why some extreme sports are seen as more fun than others.

THE THRILL OF EXTREME SPORTS

In 2014, a 57-year-old American named Alan Eustace set a world record for skydiving. He jumped from 42 kilometres above the earth, reaching a velocity of 1,322 kilometres per hour before his parachute opened and he landed safely in the desert of New Mexico. The jump received massive media coverage and was one of the most spectacular stunts ever achieved.

Of course, most extreme sports take place away from the global media spotlight. And while the majority involve people significantly younger than Alan, all involve a degree of risk. And for me this raises one question in particular: as one of our most fundamental human instincts is to protect ourselves from danger, what makes some people actively seek it out? I don't just mean the high-profile record-breaking skydivers such as Alan, but also the many ordinary men and women around the world who spend their weekends rock climbing, hang gliding or white water rafting.

It was this question that prompted researchers Erik Brymer and Lindsay Oades to conduct a research study of 15 participants in extreme sports including waterfall kayaking and big wave surfing. The aim was to investigate whether these sportspeople have a kind of 'death wish', and whether they are somehow different from those of us who find the idea of bungee jumping or other equally dangerous activities
line 29 terrifying. One of the conclusions they drew was that people are attracted to try these high-risk activities in order to conquer their fear. Some view fear as something positive; overcoming it can lead to a sense of wellbeing and increased self-esteem.

Yet motivation is a curious thing. Many people don't have a better answer than George Mallory, who took part in three mountaineering expeditions to Mount Everest back in the 1920s. His answer to the question 'Why climb Everest?' was simply 'Because it's there.' Mallory was one of the unlucky ones, who tragically died in his attempt to climb Everest in 1924, though several thousand have successfully made the ascent to the summit since then.

Other researchers, such as John Kerr and Susan Mackenzie, have found that frozen lake skaters and other athletes are driven to improve their own performance, much like practitioners of any sport. And a high proportion of wingsuit fliers, skydivers and so on don't view their sport as being particularly risky. They learn everything they can about the sport, find out about weather conditions and how this might impact them, and find the best and safest places to practise it. They actually put a huge amount of effort into minimising the risks, for example, by finding out about what wind does in and around buildings and cliffs, so that they know what they can and can't do.

In spite of the ever-increasing demands made by health and safety legislation, extreme sports from free diving to wingsuit flying are increasing in popularity. I've seen this myself; weekend white-water trips that I've been a regular on for years used to attract just a handful of people, but now they fill up without even needing to be advertised. Perhaps what drives so many of these people is the feeling that if they can ride that wave, do that jump or climb that mountain, then they can achieve whatever they want in life. But if so, it raises the question as to whether a successful bungee jump really has any influence over that job you're trying to get or exam you're aiming to pass. Maybe you're better off just sitting back and enjoying the ride.

5 Now read the rest of the article and answer questions 3–5.

3 Who does *they* refer to in line 29?

- **A** people conducting the sports research
- **B** people who consider extreme sports too dangerous
- **C** people who want to try an extreme sport for the first time
- **D** people who participated in the research study

4 Kerr and Mackenzie found that many people who do extreme sports

- **A** are highly educated.
- **B** consider their activity to be safe.
- **C** enjoy finding new locations for practising their hobby.
- **D** clearly understand the laws about their hobby.

5 What opinion does the writer express in the final paragraph?

- **A** Extreme sports need to attract the right kind of people.
- **B** Many people try extreme sports in order to understand their popularity.
- **C** People may have unrealistic expectations about extreme sports activities.
- **D** Concerns about the safety of extreme sports will make them less enjoyable.

6 Work in pairs and answer the questions.

1. Do you think people who do extreme sports are always successful in other areas of life?
2. What is the best way to conquer a fear of heights?
3. Some people think that social media and online videos have encouraged more people to try extreme sports. Do you agree?

VOCABULARY

COHESIVE DEVICES

1 Match the words (1–7) with the words (A–G) to make phrases.

1	by	***A***	balance
2	first	***B***	comparison
3	for	***C***	instance
4	having	***D***	of all
5	in	***E***	or less
6	more	***F***	particular
7	on	***G***	said that

2 Quickly read the article, ignoring the gaps. Which type of sport does the writer prefer?

From childhood, we are encouraged to take part in team sports such as football, hockey and baseball. There are many reasons for this. (1) ________ , learning to work as part of a team is an important social skill and, later in life, it is one that will help us in the workplace. Besides, team sports are enjoyed by most people who play them. (2) ________ , it is also true that playing a sport as a member of a team does involve a lot of waiting around while the ball is over at the other end of the pitch. (3) ________ , when we play a sport against an individual opponent, we are constantly active. Take racket sports, (4) ________ . The average player probably has to hit the ball once every ten seconds, (5) ________ , and so is far more involved in the game. I can see the appeal of both team and individual sports. But I'd say that (6) ________ , I much prefer taking part in individual sports, (7) ________ badminton, than in team games.

3 Complete the gaps with the phrases from Exercise 1.

4 Which of the phrases you used ...

A means 'especially'?
B means 'approximately'?
C begins a list of reasons?
D introduces an example?
E emphasises a difference between things?
F suggests you are going to contradict something you just said?
G introduces a conclusion, and shows you have considered different ideas?

5 Work in groups and talk about the advantages and disadvantages of team sports and individual sports for schoolchildren. Win one point each time you use one of the eight phrases appropriately.

WRITING PART 2: ARTICLE **TRAINING**

1 Look at the writing task below. Underline the points you must write about.

You see this announcement on an English-language website.

> **Articles wanted!**
>
> *What sport or leisure activity is currently becoming more popular in your country?*
>
> *What do you think are the reasons for this?*
>
> **We will publish the most interesting articles on our website.**

Write an article in 140–190 words.

2 Work in pairs. Tell your partner about a sport or leisure activity that is popular in your country.

3 **Read the model answer below. Put the paragraphs (A–D) of the article in the correct order.**

A COLD SPORT IN A WARM COUNTRY

A What has made ice skating so popular here is the Winter Olympics. We won two gold medals and this has inspired more people to get into it. Furthermore, going ice skating with your friends provides a great opportunity for group photos. When these are shared on social media, more people want to go.

B I first went ice skating last year with a few friends. There was a pop-up ice skating rink just outside the shopping centre, so we decided to give it a go. At first, I was terrified! I kept falling over, so I got my friend to hold my hand as we went round. It was a little embarrassing, but I soon became more relaxed and eventually managed to go round unaccompanied.

C It's a really enjoyable activity, so I'm sure it will continue to grow in popularity in the future.

D One sport that has really taken off in my country in the last few years is ice skating. Even though I live in a warm country, the number of people who are taking up this activity has certainly increased.

DID YOU KNOW?

In the UK, the place where people go shopping is called a *shopping centre*. In the USA, it is known as a *shopping mall*.

4 **Underline the words and phrases in the article which have a similar meaning to …**

1. to become interested in something
2. to try something
3. not having anyone with you
4. to become more popular
5. in addition

PUSH YOURSELF C1

CLEFT SENTENCES

5 **Circle the two sentences in the article that have the same meaning as the two sentences (1–2) below.**

1. Ice skating has really taken off in my country in the last few years.
2. Ice skating has become so popular here because of the Winter Olympics.

Cleft sentences

Look at the sentences you circled in the article. These are examples of cleft sentences. Cleft sentences are used to add emphasis to part of a sentence.

Compare:

My cousin got me interested in kayaking.

It was my cousin who got me interested in kayaking.

6 **Put the words in the correct order to form cleft sentences.**

1. about / hang gliding / views / what / the / like / most / I / is
   ……………………………………
2. father / got / it / my / tennis / me / was / into / who
   ……………………………………
3. activity / which / basketball / is / country / one / popular / my / in / is
   ……………………………………
4. I / to / why / reason / go / the / fit / gym / is / keep / to / the
   ……………………………………
5. fresh / hiking / the / about / one / is / air / love / thing / I
   ……………………………………

7 **Choose another sport or leisure activity. Write your own article to answer the exam task in Exercise 1. Use cleft sentences where appropriate.**

GRAMMAR

-ED AND -ING ADJECTIVES

GRAMMAR ON THE MOVE
Watch the video

1 **Look at the extract from the article. Answer the questions about the underlined words.**

1. Which describe how the writer felt?
2. Which describe the situation?

At first, I was terrified! I kept falling over so I got my friend to hold my hand as we went round. It was a little embarrassing, but I soon became more relaxed and eventually managed to go round unaccompanied.

➡ **GRAMMAR REFERENCE** / *-ed and -ing adjectives: Page 225*

2 **Choose the correct form of the adjective to complete the sentences.**

1. A friend of mine tried to teach me chess but I found it utterly *confused/confusing*.
2. We were both *exhausted/exhausting* after finishing the marathon.
3. I know a lot of people don't like astronomy, but I find it *fascinated/fascinating*.
4. I was *shocked/shocking* to hear about the number of people addicted to online gaming.
5. My sister is so *excited/exciting* about seeing her favourite band in concert next week.
6. My brother always wants to borrow my things. He's so *irritated/irritating*!
7. We were *thrilled/thrilling* at the prospect of studying in Spain for six months.
8. I was absolutely *petrified/petrifying* before I did my first parachute jump.

3 **Complete the sentences with the correct form of the adjectives in brackets.**

1. I found the martial arts course really ________ . (challenge)
2. I'm afraid of heights so I'm ________ by the thought of bungee jumping. (terrify)
3. I really enjoy hiking but it can be ________ at times. (tire)
4. One of the things that makes volunteering so ________ is the fact that you're making a difference in people's lives. (satisfy)
5. They were ________ to hear that their application to become a tour guide had been rejected. (disappoint)
6. I recently read about a group of people who go ice diving in the winter, which sounds ________ . (amaze)

4 **Think of one answer and make a note for each of the sentences (1–6). Then discuss your ideas in pairs and ask follow-up questions.**

Tell me about …

1. something that you're frightened of.
2. someone who you find really annoying.
3. the last time you were embarrassed about something.
4. an activity that you find relaxing.
5. a place you think is stunning.
6. something that you find fascinating.

SPEAKING PART 1 TRAINING

1 **Work in pairs. Which hobbies in the box below do you do? Which would you like to try?**

~~dancing~~ photography cookery gymnastics singing travelling acting martial arts magic tricks hiking online gaming volunteering

2 **065 Listen to Ivan, Ana and Simon answering the question below. Complete the table about each.**

Do you have any hobbies or interests?

Name	Hobby	Who with	When	Extra information
Ivan		Work colleagues		They have a picnic
Ana			Twice a week	
Simon	Online gaming		Almost every day	

*You might be asked **Yes/No** questions in Part 1 of the B2 First Speaking exam. Try to give extra information and don't just answer **Yes** or **No**. For example, if you are asked about your hobbies, say what these are, who you do them with and when you do them.*

3 **Ask three classmates the same question in Exercise 2. Remember to give extra information.**

4 **066 Listen to Ivan and Ana doing Part 1 of the B2 First Speaking exam. Write the different expressions they use to say what they like and don't like doing.**

5 **Talk to your classmates. Ask one question to each classmate you speak to.**

- What sport did you play as a child?
- Do you enjoy watching sport?
- What are the best ways to keep fit?
- Are there any sports which you would like to try in the future?
- How much exercise do you do each week?
- What do you most enjoy doing when you're at home?

VOCABULARY

SPORT AND LEISURE

1 067 **Listen to extracts from three TV sports commentaries. In each extract, which sport is being described? Write four words or phrases from each extract which helped you to identify the sport.**

1 ....
2 ....
3 ....

2 067 **Complete the table with the correct form of the words. Then listen to the sports commentaries again and check your answers.**

VERB	NOUN (THING)	NOUN (PERSON)	ADJECTIVE
compete	(1) *competition*	(2) *competitor*	competitive
decide	(3)		(4) ....
excite	(5)		exciting / excited
impress	impression		(6) ....
spectate	(7)	(8)	(9) ....
separate	(10)		(11) ....

P WORD STRESS

Type A
Sometimes, the same syllable is stressed in a group of related words:
*de**fend**; de**fen**der; de**fen**sive*

Type B
In some groups, the stress is on different syllables:
***gym**nast; gym**nas**tics*

3 **Decide whether the groups of words in Exercise 2 are Type A or Type B, and mark the stress.**

4 **Use the words in capitals at the end of some of the lines to form a word that fits the gap in the same line.**

Gregski triumphs in thriller

Silvio Gregski fought back from two sets down to claim a stunning victory over James Hodford in a hugely **(1)** .... final. The young Englishman should take great pride in his **(2)** .... , and it shouldn't be forgotten that he's only twenty years old and was making his debut in what has to be one of the most **(3)** .... tournaments we've seen for a long time. However, that's not to take anything away from Gregski, who produced one of the most **(4)** .... fightbacks of his career.

Hodford got off to an incredible start, taking the first two sets in under two hours. The **(5)** .... who were lucky enough to get tickets must have thought it would be the quickest final in history. Gregski had other ideas though. He took the next two sets, which included the shot of the match when he played a **(6)** .... back-hand lob from what looked to be an impossible angle, to set up a fifth and final set. Gregski used all of his experience and eventually beat Hodford in just under five hours.

There have been a lot of rumours that Gregski might now announce his retirement from the sport but, given the fact that he still looks incredibly **(7)** .... , I wouldn't be surprised to see him in the final again next year.

ENTERTAIN
PERFORM
COMPETE
IMPRESS
SPECTATE
THRILL
ATHLETE

5 **Work in groups. Write your own sports commentary without including the name of the sport. Then read them to your group, who must guess which sport you are talking about.**

EXAM FOCUS

READING AND USE OF ENGLISH PART 5

Who would want to be a match official?

Dennis O'Mackton, 53, is an international hockey referee, and has also worked as a match official in other sports, including tennis, football and boxing.

I've been a match official of one kind or another throughout much of my life. Hockey referee, tennis umpire, rugby linesman, I've done it all. And when I tell people, the reaction varies from pity ('Oh dear, you weren't good enough to be a player?) to disbelief ('Why on earth would anyone actually want to do that?') Actually, I think both these attitudes are mistaken for a number of reasons, and I'd like to set the record straight. For a start, many people truly prefer to be a referee or umpire than a player, and I'm one of them.

Having said that, many match officials have probably at times wondered why they bother to do it. Whatever decision you make, especially where there's been foul play, there's always going to be someone who disagrees. And sometimes in the heat of the moment, emotions can get the better of people. I've had five angry footballers all yelling at me on several occasions. You have to have thick skin – I sometimes ask myself why I am giving up my Sunday to run around a pitch in the cold rain with players who don't seem to respect me or the work I do, and who think it's their right to give the ref a load of abuse.

But despite this, I've always loved it. I now referee top-level professional hockey games. Believe me, for the couple of hours when I'm out on the pitch with the players, it's the best seat in the house. The skill of some of these top players is astounding, as are their fitness levels.

Of course, in this line of work, you don't start at the top. I oversaw something like 1,000 Sunday morning hockey games before I ever did a pro game. These were junior and adult games. I think **this** is key to a match official's *line 18* success at higher levels. There has to be enough experience for him or her to draw on, whatever the sport is. There is a concern that in some sports, young match officials are rising very quickly and officiating in a major tournament before they're ready.

I know that I've evolved in the years I've worked as a hockey referee. In the early years, I wasn't really assessed formally, not like newly qualified referees nowadays. But informally, I was being assessed by coaches, players and spectators every game. I occasionally heard criticisms in some of my matches that I was stopping play too frequently. So now I'm more reluctant to blow the whistle unless it's a more serious foul.

Unsurprisingly, I'm keen to see more young people becoming match officials. Back in the 1980's when I finished college, I was struggling to fill one page on a CV when I hadn't got any 'proper' work experience. I wasn't sure whether to include the fact that I'd been an umpire in my college tennis club, especially as one of the other umpires I knew said it wasn't relevant, and might suggest you're happy to work for a low wage (my university sports club wasn't a generous payer). Well, I put it down anyway. When I applied for a post with an ad agency, the guy who interviewed me told me later that he'd hired me because it showed that I must be 'reliable and responsible'. So for me, being a referee has had all sorts of benefits.

1 In the first paragraph, the writer says that his purpose is to
- **A** outline the characteristics of a good match official.
- **B** encourage more people to become match officials.
- **C** correct misunderstandings about being a match official.
- **D** reflect on what he has learned about being a match official.

2 According to the writer, it is impossible to
- **A** enjoy matches in bad weather.
- **B** control the behaviour of players.
- **C** always know what a referee should do.
- **D** make decisions that everyone will be happy with.

3 What does the writer mean by saying he has 'the best seat in the house'?
- **A** Lots of other people would like to do his job.
- **B** He is very tired after matches and needs to rest.
- **C** Being a referee is a great way to see the match.
- **D** He tries his hardest to be a fair referee.

4 What does *this* refer to in *line 18*?
- **A** being prepared to work at weekends
- **B** the writer's first professional game
- **C** wide experience of non-professional games
- **D** the difference between a sport at junior and adult level

5 How has the writer changed as a hockey referee?
- **A** He makes decisions less quickly than before.
- **B** He allows play to continue for longer than before.
- **C** He undertakes regular training more often than before.
- **D** He listens to feedback from other referees more willingly than before.

6 The writer said that being a tennis umpire at college helped him to
- **A** get a job.
- **B** make useful contacts.
- **C** earn a reasonable wage.
- **D** negotiate with his future employer.

EXAM CHECK

Read the sentences about Reading and Use of English Part 5 below. Decide if the sentences are true or false.

1 You must answer six questions, each of which has three answer options.
2 The text can be an article or an extract from a novel.
3 The questions are not in the same order as the information in the text.
4 You may be tested on your understanding of reference words, such as pronouns.
5 You won't be asked to work out the meaning of a word or phrase from its context.

SPEAKING PART 1

EXAM CHECK

Work in pairs. Make notes about Speaking Part 1. Then look at Unit 4 and Unit 8 and check your notes.

How often do you do exercise?
What are the sporting facilities like in your town?
Do you think you would enjoy being a famous athlete?
Where are the best places in your country for outdoor activities like mountain-biking?
Tell me about the last time you watched a sport.

➡ ***SPEAKING BANK*** / *Pages 244–245*

WRITING PART 2: ARTICLE

You see this announcement in an English-language magazine.

Articles wanted!

SPORTING EVENTS

Taking part in big sporting events is growing in popularity all around the world.

Tell us about a sporting event you have taken part in.

What might be difficult about organising events like this?

Why do you think they appeal to so many people?

We will publish the most interesting articles.

Write your **article** in **140–190** words.

➡ ***WRITING BANK*** / *Pages 240–241*

REAL WORLD

GOING ON AN ADVENTURE IN ... THE BRECON BEACONS

1 **Look at the photos of the Brecon Beacons, a national park in the UK. Describe them with a partner. Do the photos make you want to visit the Brecon Beacons? Why? / Why not?**

2 **Read the brochure on the Brecon Beacons National Park. <u>Underline</u> the different things you can see and do there. Work with a partner and talk about the things you would most like to do.**

THE BRECON BEACONS

the UK's adventure playground

Visitors to the Brecon Beacons National Park in Wales come for various reasons. For many of them, it's climbing the wild, impressive scenery of the Black Mountains, including some of the highest peaks in the southern United Kingdom. Whether you want to view them from a hang-glider or from the comfort of your own car, there's something for everyone.

Other visitors come to walk through ancient woodlands to get a glimpse of the spectacular waterfalls. It's also one of the best areas in the UK to see rare species such as the red kite, a bird whose distinctive silhouette can be seen in the skies throughout the year. The Usk valley is also filled with beautiful flowers, some of which are unique to the region.

Of the several attractive market towns, perhaps the most unusual is Hay-on-Wye. Mostly in Wales, but with a handful of streets over the border in England, this unusual town with a population of just 1500 has no fewer than 24 bookshops, and a literary and arts festival every summer. Visitors can also stay in one of the many hotels in the region, which offer breathtaking views, perfect for those on their honeymoon or celebrating an anniversary.

3 **Here are three groups who would like to visit the Brecon Beacons. Using the ideas you underlined in the brochure, choose one or two attractions that would be suitable for each group.**

1. **Martin and his friends**
   Martin, 29, is about to get married, and is travelling from Manchester with seven male friends to the Brecon Beacons for the weekend. They are looking for some adventurous activities to do while they're there.
2. **The Weifeng family**
   Zheng Weifeng is on holiday from China with his parents, his wife and their ten-year-old son. They love wildlife and would really like to see things which they can't see elsewhere.
3. **Shaun and Latifa**
   One year after their wedding, English teachers Shaun and Latifa want to get away from it all and have a peaceful, romantic break in the countryside. They've chosen the Brecon Beacons because they have never been there before.

4 **Sometimes you will read colloquial expressions in brochures. Find the words and phrases in the text that have a similar meaning to the words and phrases below.**

1. see something (often for a short period of time)
2. a small number of
3. from the more relaxed position of

5 **Work with a partner and answer the questions.**

1. What is the man in the reddish-purple T-shirt doing?
2. What is the other man doing? Why is this important?
3. Have you ever been climbing before?
4. What do climbers need to consider in order to climb safely? Write two DOs and two DON'Ts.

6 **068 Now listen to a member of staff at the Brecon Beacons Walls Climbing Centre, and write down the advice he gives for climbing safely. Which of your ideas in Exercise 5 does Jason talk about?**

You should:
You shouldn't:

7 **069 Sometimes people use colloquial expressions when giving information about health and safety. Match the underlined phrases in sentences 1–5 to the correct meanings (A–E). Then listen to the first part of the listening again and check your answers.**

PHRASES YOU MIGHT HEAR

1. I'll be telling you about the basics of climbing safely.
2. If you do see anything that doesn't look right, please let a member of staff know.
3. We'd ask you to pay attention and help us keep the Wall Climbing Centre a safe place.
4. Don't use any equipment yourself until you've checked that it's secure. It's better not to take risks even if it seems ok.
5. That might seem like something you already know, but honestly, we've had people turn up in sandals or high-heeled shoes in the past.

A common sense
B keep your eyes open
C better to be safe than sorry
D taking you through
E spot

8 **Watch the video about the Brecon Beacons. What do you learn about these things? Make notes.**

- The history of the Brecon Beacons
- Pen Y Fan
- The Brecon Beacons at night
- Water sports

WATCH

LIFE COMPETENCIES

UNDERSTANDING ISSUES, PARTICIPATING WITH CONFIDENCE

9 **Work with a partner. Go online and research one other national park in the UK. Prepare a short presentation of what people can do there and some of the health and safety information that people would need to know. Then give your presentation to the rest of the class.**

11 FACT OR FICTION?

A

GETTING STARTED

1 Write one or two examples for each of the following.

- your favourite TV programmes or series
- your favourite social media platforms for young people
- your favourite radio stations or podcasts
- your favourite local or national newspapers
- your favourite advertisements

2 Work in groups and compare your answers in Exercise 1. Try to agree on a group list to share with the class.

3 Work in pairs and answer the questions.

1. What type of media do the photos (A–E) represent?
2. Are these types of media becoming more or less popular in the world today?

B

C

D

E

VOCABULARY

THE MEDIA

1 **Match the words in bold in sentences (1–6) with their meanings (A–F). Which types of media do you think the sentences are talking about?**

1 If you ask me, it spoils the flow of **prime-time** television, especially for the most popular shows which it interrupts every 10 minutes.
2 Personally speaking, I don't mind seeing adverts from companies trying to **promote** their products in my news feed.
3 The problem is that a lot of opinions or stories posted on them are just not **credible**, don't you think?
4 They have far too much **influence** on what people are thinking, if you want my opinion.
5 To be honest, I would say their **target audience** is probably teenagers.
6 I would say that they present a version of life that is often very different from **reality**.

A situations from everyday life
B the main person or group you're aiming at
C publicise, advertise
D the power to have an effect on something or someone
E believed or trusted
F a time when the largest number of people are watching or listening

2 **Look at the sentences in Exercise 1 again and underline the six opinion phrases.**

P INTONATION WHEN GIVING AN OPINION

Generally, when we give an opinion, there is a rising intonation on the opinion phrase. For example:

If you ask me, it spoils the flow of prime-time television …

3 **Read the sentences in Exercise 1. Focus on the intonation of the opinion phrases.**

4 **Complete the sentences with some of the words in bold in Exercise 1. Then ask and answer the questions in pairs.**

1 Do you think that fast-food restaurants should use famous sports starts to .... their products?
2 Some people think that the media has too much .... on our lives. What do you think?
3 How many of the news stories that are posted on social media are .... ? How much of an issue is fake news?
4 What's your view on the standard of .... television, compared to when you were younger?

READING

1 **Work with a partner and answer the questions.**

1 What reality TV shows are famous in your country? Do you enjoy watching them?
2 Would you ever appear on a reality TV show? If so, which one?
3 Read the first part of the article (Some people believe …). Answer the question at the end of the paragraph.

Some people believe that reality TV is nothing more than fake reality, creating bad role models for young people and providing little educational benefit to society. Others, however, argue that they provide an excellent and much-needed form of entertainment on television and have the potential to turn ordinary people into superstars. Where do you stand on the topic of reality TV?

2 **Read the arguments in defence of reality TV on the next page, ignoring the gaps for now. Does the writer's opinion match your ideas from Exercise 1?**

In defence of REALITY TV

Right now, the viewing figures for such shows are among the highest around. After all, most television channels are dependent on the money they make from advertising, and the more popular the show, the more advertising revenue it can generate. So, it would be unreasonable to **(1)** ________ television programmers not to exploit this. After all, they are only giving **(2)** ________ what they clearly want to watch.

Besides, it's **(3)** ________ to watch how people react in certain situations, even if these are slightly unrealistic. Reality television is educational in that it teaches us something about human **(4)** ________ and therefore, about ourselves.

Ultimately, if we believe in **(5)** ________ of speech, then we must accept reality television is an expression of popular taste. It's also worth considering that if these kinds of TV shows fail to **(6)** ________ a big enough audience, then they'll be removed from the airwaves. Though we can't ignore the fact that their **(7)** ________ continues to grow and even those who criticise them have secretly watched them at some **(8)** ________ or another.

3 **Look either side of the gap. What collocations, or other set phrases, can you identify?**

4 **Now, complete the gaps (1–8) using the options (A–D).**

	A	B	C	D
1	expect	predict	need	assume
2	spectators	observers	supporters	viewers
3	attractive	glamorous	fascinating	breathtaking
4	character	nature	identity	species
5	independence	democracy	freedom	expression
6	attract	invite	welcome	host
7	approval	demand	admiration	popularity
8	end	point	tip	phase

5 **Think of three arguments against reality TV. Read the text and check which of your ideas are mentioned. Then discuss questions 1–4 with a partner.**

AGAINST REALITY TV

One serious problem with reality television is that often it involves putting people in horrible situations to see how they react. For example, participants may be asked to do nasty, often humiliating, things, either to themselves or each other, just for the entertainment of viewers. In doing so, it sets a poor example for society, especially for younger viewers, namely that it is fun to laugh at people and watch them suffer.

One obvious example of this is the unexpected abuse that many contestants face either during or after the programme airs, either in newspaper columns or on social media platforms such as Twitter, abuse which they are ill-prepared to cope with.

Without control, reality television is responsible for lowering social standards by making the unacceptable acceptable. It's wrong for broadcasters to claim that it is all harmless entertainment. Because their programmes are seen by millions, they have even more responsibility to promote high standards.

1 Think about reality TV shows you have seen. Can you think of any embarrassing situations you have seen on them?
2 Do you agree that reality TV sets a bad example for society and encourages unacceptable social behaviour?
3 Do you think there is a problem in your country with people using social media to bully other people? If so, should there be laws to stop this?
4 Would you say that you are for or against reality TV based on what you have read and discussed?

GRAMMAR

REPORTED SPEECH AND QUESTIONS

GRAMMAR ON THE MOVE
Watch the video

1 **Look at the two pictures and answer the questions (1–2).**

1. How does the second picture relate to the first?
2. Look at the underlined words and phrases. How do the tenses and word forms change?

GRAMMAR REFERENCE / *Reported Speech: Page 226*

2 **Change what Lucas says from direct to reported speech.**

Direct speech

1. Lucas: *"I'm not online this evening."*
2. Lucas: *"I'm starting my new social media channel tomorrow."*
3. Lucas: *"I've had a great response to my new channel."*
4. Lucas: *"I've been searching this site for new online material."*
5. Lucas: *"I went online to check how many subscribers I have."*
6. Lucas: *"I'd been working on it for a month when I started having problems."*
7. Lucas: *"I really must get it fixed as I can't upload my videos."*

DID YOU KNOW?

Prepositions and social media

- We subscribe **to** a channel or service but we unsubscribe **from** a channel or service.
- We post **on** social media but we post **about** a particular topic.

3 **Change the questions below from direct to reported speech.**

1. What were you doing last weekend?
   S/he asked me ....
2. Where do you get your news from?
   S/he asked me ....
3. Have you ever met anyone famous?
   S/he asked me ....
4. What is your dream job?
   S/he asked me ....
5. Do you enjoy watching football?
   S/he asked me ....
6. Do you have a favourite app?
   S/he asked me ....

4 **Walk around the classroom. Ask and answer the questions in Exercise 3. Then report back to your partner. Tell them the questions you were asked and what you said.**

Matt asked me what I did at the weekend and I told him that I had gone to the cinema.

WRITING

DEVELOPING YOUR WRITING

1 **Read the exam task below. Work in pairs and discuss the question.**

Some people say television has a bad influence on young people's lives. Do you agree?
Notes
Write about:
1 Education
2 Violence
3 ________ (your own idea)

2 **Read the model answer, ignoring the gaps for now. What is the writer's own idea?**

While it is true that television has potential for promoting positive effects through education, the amount of time spent viewing inappropriate programmes means young people are not only less sensitive to violence, but also spend less time doing physical activities.

(1) ________ . **(A)** ________ , programmes like documentaries have a positive impact, **(B)** ________ , by providing warnings about the effects of global warming.

(2) ________ . **(C)** ________ , excessive time spent watching television means children are not exercising and, **(D)** ________ , may become obese.

(3) ________ . Many parents feel overwhelmed by their children's internet abilities and **(E)** ________ they attempt to control viewing of violent content, they cannot do so effectively.

On balance, with limited controls possible and our increasing need for exciting and entertaining broadcasts, behaviour and health are suffering where young people are concerned.

3 **In the model answer, put the topic sentences (A–C) in the correct position (1–3).**

A Having said that, as children tend to believe what they are told, advertisements promoting unhealthy eating could lead to negative habits.
B Despite age ratings provided by broadcasters, the internet means it is increasingly difficult to limit what young people watch.
C It goes without saying that there are many educational programmes which support a child's learning, particularly when they are younger.

4 **In the model answer, put the linking words and phrases in the box below in the gaps (A–E). What other linking words and phrases has the writer used?**

furthermore	additionally	for instance
even when	as a consequence	

5 **Write your own essay for the question in Exercise 1.**

PUSH YOURSELF C1

COHESIVE PHRASES

1 **Look again at the model essay and topic sentences. Match the underlined phrases with the phrases in the box which have a similar meaning. Then complete sentences 1–4 below with the phrases in the box.**

All things considered	It speaks for itself (that)	Regardless (of the fact that)	That being said

1 ________ newspapers sometimes behave unacceptably, they often speak out against social injustice.
2 ________ , the internet is a useful source of news, yet we must be careful of inaccuracies and bias.
3 There's no denying that the new editor has improved the way we work. ________ , he can be quite difficult to work with at times.
4 ________ an increase in reality TV can be attributed to our love of others' misfortune.

SPEAKING PART 2 TRAINING

1

2

1 **Work in pairs and answer the questions.**

1. How often do you watch television and what types of programmes do you prefer?
2. Look at the photographs. What types of programmes are these? Do you enjoy watching these types of TV programmes?

2 **070 Listen to Albina and answer the questions.**

1. Which photograph, 1 or 2, is she talking about?
2. Which question, A or B, is she answering?
   - **A** What might these people enjoy about being on these television programmes?
   - **B** Why have these people decided to take part in these television programmes?

3 **070 Listen again. How well did Albina express her opinion? Which phrase does she repeat too often?**

4 **Work in pairs and make a list of opinion phrases Albina could have used instead.**

Opinion phrases

As far as I'm concerned

5 **071 Now listen to Walid talking about the other photo. Complete the extract with the words that Walid uses.**

I'd argue this would be suitable for a viewer who wants to watch something quite light-hearted because the subject matter is far from serious. It goes **(1)** .... that they would be quite competitive too. I'm not **(2)** .... what the ideal age might be, but it's **(3)** .... the person watching this would enjoy preparing delicious dishes for themselves or their family. My **(4)** .... is that they wouldn't need to watch every episode in order to understand what's going on.

6 **Work in pairs.**

Student A: Answer the Speaking Part 2 question below.
Student B: Answer the Speaking Part 2 question on page 201.

Student A

Talk about your photographs for one minute. The photographs show people who work in the media. Compare the photographs and say what you think these people might enjoy about doing these jobs?

What might these people enjoy about doing these jobs?

Student B

Would you like to work in the media?

GRAMMAR

REPORTING VERBS

GRAMMAR ON THE MOVE
Watch the video

1 When was the last time you watched something terrible on television? What was it and why?

2 Match the sentences (1–6) with the functions (A–F).

1. Thomas: It wasn't me who broke the television. *deny*
2. Maria: Would you and your sister like to come to my graduation ceremony?
3. Julia: I will cancel my subscription if they don't improve the service.
4. Simon: I am not paying them any money.
5. Dan: I will be leaving the company at the end of the month.
6. Sophie: It might rain later.

A threaten	B warn	~~C deny~~
D reveal	E invite	F refuse

→ **GRAMMAR REFERENCE** / *Reporting verbs and questions: Page 226*

3 Use the reporting verbs in Exercise 2 (A–F) to report the direct speech (1–6).

1. *Thomas denied breaking the television.*

4 Complete the second sentence so that it has a similar meaning to the first sentence, using the word given.

1. "I'll find the story online," Suzanne promised.
   WOULD
   Suzanne promised ________ online.
2. "I'm not watching this on TV," Keith said.
   REFUSED
   Keith ________ on TV.
3. "You must read the article tonight," the teacher said to me.
   TOLD
   The teacher ________ read the article that night.

VOCABULARY

PHRASES TO TALK ABOUT THE MEDIA

1 Work in pairs and answer the questions.

1. How concerned should we be about our privacy when using social networking websites?
2. Do you feel social networking websites do enough to keep your personal data safe?

2 Look at the newspaper headlines. Which stories would you be most interested in reading about?

1. Journalists **speak out** against instant messaging bullying
2. Social media giants must do more to **stamp out** social media addiction
3. Government to **tighten up** data protection laws
4. Teenagers **under pressure** to get likes

3 Read the newspaper article introduction. Which headline does it refer to?

Politicians claim social networking sites are **overstepping the mark** and should **come clean about** the tricks they use to get us hooked. From instant alerts that your message has been read, to wavy lines informing you someone is writing a message, social media creators **go to great lengths** to keep people, especially teenagers, coming back for more.

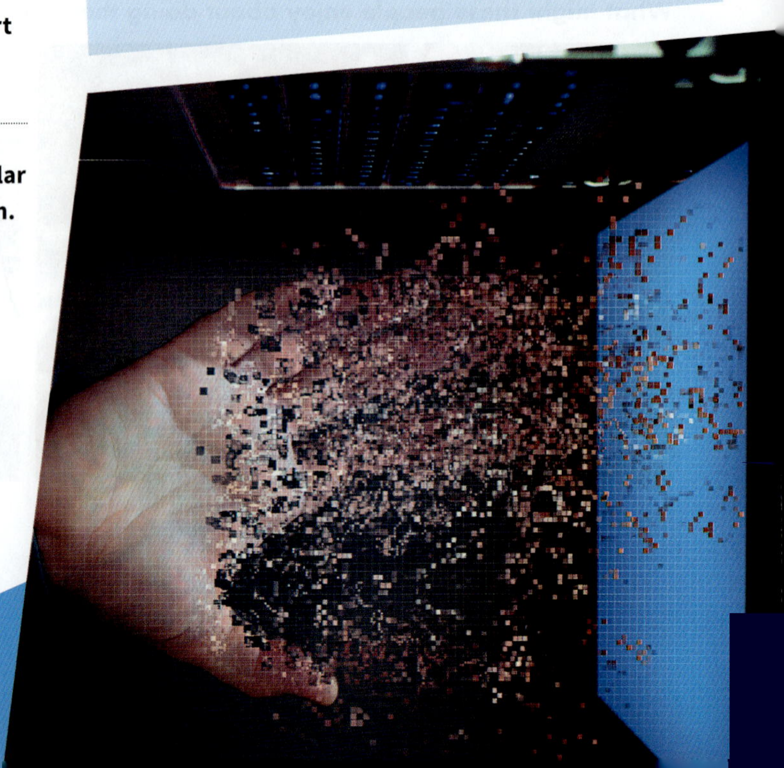

4 **Complete the definitions with the vocabulary in bold in Exercises 2 and 3.**

1 *under pressure* is when someone is being strongly persuaded to do something.
2 .... is to tell the truth about something.
3 .... is to make a great effort to achieve something.
4 .... is to give your critical opinion about something in public.
5 .... is to limit or control something.
6 .... is to behave in an unacceptable way.
7 .... is to eliminate something because it's wrong or harmful.

5 **Complete the gaps with the correct form of the phrases in Exercise 4. There is one phrase you don't need to use.**

1 The newspaper admitted to .... when they printed pictures of the celebrity's children, so they issued an apology.
2 It's important for teenagers to .... when they experience cyberbullying.
3 The journalist .... to make sure that everyone was aware of the issue.
4 The government are .... the laws to make it harder for people to share fake news.
5 It's about time the chat show host .... about his financial dealings.
6 Since the scandal was printed in the newspapers, the politician has been .... to resign.

6 **Work with a partner. Choose one of the stories in Exercise 2 and write a short news report.**

LISTENING PART 1 TRAINING

1 **What skills do you need to do the following jobs? Would you like to be one of them in the future?**

a journalist   a TV Presenter   a business owner
a photographer

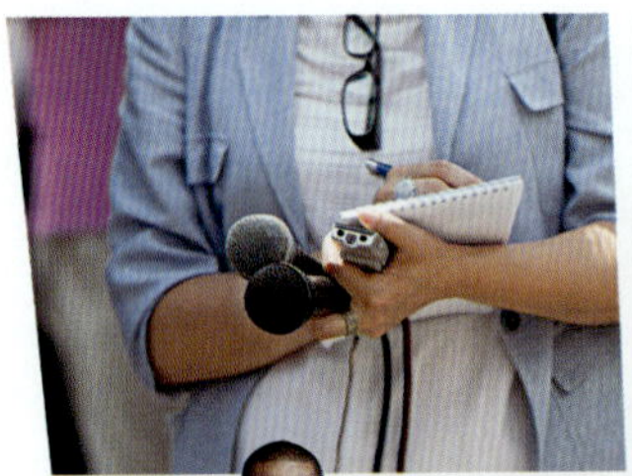

2 **Read the Listening Part 1 question, answer options and the recording script. Option C is the correct answer. Answer questions 1 and 2 to work out why Options A and B are incorrect.**

1 You hear a man talking about a job interview. How did he feel during the interview?
A worried about the questions he would be asked
B interested to find out more about the company
(C) confident that he was the right person for the job

I remember walking into the room and meeting the three people who were going to interview me for the journalist job. I was only told about the interview a day in advance, which didn't give me a lot of time to do background research on the company, and that was a little worrying to be honest. They were keen to learn more about my experience in previous roles, which I was able to provide as I'd been working in the field for over ten years. Secretly, I was certain that I would be a great fit for the role as I had all the relevant experience they were asking for.

1 What was the man worried about?
2 Who wanted to find out more information?

3 **Read the extract again and answer the questions.**

1 What phrase does the man use to say he was confident?
2 What phrase does the man use to say he was the right person for the job?

4 **072 Read the next Listening Part 1 question and listen to the recording. Option C is the correct answer. Answer questions 1 and 2 to work out why Options A and B are incorrect.**

2 You will hear two people talking about a television programme. What is the programme about?
A health   **B** finance   **(C)** travel

1 In what context is the word health mentioned?
2 What phrase does the man use to say that Bryan Stephens no longer makes shows about finance?

5 **073 You will hear people talking in three different situations. For questions 3–5, choose the best answer (A, B or C).**

3 You hear a woman talking about how her business became successful. Where did she get extra money from?
A a bank   **B** her own savings   **C** a family friend
4 You hear a journalist talking about a journey. How did he travel?
A by train   **B** by boat   **C** by plane
5 You hear two photography students talking about an assignment. What are they both unsure about?
A what photographs they need to take
B how they should submit their project
C when they need to present their findings

EXAM FOCUS

READING AND USE OF ENGLISH PART 1

For questions 1–8, read the text below and decide which answer (A, B, C or D) best first each gap. There is an example at the beginning (0).

Example: ***A*** vivid ***B*** hard ***C*** strong ***D*** serious

Reality TV

It was so long ago, it's **(0)** .... to remember a time when reality TV wasn't part of our daily television schedule. What started as the occasional fly-on-the wall documentary has now been **(1)** .... by a seemingly endless selection of shows, full of ordinary people, desperately **(2)** .... fame and attention.

What changed? **(3)** .... being incredibly cheap to produce – something which wasn't lost on television programmers and producers, some argue it was the development of digital editing. The latter made it possible to quickly **(4)** .... 30 minutes of ordinary people being interesting, from hundreds of hours of footage of them being terribly boring.

As for the viewers, there's no doubt that **(5)** .... enjoy the drama of reality TV. Perhaps it is because they feel **(6)** .... to the people they're watching. Research **(7)** .... by a team of psychologists also suggests that people enjoy watching how people behave in different situations. Love it or hate it, viewers have been **(8)** .... on reality TV for many years now. It's here to stay!

1	***A***	changed	***B***	taken	***C***	altered	***D***	replaced
2	***A***	seeking	***B***	finding	***C***	earning	***D***	obtaining
3	***A***	Apart from	***B***	Except for	***C***	Rather than	***D***	Instead of
4	***A***	withdraw	***B***	remove	***C***	leave	***D***	extract
5	***A***	spectators	***B***	audiences	***C***	observers	***D***	witnesses
6	***A***	joined	***B***	associated	***C***	connected	***D***	linked
7	***A***	directed	***B***	conducted	***C***	controlled	***D***	accompanied
8	***A***	hooked	***B***	absorbed	***C***	addicted	***D***	dedicated

LISTENING PART 1

074 **You will hear people talking in eight different situations. For questions 1–8, choose the best answer (A, B or C).**

1 You hear a journalist talking on her mobile phone about an interview. How does she feel?

A annoyed with the person she'll be seeing
B anxious about the meeting
C confident in her abilities

2 You hear two media studies students talking about their course. What do they agree about their lecturer?

A He explains his ideas clearly.
B He gives useful feedback.
C He's enthusiastic about the subject.

3 You hear a woman talking about a newspaper article. What is it about?

A a politician
B a survival story
C an award ceremony

4 You hear a weather reporter talking about his job. What is the purpose of his talk?

A to emphasise the importance of technology
B to suggest how forecasting the weather will change
C to warn about the challenges of becoming a meteorologist

5 You hear a journalist talking about his job. Why did he study journalism?

A It was challenging.
B It was worthwhile.
C It was well-paid.

6 You overhear a man talking to his colleague on the phone. What is he talking about?

A making a hotel reservation
B leaving the company he works for
C buying some new equipment

7 You hear a television actor telling a friend about an award she's just won. What is she doing?

A thanking people who helped her in the past
B explaining why she thinks she was chosen
C admitting that she is excited about her future

8 You hear two people talking about a piece of music. What does the woman say about it?

A It makes her feel happy.
B It reminds her of an old song.
C It inspired her to study music.

EXAM FOCUS

SPEAKING PART 2

Student A: Talk about your photographs for one minute. The photographs show people watching different TV programmes. Compare the photographs and say why these people might have chosen to watch these things?

Why might these people have chosen to watch these things?

Student B: Which TV programmes do you enjoy watching?

SPEAKING PART 2

Student B: Talk about your photographs for one minute. The photographs show people taking photographs in different situations. Compare the photographs and say why these people are taking photographs in these situations.

Why are these people taking photographs in these situations?

Student A: Do you enjoy taking photographs of the places you visit?

➡ ***SPEAKING BANK*** / *Pages 246–249*

REAL WORLD

HAVING FUN IN ... COPENHAGEN

1 075 **Work with a partner. Complete the fact sheet about Copenhagen. Guess the answers you don't know. Then listen and check your answers.**

COPENHAGEN

- ★ Copenhagen is the capital of **(1)** ________ .
- ★ Copenhagen has a population of approximately **(2)** ________ .
- ★ A statue of the famous author, **(3)** ________ , can be found at the City Hall Square in Copenhagen.
- ★ According to a report in 2013, Copenhagen was voted the **(4)** ________ city in the world.
- ★ Copenhagen is home to the second oldest **(5)** ________ in the world.

2 **Go online and find three more facts about Copenhagen. Then share these facts with your classmates.**

3 **Look at the two photos below. What do you think they have in common? Read the article and check your predictions.**

In the heart of Copenhagen lies the Royal Danish Opera House, considered by many to be one of the most modern opera houses in the world. Yet for a few action-packed hours the roof of this iconic structure, which also boasts a stunning panoramic view of the city, will be transformed into a giant springboard as it plays host to the Cliff Diving World Series. Watch in awe as the diving elite compete by diving some 27 metres into the harbour below. With no protection, other than skill and their own skin, divers will hit the water at over 80 kilometres per hour. It's an entertaining event and one which guarantees an electric atmosphere for spectators. Come along and prepare to be impressed by the divers' performance.

4 **Find phrases in the text which mean the following:**

1. famous building ....
2. a very attractive and far-reaching view ....
3. provides the space for ....
4. the best-trained divers ....
5. an exciting feeling ....

5 **Complete the sentences (1–6) with the correct endings (A–F). Then decide if the phrases are used for making, accepting or refusing an invitation. Which phrase is used if we are not sure if we can accept an invitation?**

PHRASES YOU MIGHT HEAR

1 Are you interested
2 Thanks for thinking
3 I'd love to but I'm supposed
4 Would you care
5 You can count
6 Could I get back

A to you later
B to come along
C in joining us
D me in
E of me
F to be doing something else

6 076 **Now listen to two friends talking about what to do over the weekend in Copenhagen and check your answers.**

7 **Which phrases in Exercise 5 have a similar meaning?**

PHRASES YOU MIGHT USE

1. I appreciate the offer. ....
2. I wouldn't miss it for the world. ....
3. I think I've got something on. ....
4. Could I check and let you know? ....

8 **Work in pairs. Read about the different things you can do in Copenhagen. Take turns inviting each other to each attraction. Use the language in Exercises 5 and 7.**

Kronborg Castle

Made famous by Shakespeare's *Hamlet*, Kronborg Castle dates back to the 1400s. It is filled with beautifully decorated rooms and historical artefacts.

Copenhagen Zoo

Home to over 3,000 animals, from snakes and crocodiles to lions and elephants.

The Botanical Garden

Covering an area of about 100,000 square metres, the Botanical Garden contains beautiful plants and flowers.

9 **Watch the video about Copenhagen. What do you learn about these things? Make notes.**

- The city of Copenhagen
- Cycling
- Nyhavn
- Shopping
- Tivoli Gardens
- Freetown Christiania
- Historical and modern buildings

WATCH

LIFE COMPETENCIES

DESCRIBING CULTURES, MANAGING CONVERSATIONS

10 **Go online and search for special events in a country of your choice. Then work in groups and invite each other to the events.**

PROGRESS CHECK 4

FUTURE PROBABILITY

1 Rearrange the words to form sentences.

1 people / planet / will / ~~it's~~ / that / in the future / likely / live / on another / more than
It's ______
2 driverless cars / in / bound / see / on the roads / to / ~~we're~~ / 20 years
We're ______
3 a new planet / is / we'll / ~~there~~ / prospect / discover / little / that
There ______
4 robot teachers / think / ~~I~~ / any / be / soon / don't / will / time / there
I ______
5 life / not / on other planets / we / ~~I'm~~ / that / find / convinced / will
I'm ______

FUTURE PERFECT AND FUTURE CONTINUOUS

2 Underline the correct phrase to complete the sentences.

1 By the year 2050, I *will have retired/will be retiring* from work.
2 It's better to phone us at 8 o'clock as we *will have finished/will be finishing* dinner by then.
3 More and more people *will have lived/will be living* in rural areas in the future.
4 Hopefully, I *will have completed/will be completing* my assignment before the deadline next week.
5 Next year, I *will have studied/will be studying* chemical engineering at university.
6 Within the next 30 years, some animals *will have become/will be becoming* extinct.
7 This time tomorrow, we *will have flown/will be flying* to the Maldives on our honeymoon.

THE WORLD AND BEYOND

3 Choose the correct word to complete the sentences.

1 There will be *dense/violent* storms in the afternoon.
2 As far as I'm *concerned/know*, Real Madrid are the best football team in the world.
3 The event was cancelled due to the *gale-force/poor* winds.
4 By February, the lake had completely frozen *through/over*.
5 The *soaring/violent* temperatures led to a water shortage in the area.
6 Personally, I wouldn't go as far *as/than* that.
7 We couldn't drive any further because of the *persistent/poor* visibility.
8 Spring is *as/by* far the best season of the year.
9 The strong winds will die *down/out* by the evening.

CAUSATIVES – *HAVE* AND *GET*

4 Complete the sentences using *have* or *get* and the words in brackets.

1 She went to the hairdresser's to ______ (hair / cut).
2 We need to ______ (passports / renew) before we go on holiday.
3 I actually prefer cleaning the windows myself rather than ______ (clean) by someone else.
4 I will ______ (eyes / test) at the opticians next week.
5 I used to ______ (car / wash) at the local garage but now I do it myself.

CAUSATIVE VERBS

5 Rewrite the sentences using the verbs in brackets.

1 My friend made me go running with him. (FORCE)
______
2 Our sports teacher allowed us to finish 30 minutes early. (LET)
______
3 My coach is supporting me in improving my tennis serve. (HELP)
______
4 I can never convince my parents to go on a camping holiday. (GET)
______

-ED AND *-ING* ADJECTIVES

6 Circle the correct word to complete the sentences.

1. We went on the new rollercoaster at the theme park and I was absolutely *terrified/terrifying.*
2. I found the ending of the film really *confused/confusing.*
3. Overall, I found the course really dull. The teacher, in particular, was really *bored/boring.*
4. The hike lasted for about seven hours in total and I was *exhausted/exhausting* after it.
5. The most *challenged/challenging* thing about tennis, I find, is serving.
6. The group were really *disappointed/disappointing* to hear that the concert had been called off.
7. I enjoy playing tennis with my brother, but he can be so *annoyed/annoying* when he wins.
8. I gave a presentation last week, and I thought I was *amazed/amazing*! I'm not sure what the audience thought, though.

SPORT AND LEISURE

7 Read the extract from a footballer's autobiography. Complete the extract with the words and phrases in the box.

autograph	compete	excitement	fan
spectators	supporters	thrilled	

I remember the morning of the cup final. I went for a walk and could feel the **(1)** ________ in the air. People were stopping me in the streets, asking for my **(2)** ________ . I even had **(3)** ________ of the other team asking me my thoughts about the match. I didn't mind that at all as I'm a big **(4)** ________ of promoting the positive side of the sport.

I have been fortunate to **(5)** ________ in some really exciting matches, but nothing compared to the moment I stepped out onto the pitch. The only thing I could hear were the sounds of the **(6)** ________ singing from their seats. After 85 minutes, it was 0–0. I received the ball just outside the penalty area, swung my foot and … scored! It turned out to be the winning goal. I was **(7)** ________ ! I still have the medal hanging up on the wall in my home today.

DIRECT AND REPORTED SPEECH

8 Change the sentences below from direct to reported speech.

1. "I will go to watch the new film", James said.
   James said (that) he ________ .
2. "I've received lots of letters from my fans", Michael explained.
   Michael explained (that) he ________ .
3. "I went to see them last weekend", said Julia.
   Julia said (that) she ________ .
4. "I must get my computer fixed", said Stephen.
   Stephen said (that) he ________ .
5. "I am going to upload a new video next week", Maria said.
   Maria said (that) she ________ .

REPORTED QUESTIONS

9 Change the sentences below from direct questions to reported questions.

1. "Where are you performing next week?", Lisa asked.
   ____
2. "Have you seen the line-up for the music festival?", Leonardo asked.
   ____
3. "How is filming on the desert island going?", Patricia asked.
   ____
4. "Can you bring me a glass of water?", Melanie asked.
   ____

ENTERTAINMENT AND THE MEDIA

10 Choose the correct words to complete the sentences below.

1. They have created an advertising campaign to *promote/target* the new TV show.
2. They *overstepped the mark/went to great lengths* to get her to perform in the film.
3. The writers are *under pressure/over pressure* to meet the deadline next week.
4. *In light of/Regardless of* the fact that he was caught cheating, he has now been thrown out of the competition.
5. The views of the mountain range from our hotel were *breathtaking/glamorous.*
6. They will have to raise more money for the show at some *phase/point* in the future.
7. I'm *addicted/hooked* to reality TV shows. I'm watching four different shows at the moment.

12 LET'S CELEBRATE

GETTING STARTED

1 **Work in pairs. Look at the advertisements for three festivals below. Which one would you be most interested in going to? Have you ever been to a festival like one of these before?**

2 **Work in pairs and answer the questions.**

1. Why do you think people go to festivals like the ones in Exercise 1?
2. What festivals and celebrations is your town, city or country famous for?
3. How do you usually celebrate the New Year?

1

International
Ice and Snow Sculpture Festival

Location: Harbin, China
Exhibits: made from snow and ice
10 to 15 million visitors annually
Event size: 750,000 square metres
Sculptures can reach up to 46 metres high

2

Location: Boom, Belgium
One of the world's largest music festivals
Over 400,000 visitors across two weekends
Watch some of the world's most famous DJs and musicians
Hurry! Tickets usually sell out in minutes

3

SUNDANCE
FILM FESTIVAL

Location: Utah, USA
Founded in 1978
Largest independent film festival in the United States
Over 40,000 visitors each year
Nearly 200 film screenings

VOCABULARY

FESTIVALS AND CELEBRATIONS

1 **Read the questions and possible answers in Listening Exercises 1 and 2. Match the words and phrases in bold with the definitions (1–10).**

1. to receive or entertain people as guests
   to host (question 4, option A)
2. a person who does something without being paid
3. easy to get to
4. the opinion that people have about someone or something
5. to interest or attract someone
6. being the only one of its type
7. happening soon
8. a place where a public event happens
9. to advertise an event
10. advice

LISTENING PART 4 TRAINING

1 077 **You will hear an interview with Martin Chase, an events manager, who organises festivals. In question 1, option A is the correct answer. Listen to the first part of the interview and work out why options B and C are incorrect.**

1 Why was Martin asked to help organise his university festival?
   A He knew people who worked at a nearby **venue**. ✓
   B He was studying hospitality management.
   C He was working as a **volunteer** at a similar event.

2 078 **Read questions 2–7 and underline the key words. Then listen to the rest of the interview. For questions 2–7, choose the best answer (A, B or C).**

2 Why does Martin think that *Street Fest* was such a success?
   A because the town already had a good **reputation** for festivals
   B because it celebrated the town's history and culture
   C because they invited famous musicians to play at the event
3 Martin believes that a good festival is one that
   A is in a location that is **easily accessible**.
   B **appeals to** a wide range of people.
   C ensures the safety of everyone attending.
4 Martin thinks the biggest challenge when organising a festival is
   A finding a place to **host** it.
   B dealing with technical issues.
   C trying not to spend too much money.
5 With his blog, Martin wants to
   A encourage more people to study event management.
   B give **guidance** to other festival organisers.
   C highlight common problems when organising festivals.
6 What does Martin say about the **upcoming** online festival in September?
   A He realised that it was a **unique** idea.
   B He was surprised by how popular the idea was.
   C He wasn't sure if the technology would work.
7 What would Martin like to do in the future?
   A **publicise** less well-known festivals
   B organise more online festivals
   C attend big music festivals

3 **Complete the extracts from the interview using the phrasal verbs in the box. You may need to change the form of the phrasal verbs.**

come up against	dress up	get into	go ahead
look after	miss out on	put on	turn down

1 First of all, tell us how you ________ organising festivals.
2 The university wanted ________ a big event for final year students …
3 … I was also volunteering at another smaller event, but I knew this was an opportunity I couldn't ________ .
4 … as well as a parade and encouraged people to ________ in costumes that best represented the town
5 One thing you've got to do though is ________ people when they're there.
6 You must have ________ a lot of challenges in your time organising these big events.
7 … it's vital that you stay within budget, which is never easy given the substantial costs involved, as this can ultimately decide whether a festival ________ or not.
8 I know there are a lot of big music events coming up, but you know, I don't want ________ the smaller events …

DID YOU KNOW?

An official holiday, when most businesses and offices are closed in the UK, is known as a ***bank holiday****. In North America, it is known as a* ***public holiday****.*

4 **Work in pairs. Ask and answer the questions below.**

Have you ever …
1 dressed up for a celebration or party? What was the occasion?
2 helped to put on a party or celebration for someone? What did you do?
3 turned down an invitation to a party or celebration? Why?
4 missed out on an event that your friends or family organised? Why?
5 come up against a problem when organising something? How did you solve it?

VOCABULARY

WORD FORMATION: SUFFIXES

1 079 **Complete the words in the extracts with the correct endings. Then listen and check your answers.**

1 *... which was big enough to hold the event and, because of these* **(1)** ***connect*** ________ *, the university invited me to join the* **(2)** ***organis*** ________ *committee.*

2 *... rather than just simply getting in bands and artists who the* **(3)** ***major*** ________ *of people had already heard of.*

3 *... one of the most important aspects of making a festival* **(4)** ***success*** ________ *as they often attract people from all over the world.*

4 *... it helps to promote them as well as the festival and this* **(5)** ***normal*** ________ *leads to a discount.*

5 *... a fast and reliable website so that people can buy tickets* **(6)** ***eas*** ________ *without the website crashing due to the high volumes of traffic ...*

P

In some word families, the stress is always on the same syllable: co**nnect**, co**nnec**tion, co**nnec**ted,
In other word families, different syllables are stressed: ***or****ganise, organi****sa****tion,* ***or****ganised*

2 079 **Mark the stress on each of the words you completed in Exercise 1. Then listen again and check.**

3 **Complete the definitions (1–10) with a word from column A and a suffix from column B. Use each word and suffix only once, and make any changes necessary to the spellings. The first one has been done for you.**

COLUMN A	COLUMN B
athlete	-able
impress	-ee
instant	-ful
interview	-ic
memory	-ion
peace	-ist
psychology	-ive
regard	-less
require	-ly
select	-ment

1 *requirement* : (noun) – something that you must do or something you need

2 ________ : (adv) – despite / not being affected by something

3 ________ : (adj) – describing something or someone that you admire or respect

4 ________ : (noun) – someone who is being asked questions (e.g. for a job)

5 ________ : (adj) – strong, healthy and good at sports

6 ________ : (adj) – quiet and calm

7 ________ : (adj) – describing something that you will remember for a long time

8 ________ : (noun) – someone who studies the human mind and feelings

9 ________ : (adverb) – immediately

10 ________ : (noun) – a group of people or things that have been chosen

GRAMMAR

EXPRESSING OBLIGATION AND PERMISSION

GRAMMAR ON THE MOVE
Watch the video

1 **Work in pairs. Ask and answer the questions about weddings around the world.**

1 What wedding traditions are shown in the photographs?

2 How are weddings in your country similar and different to the weddings shown here?

3 Would you like to have a wedding that looks like one of the weddings shown here?

2 **You are going to read about wedding traditions in three different parts of the world. Work in two groups, A and B.**

Group A: Read the texts on this page and answer three of the questions.

Group B: Turn to page 202. Read the texts and answer three of the questions.

3 **Work in pairs (one from Group A and one from Group B). Ask your partner the questions you couldn't find the answers to.**

4 **Read the texts again. Underline the words and phrases used to talk about obligation and permission.**

➜ ***GRAMMAR REFERENCE*** / *Expressing obligation and permission: Page 228*

5 **Put the words and phrases you underlined in the correct categories below. The first one has been done for you.**

NECESSARY	
NOT NECESSARY	
RECOMMENDED	
NOT RECOMMENDED	
ALLOWED	*allowed to*
NOT ALLOWED	
POSSIBLE	

6 **Complete the second sentence so that it has a similar meaning to the first, using the word given in bold. Write between 2–5 words.**

1 You should get the organiser to sign the document.
SUPPOSED
You are .... the document signed by the organiser.

2 It's not necessary to dress up for the party.
DON'T
You .... for the party.

3 Children may attend the event provided that they are accompanied by an adult.
ALLOWED
Children .... the event provided that they are accompanied by an adult.

4 In 1976, it became a requirement for all passengers in Ontario, Canada to wear a seatbelt.
COMPULSORY
It .... for all passengers in Ontario, Canada to wear a seatbelt since 1976.

GROUP A
IN WHICH COUNTRY …

1 does the bride and groom try to leave without being seen?
2 does a wedding cake tradition decide who will get married next?
3 are you allowed to kiss the bride or groom?
4 are you not allowed to smile in the wedding photos?
5 is it not allowed to go into certain rooms?
6 does the groom have to answer questions under difficult circumstances?

SWEDEN

At the wedding ceremony, if the bride leaves the room for any reason, then any of the female guests are allowed to kiss the groom. The same applies to the male guests, who may kiss the bride when the groom leaves the room.

THE TIDONG COMMUNITY (MALAYSIA, INDONESIA AND THE PHILIPPINES)

After a Tidong couple's wedding, the bride and groom cannot leave their home for three days. They are also prohibited from going to the bathroom or toilet and they are watched closely by friends and relatives to ensure that they stick to this rule. If this tradition isn't followed, it's believed that bad things might happen in the future to the couple or their children.

VENEZUELA

If you're invited to a wedding in Venezuela, it's advisable not to wait until the end of the reception before offering your congratulations to the happy couple. This is because they're actually supposed to make their getaway without being noticed before the party's over. All the guests should watch the bride and groom carefully, as it's considered good luck for the person who first sees the couple leave.

PUSH YOURSELF C1

EXPRESSING OBLIGATION AND PERMISSION IN DIFFERENT TENSES

1 **Rewrite the sentences below in the tense shown in brackets. Then decide how the meaning between the two pairs of sentences is different.**

1 All passengers must print their boarding passes in advance. (Future)

....

2 You should bring your e-ticket with you to the event. (Past)

....

3 You might be able to catch the end of the performance. (Past)

....

4 You can't bring your friends into the VIP area. (Future)

....

WRITING PART 2: REPORT TRAINING

1 **Read the exam task below. Underline the points you must write about in your answer.**

> A new festival was held for the first time in your town this year, and you attended it. The organisers now want feedback as to what worked well and why, and what aspects of the festival could be improved in the future.

2 **Work in pairs and think about a festival that you have been to or heard about. Write three things that worked well and three things that could have been improved.**

What worked well: *The festival was in a convenient location*
What could be improved: *There weren't any facilities to charge mobile phones.*

3 **Rearrange the words below to form sentences that you can use at the beginning of your report. Then choose which ending (A, B or C) is the most appropriate for an introduction to the writing task in Exercise 1. Why are the other two endings not appropriate?**

1 to / of / the / is / purpose / report / this

....

2 intended / report / to / this / is

....

3 report / aim / to / this / of / the / is

....

A discussing what was good about the festival and suggesting improvements to improve it.
B evaluate the success of the festival and make suggestions for ways to improve it in the future.
C talk about a festival that I recently organised and some of the challenges I faced.

All items in a bullet-pointed list will usually have the same grammatical structure. For example, they could all be:

- full sentences, including capital letter and full stops (e.g. *This would be much cheaper.*)
- noun phrases (e.g. *the option to buy tickets online in advance*)
- verbs in the *-ing* form (e.g. *learning about other cultures*)

4 **Now read the next two paragraphs of the review. Choose the best options for the gaps in the text. Then add one more bullet point of your own to each section.**

1 **A** the wide range of entertainment for people of all ages.
B There was a wide range of things for people to do, regardless of their age.
C having a wide range of entertainment for all visitors, whether young or old.

2 **A** the sales of additional tickets to some events.
B People had to buy an additional ticket even though they had already bought a ticket to the festival.
C not being allowed to attend some events without buying an additional ticket.

Overall, the festival was very well organised and a lot of people were very positive about their experience there, particularly with regards to

- the high standard of food and drink on offer.
- the convenient location.
- (1) ....
- ....

Although comments were overwhelmingly positive, some people expressed disappointment at

- having to queue for a long time when arriving at the venue.
- (2) ....
- ....

5 **Read the final paragraph. Underline the two phrases which the writer uses to make a recommendation.**

Looking ahead to future festivals, I would propose switching to an electronic ticketing service in order to reduce the amount of time people wait to enter the festival. In addition, I would suggest allowing attendees to access all areas of the festival with the same ticket.

6 **Write your own report for the writing task in Exercise 1. Use your ideas from Exercise 2. Write 140–190 words.**

READING AND USE OF ENGLISH PART 3 TRAINING

1 **Answer the questions about Reading and Use of English Part 3.**

1. How many questions do you need to answer?
2. How many marks do you get for each question?
3. Are you penalised for spelling a word incorrectly?
4. What changes might you need to make to the words in capital letters?

2 **Correct the mistakes these candidates have made in Reading and Use of English Part 3. Use the questions (A–D) to help you.**

A What type of word is needed?
B Is the context positive or negative?
C Do you need the singular or plural form?
D Is the word you've written spelt correctly?

1. The number of people attending the festival has increased ...significant... in recent years. (**SIGNIFICANT**)
2. The festival is ...dislike... any other celebration in the city, in that it's free to enter. (**LIKE**)
3. One of the reasons for the continued success of the museum is the organiser's ...unable... to keep the exhibitions interesting. (**ABLE**)
4. This is just one example of the many ...possibility... available to us for next year's event. (**POSSIBLE**)
5. Although profitable, the event has proven to be ...popularity... with local residents because of the noise and litter. (**POPULAR**)
6. Many of the attendees thought that it was a really ...enjoying... experience and said they would come again next year. (**ENJOY**)
7. There was a ...various... of beautiful paintings on display by artists from around the world. (**VARY**)
8. All of the solutions turned out to be ...unsuccess... so the festival was closed down permanently. (**SUCCESS**)

In Reading and Use of English Part 3, you may not only need to use a prefix or a suffix. Sometimes, a change in the middle of the word is needed. For example:
*The statue stands at a ...height... of 10 metres. (**HIGH**)*

3 **Complete the sentences with the correct form of the words in brackets.**

1. This festival is the perfect ________ for anyone who enjoys music and culture. (**CHOOSE**)
2. One of the volunteers built a stage with the ________ to support twenty people. (**STRONG**)
3. They needed to measure the ________ of the river to see if their boat would fit. (**WIDE**)
4. The residents of the town take great ________ in their annual film festival. (**PROUD**)
5. It's important to make people feel at ________ when they arrive. (**EASY**)
6. Every year, people skate on the ________ lake to mark the beginning of winter. (**FREEZE**)
7. The town's continuing ________ as a cultural centre has led to a tourist boom. (**GROW**)
8. These fish typically live at ________ of more than 400 metres. (**DEEP**)

4 **Look at the picture and read the title of the text below. Work in pairs and answer the questions.**

1. What do you think happens at this event?
2. Would you be interested in going to an event like this? Why / Why not?

5 **For questions 1–8, read the text below. Use the word given in capitals at the end of some of the lines to form a word that fits in the gap in the same line.**

SNOWBOMBING THE BEST SHOW ON SNOW

Snowbombing is a snow and music festival held **(1)** ________ in the spring in Austria. The festival attracts thousands of people from around the world, who come to enjoy the wide **(2)** ________ of snow and musical events on offer. First held in 2000, the festival was virtually **(3)** ________ until it moved to Austria in 2005. Since then it has become one of the most **(4)** ________ snow and music festivals in the world, both in terms of popularity and clothing as visitors are **(5)** ________ to dress up in fancy dress and other types of unusual clothing.

ANNUAL (1)
VARY (2)
KNOW (3)
FASHION (4)
COURAGE (5)

Getting to the festival is also an event in itself. Known as the Snowbombing Road Trip, visitors drive from the UK, stopping off in Germany for a quick break, before heading to the ski resort in the **(6)** ________ town of Mayrhofen, located near the breathtaking Hintertux glacier, which stands at a **(7)** ________ of 3,250 metres above sea level. A whole range of accommodation is available to the festival goers, including hotels, apartments and chalets, which offer **(8)** ________ views of the resort and town.

PEACE (6)
HIGH (7)
SPECTACLE (8)

6 **Go online and read some reviews of the Snowbombing festival. Decide whether you would like to go to it, or alternatively, find another festival somewhere else in the world that you would rather go to.**

GRAMMAR

EXPRESSING ABILITY AND POSSIBILITY

GRAMMAR ON THE MOVE
Watch the video

1 **Read the job description below. What do you think life as a tour manager is like? Write three good things and three bad things about being a tour manager.**

TOUR MANAGER

- Excellent organisational skills
- Experience of managing bands and artists
- Confident in booking venues and liaising with venue staff
- Must be willing to travel for long periods of time

2 **080 Listen to an interview with Chris Smith, who works as a tour manager. Complete the sentences with a word or short phrase from the recording.**

1. Chris ________ to learn more about being a tour manager by organising concerts for his band.
2. Chris ________ to put on a great show despite the low number of attendees.
3. As well as being paid more, supporting a bigger act ________ them to play to a larger audience.
4. When asked by a friend to be their tour manager, Chris agreed because he believed he was ________ doing the job well.
5. Chris and the band were ________ to go abroad last year because they had other plans.
6. Chris ________ to meet other tour managers as part of his overseas tour.

3 **Complete the rules (A–F) with your answers in sentences (1–6) above. The first one has been done for you.**

A We use *was able to* (not could) to talk about something that was possible on a specific occasion.
B We use ________ + *to* to talk about something that you did which was difficult to do.
C We use ________ + *to* to talk about something that you couldn't do.
D We use ________ + *to* to talk about something you can do in the future.
E We use ________ + object pronoun + *to* to say that something is possible because of something else.
F We use ________ + verb -*ing* to talk about something you think or believe you can do.

→ **GRAMMAR REFERENCE** / *Expressing ability: Page 229*

4 **Correct the mistakes in the sentences.**

1. I didn't know the band were capable of perform that well.
2. Unfortunately, we won't can to attend because we're away on holiday.
3. He could to play the guitar when he was only three years old.
4. I can't believe he managed putting on such a good event.
5. The organisers were unable find a solution to the problem.
6. Despite it selling out in minutes, I could get two tickets for the music festival.
7. The warm weather will enable we to host the party outside.
8. I've could swim ever since I was two years old.

5 **Using the words and phrases in Exercise 3, write one sentence about the ability shown in each picture.**

It looks as though the boy knows how to mend his bike.
I'm not so sure – he probably wouldn't be able to do it without his dad's help.

SPEAKING

SHORT RESPONSES WITH *SO*, *NEITHER*, *EITHER*, AND *TOO*

1 **How are the following events celebrated in your country?**

Weddings	Moving to a new home
A new baby	Graduation

DID YOU KNOW?

*The word **milestone** is used to describe an important event in someone's life, e.g., the day you graduate from university or when you get married.*

2 **Work in pairs. Look at the milestones in Exercise 1 and the pictures below. Predict what the connection might be between the milestones and the pictures.**

3 081 **Listen to a conversation between Alison and Marcus, talking about how the milestones are celebrated around the world. Make notes about what they say next to the pictures below. Were your predictions correct?**

4 **Work in pairs. Look at your notes in Exercise 3 again and answer the questions.**

1. Do you celebrate these milestones in similar or different ways?
2. Which do you find most interesting?

5 082 **Complete the short responses from the conversation. Then listen and check your answers.**

1 ***Marcus:*** Yes, I have. I actually read it earlier today. I found the bit about weddings in Turkey really interesting.
Alison: Yeah, ________ .

2 ***Marcus:*** It's a really interesting tradition but I can't imagine ever doing that myself, to be honest.
Alison: No, ________ .

3 ***Alison:*** I would love for that to be a tradition here!
Marcus: Yeah, ________ .

4 ***Marcus:*** I'd never heard of that one before.
Alison: No, ________ .

6 **Look at the statements below. Decide if you agree or disagree with them and why. Then work in groups and share your ideas, using the short responses in Exercise 5.**

1. Money is more important than love.
2. People shouldn't post pictures of their new-born babies on social media.
3. The best concerts are always the biggest.
4. The most important thing about a job is the salary.

I'm not convinced that money is more important than love, to be honest.
No, neither am I. I'd say it's the other way round …

7 **Work in groups. Choose one of the milestones in Exercise 1. Go online and find more information about how these milestones are celebrated in three other countries. Make notes then share what you have learnt with your group.**

WEDDINGS IN TURKEY

MOVING TO A NEW HOME IN THE PHILIPPINES

A NEW BABY IN FINLAND

GRADUATING IN ARGENTINA

EXAM FOCUS

LISTENING PART 4

EXAM FACTS

- *Part 4 of the Listening test features two speakers and is often an interview.*
- *The questions can cover specific facts and details, as well as the speakers' attitudes or opinions.*
- *You get one mark for each correct answer and no mark if an answer is wrong or missing.*

EXAM TIPS

- *Because you don't lose marks for a wrong answer, it's better to guess an answer which you don't know than to leave it blank on the question paper.*
- *Try to answer each question during the first listening. Then, during the second listening, pay attention to any questions you weren't sure about the first time.*

083 **You will hear part of a podcast with a blogger called Juanita, who has travelled all over the world. For questions 1–7, choose the best answer, A, B or C.**

1 Juanita started her blog in order to

A stay in touch with people.
B earn money while she travelled.
C help some travel destinations gain publicity.

2 The International Ice and Snow Sculpture Festival is Juanita's favourite because of the festival's

A unique style.
B beautiful location.
C impressive artwork.

3 Juanita says that the greatest achievement of the workers who build with ice is

A making the structures safe.
B collecting so much ice from a frozen river.
C designing such varied attractions.

4 Why does Juanita say the Festival in Harbin is similar to the Burning Man Festival?

A Both require skilful engineering.
B Both are worth visiting several times.
C Both involve something which is temporary.

5 What surprised Juanita about her tyre ride on the river?

A how many people she met there
B how enjoyable she found it
C how fast she travelled on it

6 Juanita emphasises the need for visitors to

A wear suitable clothing.
B arrange accommodation early.
C plan which attractions to see.

7 Juanita says that arriving in the afternoon enables visitors to

A save money on the price of the ticket.
B spend as much time there as they want.
C have a wider variety of experiences.

READING AND USE OF ENGLISH PART 3

For questions 1–8, read the text below. Use the word given in capitals at the end of some of the lines to form a word that fits in the gap in the same line.
There is an example at the beginning (0).
Write your answers IN CAPITAL LETTERS.

Example: **(0)** *significantly*

London's frost fairs

During the period between approximately 1300 and 1850, temperatures were	
(0) *significantly* lower than they are nowadays. During this 'Little Ice Age',	**SIGNIFICANT**
London's River Thames would sometimes become totally **(1)** .... ,	**FREEZE**
so that Londoners could actually walk on the ice. This was by no means an	
annual event, occurring only in **(2)** .... cold winters.	**EXCEPTION**
London was a major port, and so the fact that boats could no longer use the	
river was **(3)** .... to the local economy. However, because the ice	**HARM**
was thick enough to walk on, it meant that festivals could be held on the river.	
There were some who argued that it was **(4)** .... to hold an event on	**RESPONSIBLE**
ice as there was a danger of people falling over. However, these 'frost fairs',	
something between a Christmas market and a dance party, were extremely	
popular and highly **(5)** .... to London's business people.	**BENEFIT**
Food and drink were sold, and the **(6)** .... , such as jugglers,	**ENTERTAIN**
musicians and magicians, were able to keep the crowds amused. According to	
the **(7)** .... of historical records which gave detailed descriptions of	**SELECT**
the festival , there was a **(8)** .... range of activities on the ice, from	**THRILL**
sledging to bowling. In the 1814 frost fair, an elephant was even brought onto	
the ice.	

WRITING PART 2: REPORT

Your college recently held a party for its students. However, few people attended, and the college principal has asked for a report explaining possible reasons for this, and suggesting what can be done differently in the future.

In your report you should

- describe some of the reasons why few people attended
- suggest, with reasons, what can be done differently in the future

Write your report in **140–190** words.

➡ ***WRITING BANK*** / *Pages 242–243*

REAL WORLD

HAVING A GREAT TIME IN ... ESSAOUIRA

B

1 **Read the brochure about Essaouira. Match the paragraphs (1–4) with the photos (A–D). Then decide if sentences 1–5 are true or false.**

A

4 THINGS YOU NEVER KNEW ABOUT ESSAOUIRA

1 **While Chicago may be the USA's Windy City, Essaouira is Morocco's**, which makes it one of the best places in the world for kitesurfing. With a state-of-the-art golf course and excursions into the desert by quad bike or camel, there's loads for the outdoor enthusiast to do!

2 **Back in the late 1960s, Essaouira attracted some of the most high-profile musicians**, with rock legends Jimi Hendrix, Frank Zappa and Cat Stevens all having spent time there. It's tempting to believe the story that Hendrix wrote his song 'Castles in the Sand' about an Essaouira beach; unfortunately though, the song was recorded two years before he visited.

3 **You might have already seen Essaouira without knowing it:** the city is featured in the popular TV series *Game of Thrones*, and was used in the 1948 film version of Shakespeare's play *Othello*. With its beautiful landscapes and remarkable architecture, it's easy to see why location scouts choose Essaouira for their films.

4 **In the Essaouira area, the local goats spend much of their time up trees.** Yes, you read that correctly – goats up trees – Argania trees, to be precise. They produce a fruit that contains argan oil, which is rich in vitamins and is increasingly being used in skin care products. The local goats just can't get enough of it. What's more, they help to fertilise the soil which helps to grow more trees, something that supports both the land and the local tourism industry.

1. Essaouira has a reputation for being a windy city.
2. Jimmy Hendrix wrote the song 'Castles in the Sand' about a beach in Essaouira.
3. The city is a popular spot for actors to go on holiday.
4. Argan oil is often used in cosmetic products.
5. The only benefit of the local goats is to help fertilise the land.

2 **Match the words and phrases in the text with the meanings.**

- ***A*** new, modern (1st paragraph)
- ***B*** well-known (2nd paragraph)
- ***C*** can be seen in (3rd paragraph)
- ***D*** very impressive (3rd paragraph)
- ***E*** more and more (4th paragraph)
- ***F*** to like something a lot (4th paragraph)

3 **Work with a partner. Which of the things in the brochure do you find most interesting? Why?**

4 **084 Listen to Peter, a tourist from London, checking into his hotel in Essaouira. Which of the following three things did he <u>not</u> know?**

1. that Essaouira has a music festival
2. that the festival is about to start
3. that music will be performed at the hotel
4. that the festival attracts around 500,000 people
5. that Marrakesh is less than a three hour drive away

5 **084 Sometimes people use colloquial phrases to express surprise. Match the words below to form phrases to express surprise. Then listen again and check your answers.**

PHRASES YOU MIGHT HEAR / USE

1	How great	*A*	my lucky day!
2	That's	*B*	be amazing!
3	It must be	*C*	is that?
4	No	*D*	crazy!
5	That would	*E*	kidding!
6	You're	*F*	no idea!
7	I had	*G*	way!

6 **Work in pairs. Write down three pieces of exciting news about yourself (they can be real or made up). Take turns telling these pieces of news to your partner and reacting. Ask follow-up questions and use the phrases in Exercise 5 to help you.**

7 **Watch the video about Essaouira. What do you learn about these things? Make notes.**

- The city of Essaouira
- The Citadel du Port
- Tourism
- Agriculture
- Water sports

C

WATCH

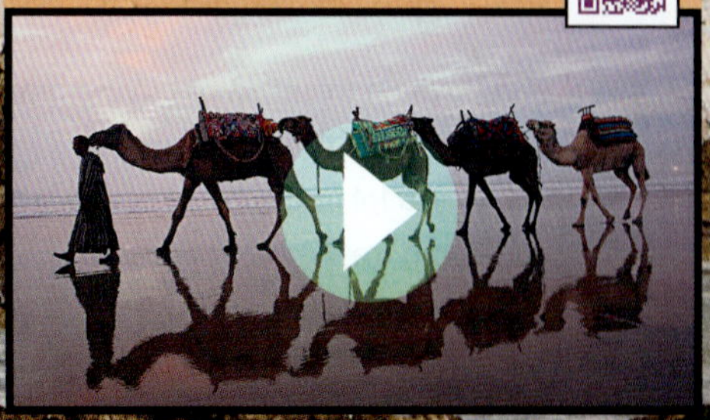

D

LIFE COMPETENCIES

ANALYSING IDEAS, MAKING DECISIONS

8 **Work in pairs. Go online and research a famous festival in the world. Create a poster using the points below. Then present your poster to your classmates and decide as a class which festival you would most like to go to.**

location	activities / events	price
accommodation	reviews from previous attendees	

13 IN FASHION, ON TREND

A

B

C

D

GETTING STARTED

1 **Match the phrases (1–4) with the correct endings (A–D). Then match the completed phrases with the photos. Which phrase(s) best describes your shopping habits?**

1 go on a spending spree
2 go window shopping
3 shop online
4 follow a popular vlogger

A and have no intention of buying anything
B and buy what they recommend
C and buy a lot in a short space of time
D and compare the best deals

2 **085 Listen to two friends doing a shopping habit quiz. Which photo best describes Andrei and why?**

3 **085 Listen again and complete the quiz items.**

Q1 When I go shopping, I always decide on a ________ and stick to it.

Q2 I avoid buying things I don't need, even if I see a ________ .

Q3 I always ________ before I buy something to make sure I get the best deal.

Q4 I don't buy ________ because the brand name isn't important.

Q5 If I can't find what I wanted to buy, I return home ________ .

4 **Match the answers from Exercise 3 with the definitions (1–5) below.**

1 without bringing or taking anything
2 the amount of money available to spend
3 a famous or fashionable label, often more expensive
4 to compare price or quality of the same, or similar, product
5 something on sale for less than its usual price or real value

5 **Do the quiz and compare your answers with a partner. Remember, 1 = Strongly disagree and 4 = Strongly agree.**

6 **Now turn to page 203 and read what your score says about your shopping habits. Do you agree?**

GRAMMAR

LIKE AND AS

GRAMMAR ON THE MOVE
Watch the video

1 **Look at Vera's response from the listening exercise. Why is the word *like* used in this sentence?**

You're just like me Andrei – I have to buy things which are on sale too.

1 to give an example
2 to make a comparison

2 **Look at the sentences (1–4) and match them with the definitions (A–D).**

1 You were in that shop for like 30 minutes.
2 My uncle works as a personal shopper.
3 My aunt treats me as her personal shopper.
4 Jane is just like me – she really enjoys shopping.

A We can use *like* + noun for making a comparison.
B We can use *like* + noun for an informal example.
C We can use *as* + noun for a job or purpose.
D We can use *as* + noun clause for manner or behaviour.

➔ **GRAMMAR REFERENCE** / *Like and as: Page 230*

3 **Complete the second sentence so that it has a similar meaning to the first sentence, using the word given.**

1 According to the magazine, the shopping centre was the 'perfect place' to find a bargain.
AS
The shopping centre was described by .... 'perfect place' to find a bargain.
2 He's a shopkeeper now and works full-time.
WORKING
He's .... shopkeeper full-time now.
3 I'm similar to you in that I can't resist buying things on offer.
JUST
I can't resist buying things on offer .... you.
4 Everybody in town used to call that shop *Jake's*.
KNOWN
That shop was .... *Jake's* by everybody in town.

4 **Complete the sentences with *like* or *as*. Then work in pairs and ask and answer the questions.**

1 Do you enjoy shopping for other people, *as/like* your friends or family?
2 Would you like to work *as/like* a shop assistant? Why / Why not?
3 Would you prefer to spend money on a shopping spree or spend it on something *as/like* travel?

LISTENING

SPEND! SPEND! SPEND!

1 **Read the signs (A–F) below. Work in pairs and answer the questions.**

1 What do the signs have in common?
2 When and why might a shop have these signs on display?

2 **086 Look at the following words which are in order and predict the context. Then, listen to the four short extracts and check your answers.**

Example
0 *food, friends, park, sunny, day:* *picnic*
1 smart clothes, good impression, early, nervous, questions, customers, experienced, shop assistant: ....
2 straightforward, selected, style, debit card, clicks, security, convenience, delivered, door: ....
3 incredible, occasion, well-dressed, elegant, dress, guests, proposed, romantic: ....
4 chocolate, tills, essentials, shops, soft music, retailers, consumers, tricks, money: ....

3 **Work with a partner and take it in turns to say why the words were mentioned in each of the recordings.**

4 **You are going to listen to a lecturer talking about how shoppers are persuaded to spend more than they had intended. Work with a partner and talk about the following:**

1 the context of the talk and how many speakers you will hear
2 if the talk will be more formal or informal
3 topic-related words or phrases that you think you'll hear

5 **087 You are going to listen to part of a radio recording which is an extension to the extract in Exercise 4 above. Answer the questions. Then listen and check your answers.**

1 What other tactics do you think retailers use to try and get people to spend money?
2 How do you think companies use digital screens in shops?
3 How has technology changed the way we shop?

VOCABULARY

GOING, GOING, GONE!

A

B

C

D

1 **Describe what you see in the photos. What do you think they have in common?**

2 088 **Listen to a conversation between two friends, Santiago and Mia. Put the photos (A–E) in the order that they are described in the listening.**

1 ______ **3** ______ **5** ______
2 ______ **4** ______

3 088 **Listen again and correct the mistakes. There is one incorrect word in each line. Before you listen, <u>underline</u> the words you think will need to change and predict what they might be. Then listen and check.**

1. Oh, you mean like an online action?
2. I might get some new running shoes after I've been paid, so I was surprising sports gear.
3. Someone had put in a bin for fifty-five thousand dollars!
4. And the gum, how on earth could anyone prove it was natural and had actually belonged to her?
5. You could hardly return it for a change if you weren't satisfied.
6. The bread's a bit steep but the cheese is good quality.

4 **Match the correct words in Exercise 3 with their meanings (1–6).**

1. exactly what it appears to be ______
2. to replace something with something else ______
3. an offer of money when competing with other people ______
4. a sale in which things are sold to the person who offers the most money ______
5. low or poor quality ______
6. looking without intending to buy ______

5 **Work in pairs. Choose one of the items below and write an online advertisement for it. Then hold an auction with your class and try to sell your item for as much money as possible.**

chewing gum	an old bicycle	a T-shirt	a guitar
a toothbrush	a half-eaten apple	a shoe	sunlight

DID YOU KNOW?

The word *advertisement* can be shortened in two ways:
1. advert
2. ad

E

SPEAKING PART 3 AND PART 4 TRAINING

1 **Work with a partner. Using the nouns in the box, talk about the advantages and disadvantages of online shopping compared to shopping in person. Which do you prefer and why? Think about:**

convenience	security	choice	availability

2 **089 Look at the Part 3 exam-style question and listen to two people, Joe and Stephanie, answering it. How well do they work together?**

3 **What would you do in the exam if your partner spoke too much or too little? Work with a partner and make a list of ideas.**

4 **090 Put the words in order to form questions that invite the other person to speak. Listen and check.**

1. about / option / what / think / do / this / you

   ....

2. this / are / thoughts / on / your / what

   ....

3. you / idea / do / another / here / have

   ....

4. that / what / you / similar / is / think / to

   ....

5. you / that / agree / would / with

   ....

P MAIN STRESS IN QUESTIONS

Sometimes speakers will emphasise certain words in questions, which can create different meanings.

5 **090 Look at your answers in Exercise 4. Listen to the questions again. Underline the word that is emphasised.**

6 **091 You will hear two other candidates, Louise and Peter, answering the exam question in Exercise 2. Listen and answer the questions below.**

1. Which option in Exercise 2 are they discussing?
2. Which phrase in Exercise 4 does Louise use to invite an answer from Peter?
3. What strategy does Louise use to encourage Peter to say more?

7 **Work with a partner. Answer the Speaking Part 3 exam question below using your own ideas. Use the questions in Exercise 4 to invite your partner to speak and the strategy in Exercise 6 to help each other. Speak for about two minutes.**

8 **Now answer the follow-up question below with your partner. Try to reach an agreement. Speak for about one minute.**

Which two things are the most important when choosing to shop in a supermarket?

9 **Read the Speaking Part 4 questions in Exercise 10. For each question, write three points to support what you are going to say.**

10 **Work with a new partner. Ask and answer the Speaking Part 4 questions below. Use your ideas in Exercises 7 and 9 to help you.**

1. Is it better to buy food online or in a shop?
2. Some people believe that one day nobody will go to shops anymore. What do you think?
3. Some people think it's better to buy things from small shops rather than big stores. Do you agree?
4. Is it true to say that people are obsessed with buying new things these days?
5. Do you think it's true that social media has had a big influence on fashion?

PUSH YOURSELF C1

DISAGREEING POLITELY

1 **Work with a partner and answer the questions.**

1. What is the sketch saying about the power of advertising?
2. Do you agree that some types of advertising should be banned?
3. Is it appropriate for people to use sports stars to advertise things such as fast food?

2 **092 Listen to two friends, Tommy and Amelia, talking about advertising. Who is in favour of banning certain types of advertising campaigns?**

3 **092 Listen again and tick the phrases you hear.**

1. That's not quite the way I see it.
2. Isn't it more a case of …
3. We don't see eye to eye.
4. I can't argue with that. However …
5. I'm afraid I just don't see it like that.
6. That's not always the case.
7. We'll just have to agree to disagree.

4 **Look at the phrases in Exercise 3 and find the following:**

A three phrases for partially disagreeing
B one phrase for accepting another's opinion
C one phrase for completely disagreeing
D two phrases when you can't reach an agreement

5 **Look at the speaking task. Work in pairs and answer the question, using the phrases from Exercise 3.**

> **How effective are these ways of promoting a new clothing range to teenagers?**
> giving away free samples
> using pop stars
> using social media
> making a fun video
> using street art

6 **Now spend one minute deciding which method would be the most effective.**

READING

1 **How important do you think the following are to help you get a job in the fashion industry? Are there any that you don't think are important or helpful?**

- doing a degree in fashion
- getting an apprenticeship or internship at a fashion company
- making your own clothes and trying to sell them
- having family who already work in fashion
- trying to make contacts in the fashion industry
- getting a job in a clothes shop

2 **Work in groups of four. Each read a different text from the article and answer the relevant questions.**

Student A – Read text A: Karthik Patel

1. What background did Karthik's family have in fashion?
2. Why did his parents think that it might not be a good idea to work in fashion?
3. How do we know he found it difficult to find a job in fashion?

Student B – Read text B: Monica Johannsson

1. When did Monica start designing clothes?
2. Why did she think she wouldn't work in fashion?
3. Why did she decide to try and become a fashion designer?

Student C – Read text C: Louis Martinez

1. What did Louis study at university?
2. How does he feel about his university studies now?
3. What does he recommend to people who want to work in fashion?

Student D – Read text D: Laura Williams

1. What discouraged Laura from studying fashion at university?
2. What benefits of her job as a shop assistant does she mention?
3. What drawback of her present job does she mention?

3 **Now, tell your group about the text you read. Were there any similarities or differences?**

4 Now you are going to read the whole article about four people who work in the fashion industry. For questions 1–10, choose from the people (A–D). The people may be chosen more than once.

Which person

1 knew what they wanted to do from a young age? ....
2 was worried about getting into debt? ....
3 was initially encouraged to do something else? ....
4 didn't think they would be successful? ....
5 thinks it's important to try and build relationships in the industry? ....
6 didn't enjoy the course that they were studying at university? ....
7 hadn't realised the hours would be so long? ....
8 says they were rejected many times? ....
9 regrets not going to work directly for a company instead of studying? ....
10 was surprised by how easy something was? ....

a career in Fashion

A Karthik Patel

It's funny, I never remember saying 'I want to work in fashion', when I was a child, but I guess I was born into it. My grandma was a dressmaker and my grandad designed children's clothing. They set up a clothes shop in New Delhi and my mum started working there when she was about 16. My parents told me it was a difficult business to make money in and so when I discussed the idea of studying marketing at university with them, they said I should go for it. I remember after I'd graduated, and was looking for my first job, something just felt wrong and so I switched back to fashion. By this point, I'd moved to Canada, so my grandparents' business wasn't an option and even though I had initially been turned down by over 20 different companies, I finally got offered a job with a local designer.

B Monica Johannsson

Although I didn't start selling anything until I was in my 20s, I was designing my own clothes at school and realised I wanted to do something like this when I grew up. I remember getting sent home on more than one occasion because my uniform didn't look like it was supposed to. After graduating from university, I wasn't sure if I would be able to make a living out of designing clothes – I guess I just wasn't that confident, but when I was approached in the street by someone asking where I'd bought my outfit from, I thought I'd give it a go. I spent the day making a couple of dresses which I put online. Well, they sold within a few minutes for far more than I'd expected, and my life changed. I feel incredibly lucky to be doing something I love.

C Louis Martinez

I was always creative and hands-on when I was a child, so it seemed likely that I would become an artist, or something like that. I studied interior design at university. My parents thought it was something which I could make a successful career from and I agreed, but even though I worked hard, I just couldn't get into it. After I'd graduated, it was hard to find work as there just weren't enough places available for the number of people who wanted them. Eventually, I managed to get an apprenticeship with a big fashion retailer, which I wish I'd done instead of going to college to be honest. I think it's much better to go direct and work your way up through different companies and that's what I would recommend to anyone who wants to work in fashion.

D Laura Williams

As well as universities which specialise in fashion, there are also private colleges, but I was put off by the fees and didn't want to borrow lots of money and then struggle to pay it back. So, when I left school, I took a job as a full-time shop assistant for a high-street brand. I knew it wasn't what I wanted, but it gave me the opportunity to make a few contacts with people working in fashion, which have since been really valuable, and it also allowed me to keep an eye on the internal job vacancies. After about six months, my efforts paid off and I managed to get a permanent role in the head office as a junior buyer. I've worked my way up and I'm a senior buyer now. There's a lot of travelling and I don't get much time off, which I wasn't prepared for, but I love what I do so I wouldn't change anything.

5 Find the words or phrases in the text with a similar meaning to the following.

1 start a company or business [Text A]
2 decide on something [Text A]
3 a choice [Text A]
4 earn enough money from your job [Text B]
5 a set of clothes [Text B]
6 try something [Text B]
7 become interested in something [Text C]
8 get better positions within the company you work for [Text C]
9 watch something carefully [Text D]
10 a period of time when you don't work [Text D]

GRAMMAR

PAST MODALS

GRAMMAR ON THE MOVE
Watch the video

1 **Work with a partner and answer the questions.**

1. How often do you buy new clothes or accessories, or gadgets, like mobile phones?
2. In your country, what kind of possessions show status?
3. Modern society is often called 'materialistic'. Why do you think that is?

2 **093 Listen to Rachida and Haruto and decide what main idea Rachida is expressing?**

1. Haruto's new, designer shirt is nice.
2. Haruto often buys stuff he doesn't need.
3. People should recycle their old phones.
4. People love the excitement of buying new things.
5. Haruto should take his cardigan back while the shops are open.

3 **093 Listen again and complete the gaps.**

1. I didn't ________ it really, but it was such a bargain.
2. The one you had was perfectly OK, so you ________ a new one.
3. Maybe, I shouldn't ________ by the special offer.

4 **Work with a partner and answer the questions.**

1. Which sentence in Exercise 3 expresses regret at doing something? What other structures can we use to express regret?
2. Which two sentences in Exercise 3 express having done something which wasn't necessary? What structures do we use to express having to do something which is necessary?

5 **Choose the correct verb forms to complete the sentences.**

1. John *shouldn't have spent/didn't need to spend* all of his money on shoes – now he can't afford to go out.
2. Mary didn't join us at the shopping centre because she *needn't have bought/didn't need to buy* a present for the party – she's already bought something online.
3. Well, that was a waste of money – I *needn't have bothered/didn't have to bother* buying that new computer as my old one is working completely fine now.
4. I *shouldn't have looked/didn't have to look* far to find the book I was looking for – they had it in the shop around the corner.
5. The local government *didn't need to build/shouldn't have built* a new shopping centre there – it was a site of historical importance.

VOCABULARY

THE BUSINESS OF SHOPPING

1 **Look at the phrases in bold in sentences 1–6 and match them with the definitions (A–F).**

1. Can you think of any products that have recently **appeared on the market** that you really want to have?
2. What changes have you seen in the types of **commerce** that your country is involved in now and in the past? Do you think that there will be any big changes in the future?
3. Do **consumers** in your country have more choice now than in the past?
4. Does your country mainly manufacture clothes or **import** them from abroad?
5. How important do you think **marketing campaigns** are in influencing people to buy a product?
6. What is the most expensive **purchase** you have ever made?

A the activities involved in the business of buying and selling things
B something that you buy
C started to become available in shops
D work that involves encouraging people to buy a product
E people who buy goods or services for their own use
F buy or bring products and/or ideas from another country

2 **Work in pairs and answer the questions in Exercise 1.**

3 **Complete the sentences (1–8) with the correct adverbs in the box.**

appropriately	carelessly	deliberately	impatiently
negatively	peacefully	simultaneously	

1. It's important that you dress ________ if you work in this shop so that you give a good impression.
2. They launched both of their new products ________ – they appeared on the market on the same day.
3. I can't wait for the new games console to come out. I've been waiting ________ for it for nearly a year!
4. I think the shop ________ puts the chocolate just where children can reach it.
5. The shop guarantees that you will sleep ________ in this bed or they will give you your money back.
6. I don't think that we should try selling the new product. We sent out a survey and most people responded ________ to the idea.
7. If you didn't behave so ________ with your money, you'd be able to afford that new jumper that you want.

➡ **GRAMMAR REFERENCE** / *Shouldn't have / Needn't have / Didn't need to / Didn't have to: Page 231*

WRITING PART 2: REVIEW TRAINING

1 **Work with a partner and decide which of the following products you wouldn't buy second hand.**

clothes a TV concert tickets a laptop a mobile phone a car / bicycle

2 **Look at the screenshot of an online store. Work with a partner and make a list of the types of information found on websites like this.**

3 **Look at the exam style question and read the model answer, ignoring the underlined words for now. In which paragraph(s) does the writer**

1 offer a recommendation?
2 make a comparison?
3 provide an explanation?

Review wanted

We are looking for reviews for online shops. Write a review of an online shop that you have used recently. Explain what type of products it sells, how easy it is to use and how it compares to other online shops. Say if you would recommend it to other people.

The best reviews will be posted on our website.

I recently purchased two rugby tickets on www.sportingticket.com, an online retailer which specialises in tickets for major sporting events.
(1) Initially, the site was straightforward to use: the range of ticket prices on offer was clearly displayed, and there was a link to a seating plan for selecting the seats. However, when I clicked on the link there was an error message and the page wouldn't open.
(2) Thankfully, I was still able to buy the tickets and went for e-tickets to avoid postage costs.
(3) Naturally, I assumed I would receive email confirmation like other sites I'd used previously.
(4) Typically, these kinds of websites deliver the tickets instantly. However, after 48 hours, I still hadn't received the tickets and so I called the helpline but (5) curiously there was no reply, even though I tried at different times of the day.
(6) Sadly, my experience with this online retailer didn't end well. Not only didn't the tickets arrive, but I was also unable to get a refund. Therefore, I would strongly discourage anyone wanting to buy sports tickets from using this site.

4 **Look at the review again and match the underlined adverbs (1–6) with their meanings (A–F).**

A strangely or unusually: ....
B obviously: ....
C firstly: ....
D luckily: ....
E normally: ....
F unfortunately: ....

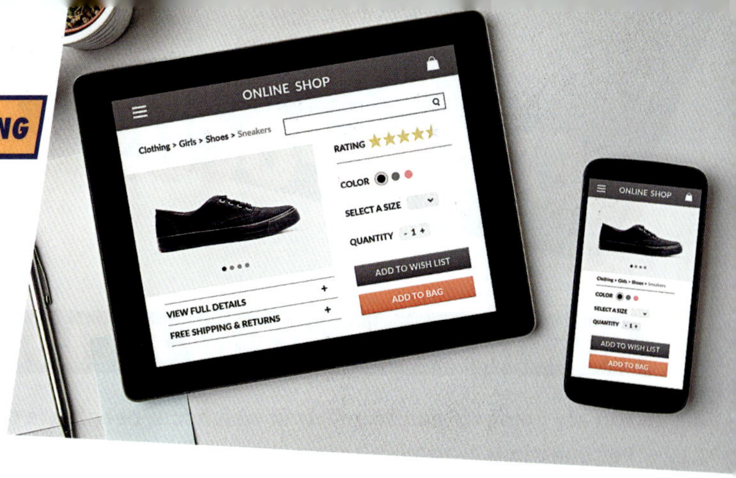

5 **Underline the correct option to complete the sentences.**

1 Shopping online was more straightforward than I'd *initially/sadly* thought.
2 *Thankfully/Curiously*, there was no option to pay for the ticket by credit card.
3 *Naturally/Sadly*, I thought they'd be delivered within a few days, or a week at most.
4 *Naturally/Typically* when you shop online, there's a search facility for finding specific models or brands.
5 *Curiously/Sadly* the gift didn't arrive in time for her birthday, which was really disappointing.
6 *Thankfully/Typically* the retailer agreed to exchange it for me, even though I hadn't kept the receipt.

6 **Look at the Writing Part 2 exam question. Write a review using at least four of the adverbs in Exercise 4.**

Review wanted

We are looking for reviews for clothes shops. Write a review of a clothes shop that you have been to recently. Explain what you bought, what the customer service was like and how it compares to other clothes shops you've been to. Say if you would recommend it to other people.

The best reviews will be posted on our website.

7 **Work in pairs and exchange reviews. Read your partner's reviews and complete the checklist below. Then give feedback to your partner.**

1 Has the candidate answered all the points in the question. **YES / NO**
2 Has the candidate written in the correct style? **YES / NO**
3 Is the review well-organised? **YES / NO**
4 Has the candidate used a variety of language accurately? **YES / NO**
5 As the reader, do you have enough information to make a decision about the product / service that has been reviewed? **YES / NO**

EXAM FOCUS

READING AND USE OF ENGLISH PART 7

You are going to read an article in which four people are talking about their job in the retail industry. For questions 1–10, choose from the people (A–D). The people may be chosen more than once.

Which person

1 hadn't originally planned to get a job in retail?
2 believes that customers can sometimes be wrong?
3 is afraid of serving customers who have a complaint?
4 thinks they could have dealt with a difficult situation better?
5 admits to not realising how their job would impact their life outside of work.
6 wishes they could improve the way they deal with customer complaints?
7 feels that they were treated badly?
8 isn't satisfied with their salary?
9 had a sudden realisation about the way they should behave?
10 accepts that their job means that they can't always do what they want?

A Elizabeth Adley

I love customer service, I really do, or I wouldn't have lasted in retail. However, over the years I've learnt there's a line between giving good customer service and letting someone get away with anything just because they're a customer. During my training, my boss told me that 'the customer is always right' but that's not always the case. I remember getting into trouble once for standing up to a shopper who was being unreasonable, which I didn't feel was right. I'm not paid any extra for dealing with rude customers. Recently, a woman started complaining to me about the price of a skirt which I thought was amusing as I don't decide what things cost. However, at that moment, I understood that people just need me to listen, like a friend I suppose, and after that, she went away quite happy in the end.

B Javier Silva

Nobody really understands why I can't come over and watch TV on a Friday or Saturday night and, when I first got the job, friends were convinced I was being anti-social or trying to be difficult when making plans. I must confess that I didn't think that my social life would be quite as affected by the job as it has been. The thing is, because people want to do their shopping when they've finished work, I'm always scheduled to work unsociable hours. I do enjoy my job in retail, but I also know that it's not as well paid as jobs in other industries. I can't always afford to get the things I want and sometimes I have to work extra shifts just to make ends meet. I guess that's the only thing I wish were different really.

C Neslihan Demir

Sometimes people look at me strangely when I tell them what I do for a living, as if it's something I should feel embarrassed about. When I started, it wasn't my dream job or even the field I wanted to work in, but I can pay my bills and I have just enough money to socialise. Of course, I'm not suggesting it's the most exciting job, but it has its moments. Like the time a woman came in to buy a dress. I was supposed to be away with friends that week but had to work at the last minute. She got really irritated because we didn't have the dress in her size and although I spent ages trying to help, I'm not sure I handled it well and felt that I could have been more polite. In the end, she went away empty-handed.

D Antonio Bianchi

People who work in retail love to complain about customers, but I know from first-hand experience that although some customers can be rude and impatient, there actually aren't that many who are. Generally, most people find what they are looking for and leave. I'm grateful, as there's nothing more terrifying than dealing with a shopper who's unhappy with a purchase. Having said that, consumers have rights and I'm the first to complain if standards are low. In actual fact, trying to resolve issues where the customer is unhappy is a big part of my job. My boss says I'll get better at handling these over time, and I really hope that's the case. Thankfully, I haven't had to deal with many, and generally I'm enjoying the job. The only downside is that I miss out on a lot of social events because of work commitments, but I guess that's just the nature of working in retail.

WRITING PART 2: REVIEW

Write your answer in 140–190 words in an appropriate style.

You recently saw this notice on an English-language website called Buy-It:

> **Reviews wanted!**
>
> We're looking for reviews of interesting things people have bought.
>
> Write a review of something interesting you've bought. Explain what it was and why you bought it. Say what you like and dislike about it and who you would recommend it to.
>
> **The best reviews will be posted on the website next month.**

➡ ***WRITING BANK*** / *Pages 238–239*

SPEAKING PART 3

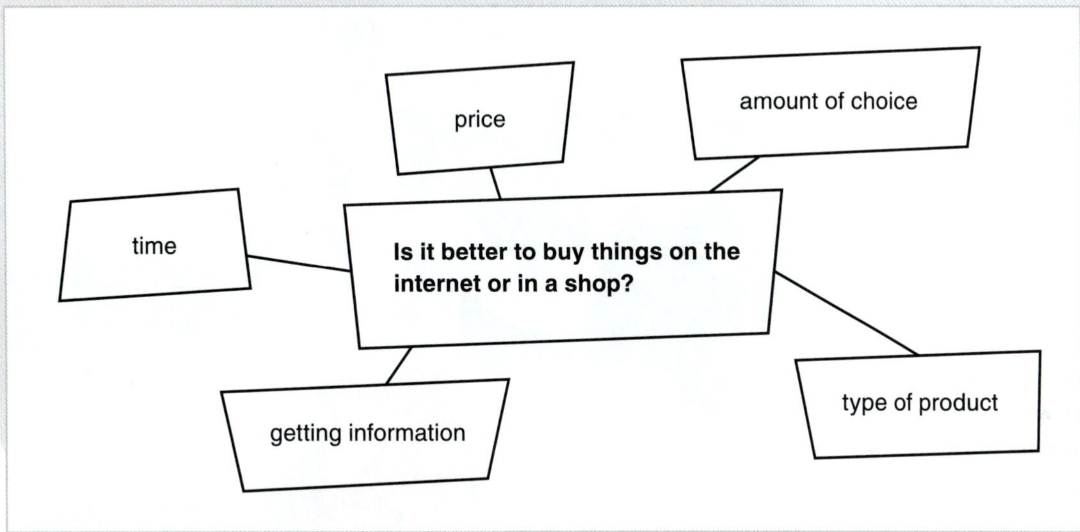

➡ ***SPEAKING BANK*** / *Pages 250–251*

SPEAKING PART 4

1 Do you think buying online will replace shops in the future? Why? / Why not?
2 Some people don't like to buy clothes online. What do you think?
3 How likely are you to buy something recommended by a friend?
4 Is it better to go shopping alone or with friends?
5 Do you think it's true that people buy too many things they don't really need?
6 Some people think that advertising encourages people to spend too much money. Do you agree?

➡ ***SPEAKING BANK*** / *Pages 252–253*

REAL WORLD

GOING SHOPPING IN ... MILAN

1 **Think about when you go shopping for new clothes. Rank the questions below in order of importance from 1 (the most important) to 7 (the least important).**

A How much does it cost?
B What is the brand name?
C Does it have a unique style?
D Is it made from quality material?
E Where was it manufactured?
F Will it match with what's in my wardrobe?
G Is it comfortable?

2 **Compare your list with a partner and explain why you have chosen this order.**

3 **Read the guidebook about places to see in Milan. Match the places (1–3) with the photos (A–C). Which places would you like to visit? Do you have anything similar in your town or city?**

A

Milan – A tourist guide for the fashionistas

1 Galleria Vittorio Emanuele II

The oldest active shopping mall in Italy and one of the most iconic landmarks in Milan, the Galleria Vittorio Emanuele II is something you just can't miss during your visit. Named after Victor Emmanuel II, the first king of Italy, this grand building was built in the 19th century. Not only can you shop to your heart's content in the vast number of luxury shops, but also admire the beautiful architecture, bathed in natural light, which gives this building its unique appeal.

2 Street Markets

Ranging from everyday household items and clothes to rare antiques, there's something for everyone in one of Milan's many street markets. Head over to the Mercato Filatelico, located in the heart of the city, for your old stamps, coins and pocket watches or the Mercato della Terra for all your organic fruit and vegetables. Find hidden gems and try your hand at bartering to get the best deals at the market stalls or just soak up the atmosphere with a coffee at one of the many restaurants or cafés in the area.

3 Milan Fashion Week

Since its creation in the 1950s, hundreds of thousands of people have flocked to the Milan Fashion week to get a glimpse of the latest trends from some of the world's most famous designers. The biannual event transforms the city into a fashion hub, with shows and events taking place all around the city. It is one of the "Big Four" fashion weeks, which takes place after New York and London, and before Paris.

4 **Find the words and phrases in the text which mean the following:**

1. very famous or popular (Text 1)
2. for as long as you want (Text 1)
3. in the centre (of the town or city) (Text 2)
4. to enjoy the experience (Text 2)
5. to see something for a short time (Text 3)
6. twice a year (Text 3)

5 **Read the texts again. Decide if the sentences are true or false.**

1. The Galleria Vittorio Emanuele II was built in the 1900s.
2. The Galleria Vittorio Emanuele II is famous for both its shops and architecture.
3. The Mercato Filatelico is located on the outskirts of the city.
4. The Milan Fashion Week takes place once a year.
5. The Milan Fashion Week takes place before the London Fashion Week.

6 094 **Match the sentence halves. Then listen to a conversation between a customer and a shop assistant and check your answers.**

PHRASES YOU MIGHT USE

1. Unfortunately, it doesn't go
2. It was a gift so I don't have
3. OK, I'll just have a browse
4. Could I try these
5. Will I be able to
6. What's your return

A the receipt, I'm afraid.
B use it online?
C with the shoes I already have.
D policy for sale items?
E on please?
F around and see if there's anything else.

7 094 **Listen again. Change the words in *italics* with the phrases the shop assistant uses.**

PHRASES YOU MIGHT HEAR

1. I see. So it's *unusable*?
2. That's fine. Have you got the *bill*?
3. Ah, in that case, I can't offer you a refund, only *a change item*.
4. Of course. Let me hang them in the *changing place* for you …
5. Just over there, madam, next to the *checkout*.
6. That's OK. I can offer you a *debit* note if you prefer?
7. Would you like to join our *customer* scheme?

8 **Work in pairs and role play the following situation:**

Student A: You are a customer and would like to return an item you recently bought.
Student B: You are a shop assistant. Listen to the customer and answer their questions.

9 **Watch the video about Milan. What do you learn about these things? Make notes.**

- The city of Milan
- The Navigli district
- Duomo di Milano
- Galleria Vittorio Emanuele II
- Piazza Gae Aulenti

WATCH

B

C

LIFE COMPETENCIES

UNDERSTANDING FINANCIAL ISSUES, REFLECTING ON OWN SUCCESS

10 **Choose a shop that you like to buy clothes from. You have a budget of €100. Visit the website and decide which clothes you would like to buy. Then compare your shopping baskets with a partner. Decide who has chosen the best clothes and who has got the best deals.**

14 NOT JUST 9–5

Underwater cameraman

Teacher

GETTING STARTED

1 Why do you think people choose to do the jobs in the photos? What skills do you need to do these jobs?

Nurse

Helicopter pilot

Lawyer

READING

1 Make a list of five perfect jobs. Then compare your list with a partner and give reasons for your answers.

2 Read the article about the perfect job quickly. Underline the three jobs mentioned. How similar are these jobs to the ones you talked about in Exercise 1?

3 **Read the article again and answer the questions.**

1. What does the writer mean by 'take a back seat' in the first paragraph?
2. What does *them* refer to in line 24 of the second paragraph?
   A developers **B** video games **C** subscribers
3. In the third paragraph we learn that
   A Martina didn't initially want to become a location scout.
   B Martina has to think about more than just finding a suitable location.
   C Martina had difficulty finding a location for the new action film.
4. What is the writer's main purpose in the final paragraph?
   A to consider why people choose a particular career
   B to praise people for the work they are doing
   C to argue that people have different attitudes to certain jobs

4 **Ask and answer the questions in pairs.**

1. What are the advantages and disadvantages of doing the jobs mentioned in the article?
2. Do you think there is such a thing as the perfect job?
3. How important is it to be happy in your job?

THE PERFECT JOB

Martin Baker ***speaks to three people doing the job of their dreams.***

Finding the job of your dreams is something that we all strive to achieve, though being happy in your profession isn't always a reality. Ultimately, many people have come to terms with the fact that, as long as they're earning enough money to get by in life, then happiness can take a back seat. After all, is there such a thing as the perfect job? Well to find out, I recently interviewed three people who claim to have found just that.

I first meet Simon Hill in a small café just outside the city. He's a young, entrepreneurial economics graduate who turned down the offer to work at a leading financial institution to pursue a career as a video games commentator. He first established his channel on a prominent video sharing website during his first year at university with the aim of walking viewers through the game he was playing and showing them how to complete it, a popular style of video known as Let's Play. His parents tried to discourage him from doing it at first. 'They just couldn't see how I would earn a living from it' Simon explains. 'It was only when I received my first pay slip that they realised it could work.' As the number of subscribers to his channel grew, he started receiving free copies of video games from developers who wanted him to review **them**. And it didn't end there. To date, he has earned an impressive £2 million through endorsements and guest appearances on TV. Not bad for someone who has only just turned 24.

I then head across town to the home of Martina Lopez. On the living room floor, there is an unpacked suitcase. She's just come back from a two-month tour of New Zealand, where, as part of her job as a location scout, she was tasked with finding appropriate locations for scenes for an upcoming action film. 'I never had any intention of doing anything else' she admits. 'What I love the most about my job is the travelling and that, coupled with my love of film, gives me the best of both worlds.' Not only does she need to find the right spots, but she also needs to work out the logistical implications of them. 'There's no point in choosing a location if it's inaccessible to the entire film crew' she concludes. She makes a valid point, particularly when you consider that there would be over a hundred people on set, not to mention all of the equipment.

My final interview takes place in the city centre, in the trendy IT district known locally as "The New Silicon Valley". Here, I meet Jason Holloway, who has one of the most interesting job titles I've ever come across, an ethical hacker. Basically, his job is to hack into computer systems on behalf of their owners in order to uncover any security vulnerabilities that other unethical hackers might try to exploit. 'People often ask me if I was ever tempted by a life of unethical hacking' he says, 'but to be honest, I much prefer being on the right side of the law.' In addition to finding flaws in these systems, Jason also works as a freelance consultant for the government. I wanted to get more information out of him about this, but I couldn't, no matter how hard I tried. 'Let's just say I really enjoy it, and, sadly, under no circumstances am I allowed to talk about the work I do for the government' he says sympathetically. Fair enough, I thought.

Meeting these three people is something that I'm really glad I did and I end the day by reflecting on what I've heard. To be honest, I had my doubts about whether the perfect job truly exists. Since they all seemed so happy, it's easy to think that it does. I guess people interpret the word perfect in different ways and what may be perfect for one person isn't necessarily the same for someone else. That being said, I wouldn't mind playing video games for a living.

READING AND USE OF ENGLISH PART 4 TRAINING

5 **Read the sentences below. Find the phrases in the article on page 185 which include the words in bold and study how they are used. Then complete the second sentence so that it has a similar meaning to the first sentence, using the word in bold. Write between 2–5 words.**

1. John offered Susan a job at the company, but she didn't accept.
   TURNED (2nd paragraph)
   Susan .... offer of a job at the company.
2. I told her that it wasn't a good idea to go to bed late.
   DISCOURAGE (2nd paragraph)
   I tried to .... to bed late.
3. 'I don't want to live in another city,' said Ellie.
   INTENTION (3rd paragraph)
   'I have .... in another city,' said Ellie.
4. It doesn't make sense to get a job that you won't enjoy doing.
   POINT (3rd paragraph)
   There's .... a job that you won't enjoy doing.
5. The company pays him to speak to potential clients for them.
   BEHALF (4th paragraph)
   He is paid to speak to potential clients .... the company.
6. Laura has to issue visitor badges and deal with enquiries as well.
   ADDITION (4th paragraph)
   Laura has to issue visitor badges .... with enquiries.
7. He just couldn't catch him, despite running really fast.
   MATTER (4th paragraph)
   He just couldn't catch him, ... ran.
8. Initially, Stefano wasn't sure whether applying for the job was a good idea.
   DOUBTS (5th paragraph)
   Initially, Stefano .... applying for the job.

GRAMMAR

ADDING EMPHASIS AND SENTENCE FRONTING

GRAMMAR ON THE MOVE
Watch the video

English sometimes uses more complex structures to add emphasis. One way is called 'sentence fronting'. This is when the part of the sentence you want to focus on is moved to the beginning. For example:
The CEO was standing in front of me.
Standing in front of me was the CEO.
Extra words are often added to make the sentence more sophisticated. For example:
She realised she was late when she looked at her watch.
It was only when she looked at her watch that she realised she was late.

1 **Read the sentences 1–6. Find the sentences in the article on page 185 which have the same meaning as these but use a more complex structure. Write the sentence from article in the gaps below.**

1. They realised it could work when I received my first pay slip.
   ....
2. There is an unpacked suitcase on the living room floor.
   ....
3. I love travelling. That's why I love my job.
   ....
4. I work for the government. I am not allowed to talk about it.
   ....
5. I'm really glad that I met these three people.
   ....
6. It's easy to think that it does because they all seemed so happy.
   ....

➜ **GRAMMAR REFERENCE** / *Adding emphasis and fronting: Page 232*

2 **Study the structures in Exercise 1. Then rewrite the sentences below using these structures.**

1. I'm really glad I went to the interview.
   Going ....
2. There is a small camera in the corner of the office above the photocopier.
   In ....
3. I had finished all of my work. I decided to leave the office for the day.
   Since ....
4. I noticed when I got home that I had left my phone at work.
   It ....
5. I really like the benefits of the job.
   What ....
6. I work for a security company. I am not allowed to talk about it.
   Under ....

3 **Imagine that you had a part-time job. Write a report about it and talk about the points below. Use the structures in Exercises 1 and 2 in your report.**

- the job you did
- a description of your working environment
- something you really liked about your job
- something you weren't allowed to do
- something you realised at the end of the job
- a reason why you're glad you did it

VOCABULARY

PHRASAL VERBS FOR BUSINESS

1 **Read the agenda and notes below from a video conference call between three employees. Check the meaning of any words you are unsure about.**

2 095 **Listen to the conference call. What roles do you think Alice, Jack and Amelia have at the company?**

3 095 **Listen to the conference call again. Complete the gaps in the agenda with the phrasal verbs you hear.**

4 **Complete the sentences with the correct form of the phrasal verbs in Exercise 3.**

1. We're going to ______ monthly team building events to improve morale in the office.
2. Due to budget restrictions, we need to ______ the amount we spend on overheads.
3. I've been in meetings all morning so I haven't ______ checking my emails yet.
4. I'd like to ______ these figures ______ the sales team to get their input.
5. We've ______ the photos ______ from the website due to customer complaints.
6. We'll have to ______ the release date as we're still trying to resolve a few bugs.
7. The IT help desk is ______ the issues that customers are having with accessing the site.
8. I've already sent him three emails but he's really slow at ______ people.

DID YOU KNOW?

The notes which are taken during a meeting are called *minutes*.

AGENDA

TIME: 10:00 am

CALL IN NUMBER: 878–1475

ATTENDEES: Alice Mayfair, Jack White, Amelia Carr

POINTS FROM PREVIOUS MEETING

1 Jack to discuss takeover offer with the board
2 Jack to **(2)** ______ meeting with sales team
3 Amelia to **(4)** ______ bugs on website

NOTES

Board to **(1)** ______ Jack next week
Jack hasn't **(3)** ______ this yet
Amelia **(5)** ______ these issues ______ the tech team.
Issues resolved

AGENDA ITEMS

1 Update budget for new financial year
2 Landing page displays outdated info

ACTIONS

Jack to **(6)** ______ overseas travel
Amelia's team to **(7)** ______ content and update

AOB

Jack has **(8)** ______ his holiday until next month

SPEAKING

EVALUATING THE ADVANTAGES AND DISADVANTAGES OF AN IDEA

1 Ask and answer the questions in pairs.

1. Would you like to run your own business? Why / Why not?
2. Do you think you would be a difficult person to work for? Why / Why not?
3. Who are the most successful entrepreneurs in your country?
4. What are the pros and cons of running your own business?

2 Put the words in order to make phrases for talking about advantages and disadvantages.

Advantages

1. product / of / is / main / the / this / advantage
2. is / the / one / of / key / of / benefits / this
3. out / makes / is / stand / this / what / the fact that

Disadvantages

4. of / the / one / is / major / of / drawbacks / this
5. this / a / is / disadvantage / major / of
6. the / downsides / product / to / this / of / is / one

3 Work in pairs. Look at the four ideas for businesses and discuss the advantages and disadvantages of each idea. Use the phrases in Exercise 2. Then decide which idea would be the most successful and why.

4 Work in pairs. Choose one of the ideas in Exercise 3 and write an online video advertisement for it. Use the questions below to help you.

Who are the main characters?
What problematic situation are they in?
How do they use the product to help them?
What is the slogan for the product?

EYE-PAY

Rather than using cash or a credit card, customers simply look at a screen which recognises their face using the latest in facial recognition software. This is linked to their bank account and payments are completed within seconds.

FLIGHT ALERT

Never miss out on the best flight deals ever again. Simply enter your email address and preferred holiday destinations and we will seek out the best and cheapest flight deals online and email a list to you. You'll be amazed at the prices on offer. One lucky customer flew from Los Angeles to London for under $150 return. $5/month subscription fee.

STYLE UP

Are you a shopaholic who wants to know if the item you've spotted in the sales looks good? Take a photo and upload it to the app and receive instant feedback and reviews from thousands of others shoppers who are on hand to tell you whether or not it's right for you. The app also stores your snaps and recommends similar items that you might also be interested in.

CLOTHES FOR PETS

You may have already moved into the world of online shopping, whereby you can place an order for items which are then delivered right to your door. But what about our beloved pets? This is a website that is dedicated to selling pet clothes and accessories that you can have delivered to your home. If you're not completely satisfied with the products, then simply post them back to us free of charge.

LISTENING

1 **Look at the list of jobs below. Put them in order from 1 (the most dangerous) to 10 (the least dangerous). Then compare your lists with a partner and say why you have chosen this order.**

chef	firefighter
journalist	lorry driver
pilot	photographer
professional footballer	stunt performer
surgeon	teacher

2 **Look at the list of jobs again. Put them in a new order from 1 (the most well-paid) to 10 (the least well-paid). Then decide if the following statement is true.**

The more dangerous the job, the better paid it is.

LISTENING PART 2 TRAINING

3 096 **You will hear a man called Harry Peterson talking about his life as a stunt performer in films. A candidate has given incorrect answers for questions 1 and 2. Listen to the extract and decide why the answers are incorrect. Then write the correct answers.**

1 Harry describes himself as **1** *irresponsible* when he was a child.

2 At first, Harry was surprised by the lack of **2** *qualifications* available.

4 097 **Now listen to the next extract. Choose the correct word from the box that fits the gap. Then decide why the other two words are incorrect.**

ambitious extraordinary fantastic

3 Harry uses the word **3** ______ to describe the film set.

5 098 **Read questions 4–8 below. Check the meaning of any words that you are unsure about. Then listen and complete the sentences with a word from the recording.**

4 Harry felt a great sense of **4** ______ when he finished his first film.

5 Harry compares the injuries he gets to those of a **5** ______ .

6 One of Harry's colleagues suffered a serious injury when he jumped off a **6** ______ and onto a moving vehicle.

7 The thing that concerns Harry the most about the job is being **7** ______ for long periods of time.

8 Harry is trying to persuade his **8** ______ to become a stuntman one day.

6 **Ask and answer the questions in pairs.**

1 Would you like to be a stunt performer? Why / Why not?
2 Why do you think people do jobs that they know are dangerous?

VOCABULARY

JOBS AND CAREERS

1 **What types of jobs do you think the people in the photos do?**

2 **Underline the odd word out in each row.**

1. made redundant promoted retired sacked
2. corporation firm headquarters institution
3. expand decline rise surge
4. assignment deadline project task
5. employee staff personnel workforce
6. earnings income overtime salary
7. appoint hire fire recruit
8. board committee CEO panel

3 **Use some of the words in Exercise 2 to complete the questions. There may be more than one correct answer.**

1. For what reasons can someone be ________ from their job?
2. Would you prefer to work for a big ________ or a small start-up?
3. What three things are most likely to keep an ________ happy and motivated at work?
4. For what reasons does a ________ go on strike? Is this common in your country?
5. Do you think that the number of people using cash will increase or ________ in the future? Why?

P AUXILIARY VERB STRESS

In *wh-* questions, auxiliary verbs are often unstressed. For example:

For what reasons can (kən)

What three things are (ə)

4 **Work with a partner and answer the questions in Exercise 3. Focus on your pronunciation.**

PUSH YOURSELF C1

COMPOUND WORDS WITH *WORK*

1 **Look at the extracts from SmartCorp's Handbook for New Employees. Choose the correct definition of the underlined words in this context.**

1. SmartCorp Limited is proud of its ethnically diverse workforce in all its sites across the country.
   - **A** whole group of workers
   - **B** ability to work well
2. We don't expect our employees to be workaholics and to take work home every weekend.
   - **A** people who enjoy their work
   - **B** people who are addicted to working
3. However, staff are expected to be flexible and recognise that the workload may increase during busy times; at such times, staff may be asked to remain at work for slightly longer than usual.
   - **A** amount of work
   - **B** weight of things to be carried
4. Abusive behaviour in the workplace will not be tolerated under any circumstances; if you have any concerns about the conduct of colleagues and managers, please arrange to discuss them in confidence with human resources.
   - **A** business meeting
   - **B** building, office or other location where people work
5. All staff are required to attend an annual health and safety workshop, covering areas such as safe lifting and healthy desk posture in order to avoid health problems such as back injuries.
   - **A** room with special equipment
   - **B** session involving practical training
6. SmartCorp staff enjoy a 50% discount on membership of Smiley's Gym. SmartCorp acknowledge the health benefits of a daily 20-minute workout, and encourages staff to take advantage.
   - **A** period of physical exercise
   - **B** friendly time with work colleagues

2 **Based on the extracts above, do you think you would like to work for SmartCorp? Why? / Why not?**

WRITING PART 2: LETTER OF APPLICATION TRAINING

1 **Read the job advertisement below. Underline the key points that you must write about in your letter of application.**

You see this advertisement in the college magazine:

Tour guides wanted

We are looking for English-speaking tour guides to work at the university, showing visitors around the campus and telling them about the university. Write a letter to Mrs Sandra Jones, the communications director, giving details of:

- Your experience of working as a tour guide
- Your knowledge of English
- What skills you have that will be useful for this role.

2 **Underline the correct greeting for a letter applying for the job in Exercise 1.**

Hello Sandra Jones   Hi Sandra
Dear Mrs Jones   Dear Sir / Madam

3 **Read the opening sentences written by candidates who are applying for the job in Exercise 1. Choose the most appropriate opening sentence. Decide why the others aren't appropriate.**

1 I am writing to apply for the position of tour guide, as advertised in the college magazine.
2 I've just seen the job advert and I'd like to give it a try.
3 I would like to apply for the role of tour guide which I have seen advertised in the local newspaper.
4 I have recently seen the advertisement for the job of tour guide and I would like to be considering for the role.

4 **Read the part of the model answer which covers the first bullet point. Find the two grammatical errors and the four spelling mistakes.**

For the past year, I am working as a tour guide in my hometown. This involves talking about the varius historical and cultural landmarks of the town in adition to hand out leaflets which explain some of the best things to do there. I am also responsable for making sure that the group stays together and is safe untill the end of the tour.

5 **Read the next part of the model answer which covers the second bullet point. Complete the sentences with the correct form of the verbs in the box.**

be   obtain   pass   spend

I have recently **(1)** .... all of my English exams, **(2)** .... a B2-level certificate. I also **(3)** .... six months in London on a language exchange so my speaking skills **(4)** .... my greatest strength.

6 **Change the form of the words below from nouns to adjectives that you can use in a letter of application. Then rank them in order of importance for the role of a tour guide from 1 (the most important) to 7 (the least important).**

NOUN	ADJECTIVE
energy	
enthusiasm	
humour	
knowledge	
organisation	
patience	
punctuality	

7 **Read the part of the model answer which covers the third bullet point in the exam question in Exercise 1. What is the structure of the first sentence? Rewrite sentences 1–3 using the same structure.**

Having studied at the university for the past two years, I am very familiar with the layout of the campus as well as the history of the university. This knowledge would enable me to answer any questions that the visitors may have and lead the tours in an organised way. Furthermore, I am a very enthusiastic person, meaning that the tours will be interesting and entertaining.

1 I am very good at speaking to customers because I've worked as a waiter for three years.

....

2 I am available to work for the whole summer as I have already passed all of my exams.

....

3 Because I've lived in England for three years, I am able to speak English fluently.

....

Make sure that you end your letter of application with a closing remark. For example:
Thank you for your careful consideration of my application.
I look forward to hearing from you soon.
Yours sincerely, / Yours faithfully,

8 **Write an answer for the exam question below. Write your answer in 140–190 words.**

You see this advertisement in the local newspaper:

Organisers wanted

We are looking for people to work as organisers at a summer camp for English-speaking children. Write a letter of application to Mr Stephen Barnes, the camp organiser, which includes:

- Your experience of working with children
- Your ability to communicate in English
- The skills you have that will be useful for the role

EXAM FOCUS

READING AND USE OF ENGLISH PART 4

For questions 1–6, complete the second sentence so that it has a similar meaning to the first sentence, using the word given. Do not change the word given. You must use between two and five words, including the word given.

0 We didn't go on the tour because there wasn't enough time.
LACK
Due *to the lack of time*, we didn't go on the tour.

1 The job interview took much longer than he had expected.
SUCH
He hadn't expected the job interview ______ long time.

2 The person who succeeded in solving the computer issue was Helen.
MANAGED
It was Helen ______ the computer issue.

3 Howard suggested a brilliant idea for our new advertising campaign.
UP
Howard ______ a brilliant suggestion for our new advertising campaign.

4 I found it hard to get a job because I didn't have the right experience.
DIFFICULTY
I ______ a job because I didn't have the right experience.

5 The number of people applying for jobs rose last month.
INCREASE
There ______ the number of people applying for jobs last month.

6 I began to cook when I was sixteen years old.
TOOK
I ______ the age of sixteen.

LISTENING PART 2

099 **You will hear a woman called Elizabeth Moore talking about a filmmaking course she attended. For questions 1–10, complete the sentences with a word or short phrase.**

Filmaking course

Elizabeth heard about the filmmaking course from her **(1)** ....

Elizabeth learnt how to use **(2)** .... on her first day.

Elizabeth's tutor made an award-winning series about **(3)** ....

For her first assignment, Elizabeth had to write a **(4)** .... for an opening scene of a film.

Elizabeth had the idea of making a film about **(5)** .... after watching an interesting talk.

While shooting her short film, Elizabeth had the opportunity to work with **(6)** ....

Elizabeth had the opportunity to develop her **(7)** .... throughout the course.

One of the sections of the course that Elizabeth didn't enjoy was the **(8)** .... classes.

At the end of the course, all participants were given a **(9)** ....

In the future, Elizabeth hopes to make more films about **(10)** ....

WRITING PART 2: LETTER OF APPLICATION

1 **Write an answer to the question below. Write your answer in 140–190 words in an appropriate style.**

You see this notice in your local newspaper:

Staff wanted

The new Hotel International is opening in three months and is recruiting staff to fill a wide range of positions, including:

- Managing Director
- Waiting staff
- Accountant
- Receptionists

If interested, please write to Vacancies@Hotelinternational.com, stating which vacancy you are applying for, explaining how your skills make you suitable for the position, and suggesting what training you would like to receive before starting the job if you are successful.

Write your **letter of application**.

➔ **WRITING BANK** / Pages 236–237

GOING FOR A JOB IN ... FRANKFURT

1 **Look at the photos of Frankfurt. What type of jobs do you think are most common in the city?**

2 **Read the three job advertisements below. Which advertisement(s) mention(s) the following?**

1. Salary
2. Working hours
3. Location
4. Work benefits
5. Language skills
6. Type of contract
7. Closing date
8. Essential skills and experience
9. Desirable skills and experience

3 **Work in pairs and answer the questions. Which job do you think ...**

1. you would be good at?
2. would be the most well-paid?
3. would be the most stressful?
4. would offer the best career progression?
5. would offer the best work-life balance?

4 **Read Ricardo's CV on page 195. Which job in the box below do you think he might be applying for?**

salesperson	social media manager	team leader	office administrator	computer programmer

A BBA

One of the leaders in Germany's financial services industry has an exciting opportunity for a resourceful and diligent financial lawyer to join an established team in our new offices in the heart of the city. The successful candidate will be responsible for drawing up and negotiating multi-million Euro(€) contracts with key clients. Excellent communication skills in English are a must in addition to five years' experience and a university degree in a relevant field.

B FRANKFURT TOURS

We are looking for a sociable and enthusiastic multilingual tour guide to lead tours. The ideal candidate will have excellent people skills and previous experience of giving tours would be an advantage but not a must. Both permanent and temporary roles are available. We offer excellent hourly rates. The workload varies with peaks in July and August and candidates will be expected to work some evenings and weekends.

C FRANKFURT AIRPORT

We are currently recruiting experience[d] baggage handlers at Frankfurt Airport. Duties will include collecting, transporting and loading passenger luggage as well as operating specialis[t] machinery. This is a 24/7 operation and you will be required to work shifts. Free on-site parking is available and we offer a competitive holiday and sick pay package as well as discounts of u[p] to 80% in most of the airport's retail outlets. Please submit your application via the link provided before the end of the month.

5 **Read Ricardo's CV again. Find the following information:**

1. an abbreviation for the date he was born
2. two university qualifications
3. a word which says he is still working at AB Associates
4. a verb which means *make sure*
5. an adjective which means *containing the latest information*
6. a word which means *a large amount of*
7. two adjectives which mean *really good*
8. a phrase to talk about references

Ricardo Costa

DOB: 17/04/1990

Contact information: ricardo_costa@gomail.com

Academic experience

- Bachelor's degree in communications and marketing – Sept 2011
- Master's degree in business administration – Sept 2013

Work Experience

AB Associates

January 2017 – Present

- Responsible for overseeing the development and maintenance of the business's social media pages
- Lead multi-platform marketing strategy, contributing to the business's aim of appealing to a younger demographic
- Ensure all social media content is relevant and up-to-date

Brighter Together

September 2013 – January 2017

- Worked as part of a team to design and manage the company's social network pages

Key skills

- Extensive knowledge of social media platforms
- Excellent attention to detail
- Able to work well in teams and independently
- Self-motivated with a positive work ethic
- Exceptional communication skills

References

References are available upon request.

6 **100 You will hear an interview between Ricardo and a recruiter. Put the questions below in the order that you think the recruiter will ask them. Then listen and check.**

QUESTIONS YOU MIGHT HEAR IN AN INTERVIEW

1. Where do you see yourself in five years' time?
2. What do you think the main challenges of the job will be?
3. What are your salary expectations?
4. What experience do you have in this field?
5. Why did you apply for this role?
6. What do you think makes a good team member?
7. What skills do you have that will help you succeed in this role?

7 **100 Listen again. Complete the phrases with the words that Ricardo uses.**

PHRASES YOU MIGHT USE IN AN INTERVIEW

1. I've been really impressed with the ________ work that the company has been doing …
2. … making sure that they reflect the key USPs of our products. ________ to this, I worked at …
3. In my opinion, the ________ of a good team member are …
4. One challenge that I would expect to ________ in the role would be …
5. Personally, I believe that I am well-organised, diligent and have a ________ .
6. in five years, it is my ________ to become a …
7. I am looking to ________ my skills as a …
8. I would be happy to consider an offer in the ________ of …

8 **Watch the video about Frankfurt. What do you learn about these things? Make notes.**

- Frankfurt Airport
- The Opera House
- The Christmas market
- The business district

WATCH

LIFE COMPETENCIES

USING APPROPRIATE REGISTER, PRACTICAL SKILLS FOR LEARNING

9 **Work in pairs. Choose one job advertisement in Exercise 2 for each person. Write four questions that you might be asked in an interview for these jobs then give the questions to your partner. Add two more questions to your partner's list. Then conduct an interview.**

PROGRESS CHECK 5

EXPRESSING OBLIGATION AND PERMISSION

1 Complete the second sentence so that it has a similar meaning to the first sentence, using the word in bold.

1 Students must wear a uniform at schools in the UK.
COMPULSORY
It's ________ a uniform at most schools in the UK.

2 It's isn't necessary to bring a gift if you don't want to.
HAVE
You ________ a gift if you don't want to.

3 Smoking is prohibited in most restaurants nowadays.
ALLOWED
You ________ in most restaurants nowadays.

4 You shouldn't buy second-hand tickets online but it's hard not to sometimes.
SUPPOSED
You ________ second-hand tickets online but it's hard not to sometimes.

5 Guests should arrive at least one hour in advance to avoid long queues.
ADVISABLE
It's ________ at least one hour in advance to avoid long queues.

EXPRESSING ABILITY

2 Choose the correct option to complete the sentences.

able to	be able	capable	could
enable	managed	unable	

1 We ________ to get the last pair of tickets for the rock concert.
2 Sadly, I won't ________ to attend your wedding next year.
3 The new ticketing system should ________ guests to enter the festival much quicker.
4 The band pulled out of the festival and sadly they were ________ to find a replacement.
5 My sister ________ play the piano when she was four years old.
6 I told my friend that I wasn't ________ make his graduation ceremony.
7 I think I'm ________ of doing a fantastic job on the project.

FESTIVALS AND CELEBRATIONS

3 Choose the correct option (A–D) to complete the sentences.

1 The festival has a ________ for being one of the best in the world. Everyone knows it!
A connection **B** requirement
C reputation **D** purpose

2 I had to ________ the invitation because I had already made plans that weekend.
A put on **B** turn down
C miss out on **D** call off

3 This event would really appeal ________ someone who loves modern art.
A for **B** to
C on **D** with

4 The venue has agreed to ________ the event as long as we pay them in advance.
A give **B** provide
C make **D** host

5 We're doing everything we can to make sure the gig goes ________ .
A ahead **B** up
C over **D** down

6 The host was fantastic and really made us feel at ________ .
A easy **B** easily
C ease **D** uneasy

LIKE VS *AS*

4 Complete the sentences with *like* or *as*.

1 It looks ________ though you've gone on a massive spending spree.
2 My best friend is just ________ me in that we both do all our shopping online.
3 I'm telling you this ________ a friend when I say that shirt doesn't suit you.
4 The fashion show wasn't as well-organised ________ last year.
5 Jane is just ________ her sister – they both love buying new clothes.
6 He works ________ an advisor for one of the big fashion brands.
7 I don't know why, but I really don't enjoy shopping ________ I used to.
8 It seems ________ they're really enjoying their day out together.

PAST MODALS

5 Complete the second sentence so that it has a similar meaning to the first sentence, using the word in bold.

1 I regret not buying a new jacket in the sale yesterday.
SHOULD
I ________ a new jacket in the sale yesterday.

2 In the end, there was no point in us bringing the extra pair of shoes.
NEED
In the end, ________ the extra pair of shoes.

3 It wasn't a good idea to spend all my money on clothes.
SHOULD
I ________ all my money on clothes.

4 Thankfully, it wasn't compulsory for him to have his photo taken.
DIDN'T
Thankfully, ________ his photo taken.

5 It wasn't necessary for me to buy a new jumper as my old one still fits me.
NEED
________ a new jumper as my old one still fits me.

SHOPPING AND FASHION

6 Find and correct the spelling mistake in each of the sentences below.

1 They created a huge marketing campane to promote their new line of shoes.
2 You don't need to perchase an extra ticket as my friend can no longer make it.
3 The group was formed to promote comerce and industry.
4 A lot of travel companies delibarately increase the price of holidays during the school holidays.
5 There seems to be a lot of jelousy in the fashion industry these days.
6 I recently won two tickets for a luxury spa weekend in an online ouction.
7 They have installed a ramp outside the shop to increase acessibility for wheelchair users.
8 Initialy, most people rejected the plans to build a new shopping centre in the town.

JOBS AND CAREERS

7 Complete the sentences with the words and phrases in the box. You may need to change the form of the words and phrases.

employee	get back to	headquarters	hire
look into	make redundant	set up	surge

1 I'm sorry I haven't replied yet. I will ________ you later this afternoon.
2 The company has ________ a new sales manager, who will begin next month.
3 There has been a ________ in the number of people visiting the website.
4 ________ are advised to carry their swipe cards with them at all times.
5 Due to recent financial losses, the company has had ________ fifty members of staff ________ .
6 We are currently ________ your IT issue and will be in touch shortly.
7 The board made the decision to move the company's ________ overseas.
8 After quitting his job as a lawyer, Martin decided ________ his own business.

ADDING EMPHASIS AND SENTENCE FRONTING

8 Rearrange the words to form sentences. The first word has been given for you.

1 the / talk / must / you / ~~under~~ / exam / no / in / circumstances
Under ________ .
2 go / the / had / them / I / to / seen / film, / I / with / decided / already / ~~since~~ / not
Since ________ .
3 like / ~~what~~ / is / really / the / salary / my / about / I / job
What ________ .
4 in / of / the / meeting / room / the / ~~waiting~~ / was / organisation / head / the
Waiting ________ .
5 the / I / something / ~~going~~ / did / really / was / happy / presentation / I'm / to
Going ________ .

COMMUNICATION ACTIVITIES

UNIT 1: WRITING PART 1 – TRAINING, EXERCISE 2

Mostly As = Oh dear! Healthy living clearly isn't a priority for you and it may be time to think seriously about shaping up. Try getting more sleep at night so you're not napping in the day and do it before your boss or teacher catch you sleeping at your desk! And think about what you're consuming – all that sugar isn't good for your teeth you know!

Mostly Bs = Not bad! While you're not going to run any marathons any time soon, you are at least getting your heart pumping a few times a week. Keep an eye on your caffeine consumption and try turning off the TV once in a while. You could even consider actually going out with your friends rather than messaging them!

Mostly Cs = Excellent! Your health is clearly important to you. You take every opportunity to exercise and always choose the healthiest eating option. Be careful though, you could be taking things too seriously – make sure you are not annoying your friends and family with all your healthy activities and advice!

UNIT 1: SPEAKING PART 2 – TRAINING, EXERCISE 5

Student B

Talk about your two photographs for one minute and answer a short question about your partner's photographs. The photographs show people eating different types of food. Compare the photographs and say what you think these people like about eating these types of food.

What do you think these people like about eating these types of food?

Student A

Which type of food would you prefer eating?

UNIT 1: SPEAKING PART 2 – TRAINING, EXERCISE 5

Student A

Talk about your two photographs for one minute and answer a short question about your partner's photographs. The photographs show people exercising. Compare the photographs and say why you think the people have decided to exercise in these ways.

Why have these people chosen to exercise in these ways?

Student B

Which of these exercises would you prefer?

UNIT 6: SPEAKING PART 2 – TRAINING, EXERCISE 7

Student B

Talk about your two photographs for one minute. The photographs show people spending time in nature. Compare the photographs and say how you think these people feel about being in these places?

How do you think these people feel about being in these places?

Student A

Do you enjoy spending time in nature?

UNIT 6: SPEAKING PART 2 – TRAINING, EXERCISE 7

Student A

Talk about your two photographs for one minute. The photographs show people spending time with animals. Compare the photographs and say what you think the people are enjoying about being with these animals.

What are these people enjoying about being with these animals?

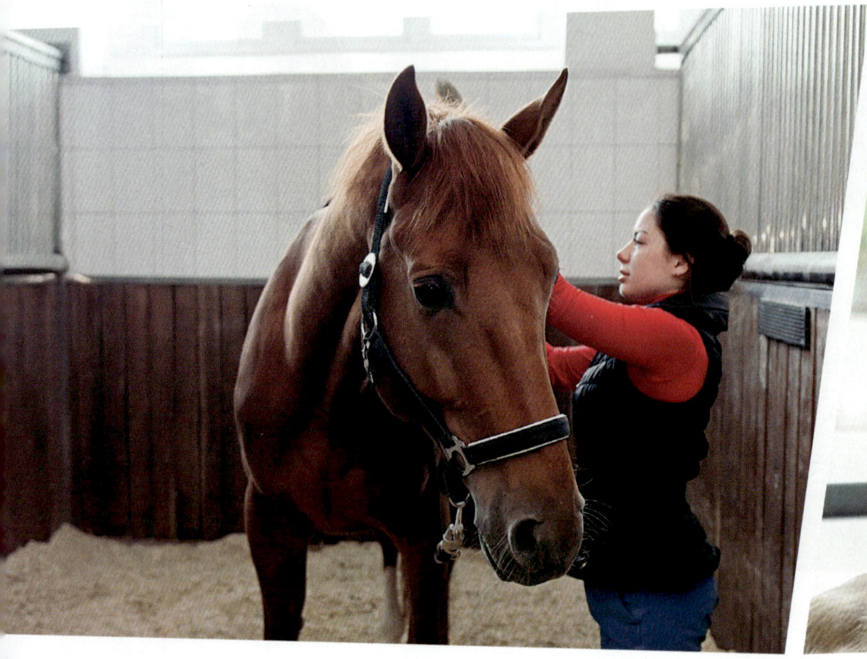

Student B

Do you spend much time with animals?

UNIT 7: WARMER – ANSWERS TO QUIZ, EXERCISE 2

1. second
2. tomato ketchup
3. 95%
4. peanut butter
5. honey
6. All of them

UNIT 7: GRAMMAR – *WISH* AND *IF ONLY*, EXERCISE 6

A - JAKE

Your friend made you a generous portion of baked aubergine last month. You thought it was overly salty and too rich, but you pretended it was delicious, so you didn't hurt her feelings. Not only that, but you suspect the oil your friend used was a bit rancid as there was an unpleasant smell to it. Now your friend is making the dish for you twice a week. Your friend has offered to show you how to make it but as you are a much better cook and don't want to offend them, you've been avoiding going into the kitchen unless your friend is out.

You managed to throw some of the revolting baked aubergine out of the window when your friend wasn't looking last week to avoid eating it. But you then had to sneak out to buy a takeaway as you were starving. You feel guilty about this and have noticed your friend has been a bit cold and distant toward you over the past few days.

You don't want to fall out with your friend.

It's time to talk.

UNIT 7: WRITING PART 2 – TRAINING, EXERCISE 5

You have received an email from your English-speaking friend, Joanna:

Hi!

Guess what? I'm coming to your city next month with my friend. Can you recommend one of your favourite restaurants for us to try? Please tell me what you like about it and if there are any problems with it as well.

Thanks,

Joanna

Write your **email**.

UNIT 11: SPEAKING PART 2 – TRAINING, EXERCISE 6

Student B

Talk about your photographs for one minute. The photographs show people using computers. Compare the photographs and say why you think these people are using their computers.

Why do you think these people are using their computers?

Student A

What do you use your computer for?

UNIT 12: GRAMMAR – EXPRESSING OBLIGATION AND PERMISSION, EXERCISE 2

GROUP B

IN WHICH COUNTRY ...

1 does the bride and groom try to leave without being seen?
2 does a wedding cake tradition decide who will get married next?
3 are you allowed to kiss the bride or groom?
4 are you not allowed to smile in the wedding photos?
5 is it not allowed to go into certain rooms?
6 does the groom have to answer questions under difficult circumstances?

SOUTH KOREA

Before leaving the wedding venue with his new bride, a Korean husband must have his shoes and socks removed by his friends and relatives, who then hit the groom's feet with a stick or even a fish. It's a light-hearted event. While this is happening, it's compulsory for the groom to answer questions that his friends and relatives ask him. After he has answered all the questions, he is permitted to leave.

PERU

The hosts at a Peruvian wedding are expected to prepare a cake with ribbons. Attached to one of the ribbons is a wedding ring, which is hidden inside the cake. After the wedding ceremony, the female wedding guests have to pull out one of the ribbons. If the ring is attached to their ribbon, then they are considered to be the next person to get married. But don't worry, you don't have to join in if you don't want to.

CONGO

Marriage is usually a joyful time, and smiling in your wedding photos is essential! But this isn't the case everywhere. A wedding tradition in Congo states that the wedding couple shouldn't smile under any circumstances on their wedding day, even for their wedding photographer! Smiling indicates that they are not serious about marriage.

UNIT 7: GRAMMAR – *WISH* AND *IF ONLY*, EXERCISE 6

B – KRISTI

You were thrilled that your friend thought the baked aubergine dish you prepared last month was delicious – it was your grandma's recipe and she was a highly-skilled cook. You feel a bit guilty that you had to use oil which was slightly off; however, your friend didn't appear to notice. This is probably because your friend's cooking is tasteless and almost inedible, although you haven't wanted to hurt his feelings by saying anything before. Recently, however, your friend has been taking you for granted. Not only did he show no interest in your offer to share your grandma's recipe, preferring instead for you to make the dish for him twice a week, but he's also stopped helping you tidy the kitchen.

Last week, you found what looked like baked aubergine in the garden below the kitchen window and a takeaway box hidden in the bin. You have become suspicious that your friend's been lying to you.

You don't want to fall out with your friend.

It's time to talk.

UNIT 13: GETTING STARTED – WHAT TYPE OF SHOPPER ARE YOU?, EXERCISE 6

BETWEEN 5–10

Oh dear. You generally overspend, and your shopping habits could get you into trouble if you're not careful. You probably have a wardrobe full of things you don't wear, and your friends might say you're a shopaholic. Buy things which are good value, rather than brand names, and, if you can't stick to your budget, stop going to the sales.

BETWEEN 11–15

Not bad. You are generally a sensible shopper, although sometimes you make silly mistakes if you come across a bargain or special offer. Try to shop around a bit more and plan what you are going to buy before you go shopping. The occasional spending spree is fine though, as long as you can afford it.

OVER 16

Well done. You are a careful shopper and generally only buy what you need. You are very good at shopping around for the best price and aren't easily persuaded by offers or deals. You don't overspend on designer labels or the latest smartphone, and you spend a lot of time doing research before you buy anything.

GRAMMAR REFERENCE

STARTER

THE PRESENT PERFECT SIMPLE AND CONTINUOUS

PRESENT PERFECT SIMPLE: *HAVE* + PAST PARTICIPLE

POSITIVE	NEGATIVE	QUESTION
I've read *the article in a newspaper.*	*She hasn't had lunch.*	*Have they arrived yet?*

THE PRESENT PERFECT CONTINUOUS: *HAVE BEEN* + PRESENT PARTICIPLE

POSITIVE	NEGATIVE	QUESTION
I've been watching *the match.*	*She* ***hasn't been waiting*** *long.*	***Have*** *they* ***been working*** *with you?*

Both the **present perfect simple** and **present perfect continuous** talk about something which started in the past.

- The present perfect simple is a completed action which has a result in the present:
  She's passed her driving test, so now she can take the children to the day care centre herself.
- The present perfect continuous is an action which is still happening now:
  They've been working hard on their presentation, but it isn't finished yet.

The two tenses are often very similar in their usage. However:

PRESENT PERFECT SIMPLE	PRESENT PERFECT CONTINUOUS
emphasises the result: *They've worked on the environmental project all week and they're going to present the final version tomorrow.* focuses on how much of an activity is complete: *I've listened to all of the audio novels you recommended.* focuses on how many times an action has been repeated: *We've watched that programme about celebrities several times.*	emphasises the action: *They've been working on the environmental project all week, but they've still got some way to go.* focuses on how long an activity has been in progress: *I've been listening to the audio novels you recommended and I've still got two left.* focuses on the process of change over a period of time and that the changes are not finished: *My use of grammar has been getting more accurate since I started testing myself.*

Note:

Some verbs are not used in the continuous form, e.g. *know, hate, understand, want.*
I've known Guy for a long time. (NOT: ~~*I've been knowing*~~ *Guy for a long time.*)
I've understood everything you've outlined. (NOT: ~~*I've been understanding*~~ everything you've outlined.)

PRACTICE

1 Complete the sentences with either the present perfect simple or continuous.

1. I ________ (prepare) my presentation on mammals all week, but I ________ (not finish) it yet.
2. What ________ (you do)? Your hands are covered in dirt.
3. Your parents ________ (look) exhausted recently. Have they ________ (work) too much?
4. I ________ (not complete) my essay yet, because I ________ (chill out) in the garden for over an hour.
5. Have you got a plaster? I ________ (do) some work around the house and I ________ (damage) the nail on my thumb quite badly.
6. I ________ (be) to Spain several times this year. Every visit was really outstanding.
7. Recently the government ________ (become) more aware of the need to promote music education.
8. I ________ (change) a wheel on my car, so I'm not really in the mood to go out.

2 Tick the correct sentences. Correct the sentences with mistakes.

1. The surgeon has just finished a nine-hour operation, so he's exhausted.
2. I have finally been learning how to use the passive in English. I feel over the moon that I can do it at last.
3. I can see that he has eaten too much recently. He's gained a lot of weight.
4. The rain has been pouring down all day, so I chose to stay indoors.
5. They haven't mastered Chinese, but they can communicate at a basic level. That's an incredible achievement!
6. They have browsed for jobs in sport management for over four hours and still haven't found anything.
7. I have gone to the weight lifting session every weekend for years.

3 Make sentences with either the present perfect simple or continuous.

1 Scientists / discover / vaccines / to cure / many fatal illnesses
2 He / not put / his recent qualifications on his CV / yet
3 Wake up! You / sleep for / over two hours now.
4 We all feel thirsty, / because / as usual / not / drink enough / during training.
5 She / know him / since / he was a small child.
6 It snow / heavily / all morning / and as a result / the roads / are slippery now.

COMPARATIVES AND SUPERLATIVES

The form of comparatives and superlatives depends on the number of syllables in the original adjective or adverb.

ONE-SYLLABLE ADJECTIVES

ADJECTIVE	COMPARATIVE	SUPERLATIVE
high	high**er**	high**est**
small	small**er**	small**est**

ADJECTIVE ENDING IN A SINGLE CONSONANT

ADJECTIVE	COMPARATIVE	SUPERLATIVE
fa**t**	fat**ter**	fat**test**
sa**d**	sad**der**	sad**dest**

ADJECTIVES WITH TWO SYLLABLES

ADJECTIVE	COMPARATIVE	SUPERLATIVE
clever	cleverer / more clever	cleverest / most clever
narrow	narrower / more narrow	narrowest / most narrow

ADJECTIVES WITH THREE OR MORE SYLLABLES

ADJECTIVE	COMPARATIVE	SUPERLATIVE
experienced	more experienced	most experienced
inconvenient	more inconvenient	most inconvenient

Note:

Adjectives with two syllables, ending in *-y*, replace the *y* with *i*:

easy *easier* *easiest*
happy *happier* *happiest*

These very common adjectives have irregular comparative and superlative forms.

ADJECTIVE	COMPARATIVE	SUPERLATIVE
good	better	best
bad	worse	worst
little	less	least
much	more	most
far	further / farther	furthest / farthest

PRACTICE

1 Complete the sentences with the correct comparative or superlative.

1 Today is the ________ (bad) day I've had this year.
2 You call in sick ________ (often) than everybody else in the class.
3 This questionnaire about energy use is the ________ (complicated) I've ever completed.
4 The conference on tropical diseases was the ________ (memorable) I've ever attended.
5 The ferry from Staten Island to Manhattan is the ________ (cheap) in the world. It's free!
6 This shape is much ________ (irregular) than the other one.

2 Put the words in order to make sentences with the comparative or superlative.

1 His ambition / than / has always / his brother's. / greater / been /
2 was as accurate / the report / Her analysis / the financial situation / as / in the magazine. / of /
3 The lecturer is / since she started / less / work on her / available to her students / thesis.
4 His skills / are not / as fast / as people predicted. / developing /
5 My interest in / considerably / than / the project is / greater now / it was / at the beginning.
6 ideally want. / high / My motivation is / as / not quite / as I would /
7 than / There are slightly / living in / fewer people / ten years ago. / the town /
8 more / than by train. / It's / to travel by car / considerably / exhausting /

UNIT 1

GERUNDS AND INFINITIVES

INFINITIVE

We use the infinitive:

- to say why we do something:
  *She put a tick **to accept** the terms and conditions.*
  *He's taken up long-distance running **to improve** his health.*
- to say why something exists:
  *They've erected the metal barrier on that sharp bend **to reduce** accidents.*
- after *too* and *enough*:
  *It was too late **to express** my opinion because the professor had already moved on to another topic.*
  *The image wasn't clear enough **to illustrate** clearly what it was supposed to depict.*

We use the infinitive in the following verb patterns:

verb + *to* infinitive	*agree, appear, bother, decide, demand, fail, hope, learn, manage, offer, plan, refuse, seem, be, supposed, threaten*	*They agreed to vote on the new reform.*
verb + (*somebody/something*) + *to* infinitive	*ask, choose, expect, help, intend, promise, want*	*He expected to do well in the test.* *I expect you to do well in the test.*
verb + *somebody/something* + *to* infinitive	*advise, allow, enable, encourage, forbid, force, invite, order, permit, persuade, recommend, remind, teach, tell, warn*	*My parents forbade me to boast about my academic achievements.*

We use the verbs in the lists above to report speech.

VERB + *-ING*

We use a verb + *-ing*, e.g. *I can't stop **yawning***:

- after prepositions:
  He's improved his English **by reading** extensively.
  Note: We also use a verb + *-ing* after *to* when *to* is a preposition:
  *I'm looking forward to **receiving** a detailed reply to my letter of complaint.*
- as subjects or objects of a sentence:
  ***Correcting** mistakes is a crucial part of the learning process.*
  *When he was fully recovered after the operation, he decided to take up **wrestling**.*
- after the verbs *admit, appreciate, avoid, celebrate, consider, delay, deny, dislike, enjoy, finish, imagine, involve, keep, mind, miss, postpone, practise, regret, risk, stop, suggest*:
  *I considered **swapping** this task for another one.*
  *She celebrated **passing** all her exams by going on a trip to Thailand.*
  *I now regret **borrowing** money from my grandparents.*
- after the expressions *it's no good, it's not worth, it's no use, it's a waste of time, can't stand, can't bear, can't help*
  *It's a waste of time **trying** to increase the bee population.*
  *It's not worth **buying** expensive ski gear – you can hire it.*
  *I can't bear **seeing** my best friend making such a fool of herself.*

VERBS FOLLOWED BY EITHER AN INFINITIVE OR A VERB + *-ING* WITH ALMOST THE SAME MEANING

I hate criticising people. I hate to criticise people.
It continued being foggy all morning. It continued to be foggy all morning.
Note: When *love, hate, prefer* and *like* are used with *would*, they are **always** followed by the infinitive:
We would like to devote more time to our exam preparation.

VERBS FOLLOWED BY EITHER AN INFINITIVE OR A VERB + *-ING* WITH A DIFFERENCE IN MEANING

	VERB + INFINITIVE	VERB + -ING
remember	*Did you remember to bring your running shoes?* (an action you have to do)	*I remember wondering if I would ever get down off the summit of the mountain.* (a memory of something in the past)
forget	*Don't forget to complete your physics presentation.* (an action you have to do)	*I'll never forget seeing my wife for the first time at my best friend's wedding.* (a memory of something in the past)
regret	*I regret to tell you that the room you booked is no longer available.* (I'm sorry to give you this information.)	*I regret not arriving at the hotel at the agreed time.* (I'm sorry I didn't do this.)
try	*I'm mailing my CV every day to IT companies to try and get a job.* (My objective is to get a job in IT.)	*If you want to get a job in IT, why don't you try phoning the companies?* (Phoning is a method to reach your objective.)
mean	*Martin means to get a scholarship to cover some of the costs of his college course.* (This is his intention.)	*He wanted to get a scholarship to cover some of the costs of his college course, but it meant getting top grades in all his subjects.* (it involved)
stop	*She stopped playing the game of chess to phone her mother.* (in order to phone her mother)	*When her opponent made a winning move, she stopped playing the game of chess.* (She didn't continue.)

Note: The form *forget* + verb + *-ing* is unusual. It is more normal to use *(not) remember*: *I don't remember being three years old.* ~~(NOT I forget being three years old.)~~

PRACTICE

1 Tick the correct sentences. Correct the sentences with mistakes.

1. He decided make a high offer to be sure he could buy the second-hand car.
2. I intend to continue to improve my level of spoken English.
3. They persuaded me applying for the position of assistant manager.
4. It's recommended to book a table in advance.
5. Can I remind you not driving without having your licence on you.
6. The lawyers advised him say he was guilty of the crime.

2 Choose the correct option in *italics*.

1. I can't stop *to speak/speaking*. I'm in a hurry.
2. He's completed the design on time by closely *follow/following* the brief he was given.
3. I'm looking forward to *joining/join* the expedition to the North Pole.
4. I admit to foolishly *celebrate/celebrating* victory before the game was over.
5. I regret not *taking up/take up* the place I was offered at university.
6. I can't bear *watching/watch* politicians being dishonest.
7. If you forget *to do/doing* the homework, you will have problems with the teacher.

3 Match the beginnings and endings of these sentences.

1. It's not
2. It's a waste of
3. It's no use
4. I can't stand
5. She prefers to
6. I very much regret

a. not taking driving lessons.
b. people talking about money all the time.
c. time learning foreign languages.
d. worth complaining to the manager.
e. eat fish rather than seafood.
f. buying property. It's better to rent.

4 Complete the sentence with the correct form of the verbs in brackets. In which sentence are two answers possible?

1. I meant ________ (buy) my grandfather a birthday present, but I forgot.
2. I remember ________ (carry) the painting I bought you all round Mexico!
3. She's stopped ________ (take) sandwiches to work. She eats in the canteen now.
4. Camping isn't for me. I prefer ________ (stay) in a comfortable hotel.
5. ________ (analyse) the problem is not enough – what we need is a solution.
6. Tom doesn't believe in ________ (pay) for anything if he can get it for free.

UNIT 2

THE PASSIVE

The passive is formed from the verb *to be* + past participle (*done/eaten/cleaned*, etc.).

ACTIVE	PASSIVE
They washed all the dirty plates by hand. *We've packed all our cases ready for the move.* *It's helpful when people keep you well informed* *The walls are not soundproof, so you can hear the neighbour's alarm in the morning.*	*All the dirty plates were washed by hand.* *Our cases have all been packed ready for the move.* *It's helpful when I'm kept well informed.* *The neighbour's alarm can be heard in the morning, as the walls are not soundproof.*

We use the passive when:

- what happens is more important than who does it:
  The roof on our holiday cottage has been replaced, so we can stay there in the spring now.
- we don't know who or what does/did something:
  My passport and my driving licence have been removed from the safe in my hotel room.
- we don't need to say who or what does/did something because it's obvious from the situation or context:
  Finally, the new international fishing regulations were accepted. (obviously by a government or by the fishing industry)
- when writing in an official style:
  A double room has been reserved for you for two nights on the 14th and 15th of May. We respectfully inform you that the room must be vacated at 11 am on the day of departure.

THE PASSIVE WITH GET

In informal English we can sometimes use *get* instead of *be* to form the passive, especially when we want to say that something bad happened to someone or something:
Our fridge-freezer got damaged during the move. (Formal: *Our fridge-freezer was damaged.*)
She got seriously injured while climbing in the Alps. (She was seriously injured.)
He got fined £100 for speeding.
The passive with *get* is not possible with state verbs: ~~*The chalet in the Swiss Alps got owned by a famous footballer.*~~
The chalet is owned by a famous footballer.

PRACTICE

1 Make the sentences passive.

1 A member of the hotel staff opened the safe in my room for me.
2 You can find lots of bargains on the market.
3 You can buy tickets for the event online.
4 People thought that children were to blame for the damage to the trees.
5 Someone took my phone out of my jacket pocket.
6 They've replaced the winter tyres on my car.

2 Choose the correct option.

1 Our antique armchairs and sofa ________ using high quality materials.
A were restored B was restored C been restored
2 My wallet with all my money and credit cards ________ at the railway station.
A been stolen B were stolen C was stolen
3 The man in the picture ________ for questioning by the police.
A had wanted B gets wanted C is wanted
4 Your train tickets ________ and you can collect them from a ticket machine at any mainline station.
A had been reserved B have been reserved C have reserved
5 Their car ________ badly damaged in the collision.
A been B had C got
6 They ________ for theft.
A were arrested B been arrested C arrested

USED TO, GET/BE USED TO

POSITIVE	NEGATIVE	QUESTION
used to + infinitive verb	*did not / didn't use to* + infinitive verb	*Did … use to* + infinitive verb?

- We use *used to* when we refer to things in the past which are no longer true. It refers to:
  - repeated actions
    I used to eat in the college cafeteria, but now I bring a packed lunch.
  - a state or situation
    That mountain bike used to belong to my best friend. (It belonged to my best friend in the past, but not anymore.)
- In **positive** statements, the form *used to* does not change. We do not use the verb *be* before *it* and *it* always refers to the past:
  *They **used to** go to the sports club three times a week when they lived in London.*
  Not: ~~They are used to go~~ … or ~~They use to go~~ …
- In **negative** statements we use *didn't use to*:
  *I **didn't use to** get very good marks in exams, but this term I'm really pleased with my results.*
- If we want to be very formal, we can use the negative form *used not to*:
  She used not to be as wealthy as she is now.

QUESTIONS

In questions we use *did* + *use to*:
You look familiar. Did you use to be in the same class as me in primary school?

USED TO OR WOULD?

We can use both *used to* and *would* to talk about people's habits in the past. When we use them both together, *used to* generally comes first, because it sets the scene for what follows:
When I was about twelve, I used to create amazing models. I would make steam engines that really worked and I would fold ordinary paper to produce boomerangs that actually flew back to you.
However, you CAN'T use *would* to describe a state or situation, which is no longer true:
We used to work in Chicago. Not: ~~*We would work in Chicago.*~~

BE USED TO

Be used to can refer to the past, present or future. It means 'be accustomed to' or 'be familiar with'.

- *be used to* + noun or noun phrase:
  I work in a fast food restaurant, so I'm used to lots of customers.
- *be used to* + pronoun:
  She was brought up in the countryside and hates pollution. She's not used to it.
- *be used to* + the *-ing* form of a verb:
  He was a surgeon until he retired, so he was used to working in demanding situations.

GET/BECOME USED TO

College life can be very stressful, but don't worry. You'll soon get used to it. (Or, more formally, *You'll soon become used to it.*)

PRACTICE

1 Complete the sentences with the correct form of *used to* and the verb in brackets.

1. I ________ eating olives when I was a child, but I can't resist them now. (– / enjoy)
2. Her friends ________ online shopping, but now they think it's great. (– / do)
3. They ________ hours playing an addictive video game. (+ / spend)
4. My father ________ a vintage Italian sports car. (+ / own)
5. ________ he ________ in touch with his relatives before they emigrated to Australia? (? / keep)
6. I ________ being alone in the dark when I was young. (– / like)

2 Tick the correct sentences. Correct the sentences with mistakes.

1. My dad would tour with a circus as an acrobat before he got married.
2. I would work in a steel factory for many years in my youth.
3. When she was younger, she would enjoy riding horses and would visit the stables every day.
4. I would live in New York State near the Great Lakes until I left to go to university in Washington.
5. When I was a kid I would play outside with my friends until it was quite dark and my mother called me to go in.
6. I didn't use to enjoy the taste of caviar, until I had the chance to eat it at a reception in Russia last year.

3 Complete the sentences with the correct form of *be/get used to*.

1. Having lived in Alaska all of her life, she ________ the extremely low temperatures during the winter months.
2. He has just started work on a construction site. It's taken him a long time ________ the noise and dust.
3. I'm completely exhausted. I ________ working such long hours.
4. We've just started our university course. It's hard for us ________ writing a 5,000-word essay every week.
5. I've just started a new job and everything is new and pretty confusing, but I ________ the systems and routines.
6. Living on your own for the first time can be very demanding, but just relax. You'll soon ________ coping with everything.

UNIT 3

ZERO, FIRST AND SECOND CONDITIONAL

CONDITIONALS

Conditional sentences express a condition (*If …*) and the consequence of the condition. The consequence can be expressed before or after the condition:
If you win a sport scholarship, you can study at that American university.
You can study at that American university if you win a sport scholarship.
Note: If the condition comes first, a comma is used.

ZERO CONDITIONAL

We use the zero conditional to express things that are generally or always true (e.g. scientific facts).
If you heat water to 100 degrees centigrade, it boils.
Most people tend to be extremely aggressive if you accuse them of lying.
Note: In zero conditionals, *when* and *if* are often interchangeable.
The present simple is used in both clauses.

FIRST CONDITIONAL

We use the first conditional to express a future situation which we think is real or possible:
I'll research that topic today, if I remember to take my laptop with me.
If it's not raining, we will go to the beach.
If there isn't a sand storm again tomorrow, we'll go hiking in the desert.
Unless my local team loses their next match, they'll be top of the championship league.
Note: In first conditional sentences, it's not important which clause comes first.
The structure is usually *if* + present simple and *will* + infinitive.
We can often use *unless* instead of *if not*:
I won't be able to go snowboarding, unless I get all my gear sorted out.
(If I don't get all my gear sorted out, I won't be able to go snowboarding.)

SECOND CONDITIONAL

We use the second conditional to express things which are imaginary, contrary to the facts, impossible or improbable:
If I won something like an international golf tournament, I'd probably spend my winnings on buying a luxury yacht.
If you reduced your calorie intake and joined a gym, you would easily lose all your excess weight.
Note: In second conditional sentences, it's not important which clause comes first.
The structure is *if* + past simple and *would* + infinitive.
Although many conditional sentences use *if* + *will/would*, conditional sentences can also use other words instead of *if*, for example *when*, *as soon as*, and *in case*. Other modal verbs can be used instead of *will/would*, for example *can/could*, *may* and *might*.

PROVIDED

Provided can sometimes be used instead of if.
Provided *the weather is fine, you could take a tour around the city.*

PRACTICE

1 Choose the correct option in *italics*.

1 The sun's very strong today, so if you don't sit in the shade, you *get/will get* badly burnt.
2 If you mix oxygen and hydrogen together, you *get/will get* water.
3 A lot of wild animals tend to attack if they *are/will be* scared.
4 When the manager is out of the office, her personal assistant *takes/will take* all her calls.
5 *If/Unless* the weather doesn't improve significantly, we'll have to postpone the barbecue.
6 You *won't win/will win* a fortune in the lottery unless you buy a ticket.

2 Complete the sentences with the first or second conditional.

1 If he ________ (be) late, we ________ (have to) leave without him.
2 If I ________ (be) you, I ________ (buy) that computer.
3 If you ________ (come) this way, the doctor ________ (see) you now.
4 If I ________ (have) more money, I ________ (not be) here now.
5 Provided you ________ (study) hard, you ________ (pass) the exam.
6 I ________ (buy) a new Ferrari, if I ________ (win) the lottery.

3 Tick the correct sentences. Correct the sentences with mistakes.

1 I would sleep more peacefully, if the neighbours stop having parties late at night.
2 We hire a car to get to the hotel from the airport, unless the flight is delayed.
3 Babies usually only cry when they are hungry, thirsty or wet.
4 If she doesn't go on the excursion, I will either.
5 We definitely will cancel the beach party, unless it pours with rain.
6 If you weren't so stubborn, we wouldn't have so many massive rows.

GIVING ADVICE

When giving advice or making recommendations, we can use the modal verb *should* + infinitive without *to*. For example:
You should ask your tutor to read through your dissertation before you submit it.
We can also use the following words and phrases to give advice and make recommendations. Pay attention to the grammatical structure of these words and phrases.

MIGHT WANT / LIKE + *TO-* INFINITIVE

You might want to book a table in advance as the restaurant can get very busy at weekends.

MAKE SURE + PRONOUN

Make sure you take an umbrella with you. It's supposed to rain.

OUGHT + *TO-* INFINITIVE

You ought to do more exercise.

RECOMMEND + VERB *-ING*

I'd recommend writing a blog of your travel adventures.

WOULD + INFINITIVE WITHOUT *TO*

I would speak to someone who has already taken the exam.

HAD BETTER + INFINITIVE WITHOUT *TO*

You had better ask your boss for an extension to the deadline.

WHATEVER YOU DO

Whatever you do, don't forget to turn your phone off before you go into the interview.

COMMON MISTAKES

Remember to include ***had*** or ***'d*** in the phrase ***had better***
You'd / You had better start revising for your exam.
Had better is often used to warn someone or give strong advice. Use ***should*** when you want to be less strong with the advice you give.
You're very good at drawing. You ~~had better~~ should study to be an artist.
We use ***might not want to*** in negative situations.
We don't use ***could not***.
You ~~could not~~ might not want to accept the job offer if the salary is low.
We don't use the ***to*** + infinitive form after ***Why not***.
We can also use ***Why don't you***
Why not ~~to~~ include a paragraph about the role of technology in education.
Why don't you include a paragraph about the role of technology in education.

PRACTICE

1 Find and correct the mistake in each of the sentences below.

1. I'd recommend to speak to your teacher about the problem.
2. He ought get more exercise otherwise he'll have health issues later in life.
3. You might want finding another person to go with you on the trip.
4. You had better to send your application in soon or you'll miss the deadline.
5. Make sure take you a jumper when you go out this afternoon.
6. I will delete this sentence from your essay if I were you.

2 Choose the correct option in *italics*.

1. You *had better/ought to* study physics at university. You're really good at it.
2. Whatever you do, *don't/not* cheat in your exam tomorrow.
3. You *could not/might not* want to go to the party if you're feeling unwell.
4. *Why not/Why not you* include a few images in your presentation.
5. *Make sure/Whatever you do,* you leave enough time at the end of the exam to check your answers.

UNIT 4

COUNTABLE AND UNCOUNTABLE NOUNS

Nouns can be either **countable** [C] or **uncountable** [U]. However, some nouns can be both countable [C] and uncountable [U], but with a difference in meaning:

Most people claim that it's healthy to drink tea regularly. (uncountable, because it's tea in general)

She ordered a tea with a slice of lemon. (countable, because it's a cup of tea)

Preparing for a major exam is an enormous amount of work. (uncountable, because it's work in general)

That sculpture is a famous work of art. (countable, because it's a particular work)

The grammar for countable nouns is different from the grammar for uncountable nouns.

COUNTABLE NOUNS

- use *a* or *an* in the singular: *a firefighter, an accountant*
- can be made plural: *platform – platforms, portrait – portraits*
- use *some* and *any* in the plural: *some ponds, any replies*
- use *few* and *many* in the plural: *few mayors, many manufacturers*

UNCOUNTABLE NOUNS

- do not use *a* or *an*
- cannot be made plural: *pollution, behaviour*
- use verbs in the singular: *The BBC news is independent.*
- use *some* and *any* in the singular: *Some student accommodation is available.* *He wasn't seeking any help or advice.*
- use *little* and *much* in the singular: *There was little information available on the website.*
- use other words to refer to a quantity: *I gave her* ***a piece of*** *advice about getting a bank loan.* *He wanted to borrow* ***a small amount of*** *money*

SOME COMMON UNCOUNTABLE NOUNS IN ENGLISH

accommodation, advice, behaviour, cardboard, countryside, damage, equipment, experience, food, furniture, homework, housework, information, knowledge, luggage, media, music, newspaper, pollution, research, scenery, smoke, software, stuff, transport, work

PRACTICE

1 Tick the correct sentences. Correct the sentences with mistakes.

1. The students finally found some suitable accommodations at a reasonable rent.
2. We were astonished to discover that the airline charged us extra for our luggages.
3. A pollution caused by plastic in the ocean is responsible for the death of marine life.
4. I usually reject an advice from my doctor.
5. The company's brochure contained little information about prices and delivery dates.
6. All of the paintings in the art gallery are extremely valuable work of art.

2 Choose the correct option in *italics*.

1. Many experts argue that it is not wise to drink *coffee/coffees* just before going to bed.
2. He considered going to the citizen's advice centre, but finally decided he didn't need to ask for *some/any* help.
3. There's a container for recycling *cardboards/cardboard* and waste *papers/paper* behind our block of flats.
4. Some of the news about the political situation *were/was* very upsetting.
5. The cost of the *equipment/equipments* needed to play golf *is/are* beyond the reach of most people.
6. The engineers were desperately struggling to repair the *damages/damage* caused to the bridge by the explosion.

ARTICLES

THE INDEFINITE ARTICLE

We use ***a*** or ***an***:

- with singular, countable nouns mentioned for the first time: ***A*** *new car loses ten percent of its value as soon as you drive it out of the showroom.*
- to talk about jobs: *My ambition is to become **a** surgeon.*

We do not use ***a*** or ***an*** with uncountable nouns or plural countable nouns:
If you have knowledge and experience you have power.
More women than men gain top university degrees.

We use ***an*** before words beginning with a vowel sound (including words with a silent 'h'):
*I've just downloaded **an** app, but I'm worried now about the security of my data.*
*Let's meet up in **an** hour.*

Note:
We don't use **an** when the letters 'u' or 'e' are pronounced with a 'y' sound:
That Swiss army knife is a useful tool.

THE DEFINITE ARTICLE

The is used:

- with things we have mentioned before, or when it's clear who or what we are referring to from the context: *Two experienced trainers – one for tennis and one for martial arts – have just joined **the** club. **The** tennis coach is from Spain and **the** Judo black belt is from Japan.* *Could you get me some detergent and some flour from **the** shop, please?* (i.e. the shop we always go to)
- when referring to particular things: *I love most sci-fi, but I don't like **the** science fiction written by that new, best-selling, American author.*
- with things which are unique: *Since I bought a telescope, I spend hours studying **the** sky at night. **The** moon and **the** stars fascinate me.*
- with adjectives to express groups: *In Europe, **the** wealthy are investing heavily in property, especially in second homes in coastal areas.*
- with nationalities: ***The*** *French tend to spend their summer holidays in their own country rather than travelling abroad.*
- with superlative adjectives: *The ferry from Staten Island to New York provides **the** cheapest service for commuters in the world. It's free!*

PRACTICE

1 Complete the sentences with definite or indefinite articles.

1. I heard ________ loud noise in ________ basement.
2. I think that ________ woman riding ________ bicycle is ________ member of ________ Dutch royal family.
3. We are looking for ________ apartment in ________ centre of ________ town.
4. What's ________ longest bridge in Europe?
5. ________ poor in many towns are having to feed themselves from food banks.
6. He's ________ university student in one of ________ most historic towns in Europe.

2 Choose the correct option in *italics*.

1. Could you go to *the/a* chemist's and get my prescription?
2. The company has bought two new vehicles for its car fleet. *The/A* luxury, three-litre car is for *the/a* CEO and *the/a* Mini is for her assistant.
3. *The/A* French and *the/a* Welsh are very protective of their national languages.
4. *The/A* window in *the/a* sitting room is *the/a* largest in *the/a* whole house.
5. She's just been awarded *a/an* university degree in modern foreign languages.
6. *The/an/–* accommodation can be quite cheap in some parts of *the/an/–* Ireland.

UNIT 5

PAST PERFECT SIMPLE AND CONTINUOUS

THE PAST PERFECT SIMPLE: SUBJECT + *HAD* + PAST PARTICIPLE

POSITIVE	NEGATIVE	QUESTION
I'd read *her dissertation in a professional journal.*	***She hadn't had*** *her packed lunch.*	***Had*** *they* ***arrived*** *at the ice rink?*

THE PAST PERFECT CONTINUOUS: SUBJECT + *HAD BEEN* + PRESENT PARTICIPLE

POSITIVE	NEGATIVE	QUESTION
I'd been considering *all the possibilities.*	*She* ***hadn't been*** *to France before her trip to Paris.*	***Had*** *they* ***been working*** *with you?*

PAST PERFECT SIMPLE

We use the past perfect simple to describe something which happened before a single event in the past:
The police arrested him, even though he had not done anything illegal.
When he opened the safe, the top-secret documents had already disappeared.
The trainee pilot in the light aircraft took off before everybody had fastened their seatbelts.
Note: We often use the past perfect simple with *already, just* and *never.*

PAST PERFECT CONTINUOUS

We also use the past perfect continuous to describe something which happened before a single event in the past, but the continuous tense focuses on the length of time:
She needed to start to do some very gentle exercise, because she'd been lying in bed for nearly a month after the operation on her spine.
It was nearly a year before his boss realised that he had been leaving the office early every Friday afternoon.

PRACTICE

1 **Complete the sentences with the past perfect simple or continuous form of the verbs in brackets.**

1. We were furious, because we ________ (wait) for over five hours before the plane got permission to take off.
2. He ________ (cheat) for over a year in all his exams before one of the teachers finally found evidence to prove it.
3. The hurricane completely destroyed the cottage that they ________ (build) only a year ago.
4. I must have dropped the confidential documents that he ________ (hand) to me.
5. When they got home, they discovered that their baby sitter ________ (already put) their toddler to bed.
6. When I finally reached the end of the queue, I found out that my colleague ________ (pick up) the tickets an hour earlier.

2 **Complete the sentences with the past perfect simple or continuous form of the verbs in brackets.**

1. The waiter, who was under a lot of pressure, brought a fruit drink that I ________ (not order).
2. I had enormous difficulty recalling the complex password I ________ (commit) to memory the previous night.
3. The children excitedly collected the nuts that ________ (fall) from the trees.
4. She ________ (ride) her pony all afternoon when we glimpsed her briefly as she went into the wood.
5. I ________ (watch) the programme every week for nearly two months, but to my horror I had to miss the last episode.
6. She ________ (live) in London all her life and was reluctant to move, even when she got married.

UNIT 6

PREPOSITIONS

AT

We use *at*:

- when we think of a place as a point, not an area (including at home, at school, at work, at university):
  The delivery man is at the back door.
  The cars were waiting at the barrier.
- to talk about an event with a number of people:
  We'll both be at the reception this evening.
  The students were at the seminar about virtual reality.

IN

We use *in*:

- when we think of a place as an area or space:
  He had his workshop in the basement of his house.
  The headquarters of the company are located in Silicon Valley.
  Many British criminals try to escape the law by living in villas in the south of Spain.
- for cars and taxis:
  He spent two hours in a taxi because of the rush hour.
  I keep up to date with the news by listening to the radio in the car.
- normally with in class, in hospital, in prison, in court:
  My partner is still in hospital after the accident in the warehouse at work.
  He defended his client in court.
- with people or things which form lines:
  She was prepared to wait in a queue for hours for a bargain.
- for the world:
  There's a lot of competition between Dubai and Saudi Arabia to construct the tallest building in the world.

ON

We use *on*:

- to talk about a position in contact with a surface:
  They posted announcements on the walls of the building.
  The frying pan is on the cooker.
  She was relaxing on the terrace all afternoon.
- with border, coast, road to, the outskirts of, the edge of, the way to/from, etc:
  On the border between France and Germany, there was a bakery selling typical bread and pastry.
- with means of transport apart from cars and taxis:
  The wind demolished the sail on our yacht.
- for technology:
  He denies that he spends hours on the phone.
  I rediscovered a friend from school on Facebook.
- with left and right:
  There was a sharp bend in the road on the left.
  Can you see the man in shorts leaning against the door over there on your right?

PRACTICE

1 Complete the sentences with the correct preposition.

1. In old spy films they often exchanged prisoners ________ the border.
2. Over two hundred guests were ________ the wedding reception.
3. He kept all his rubbish ________ his attic rather than getting rid of it.
4. Their head office is ________ a prestigious part of the capital.
5. The criminals who burgled my flat will be ________ court tomorrow.
6. We played football all day ________ the new pitch.

2 Tick the correct sentences. Correct the sentences with mistakes.

1. They waited patiently on the back door for him to come back.
2. They had to wait all afternoon at the queue for the opera tickets.
3. That snake is reputed to be the most poisonous on the world.
4. All the cutlery is on the tray ready to be carried into the dining room.
5. He used to own a luxury villa on the outskirts of that medieval town.
6. The facilities in that cruise ship are incredible.

3 Choose the correct preposition in *italics*.

1. There are lots of fortified castles *on/in/at* the border between Spain and Portugal.
2. A lot of children are failing to achieve at school because they are spending too much time *on/in/at* their phones.
3. He damaged his car quite badly because he didn't see the vehicle parked *on/in/at* the left until too late.
4. I saw several old friends and acquaintances *on/in/at* the festival.
5. I didn't set out early enough and got stuck *on/in/at* a traffic jam *on/in/at* the M25 ring road.
6. The last time I saw that talented young actor was on the stage *on/in/at* the Royal Shakespeare Theatre.

RELATIVE PRONOUNS AND RELATIVE CLAUSES

A clause is a group of words containing a subject and a verb in a tense which form a sentence or part of a sentence. Relative clauses start with these relative pronouns:
who, which, that, whose, where, when and *why*.

DEFINING RELATIVE CLAUSES

- Relative clauses which tell us which particular person or thing the speaker is talking about are called defining relative clauses. They give essential information:
  The optician who tested my eyes is my cousin.
  The relative clause tells us which optician we are talking about.

NON-DEFINING RELATIVE CLAUSES

- Relative clauses which give us extra information are called non-defining relative clauses:
  My cousin is an optician, who is a member of your golf club.
  We already know which optician (it's my cousin); *who is a member of your golf club* does not tell us which optician we are talking about; it just adds extra information.
  There are differences in grammar:

DEFINING RELATIVE CLAUSES ...	NON-DEFINING RELATIVE CLAUSES ...
don't have commas use the following relative pronouns: *who, which, whose, where, when* and *why* can use *that* instead of *who* or *which*. *Who, which* or *that* can be omitted when they are the object of the clause: *The eye drops (–/which/that) the optician gave me should be used twice a day.*	use commas (or pauses in spoken English) use the following relative pronouns: *who, which, whose, where* and *when* don't use *that*. The relative pronoun cannot be omitted.

PRACTICE

1 Choose the correct relative pronoun.

1. Vienna, *which/where/whose* is the capital of Austria, is a city famous for its history and culture.
2. Melanie, *who/whose/which* mother is from Kyoto, speaks English and Japanese fluently.
3. This phone, *who/which/where* I bought on holiday, takes absolutely superb photos.
4. Buckingham Palace, *which/where/whose* members of the British royal family live, is located in the centre of London.
5. Ms Wilde, *who/which/where* is my physics teacher, is going to retire in the near future.
6. The film star Russell Crowe, *which/who/whose* has starred in numerous successful films, was born in New Zealand.

2 Complete the sentences with a relative pronoun.

1. The abstract painting __________ was damaged by yesterday's fire is being repaired.
2. The place __________ the lorry had been abandoned was a pedestrian precinct.
3. The reason __________ I came here early this morning is not of any significance.
4. The doctor __________ I was hoping to see wasn't on duty when I arrived at the medical centre.
5. The woman __________ spoke at the meeting was very knowledgeable.
6. That's the owner __________ vicious dog ferociously attacked the postman.

UNIT 7

WISH, IF ONLY AND HOPE

WISH, IF ONLY

- We use *wish* / *if only* + past simple to say we would like a present situation to be different:
  I wish I lived in a villa overlooking the sea. (I don't live in a villa overlooking the sea now.)
  If only it was the end of the summer term! (But it isn't – it's the middle of the summer term.)
  Note: This use of *wish* / *if only* is similar to the second conditional, as it uses a past tense to refer to something which is contrary to the facts in the present.
- We use *wish* / *if only* + *would* to say if we want:
  - something to happen:
    I wish that terrible noise would stop. (I can't make it stop and I want it to stop.)
  - someone to start doing something they don't do:
    If only you'd stop wasting my precious time!
  - someone to stop doing something which annoys us:
    If only friends wouldn't keep asking me to go out when I'm trying to revise!
- We use *wish* / *if only* + past perfect to talk about things which we are unhappy about which happened in the past:
  He wishes he had completed the project by the deadline. (He didn't complete the project by the deadline – perhaps if he had completed it, he would have been promoted.)
  Note: This use of *wish* / *if only* is similar to the third conditional, i.e. it uses a past perfect tense to refer to something which is contrary to the facts in the past.
- *If only* means 'I wish'. When talking about other people, we use *he wishes, they wish*, etc. We use *if only* when we feel something very strongly. Otherwise we use *I wish*.

HOPE

- We use hope when we want something to happen or to be true, and usually have a good reason to think that it might:
  I hope you make lots of friends when you are abroad.
  She hopes her parents will enjoy themselves on their world cruise.
  Note: We use hope + present/future tense with a future meaning, especially when the subject of the two clauses is different, i.e. I and you in ***I** hope you make lots of friends when **you** are abroad.*
- We often use *hope* + infinitive when there is only one subject to the sentence:
  She hopes to work in the field of entertainment after college.
- We can use *hope* when we want something to be true about the past, but we don't know if it is true:
  I hope you had a brilliant honeymoon. (But I don't know if you had a brilliant honeymoon.)

PRACTICE

1 Complete the sentences with verbs in the simple past or with *would*.

1. I wish I ________ (had) a really well-paid job in the tech industry.
2. If only I ________ (can) meet some people who are more motivating.
3. I wish that tap in the kitchen ________ (stop) dripping. It's driving me crazy!
4. If only he ________ (start) being more responsible.
5. I wish I ________ (weigh) a little bit less.
6. If only my mother ________ (not keep) texting me asking if I'm alright.

2 Tick the correct sentences. Correct the sentences with mistakes.

1. He wishes he has chosen to do a different course at college.
2. I hope you made lots of money when you start your new business.
3. They really hope their children will behave well at school next term.
4. He hopes get a job in the field of entertainment after college.
5. We all hope you had managed to get a visa for your trip to the USA.
6. He hopes he will have success with his job application.

THIRD CONDITIONAL

We use the third conditional to talk about:

- something which did not happen in the past and its results, which are imaginary.
  If you had texted me yesterday, I would not have forgotten that I had an appointment at the hospital. (You didn't text me yesterday and I forgot I had an appointment at the hospital.)
  If he hadn't jumped out of the way of the speeding car, it would have run him over. (He jumped out of the way of the speeding car, so it didn't run him over.)

Notes

- We can contract the third conditional as follows:
  If you'd texted me yesterday, I wouldn't have forgotten that I had an appointment at the hospital.
- We can use *could* and *might* instead of *would*:
  If I had revised better for the exam, I could have passed it. (I had the ability to pass the exam, but I didn't pass it, because I didn't revise well enough.)
  If the temperature had been slightly higher, we might have had a picnic in the countryside. (The picnic was a possibility.)
  If the temperature had been slightly higher, we would have had a picnic in the countryside. (The picnic was a certainty.)

MIXED CONDITIONALS

- When we want to use a conditional sentence to talk about both the past and the present, we can use the second conditional in one part of the sentence and third conditional in the other:
  If the cost of even the cheapest seats wasn't so high (2nd conditional, present time), *we'd have gone to see the opera* (3rd conditional, past time).
  The cost of even the cheapest seats is high and that is why the speaker didn't go to see the opera.
  If the runner hadn't collapsed fifty metres from the finishing line (3rd conditional, past time), *she would be the winner* (2nd conditional, present time).
  The runner collapsed fifty metres from the finishing line and that is why she isn't the winner.
  Note: You cannot use zero or first conditionals in mixed conditional sentences.

PRACTICE

1 Choose the correct verb tense.

1 If the bank ________ to give me a loan, I wouldn't have bought that expensive motorbike.
A didn't agree **B** doesn't agree **C** hadn't agreed
2 I wouldn't have stayed at that luxury resort, if you ________ it to me.
A didn't recommend **B** don't recommend **C** hadn't recommended
3 She would have been seriously injured in that multiple car crash if she ________ her seat belt.
A wouldn't wear **B** didn't wear **C** hadn't worn
4 If you ________ for my support, I would have willingly helped you in any way I could.
A had asked **B** asked **C** ask
5 I would have been extremely disappointed, if you ________ with us on holiday.
A don't come **B** hadn't come **C** wouldn't have come
6 If he ________ rushing to take his pregnant wife to the maternity clinic, he wouldn't have driven through the traffic light on red.
A wasn't **B** hadn't been **C** wouldn't be

2 Complete the third conditional sentences with the verbs in brackets.

1 If you ________ (not / arrive) late at the check-in desk, we ________ (not / miss) our international flight.
2 If they ________ (go) to bed at a reasonable time, they ________ (not / wake up) so late.
3 If she ________ (enrol) in the advanced course at art school, she ________ (might get) that fabulous job as a fashion designer.
4 If you ________ (be) born in that part of Switzerland, you probably ________ (learn) to speak three languages.
5 If he ________ (not go) on that coach trip round Europe, he ________ (never meet) his future wife.
6 She ________ (catch) a taxi from the railway station, if she ________ (have) enough money.

UNIT 8

DIRECT AND INDIRECT OBJECTS

The object of a sentence normally comes after the verb. It is the person or thing which is affected by the verb.

Sarah wrote a letter.

In the sentence above, *a letter* is the object. There are two different types of object in English, a direct object and an indirect object. A direct object shows who or what the action of the verb affects.

James bought a new computer game.

In the sentence above, *a new computer game* is the direct object. An indirect object is usually a person or animal and is the recipient of or is affected by the direct object.

James bought his brother a new computer game.

In the sentence above, *his brother* is the indirect object. The indirect object always comes before the direct object in a sentence.

~~James bought a new computer game his brother.~~

The exception to this rule is when we use *to* or *for*.

James bought a new computer game for his brother.

Sarah wrote a letter to her friend.

In the sentences above, the direct object comes first, followed by the indirect object.

The following verbs often take a direct and indirect object with *to*:

bring	give	lend	offer	owe	show	teach	tell	write

Lucas wrote an email to his cousin.

Louisa gave a presentation to the class.

The following verbs often take a direct and indirect object with *for*:

buy	find	get	make	order	save

Maria bought a new jumper for her husband.

Simon ordered a new computer for his son.

PRACTICE

1 Rewrite the sentences using *to* or *for*

1. I've just bought my brother a new computer.
2. I lent my friend my new phone and she broke it!
3. They offered her the role of assistant at the company.
4. I ordered my wife the new Taylor Swift album.
5. I made my sister a cake for her birthday.
6. I will bring her some flowers when I visit next week.
7. I found her a new dress in the end-of-season sales.
8. I would like to show them the photographs from our honeymoon.

MODALS OF SPECULATION AND DEDUCTION

To make speculations or deductions, we use *must, might* and *can't.*

In the **present**, we use:

- **must** to say that we are sure that something is true :
  The letter must be from Simon because that's his handwriting.
- **might / may / could** to say that we think that something is true but we're not sure.
  The workers might go on strike soon because they're unhappy with their salary.
- **can't** to say that we are sure that something is not true.
  Sarah can't be a vegetarian because she ate a kebab with me yesterday.

  Note that *could* means the same as *might* or *may* but *couldn't* has a different meaning to *might not* and *may not.*

  They may / might not be at home.

  ~~*They couldn't be at home.*~~

  We can also use these modal verbs in the present continuous form to talk about a situation we think is happening now.

  Daniel might be working at the moment.

In the **past**, we use:

- **must have + past participle** to say that we are sure that something is true :
  He must have left early because his car isn't here.
- **might / may / could have + past participle** to say that we think that something is true but we're not sure.
  Lucy wasn't feeling very well this morning so she might have gone home.
- **can't have + past participle** to say that we are sure that something is not true.
  Paulo can't have gone shopping because he's left his wallet on the table.

PRACTICE

1 Complete the dialogues with a modal verb and the correct form of the verb in brackets.

1 **A:** I think I saw Charlotte at the supermarket today.
B: It ________ (be) her. She's in Italy at the moment.

2 **A:** I feel really sleepy.
B: You ________ (be) tired. You've only just woken up!

3 **A:** I don't know where Eleonore and Camilla are.
B: They ________ (go) to the cinema but I'm not sure.

4 **A:** Sarah looks really stressed.
B: She ________ (revise) for her exams at the moment. They start next week.

5 **A:** I can't find my keys anywhere.
B: Let's ask reception. Someone ________ (hand) them in.

6 **A:** Someone's at the door.
B: It ________ (be) Joe. He said he was going to come round.

2 Tick the correct sentences. Correct the sentences with mistakes.

1 My feet can't have grown because my shoes don't fit me anymore.
2 I can't find my watch anywhere. I must have leave it at the gym.
3 They're not answering their phone. They couldn't be at home.
4 They might have changed the date of the presentation but I'm not sure.
5 There's a strange smell coming from the fridge. The milk must be gone off.
6 The burglars can't have climbed through the window of the flat. It is on the 18th floor.
7 My door to my flat was unlocked. I must have forgot to lock it.

UNIT 9

FUTURE FORMS (WILL, BE GOING TO)

THE FUTURE WITH *WILL*

POSITIVE	NEGATIVE	QUESTION
I'll call *the restaurant now and make a reservation.*	*Unfortunately,* ***I won't be able to come*** *to the party tonight.*	***Will you be*** *there on Saturday?*

The future with ***be going to***

POSITIVE	NEGATIVE	QUESTION
I'm going to buy *a new car at the weekend.*	***They're not going to arrive*** *until later this afternoon.*	***Are you going*** *to the cinema later?*

The future with ***will***

1 We use *will* to talk about decisions made at the time of speaking.
This room is very untidy. I will clean it this afternoon.

2 We use *will* to make predictions about the future. These sentences often include words and phrases such as *I think, probably, in all probability, It's likely that, there is little prospect that*
I think there will be driverless cars on the roads in the future.
It's likely that people will live on Mars at some point in the future.

THE FUTURE WITH *BE GOING TO*

1 We use *be going to* to talk about future actions that have already been decided.
We're going to stay with my cousin. We arranged it last week.

2 *Gonna* is often used instead of *going to* in spoken, informal English.
I'm gonna try and get in touch with him tomorrow.

BOUND TO

We use *bound to* to say that something is almost certain to happen in the future.
Engineers are bound to develop a mobile phone that can be fully charged in ten minutes.

PRACTICE

1 **Complete the sentences with the correct form of *be going to* and a verb from the box.**

apply	order	see	visit	watch	write

1 They ________ a pizza for dinner tonight.
2 ________ the new James Bond film at the weekend?
3 I ________ for a job at the local zoo during the semester break.
4 We ________ her in concert anymore as they've cancelled the show.
5 Susan and Alison ________ their sister in Canada next week.
6 I ________ a letter of complaint about the service at the restaurant.

2 **Change the meaning of the second sentence so that it has a similar meaning to the first. You must use the word in capital letters. Write between three and five words.**

1 I don't think that Martin will pass his exams.
UNLIKELY
It ________________ pass his exams.

2 I'm almost certain that scientists will discover a cure for the common cold.
BOUND
Scientists ________________ a cure for the common cold.

3 We are staying with my sister when we visit her next week.
GOING
We ________________ with my sister when we visit her next week.

4 I think it's very unlikely that people will stop using social media in the future.
PROSPECT
There ________________ that people will stop using social media in the future.

FUTURE PERFECT, FUTURE CONTINUOUS

FUTURE CONTINUOUS: *WILL BE* + VERB *-ING*

POSITIVE	NEGATIVE	QUESTION
I will be flying *to Thailand this time next week.*	***I won't be staying*** with you when I visit next week.	***Will you be joining*** *us for the conference next week?*

FUTURE PERFECT SIMPLE: *WILL HAVE* + PAST PARTICIPLE

POSITIVE	NEGATIVE	QUESTION
I will have left *by the time you read this note.*	***She won't have finished the project*** *by next week, in my opinion.*	***Will you have had*** *breakfast by the time I arrive?*

FUTURE PERFECT CONTINUOUS: *WILL HAVE BEEN* + PRESENT PARTICIPLE

POSITIVE	NEGATIVE	QUESTION
I will have been working *here for ten years by 2022.*	***She won't have been waiting*** *for more than ten minutes, by the time we get there.*	***Will they really have been learning*** *English for five years, when they take the exam?*

We use the future continuous to talk about actions and events that will be in progress at a particular time in the future.

We also use the future continuous to talk about something that we think is happening at the time of speaking. For example:

Elizabeth will be having dinner now so there's no point calling her.

The future continuous can also be used in the question form to ask politely for information about the future.

Will Sarah be joining us for dinner tonight?

We use both the future perfect simple and the future perfect continuous to project ourselves forward in time and to look back. The future perfect simple tense refers to a completed action in the future and the future perfect continuous refers to events or actions that are currently unfinished, but will be finished at some future time. Both tenses are usually used with time expressions.

FUTURE PERFECT SIMPLE	FUTURE PERFECT CONTINUOUS
refers to a completed action in the future. *Hurry up, or the concert will have started by the time we get there.* *She will have eaten all her sandwiches by the time she gets to the top of the hill.* *They will have finished the new road by this time next month.*	refers to actions that are currently unfinished but will be finished in the future: *At six o'clock, we will have been waiting for the bus for half an hour.* *She will be exhausted when she gets home because she will have been running for over two hours.* *They will have been building that road for over a year by the time it's finished.*

PRACTICE

1 Choose the correct option to complete the sentences.

1. By the time I'm 65 years old, I will *be stopping/have stopped* working.
2. This time next week, we will *be sitting/have sat* on a beach in the Maldives.
3. Will you *be coming/have come* to my birthday party next week?
4. Hopefully, I will *be having/have had* the chance to travel around South America by the time I'm forty years old.
5. There's no point phoning them now as they'll *be watching/have watched* the final
6. I will *be finishing/have finished* the report in time for the meeting tomorrow.

2 Complete the sentences with the future perfect simple or continuous form of the verbs in brackets.

1. By the end of the next decade most people in America ________ (drive) hybrid cars for years.
2. Next week my best friends ________ (be) married for a year.
3. I ________ (live) in London for nearly two years when I finish my training course.
4. Next month Sylvia ________ (work) here for 20 years, so she can answer all your questions.
5. I think they ________ (reach) their hotel by now.
6. My grandfather ________ (retire) by the end of the year at the age of 75!
7. I bet there will be some great food at the party. My mum ________ (cook) all day.
8. How long ________ (study) when you finally get your master's degree?
9. Next week we ________ (know) each other for exactly ten years. We should celebrate!
10. How much do you think you ________ (earn) by the end of the year?

3 Tick the correct sentences. Correct the sentences with mistakes.

1. By the end of the day, I will have been learning all the new words on that list.
2. This time tomorrow we will have been working here for exactly a month.
3. Sorry, I'm late. How long have you waited for me?
4. I think she will have been playing tennis all morning, so she'll be pretty tired.
5. By the time we get home we will have been walking 20 miles. That's quite impressive!
6. They will have travelled all day so they'll want to go to bed early.

UNIT 10

CAUSATIVES

- We use **have/get + something + done** (*cleaned/fixed/made/repaired* etc.), when we ask someone else to do something for us:
  I've just had my car serviced. (i.e. Someone has serviced my car.)
- *get* is less formal than *have*:
  I usually get my car washed at the weekend.
  We have just got the week's shopping delivered from the supermarket.
- It's not usually necessary to say who did it for us, but it is possible:
  I'm going to get the light fixed by an electrician.
- *have/get + something + done* can be used in any tense or form:
  I'm going to get the trouser bottoms of my new suit shortened for the interview.
- We can also use this structure with *have* to say we have been the victim of something:
  I had my passport and driving licence stolen while I was travelling on the underground.

PRACTICE

1 Complete the sentences with the correct form of *have* or *get*.

1. I've just ________ my hair styled at that new salon near the station.
2. We have just ________ a supply of logs delivered for the wood burner.
3. I'm going to ________ my suit dry cleaned for the wedding.
4. She ________ her handbag stolen while she was on the bus.
5. The police ________ to treat all members of the public fairly.
6. She ________ her son to do his homework by giving him pocket money.

CAUSATIVE VERBS

In addition to *have*, we can also use other causative verbs to express the idea that something is caused by something else or that something or someone causes something else to happen. Some of the most common causative verbs are *let*, *make*, *help* and *get*. Notice how the structure of the sentence changes slightly depending on the causative verb used.

*My parents **let me stay up** to watch the end of the film.*
*I broke a glass statue in the shop and they **made me buy** it.*
*My friend **helped me (to) write** my essay.*
*I usually **get my brother to read** through my presentations before I deliver them.*

PRACTICE

1 Correct the mistakes in the sentences below.

1. My friends made myself sit through the whole film even though it wasn't very good.
2. I can never get my sister come to the dentist with me. She really hates going there.
3. The shop assistants are really helpful. They always help me to finding the right clothes.
4. It's not unusual for my boss to let me to finish work early provided that I've completed all my tasks.
5. I always find it difficult to get more than ten people like my social media posts.
6. Even though we had priority boarding, they still made we queue up with the other passengers.
7. Getting my children do their homework is something that I find really challenging.
8. If he had helped us for solve the computer issue, we would have handed the report over on time.

ADJECTIVES WITH -ING AND -ED

People often confuse adjectives that end in *-ed*, like ***bored*** or ***excited***, with adjectives that end in *-ing*, for example, ***boring*** or ***exciting***.

The difference is that:

- adjectives that end in *-ed* describe emotions – they tell us how people feel about something.
  *Did you see that video about spiders? Yes, I was **terrified** by it.*
- adjectives that end in *-ing* describe the thing that produces the feeling.
  *I watched a **terrifying** video about spiders on YouTube.*

SPELLING CHANGES WHEN ADDING *-ED* AND *-ING*

-ed

If the base word ends in an 'e', just add 'd':

surpris**e** → surprise**d**   amus**e** → amuse**d**

-ing

If the base word ends in an 'e', remove the 'e' and add 'ing':

surpris**e** → surpris**ing**   amus**e** → amus**ing**

PRACTICE

1 Choose the correct adjective.

1. I was *fascinated/fascinating* by the presentation.
2. He was *irritated/irritating* to meet Milly in town after they had had an argument.
3. She talks a lot about the time she worked in a circus. She's so *amused/amusing*.
4. You look *exhausted/exhausting*. Why don't you lie down for a bit?
5. Feeling *tired/tiring* and *depressed/depressing*, she phoned her best friend for a chat.
6. I really can't eat this! It smells *disgusting/disgusted*! What is it?

2 Complete the sentences with the correct form of the adjectives.

1. The plot of the story was really interesting and the characters were very ________ (appeal).
2. I could listen to her all night. She's one of the most ________ (fascinate) people I know.
3. Although some people are not directly ________ (involve) in education, they can still be very influential.
4. Put your notebook down and listen. I've got some ________ (astonish) news for you.
5. His parents were very ________ (dissatisfy) by his result in the test.
6. She's got the ________ (irritate) habit of speaking with her mouth full.
7. Children! Your behaviour is ________ (disgust)! Don't eat without washing your hands!
8. The new Professor of Politics is very ________ (prejudice). Very few students attend his lectures.

UNIT 11

REPORTED SPEECH

We change tenses in reported speech. If the reporting verb (*said, told, admitted, warned*, etc.) is in the past, we tend to change the original verb to a past form as well. Here are some changes we make:

	DIRECT SPEECH	**REPORTED SPEECH**
present simple → past simple	*'I am a sales representative for a steel company.'*	*She said she was a sales representative for a steel company.*
present continuous → past continuous	*'I'm filing this correspondence.'*	*He said he was filing the correspondence.*
present perfect → past perfect	*'I've tried eating insects in Asia.'*	*She said she had tried eating insects in Asia.*
past simple → past perfect	*'I missed the last flight.'*	*He told me he had missed the last flight.*
will → *would*	*'I'll reply to your email tomorrow.'*	*She promised she would reply to my email tomorrow.*

Modal verbs change in the following way:

can → *could*	*'I can gently jog for long periods, but I can't run fast.'*	*She said she could gently jog for long periods, but she couldn't run fast.*
may → *might*	*'I may let you use the calculators to solve the problems later.'*	*The teacher suggested he might let us use the calculators to solve the problems later.*
must → *had to*	*'I must sort out my financial difficulty.'*	*She said she had to sort out her financial difficulty.*

We do **not** change:

- modal verbs *could, would, should, might, ought to* and *used to* in reported speech:
  'I would prefer to have two starters rather than a main course.' → *She said she would prefer to have two starters rather than a main course.*
- must when it's negative:
  'You mustn't open the files relating to the new product launch.' → *Her boss told her she mustn't open the files relating to the new product launch.*
- must when it expresses a deduction:
  'The candidates must still be waiting in reception.' → *She said that the candidates must still be waiting in reception.*

Note: If the reporting verb is in a present tense, no tense changes are necessary:
'I'll help you when you move into your new flat.' → *She says she'll help me when I move into my new flat.*

QUESTIONS IN REPORTED SPEECH.

- We change the word order in the question to the same as a normal sentence.
- We make the same tense changes as in reported speech (see above).
- We use the same question words (*when, how*, etc.).
- We use a full stop (.), not a question mark (?).
  'How long have you been working in the marketing department?' → *She asked me how long I had been working in the marketing department.*
  'When can I interview you?' → *The researcher asked the students when he could interview them.*
- We do not use the auxiliary verbs do, does and did; the question has the same form as a normal sentence:
  'What time do you take a coffee break?' → *The new employee asked what time we took a coffee break.*
- We use *if* or *whether* with Yes/No questions:
  'Can I wear casual clothes at the presentation tomorrow ?' → *He wanted to know whether he could wear casual clothes at the presentation the following day.*
- We often use these verbs and phrases to introduce reported questions: *ask, wonder, want to know, enquire.*

PRONOUN, ADJECTIVE AND ADVERB CHANGES IN REPORTED SPEECH

We usually make the following changes:

you → he/she/they	*'I warned **you** earlier.'*	*He said he had warned **her** earlier.*
your → his/her/their *our* → their	*'I noticed **your** grammar mistake earlier.'*	*He mentioned that he had noticed **her** grammar mistake earlier.*
this/that (as pronouns) → *it*	*'You should erase **this** from your memory.'*	*She told him he should erase **it** from his memory.*
this/that/these/those + noun → *the* + noun	*'**This** report is very detailed.'*	*She told him **the** report was very detailed.*

Remember that references to times also need to change in reported speech:
'I delivered the package this morning.' → She said she had delivered the package that morning.
Other changes include:

present reference	*today* *this week/month/year*	*that day* *that week/month/year*
future reference	*tomorrow* *next week/month/year*	*the next /the following day* *the next / the following week/month/year*
past reference	*yesterday* *last week/month/year*	*the day before* OR *the previous day* *the previous week/month/year* OR *the week/month/year before*

Descriptions of place also frequently change:
'Did the courier service deliver the package here?' → He asked if the courier service had delivered the package there.

PRACTICE

1 Complete the reported speech with the verbs in the correct tense and any other words necessary.

1 'I work in the human resources department.' → She said she ________ in the human resources department.
2 'I'm having a late breakfast.' → He phoned to say that he ________ a late breakfast.
3 'I've never done anything adventurous or dangerous.' → He wrote to tell me that he ________ anything adventurous or dangerous.
4 'I got food poisoning from the fish I ate.' → She suggested that she ________ food poisoning from the fish she ________.
5 'I'll ring as soon as I wake up.' → She promised that ________ as soon as she ________.
6 I can speak and understand Chinese but I can't write it.' → He told me that he ________ speak and understand Chinese but that he ________ write it.

2 Choose the correct option, A or B.

1 She shouted that she ________ into the river from the top of the cliff.
A could jump **B** can jump
2 The waiter said that he ________ an extra portion of cheesecake, if we wanted it.
A might bring **B** may bring
3 She whispered that she ________ pay the bill.
A can't **B** couldn't
4 She told them that they ________ better in the tests this year.
A must do **B** had to do
5 She stated that she ________ to travel by ferry rather than by plane.
A would prefer **B** will prefer
6 The lecturer told the students they ________ at the exam questions until ten o'clock exactly.
A mustn't look **B** had not to look

3 Complete the sentences in reported speech. Pay particular attention to the correct pronouns, adjectives and adverbs.

1 'Martin, I gave you clear instructions about what to do yesterday.'
He told Martin that he had ________
2 'Cynthia, we discovered your missing sports gear in the washing machine this morning.'
They told Cynthia that ________
3 'What project are you working on tomorrow, Jack?'
I asked Jack what project ________
4 'Tom, your essay is extremely confusing.'
The lecturer told Tom that ________
5 'What did you do yesterday, Maria?'
He asked Maria what ________
6 'Have you noticed any of my belongings here?'
He asked if she ________

UNIT 12

EXPRESSING OBLIGATION AND PERMISSION

OBLIGATION – *MUST* AND *HAVE TO*

- We can often use *must* and *have to* without any difference in meaning:
  Surgeons have to / must perform operations conscientiously and professionally to ensure their patients make a swift recovery.
- We use *must* + infinitive without *to* in the present tense. For other tenses, we use *have to* + infinitive:
  I'd love to go on an adventure holiday, but I'll have to save up enough money first.
  In order to get a tourist visa for the USA, I had to fill in an online application form and make an online payment.
- We use *have to* more often in questions:
  Do we have to complete all sections in the survey?
- We use *must* for a goal (or an obligation) that we give ourselves:
  I must make a bigger effort to meet the targets I set myself.
- We use *have to* when the obligation comes from someone else:
  My manager has just handed me a list of jobs that I have to complete by Friday at the latest.
- We use *must* for strong advice:
  You must be extremely attentive when you start learning how to handle birds of prey.

OTHER WAYS OF EXPRESSING OBLIGATION

- We use *be supposed to* + infinitive to talk about an obligation which is different from what really happens:
  We're supposed to do circuit training for two hours a day. (But most people do much less.)
  Aren't you supposed to be doing group work now? (i.e. not chatting with friends over coffee)
- We use *should* + infinitive without *to* to talk about the right thing to do, but which is different from what really happens:
  You should always use your own words when you write an essay, not copy texts you have found on the internet.
- The past of *should* is *should have* + past participle:
  You shouldn't have answered that question in only 150 words!
- We can use *ought to* to mean 'should':
  In some cultures, young people are taught that they ought to be especially respectful towards older people.

PERMISSION

- To express permission, we use *can* (past *could*), *let*, *allowed to* and *may* (past *was/were allowed to*).
  You can drive to college, but you must park your vehicles in the spaces allocated to students.
  Am I allowed to use my student identity card to get reduced fares on public transport?
  She let him copy her notes before the exam.
- We use *may* in formal situations:
  You may go and wait outside the interview room when you have completed the questionnaire.
- To say that there is no obligation, or it's not necessary, we use: *don't have to, don't need to* and *needn't*:
  You don't have to take your shoes off, if you don't want to, but it is expected when you are invited into most homes in Sweden.
  You needn't wear a suit and tie for this job, but it's important to dress smartly.
- *I didn't need to* means 'It wasn't necessary and I didn't do it'; *I needn't have* means 'It wasn't necessary but I did it':
  I didn't need to read the novel to find out about the plot of the story because I'd already seen the film.
  You needn't have bothered to bring a present, but thanks very much anyway. It's much appreciated.

PRACTICE

1 Choose the correct verb in *italics*.

1. Do we *have to/must* leave now?
2. I *must/have* try to modify my behaviour and be more punctual.
3. The police warned me that I *might/must* never drive without insurance again.
4. We're *supposed to/should* follow all of the club rules.
5. You *should/supposed to* never cheat in an exam or copy other students' homework.
6. In my country, men accept that they *may/ought* to offer their seat to women in public transport.
7. You *can/must* buy lunch in the canteen or bring a sandwich if you prefer.

2 Tick the correct sentences. Correct the sentences with mistakes.

1. You are not let to park in front of the entrance.
2. The teacher allowed them to use calculators in the maths test.
3. You may leave the room when you have finished the exam.
4. I wish I hadn't put a coat on. I didn't need to do as now I'm too hot.
5. You needn't wear casual clothes on 'dress-down Friday', but most people do.
6. I needn't have bothered to buy a return ticket because my friend offered me a lift home.

EXPRESSING ABILITY

To say someone has an ability, we use *can, can't, could, couldn't,* and *be able to.*

In the **present**, we use:

- *can* or *am/is/are able to* to express ability:
  That athlete can run at a steady pace over long distances, but she can't sprint on the last lap.
- *can't* or *am not/isn't/aren't able to* for things which are not possible:
  The bank manager isn't able to discuss your loan today, but is able to see you tomorrow morning.

Note: We usually use *can* and *can't* when speaking because they are shorter and less formal than *able to.*

In the **past**, we use:

- *could*, but only when speaking in general:
  When she was at primary school , she could recite several lengthy poems off by heart. (NOT ~~was able to recite~~ several lengthy poems off by heart.)
- *was/were able to* when speaking about one particular occasion when someone succeeded in doing something:
  When the waiter brought the bill, I realised that I didn't have enough cash on me to pay, but I was able to ring a friend who came and paid it. (NOT ~~I could ring~~ a friend who came and paid it.)
- *couldn't* and *wasn't/weren't able to* when speaking in general and also when speaking about one particular occasion:
  I wasn't able to / couldn't calculate the exact dimensions of the store room from the office plan.
  He couldn't / wasn't able to understand many of the formulas in chemistry until he started to revise seriously for his exam.
- when talking about ability, we use *can* only in the present and *could* only in the past. For perfect and future tenses, we use *able to*:
  He's been under a lot of pressure at work, so he hasn't been able to go out much recently. (present perfect)
  When you finally get the job, you'll be able to organise your daily routine as you wish. (future simple)

We use *be able to*:

- after an infinitive:
  She hopes to be able to study tropical medicine when she goes to university.
- after modal verbs (*might, should, may,* etc.):
  I've got some free time at the weekend, so I might be able to help you fix the dent in your car.
  When you've completed this assignment, you should be able to start the advanced course.
- We usually use *can* and *could* with *see, hear, smell, feel* and *taste*:
  From upstairs we could smell the eggs burning in the frying pan on the stove in the kitchen.
  I can hear a strange, scratching noise coming from in the chimney.

However, we use *manage* when we succeed in doing something which is quite difficult to do:

Did you manage to run the marathon in less than two and a half hours?
She managed to get the top grade in the chemistry exam, although she had not attended sessions in the lab for some time.

Note: *could* is not possible in this example:
~~*He could get the top grade in the chemistry exam, although he had not been to the lab to do experiments for some time.*~~

Note: We do not use *be able to* in continuous forms.

PRACTICE

1 Complete the sentences with a modal verb from the box. One of the modal verbs is used twice.

can	can't	could	couldn't	was able to

1 ______ you understand basic economics when you were eight?
2 He ______ get to the meeting on time yesterday, because his car broke down.
3 She's absolutely amazing – she's only seven and she ______ speak five languages, including Japanese.
4 He was delighted, because he ______ find a taxi and get to the party on time.
5 I've searched everywhere for my car keys, but I ______ find them anywhere.
6 I ______ lift this armchair – it's so heavy! Could you help me, please?

2 Tick the correct sentences. Correct the sentences with mistakes.

1 I wasn't able translate the text into French, because it contained too many unfamiliar expressions.
2 When the garage mechanic showed me the bill for the repair, I didn't have enough money on me to pay for it, but fortunately I could use my credit card this time.
3 Thank you for your job offer, but I am afraid I couldn't accept it.
4 When you finally move into your new flat, you'll be able to decorate it as you wish.
5 I could taste and smell the garlic for hours after the meal.
6 He could run the marathon in less than three hours, although he had not been training regularly for ten days.

UNIT 13

LIKE AND AS

AS

We use as:

- to say someone or something is that thing, or has that function:
  He is employed part-time as a lorry driver.
  She uses social media and text messaging as a means of communication.
  The role of a financial adviser is to act as a critical friend.
- to express the same as was predicted, expected, imagined, promised, etc.
  He did exactly as he had promised.
  As expected, the driving test was very stressful.
- to mean 'because':
  As this is an official written examination, I must warn all candidates that no talking is allowed.
  As he exceeded the speed limit, he has to pay a fine.
- after certain verbs, e.g. *describe* and *regard*:
  The police regard these criminals as potentially very dangerous.
  The staff at the zoo are describing the escaped monkey as a risk to the public.
- with adjectives and adverbs to make comparisons:
  The waltz is nowhere near as dramatic as the tango.
- to mean 'for example' in the phrase *such as*:
  We have been trying out lots of different activities at the gym, such as aerobics, yoga and cycling.
- with *the same … as*:
  There's a Russian joke about two men who met each other after fifty years. The one said to the other: 'How did you recognise me after all this time?' The other replied: 'It was easy, you're still wearing the same jacket as when we last met.'
- in the following phrases:
  as far as I know (I think it's true but I don't know all the facts)
  As far as I know, my wife's grandparents originally came from Poland.
  as far as I'm concerned (this is my personal opinion)
  As far as I'm concerned, you can continue wasting your time trying to finish that 5000-piece jigsaw puzzle.
  as far as I can see/tell (this is what I've noticed or understood):
  As far as I can see, he'll be lucky to pass his exams if he doesn't study more.

LIKE

We use like:

- to mean 'similar to' (especially after the verbs be, seem, feel, look, sound, smell and taste):
  When he plays the violin, it sounds like a cat out on the roof at night.
- to mean 'for example':
  He takes part in a wide range of cultural activities like singing in a choir, modern dance and classical ballet.

PRACTICE

1 Tick the correct sentences. Correct the sentences with mistakes.

1. He works full-time like a dental receptionist.
2. When he serves in badminton, he looks as a professional player.
3. By far as I can tell she has probably twisted her ankle.
4. They've added a lot of traditional dishes, such like onion soup and Irish stew, to the restaurant's specials' menu.
5. The customs officers at the airport regard men on their own with large suitcases as highly suspicious.
6. Like she stole a bottle of expensive perfume from the duty free shop, she was arrested and missed her flight.

2 Complete the sentences with *as* or *like*.

1. There's really no point in learning to bake pastry ______ far ______ I'm concerned.
2. She's actively involved in lots of extreme sports, ______ rock climbing and white-water rafting.
3. She gave her husband a sports car for their wedding anniversary, ______ promised.
4. He uses his Swiss army knife ______ a bottle and can opener.
5. That teenager's bedroom looks ______ the inside of a recording studio.
6. The new Professor of History is not ______ entertaining ______ the person who held the post before her.

SHOULDN'T HAVE / NEEDN'T HAVE / DIDN'T NEED TO / DIDN'T HAVE TO

SHOULD / SHOULDN'T HAVE

Should have + past participle is used to talk about events in the past which did not happen. It is typically used to express regret about something that didn't happen. For example:

I should have studied computer science at school

In the sentence above, the speaker didn't study computer science at school but wishes that they had.

Shouldn't have + past participle is used to talk about events in the past which did happen. It is often used to express regret about something that happened.

I shouldn't have eaten the whole cake

In the sentence above, the speaker ate the whole cake but wishes that they hadn't.

We can also use both *should have* + past participle and *shouldn't have* + past participle to speculate about events that might or might not have happened.

Their plane should have landed by now

She shouldn't have left the office yet

NEEDN'T HAVE / DIDN'T NEED TO

Both *needn't have* + past participle and *didn't need to* + infinitive are used to talk about events in the past. For example:

I needn't have taken an umbrella because it was sunny

I didn't need to take an umbrella because it was sunny

There is a small difference in meaning between the two sentences:

- In the first sentence, the speaker took an umbrella but it wasn't necessary
(the meaning here is that the speaker didn't know that it was unnecessary at the time)
- In the second sentence, the speaker didn't take an umbrella because it wasn't necessary (the meaning here is that the speaker knew it was unnecessary at the time)

DIDN'T HAVE TO

Didn't have to + infinitive and *didn't need to* + infinitive have a similar meaning. Both are used to talk about an action or event that wasn't necessary.

I didn't need to buy a ticket because it was free to enter

I didn't have to buy a ticket because it was free to enter

PRACTICE

1 Find and correct the mistake in each sentence below.

1 I didn't had to wear a uniform when I was at school.
2 He shouldn't have ate all those sweets.
3 I didn't need have brought my jumper with me. It's boiling!
4 Their train should arrived by now.
5 I should listened to my teacher this morning. I don't understand any of this.
6 I needn't have filled my car with petrol because it was already full.
7 He didn't has to buy a ticket because he's a student.
8 He didn't need to use his phone while driving. It's against the law.

2 Complete the second sentence so that it has a similar meaning to the first. You must use the word in bold. Write between two and five words.

1 It wasn't necessary for me to update my password.
NEEDN'T
I ______________________________
my password.

2 I regret not going to bed earlier last night.
SHOULD
I ______________________________
to bed earlier last night.

3 There was no point in taking a jacket with me this morning.
NEED
I ______________________________
a jacket with me this morning.

4 I regret shouting at him this morning.
HAVE
I ______________________________
at him this morning.

UNIT 14

ADDING EMPHASIS AND FRONTING

When we want to focus on a particular piece of information or emphasise how important it is, we can bring it to the front of the clause. This is known as 'fronting'. Fronting often makes a piece of writing or speech sound more natural. Compare the pairs of sentences below.

QUESTION WORDS

Nobody knows when he left the party
(fronting) *When he left the party nobody knows*

PREPOSITIONAL PHRASE

A young man stood at the side of the river
(fronting) *At the side of the river stood a young man*

INVERSION WITH *SINCE*

I went out with my friends since I had finished all my homework
(fronting) *Since I had finished all my homework, I went out with my friends*

PARTICIPLES

I'm really glad I applied for the job
(fronting) *Applying for the job is something that I'm really glad I did*

We can also add emphasis by forming cleft sentences. A cleft sentence is a sentence in which something is emphasised by being put in a separate clause. These can be formed by using a kind of relative clause with the information we want to emphasise joined to it. Read the main sentence then study how each component is emphasised.

<u>Main sentence</u>
Sarah went to the shops on Wednesday to buy some milk.
SARAH went to the shops on Wednesday to buy some milk.
It was Sarah who *went to the shops on Wednesday to buy some milk.*
(Emphasising that it was Sarah who went to the shops)
Sarah went to the shops ON WEDNESDAY to buy some milk.
Wednesday was the day when *Sarah went to the shops to buy some milk.*
(Emphasising the day when Sarah went to the shops)
Sarah went to the shops on Wednesday TO BUY SOME MILK.
The reason why *Sarah went to the shops on Wednesday was to buy some milk.*
(Emphasising why Sarah went to the shops)
We can also use *what* to emphasise things and *where* to emphasise places.
The money is what I really like about my job.
The beach is where I spend most of my summer holiday.

PREPARATORY *IT*

Sarah realised she had forgotten to buy some milk when she got home.
It was only when *Sarah got home that she realised that she had forgotten to buy some milk.*

PRACTICE

1 Rewrite the sentences using fronting.

1 I will choose the vegetarian option since I don't eat meat.

....

2 I'm really happy that I passed my driving test.

....

3 Amy didn't know why she had received the letter.

....

4 There was a small, dark object in the corner of the room.

....

5 Sarah realised she had left her phone at work when she got home.

....

6 Julie wasn't sure when she was going to receive her results.

....

2 Emphasise the part of the sentence in capital letters using a cleft sentence.

1 Stephanie went to visit her friend ON SATURDAY.
2 DAVID had problems with his car last week.
3 I spend most of my pocket money at THE CINEMA.
4 Mark went to the dentist TO HAVE A TOOTH REMOVED.
5 ALISON won the competition and received two tickets to a music festival.
6 I signed up to private English classes TO IMPROVE MY READING SKILLS.

WRITING BANK

WRITING PART 1: AN ESSAY

1 Read the exam task. What question should you answer? What ideas should you include?

In your English class you have been talking about the environment. Now, your English teacher has asked you to write an essay.

Write your essay using **all** the notes and giving reasons for your point of view.

Will environmental problems be worse in 20 years?

Notes

Write about:
1. pollution
2. climate change
3. .... (your own idea)

2 Study the model answer. What extra idea does it include?

3 Read the essay question. Then decide which ideas would be relevant to include in the essay.

We shouldn't spend so much money on exploring space. Do you agree?

1. It costs a huge amount of money to send rockets into space.
2. Rockets have extremely powerful engines.
3. There are more important problems in the world that we should spend money on.
4. We can learn a lot about our own planet and solar system.
5. People first landed on the moon in 1969.
6. A lot of people in the world don't have food or shelter.
7. I would love to go into space one day.
8. Some important scientific experiments can be carried out in space.

4 Look at the plan for a student's essay on the question in Exercise 5. Decide which paragraph the correct sentences from Exercise 5 could go in.

Introduction
[1] .... Is it worth the money?

Arguments against exploring space
[2] .... , ...

Arguments for exploring space
[3] .... , ...

Conclusion
We can learn things from exploring space, but it's probably a luxury the world can't afford.

MODEL ANSWER

[1]Use phrases to express your own opinion.

[2]Start with a general introduction to the topic.

[3]Use words and phrases to organise your essay and make it clear when you are introducing a new topic.

[4]Give information which is relevant to the topic.

[5]Give reasons to support your arguments and opinions.

[6]End with a clear conclusion.

[7]Use linking words to add similar or contrasting ideas.

[1]In my opinion, [2]it is possible that environmental problems will be worse in 20 years. We already face a large number of serious environmental problems and, if steps are not taken to tackle them, they will become even more serious.

[3]Firstly, there is already a huge amount of pollution in the world, for example from cars, lorries and planes. There is also a big problem with the amount of rubbish that we produce, which often ends up in the sea.

Secondly, [4]our modern way of life produces harmful gases which are causing the planet to become warmer. This is a very serious problem for animals such as polar bears, [5]which may die out if the ice that they live on melts.

Finally, the world's population is growing rapidly and this will put even more pressure on the Earth's resources. More people means more food production, more pollution and more waste.

[6]In conclusion, the world faces some very serious environmental problems which will definitely be worse in 20 years if nothing is done to solve them. [7]However, I am optimistic that scientists and politicians will find ways to improve the situation.

5 **Read the essay question. Then choose the best introduction and conclusion. Why is it the best one?**

Do you think it is better to watch films in the cinema or at home?

1 Introductions

A There are loads of amazing films nowadays. Personally, I love science fiction films and I often watch them with my friends.

B Watching a film on the big screen at the cinema is certainly very impressive. But in my opinion, there are also advantages to watching films at home, with friends.

C Going to the cinema is quite expensive, and some people can't afford it. Also, some small towns don't have a cinema.

2 Conclusions

A To sum up, I hardly ever go to the cinema because there isn't one very close to where I live. But I often watch movies with my friends at the weekend.

B On balance, some people prefer going to the cinema to watch films, and some people prefer to watch films at home. There are lots of different reasons for this, for example some people can't afford to go to the cinema.

C In conclusion, I would say that for most films, it is more enjoyable to watch at home, with a few friends. However, for films with a lot of special effects, it is worth the trip to a cinema to see these on the big screen.

6 **Study the words and expressions in the *Key language* box.**

KEY LANGUAGE FOR ESSAYS

Ordering your ideas: *firstly, secondly, finally*

Expressing your opinion: *in my opinion, in my view, I would say that, Personally, I think*

Giving reasons: *because, as, since*

Giving results or consequences: *consequently, as a result, therefore, for this reason*

Giving examples: *for example, for instance, such as, one example of this is*

Linking similar ideas: *in addition to this, furthermore, moreover*

Linking contrasting ideas: *however, on the one hand / on the other hand, in contrast, although, whereas*

Giving a conclusion: *in conclusion, to sum up, on balance*

7 **Choose the correct words and phrases in *italics*.**

1 In my opinion, computers are essential in schools *as/for this reason* students need them to find information on the internet.

2 It is clearly necessary to test new medicines, but *in my opinion/therefore* this doesn't justify causing animals to suffer.

3 Cars create a lot of pollution in city centres. *In addition to this/Consequently,* they can cause accidents and injure or kill pedestrians.

4 There are several reasons why I am against exams. *Finally/Firstly,* they only test what someone can remember on one particular day.

5 Sports *such as/furthermore* tennis and football are more sociable than running.

6 *To sum up/One example of this is,* I would say that university should be free for anyone who wants to study there.

7 Trains are much better for the environment. *In addition to this/On the other hand,* they are much slower than planes, so they are much less convenient.

8 The climate is becoming warmer and *in contrast/as a result* a lot of animals are now in danger of dying out.

8 **Read the exam task and use the table to plan your essay.**

In your English class you have been talking about city life. Now, your English teacher has asked you to write an essay.

Write an essay using **all** the notes and giving reasons for your point of view.

Some people believe that cycling is the best way to travel around cities. Do you agree?

Notes

Write about:

1. health
2. safety
3. .... (your own idea)

	IDEAS	*USEFUL PHRASES*
Introduction		
Paragraph 1		
Paragraph 2		
Paragraph 3		
Conclusion		

9 **Write your essay. Remember to write between 140 and 190 words.**

10 **Check your essay and make changes if necessary.**

- Have you answered the question in the task?
- Have you included the two ideas in the task and added your own idea?
- Have you included only relevant information?
- Have you started with an introduction and ended with a conclusion?
- Have you ordered your ideas into paragraphs?
- Have you given reasons for your ideas and opinions?
- Have you used words and phrases to link ideas?
- Have you used between 140 and 190 words?

WRITING PART 2: AN EMAIL / LETTER

1 **Read the exam task. Who should you write an email to? What should you write about in your email? What questions should you answer?**

You have received this email from your English-speaking friend, Jo.

> I guess you've been in your new home for about a month now. All your old friends are really keen to know how you're getting on. What's your new home like? And are there lots of exciting things to do in the city? Also, have you made plenty of new friends?
>
> Write and tell me all about it!
>
> Jo

Write your **email** in 140–190 words.

2 **Study the model answer. Does it answer all the questions in Jo's email? Is the tone formal or informal?**

MODEL ANSWER

[1]Hi Jo,

[2]It was great to hear from you! I miss all my old friends, but I'm getting used to living here in Manchester now.

[3]My new flat is amazing! It's modern and quite big, and it's got a lovely balcony which looks out over a park. There's also a large living room with comfortable sofas and our new huge TV! My room's quite small, but I don't mind that because I'm out during the day, so I only use it for sleeping.

[4]Manchester's a really lively city. Did you know it's the biggest university city in Britain, so there are loads of young people here. There's always something new and exciting to do. I've discovered some amazing music venues where there are live bands.

[5]I've been lucky with friends and I've met some really nice people here. I'm seeing some of them this evening, to go to the cinema, and I know [6]you'll get on with them when you meet them. When are you going to come and visit me? Let me know when you're free and we can fix a date.

[7]See you soon,

Ali

[1]Use a suitable greeting.

[2]Give a reason for writing.

[3]Answer the first question.

[4]Answer the second question.

[5]Answer the third question.

[6]In an informal email/letter, use informal words and phrases.

[7]Use a suitable ending phrase.

3 **Read this task. Then decide if the sentences below are true or false.**

You see this notice in your college.

> Our college wants to organise an event this summer to raise money for schools in developing countries. Below are some of our ideas. Please email me to let me know which you think is the best idea and why. Please also tell us how we should organise the event, to make sure it is a success.
>
> 1 a fun sports day
> 2 a quiz evening
> 3 a concert
>
> Thank you for your help.
>
> Anna Bradley, Principal

Write your **email**.

1 You need to write a notice about the event.
2 You have to choose one idea.
3 You should explain your reasons for choosing this.
4 You should suggest a date for the event.
5 Your email is to the college principal.
6 You should use an informal tone.

4 **Choose the four sentences that are suitable to include in your email to the principal in Exercise 3. Why are they suitable?**

1 I think it's a great idea to raise money for schools in developing countries.
2 I would suggest that a fun sports day would be the best option.
3 I think a quiz evening would be amazing!
4 Loads of people enjoy listening to live music.
5 Concerts are extremely popular with lots of people of different ages.
6 I think it would be a good idea to keep the ticket price fairly low.
7 Why don't you serve food during the event, too?
8 I'm sure that the event will be a huge success and hopefully it will raise a large amount of money.

5 **Choose the correct option in *italics* in this formal email.**

(1) *Dear Ms Copeland,/Hi Anne,*

I am writing **(2)** *because of/in response to* your advertisement for staff to work in your hotel this summer. I am **(3)** *currently/at the moment* studying hotel management at college and **(4)** *would love to work/would be interested in working* in your hotel.

I have **(5)** *learned all about/studied different aspects of* hotel work as part of my course, and I also have some experience of hotel work as I **(6)** *was employed/had a job* in a large international hotel in Spain for six weeks last summer. I worked mainly as a waiter, but also **(7)** *gained some experience as/had a go as* a receptionist when the regular receptionist was ill.

I am friendly and hardworking, and work well as part of a team. I also understand that in a hotel, **(8)** *keeping the customer happy/customer satisfaction* is the most important thing.

(9) *I would be grateful if you would/Please will you* consider me for a position in your hotel.

(10) *I look forward to hearing from you./Write soon!*

Joseph Brown

6 **Study the words and expressions in the *Key language* box.**

KEY LANGUAGE FOR FORMAL EMAILS AND LETTERS

Opening a formal email/letter: *Dear (Mr/Mrs/Ms Edwards), Dear Sir/Madam,*

Giving reasons for writing: *I am writing in response to … I saw your notice/advert in …*

Referring to something mentioned in the letter/notice/advert: *Your letter/notice/advert mentioned that … Your letter/notice/advert asked for …*

Making suggestions / giving advice: *It would be a good idea to … It might be sensible to … You might like to consider …*

Offering to do something: *I would be able/willing to … if necessary.*

Making requests: *Would it be possible for you to …?*

Asking for information: *Could you give me some information on …? Could you let me have more details about …?*

Apologising: *I would like to apologise for …*

Closing an informal email: *Yours sincerely (after Dear Mr Edwards), Yours faithfully (after Dear Sir/Madam), I look forward to hearing from you, Kind regards.*

Tip: Only use *Mrs* if you are sure that the woman you are writing to is married. Otherwise, use *Ms*.

7 **Correct the mistakes in the letters from formal and informal letters/emails.**

1. It was great hear from you.
2. Why you don't come and visit me in the summer?
3. It would be good idea to invite people from outside the college, too.
4. I would able to help with the arrangements on the day.
5. Could you give to me some information on the different courses that you offer?
6. I look forward hearing from you.

8 **Read the exam task and use the table to plan your letter.**

You see this advertisement in your local English-language newspaper.

Staff wanted for summer work

We require staff to work with our English-speaking guests in our busy hotel this summer.

We are looking for people for the following roles:
- Waiter
- Coffee bar assistant
- Receptionist

Write to Maria Simpson at Top Beach Hotel saying which job interests you and why, and explain why you would be suitable for the job.

Write to Maria Simpson at Top Beach Hotel saying which job interests you and why, and explain why you would be suitable for the job.

Write your **letter** in 140–190 words.

	IDEAS	***USEFUL PHRASES***
Writing to?		
Formal or informal?		
Opening phrase		
Point 1		
Point 2		
Point 3		
Ending		

9 **Write your letter. Remember to write between 140 and 190 words.**

10 **Check your letter and make changes if necessary.**

- Have you covered all the points in the task?
- Have you used an appropriate formal or informal tone?
- Have you used a range of phrases for giving advice, making suggestions, etc.?
- Have you used a suitable opening phrase, and a suitable ending?
- Have you used a wide range of language?
- Have you used between 140 and 190 words?

WRITING PART 2: A REVIEW

1 **Read the exam task. What should you write a review of? What points should you include? Where will people read your review?**

> You see this notice in an English-language magazine.
>
> **Film reviews wanted**
>
> What films have you seen recently? Write a review of a film you have seen, explaining what it was about and whether you enjoyed it or not. Tell us whether or not you think other people would enjoy it.
>
> The best reviews will be published in next month's magazine.
>
> Write your **review**.

2 **Study the model answer and answer the questions.**

1. Does the review cover all the points in the task?
2. Did the writer enjoy the film?
3. Who does the writer think will enjoy the film?
4. Is the language in the review formal and neutral, or informal and friendly?

MODEL ANSWER

[1]includes the name of the film as the title

[2]briefly describes the film in the introduction

[3]is organised into clear paragraphs, which focus on positive and negative aspects

[7]clearly states the writer's opinion in the conclusion

[1]Black Panther

I watched the film 'Black Panther' for the first time last week. [2]It's a superhero film, in the same genre as 'Superman' and 'Spiderman', and has been extremely popular around the world.

[3]Although I am not usually a big fan of superhero films, [4]I was really impressed with this one. The story is fairly traditional, with the hero T'Challa (Black Panther) defeating the evil Killmonger, who is trying to gain power over the whole world. [5]But the action is gripping and the special effects are spectacular. Chadwick Boseman, who plays T'Challa, acts superbly, and really brings the comic-book character to life. The brilliant costumes and music also really help make the film a great spectacle.

[3]On the negative side, [6]I felt that there was sometimes a bit too much violence, which makes it unsuitable for young children, and of course you have to accept that the plot is slightly predictable because the good guy will always win.

In spite of this, [7]I loved the film and [8]anyone who enjoys fantasy movies will definitely like it.

[4]uses a range of phrases to express a personal opinion

[5]praises positive features and says why the film is good

[6]includes some negative features, to give a balanced view

[8]includes a recommendation, saying who would enjoy the film

3 **Read the review task. Then look at the two student plans. Which plan is better? Why?**

> **Reviews wanted!**
>
> What shopping websites have you used recently? Write a review of a shopping website that you have used. Say what you bought, how pleased you were with the product, and talk about any problems you experienced. Say whether you would recommend the site to others.

A

Introduction
name of website *TechWorld*, and basic information (what they sell).
What I bought (a new tablet)

My experience
The website – why I like it (easy to use – good prices)
The product – why I was pleased with it (good quality)

A few problems
slow delivery, missing case, but they dealt with this quickly

Recommendation
great website for anyone who is looking for a low-priced tablet or other device

B

Introduction
why I chose to use this website (looking for a cheap tablet, easier to buy online than go into town)

The website
how I found out about it, how I chose my tablet, problem of slow delivery

Games
why I like it (I needed a new tablet for playing games)

Conclusion
I'm very pleased with my new tablet and it was very cheap

4 **Using descriptive adjectives and adverbs in a review makes it interesting to read. Choose the best adverbs to go with the descriptive adjectives.**

1 The action scenes in the film were *a little/incredibly* gripping.
2 The food in the restaurant is lovely, but it is *absolutely/ridiculously* expensive.
3 The basic plot of the book is *rather/mildly* predictable.
4 This is *a completely/a brilliantly* entertaining show.
5 The device that I bought is *totally/extremely* useful.
6 The holiday flat is small but *very/highly* well-equipped.
7 Our hotel room was *absolutely/very* perfect.
8 All the staff were *a bit/really* welcoming.

5 **We often use adjectives or phrases to give our opinion about something in an indirect way. Match the beginnings and endings of the sentences.**

1 I was disappointed to
2 We were delighted that
3 I'm absolutely thrilled with
4 The tent isn't as big
5 The food was even better
6 There weren't enough

a my new camera.
b seats around the pool for all the guests.
c find that the screen was cracked.
d than I expected.
e as it looked on the website.
f we had a room with a view of the sea.

6 **In a review we often use words to express contrast. Complete the sentences with words from the box.**

although	despite	however	though	spite

1 The weather was terrible, but in .... of this, we thoroughly enjoyed our stay at the resort.
2 Even .... it was rather expensive, we really enjoyed our time at the museum.
3 I would advise anyone to check out this website, ... the problems that I experienced.
4 .... the service was quick and friendly, the food was a little disappointing.
5 The website stated that the bag was made of leather. .... when it arrived it was clear that it was not genuine leather.

7 **Study the words and expressions in the *Key language* box.**

KEY LANGUAGE FOR REVIEWS

Praising something: *It is one of the best … I have ever …, the … was absolutely perfect, the … was even better than I expected, I was pleased/delighted to find that …, It was a nice surprise to find that …,*
Criticising: *The … was rather disappointing, The advertisement said …, but in fact …, I was a little disappointed to find …, There weren't enough …*
Recommending: *Anyone who likes … will really enjoy …, Don't miss the chance/opportunity to …, I'm sure everyone will really enjoy …, If you get the chance to see/buy/try …, you should definitely do it, I would advise anyone to …*
Advising someone against something: *I would suggest finding a better … than this. I would strongly advise against eating/reading/watching/buying this …, My advice is to avoid this …*

8 **Choose the correct words in the sentences.**

1 This show was even better *than/as* I expected.
2 The dessert was rather *disappointed/disappointing*.
3 Anyone who enjoys crime novels *will/can* love this book.
4 Don't *lose/miss* the opportunity to visit this theme park.
5 I would suggest *using/to use* a different website.
6 I would strongly *advise/suggest* against staying at this campsite.

9 **Read the exam task and use the table to plan your review.**

> You see this advertisement on a travel website.
>
> **Reviews wanted!**
>
> What holiday resorts have you been to recently?
>
> Write a review describing the resort, explaining why you did or didn't enjoy your stay there and saying whether it is good value for money.
>
> The best reviews will be published on our website.
>
> Write your **review**.

PARAGRAPHS	*IDEAS*	*USEFUL PHRASES*
Description of the resort		
Why I enjoyed/didn't enjoy it		
Good value for money?		
Recommendation		

10 **Write your review. Remember to write between 140 and 190 words.**

11 **Check your review and make changes if necessary.**

- Have you covered all the points in the task?
- Have you organised your ideas clearly into paragraphs?
- Have you given your own opinion clearly?
- Have you ended with a recommendation?
- Have you used descriptive adjectives and adverbs to make your writing interesting?
- Have you used a friendly tone?
- Have you used between 140 and 190 words?

WRITING PART 2: AN ARTICLE

1 **Read the exam task. What should you write an article about? What points should you include? Where will people read your article?**

> You see this notice in an English-language magazine.
>
> **Articles wanted**
>
> My hobby
>
> Write an article about your hobby. Say what it is, how you started doing it, and why you enjoy it.
>
> The best articles will appear in our magazine next week.
>
> Write your **article**.

2 **Study the model answer and answer the questions.**

1 Does the article cover all the points in the task?
2 How many paragraphs does it have?
3 How many direct questions does it ask the reader?
4 Is it written in a formal or an informal style?

MODEL ANSWER

[1]The thrill of the stage

[2]I'll never forget the first day I stepped onto a real theatre stage. I knew immediately that this was my hobby for life! I'm now a member of my local drama club. We put on two shows every year and have a lot of fun while doing so!

[3]I first started acting by chance. A friend of mine was interested in joining a drama club, and I agreed to go along with her, to give her a bit of support. [4]And I loved it from the first day!

First, drama is [5]incredibly challenging. [6]Not only do you have to learn what you're going to say, but also understand the character you're playing, their role in the play, and then communicate that to the audience.

[7]Another thing I love about drama is how sociable it is. I've made so many good friends at the drama club, and spending time with them working towards a shared goal is extremely rewarding. And in addition to all of this, [8]what could beat the thrill of appearing under the lights, in front of a cheering crowd?

[1]has an interesting title

[2]has a first sentence which interests the reader and encourages them to read more

[3]is organised into clear paragraphs, each with a topic sentence

[4]gives the writer's opinions

[5]uses creative language with strong meanings

[6]gives examples to support the ideas

[7]uses structures to add emphasis

[8]ends with a question or a lively final sentence

3 **It is important to choose a title and first sentence which will engage your reader and encourage them to read more. Choose the best title and first sentence for an article about Nelson Mandela. Why is it the best?**

A Nelson Mandela
I really admire Nelson Mandela because of everything he achieved in South Africa.

B A peaceful transformation
Can you imagine one person bringing peaceful change to a whole country?

C An important figure in South Africa
Nelson Mandela is a very important figure in the history of South Africa.

4 **The first sentence in each paragraph (the topic sentence) gives the topic of the paragraph. Match the topic sentences (a–e) to the paragraphs from an article about a favourite place to visit. There are two topic sentences you don't need.**

a The people here are incredibly warm and welcoming.
b This is a lovely, relaxing place.
c I first discovered this place about five years ago.
d One thing I really love is the stunning scenery.
e If you love good food, this is a great place to visit.

1 ________ When you look in one direction, you can see the beautiful beach and the clear blue sea. In the opposite direction, there are lovely views of the mountains, which have snow on their peaks all year round.

2 ________ You can find delicious local cheeses, and plenty of fresh fruit and vegetables. And of course there's fresh fish which the fishing boats bring in each day, and which is perfectly cooked in the restaurants by the beach.

3 ________ They always have time to stop and chat and they seem genuinely keen for you to enjoy your stay. You can always find someone to help if you have any problems, too.

5 **In an article, it is important to use creative words with strong meanings, to make your writing more interesting. Replace the bold words and expressions in the sentences with the creative words with similar meanings from the box.**

absolutely	essential	freezing	fascinated by	huge	packed	terrifying

1 Like a lot of people, I was **interested in** the castle's history.
2 The city centre is always **crowded** with tourists.
3 His first film was a **big** success.
4 I always enjoy watching my local football team play, even when the weather's **cold**.
5 The drive up the narrow mountain road was quite **scary** at times.
6 A good fitness programme is **really necessary** if you're serious about losing weight.

6 **You can use structures to emphasise your ideas and opinions in an article. Complete each second sentence so it has a similar meaning but has more emphasis.**

1 I admire his determination.
What _I admire is_ his determination.
2 I like the freedom you get when you go hiking.
The thing ______ the freedom you get when you go hiking.
3 Her honesty really surprised me.
One thing ______ her honesty.
4 I will never forget our evening barbecues on the beach.
What ______ our evening barbecues on the beach.
5 I noticed how happy everyone looked.
The thing ______ how happy everyone looked.

7 **Study the words and expressions in the *Key language* box.**

KEY LANGUAGE FOR ARTICLES

Catching the reader's attention: *Have you ever …? I want to tell you about … It's the best …*
Ordering ideas: *First(ly), Second(ly), Finally,*
Linking similar ideas: *moreover, in addition to this*
Linking contrasting ideas: *while, whereas*
Linking results: *therefore, which means*
Emphasising ideas: *What I love/admire the most is …, The thing I like best is …*
Giving your opinion: *In my opinion, For me, as far as I'm concerned*

8 **Complete the sentences with one word in each space.**

1 ______ me, sailing is the best sport in the world!
2 Painting is relaxing, creative and fun, and ______ addition to this, you can earn a bit of money by selling your paintings.
3 As far ______ I'm concerned, cooking is the best hobby
4 Hiking isn't expensive which ______ means that anyone can do it.
5 I want to ______ you about something amazing that happened to me last year.
6 ______ I love most is watching live shows in a theatre.

9 **Read the exam task and use the table to plan your article.**

You see this notice on an English-language fitness website.

Articles wanted

Staying healthy

How important is your health to you? What do you think are some of the best ways to stay fit and healthy?

The best articles will appear on our website next month.

Write your **article**.

	IDEAS	***USEFUL PHRASES***
How important is health to me?		
Good diet		
Exercise		

10 **Write your article. Remember to write between 140 and 190 words.**

11 **Check your article and make changes if necessary.**

- Have you covered all the points in the task?
- Have you organised your ideas clearly into paragraphs?
- Have you got an interesting title and first sentence?
- Have you given your own opinions clearly?
- Have you used creative vocabulary with strong meanings?
- Have you used structures to add emphasis?
- Have you used between 140 and 190 words?

WRITING PART 2: A REPORT

1 Read the exam task. Who is the report for? What points should you include?

A group of English-speaking students wants to visit your city. The group leader has asked you to write a report that includes the following information:

- the best time of year to visit
- some interesting places to visit in your city
- the best way to get around the city

Write your **report**.

2 Study the model answer. Does it cover all the points in the exam task?

MODEL ANSWER

Introduction

[1]The aim of this report is to make recommendations for a group of students who are interested in visiting York.

[2]The best time of year to visit

York can be cold during the winter, and extremely busy with tourists during the summer. However, the spring is often warm and the city is quiet, so this is a good time to visit. [3]For this reason, I usually encourage my friends to visit in April or May.

[4]Places of interest

The city has numerous attractions which reflect its long and fascinating history. [5]The must-see places are the city walls, the tiny streets in the Shambles area of the old city and the Castle Museum.

Transport

York is a small city, and easy to get around on foot. However, [6]I would strongly recommend buying a York Pass, which not only includes entry to the top attractions, but also allows travel on the Hop-on, Hop-off tourist bus. It therefore offers [7]a practical and good value transport option.

[7]Conclusion

To sum up, I am sure the students will enjoy seeing the sights in York and I look forward to welcoming them when they come.

[1]Start with a general introduction which gives the aim of the report

[2]Use clear headings for the different points

[3]Include a small amount of personal information to make the report interesting to read

[4]Avoid repeating the exact words in the input

[5]Use a neutral tone for most of the report, and avoid expressing your feelings

[6]Make recommendations

[7]End with a conclusion

3 Read the exam task. Then match the headings with three paragraphs from the report.

Your English teacher wants to take your class for a meal to celebrate the end of the year and has asked you to suggest a restaurant in your area. Describe a restaurant that you know and say why it would be popular with your classmates.

1 The restaurant
2 Advantages of this restaurant
3 Why it would be popular

a
The food is all freshly cooked and the dishes are reasonably priced. There are often daily specials, which are especially good value.
In addition to this, there is a separate room at the back of the restaurant which is excellent for large groups.

b
Students will like it because the staff are always welcoming and there is an informal, friendly atmosphere. People in the class have different likes and needs, and there is a good choice of dishes for everyone, including some excellent vegetarian options. Most people will also be unable to resist the delicious desserts.

c
The restaurant is called Dario's and is located on North Street, quite close to the college.
It serves a range of Italian food, including pizzas and pasta.

4 Which personal information would it be useful to include in the report in Exercise 3? Why?

A My cousin doesn't usually like Italian food, but he enjoyed his meal there.
B I eat there quite frequently and am always surprised at how low the final bill is.
C I can get there quite easily from my flat because the bus service is excellent.
D I know one of the waiters who works there, and he has confirmed that the food is excellent.

5 **Choose the best introduction and conclusion for the report in exercise 5. Why is it the best one?**

Introduction

A In this report I'm going to recommend the best Italian restaurant for our class meal.

B This report describes the advantages and disadvantages of a particular restaurant and discusses whether it would be suitable for a class meal.

C This report aims to give information about a restaurant that I know and explain why it would be a good choice for a class meal.

Conclusion

A In conclusion, I strongly recommend Dario's because it offers a range of tasty food at good prices and has adequate space to cope with a large group.

B To sum up, Dario's is my favourite restaurant and I'd love to go there with the class.

C On balance, Dario's offers several advantages, especially the desserts, but it also has a few disadvantages.

6 **We often use passive forms in reports to make the tone neutral. Complete the passive sentences with the correct words.**

1. People often recommend this restaurant for large groups.
   This restaurant ....
   for large groups.
2. People consider this hotel to be one of the best in the area.
   This hotel ....
   one of the best in the area.
3. We expect that around 30 students will attend this event.
   It ....
   that around 30 students will attend this event.
4. People have suggested that a new sports centre should be built.
   It ....
   that a new sports centre should be built.
5. We recommend waterproof clothes for the hiking trip.
   Waterproof clothes ....
   for the hiking trip.

7 **Study the words and expressions in the *Key Language* box.**

KEY LANGUAGE FOR REPORTS

Introductions: *The aim/purpose of this report is to …, This report aims to …, This report looks at …*

Giving advantages and disadvantages: *One advantage is …, One disadvantage is …, One problem with this is …*

Linking similar ideas: *in addition to this, furthermore, moreover*

Linking contrasting ideas: *however, on the one hand / on the other hand, in contrast, although, whereas*

Making recommendations: *I would recommend …, I strongly recommend …, I have no hesitation in recommending …*

Giving a conclusion: *in conclusion, to sum up, on balance, all things considered,*

8 **Correct the mistakes in the sentences. Look at punctuation and spelling as well as language mistakes.**

1. The aim for this report is to discuss the problems with public transport in Leeds.
2. There are some excellent shops in the shopping centre. In adition to this, there are a number of very good cafés and restaurants.
3. There are very few buses that come to the college moreover the ones that do come are expensive.
4. I have no hesitation in recomending the New Forest for a walking trip.
5. All things consider, the *Old Duck* would be an excellent choice of hotel.
6. In conclusion I would strongly recommend a new car park in the city centre.

9 **Read the exam task and use the table to plan your report.**

> The local council wants to improve the shopping centre in your town. Your English teacher has asked students to write a report about the shopping centre, explaining which shops are popular and why, and recommending ways to improve it.

HEADING	***IDEAS***	***USEFUL PHRASES***
Introduction		
Conclusion		

10 **Write your report. Remember to write between 140 and 190 words.**

11 **Check your report and make changes if necessary.**

- Have you covered all the points in the task?
- Have you organised your ideas under clear headings?
- Have you included only relevant information?
- Have you started with an introduction and ended with a conclusion?
- Have you used words and phrases to link ideas?
- Have you used a formal, neutral tone?
- Have you used between 140 and 190 words?

SPEAKING BANK

SPEAKING PART 1

1 **Read about Part 1 of the Speaking paper.**

In Part 1 of the Speaking paper, an examiner asks you personal questions about familiar topics. In Part 1:

- you are with another candidate, but you only speak to the examiner, not the other candidate
- an examiner asks you questions about yourself, and you answer
- the questions are about everyday topics such as your family, your home town, likes and dislikes, your work or studies, free time, travel, celebrations and your future plans.

2 **Read the tips.**

To get a good mark in Part 1 of the Speaking paper:

- you should listen to the questions carefully and make sure you answer the exact questions the examiner asks you
- you should use full sentences to answer the questions
- you should add reasons, examples or extra information to support your answers
- you should express your own opinions
- if you don't understand a question, you can ask the examiner to repeat it
- you should try to relax and answer the questions in a natural way.

3 **Read some typical Part 1 questions. Match each question with a topic (a–e).**

1 What do you like about your home town?
2 What kind of job would you like to do in the future?
3 How do people usually celebrate New Year in your country?
4 When do you usually spend time with your family?
5 What do you normally do at the weekend?
6 Tell us about an enjoyable trip that you went on.
7 Which country would you most like to visit?
8 Which subject did you most enjoy when you were at school?
9 What's the most important festival in your country?
10 What do you enjoy doing in your free time?

a Personal and family life
b Hobbies and free time
c Work and studies
d Travel
e Celebrations

4 **101 Read and listen to Sofia's answers to four of the questions in Exercise 3. Does she add more information to every answer?**

MODEL ANSWER

Examiner: What do you like about your home town?
Sofia: [1]Well, I'm from Milan, in the north of Italy. It's a big city, and I enjoy living there because there's always lots to do, like going to the cinema or music concerts. There are also a lot of young people there, [2]so I like that as well.
Examiner: What do you enjoy doing in your free time?
Sofia: Well, I'm quite a sporty person, so I do a lot of exercise. [3]For example, I go to the gym two or three times a week, and I play tennis. I also enjoy spending time with my friends.
Examiner: Which country would you most like to visit?
Sofia: I would love to go to Australia. [4]The reason for this is that I like hot weather and I love going to the beach. The beaches in Australia look amazing. I also think the way of life in Australia is quite relaxed, having barbecues and things like that, so I think I'd enjoy that.
Examiner: Which subject did you most enjoy when you were at school?
Sofia: [5]Could you repeat that, please?
Examiner: Yes. Which subject did you most enjoy when you were at school?
Sofia: That was definitely geography, because I'm really interested in different countries, and I love learning about how people live in other parts of the world. [6]I had a very good geography teacher at school too, and I think he made the subject very interesting.

[1]use full sentences in your answer

[2]give your own opinions

[3]add examples to support your answers

[4]add reasons to support your opinions

[5]ask the examiner to repeat a question if necessary

[6]add extra information to make your answer longer

5 **The questions the examiner asks may be about the past, present and future, and it is important to listen carefully and answer correctly. Read six more questions. What do they ask about? Write *past*, *present* or *future*.**

1. Tell us about your last holiday or trip. ....
2. How often do you watch TV? ....
3. Which sport would you like to try? ....
4. What things do you usually buy online? ....
5. Which famous person would you most like to meet? ....
6. What kinds of food did you dislike when you were younger? ....

6 **Choose the most suitable verb form to complete the answers to the questions in Exercise 5.**

1. I .... to Spain last month with some friends.
   A 've been **B** would love to go **C** went
2. I .... TV very often.
   A don't watch **B** didn't watch **C** 'm not going to watch
3. I .... skiing because I think it's really good fun.
   A once tried **B** 'd like to try **C** love
4. I usually .... clothes online.
   A bought some **B** buy my **C** didn't buy many
5. I .... Ariana Grande because I think she's an amazing singer.
   A 've never met **B** meet **C** 'd love to meet
6. I .... ice cream!
   A hated **B** hate **C** 'd hate

7 **Write the words and expressions in the box next to the correct function.**

also	as well	because	for example	for instance
like	plus	such as	too	the reason for this is that

1. adding extra information ....
2. giving a reason ....
3. giving an example ....

8 102 **Choose the correct options in *italics* to complete Dan's answers to three more questions. Listen and check.**

Examiner: In what ways do you think you will use English in the future?

Dan: I think I'll use English for my job in the future. **(1)** *The reason for this is that/Such as* I want to work for an international company, so probably everyone will speak English to each other. I'll probably use it for travelling **(2)** *too/also,* because I'd like to travel and visit lots of different countries.

Examiner: What do you usually do on your birthday?

Dan: I usually see my family on my birthday **(3)** *also/because* they like to wish me a happy birthday and they might have presents for me. Then in the evening I usually get together with some friends and do something, **(4)** *as well/like* go for a meal together.

Examiner: What kind of music do you enjoy listening to?

Dan: I really enjoy R&B music. **(5)** *For instance/Too* I like American singers like Rihanna. I'm **(6)** *as well/also* keen on classical music because I find it very relaxing.

9 **Practise answering some of the Part 1 questions in this section. Try to relax and talk about yourself in a natural way.**

SPEAKING PART 2

1 Read about Part 2 of the Speaking paper.

In Part 2 of the Speaking paper, you are given a one-minute 'long turn'. In Part 2:

- the examiner will give you two photographs on a similar topic and ask you to compare them and answer a question
- the question you have to answer is written above the photographs
- you speak on your own for around one minute, and no one will interrupt you
- your partner will talk about a different set of photographs
- when your partner has finished speaking, the examiner will ask you a question about your partner's photographs. You will have around 30 seconds to answer this question.

2 Read the tips.

To get a good mark in Part 2 of the Speaking paper:

- you should compare the two photographs and say what is similar and different about them, rather than just describing them
- you should always make it clear which photograph you are talking about
- you should focus equally on both photographs, rather than just talking about one of them
- you should speculate about what is happening in the photographs and how the people are feeling
- you should make sure you allow enough time to answer the question after you have finished comparing the photographs
- you should listen carefully while your partner is answering, so you can answer the question the examiner will ask you.

3 Read the exam task and look at the photographs. What topic connects the two photographs? What question do you have to answer?

Examiner: In this part of the test I'm going to give each of you two photographs. I'd like you to talk about your photographs on your own for about a minute, and also to answer a question about your partner's photographs. Ana, it's your turn first. Here are your photographs. They show people on holiday. I'd like you to compare the photographs and say why you think the people chose these holidays.

4 103 **Read and listen to the model answer. Does the student say why the people have chosen the holidays?**

MODEL ANSWER

[1] Say what is similar about the two photos.

[3] Use linking words to compare the photos and say what is different about them.

[5] Say how you think the people are feeling.

[1] Both pictures show people on holiday, but they're different kinds of holidays. [2] The people in the first photo are in the countryside, [3] whereas the second photo shows a big city. [4] It looks as if the people in the first photo are on a walking holiday, because they've got backpacks and a map. [3] On the other hand, the other people are probably doing some sightseeing. They seem to be up in a tower, and they're taking a selfie. Another difference is that the people in the city [5] look happy and relaxed, whereas the people in the countryside look worried. I think they might be lost. They don't look as happy as the people on the city break. I think the people in the first photo must enjoy walking. [6] Maybe they chose this holiday because they enjoy being in the countryside. I think the people in the second photo enjoy city life, so [6] I guess they probably chose to visit this city because there are lots of interesting things to see.

[2] Make it clear which photo you are talking about.

[4] Speculate about what the people are doing.

[6] Answer the question when you have finished comparing the photos.

5 104 **Complete the sentences for comparing and contrasting photographs with the words in the box. Listen and check.**

as both difference different other whereas

1 ________ pictures show people on holiday.
2 They're ________ kinds of holidays.
3 The people in the first photo are in the countryside, ________ the second photo shows a big city.
4 On the ________ hand, the other people are probably doing some sightseeing.
5 Another ________ is that the people in the city look happy and relaxed.
6 They don't look ________ happy as the people on the city break.

6 105 **Match the beginnings and endings of sentences for speculating about photos. Listen and check.**

1 It looks as
2 They're probably doing
3 They seem to
4 They look
5 I
6 They must enjoy
7 Maybe they
8 I guess

a be up in a tower.
b think they might be lost.
c if they're on a walking holiday.
d walking.
e some sightseeing.
f happy and relaxed.
g they probably chose to visit this city because there are lots of interesting things to see.
h chose this holiday because they enjoy being in the countryside.

7 106 **Look at the exam task question and the two photographs on page 248. Then listen to three students making mistakes when they complete the task. Match each speaker (1–3) with the mistake that they make (A–D). There is one answer you don't need.**

A describes what they can see in both photos, but doesn't compare and contrast them
B focuses too much on one photo
C doesn't give any personal opinions about the photos
D compares and contrasts the photos but doesn't answer the question

Here are your photographs. They show people preparing food. I'd like you to compare the photographs and say how the people might be feeling about the food they are preparing.

How might the people be feeling about the food they are preparing?

8 107 **Read the task and look at the photographs. Complete the task, then listen to the model answer and compare your answers.**

Here are your photographs. They show people working. I'd like you to compare the photographs and say what you think might be difficult about the people's jobs.

What might be difficult about the people's jobs?

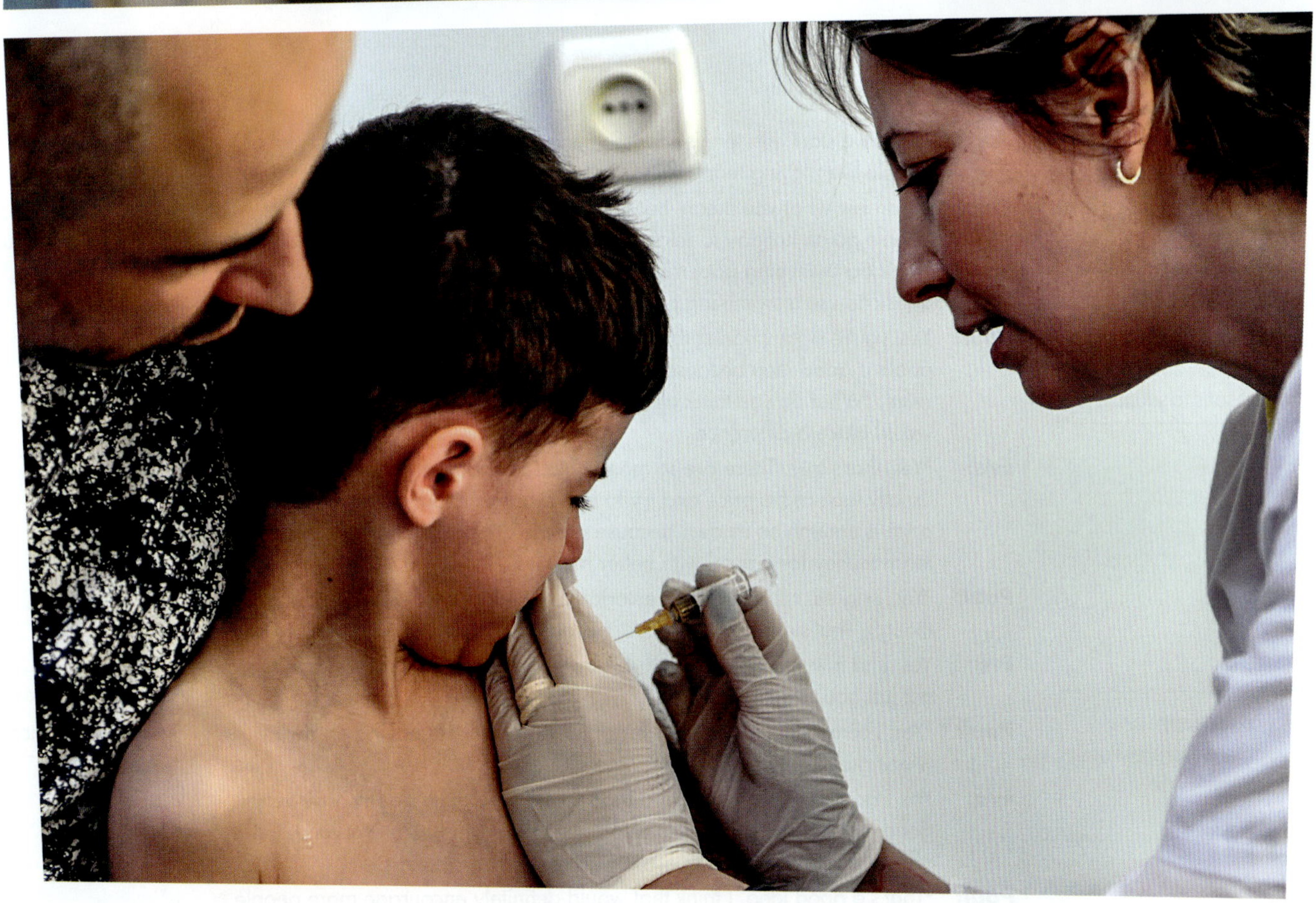

SPEAKING PART 3

1 Read about Part 3 of the Speaking paper.

Part 3 of the Speaking paper lasts for about three minutes, and you work with a partner. In Part 3:

- the examiner will explain an imaginary situation to you, then give you a piece of paper with written prompts that show different ideas or possibilities
- you must talk with your partner and discuss the prompts, giving your opinions about the different prompts
- you do not have to discuss all the prompts, but you should discuss most of them
- there is no right or wrong answer to the task
- the examiner will then ask you to try to reach agreement about something, and you do this with your partner
- you do not *have* to reach agreement with your partner, but you should try.

2 Read the tips.

To get a good mark in Part 3 of the Speaking paper:

- you should talk to your partner and listen to your partner – it is important to have a conversation with your partner, rather than just expressing your own ideas
- you should make suggestions and respond to suggestions that your partner makes
- you should express your own opinions on the different prompts and respond to your partner's opinions
- you should give reasons for your opinions
- you should try to reach agreement with your partner when the examiner asks you to.

3 Read the exam task and read how the examiner will introduce it. What question do you have to discuss? How many prompts are there for you to discuss?

I'd like you to imagine that a hotel wants to attract more guests. Here are some ideas they're thinking about. Talk to each other about why these ideas would attract more guests to the hotel.

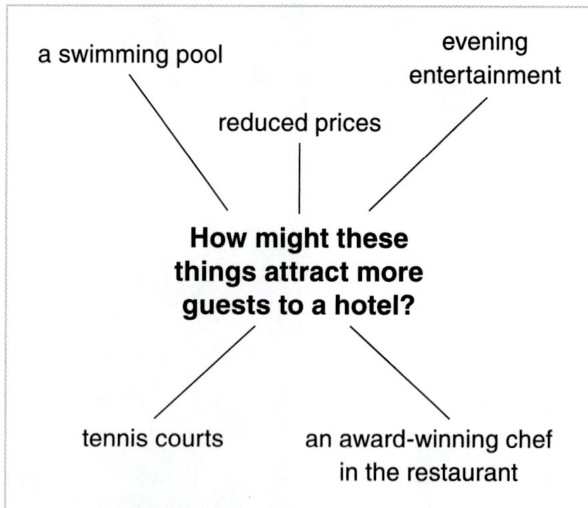

4 108 Read and listen to Paul and Eva completing the task. How many of the prompts do they discuss? Do they both express their opinions?

MODEL ANSWER

Paul: [1]Shall we start with tennis courts? This sounds like a good idea. A lot of people like playing tennis.

Eva: [2]I can see what you mean, but not everyone likes tennis, and a lot of people go on holiday to relax, so they perhaps don't want to do sport. [3]I think a swimming pool might be a better idea, because people of all ages can use a swimming pool. Do you agree?

Paul: Yes, you're right. I hadn't thought about that. I agree that a swimming pool's a good idea because people like to sit by it even if they don't swim. [1]What do you think about the idea of reduced prices? I think that would make a difference.

Eva: [5]Yes, that's true. There are so many hotels to choose from, and people usually look at the price and try to find a bargain. But I'm not sure that price is enough on its own because people are often happy to pay a bit more money for a hotel with better facilities.

Paul: [5]Yes, I agree. I think evening entertainment might be a good idea, though. That's a bit different, too, because not many hotels offer it.

Eva: Yes, and it would be good if they offered entertainment for children too, not just adults.

Paul: [5]Yes, I completely agree with you. [4]Do you think that having an award-winning chef would attract customers?

Eva: Yes, I do. Everyone loves good food, but a lot of hotels don't have very good restaurants. They could also open the restaurant to everyone, but offer cheaper prices for guests.

Paul: [5]That's a good idea. I think that would definitely encourage more people to stay at the hotel.

[1]Make suggestions to move the discussion to the different prompts.

[2]Use polite expressions if you disagree with your partner.

[3]Give your own opinion, and give reasons to support it.

[4]Ask for your partner's opinion.

[5]Use a range of different expressions to agree with your partner.

5 109 **Read the second task that the examiner gives the students, then read and listen to the students completing the task. Do they reach agreement?**

Examiner: Now you have about a minute to decide which idea would be best for the hotel.

Eva: So, what do you think would be best for the hotel?

Paul: I'd suggest either the swimming pool or the evening entertainment. Both those things are easy for people to see when they look on the website, and I think they would both be popular with guests.

Eva: Well, I think everyone enjoys a swimming pool, especially children and young people. But on the other hand, most people only use a swimming pool in the summer, whereas evening entertainment can continue all year, and, like we said, they could offer different entertainment for different ages.

Eva: That's true, so shall we choose the evening entertainment?

Paul: Yes, let's go for that.

6 110 **Listen to extracts from three more pairs of students completing the task in Exercise 3. What mistakes do the students make? Match each pair (1–3) with a common mistake (A–D). There is one mistake you don't need.**

A The students talk about one prompt for too long, so don't have enough time to talk about the other prompts.
B The students talk for too long individually, don't listen to each other, and don't ask for each other's opinions.
C The students interrupt each other.
D The students talk about things that are not relevant to the task.

7 111 **Match the beginnings and endings of the sentences to make suggestions. Listen and check.**

1 It might be a good
2 Perhaps they
3 Tennis courts sound
4 They could
5 I would say that

a like a good idea.
b idea to offer reduced prices.
c offer entertainment for children, too.
d an award-winning chef would be a good idea.
e should have a swimming pool.

8 112 **Choose the correct words to complete the questions you can use to ask your partner's opinion. Listen and check.**

1 *Do/Are* you agree?
2 What *are/do* you think about the idea of a swimming pool?
3 *Will/Would* you agree with that?
4 *Do/May* you think that's true?

9 113 **Complete the expressions for agreeing and disagreeing with words from the box. Listen and check.**

agree	better	but	mean
right	sure	that's	think

1 I ______ so, too.
2 Yes, ______ true.
3 Yes, you're ______ .
4 I ______ with you.
5 I can see what you ______ but I think a swimming pool might be a ______ idea.
6 I'm not ______ about that.
7 Yes, that's true, ______ on the other hand, entertainment would also be popular.

10 114 **Read and listen to the expressions for reaching agreement. (a) Which two expressions can you use to encourage your partner to reach agreement with you? (b) Which expression shows that you have reached an agreement.**

1 I'd suggest either the swimming pool or the evening entertainment.
2 Are you OK with that?
3 My choice would be the reduced prices.
4 So, shall we choose the evening entertainment?
5 Yes, let's go for that.

11 115 **Read an exam task and practise answering it with a partner. Listen and compare your ideas.**

I'd like you to imagine that some people are discussing modern technology. Here are things that some people say it would be difficult to live without. Talk to each other about why it would be difficult to live without these things.

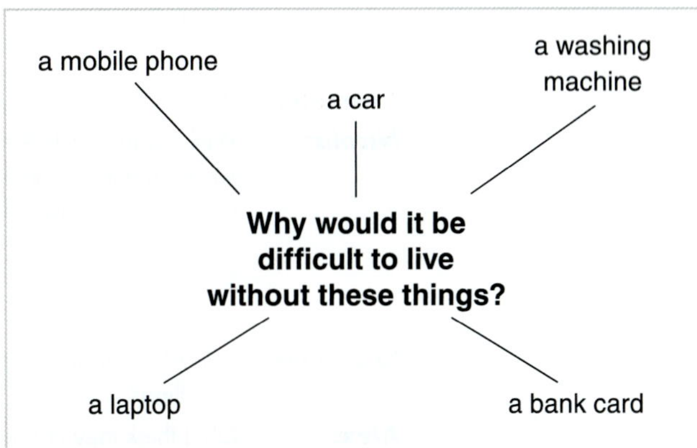

12 116 **Read the second part of the exam task and practise answering it with a partner. Listen and compare your ideas.**

Now you have about a minute to decide which thing people would find it the most difficult to live without.

SPEAKING PART 4

1 Read about Part 4 of the Speaking paper.

Part 4 of the Speaking paper lasts for about four minutes, and you work with a partner. In Part 4:

- the examiner will ask you questions on the general topic that you have talked about in Part 3
- the questions ask you to express your opinion rather than give information
- the examiner will ask you questions individually, but they may also bring your partner into the discussion after you have answered a question
- the examiner may also ask you to reply to your partner's opinions.

2 Read the tips.

To get a good mark in Part 4 of the Speaking paper:
- you should express your opinions and give reasons and examples to support your opinions
- you should avoid giving short answers and should always give more information to expand your answers
- you should listen carefully when your partner is speaking, so that you can give your opinion on what they have said if you are asked.

3 Read some typical Part 4 questions on the topic of travel and holidays. Do all the questions ask about opinions?

What is the advantage of going on holiday with friends, rather than with family?
Some people say that tourism is bad for an area. What do you think?
What places are popular for holidays in your country?
Some people say travel is bad for the environment. Do you agree?
What do you think young people can learn by going travelling?

4 117 Read and listen to Alex and Nicola discussing two of the questions in Exercise 3. Choose the sentence which describes how they answer.

A They each give their own opinions, but don't listen to each other.
B They listen to each other and respond to what the other says.

MODEL ANSWER

[1] Make suggestions to move the discussion to the different prompts.

[2] Give reasons and examples to support your opinions.

[3] Talk about your own likes, dislikes and preferences.

[4] Agree and disagree with your partner, and respond to what they say.

Examiner: Alex, some people say that travel is bad for the environment. Do you agree?

Alex: Yes, I do because [1] I think that when people travel they use fuel, for example in a plane or a car, and that's very bad for the environment. [2] They also create a lot of rubbish, for example if they have a picnic on the beach, and that's bad for the environment too.

Examiner: What do you think, Nicola?

Nicola: Well, I agree with Alex that travel can be bad for the environment, but on the other hand, I'd say that you *can* be a responsible tourist. [3] For example, I prefer to travel by train because it's better for the environment, and I never leave rubbish. So I think it's possible to travel in a way that isn't bad for the environment.

Examiner: OK. Alex, what do you think young people can learn by going travelling?

Alex: Oh, I think they can learn a lot. For example, they can learn about other cultures and ways of life, and they can also see some of the problems that exist in other parts of the world. I think that travelling is very good for young people.

Examiner: What do you think about this, Nicola?

Nicola: [4] I completely agree with Alex, and I also think that young people can benefit personally by becoming more independent when they go travelling. For example, when you're travelling you might have to deal with some difficult situations, and if you do this successfully, it can give you a lot of confidence.

5 118 **Listen to three more pairs of students answering Part 4 questions. What mistakes do the students make? Match each pair (1–3) with a common mistake (A–D). There is one mistake you don't need.**

A The students' answers are too short, and they don't add more information.
B The students don't listen to each other, so they can't respond to what the other says.
C The students talk about things that are not relevant to the task.
D The students interrupt each other.

6 119 **Read the tip. Then listen to three students answering Part 4 questions on the topic of food. What extra question does each student have in their mind?**

- Sometimes it can be difficult to think of things to say in answer to a Part 4 question. To help, it can be useful to keep question words in your mind: Why? How? When? Where? Asking these questions to yourself can help you think of extra things to say.

7 **Sometimes the examiner might ask you a question that you haven't thought about before. Look at the model answers and notice the strategies that the students use.**

MODEL ANSWER

1

Examiner: Do you think online shopping will ever replace going to shops?
Student: [1]Hmm, let me think. That's an interesting question. I'm not sure that online shopping will ever replace going to the shops because there are some things that people like to see or try before they buy them.

[1]Use expressions to give yourself time to think about your ideas, then give your opinion.

2

Examiner: Do you think that some people spend too much time shopping?
Student: [2]Well, it's true that some people spend quite a lot of time shopping. I guess for some people shopping is almost like a hobby. But I think that if they've got plenty of money to spend, then it isn't a problem for them to spend a lot of time in the shops. But I think it's a problem for people who don't have much money, because they might spend too much if they spend a lot of time shopping.

[2]Start with a general statement about the topic of the question, then develop the idea and give your opinion.

3

Examiner: Is it better to go shopping alone or with friends?
Student: [3]I think that there are some advantages to shopping alone, for example you can find things more quickly and you probably don't spend as much money. On the other hand, shopping with friends is more fun because you can chat about things and go for a coffee together. So I think I would probably say that shopping with friends is better for this reason.

[3]Give one point of view and then the opposite point of view, then give your own opinion.

8 120 **Listen to three students answering Part 4 questions about health and fitness. Match each student with the strategy (1–3) from Exercise 7 that they use.**

9 121 **Practise answering these Part 4 questions. Listen and compare your answers.**

1. Some people say that there will be no shops in 20 years because people will buy everything online. Do you agree?
2. Are there advantages to living in the countryside rather than a big city?
3. Why do you think that so many people dream of becoming a celebrity?
4. How do you think people benefit from going on holiday?

PHRASAL VERB BUILDER

Phrasal verbs consist of a verb with a preposition or adverb or both. The meaning of the phrasal verb is different from the meaning of its separate parts. The following are all phrasal verbs:

PHRASAL VERB	DEFINITION
to be into sth	to be interested in something
to book sb into	to reserve a place for somebody at a hotel/event
to break up	to finish school/college at the end of the term/year
to bring up	to introduce (a topic in a discussion)
to burst out	to suddenly start doing something (laughing/crying)
to calm sb down	to stop somebody feeling angry, upset or excited
to check in	to arrive and register at a hotel or airport
to check out	to leave a hotel after paying and returning your room key
to cheer up	to become happy
to copy out	to write a written text again on a piece of paper
to devote sth to sb	to use time, energy, etc. for a particular purpose
to drop out	to fail to complete something (a university course / a race)
to fall behind	to not make progress
to get away	to leave or escape from a person or place
to get back	to return
to get on	to board a plane/train/ferry/bus
to get through	to complete successfully
to go away	to go on holiday
to go over	to examine or look at something in a careful or detailed way
to hand in	to give something (homework) to a teacher
to hand out	to give something (worksheet) to each of a number of people
to keep up with	to progress or travel at the same rate/speed as others
to listen up	to pay attention
to look through	to quickly read
to make up	to invent
to pick out	to identify (details)
to point out	to direct someone's attention to someone or something
to pull out	to drive from the side of the road onto a different part of the road
to pull over	to drive to the side of the road and stop
to pull up	to stop in a vehicle
to read out	to read words aloud so that other people can hear
to read up	to spend time reading in order to find out information about something
to refer to	to talk or write about somebody or something, especially briefly
to rub out	to erase
to run into sb	to meet someone you know when you are not expecting to
to run into sth	to crash into something (in a vehicle or on a bike)
to set out	to start a journey
to shut up	to stop talking or making a noise, or to make somebody stop doing this
to speak up	to speak loudly and distinctly OR to express an opinion freely
to stand for	to mean
to stand up for	to defend
to stay over	to sleep overnight (often at someone's house)
to stop over	to stay somewhere for one night or more when you are travelling to somewhere else
to take off	to leave the ground and fly (of an aircraft)
to take up	to become interested or engaged in a pursuit
to talk sb into sth	to persuade someone to do something
to talk sth over	to discuss a problem or situation with someone, often to find out their opinion or to get advice before making a decision about it
to tell sb off	to express disapproval to someone for doing something bad
to turn up	to arrive or appear somewhere, usually unexpectedly

B2 FIRST EXAM INFORMATION

PART/TIMING	CONTENT	EXAM FOCUS
Reading and Use of English 1 hour 15 minutes	**Part 1** A modified cloze text containing eight gaps and followed by eight multiple-choice items **Part 2** A modified open cloze text containing eight gaps **Part 3** A text containing eight gaps. Each gap corresponds to a word. The stems of the missing words are given beside the text and must be changed to form the missing word. **Part 4** Six separate questions, each with a lead-in sentence and a gapped second sentence to be completed in two to five words, one of which is given as a 'key word' **Part 5** A text followed by six multiple-choice questions **Part 6** A text from which six sentences have been removed and placed in a jumbled order after the text. A seventh sentence, which does not need to be used, is also included. **Part 7** A text, or several short texts, preceded by ten multiple-matching questions	Candidates are expected to demonstrate the ability to apply their knowledge of the language system by completing the first four tasks; candidates are also expected to show understanding of specific information, text organisation features, tone, and text structure.
Writing 1 hour 20 minutes	**Part 1** One compulsory essay question presented through a rubric and short notes **Part 2** Candidates choose one task from a choice of three task types. The tasks are situationally based and presented through a rubric and possibly a short input text. The task types are: • an essay • an article • a letter or email • a review • a report	Candidates are expected to be able to write using different degrees of formality and different functions: advising, comparing, describing, explaining, expressing opinions, justifying, persuading, recommending and suggesting.
Listening Approximately 40 minutes	**Part 1** A series of eight short unrelated extracts from monologues or exchanges between interacting speakers. There is one three-option multiple-choice question per extract. **Part 2** A short talk or lecture on a topic, with a sentence completion task which has ten items **Part 3** Five short related monologues, with five multiple matching questions **Part 4** An interview or conversation, with seven multiple choice questions	Candidates are expected to be able to show understanding of attitude, detail, function, genre, gist, main idea, opinion, place, purpose, situation, specific information, relationship, topic, agreement, etc.
Speaking 14 minutes	**Part 1** A conversation between the examiner (the 'interlocutor') and each candidate (spoken questions) **Part 2** An individual 'long turn' for each candidate, with a brief response from the second candidate (visual and written stimuli, with spoken instructions) **Part 3** A discussion question with five written prompts **Part 4** A discussion on topics related to Part 3 (spoken questions)	Candidates are expected to be able to respond to questions and to interact in conversational English.

ANSWERS AND AUDIOSCRIPTS

STARTER

Page 8

SPEAKING

Exercise 1

2 Education and work
3 Hobbies and interests
4 Family and friends
5 Daily life
6 Hobbies and interests
7 Education and work
8 Where you're from
9 Daily life
10 Family and friends

Page 9

Exercise 2

1 Where are you from?
2 How many brothers and sisters do you have?
3 What's your favourite subject?
4 What's your favourite part of the day?
5 What do you like most about your hometown?
6 What job would you like to have in the future?
7 What do you like to do at weekends?
8 What's your favourite hobby?
9 Who are the most important people in your life?
10 What's your favourite kind of food?

VOCABULARY

Exercise 2

1 F
2 D
3 C
4 E
5 A
6 B

Page 10

READING

Exercise 1

1 D
2 A
3 E
4 B
5 C

Exercise 2

Suggested answers:

A – We danced all evening. It was great!

B – Yes! I've just bought a new pair of shoes. Do you like them?

C – Thanks for the reminder. I can't believe they've been married for 30 years!

D – I've been running all day. I'm so tired!

E – No! I've lost my keys and now I can't get into my car.

Exercise 3

2 There are a lot of benefits to using emojis.

Page 11

1 False
2 True
3 True
4 False
5 True
6 False

GRAMMAR

Exercise 1

1 A We danced all evening. It was great!
2 E No! I've lost my keys and now I can't get into my car.
3 C Thanks for the reminder. I can't believe they've been married for 50 years!
4 D I've been running all day. I'm so tired!
5 B Yes! I've just bought a new pair of shoes. Do you like them?

Exercise 2

1 I've ~~been knowing~~ **known** Richard for about ten years.
2 I~~'ve~~ sent him a message yesterday.
3 A You look really tired. B Yes, I am. I've ~~painted~~ **been painting** the flat all afternoon.
4 I~~'ve~~ got my first phone when I was eighteen years old.
5 I ~~didn't see~~ **haven't seen** the new film yet.
6 ~~Have you watched~~ **Did you watch** the documentary on TV last night?
7 I ~~lived~~ **have been living** in London for the past five months.
8 I've already ~~been drinking~~ **drunk** three cups of coffee this morning.

Exercise 3

1 have been living here
2 have you been doing
3 have never eaten
4 seen each other for
5 have been married

Exercise 4

2 How long have you been learning English?
3 Have you ever visited another continent?
4 How long have you been living / have you lived in your present home?
5 What blogs have you read / have you been reading recently?
6 What's the most exciting thing you've ever done?
7 Have you ever met a famous person?

Page 12

LISTENING

Exercise 2

1 B
2 A
3 B
4 B
5 A

Track 002

Andrew: A funny thing happened to me when I was living in Poland. When I arrived there, I didn't know any Polish, and so my Polish flatmates always helped me, like when I needed to buy something. Anyway, one day I needed to go into the city centre. As my flatmates were all watching a film on TV – and it was raining – I didn't want to ask them to come outside with me and help me buy a ticket for the tram into town. So instead I asked them to tell me what to say at the street kiosk to buy tickets into town and back. I practised saying it a couple of times, and they wrote it down on a piece of paper for me so I'd remember.

I left the flat and went to the kiosk. An old woman was sitting inside, so I asked for two tram tickets in Polish. She said something and made a face at me which told me that she had no idea what I was saying. So I said it again. Still no luck.

I realised I probably wasn't pronouncing it very well, but I was determined to buy those tickets. And when she saw that I was holding a piece of paper, she pointed at it so that she could see what I wanted.

I didn't give it to her, but instead, tried one more time to ask for the tickets.

Finally, she gave a big smile and her eyes opened wide. 'At last' I thought, 'she understands me! I'm going to get my tickets after all.' She then gave me a magazine, a chocolate bar and a packet of toothpaste! I had to laugh, as my attempts to speak Polish had gone badly wrong. So in the end I showed her my piece of paper.

I thought that if I wasn't able to make myself understood, then it was time to take a Polish language course. So I did. And I'm pleased to say that I can now buy tickets for the tram!

GRAMMAR

Exercise 2

The funniest thing happened to me and my friend on a recent trip to Germany. We went to Berlin, which is the biggest city in Germany. Actually, it's as big as my home city in terms of land area, but it has a smaller population.

After a few days of exploring the city, we wanted to take the train to Hannover, which is about an hour and a half away from Berlin. My friend is much more confident than me and actually speaks better German, so she went to the ticket office to buy two train tickets. We decided to take the express train as it was faster than the regional train. It was nicer and more relaxing, too. We sat down in our seats and the train departed. We chatted the whole way and admired the beautiful view from the train window.

After an hour and a half, we arrived at our final destination. Hamburg! We realised then that we had somehow got on the wrong train. I couldn't believe it! We ended up having a great time, even though we had originally planned to visit Hannover.

Page 13

Exercise 3

1. faster, smaller
2. nicer
3. funniest
4. more confident, more relaxing
5. the biggest
6. better
7. as big as

Exercise 4

1. What is the ~~better~~ **best** film you have ever seen?
2. What is the ~~difficultest~~ **most difficult** thing about learning English?
3. Would you prefer to live in the coldest or ~~hotest~~ **hottest** place on earth?
4. Is it ~~easyer~~ **easier** to learn a musical instrument or learn a new language?
5. Do you think that nurses should be paid as much money ~~than~~ **as** footballers?
6. What's the ~~more~~ **most** expensive thing you have ever bought?

WRITING

Exercise 2

While I was walking back home, I came across a ~~brite~~ **bright** blue suitcase just behind a café next to my house. It was quite large and had a pink ribbon on the side of it. I looked for a label to see who it belonged to but it didn't have one. As I only lived next door, I ~~desided~~ **decided** to take it home, open it up and see if there was a name or ~~adress~~ **address**, anything that would help me to find the owner.

The first thing I noticed when I opened it was a ~~gorgous~~ **gorgeous** green dress. It was beautiful. So beautiful, in fact, that I tried it on!

I went back out, still wearing the dress. I was just turning the corner when I bumped into an old ~~frend~~ **friend**, who I hadn't seen for a while. She was in town visiting her sister.

"Hey, nice dress!" she said. "I have one just like that. Well, ~~actualy~~ **actually**, I had one just like that."

"What do you mean?" I asked.

"I left my suitcase here about 15 minutes ago. I walked off and just ~~completly~~ **completely** forgot about it. I don't know where it is!"

"I think I know where it might be." I said, feeling extremely ~~embarassed~~ **embarrassed**.

Exercise 3

1. was watching, rang
2. was sitting, was
3. walked, was talking
4. broke, was preparing

UNIT 1

Page 14

GETTING STARTED

Exercise 2

No prize for finishing first

Track 003

Matt: Hey Daniel, I thought the plan was to wander around the park, sit down and enjoy our lunch. We've got plenty of time.
Daniel: Yeah, I know, Matt. I just can't help it. Even when I was younger, I always ate too quickly.
Matt: Don't you get indigestion?
Daniel: Sometimes, though I think that depends on what I'm eating to be honest. I get a bit of heartburn if I eat too much junk food.
Matt: You know that speed-eating's not good for your health, right?
Daniel: Oh? Why not?
Matt: Well, research suggests there's a link between obesity and eating quickly.
Daniel: I don't believe you!
Matt: It's true! Your brain doesn't get the chance to tell your stomach it's full.
Daniel: That sounds ridiculous!
Matt: No, really! It takes a while for your stomach to send messages to your brain that you've had enough. Therefore, the quicker you eat, the more calories you'll consume.
Daniel: Oh!
Matt: Yeah. You might clear your plate quickly, Daniel, but in the long run, it could harm your health!
Daniel: Hmm… Matt? Are you going to eat that sandwich? I'm still hungry!

Exercise 3

1. plenty of
2. junk food
3. obesity
4. calories, consume

Page 15

Exercise 5

(The sounds in bold are weak)

1. It's time **for** dinner.
2. It's **a** health **and** fitness book.
3. How long **has** she worked there?
4. I **can** play tennis on Saturday.
5. We've got quite **a** lot **of** work **to** do.

Track 004

1. It's time for dinner.
2. It's a health and fitness book.
3. How long has she worked there?
4. I can play tennis on Saturday.
5. We've got quite a lot of work to do.

VOCABULARY

Exercise 1

Suggested answer:
healthy (Mauro used to live an unhealthy lifestyle, but now he leads a healthy lifestyle.)

Exercise 2

1. cut down
2. keep up
3. keeping track
4. overweight
5. overdid
6. rate
7. aching

Exercise 3

1. overdoing (verb – *-ing* form)
2. overweight (adjective)
3. keep up (verb – base form)
4. ache (verb – base form form)
5. cutting down (verb – *-ing* form)
6. keep track (verb – base form)
7. rate (noun)

Exercise 4

Example questions:
Was it difficult to **keep track of** what you were eating?
What type of food did you **cut down** on?
Did you use an app to **monitor** your progress?
How did you cope with muscle **ache**?
Did you ever **overdo** it at the gym?

Page 16

READING AND USE OF ENGLISH PART 7 TRAINING

Exercise 2

Photo 1: Text D
Photo 2: Text C
Photo 3: Text A
Dr Allan Stewart is not shown in the photos.

Exercise 3

1 D
2 B
3 B
4 A
5 C

Page 17

VOCABULARY

Exercise 1

touch and go – C
keep his brain sharp – E
back on her feet – A
keeps in shape – B
recharge his batteries – D

Exercise 2

2 keeping my brain sharp
3 recharging her batteries
4 to keep in shape

SPEAKING PART 2 TRAINING

Exercise 2

2

Track 005

Maria: Well, in both photos, food is being consumed. The first photo shows two women sitting in a restaurant or café, enjoying what looks to be fast food, while the second photo shows a woman eating on the move. I think the women in the first photo have decided to eat this type of meal because they enjoy it. Even though they look happy, it doesn't look as though the food they're eating is too healthy. The woman in the second photo appears to be eating fast food, possibly a burger or a sandwich. It looks like she's commuting to or from work and so it's possible that she doesn't have the time to sit down and enjoy her meal. Personally, I think the women in both photos should try to eat a more balanced meal rather than food which is high in salt and fat.

Exercise 3

both, while, looks like, rather than, look as though, even though

Exercise 4

1 <u>In</u> the first photograph, you can see a picture of two people eating in a restaurant.
2 The second photo appears to show a woman <u>eating</u> on a bus.
3 It looks <u>like / as though</u> two people are enjoying a meal together in the first photo.
4 I think the woman <u>is eating</u> a burger or a sandwich in the second photo.
5 A lot of people tend <u>to be</u> quite busy at work, so they don't have much time to eat.

Page 18

LISTENING

Exercise 2

A

Track 006

Chloe: Hello Ali.
Ali: Hi Chloe.
Chloe: Ali, I'm going to get myself in shape!
Ali: But you're not overweight.
Chloe: Well, I do need to slim down a little. Anyway, as you know, I've wanted to buy a smart watch for ages.
Ali: Yep. You said they were too expensive and that you decided not to get one.
Chloe: True. I was thinking about a cheaper option. I know they have lots of free apps you can download, like the ones some people use to measure whether they're getting a good night's sleep.
Ali: Yes. That's a great idea, though you never get up until mid-morning, so I don't think you really need that one.
Chloe: I agree. You can also get one that checks your pulse. You know, measures your heart rate. I thought about downloading it but I don't think I have any problems with my blood pressure and anyway, it isn't very user-friendly.
Ali: I see.
Chloe: There's even one where you type in what you're eating and it tells you how much fat, protein and carbohydrates you've consumed. Brilliant if you're trying to cut down on calories.
Ali: So, you're getting that one then?
Chloe: Err no, it's far too time-consuming entering all that data. I'd be bored after a few days.
Ali: So…?
Chloe: I've discovered a great app for cyclists.
Ali: Hold on a second, I thought you hated cycling?
Chloe: I know. But it includes other physical activities too, like walking, running and swimming. So, I've downloaded it and I'm starting now.
Ali: Err, Chloe, was that you? I think someone's calling you.
Chloe: Nope, that's just my phone telling me to get moving. See you, Ali. I'm off to get fit…

Exercise 3

1 They are too expensive.
2 The app that measures your sleep
3 The app that measures your heart rate
4 The app that measures your food intake
5 Ali is surprised because he thought Chloe hated cycling.

Exercise 4

didn't lose weight

Track 007

Chloe: Hey Ali, how's it going?
Ali: Oh, hi Chloe. Good, thanks. How are you getting on with the app?
Chloe: I'm a bit stressed to be honest.
Ali: Really? Why's that?
Chloe: Well, you know I've been using it to keep track of the number of steps I've been taking. I mean, I wasn't obese, but I'd put on a few kilos and I thought I was a little overweight.
Ali: Yeah. I remember you telling me you were giving it a go. You said it was your favourite app.
Chloe: Not anymore. At first, everything was great. It monitored my steps and sent me little reminders when I'd stopped moving for longer than 30 minutes or so, to help with the weight loss and keep my heart rate up. It even had me running up and down the stairs once. My legs didn't stop aching for days after that, which wasn't really an issue. It just took me much longer to get around.
Ali: Ha! I'd like to have seen that. You told me to download it if I remember rightly. Several times!
Chloe: Don't remind me. Anyway that's not why I've given it up. I mean. I could put up with being out of breath from time to time. And I never hurt myself or anything like that, though my friend Sunita hurt her ankle when she tried. The thing is, I was starving. All the time!
Ali: Well, I guess your metabolism was working harder, so I'd expect you to eat more.
Chloe: Actually, I didn't mind that bit and I could deal with being hungry, but guess what? I actually put on weight which put me off the app completely.
Ali: Oh no! Not really what you wanted was it? I guess…

Exercise 5

Reasons why they are distractors:
sore muscles: Chloe says that her legs aching wasn't really an issue.
an injury: Chloe says she never hurt herself, but her friend Sunita hurt her ankle.
extremely hungry: Chloe says that she could deal with being hungry.
too tired: Chloe says that she could put up with being out of breath from time to time.

Page 19

GRAMMAR

Exercise 1

1 infinitive form
2 -ing form (gerund)

Exercise 2

1 to be
2 to skip
3 using
4 harming
5 to drink
6 eating
7 playing

Exercise 4

1 stopped to take
2 stopped eating
3 remember telling
4 remember to give
5 try cutting out
6 tried to book

Track 008

Matilde: Well, when I saw the poster at the food market, I stopped to take a look. I wanted to get more information. You'd said more and more people have stopped eating meat these days.

Franco: Yes, I remember telling you about the benefits of vegetarianism when we met in the café last week. Although, I didn't remember to give you the address of the food market, so I'm glad you found it.

Matilde: No problem. It was really interesting and I loved the variety of fruit and vegetables on offer. A friend of mine also told me that I should try cutting out meat and fish from my diet. I wanted to speak to a professional so I tried to book a meeting with a nutritionist but sadly no-one was available.

Franco: That's a shame.

Exercise 5

1 We use the *-ing* form after *stop* to show that an action or event is no longer continuing. We use the infinitive form after *stop* to show that someone has stopped doing something in order to do something else.
2 We use the *-ing* form after *remember* to show that the action comes first and then you *remember* it. We use the infinitive form after *remember* to show that you remember something first, and the action comes after.
3 We use the *-ing* form after *try* to show that you do something to see if you like it or not or to show that someone has recommended that you try it (e.g. a doctor or a friend). We use the infinitive form after *try* to emphasise that something is difficult to achieve.

Exercise 6

1 consuming
2 to cut out
3 to grab
4 to eat
5 trying
6 putting

Page 20

WRITING PART 1 TRAINING

Focus on structure

1 yes
2 work – the writer talks about how working longer hours is affecting our health.
3 the final paragraph – the writer says *I agree that it is more difficult to be fit and healthy in modern society …*
4 *To sum up* – other words and phrases that can be used are: *In conclusion, In summary, Overall*

Page 21

GRAMMAR

Exercise 1

1 Even though
2 instead of / rather than
3 Despite
4 instead of / rather than
5 However
6 than ever before

Exercise 2

1 Despite **hating** carrots …
2 … to walk to school, **even though** it might take … / … to walk to school. However, it might take …
3 ✓
4 … rather **than** pay money …
5 **Instead of** writing down …

PUSH YOURSELF C1

Exercise 2

Day 1: Digestion
Day 2: Stamina
Day 3: Posture
Day 4: Nutrition
Day 5: Well-being

Track 009

Gavin: Good evening and welcome everyone. I'm Gavin and thanks for signing up for First Fit Boot Camp. I'm sure you'll love every minute of it. Ok, perhaps not every minute. I'm going to work you guys hard – but if you stick with it, I guarantee that, by the end, you're going to feel amazing!

Right guys, so what have we got in store? Day one starts at five am with a quick dip in the lake to help wake us all up. Then at seven am, you're going to have a body assessment with some of the country's leading nutritionists. Fitness begins in the kitchen and that's why they'll be advising you on how to manage your metabolism. After your assessment, they'll be teaching you a bit about the science of food and how your body breaks it down. I know some of you have allergies to certain foods and in a later session we'll talk all about how to fuel our bodies by eating clean.

Ok, so day two is another five am start, but this morning we're off for a five-mile run around the lake, followed by a workout in the field behind the gym. Here we're going to focus on extending your energy levels and your ability to work out for longer by doing intensive interval training. And when I say intensive, I mean you're going to feel exhausted by the end of it, but I can assure you that intense workouts followed by short periods of rest will encourage you to burn more calories and build endurance.

Now, in your pre-boot camp questionnaire, many of you mentioned suffering from aches and pains associated with your study or work habits, and this is our focus on day three. As we get older, bad habits like not sitting up straight, crossing our legs and inactivity can lead to back and shoulder problems. We'll be splitting you into small groups to work with our Pilates experts. You might find some of the positions uncomfortable to start with, but they'll become natural with practice.

Day four is the follow-up from the first day and this is where we're going to focus on how to fuel your body to give you sufficient energy and to promote weight loss. Of course, while you're here our exceptionally talented chefs are preparing what you need, but it's important that you know how to give your bodies the right vitamins and minerals and how to prepare a healthy, balanced meal. This will take place after the ten-mile hike which will start slightly later than usual, at five thirty am.

That leads us to the final day. We're going to start with meditation at five thirty am, followed by a quick swim in the lake. Then we're going to spend the rest of the morning looking at the damaging effects of stress on long-term mental health. We know that keeping fit and active can help to reduce anxiety. However, everyone is different and that's why we're adopting a tailored approach to this session. We'll look at your lifestyle, eating habits and personal relationships. You'll then be given personal guidance from an expert in the field.

Right, so welcome again and, well, as it's nine pm, I suggest we all get an early night and I'll see you at five am sharp!

Any questions …

Exercise 3

Suggested answers:

Day 1: 5 am swim. 7 am body assessment. Manage Metabolism. How food is broken down

Day 2: 5 am 5-mile run. Work out in field behind gym. Ability to work out for longer. Intensive workout / interval training. Build endurance.

Day 3: Looking at bad habits from sitting, slouching. Working with Pilates expert.

Day 4: Fuelling body to get energy and weight loss. Learn how to nourish our bodies after the course. 5.30 am 10-mile hike.

Day 5: 5:30 am meditation. Swim in the lake. Damaging effects of stress on long-term mental health. Looking at lifestyle, eating habits and personal relationships. Personal guidance from an expert.

Page 22

EXAM FOCUS
READING AND USE OF ENGLISH PART 7

1 A
2 D
3 A
4 D
5 C
6 D
7 B
8 A
9 B
10 C

Page 23

WRITING PART 1

Students' own answers

Pages 24 and 25

SPEAKING PART 2

Students' own answers

Page 26

REAL WORLD

Exercise 1

1 Take out
2 Refer to
3 Read
4 Make sure
5 Subscribe
6 need
7 Find
8 Pack

Page 27

Exercise 2

1 vaccination
2 policy
3 roaming charges
4 carry-on (luggage)
5 visa / passport
6 alerts

Exercise 3

Gina and Pierre talk about points 1 and 2.

Track 010

Gina: Hello Pierre, did you manage to find some low-cost travel insurance for our trip to Zurich?

Pierre: Oh, hi Gina. Yes, I did. And as we're planning on taking a few trips this year, I've taken out an annual policy. Medical expenses are covered for up to 5 million pounds.

Gina: That's great. I'm sure we won't need to make an insurance claim while we're there, but it's better to be safe than sorry. Prescription charges can be high, wherever you travel.

Pierre: Yes, they can. I remember I was prescribed a course of antibiotics when I got an infection in Finland last year and was surprised how much it cost.

Gina: Weren't you covered by insurance?

Pierre: I'd forgotten to take any out!

Exercise 4

1 didn't agree with me
2 an upset stomach
3 under the weather
4 quite light-headed
5 coming down with something
6 do you good to get

Track 011

Gina: Oooh …

Pierre: What's up, Gina?

Gina: I think I've eaten something which didn't agree with me.

Pierre: Are you sure? We ate the same for dinner last night and I feel fine.

Gina: Well, I've got a bit of an upset stomach and I feel quite weak.

Pierre: Oh dear. You do look a little under the weather. Do you have any other symptoms?

Gina: Yes, I do. I think I've got a slight temperature and I'm feeling quite light-headed when I stand up.

Pierre: I'm sure it's nothing serious but maybe you're coming down with something. That guy on the bus from the airport was coughing and sneezing, so perhaps you've caught whatever he had.

Gina: Maybe you're right.

Pierre: It's probably just a cold but it might do you good to get some sleep for a few hours and then if you feel worse, perhaps we should go to the doctor?

Gina: That's a good idea. I might feel better after some rest.

Exercise 5

1 May cause drowsiness
2 One capsule twice daily
3 If symptoms persist, consult your physician
4 Only to be taken as directed
5 Side effects may include nausea and vomiting

UNIT 2

Page 28

READING AND USE OF ENGLISH PART 6 TRAINING

Exercise 1

1 A
2 B
3 A
4 B
5 B
6 B

Page 29

Exercise 3

B

Exercise 4

Read the information before and after each gap carefully to see what kind of information would fit.

Track 012

Jan Did you enjoy the text on social media and friendship, Anna?

Anna I did, Jan. I thought it raised some very interesting ideas about how social media has changed the way we form and maintain friendships.

Jan Absolutely! So now we have to choose which sentences best fit each gap from this list of six. I'm not too sure how to approach this.

Anna Ok, well what I've found most useful is to read the information before and after each gap carefully.

Jan How do you mean?

Anna Ok, well if we look at the bit surrounding gap 1 first: *According to the latest figures, the average number of friends people have on social media is somewhere between 200 and 300.* And then we have the gap.

Jan Right, so the missing sentence has got to follow on from that, hasn't it? I guess it will say something about the number of friends people have on social media, so it's still talking about the same thing.

Anna Yeah. I mean the missing sentence has to be connected to the text next to it.

Jan That's right. Let's look at the information after the gap then. *But is this a realistic amount? Is it feasible to maintain meaningful relationships with so many people…?* Right. Ok… It sounds as though the writer is still talking about the same thing because it says 'realistic amount' after the gap …

Anna Ok, so let's look through the list of six sentences, A–F, and see which one talks about this.

Jan Good idea!

Exercise 5

1 B

Exercise 6

1 How easy it is to make friends on social media

2 E

Exercise 7

3 F

4 D

5 A

Page 30

GRAMMAR

Exercise 3

present simple passive	is included
present continuous passive	is being used
present perfect passive	has been done haven't been taken
modal verb + passive	might not be liked
passive infinitive (with *to*)	*to be seen* to be heard

Exercise 4

1 being taken out

2 has already been shared

3 is being looked after

4 have been sold, was published

5 is updated / has been updated / is being updated

6 be switched off

7 is owned

8 to be cleaned / to have been cleaned

Page 31

PUSH YOURSELF C1

Exercise 1

It has been suggested that

It could be argued that

Exercise 2

1 It could be argued that friends are more important than family.

2 It has been suggested that friendships are less sincere than in the past.

3 It is said that social media has made people more lonely.

VOCABULARY

Exercise 3

From left to right:

Faye, Desmond, Sandra, Tiffany, Chantelle, Anthony, Jackson, Leonard

Page 32

SPEAKING

Exercise 2

1 They must be at a fancy-dress party.

2 It looks as though the women are at a spa.

3 This could be a party at someone's home.

4 It looks like they are dancing to some music.

5 The girl might have had an argument with someone.

Exercise 3

1 B

2 A

3 B, D

4 B, D

5 C

Exercise 4

Almost certainly true	**Likely**	**Possible**
it's obvious that	it looks as though	I guess that
I can tell that	likely to be	might be
must be		there's a chance that

Page 33

GRAMMAR

Exercise 2

1 Mexico

2 Spain

3 Mexico

4 Mexico

5 Spain

Track 013

Maribel: I was born in Mexico City and lived there until I was 18 years old, when my family relocated to Spain after my dad was offered a job there. I loved my life in Mexico. I remember during my early childhood, my family and I used to travel a lot around the city, exploring the beautiful parks. These are some of my earliest childhood memories. We never had bikes, so I didn't use to cycle at all back then in Mexico, whereas now in Spain I do it almost every day. I've always been really into Norteño, which is a style of music popular in parts of Mexico. And during my teenage years, I used to hang out with my friends in the local shopping mall and listen to it a lot. My life in Spain is different, but just as fun, although it took me a while to get used to eating the different types of food! We live about 30 kilometres north of Valencia, in a coastal town called Sagunto. It's close to the sea so I spend a lot of time at the beach with my friends, which is something I didn't use to do in Mexico. I'm used to my new life in Spain now and I'm very lucky to have lived in two beautiful countries. Did you use to do any of the same things as me?

Exercise 3

1 used to travel

2 didn't use to cycle

3 used to hang out

4 get used to eating

5 didn't use to do

6 'm used to, Did you use to do

Exercise 4

1 used to

2 used to / would

3 used to / would

4 used to

5 used to / would

6 used to

Exercise 5

We use *be used to* to talk about a situation that is no longer new or strange. We use *get used to* to talk about a situation that has become less new or strange or has become more comfortable. We use *used to* to talk about the past.

Exercise 6

1 getting used to

2 to get used to

3 isn't used to

4 to get used to

5 is used to

Exercise 7

1 to be employed as

2 getting used to living

3 not used to working

4 to hang out with

Page 34

LISTENING PART 4 TRAINING

Exercise 2

A iii

B i

C ii

Exercise 3

A

Track 014

Maya: I'm here today with Aidan Reed, who is going to talk to us about his family, and the relationships he has with different members of his family, both past and present. Welcome, Aidan. Who would you like to talk about first?

Aidan: I'd like to start with my grandad.

Sadly, he passed away about three years ago now. He was a great guy, and although he lived quite a long way away, so we didn't have a lot of face-to-face contact, I was always close to him. We had a great bond and I really looked up to him when I was growing up. I sort of wanted to be like him when I was older. He used to call me a lot and he always wanted to find out what I'd been up to at school, always asking lots of questions, that kind of thing.

Exercise 4

Suggested answers:

2

optimism – positivity

sense of humour – funny

intelligence – smart / clever

3

is most similar to – is like / takes after

4

fell out – argued

moved away – moved out

stopped seeing each other – stopped spending time together

5

influenced – affected

Exercise 5

2 A
3 B
4 C
5 B

Track 015

Maya: That's great. It sounds like you had a very close relationship with your grandfather. Who would you like to talk about next?

Aidan: I'd like to tell you more about Dilys. We've been going out for just over a year and I actually proposed to her quite recently. Everyone knows how smart she is, so I'm surprised she said yes! I'm just kidding of course, but I really do think I'm the luckiest guy alive. I mean, she's such a wonderful woman. She's got a really positive attitude, she never seems to be down at all – I really envy that quality. She takes the view that worrying about things is pointless, and even when we find ourselves in difficult situations we usually manage to have a laugh together. I like to think that I'm quite a funny person, so I try to make her laugh as much as I can, not always successfully I should add, but I think she's used to my jokes by now.

Maya: Are you and Dilys very similar?

Aidan: I'd say we're... compatible. We have the same point of view about many issues and we enjoy doing the same things. But in terms of personality, we differ a lot. Regarding my more immediate family, I'd say that I probably take after my dad more than anyone else, both in personality and appearance. With my mum, well, we both have a similar hair colour, but she's far more laid-back than I am and never gets stressed.

Maya: And do you and your father still get along today?

Aidan: Well, we're still pretty close, but I think we have grown apart in recent years. It's a long story but basically my parents used to argue a lot and eventually they split up. My dad moved out of the house and, although he still lived locally, he worked evenings which made finding time together difficult. My parents managed to patch things up and they're on good terms, and even though they didn't get back together as a couple, we still all get on well when we get together.

Maya: Overall, what effect would you say social media has had on your family relationships?

Aidan: Well, neither my mum or dad use social media which, to be honest, is probably a good thing as I don't think they would necessarily agree with some of the things I post. I do, however, get a lot of updates from my aunt, uncle and their children who live in Australia. I can see what they're up to and even chat to them from time to time so I feel much more connected to them than I used to, all thanks to social media. As for Dilys and I, well, while we both have social media accounts, we have an agreement not to talk to each other online as we already have such a strong bond offline, which we don't want to change.

VOCABULARY

Exercise 2

1 D
2 E
3 A
4 C
5 B
6 G
7 F

Page 35

Exercise 3 and 4

1 grew **apart**
2 getting **on**
3 takes **after**
4 fell **out**
5 split **up**
6 looked **up** to
7 hanging **out**

WRITING PART 1 TRAINING

Exercise 2

Suggested answers:

A and E

Reasons why the others are not appropriate:

B This would usually be more effective in the final paragraph.

C The word count would not allow this.

D Students should paraphrase the question to demonstrate their writing ability and make it more interesting

Exercise 3

Suggested answer:

3

Exercise 4

A 4
B 2
C 1
D 3

Page 36

EXAM FOCUS

READING AND USE OF ENGLISH PART 6

1 E
2 F
3 G
4 C
5 D
6 A

Page 37

LISTENING PART 4

1 C
2 A
3 C
4 B
5 C
6 B
7 C

Track 016

Narrator: You will hear part of a radio interview with Dr Leonora Stockley, an expert in communication, talking about her research. For questions 1–7, choose the best answer (A, B or C).

Presenter: In today's show, I'm delighted to be joined by Doctor Leonora Stockley, author of the new book *Human Relationships and Communication in the 21st Century*. Doctor Stockley, welcome.

Dr Stockley: Hello!

Presenter: Now, you've been doing research into how technology affects human relationships. Could you tell us more about why you chose to research this and how you collected your data?

Dr Stockley: Sure. Well, this arose out of a discussion my colleagues and I were having at the university where I work. We already knew how we ourselves interact with our family and friends but I wanted to see how a wider sample of people reported their own behaviour, so I sent out a questionnaire to people within my own online networks. I asked them to consider how technology affects human relationships.

Presenter: And what did you find out from the responses to the questionnaire? Was this what you were expecting?

Dr Stockley: Well, initially, I thought people would comment on how easy it can be to share information online which isn't always factually correct, but this wasn't one of the issues people raised. One theme that emerged repeatedly was that, while many people have an internet connection that's good enough to connect with anyone anywhere in the world, there are drawbacks. For instance, whenever someone's using an internet-enabled device, such as a phone or tablet, people in their immediate environment, like colleagues or friends, tend not to get their full attention.

Presenter: Well, I think we've all experienced that at some point. In the book, you give an example from one of the people you surveyed, Fred. What does he find challenging when talking to people online?

Dr Stockley: Well, Fred explained to me that even when he's using some form of written communication online with people he knows really well, and has a bond with, he finds it really difficult to tell if someone is, you know, expressing admiration, despair or relief, which is something I think a lot of people have trouble with. It's interesting, though, because he also insists that he doesn't have an issue with saying how he feels himself.

Presenter: What do you think about humour in online communication?

Dr Stockley: Well, humour is another very interesting area. The internet is a great way to share things that have amused us. And of course, we can respond to a friend's amusing post with a positive comment. Actually, it's always been known that sharing a laugh, I mean actually hearing and seeing people laugh, does a lot of good, in terms of lowering your blood pressure, and giving you a general sense of well-being. But we're still waiting to see if the same is true when a person is sitting at their computer watching funny videos and reading humorous articles.

Presenter: I see. You also include an example from your interview with Josephine. What opinions did you form from interviewing her?

Dr Stockley: Well, Josephine was a huge fan of social media. I didn't collect enough data to know if she can be described as having an addiction though. But it's clear that conversations through social media can start to take the place of conversations in real life. In Josephine's case, she was finding that she didn't need to leave her home in order to communicate with people. So she didn't. However, the longer she stayed at home, the more she missed the company of other people. This was very much my impression, from our discussions. And so that's the reason why she decided to cut down on how much she used social media.

Presenter: Now these days, we hear so much about people falling for someone they met online, and real-life relationships failing as a result. Would you say that social media is essentially a bad thing for romantic relationships?

Dr Stockley: I wouldn't go so far as to say that. The internet offers us so much, but I know that for the older generation at least, the thought of people getting together and breaking up, all online, is a very strange concept. What I would say is that if two people who may or may not be in love feel that there's an issue in their relationship, this needs sorting out by sitting down together in person, rather than say, finding the solution to their problem on the internet, which is what a lot of people do nowadays.

Presenter: And finally, can you summarise what you feel online communication is most useful for?

Dr Stockley: Well, I think it's ideal for staying up-to-date with what people are up to, you know, the people you're close to, just maintaining the channel of communication… although, I do think that it can all get very complicated when trying to organise some sort of meeting, such as a day out. And getting things done – especially when other people need to know what's expected of them, that can be tricky too, because some things, practical details, often need to be checked and confirmed.

Presenter: Dr Stockley, thank you very much for talking to us.

WRITING PART 1

Model answer

Traditionally, families were not limited to just parents and children. People lived with other members of their extended family, including grandparents, aunts, uncles and cousins. Many of these relatives shared responsibility for raising the children, which some argue was beneficial to everyone.

Although many families no longer live in close proximity to their relations, having a strong connection between them is usually positive for all generations. Grandparents can help out with childcare, albeit occasionally, and family members can offer financial support as needed.

Clearly, spending time with the extended family brings benefits to old and young alike. Children may develop a wider range of interests and get more attention when they have frequent contact with grandparents, aunts, uncles and cousins.

On the other hand, nowadays people have different expectations of family relationships. Young parents may not value the advice of their elders, and grandparents now expect to spend their retirement pursuing their own interests rather than caring for their grandchildren.

Personally, I believe that parents are responsible for their children. Other family members may help but do not, in my view, have any obligation to do so.

REAL WORLD

Page 39

Exercise 3

1 pick up
2 come across
3 are held in
4 benefit
5 bound to
6 tons of
7 ideal
8 hotspots
9 tip

Exercise 4

1 Hometown
2 Family
3 Hobbies and interests

Track 017

Eun-ju: Hi, are you Simon?

Simon: Yes, you must be Eun-ju.

Eun-ju: That's right! It's nice to meet you.

Simon: Likewise. Where are you from?

Eun-ju: I'm from Seoul.

Simon: No way! I've just got back from there.

Eun-ju: Really?

Simon: Yeah, I was visiting my brother there.

Eun-ju: What does he do?

Simon: He works as a sports coach at the National Sport University.

Eun-ju: That's incredible! I used to play tennis there.

Simon: What a small world! What other sports are you into?

Eun-ju: I love playing badminton but I haven't met anyone else who does yet.

Simon: I play! We actually meet up every Thursday and play at the sports centre. You can join us if you like.

Eun-ju: That sounds good. Thank you so much.

Simon: No worries. Just give me your email address and I'll be in touch.

Eun-ju: Great!

Exercise 5

1 Likewise.
2 No way!
3 What other sports are you into?
4 No worries.
5 I'll be in touch.

Exercise 6

Said to show surprise when someone you meet knows someone or something that you do, often unexpectedly.

Exercise 7

1 C
2 E
3 B
4 A
5 D

Exercise 8

1 G
2 D
3 A
4 C
5 F
6 B
7 E

Track 018

George: Hey, how's it going?
William: Good, thanks! It's been a while!
George: Tell me about it. What have you been up to?
William: This and that. I'm doing a bit of volunteering at the moment.
George: No way! Whereabouts?
William: At the local animal shelter. It's been really enjoyable so far.
George: I bet it has. Do you know if they're looking for any more volunteers?
William: As a matter of fact, they are. Shall I pass your name on?
George: That would be great, cheers!

PROGRESS CHECK 1

Page 40

Exercise 1

1 went
2 has been
3 hasn't replied
4 Have you been running?
5 bought
6 has known
7 graduated
8 have never met / haven't met

Exercise 2

1 hotter
2 good
3 easier
4 the worst
5 more difficult
6 later
7 the funniest
8 the best

Exercise 3

1 shocked
2 disappointed
3 worried
4 delighted
5 upset

Exercise 4

1 cut down on
2 keep track of
3 keep in shape
4 ache
5 touch and go
6 stamina

Exercise 5

1 to run
2 eating
3 playing
4 to buy
5 to open
6 developing
7 to see
8 to take

Page 41

Exercise 6

1 rather than
2 despite
3 Even though
4 However
5 Instead of

Exercise 7

1 as
2 keep
3 However
4 before
5 used
6 to
7 addition
8 more
9 only
10 Even

Exercise 8

1 The book was written in 2009 (by James Richardson).
2 The car hasn't been cleaned yet.
3 My bike is being fixed (by my dad).
4 The window might have been broken (by Peter).
5 She has been offered a job in New York (by the company).
6 Despite the good weather, the concert was cancelled (by the organisers).
7 Your contact information was given to me (by a friend of mine).
8 The training is supposed to be given tomorrow (by the consultant).

Exercise 9

1 I used **to** go with my family to the park every weekend.
2 My friends and I would **to** meet in the shopping centre close to my house.
3 I'm not used to **living** in a big city as I grew up in a small village.
4 I didn't **use** to like mushrooms, but now I love them.
5 Did **you** use to have a pet when you were younger?
6 We ~~would~~ **used to** live in New York when I was a kid.
7 I am slowly **getting** used to my new life in Spain.

Exercise 10

1 stepdaughter / stepson
2 widow
3 half-sister / half-brother
4 extended family
5 father / mother-in-law
6 niece / nephew

UNIT 3

Page 42

READING AND USE OF ENGLISH PART 5 TRAINING

Exercise 1

Virtual reality learning, On-the-job training

Exercise 2

Paragraph 1 introduces Ted Milmorrow.
Option B is correct
Option A: Ted is smiling when he says *'Oh don't worry, it only looks realistic'*. This isn't *showing concern*.
Option B: Ted uses the word *irritatingly* to describe how it started. This is similar to the word *frustrated*.
Option C: Ted uses the phrase *passionate about* to describe the surgeon's attitude. This isn't the same as *worried*.
Option D: Ted uses the adjective *invaluable* which means extremely useful. This isn't similar to *being unsure*.

Page 43

Exercise 3

2 C
3 D
4 A
5 C
6 D

Page 44

GRAMMAR

Exercise 1

1 A D
2 B C

Exercise 2

1 'll / will lose
2 wouldn't drop out / would not drop out
3 'd / would teach
4 'll / will graduate
5 'll / will retake
6 'd / would support

Exercise 3

1 If I listen to music, it**'ll** / **will** distract me from my studies. / If I listen**ed** to music, it would distract me from my studies.
2 If the research was underfunded, I think it **would** be criticised by the academic world / If the research **is** underfunded, I think it **will** be criticised by the academic world.
3 If no formal training is given, I'll **try** and get on an apprenticeship scheme.
4 I'll become a fully qualified electrical engineer if I **can** pass the final exam. / I**'d** become a fully qualified electrical engineer if I **could** pass the final exam.
5 I'll become rich and famous if I **~~will~~** manage to start selling my artwork.
6 If the lessons were more interesting, I'd **study** / **be studying** a bit harder.

Exercise 4

1 C
2 D
3 E
4 A
5 B

PUSH YOURSELF C1

Exercise 1

1 Should you decide
2 If the government reduced
3 unless you get
4 If you were to get / Were you to get
5 Should she pass

Page 45

VOCABULARY

Exercise 1

1 B
2 D
3 E
4 C
5 F
6 H
7 A
8 G

PRONUNCIATION

Exercise 1

1 Where's the address?
2 That's a slow car.
3 I liked the support.
4 I had an ice cream.
5 There's a spot over there.

Track 019

1 Where's the address?
2 That's a slow car.
3 I liked the support.
4 I had an ice cream.
5 There's a spot over there.

Page 46

WRITING

Exercise 1

1 False – You are also assessed on your writing style, relevance and organisation.
2 False – You must cover all the points on the exam card.
3 True
4 False – You must write in the correct register.

Exercise 2

1 D
2 C
3 B
4 A

Exercise 3

Dear Mrs Jones, [*communicative achievement – the register is too formal*]
If you **~~don't~~** like [*language*] watching television, I would certainly recommend it to help improve your English. **Moreover**, [*communicative achievement – the register is too formal – you can also*] you can watch shows with English subtitles which will also help you with difficult words and phrases. ~~My mum actually bought a new television last week, which is great.~~ [*content – this does not connect to the task in the question*]
With reference to [*communicative achievement – the register is too formal*] practice, I would definitely suggest **sign** [*language – signing*] up to language learning websites. They give you the chance to **practice** [*language – practise*] your listening skills through **webiners** [*language – webinars*] and check your written work with native speakers and practise your reading skills with daily articles. ~~A friend of mine has been doing this for the past two months and she loves it!~~ [*content – this does not connect to the task in the question*]
Let me know how you get on. **It's great to hear from you and I'd be more than happy**
to give you some <u>advise</u> [*language – advice*] [organisation – the second sentence should be at the beginning of the email.
Yours sincerely, [*communicative achievement – the register is too formal – Bye for now*]
Marcello Pinotti [*communicative achievement – the register is too formal – Marcello*]
[content – the answer does not include information about how the writer's studies are going which was asked in Annie's email.]

Page 47

LISTENING PART 1 TRAINING

Exercise 1

1 Students' own answers
2 *complain to* is the person you are talking to, *complain about* is the topic you are unhappy with.

Exercise 2

B

Veronica: Hey Adira, how did it go?
Adira: Not good. I just couldn't follow her ideas.
Veronica: Why not?
Adira: Well, it's not just me; the other students on the course didn't understand her either. I know she's supposed to be an expert in her field, and she's carried out loads of research, but nevertheless …
Veronica: Have you spoken to your tutor about her?
Adira: Yes, I told her I wasn't happy, and she was helpful. She gave me some useful websites, where I could look the subject up online, and suggested that might help me understand more clearly. I'm going to try it.

Exercise 3

1 A
2 A
3 C

Track 020

Antonella: Can you help me, Frank? I need to make a decision about my next training course.
Frank: Sure, Antonella. I will if I can.
Antonella: Well, I like the idea of studying at college, providing I can find something suitable.
Frank: I tried that. Face-to-face interaction can be very motivating, but it's not that flexible if you're working at the same time.
Antonella: Hmm. What if I worked from home? Maybe did some self-study?
Frank: You could try that, but unless you're disciplined, it's easy to get distracted. You might want to think about something which combines both.

Track 021

Male student: So what do you think of the university?
Female student: I really like it, to be honest, although I do think the fees are quite high.
Male student: I actually think they're pretty reasonable, particularly in

comparison to the other universities we've seen. I'm not so keen on the lecture theatres though – I thought they were a bit old-fashioned.

Female student: Really? I thought they were impressive from the outside and smart and modern on the inside. I was disappointed to see that they don't have any places to stay on campus, though.

Male student: Yes, that is quite annoying. It will take us at least 30 minutes to walk to classes every day, which isn't ideal.

Track 022

Man: Hey. So, it's graduation soon, how're you feeling? It seems like I've been planning the party for ages!

Woman: I know. It's a bit weird to be honest. We've been studying for three years – I can't believe it's all going to come to an end after next week.

Man: I know, as soon as it's over, I'm taking a year out. I've already arranged it so I can't back out now.

Woman: That's brilliant.

Man: Yeah, I wanted to make sure you were still coming on Saturday, so I can tell you all about it. You really ought to join me on my trip, you know. I'm sure you'd love the experience.

Woman: Sounds great. I might just do that.

VOCABULARY

Exercise 2

1 achieve high grades
2 really happy about something
3 work through the night without going to bed
4 memorise something
5 old-fashioned
6 someone who really enjoys reading
7 someone who copies someone else's work or actions
8 be obviously better than others
9 someone who is the teacher's favourite
10 do more than is necessary

Exercise 3

1 go the extra mile / learn something by heart / pull an all-nighter
2 old-school
3 the extra mile
4 with flying colours
5 bookworm / copycat / teacher's pet
6 stood-out

Page 48

GRAMMAR

Exercise 1

1 ought to
2 Make sure
3 would / 'd
4 might want / like
5 recommend
6 could try

Exercise 2

1 You might want to use a spell checker on your report.
2 You ought to specialise in a particular field of education.
3 You *had* / *'d* better check with your lecturer first.
4 Whatever you do, *don't* / *you shouldn't* miss the cut-off date for your coursework submission.
5 What if we highlighted the effect of using virtual reality in the classroom?

Exercise 3

1 **Why not to** create a poll … → Why not create a poll …
2 You **ought look** at … → You ought to look at …
3 … **made sure** you don't book … → … make sure you don't book …
4 … you **better ask** the students. → You'd / You had better ask the students...
5 **Should you thinking** about a career … → you should think about a career…

Page 49

SPEAKING PART 3 TRAINING

Exercise 2

Distance learning

Exercise 3

Shall we start with this one? / Shall we move onto the next one?
Yes, that's a good point.

Exercise 4

traditional education,
volunteering
on-the-job training
an apprenticeship

Track 023

Faye: Ok, so unlike the last one, this would suit someone who preferred a conventional classroom environment. Perhaps someone younger.

Ryan: Hmm, I'm not sure I'm in complete agreement. Provided a mature student had time on their hands, it would suit them too. For example, if they were retired.

Faye: Yes, I take your point. What about this one? I think someone who'd just finished full-time study but who needed experience would find this useful.

Ryan: I couldn't agree more. Although, I'd add that if it's unpaid, the person who did this would need to have an alternative income or maybe still live at home with their parents. Ok, what's your view on this one?

Faye: Well, I'd suggest this would be brilliant for someone who was in employment but who needed to develop new skills as they did their work. Sort of like learning on the job.

Ryan: I think you're absolutely right about that. It would definitely suit someone who prefers to learn from experiences. If someone were inexperienced and had to learn at the same time, this would be a great way of doing it. Ok, we're running short of time, so let's move on. This one's similar to the last in that it's work-based.

Faye: I agree up to a point; however, it might be more specifically suited to someone who had decided not to attend university and wanted to learn practical skills, while getting paid.

Ryan: I'd go along with that, although the pay is typically low, so it would only really suit someone who's just left school.

Exercise 5

1 Ryan
2 Faye
3 Ryan
4 Ryan
5 Faye
6 Ryan

Exercise 6

1 taking everything into account
2 as you mentioned before
3 why don't we agree to disagree, that makes sense, let's do that

Track 024

Faye: So, I think taking everything into account, a mature student would find distance learning the most beneficial. As you mentioned before, it offers a lot of flexibility for those who have jobs or families.

Ryan: I'm not so sure. I think a traditional education would be better in most circumstances.

Faye: Ok, why don't we agree to disagree on this occasion?

Ryan: Yes, that makes sense – let's do that.

Pages 50 and 51

EXAM FOCUS READING AND USE OF ENGLISH PART 5

1 B
2 C
3 C
4 A
5 B
6 D

Page 52

LISTENING PART 1

1 A
2 B
3 A
4 B
5 C
6 B
7 A
8 C

Track 025

Narrator: 1 You overhear two friends talking in a corridor. What did the man find difficult when he was studying Arabic?
Woman: You've finished your Arabic lessons now, haven't you? How did it go?
Man: I really enjoyed it, although there was a lot of writing to do toward the end of the course, plus it was a bit of a challenge finding enough time to study after work.
Woman: I bet. I've heard the pronunciation is quite difficult too.
Man: Well, there are a few sounds not made in my first language, so it took a while for me to get used to it, but overall, I think I managed it quite well. This time though, it was the sentence structures and tenses which I didn't find clear. I only just passed in the end.
Narrator: 2 You hear a student talking about his future plans. What is he going to do when he leaves university?
Man: I've always wanted to work with children. During my research, I discovered, though, that it wasn't as easy as that. I mean there was so much planning, marking and paperwork to do. I'm still interested in working with them, though, and I'm fascinated by the research I've read about human emotions and behaviours. Unless I'm prepared to do more studying, it'll be more of a hobby than anything else. My tutor suggested I gain some experience after graduation and I can see her point. Working long hours without being paid wasn't my first choice, but if I don't, I just won't get a job in my chosen field.
Narrator: 3 You hear a man and a woman discussing the qualities of a traditional education. What does the woman think?
Man: I think that without an educated population, society just won't work as effectively.
Woman: Perhaps, though I disagree that the aim of school is to set boundaries and teach rules. Providing there are close family and friends who can set a good example, children could learn those things at home.
Man: What about getting a job?
Woman: Well, getting a good education does indeed give people more options in life although that doesn't always come from conventional teaching methods. It's important to remember that education doesn't end after graduation, does it?
Man: I guess not.
Narrator: 4 You hear two students talking about one of their university courses. What do they agree about?
Man: What do you think about the course?
Woman: I'm really enjoying the course at the moment.
Man: I'm not surprised, you've been getting full marks in every test we've done. It's not really my area of interest.
Woman: Well, I must admit that it's a really complex topic so I do think we need to spend a lot of time on it.
Man: That's true. I don't really get it to be honest.
Woman: Do you think it would be useful if we arranged to meet the tutor to talk about the course?
Man: Not really, she's always so busy. I've been trying for months to set up a meeting now and haven't had any luck. It's probably best to keep going as we are.
Narrator: 5 You hear two friends talking at a graduation ceremony. Why didn't the woman want to attend?
Man: Hey, isn't this brilliant? I never thought we'd do it.
Woman: Any excuse for a party where you're concerned! But I know what you mean – it's been hard work but we made it in the end.
Man: Are your parents here?
Woman: They're away for their anniversary – somewhere exotic. They were going to cancel, you know, but I didn't want them to miss their holiday.
Man: Unlucky timing. How are you feeling now?
Woman: Well, I am a bit stressed but that's only because I'm not really into big social events. I'd have preferred to have just gone out for dinner with a few friends.
Narrator: 6 You hear a woman talking on the phone to her son. What does she suggest?
Mother: How did your lessons go?
Son: Yeah, good thanks. We got our maths assignment back today. I got 80%!
Mother: That's great. I'm so proud of you. You must be over the moon. I know how much effort you put into that.
Son: Thanks, Mum.
Mother: Why don't you see what Matt and Luke are up to? I could take you all bowling if you'd like.
Son: That sounds great! I'll give them a call now.
Mother: Well, I'll be back from work at 6. Remember that you need to finish your school work before going, though, ok?
Son: Ok, Ok.
Narrator: 7 You hear a man talking on the radio about his job. What disappoints him about being a lecturer?
Man: I've been lecturing for ten years now. It has its downsides, like all jobs, but I wouldn't change what I do. Starting out, I wasn't aware just how long my working day would be. It's not just about the lectures themselves, there's all the preparation involved. Now though, it's something I'm used to. These days, I've got a different set of challenges. I mean, we're not highly paid in this profession, although that's never been my motivation! I realise things change, but it's not always for the best, is it? I've got an issue with how assignments have to be graded these days. Though I admit, the topics are far more interesting than when I was studying.
Narrator: 8 You hear a teacher talking about a colleague at work. What does she admire most about her colleague?
Woman: I don't know how he does it. It's a challenging job but he manages to stay motivated no matter what and seems to really like his job. For one, he's really good at creating fun and exciting lessons in what seems like no time at all. The students always seem to look forward to them and I can often hear lots of laughter coming from his classroom. The other thing is that he acts fairly with the students and never makes any judgements. I think they look up to him for that and that's what I think is really impressive about him. He says he took inspiration from a tutor when he was studying at university.

Page 53

SPEAKING PARTS 3 AND 4

Students' own answers

Page 55

REAL WORLD

Exercise 3

1 sign up to
2 master
3 authentic
4 to impress
5 workout
6 unique
7 capture
8 suitable for

Exercise 4

Start date: April 15th (3-week intensive programme)
Course details:

- Introduction to coding
- Learning to build a basic website
- Introduction to Python (optional)

Location: Room 14A
Price: $350 (price excludes lunch)
Exam: No
Accredited by the school

Track 026

Student: Good morning. I've got a few questions about the coding for beginners course.

Teacher: Sure, go ahead

Student: What's the start date of the course?

Teacher: Well, it was originally going to start on March 15th, but we've now pushed it back by a month to April 15th. It's also a three-week intensive course instead of four.

Student: Ah ok. What modules are included in the course?

Teacher: We'll start with an introduction to coding and then move on to creating a basic website, using HTML and CSS. There is also a module which looks at Python, but this is optional.

Student: That sounds great. Where are the classes held?

Teacher: They will be in room 14A, which is on the second floor of this building.

Student: And how much does it cost to enrol?

Teacher: The price of the course is $350. The price excludes lunch so you'll need to pay for that yourself.

Student: That's good to know. Is there an end-of-course exam?

Teacher: No, there isn't for this course as we don't want to put too much pressure on the students.

Student: I see. One last question. Will I receive a certificate at the end of the course?

Teacher: Yes, you will. It's accredited by the school and you'll receive it in the post a week after the course has finished

Student: Thank you! I think I'll go and sign up …

Exercise 5

1 start date
2 modules
3 held
4 enrol
5 end-of-course
6 certificate

Exercise 7

1 F
2 A
3 D
4 E
5 B
6 C

UNIT 4

Page 56

VOCABULARY

Exercise 1

steering wheel – photo C
departure lounge – photo A
commuters – photos A, D, F
runway – photo A
handlebars – photo D
cockpit – photo E
motorist – photo C
backpackers – photo B
rush hour – photos C, F

Exercise 3

Possible answers:

1 aeroplane, train, boat
2 car, van
3 car, taxi, van
4 bicycle, car, taxi, van
5 bicycle
6 aeroplane, jet
7 metro/subway/underground, train
8 aeroplane
9 aeroplane
10 bicycle, motorbike

Page 57

Exercise 4 and 5:

1 runway (true)
2 cockpit (true)
3 motorists (false, this is the predicted number of vehicles; the number of motorists will be higher because of car sharing)
4 commuter (false – 42 hours)
5 diesel (true)
6 overtaking (false – distracted driving is said to be the most common cause)
7 jet lag (false – it's worse going from west to east)
8 departure lounge (true)

LISTENING

Exercise 3

The Agrojet
Swoop
Freefall Xtreme

Track 027

Jill: Hello, I'm Jill, and I'm a member of staff at the Velocity Valley Adventure Park. We're on the North Island of New Zealand in the city of Rotorua. Actually, we're just outside the city, and the easiest way to find us if you're coming by car is to come off State Highway 5 and take Paradise Valley Road. If you don't have your own transport, we can pick you up, as we have a complimentary shuttle service which transports you between Rotorua CBD and Velocity Valley.

One great experience we've got is called The Agrojet, that's A-G-R-O-J-E-T. I expect you've been on a nice leisurely cruise before, but this is completely different. It's a boat ride at extreme speeds. You'll be in the capable hands of a fully trained driver who remains in control of the boat as you accelerate up to 100 kilometres an hour in a matter of seconds, and then takes you around the course with some pretty sharp bends!

Extreme speed of course features in many of our rides; Swoop, spelt S-W-O-O-P, is no exception. It's essentially a huge swing, which you and up to two friends are strapped into wearing a harness. You are then lifted up to a height of 40 metres. When you're ready, you release the cord, which sends you into a giant pendulum swing. And when you think that the speed limit on New Zealand's fastest roads is one hundred and ten kilometres an hour and yet you accelerate up to a hundred and thirty on this after about four seconds, well, that just shows how incredible this ride is!

Now, we also have Freefall Xtreme, spelt without the first letter E on 'extreme'. This doesn't have you travelling fast, although you do get the impression of extreme speed. It's essentially a flight, at least, that's what we call it, rather than a ride. It's a wind tunnel; wind blasts at you with such force that you are able to float in the air. People often wonder if you can be blown away, which of course you can't, as there's a net to keep flyers inside the wind tunnel. Of course, there are age and height restrictions on this and everything else in Velocity Valley to ensure that it's absolutely safe.

Exercise 4

1 Paradise
2 driver
3 40
4 130
5 flight
6 net
7 height

Page 58

Exercise 6

If you don't have your own <u>**tran**sport</u> *(noun)*, we can pick you up, as we have a complimentary shuttle service which <u>trans**ports**</u> *(verb)* you between Rotorua CBD and Velocity Valley.

Track 028

Jill: If you don't have your own transport, we can pick you up, as we have a complimentary shuttle service which transports you between Rotorua CBD and Velocity Valley.

Exercise 7

1 The travel agency has recently in**creased** (*verb*) their prices. Because of this **in**crease (*noun*), many people have decided to book their holidays themselves.
2 Usain Bolt re**corded** (*verb*) a time of 9.58 seconds in the 100 metres sprint in 2009. This is still the world **re**cord (*noun*) today.
3 The airport **trans**fer (*noun*) costs 10€. It takes about an hour to trans**fer** (*verb*) you from the airport to the city centre.

Track 029

1 The travel agency has recently increased their prices. Because of this increase, many people have decided to book their holidays themselves.
2 Usain Bolt recorded a time of 9.58 seconds in the 100 metres sprint in 2009. This is still the world record today.
3 The airport transfer costs 10€. It takes about an hour to transfer you from the airport to the city centre.

GRAMMAR

Exercise 1

1 My advice to travellers has always been to take out comprehensive travel insurance.
2 The last time we went away, we left it too late to find a self-catering accommodation.
3 We tried to find a / the subway station.
4 The latest news **is** that the travel company has gone bankrupt.
5 I couldn't believe it when the airline told us that they had lost our luggage.
6 Our tour guide gave us some / – advice about the best places to visit.
7 Travel has always been a passion for me.
8 There's often a traffic jam in my neighbourhood.

Exercise 2

Uncountable: advice, travel insurance, accommodation, news, luggage, travel
Countable: travellers, subway station, travel company, airline, tour guide, places, passion, traffic jam, neighbourhood

Exercise 3

congestion (U) – traffic jam (C)
scenery (U) – view (C)
transport (U) – vehicle (C)
money (U) – dollars (C)
luggage (U) – backpack (C)
advice (U) – suggestions (C)

Page 59

Exercise 4

1 scenery, view
2 dollars, money
3 congestion, traffic jam
4 vehicle, transport
5 advice, suggestions
6 luggage, backpack

Exercise 5

1 much
2 several / many
3 fewer and fewer
4 less
5 many

PUSH YOURSELF C1

Exercise 1

1 A business, B a business
2 A a room, B room
3 A noise, B a noise
4 A competition, B a competition
5 A a paper, B paper
6 A time, B times

Exercise 2

1 A uncountable, B countable
2 A countable, B uncountable
3 A uncountable, B countable
4 A uncountable, B countable
5 A countable, B uncountable
6 A uncountable, B countable

Page 60

READING AND USE OF ENGLISH PART 1 TRAINING

Exercise 4

Members

Exercise 5

1 C
2 D
3 A
4 B

the word *ideas* has a similar meaning to *suggestions*. The verb *submit* collocates with the word *ideas*.

Exercise 6

2 C
3 D
4 C
5 B
6 A
7 D
8 B

Track 030

Speaker: To celebrate Google's 10th birthday in 2008, Google launched a competition which it called 10^{100}. Members of the public were asked to take part and submit suggestions for projects which they wanted to bring to life in order to make the world a better place. One of the winning proposals was from a company in New Zealand called Shweeb. Their aim was to combine elements of the monorail together with those of the bicycle, and to produce a clean and fast vehicle, which could reduce congestion. In the end, Google invested $1 million in Shweeb's research and development.

The world's first Shweeb was built at the Velocity Valley Adventure Park in New Zealand. Riders sit in a capsule suspended from a rail, and pedal as fast as they can for three laps around a 200-metre track. In the past, prizes were awarded to anyone who broke a speed record, such as being the fastest rider from their country. However, the adventure park has recently stopped these records after upgrading the capsules to have electric assistance.

Shweeb has become a very popular visitor attraction and time will tell if it may also be the transport of the future for commuters, business travellers and tourists.

Page 61

GRAMMAR

Exercise 1

1 F
2 B
3 D
4 A
5 G
6 C
7 E

Exercise 2

1 a
2 a
3 the
4 the
5 a
6 The
7 a
8 –
9 a
10 –
11 the
12 the
13 –

Exercise 4

1 the
2 the
3 –
4 a
5 –
6 a
7 the
8 –

Page 62

VOCABULARY

Exercise 1

world-famous

Exercise 2

air-conditioned
cut-price
duty-free
last-minute
long-distance
part-time

Exercise 3

1 air-conditioned
2 duty-free
3 last-minute
4 part-time
5 long-distance
6 cut-price

SPEAKING PART 1 TRAINING

Exercise 1

Olek – A, B, D
Anna – A, C

Both candidates perform well. However, Olek's answers are fully developed; Anna makes rather minimal contributions, leading the examiner to ask 'Why?' in order to encourage Anna to speak more.

Track 031

Examiner: Hello, my name is Sandra Howardson. And your names are….?
Olek: My name is Aleksander, but everyone just calls me Olek.
Anna: My name's Anna Kapuch.
Examiner: Thank you. Can I have your mark sheets, please? Thank you. Where are you from, Anna?
Anna: I'm from Poland.
Examiner: And Olek, where are you from?
Olek: I come from Poland as well, from a small town in the centre of the country called Pabianice.
Examiner: First, we'd like to know something about you. Olek, what's the best way to travel to and from work or college in your hometown?
Olek: The best way of getting around is definitely by tram. It's far quicker than the bus because we don't have many bus lanes so buses tend to get stuck in traffic jams. Trams run on their own tracks alongside bus routes so they don't have this problem.
Examiner: Thank you. Anna, what sort of holidays do you enjoy most?
Anna: For me, just being on the beach is my favourite kind of holiday.
Examiner: Why?
Anna: Well, I work hard all year, so when I get some time off, I just like to rest!
Examiner: Olek, did you use to have enjoyable holidays when you were a child?
Olek: I certainly did. My parents have always been really into trekking in the mountains, so even when I was a child, we'd spend time in the Tatra Mountains whenever we could.

Exercise 2

2 way to travel to and from work or college in your hometown
3 holidays do you enjoy most
4 use to have enjoyable holidays when you were a child

Exercise 4

Suggested answers

Holidays and travel
What's your favourite kind of holiday?
Have you ever been to….?
Do you like trying different types of food on holiday?
Home / Daily life
What's your favourite part of the day?
Can you tell me about your house or flat?
What household chores do you usually do?
Friends and family
What kind of things do you enjoy doing with your friends?
Who are you closest to in your family? Why?
Where did you meet your best friend?

Page 63

WRITING PART 2: ARTICLE TRAINING

Exercise 1

Suggested answers:

Statements 1, 4 and 6 are true.

Exercise 2

Terrible Holidays

Have you had a holiday where something went wrong? What happened? How can people avoid having a problem like this when they go on holiday? We will publish the best articles on our website.

Write your article.

Exercise 4

Suggested answer:

Georgina's plan is better, as it addresses the questions more fully. Alex should rewrite his plan to ensure that he addresses each of the questions in the exam task, rather than just discussing and describing holidays in general terms.

Exercise 5

1 D
2 A
3 B
4 C

Exercise 6

1 All sorts of things can go wrong when you're on holiday.
2 Some of my holidays have been fantastic; others have been a disaster
3 It's always worth doing thorough research before you book a holiday.
4 It's vital that you have the chance to take a break from your work or studies.

Page 64

EXAM FOCUS READING AND USE OF ENGLISH PART 1

1 C
2 C
3 D
4 B
5 A
6 B
7 C
8 A

Page 65

SPEAKING PART 1

Students' own answers

WRITING PART 2: ARTICLE

Model answer

Last summer, my family and I broke with our usual tradition of taking beach holidays to have a more cultural, city-based vacation. We chose the Hungarian capital, Budapest, and it turned out to be one of the best trips of my life.

Budapest is an absolutely stunning city, divided into two parts by the majestic River Danube. The city is steeped in history, crammed full of breathtakingly beautiful buildings in different architectural styles.

I was pleasantly surprised by how much there was to do. We took a relaxing river trip to Margaret Island, where we hired bicycles for a leisurely ride around. We saw a couple of classical music concerts at the opera house, which we loved.

What I enjoyed most about this holiday was that every day was different. We went to the public spa baths to relax, went sightseeing, visited art galleries, shopped and ate food from all over the world. The people were friendly and helpful, and our hotel was spectacular. All in all, it had all the elements needed for a perfect getaway.

Page 66

REAL WORLD

Exercise 2

1 C (Casa Rosada)
2 B (Caminito Street)
3 A (Palacio Barolo)
4 C (Casa Rosada)
5 A (Palacio Barolo)
6 B (Caminito Street)

Page 67

Exercise 4

1 trouble
2 jumped
3 hard to miss
4 a handful of
5 got chatting
6 bumped into

Exercise 5

Announcement	Maddie / someone else	Maddie needs to ...
1	someone else	–
2	Maddie	proceed to Gate 14.
3	someone else	–
4	Maddie	make herself known to a member of staff as soon as possible.

Track 032

1 This is an announcement for passengers on flight FA6590. We regret to announce that this flight has now been cancelled. Please make your way to the check-in desk for further information.
2 This is an announcement for all passengers on flight FA6509 to Santiago. Please proceed to Gate 14.
3 Calling all passengers on flight FA6509 to Santiago. We are pleased to announce that this flight is now ready for boarding. Could passengers seated in rows 15–30 please come to the desk with your boarding passes and passports open at the photo page.
4 This is a special announcement for passenger Maddie Jones, travelling to Santiago on flight FA6509, that's Maddie Jones travelling to Santiago. Please make yourself known to a member of staff as soon as possible.

Exercise 6

1 announce, make your way
2 passengers
3 seated
4 special

Exercise 7

1 C
2 E
3 D
4 A
5 F
6 B

UNIT 5

Page 68

LISTENING PART 3 TRAINING

Exercise 1

1 music
2 the benefits of listening to music
3 three – you don't need to use two letters

Exercise 2

A It has increased (improved, raised) my creativity (imagination).
B It has improved (made better) my concentration (focus).
C It has made (I have become) me a happier (more contented) person.
D It has helped (encouraged) me to make more friends (get to know more people).
E It has reduced (decreased) my stress levels (tension).

Exercise 3

Speaker 1 – E
Speaker 2 – C
Speaker 3 – B

Track 033

Narrator: Speaker 1

I'm lucky with my job because I can do the majority of tasks independently, which means I can listen to a lot of music while I work. I can't say it's actually made me a more creative person or anything like that though. Friends tell me listening to music will enable me to not lose concentration while studying, but I've found the opposite to be true. I actually think the more I listen to music, the less worried I am about things. That doesn't mean to say that I don't work as hard on a particular project, it's just that I tend to feel more relaxed about the work I'm doing, which keeps me, and my boss, very happy.

Narrator: Speaker 2

If you've ever met someone from another country you'll know that, more often than not, you'll probably end up talking about the different kinds of music you like. In the job I'm currently doing, I've been fortunate enough to make many friends from around the world – we spend our evenings introducing each other to the music we like, and it's a great way to discover new music from other countries! I think music has helped me to be a more cheerful person. I just hope music can have the same effect on more people in the future.

Narrator: Speaker 3

I'm currently in my final year at university and I must admit that it's been one of the most difficult years of my life. One of my friends suggested that I try listening to classical music to reduce stress while studying. I was a little pessimistic at first because I always thought it would be more distracting than helpful. What I did find though was that I was much more focused on my work. I mean, I'm still stressed about my end-of-year exams but at least I feel better prepared for them now.

Page 69

READING

Exercise 2

The writer will go to a type of cinema where the audience also participate in the film.

Exercise 3

the big screen – the cinema
blockbuster – a film that is very successful
cast – the actors and actresses in a film
remake – a new version of an old film
non-refundable – money that you pay that you cannot get back
set – the place where a film is performed or recorded

outfits – a set of clothes worn by actors and actresses
roles – the actors' and actresses' parts in a film

Exercise 4

1 C
2 B
3 A

Page 70

READING AND USE OF ENGLISH PART 7 TRAINING

Exercise 6

1 was recently asked by a
2 'm / am used to spending
3 'd / would rather watch films than

Exercise 7

1 even though the weather was / even though it was
2 looked up to
3 was better than
4 prevented us (from) going
5 anyone came to / anybody came to

VOCABULARY

Exercise 2

2 from cover to cover
3 best-selling
4 page-turner
5 had me in stitches
6 heavy-going
7 flick through
8 hooked
9 bedtime reading

Page 71

Exercise 3

1 to flick through
2 had me in stitches
3 heavy-going
4 best-selling
5 from cover to cover
6 page-turner
7 hooked
8 bedtime reading
9 I couldn't put it down

Exercise 4

Suggested answers:

I'd wanted to read some of the author's best-selling work for a while, so when I came across a little bookshop on holiday, which had a reasonably priced signed copy, I bought it immediately. I hadn't thought it'd make great bedtime reading – my friend said it was heavy-going when she'd read her copy on holiday recently, but not for me. I found it to be such a thrilling page-turner, I couldn't put it down. I remember I'd gone to bed at 10 pm, intending to flick through a magazine for 30 minutes, but once I'd picked it up, I was hooked. I read it from cover to cover, turning the last page at 3 am! I couldn't believe it! I had no idea I'd been reading for so long and it was so late – or early! The book has it all. It's not only exciting, it's sensitively written and funny too: the humour had me in stitches at times. Having said that, make sure you have plenty of tissues handy: the ending is a real tearjerker.

Page 72

GRAMMAR

Exercise 1

1

(A) *I'd wanted to read some of the author's best-selling work for a while, so when* (B) *I came across a little bookshop on holiday, which* (C) *had a reasonably priced signed copy,* (D) *I bought it immediately.*

A past perfect simple
B past simple
C past simple
D past simple

2 A

Exercise 2

I was bored yesterday afternoon. I had already been to the supermarket, cleaned the house and cooked lunch so I decided to go for a walk around the park.

Order of events:

1 I had already been to the supermarket
2 cleaned the house
3 cooked lunch
4 I was bored yesterday afternoon
5 I decided to go for a walk around the park

Exercise 3

1 had never been, went
2 had been thinking, bought
3 arrived, had already started
4 discovered, had thought
5 had been waiting, started
6 (had) recommended, had already read
7 got, had been cycling

Exercise 4

1 had sold out
2 had booked
3 managed
4 had been reading
5 started
6 had been

Page 73

WRITING PART 2: REVIEW TRAINING

Exercise 2

1 best, perfect, spectacular, first-rate, marvellous
2 monotonous
3 frustrated
4 absurd

Exercise 3

1 D
2 A
3 B
4 C

Exercise 4

Sentence **3** is correct.

1 I suggest you go out and see the film. / I suggest that you go out and see the film.
2 I would highly recommend this book to anyone who enjoys thrillers.
4 I advise you to go and watch the play.

Page 74

VOCABULARY

Exercise 1

Positive: appealing; delightful; entertaining; gripping; hilarious; impressive; informative; stunning

Negative: average; confusing; dense; predictable

Exercise 2

2 dense
3 predictable
4 average
5 gripping
6 informative
7 hilarious
8 confusing
9 impressive

PUSH YOURSELF C1

Exercise 1

1 film
2 feel
3 imagination
4 novel
5 personal
6 at the end
7 article
8 complicated

Exercise 2

1 tragedy
2 plot
3 centres around
4 must-read
5 twist
6 contemporary
7 absorbing
8 vivid

Page 75

SPEAKING

Exercise 2

D

Track 034

A: It's almost closing time. We need to reach a decision about which one to buy.

B: It's hard now we're standing in the gift shop. We've seen some really creative pieces of art today. I thought I'd made up my mind but I'm no longer sure.

A: Really? It's getting late, so we've got to be quick. You've changed your mind several times. What's the problem?

B: I don't know. I'm stuck between these two. What do you think about that one? What's that in the foreground?

A: I'm not sure, but I like the contrast between the colours.

B: I agree. I think the landscape is quite complex but it isn't really that contemporary. What about this one?

A: Well, I must admit that it is distinctive, though I'm not in favour of that one because the colours are too vibrant for my taste and it's far too abstract. And, as it's a limited edition, it's quite expensive.

B: I disagree with you about the colours – I think they're really nice, but I'm with you on the price.

A: So should we forget about that one then?

B: Yes, I think so.

A: I know you ruled this one out, but I think it's an incredible piece. The fact that the artist isn't human makes it unique.

B: That's true. It also says here that with every purchase, a donation is made to the wildlife trust, which is really nice.

A: So, we're settled?

B: Yes. Let's go for that one. I think it'll look great on the wall at home.

Exercise 3

1 reach a decision
2 made up my mind
3 changed your mind
4 stuck between
5 agree
6 in favour of
7 with you
8 about that one
9 settled

Exercise 4

1 G
2 A
3 F
4 C
5 B
6 H
7 E
8 D

Exercise 5

1 C
2 A
3 E
4 F
5 B
6 D

Page 76

EXAM FOCUS
READING AND USE OF ENGLISH PART 4

1 only does he sing
2 used to write better than
3 were shown around by
4 the only / one person who did
5 one of the hardest
6 reminded her to pick up

Page 77

WRITING PART 2: REVIEW

Model answer

Recently, my friends and I were lucky enough to get tickets to see an Ed Sheeran concert at the Manchester Arena. Ed is our favourite singer, so we were thrilled to be seeing him live at last, and he didn't disappoint. The Arena is an iconic venue, having hosted all the most talented music stars of our time, and it is always a delight to be there, soaking up the atmosphere.

What I loved most about this concert was that Ed appeals to young and old. It was a real mix of people, from mums and grandmas to teenagers and younger kids. He performed songs from all his albums, including my absolute favourite, 'Perfect'. Everyone was swaying and singing along with the lights on their phones shining in the darkness.

Even if you are not usually a concert-goer, I would recommend going to see Ed Sheeran live. Whoever you are, if you love romantic songs with meaningful lyrics, try to catch Ed on his next tour. You won't regret it!

LISTENING PART 3

Speaker 1 – C
Speaker 2 – D
Speaker 3 – G
Speaker 4 – A
Speaker 5 – E

Track 035

Narrator: Speaker 1

The first thing you often learn in any acting class is that acting isn't just about learning your lines. I actually didn't take many classes myself, but I know a lot of people who did and put much of their success down to having taken these classes. More useful, I found, was meeting with as many people as possible who shared my passion for acting. It was actually through a friend that I got my first job in acting, after he recommended me to the director. Some people find this quite difficult to do, so work hard at it and I'm sure you'll be a star in no time.

Narrator: Speaker 2

Some people think that the life of a professional actor is only about attending film premieres and hanging out with celebrities at parties. People don't really understand how difficult the job is and how much stress and disappointment an actor goes through, particularly at the beginning. It's important to understand that you won't always be successful at your first attempt. I was turned down twenty times before I landed my first role, and I even started to question my choice of career, but I stuck with it and I'm pleased to say that all that hard work is now paying off.

Narrator: Speaker 3

In my opinion, becoming a successful actor isn't necessarily something that can be achieved by spending lots of money.
Of course, there will be things you need to pay for along the way, such as acting classes, and don't forget that your agent will take a share of your fee. I've always thought that it's more important to focus on yourself. Think about the kind of films you want to star in and the parts in films that might be of interest to you. Once you've figured this out, you'll be much more focused and this will really help you in the long run.

Narrator: Speaker 4

I remember a good friend of mine telling me about a time he was asked to play a role that he didn't feel entirely comfortable with. He ended up turning it down and felt much better because of it. I realised that I wasn't alone and that there were plenty of other actors out there with stories to tell. I found a lot of online articles written by actors which went into a lot of detail about how they achieved success in the film industry. I strongly recommend doing this as I found that the advice was invaluable.

Narrator: Speaker 5

When I was starting out, I spent a lot of time researching how to make a living as an actor online. I was always keen to find out more about other actors' experiences, especially how they supported themselves when there wasn't much work. I then went on to email some of the directors I particularly admired to get a different perspective on life in the film industry.
I was a little nervous at first because I didn't think they would appreciate being contacted directly, but it turned out to be one of the best decisions I ever made. They were really supportive and I really learnt a lot from them.

REAL WORLD

Page 79

Exercise 3

1 must-see
2 annual
3 world-famous

4 picturesque
5 spot
6 numerous
7 lively

Exercise 4

2 plans for
3 in mind
4 are you sure
5 say

Track 036

Joe: Hey Olivia, what are you up to this weekend? I thought we might do something.
Olivia: Yes, that would be great – though I'm tied up on Friday night. It's my sister's birthday, remember?
Joe: Ah that's right. Have you got any plans for Saturday? I thought we might go to the balloon fiesta. I've always wanted to see it.
Olivia: I've got a few things planned but I'm sure I could make time for it. What did you have in mind?
Joe: I wanted to see the nightglow.
Olivia: What's a nightglow?
Joe: It's where a lot of the hot air balloons turn on their flames at night. It's supposed to be quite spectacular, with a really vivid display of colour. It starts at 9 pm.
Olivia: It sounds amazing, especially against the night sky, but I'm afraid I've got something on between 8 and 8:30 pm so I don't think I can make it for 9.
Joe: Ah, that's a shame. I guess I could go with Tom. Are you sure you can't get out of it?
Olivia: Well, if I can, I'll let you know. Otherwise, I can meet you there a bit later, say 9:30?
Joe: Ok. That would be great. I'm sure you won't have missed much by then.

Exercise 5

1 E
2 F
3 A
4 B
5 D
6 C

PROGRESS CHECK 2

Page 80

Exercise 1

1 will not / won't graduate
2 had
3 would join
4 will / 'll come
5 will / 'll go
6 will not / won't be able to

Exercise 2

1 You ought to ask your teacher for advice.
2 You could to try doing an online class for extra practice.
3 He had better arrive soon or we'll be late for the seminar.
4 Whatever you do, don't cheat in your exam.
5 You might want to try using a spellchecker to check your spelling.
6 I wouldn't to ask him, if I were you. He's in a bad mood.

Exercise 3

1 over the moon
2 dissertation
3 tutor
4 pull a few all-nighters
5 graduation ceremony
6 lecture theatre
7 campus
8 volunteering

Exercise 4

1 We had a really great trip to Prague last month.
2 Dubrovnik is a beautiful city, located in the south of Croatia.
3 Correct
4 The advice the tourist guide gave us was really useful.
5 My city has a big problem with the congestion.
6 Correct
7 I've been thinking about starting an ice cream business.
8 Spanish is one of the most widely spoken languages in world.

Exercise 5

Countable: backpack, traffic jam, vehicle, view
Uncountable: advice, luggage, money, scenery
Both: business, competition, congestion, noise, paper

Page 81

Exercise 6

Across

1 jam
7 helmet
8 departure lounge
9 rush hour
10 cockpit

Down

2 motorist
3 announcement
4 commuter
5 steering
6 jet lag

Exercise 7

1 arrived / had already started
2 had never been / was / bought
3 had been sleeping / woke
4 told / had seen
5 were / had been cancelled
6 were / had been helping out
7 visited / had told
8 became / had been working

Exercise 8

1 best-selling
2 hilarious
3 confusing
4 set
5 compelling
6 awful
7 contemporary
8 twist

Exercise 9

1 cast = line-up
2 costumes = outfits
3 critics = reviewers
4 entertaining = enjoyable
5 lead = main

UNIT 6

Page 82

GETTING STARTED

Exercise 2

Suggested answers:

1 B
2 C or A
3 D
4 A, D or E
5 F
6 A or E

READING

Exercise 3

Suggested answers:

A sea anemone is an animal that looks like a plant.
It can grow up to two metres in diameter.
It is found in shallow coastal waters and above water level at low tide.

Page 83

READING AND USE OF ENGLISH PART 2 TRAINING

Exercise 4

1 between
2 where
3 only

Exercise 5

4 though
5 to
6 up
7 spite
8 for

VOCABULARY

Exercise 1

1 B
2 C
3 A

Exercise 2

1 issue – C
2 footprint – A
3 warming – B
4 energy – E
5 documentaries – F
6 range – D

Page 84

GRAMMAR

Exercise 1

1 Bats are nocturnal, which means they only come out at night.
2 The scientists have now arrived at the venue for the annual conference.
3 We travelled across the mountain range by train / in a train.
4 The seminar on animal welfare will be held at 32 Main Street.
5 We are planning to go back to the beach next week.
6 When you walk over / across the bridge, you get a better view of the river.

Exercise 2

1 approve of
2 depends on
3 capable of
4 insist on
5 regarded as
6 enquire about
7 looking forward to
8 succeeded in

Exercise 3

1 The visitors congratulated the tour guide on a very informative tour.
2 The closure of the lion exhibit hasn't prevented people from visiting the zoo.
3 The guide has warned visitors against taking photographs of the animals.
4 The security guard stopped everyone from entering the museum.
5 The researcher was accused of stealing the money from the office.

PUSH YOURSELF C1

Exercise 1

Complex prepositions

Exercise 2

with the exception of
Ahead of
in the event of
in the hope of
along with

Exercise 3

1 in the hope of
2 in the event of
3 ahead of
4 with the exception of
5 along with

Page 85

SPEAKING PART 2 TRAINING

Exercise 2

guide – picture A
camels – picture A
desert – picture A
crops – picture B
hikers – picture C
mountain range – picture C
waterfall – picture D

Exercise 3

1 similarity
2 In the same way
3 in this case
4 obvious
5 In contrast
6 safe to

Exercise 4

Student A:
A depends on
B earn (a living)
C transporting
Student B:
D huge
E magnificent
F presumably

Exercise 5

Student A:
2 How do these people feel about the animals they are with?
Student B:
1 Why have these people chosen to visit these places?

Page 86

LISTENING

Exercise 3

1 Liz
2 Joey
3 Isaac
4 Liz
5 Isaac

Track 037

Presenter: And now, in the final two minutes of the Breakfast Show here on Radio Talk FM, I'd like to tell you about a news story that's just coming in. In France, researchers claim that they have trained an orca to copy the sound of a human. Isn't that amazing? Apparently, the orca can say several words, which is just unbelievable! And the orca has also been able to mimic various sounds that it hears, like the howl of a wolf. Well, I'd love to hear from our listeners. Call in now on the usual number if you'd like to take part in the show. And now we can go straight to our first caller, Joey.
Joey: Hi.
Presenter: Hello Joey, thanks for speaking to us today. So, what do you make of it?
Joey: Well, we've always known that animals like orcas, you know, whales and dolphins, are really smart.
Presenter: Sure.
Joey: And this makes me think that with this orca, there must be something that she's desperate to get across to people.
Presenter: Go on.
Joey: And in the future, I mean with science, and all the stuff they can find out, I bet people will be able to interpret most of the sounds that animals make. It's just that we haven't quite got there yet.
Presenter: I see. Well, thanks for your call Joey. Next on the line we have Liz.
Liz: Hello there.
Presenter: What would you like to say?
Liz: Well, it's certainly an intriguing story. But I think we need to be sensible, and not jump to the wrong conclusion. It's very easy to believe that we have an orca that can actually hold a conversation with a human. It would of course be wonderful if that were true but, in reality, I don't think the orca has really accomplished anything particularly remarkable.
Presenter: How do you mean?
Liz: Well, lots of animals, and parrots are a good example, can imitate people's speech reasonably well, which is certainly a remarkable achievement.
Presenter: Sure.
Liz: The whole question of how other species communicate is something we're only just beginning to understand. And we don't really have enough evidence yet, but hopefully this will come in time.
Presenter: Ok, great, Liz, thank you for calling. Our next caller is Isaac. What are your thoughts on this?
Isaac: Well, to consider whether an orca making a few noises, and then being rewarded by a trainer… I mean, does that count as actually trying to express some sort of meaning, a message for another individual to receive? I would argue that it doesn't.
Presenter: Right, well, in the recording you can hear the trainer saying her name, and that has the effect of making the orca say the same thing… at least, that's what it sounds like to me.
Isaac: But there's no indication that the orca has any idea of what the trainer is saying. And I find it highly unlikely that she does.

Presenter: Isaac, thank you for joining us. It's been really interesting, but that's all we have time for this week.

Exercise 4

Presenter: And now, in the final two minutes of the Breakfast Show here on Radio Talk FM, I'd like to tell you about a news story that's just coming in. In France, researchers claim that they have trained an orca to copy the sound of a human. Isn't that amazing? Apparently, the orca can say several words, which is just unbelievable! And the orca has also been able to mimic various sounds that it hears, like the howl of a wolf. Well, I'd love to hear from our listeners. Call in now if you'd like to take part in the show on the usual number. And now we can go straight to our first caller, Joey.

Joey: Hi.

Presenter: Hello Joey, thanks for speaking to us today. So, what do you make of it?

Joey: Well, you know, we've always known that animals like orcas, you know, whales and dolphins, are really smart.

Presenter: Sure.

Joey: And this makes me think that with this orca, there must be something that she's desperate to get across to people.

Presenter: You think?

Joey: Sure. And in the future, I mean with science, and all the stuff they can find out, I bet people will be able to interpret most of the sounds that animals make. It's just that we haven't quite got there yet.

Presenter: I see. Well, thanks for your call Joey. Next on the line we have Liz.

Liz: Hello there.

Presenter: What would you like to say?

Liz: Well, it's certainly an intriguing story. But I think we need to be sensible, and not jump to the wrong conclusion. It's very easy to believe that we have an orca that can actually hold a conversation with a human. It would of course be wonderful if that were true but, in reality, I don't think the orca has really accomplished anything particularly remarkable.

Presenter: How do you mean?

Liz: Well, lots of animals, and parrots are a good example, can imitate people's speech reasonably well, which is certainly a remarkable achievement.

Presenter: Sure.

Liz: The whole question of how other species communicate is something we're only just beginning to understand. And we don't really have enough evidence yet, but hopefully this will come in time.

Presenter: Ok, great, Liz, thank you for calling. Our next caller is Isaac. What are your thoughts on this?

Isaac: Well, to consider whether an orca making a few noises, and then being rewarded by a trainer… I mean, does that count as actually trying to express some sort of meaning, a message for another individual to receive? I would argue that it doesn't.

Presenter: Right, well, in the recording you can hear the trainer saying her name, and that has the effect of making the orca say the same thing… at least, that's what it sounds like to me.

Isaac: But there's no indication that the orca has any idea of what the trainer is saying. And I find it highly unlikely that she does.

Presenter: Isaac, thank you for joining us. It's been really interesting, but that's all we have time for this week.

1 Liz
2 Isaac

Page 87

GRAMMAR

Exercise 1

defining: B
non-defining: A

Exercise 2

1 D
2 ND
3 D
4 ND
5 ND
6 D

Exercise 3

1 Giraffes, **which** are the tallest mammals on earth, are able to run up to 55 kilometres per hour. (ND)
2 Edmund Hillary and Tenzing Norgay were the two explorers **who** / **that** first climbed Mount Everest back in 1953 (D)
3 The scientist Stephen Hawking, **whose** work greatly enhanced our understanding of the universe, died aged 76. (ND)
4 The North Pole is the one place **where** you can go 1km south, 1km east and 1km north, and be back at your starting position. (D)
5 That's the book **which** / **that** / – I was telling you about last week. (D)
6 1752 was the year **when** / **that** the world's first zoo opened in Vienna. (D)
7 There's a river in Peru **where** the water is so hot that any animals **which** / **that** fall in are quickly killed. (D, D)

Exercise 4

2 who … from
3 (that / which) … to
4 which … about
5 who / whom… with
6 which … on

Exercise 5

2 both of whom
3 neither of which
4 all of which
5 one of whom
6 most of which

Page 88

VOCABULARY

Exercise 2

1 trip
2 lend
3 sensible
4 loose
5 advice
6 choose
7 sight
8 rise
9 affect
10 Tell

Page 89

WRITING PART 2: REPORT TRAINING

Exercise 2

1 for the teacher
2 what the zoo is like; what students can learn from a visit; whether you would recommend it

Exercise 3

relevant = **2**, **4**, **7**

Exercise 4

1 B
2 C
3 E

Exercise 5

A The aim of this report is to …
B In order to prepare this report …
C They described the facilities of the zoo as …
D For these reasons, I am certainly in favour of …

Page 90

EXAM FOCUS READING AND USE OF ENGLISH PART 2

1 when / that
2 on
3 by
4 with
5 which
6 terms
7 fact
8 like

WRITING PART 2: REPORT

Model answer

Purpose

The aim of this report is to evaluate the Animal Kingdom Wildlife Park and make recommendations as to how it could be improved.

Attractions

The Park is home to a range of animals, including penguins, lemurs, wallabies, zebras and giant tortoises. There are several 'walkthroughs', which enable visitors to get close to the animals. There are also 'be a keeper' experiences, for both adults and children, where guests can see what it is like to work at a wildlife park.

Evaluation

The Park has excellent enclosures, where animals can live in an environment which is as close as possible to their natural one. It provides a very educational experience for visitors of all ages. While the price of admission is reasonable, the 'experiences' are a little over-priced, as are the cafes and gift shops. The population of some of the species has diminished in recent years.

Recommendations

- Introduce a breeding programme to maintain animal populations.
- Review pricing to make it affordable for all visitors.
- Consider introducing 'family tickets', off-peak discounts and special offers.

Page 91

SPEAKING PART 2

Students' own answers

Page 92

REAL WORLD

Exercise 2

1 C
2 A
3 B

Exercise 3

1 a whole host of / a wide variety of
2 in advance of
3 a popular spot for
4 from far and wide

Page 93

Exercise 5

Spring / manatee / swim
turtle / moonlight

Track 038

Jack: Hello.
Matt: Oh hello, are you enjoying your stay with us so far?
Jack: Yes, thanks. Actually, I was wondering if I could ask you a few questions about the different things we can do here.
Matt: Sure.
Jack: We want to make sure we get to see some of the wildlife while we're here. I mean, I know you guys here have animals that we never see in England.
Matt: Ok.
Jack: I was hoping you could recommend somewhere we can see some of the animals up close.
Matt: No problem. There are various wildlife reserves around the state. There's one called Blue Spring quite close to here, for example.
Jack: Right, I'll just make a note of that. Am I right in saying it's on the coast?
Matt: No, it's inland, and the freshwater habitat is ideal for one of Florida's best-known species, the manatee.
Jack: Oh – sorry, would you mind spelling that for me?
Matt: M-A-N-A-T double E.
Jack: That's the animal also called the sea-cow, isn't it?
Matt: That's it. And visitors always love seeing them.
Jack: I'm sure. I've always wanted to see them myself.
Matt: Well, you should get a pretty good view of them, because although you can actually swim there some of the time, it's not allowed at the present time because the manatees are around. But they do come right up beneath the wooden platforms you'll be on. So you'll get a good view. And it shouldn't be too hard to photograph them.
Jack: That sounds excellent. Is there any particular animal that we should try and see on the coast?
Matt: Well, one obvious one, which you should be able to catch sight of on several of the beaches throughout Florida, is the turtle.
Jack: Right, I don't think I've ever actually seen one. Aren't they endangered?
Matt: Yes, I believe they are. But you still have a chance of seeing quite a large group if you're there at the right time.
Jack: So I suppose you have to get up at dawn, do you?
Matt: Well, apparently, although I haven't done this myself, they say the ideal time to see them is in the moonlight, when they come to lay eggs.
Jack: That's sounds amazing! We'll definitely make time to go and see them.

Exercise 6

1 F
2 A
3 E
4 C
5 B
6 D

Track 039

1 Actually, I was wondering if I could ask you a few questions about the different things we can do here.
2 I was hoping you could recommend somewhere we can see some of the animals up close?
3 Right, I'll just make a note of that. Am I right in thinking it's on the coast?
4 Oh – sorry, would you mind spelling that for me.
5 Is there any particular animal we should try and see on the coast?
6 So I suppose you have to get up at dawn?

Exercise 7

1 F
2 A
3 E
4 D
5 C
6 B

UNIT 7

Page 94

GETTING STARTED

Exercise 2

1 A
2 C
3 C
4 B
5 A
6 A, B and C

Exercise 3

3

Track 040

Narrator: Speaker 1
I love my food, but I was worried about food miles – you know, how far food has travelled before it reaches my plate, especially things like meat and cheese. It's great that nowadays most things are available on supermarket shelves, but that comes at a cost to the environment, right? Now, I mostly eat what's in season – either I've planted it myself or I buy it from a nearby market. It's hard sometimes because I can't always have what I want, when I want it, but I'm pleased I'm doing my bit to save the planet, and I'm sure I'm eating more healthily too.

Page 95

Exercise 4

1 F
2 E
3 C
4 B
5 G

Track 041

Narrator: Speaker 1

I love my food, but I was worried about food miles – you know, how far food has travelled before it reaches my plate, especially things like meat and cheese. It's great that nowadays most things are available on supermarket shelves, but that comes at a cost to the environment, right? Now, I mostly eat what's in season – either I've planted it myself or I buy it from a nearby market. It's hard sometimes because I can't always have what I want, when I want it, but I'm pleased I'm doing my bit to save the planet, and I'm sure I'm eating more healthily too.

Narrator: Speaker 2

I remember my mum would always give me large plates of food. At least I thought she did, but when I went to university and compared what I was eating to my friends' portion sizes, I realised they hadn't been big after all. For me, it was more about having a small appetite. I had some problems with my health and I found out I was lacking in certain vitamins because I wasn't eating enough oily fish. I'm changing my diet slightly and, in the meantime, my doctor has recommended some tablets to help with nutrition.

Narrator: Speaker 3

I used to be a food critic so I was eating out in expensive restaurants on a regular basis. Of course, it was great as I was eating good food – most of the time – without having to pay for it, but it can get rather tedious after a while. For example, I've never been keen on rich, cream-based food, and I had to eat a lot of that. I'm retired now and I'm happy about this because I was having too many sweet things, like pastries, at the end of meals. I've cut those out of my diet completely now and I feel much better for it.

Narrator: Speaker 4

I used to eat out a lot because of my job as a salesman. It was fun to start with; my expenses were paid for by the company so I ate in high-end restaurants. But even though I tried to eat a balanced diet, with lots of vitamins and minerals, and limit the number of savoury snacks I consumed, I still started to gain weight. A close friend, who works at my local market, told me she eats smaller portions, but I'm not sure I could do that. Instead, I finish eating before I'm full because I know it can take up to thirty minutes for my body to realise I'm not hungry anymore.

Narrator: Speaker 5

Speaker 5: I used to have some difficulties swallowing because of a problem with my throat. It meant that for a while I hardly ate anything that needed a lot of chewing and had to stick to soft things, like potato and eggs. I was worried I'd go off my food. I've actually been told that I should eat bigger portions because I've got a fast metabolism and burn off a lot of calories. I invested in a blender and made a generous amount of healthy soup which I had about four or five times a day. It was a bit boring, but at least I could consume the quantity my body needed, without it being in too much pain.

VOCABULARY

Exercise 1

1 savoury
2 full
3 in season
4 vitamins
5 appetite
6 gone off
7 stick to
8 portions

Exercise 2

1 gone off
2 vitamins
3 savoury
4 appetite
5 stick to
6 portions
7 full
8 in season

Page 96

GRAMMAR

Exercise 1

1 B
2 C
3 A

Exercise 2

1 <u>could go</u>
2 <u>didn't have</u>
3 <u>hadn't eaten</u>
1 the past perfect (B)
2 the past simple (C)
3 could (A)

Exercise 3

A I wish you would stop borrowing my clothes = Box 2
B I hope the food will be good tonight. = Box 4
C I wish I were a famous chef. = Box 1
D I regret not going to the restaurant last night. = Box 3

Exercise 4

2 It was great seeing you yesterday and I <u>hope</u> to see you again soon.
3 I regret <u>not</u> choosing the pasta dish. It looks delicious.
4 I wish I <u>could</u> come to dinner with you tomorrow but I already have other plans.
5 I really wish that person at the other table <u>would talk</u> more quietly. It's driving me up the wall.
6 I was in Venice last week and had trouble ordering in a restaurant. If only I <u>could</u> speak Italian.
7 I wish I <u>had paid</u> more attention to the teacher yesterday. I don't understand any of this.

Exercise 5

1 wish I had done
2 I had applied for
3 regret not learning
4 If only I was / were
5 wished they hadn't tried
6 I had eaten less

Exercise 6

Example answers:

Jake: I regret not saying anything, but I thought the aubergine was too salty. I'm sorry. I didn't want to upset you. Not only that but the oil was rancid.

Kristi: You should have told me. I wish I hadn't given you the oil. I thought it was off but thought you wouldn't notice.

Jake: Why's that?

Kristi: Well, I wish I'd mentioned it earlier, but I don't think you're a very good cook.

Page 97

READING

Exercise 1

The photos all show poisonous plants or animals.

Exercise 2

The writer feels nervous about eating pufferfish.

READING AND USE OF ENGLISH PART 3 TRAINING

Exercise 3

Answers to tips

1 -ly
2 adjective
3 -less

Answers to gaps

1 Recently
2 enthusiastic
3 harmless

Exercise 4

4 noun – ability
5 noun – length
6 adverb – widely
7 adjective – unaware
8 noun – ease

Exercise 5

1 Students' own answers.

2 *Suggested answer:* Because the guide knows that as long as the dish is prepared carefully, it isn't harmful. This is confirmed in the final line of the first paragraph *'The guide reassured me though and said that as long as the preparation is carried out carefully, fugu is quite delicious and harmless.'*
3 Students' own answers

Page 98

PUSH YOURSELF C1

Exercise 1

1 something is true

Exercise 2

A inevitably
B apparently
C ultimately
D remarkably
E supposedly

Exercise 3

1 Ultimately
2 Apparently
3 Remarkably
4 Supposedly
5 Inevitably

Track 042

1 Ultimately, it's the food industry who have the money and who will therefore drive the development of genetically modified food.
2 Apparently, the colour of your plate influences the amount of food you put on it and therefore eat. While I can see this might be the case, I won't be convinced until I see more evidence.
3 Remarkably, I actually lost weight when I started eating dessert from a spoon made with zinc. I'd been doubtful at first but realised after a while, I'd cut down on sugar consumption.
4 Supposedly, the new chef is a scientific genius, but I can't see how combining sweet ice cream with a savoury meat pie is ever going to work!
5 Inevitably, the government will have to tackle growing concerns over the link between processed food and obesity. Rising rates of related illnesses simply cannot be ignored.

Exercise 4

See pronunciation box on page 98

Page 99

LISTENING PART 2 TRAINING

Exercise 3

1 *waitress* is incorrect because this was Lucy's job during her studies.
2 *analyst for a global chocolate company* is incorrect because it exceeds the word limit.
3 *analyser* is incorrect because it doesn't use the same word as in the recording.

Exercise 4

1 analyst

Exercise 5

Suggested answers:

2 a negative aspect of Lucy's job
3 a positive aspect of Lucy's job
4 a person / group of people
5 something negative about the information on food packaging
6 Lucy's attitude to processed foods
7 a negative aspect of the production process

Exercise 6

2 processes
3 technology
4 scientists
5 complicated
6 avoid
7 soil

Track 043

Lucy: My job is varied and no two days are the same. In addition to developing flavours, which can be unbelievably difficult to get right at times, there are a range of issues relating to processes that I have to work on every day. Occasionally, there are a few problems with suppliers but, as we've developed good working relationships with them, these are rare.
People often ask me about the perks of being a food scientist. They presume that, as a food scientist, I get to eat lots of delicious food but we actually have a group of taste testers who do this for us. For me, it's more about the technology, which makes all the difference when analysing food. There's quite a lot of travelling involved, visiting clients, and I really enjoy that aspect of the work too, though it's not what motivates me the most.
Speaking of travel, our department is embarking on a three-week worldwide research trip in September. A few people I work with are travelling to Asia to speak to the cacao farmers there and find out more about how they grow and harvest their crop. I'm off to South America to meet scientists and discuss new ways of working, which I hope will be really beneficial. I'm also hoping to visit North America as part of the trip to meet suppliers, although this hasn't been confirmed yet.
Next year, I'm moving more into the nutritional side of things and I'm really looking forward to the challenge. For this, I'll need to analyse the content of food to establish its nutritional value so that it can be included on food labels. I know not everyone looks at these when buying food in the supermarket as they can seem a little complicated, but I think it's important to display the information.
I'll also be working with a range of processed foods and researching ways to make them healthier. Generally, as I prefer to cook everything fresh, I avoid eating processed food as much as I can but I've tried one or two things I really like and my flatmate adores those ready-made soups you can get in the supermarket.
One of my colleagues works on the agricultural side of things. We always joke about it being a dirty job, but it's very important. He spends a lot of time analysing different chemicals and how they affect crop growth. He recently found that, as a result of a strong chemical substance used by a crop grower, there was an issue with the soil. As a result of this, production had to be stopped for six months. I think what he does is closely related to conservation and environmental science. It's not an area that I want to get into at the moment but in the future, who knows?

VOCABULARY

Exercise 2

1 C
2 E
3 B
4 A
5 F
6 D

Exercise 3

1 **dis**like
2 **re**placed
3 **ir**responsible
4 **un**acceptable
5 **il**legal
6 **im**polite

Page 100

SPEAKING

Exercise 1

2 value for money
3 service
4 location
5 decor
6 ambience
7 hygiene

Exercise 3

1 the interior
2 reasonably priced
3 specialises in Mediterranean food
4 efficient
5 situated

GRAMMAR

Exercise 1

Sentence **1**

A False
B True
C True

Sentence **2**

A True
B False
C False (first part is in the past, second part is in the present)

Exercise 2

Suggested answers:

1 If Tonya were a better cook, she would have attempted to make a dessert. / If Tonya hadn't been (such) a terrible cook, she would have attempted to make a dessert.
2 If Rebecca hadn't been in Japan, she wouldn't have tried the pufferfish.
3 If Peter didn't have / hadn't had an allergy, he would have eaten the nut cake.
4 If Kim had realised the meat was off, she wouldn't have used it to cook with.
5 If Leonardo hadn't eaten so much ice cream, he wouldn't feel sick.

Page 101

WRITING PART 2: LETTER / EMAIL TRAINING

Exercise 2

What kind of restaurant did you go to?
What was the food like?
Who did you invite and how did it go?

Exercise 3

1 A
2 B
3 B
4 C
5 B
6 A
7 A
8 C
9 B
10 C

Exercise 4

1 G
2 E
3 A
4 B
5 C
6 D
7 F

Used at the beginning: 2/E, 4/B, 5/C, 7/F
Used at the end: 1/G, 3/A, 5/C, 6/D

Page 102

EXAM FOCUS
READING AND USE OF ENGLISH PART 3

1 throughout
2 originally
3 poisonous
4 unlike
5 illnesses
6 rapidly
7 dishonest
8 growth

Page 103

WRITING PART 2: LETTER / EMAIL

Model answer

Hi Sonya,

Great to hear from you! I'd be glad to tell you more about the surprise meal I've organised for my sister's graduation next week.

We're planning to go to the new Italian restaurant in the city centre, just around the corner from the main square. It's an ideal spot because they have two large function rooms which seat up to thirty people each. This was one of the reasons why I chose it actually. I've also heard great things about the food and they have both gluten-free and vegan menus, which is perfect for us!

I'm a little concerned about my sister finding out. I sent the invitations out online via a special group I set up on social media. I just hope nobody accidentally posts or shares anything about it on their own timelines that she might see. I've told everyone to be careful so I'm sure it'll be fine.

Let's catch up soon! I'd love to hear all your news.

Speak soon,
Alicia

LISTENING PART 2

1 geography
2 charity
3 villagers (preparing food)
4 retired
5 delicious
6 doctor
7 November
8 unhealthy eating
9 *In Season*
10 recipes

Track 044

Narrator: You will hear a chef called Tobias Stewart talking about his career and new book. For questions 1–10, complete the sentences with a word or short phrase.

Tobias: Hi, my name's Tobias Stewart and I'm here today to talk about my experiences as a chef and to talk a little bit about my new book.

It all started when I was choosing what to do at university. I'd intended to study history, having always loved how the past influences the present. I decided to go for geography in the end though – my uncle was an environmental consultant and he got me interested in the importance of conservation.

As part of my course, I'd taken an internship in Hungary and was planning to go back after I'd graduated but it wasn't to be. I looked for opportunities closer to home but I couldn't find anything paid at the time, so I offered my support to a charity that sent me to Africa where I stayed for six months.

There, I helped local farming communities with new farming techniques. I spent quite a bit of time with a local guide. He was really knowledgeable, and I learned a lot from him about harvesting fruits. We picked papayas together when they were ripe. In the evenings, I used to watch the villagers preparing food and was fascinated by their understanding of flavours and ingredients. It was then that I realised I wanted a change of career.

When I returned home, my cousin put me in touch with a chef he knew and I begged him to give me a job in his new restaurant. Initially, I found it exhausting – I hadn't realised he'd want me there at 7 am, hours before the restaurant actually opened. But I'd found my passion and took over from him seven years later after he retired to spend more time with his family.

I remember not long after that, a food critic arrived during a busy service. He was fierce – his last review had closed a restaurant because he'd reported that the starter had been too salty, and that the meat in the main course was too tough. I was nervous; however, on the night we pulled it off and the opinion he gave in one word was 'delicious'.

As I said, the hours are long, and some friends find it hard to understand that I'm not available in the evenings or at weekends. Luckily, I married a doctor who accepts that being a chef isn't a nine to five job, but I know another chef, whose partner is a finance manager, and for them it's a real struggle.

It was following my trip to Thailand to research the latest menu for my second restaurant, The Spices of Life, that I decided to write a book about the different cuisines I'd been exposed to there. The trip lasted for about three months and I started writing when I returned in February. If it hadn't been for the opening of my restaurant, I'd have completed it by August.

Finally, though, I got it done in November, exactly a year after my trip.

The book centres around dishes which are both full of flavour and healthy. I think chefs have a responsibility not to go on reality TV which is all about ratings in my opinion, but instead to fight the problem of unhealthy eating at all costs. I know many disagree and think it's about making money, but I don't go along with that line of thought at all.

Originally, I wanted to call my book *Good Taste*, but there was already a cookery book with the same name. I ended up calling it *In Season*, which I think is a really nice title. My publisher wanted me to call it *Green Food*, because I use a lot of that in my cooking, but the sound of that wasn't very appealing, I thought.

At the book signing we're giving away three signed copies to three lucky competition winners. To be in with a chance, simply sign up for my weekly blogpost which you can find on my website. You can also find the latest recipes, which are available to download for free.

Well, I think that's all from me …

REAL WORLD

Page 105

Exercise 3

Text A

1 mouth-watering cuisine
2 generous portions

Text B

3 breathtaking views
4 foodies

Text C

5 being (incredibly) hospitable
6 genuine dining experiences

Exercise 4

1 C
2 D
3 B
4 A

Exercise 5

1
1 of us
2
2 the sound of
3 of the house
4 not allergic to
3
5 I ordered
6 same again
4
7 credit card
8 tip included

Track 045

Narrator: 1 Asking for a table

Waiter: Good evening, madam. Have you already booked a table?

Marianne: No, I haven't but I was wondering if you could squeeze us in?

Waiter: How many of you are there?

Marianne: There's four of us.

Waiter: Yes, of course. Follow me. Is the table next to the window ok?

Narrator: 2 Asking about the menu

Waiter: Are you ready to order?

Marianne: Almost. I like the sound of the Moussaka, but I wanted to know if it's suitable for vegetarians?

Waiter: I'm afraid not but the Briam is. It's an oven-baked dish of mixed vegetables which I highly recommend.

Marianne: Is that a speciality of the house?

Waiter: Yes, it is and very delicious. Do you have any allergies?

Marianne: No. I'm not allergic to anything but my friend is gluten intolerant. He can't eat wheat.

Waiter: Right. Well, for your friend I can recommend the …

Narrator: 3 Talking about dietary requirements

Marianne: Excuse me, I think this might be someone else's. It's not what I ordered.

Waiter: Oh, I'm very sorry, madam, let me take it back to the kitchen and change it.

Marianne: Thank you. Oh, and I'm sorry, but my cutlery is a little dirty. Could you bring me a clean knife, please?

Waiter: Yes, of course. Is there anything else? Would you like any more drinks?

Marianne: Yes. The same again for me, please. Plus, a jug of tap water.

Waiter: Certainly, madam, I'll be right back with the correct dish, a clean knife and the drinks.

Narrator: 4 Asking about payment

Waiter: Can I take your plates away?

Marianne: Yes. Thank you. The food was excellent. Could we pay separately, if that's ok?

Waiter: Of course. I can bring you separate bills if you like? How do you wish to pay?

Marianne: Is it possible to pay by credit card?

Waiter: Yes, we accept all major credit cards. Here you go, madam.

Marianne: Thank you. Is the tip included?

Waiter: No, it isn't. It's up to you how much you would like to leave.

Marianne: OK, thank you …

UNIT 8

Page 107

LISTENING PART 3 TRAINING

Exercise 2

1 economical (H)
2 schedule (B)
3 individual needs (G)
4 assistance (E)
5 boosted; developed (C, F)

Exercise 3

1 D
2 H
3 G
4 B
5 F

Track 046

Narrator: Speaker 1

I work as a sales manager for an international company, so learning a language was vital for me to do my job properly. I decided to learn Chinese online having spoken to a friend who was telling me about how much she improved her language skills after doing a 4-week intensive course online. I thought it would be difficult to find a good teacher, but I was really surprised to see just how many there were. This meant that I could select the teacher that was right for me and I ended up having over 30 hours of lessons.

Narrator: Speaker 2

I have always struggled with languages and I was worried that I would end up failing my French exam. My teacher suggested that I try doing extra classes online to help with the preparation. I thought it was a great idea, even if I'm not very good at using computers. Being a student, I wasn't sure if I could afford it, but it turned out to be much less than it would have been if I'd gone to the language centre in town. In the end, I passed my exam, so it was definitely worthwhile.

Narrator: Speaker 3

I've always been passionate about learning languages. I'm fluent in English, Spanish, French and Italian, and I've just completed a one-to-one German course online. I really enjoyed the fact that during the lessons we were able to work on the problems that were specific to me, rather than more general issues. I still go to language classes at the local college close to where I live. These are great because you have the chance to meet and interact with other language learners, which I think is important for developing language skills.

Narrator: Speaker 4

One of the best things about learning a language online is how convenient it is. I found a really good Italian teacher who was based just outside Naples in southern

Italy. As a full-time teacher myself, it was always difficult getting to classes. This isn't an issue with online learning as I'm able to book lessons at a time when I'm not teaching. It was quite expensive, though. It worked out at around 30 euros per lesson, but I learned a lot from my teacher so it was certainly value for money. I just need to build up my vocabulary more.

Narrator: Speaker 5

I recently retired from my job as a doctor and I was looking for a new hobby. I have a few Brazilian friends and so I decided to learn Portuguese online. I was a little nervous at first as I'm not exactly an expert in using technology. It was interesting – the more I learned the language, the better I became at getting my laptop to do what I want it to! My friends in Brazil have been really supportive, too, and I can now write them an email telling them all about my day. They write back to me in English so I guess it's a kind of language exchange.

GRAMMAR

Exercise 1

Suggested answers:

offered, bought, brought, lent, threw, passed, found, ordered

Exercise 2a

2 lend someone some money
3 buy someone a present / a meal
4 cook someone a meal
5 tell someone a story
6 sing someone a song
7 do someone a favour

Exercise 2b

Phrases with *to*	Phrases with *for*
forward an email to someone lend some money to someone tell a story to someone sing a song to someone	buy a present for someone cook a meal for someone do a favour for someone

Exercise 3

1 bought, for
2 lent, to
3 pre-ordered, for
4 forwarded, to

Exercise 4

1 ✓
2 Is there any chance you could lend me your mobile phone? / lend your mobile phone **to** me?
3 I can't believe you cooked that meal for me using only a microwave – it was really good!
4 ✓
5 I downloaded the instruction manual for my grandfather.
6 ✓
7 ✓
8 My phone tells ~~to~~ me the temperature inside and outside my home.

Page 108

VOCABULARY

Exercise 1

Suggested answer:

Aziz's boss may have been delighted that Aziz's screenshot helped the engineer to solve the problem. However, they may also have been puzzled as to why Aziz made screenshots of company data in the first place.

Track 047

Aziz: A few years ago, I got a job during the summer holidays while I was a student. It was doing some office admin work, basically filling in spreadsheets and that kind of thing. It was a really small company, and maybe just to save money, the boss didn't always upgrade the software. Anyway, one day the inevitable happened, the office's computer system died, and all the files – you know, customer contact details, invoices, etc. – it all went. They got an engineer in to see if he could get it back, but the problem is that no-one ever made backups of all the files. And so he didn't even know the names of the files he needed to find. But a breakthrough came when I realised that I might be able to help. When I started at the office, I had taken a screenshot of loads of the filenames in a list, just to learn my way round. For some reason I'd emailed it to myself, so I still had it. Anyway, to cut a long story short, the engineer was able to use my list and get at least some of the data back. It just goes to show – always back your files up!

Exercise 2

backup
breakthrough
filename
screenshot
spreadsheet
upgrade

Exercise 3

1 upgrade
2 spreadsheet
3 screenshot
4 breakthrough
5 backup
6 filename

Exercise 4

1 bug
2 icon
3 browse
4 run
5 bookmark
6 network
7 crash

Exercise 5

1 icon (old)
2 bookmark (new)
3 crashed (new)
4 network (old)
5 icon (new)
6 browsing (new)
7 bug (old)
8 run (old)
9 bookmark (old)
10 bug (new)

Page 109

WRITING

Exercise 1a

1 formal
2 informal
3 formal
4 informal
5 informal
6 formal

Exercise 1b

Students' own answers

Exercise 2

	Formal	Informal
Beginning	Sentence 3	Sentence 5
Requesting	Sentence 6	Sentence 2
Suggesting	Sentence 8	Sentence 9
Apologising	Sentence 1	Sentence 7
Complaining	Sentence 4	Sentence 10

Exercise 3

B

Exercise 4

1 C
2 D
3 F
4 B
5 H
6 A
7 G
8 E
9 I

Page 110

READING AND USE OF ENGLISH PART 6 TRAINING

Exercise 3

A i
B ii
C i
D ii
E i

Page 111

Exercise 4

1 C
2 G
3 E
4 F
5 D

VOCABULARY

Exercise 1

1a on the cutting edge
1b not the sharpest tool in the box (3rd paragraph): not very intelligent
stand the test of time (final paragraph): be popular for a long time

Exercise 2

fuse – picture 5
light bulb – picture 6
plug – picture 2
rocket – picture 3
steam – picture 1
wires – picture 4

Exercise 3

1 run out of steam
2 pull the plug on something
3 it's not rocket science
4 get your wires crossed
5 have a short fuse
6 have a light-bulb moment

Exercise 4

1 run out of (D)
2 pull the (A)
3 exactly, science (F)
4 getting, crossed (B)
5 a short (C)
6 a, moment (E)

Track 048

Ricardo: Louise?
Louise: Hey, what's up?
Ricardo: You know how you're really smart, intelligent, and –
Louise: Yeah, yeah, alright! What do you want?
Ricardo: Well, someone's just sent me a link to this quiz.
Louise: A sort of brain-teaser, is it?
Ricardo: Kind of. So, basically, you've got these six pictures. And there's an idiom connected to each one.
Louise: Let's have a look then....
Ricardo: So, what have we got – looks like a machine. I can't think of an idiom there.
Louise: Is that steam coming out the top?
Ricardo: Got it! Yeah, this is what you do after you've been at work for a whole five minutes – you run out of steam.
Louise: Very funny!
Ricardo: You do. You stop work and start doing quizzes!
Louise: Alright! What's next: plugs, sockets, take the plug out...
Ricardo: Not really an idiom though, is it?
Louise: No, guess not. What about pull the plug on something?
Ricardo: That's the one! I always think, you know, if you pull the plug on something, like you stop doing it, that it comes from a bath plug.
Louise: Pull the plug, let all the water out.
Ricardo: Yeah.
Louise: Or it could be the idea that if you pull out an electric plug, then it would stop working.
Ricardo: Hey, we're doing well, aren't we? Geniuses!
Louise: Yeah, but come on, it's not exactly rocket science is it? Hey – did you see what I just did there?
Ricardo: What?
Louise: Not exactly rocket science!
Ricardo: Oh, another answer!
Louise: Yeah, come on, Ricardo. Keep up!
Ricardo: What about all those cables? What could that be?
Louise: Cables... or wires.
Ricardo: Oh, I know, getting your wires crossed.
Louise: Right, for like, a misunderstanding. That must have come from, like in the olden days, if you wanted to make a phone call, you had to phone an operator and they would literally plug your line into someone else's, to connect your line to theirs.
Ricardo: Right, so getting your wires crossed would be like, being connected to the wrong person, so you wouldn't know what they were talking about.
Louise: Yeah, makes sense.
Ricardo: What about the fuses? Oh I know, to have a short fuse.
Louise: Have a short fuse. Like our supervisor, who gets angry at the smallest thing!
Ricardo: I was thinking more like you, actually.
Louise: Hilarious!
Ricardo: OK, one more to get then. With this bulb. Come on, Louise, we need a moment of inspiration here, a sudden brilliant idea.
Louise: A light-bulb moment, you mean!
Ricardo: A light-bulb moment, that's it, look at you. Not as daft as you look, are you?
Louise: Watch it!
Ricardo: Oh well, now that we've done them all, I guess we should get back to those spreadsheets.
Louise: What? Don't be ridiculous – it's coffee time!
Ricardo: Oh, alright, go on then.

Exercise 5

1 got my wires crossed
2 has a short fuse
3 isn't (exactly) rocket science
4 pulled the plug
5 a light-bulb moment
6 ran out of steam

Page 112

GRAMMAR

Exercise 1

1 A
2 C
3 B
4 A
5 B
6 C

Exercise 2

	Present	Past
Certainly true	**1** *He must be stuck in traffic.*	**4** He must have been delayed.
Certainly not true	**5** He can't be making a phone call.	**3** He can't have gone to another room because they're all full.
Possibly true	**6** He could be in the wrong meeting room.	**2** He may have gone to the bathroom prior to the meeting.

Exercise 3

Suggested answers:

1 can't have seen
2 must have forgotten
3 might / may / could be
4 must have received
5 can't possibly be
6 must be held up / must have got held up

Exercise 4

1 must be stuck
2 might not have been
3 have run out of
4 might have pulled the plug

PUSH YOURSELF C1

Exercise 1

1 It looks as though the software installation might have failed.
2 My laptop can't possibly be fully charged yet.
3 Research suggests that the drug might be effective.
4 Is there a possibility that the device might need an update?
5 In all likelihood, the machinery must have been damaged in transit.
6 Scientists believe they may well have made a major breakthrough.

Page 113

SPEAKING PART 1 TRAINING

Exercise 1

1 more personal topics
2 no
3 both

Exercise 2

1 B
2 D
3 A
4 C

Track 049

1 Well, I'm a student, so I find that my phone is really handy for making notes or taking photographs of slides during lectures. I suppose the other main thing I do with it is read the latest news or catch up with my friends on social media, especially before going to bed.
2 I'm not sure I could to be honest. I'm so reliant on my mobile phone, whether it's keeping in touch with my friends or using the latest apps to help me with learning French, that I can't really imagine my life without it.
3 Yes, I do. I travel abroad a lot and having all my favourite tracks with me on the go is a lifesaver. The only issue I have is that I'm always running out of storage space, so I can't store all of my albums on my phone.
4 Actually, no. I don't use my phone very much so I'm not too bothered whether it's the fastest or has a cutting-edge camera, for example. As long as I can make and receive calls, then I'm happy.

Exercise 3

1 notes
2 slides
3 it
4 read
5 media

Track 050

Well, I'm a student, so I find that my phone is really handy for making notes or taking photographs of slides during lectures.
I suppose the other main thing I do with it is read the latest news or catch up with my friends on social media, especially before going to bed.

Track 051

I'm not sure I could to be honest. I'm so reliant on my mobile phone, whether it's keeping in touch with my friends or using the latest apps to help me with learning French, that I can't really imagine my life without it.

Exercise 5

Suggested answers:

Yes, I do. I travel abroad a lot and having all my favourite tracks with me on the go is a lifesaver. The only issue I have is that I'm always running out of storage space, so I can't store all of my albums on my phone.

Track 052

Yes, I do. I travel abroad a lot and having all my favourite tracks with me on the go is a lifesaver. The only issue I have is that I'm always running out of storage space, so I can't store all of my albums on my phone.

Page 114

EXAM FOCUS

READING AND USE OF ENGLISH PART 6

1 A
2 G
3 E
4 F
5 C
6 D

EXAM CHECK

The texts in Reading and Use of English Part 6 are usually articles from magazines, newspapers or informative texts. The text will contain six gaps and you must choose from a list of seven sentences the sentence that fits each gap. There is one sentences that you don't need to use. You can't use one sentence more than once.

Page 115

LISTENING PART 3

EXAM CHECK

1 False (five people)
2 False (for about 30 seconds)
3 True
4 False (three options)
5 True

1 C
2 E
3 H
4 F
5 G

Track 053

Narrator: You will hear five short extracts in which people are talking about their experience of going for a ride in a driverless car. For Speakers 1–5, choose from the list (A–H) how each speaker felt about their experience. Use the letters only once. There are three extra letters which you do not need to use.
Narrator: Speaker 1
I've always been fascinated by driverless cars. I'd seen loads of pictures of them in magazines and I always thought they looked really cool. I certainly wasn't disappointed when I saw one in real life. Prior to getting in, I wasn't sure if I would feel as safe as I did in a regular car, which didn't surprise the engineer with me who said that this was a normal feeling to have. I was interested to see how it would react when it came up against obstacles, like pedestrians or traffic lights and, by the end of the drive, I was happy that we didn't hit anyone or crash into anything.
Narrator: Speaker 2
I've always been slightly against the development of driverless cars, mainly because I love being able to control a car myself. It's not that I didn't enjoy the ride, quite the opposite in fact; it was really comfortable and incredibly secure, which was something I wasn't expecting to feel before getting in. What I didn't realise was how much less risky it is than having human drivers. As well as telling me about how straightforward they are to operate, the engineer also told me the price.
It wasn't cheap but that's hardly surprising, I suppose, given just how much money the car and software industries have invested in driverless technology.
Narrator: Speaker 3
I'll be the first to admit that I'm not very good at using technology and the concept of driverless cars had always terrified me. I was invited to try it out by a friend of mine who works at one of the companies developing driverless cars. While driving along, he did his best to convince me that they're completely safe and that I should be enthusiastic about the benefits it would bring to society. Before all that though, they need to work on making the car look more attractive, as this didn't impress me at all. If they fixed this, I might then be persuaded to buy one in the future.
Narrator: Speaker 4
The number of accidents caused by human error while driving is really alarming.

So I've always felt confident that driverless cars would be safer. And having now been in a driverless car myself, I've got to say that I can see a very bright future for road users. My experience was like being driven around by the most considerate driver you can imagine. So if there are to be more driverless cars in the future, I think we can expect a transport system that's in everyone's best interests, with fewer delays and less vehicle pollution. So I'm definitely optimistic.

Narrator: Speaker 5

Before I went for a ride myself, I did quite a bit of research into the driverless car industry as a whole. What I found was that the level of investment that's gone into getting the whole thing started is absolutely staggering. Amazing really. I mean, obviously they wouldn't have done it if they didn't think the whole thing had great potential. But unless there are millions of driverless cars on our roads in a relatively short space of time, I can't see that they're going to get any of it back. Furthermore, if the cars don't sell, then the development of driverless technology will go down as one of the most unwise enterprises of all time!

SPEAKING PART 1

Students' own answers

EXAM CHECK

1 The examiner
2 with
3 don't need
4 two

Page 117

REAL WORLD

Exercise 3

1 must-have
2 get from A to B
3 lost your bearings
4 star ratings

Exercise 5

1 Ethan cannot download images from his camera to his laptop.
2 Jasmine asks Ethan to restart his laptop.
3 Jasmine recommends that Ethan installs the latest software on his laptop.

Track 054

Jasmine: Hello sir, how may I help?

Ethan: Oh hello, I bought this digital camera here yesterday. But the thing is, it doesn't seem to be working properly.

Jasmine: Oh dear.

Ethan: I thought it might be damaged, so I thought you might be able to take a look at it.

Jasmine: Sure. So, what appears to be the issue?

Ethan: Well, it takes photos, which I can view on the screen without a problem. But the issue is that when I connect the camera to my laptop, nothing happens. So I can't get it to download the photos from the camera.

Jasmine: I see. Have you tried restarting the laptop?

Ethan: Yes, I tried that, but it didn't make any difference. And I checked out the troubleshooting menu online, but I couldn't find anything that worked. So I guess it must have a fault. The camera's still under warranty, so can I exchange it?

Jasmine: Well, I just need to see if I can get to the bottom of it myself first… Did anything else happen when you connected the camera?

Ethan: Yes, it did. I received an error message on the screen of my camera. It said 'this device isn't compatible with the camera; please connect another device'. I don't really want to buy another laptop, because there's nothing wrong with this one.

Jasmine: How long have you had the laptop?

Ethan: About six years.

Jasmine: And have you ever updated the software?

Ethan: Well, no, not recently

Jasmine: OK, well, what I'd recommend is that you install the latest software on your laptop. And then hopefully, that should do the trick.

Ethan: OK, great, I'll give that a go and hope for the best.

Exercise 6

1 E
2 A
3 F
4 B
5 D
6 C

PROGRESS CHECK 3

Page 118

Exercise 1

1 at
2 by
3 on
4 as
5 from
6 of
7 with
8 of

Exercise 2

1 Charles Dickens, who wrote the book "Great Expectations", died in 1870.
2 There used to be two lions in the zoo, both of which were male.
3 The concert, which I have tickets for, starts at 7 pm.
4 John Forrest, who(m) I met last year, is an award-winning actor.
5 The dishes, all of which are suitable for vegetarians, use ingredients grown on the local farm.
6 Unfortunately, the market, which I buy my food from, has closed down.

Exercise 3

1 endangered
2 environmental
3 renewable
4 astonishing
5 coastal
6 sightseeing

Exercise 4

1 dislike
2 unaware
3 reapply
4 irresponsible
5 impolite
6 illegal

Exercise 5

1 If I had known that you were hungry, I would <u>have</u> prepared dinner.
2 I wish I hadn't <u>eaten</u> all that ice-cream. I feel really sick now.
3 I really regret not <u>going</u> to the restaurant with my friends last night. Apparently they met Ed Sheeran!
4 I would love to go on a road trip around Europe. <u>If only</u> I could drive!
5 If I hadn't gone to the concert last night, I wouldn't <u>be</u> so tired now.
6 I <u>hope</u> the meal will be good tonight.
7 I wish the man would <u>stop</u> smoking. It's so annoying.
8 I can't understand anything on the menu, sadly. If only I <u>could</u> speak French.

Page 119

Exercise 6

1 portions
2 gone off
3 vitamins
4 in season
5 savoury
6 appetite
7 sticking to
8 hygiene
9 cuisine
10 split the bill

Exercise 7

1 They must have bought their son a new car.
2 Stephanie might be cooking a meal for him because it's his birthday.
3 He couldn't have written her a song because he can't play any musical instruments.

4 Mary can't have lent her friend some money because she doesn't have any herself.
5 Simon must have forgotten to send me the email.

Exercise 8

1 must have forgotten
2 might have been backed up
3 (might/may/could) be able to fix
4 (might/may/could) be making

Exercise 9

1 up
2 back
3 bugs
4 short
5 pull the plug
6 compatible
7 load
8 breakthrough

UNIT 9

Page 120

GETTING STARTED

Exercise 1

1 1 Mandarin Chinese, 2 Spanish, 3 English
2 1 China (approx. 1.4 billion), 2 India (approx. 1.3 billion), 3 U.S.A. (approx. 325 million)
3 56.7 °C (134.1 °F) – recorded at Death Valley, California, USA in 1913
4 (African) Elephant which can weigh 4,500–5,900 kg
5 122 years, 164 days (Jeanne Calment – 1875–1997)

READING

Exercise 1

A Tornado rips through rural farmland
B Stormy tropics cut off travellers
C Double rainbow delights in daylight
D Sinking soil as earthquake strikes
E Selfie-takers flee as volcano erupts
F Falling amphibians cause confusion
G Coastal darkness lit up by breath-taking night sky

Page 121

Exercise 3

Falling amphibians cause confusion

READING AND USE OF ENGLISH PART 2 TRAINING

Exercise 5

1 by / at
2 are
3 whom
4 of
5 with
6 to
7 them
8 have

VOCABULARY

Exercise 1

Today
1 Late morning / afternoon: rain
2 Temperature: above average
Tomorrow
3 Morning: rain moving north
4 Lunchtime: storm
5 Afternoon: winds up to 65 km/h
Day after tomorrow
6 Afternoon: hazy sunshine
7 Night: damp and misty

Track 055

Today

We can expect a gusty start to the day with wind speeds reaching 40 kilometres per hour at times. It will cloud over by mid-morning leading to rain which will be persistent through the afternoon, and heavy in places, particularly across the southwest corner of the country. Fortunately, the hard frosts and freezing conditions experienced last week when many lakes froze over will have been replaced by mild temperatures which will be above average for the time of year.

Tomorrow

Brightening up in the west as rain pushes north; however, expect wind speeds to pick up along the northeast coast. There's a possibility of a storm developing around lunchtime, becoming quite violent by mid-afternoon. Gale force winds reaching 65 kilometres per hour are expected to rip through coastal regions where seas will be rough particularly around high tide times. The worst of the wind will have died down by early evening, however, leading to more settled weather overnight.

The day after tomorrow

In the southern hills, dawn will be greeted with dense fog. Please take care if you are on the roads as visibility will be poor. By mid-afternoon, however, the worst of the fog will have lifted, and we can expect some pleasant hazy sunshine. It will remain damp and misty overnight but with improved visibility and, by the time the sun comes up on Friday, we can expect the mist to have completely cleared and the temperatures will have warmed up by the early afternoon.

Exercise 2

persistent rain
mild temperatures
violent storms
gale-force winds
dense fog
poor visibility

Exercise 3

1 over
2 over
3 up
4 up
5 through
6 down
7 up

Exercise 4

Example answer:

Today
A bitterly cold start with dense fog and poor visibility. By late afternoon, the wind will have picked up and it will have clouded over. We can expect heavy rain by early evening and strong winds reaching 30mph.
Tomorrow
Overnight we can expect thunder storms followed by persistent rain all morning. Wind speeds will reach 50mph and there is a risk of floods in some areas. However, after the heavy downpour it will brighten up and temperatures will rise to 20 degrees.
Outlook
The outlook is good. The wind will die out and temperatures will soar. By Friday the weather will be scorching with temperatures set to reach 30 degrees.

Page 122

SPEAKING PARTS 3 AND 4 TRAINING

Exercise 1

A littering
B deforestation
C coastal erosion
D oil spills
E urban sprawl
F toxic waste
G greenhouse gas emissions
H rising sea levels

Exercise 2

1 oil spills
2 urban sprawl
3 deforestation
4 costal erosion
5 littering
6 rising sea levels
7 toxic waste
8 greenhouse gas emissions

SPEAKING PART 3 TRAINING

Exercise 1

1 Not talked about
2 D
3 E
4 C
5 A

Track 056

Examiner: Now I'd like you to talk about something together for about two minutes. Here are some of the issues that affect the environment and a question for you to discuss. First you have some time to look at the task. Now talk to each other about how these issues affect the environment.

Harry: Shall I start?

Emma: Yes, go ahead.

Harry: OK, let's start with this one, oil spills. I think this can really harm the animals that live in and around the sea, such as birds, whose feathers get covered in oil which can prevent them from flying.

Emma: I agree. It's not just birds that are affected, but fish as well. Oil spills can lead to the death of hundreds and thousands of fish which also has a huge impact on the fishing industry as it depends on them to make a living. How about this next one, littering?

Harry: Yes, this is a big problem in my city. People throw litter on the floor or leave it in the street and don't think about the consequences, one of which is the health risks, such as the spreading of bacteria.

Emma: You're right! Not to mention broken glass, which can lead to infections if it cuts the skin.

Harry: Exactly. Shall we move on to the next topic? What about the effect of deforestation on the environment?

Emma: Well, this is a big problem in places like South America. I think that by cutting down large numbers of trees, you reduce the number of green spaces in that area.

Harry: Yes and, in a lot of cases, it can actually cause more harm to the environment because they often burn the trees. What do you think about urban sprawl?

Emma: Well, where I live, many people have moved out of the city centre to the suburbs, and more and more people are driving because the transport isn't as good in these areas.

Harry: It's the same in my city. The traffic is terrible and it often takes me over an hour to reach the city centre. I would love to use public transport but, as you say, it isn't always available, so I use my car instead.

Examiner: Thank you.

Exercise 2

1. Shall I start?, Yes go ahead.
2. How about this next one, littering?
3. You're right!
4. What do you think about urban sprawl?
5. but, as you say, …

Exercise 3

Track 057

It's the same in my city. The traffic is terrible and it often takes me over an hour to reach the city centre. I would love to use public transport but, as you say, it isn't always available, so I use my car instead.

Page 123

Exercise 4

1. as far as I'm concerned …
2. don't you think that …
3. That's a valid point, but …
4. Perhaps we can agree to disagree …
5. Almost (they agree on the top 3.)

Track 058

Examiner: Now you have about a minute to decide which two issues you think are the most serious and why.

Emma: OK, as far as I'm concerned, the two most serious issues are deforestation and oil spills because these are two things that affect animals as well as humans.

Harry: I agree with you about oil spills, but don't you think that urban sprawl is more serious because it affects a wider number of people across the world?

Emma: That's a valid point, but I would argue that deforestation is more dangerous for the planet.

Harry: Perhaps we can agree to disagree on deforestation and urban sprawl. It looks as though we can rule out the other two options, coastal erosion and littering.

Emma: Yes, I think so. They are both important issues but perhaps they aren't as serious as the other three we've already discussed.

Harry: That's true.

Examiner: Thank you.

SPEAKING PART 4 TRAINING

Exercise 1 and 2

1. I've never really **thought** about that**,** but if I **had** to express an **opinion**, I'd say …
2. **Actually,** I've **thought** about **this** before and I think …
3. It's quite **difficult** to **say** but I guess …
4. That's an **interesting question** to answer. I reckon …
5. That's a **difficult question**. Let me **consider** that for a moment. Ok, I think …
6. That's an **interesting question** and something I have **strong views** about. I **firmly believe** …

Track 059

Narrator: 1

Examiner: Is littering a problem where you live?

Emma: I've never really thought about that, but if I had to express an opinion, I'd say …

Narrator: 2

Examiner: Do you think the amount of pollution in cities has increased in recent years?

Harry: Actually, I've thought about this before and I think …

Narrator: 3

Examiner: Some people think that cars should be banned from city centres. Do you agree?

Emma: It's quite difficult to say but I guess …

Narrator: 4

Examiner: Do older people care more about the environment than younger people?

Harry: That's an interesting question to answer. I reckon …

Narrator: 5

Examiner: Do you think it would be possible to recycle everything that people throw away?

Emma: That's a difficult question. Let me consider that for a moment. OK, I think …

Narrator: 6

Examiner: Do you think people should do more to help protect the environment?

Harry: That's an interesting question and something I have strong views about. I firmly believe …

Page 124

GRAMMAR

Exercise 4

1. **A** I think it's more than likely that <u>we will try</u> and get nearer the sun.
   B In all probability, <u>space tourism will become</u> a reality in my lifetime.
   C I'm doubtful though that <u>it will be</u> affordable for the majority of people at first
   D I'm sure <u>it won't be</u> long before the rich and famous …
2. <u>they're going to build</u> a prototype in the near future.
3. <u>engineers are bound to</u> develop a probe that can …
4. <u>We'll have to wait</u> and see if it becomes a reality.
5. in the near future, it won't be long …
6. I'm on the fence …

Exercise 5

1. In all probability, we'll continue to spend vast amounts of money on space exploration.
2. It's more than likely that people will settle on Mars.
3. There's little prospect of finding life on another planet.
4. I'm almost certain that tourists will go to space in my lifetime.

PUSH YOURSELF C1

Exercise 1

1 B
2 D
3 E
4 C
5 A

Page 125

LISTENING

Exercise 2

1 A (photo D)
2 A (photo C)
3 C (photo B)
4 A (photo A)

Exercise 3

4 Challenger Deep

Track 060

Abeer: What about this one. Explorations here are expensive, aren't they?
Omera: Yes. As far as I know, a trip costs on average eight million dollars. Don't you think the expense is outweighed by the scientific benefits though?
Abeer: To be honest, I'm not convinced it is. I can't see the point of exploring somewhere where the probability of finding anything living is pretty much zero. I'm not sure what we can learn from that.
Omera: So, you think it's a complete waste of time?
Abeer: Well, I wouldn't go as far as that, but I think it's far too costly. In my view there are more worthwhile things to spend our money on, above the surface, like hospitals and education, don't you agree?
Omera: Hmm. As a matter of fact, I don't. I think the costs are relatively cheap.
Abeer: Really? How come?
Omera: Well, you need to take into account that the ocean regulates temperatures and drives weather. Not only that, but throughout history it's been a vital source of sustenance, transport and growth. So, as far as I'm concerned, the money is well-spent and the deeper the dive the better!
Abeer: I agree up to a point. OK, we don't have much time …

Exercise 4

1 **Don't** you think
2 I'm **not** convinced it is
3 **total** waste of time
4 as far **as** that
5 **As a matter of fact**
6 How **come**?
7 you need to take **into** account that
8 **as** far as

VOCABULARY

Exercise 1

1 C
2 F
3 D
4 A
5 E
6 B

Exercise 2

1 by far
2 I wouldn't go that far
3 far too
4 As far as I'm concerned,
5 Far from it
6 As far as I know

Page 126

GRAMMAR

Exercise 3

D enthusiastic

Track 061

Josh: Hey Angeline. So, it's an early start in the morning. I think we're heading off at 6am. No more supermarkets or eating out for us for a while. Just think, by this time next week, we'll have caught our own lunch!
Angeline: Hmm, I know. This time tomorrow, we'll be learning about how to keep warm in the wild. I bet by the end of the day we'll have successfully learnt how to build a fire from scratch.
Josh: I hope so, though I'm not sure those are skills I'll be taking advantage of once I get home. I have central heating and a supermarket round the corner! How're you feeling about the expedition?
Angeline: I don't know what to expect to be honest. I'm a bit anxious that I'll have injured myself before the week's out.
Josh: Oh, I'm sure the group leaders will have taken everything into account when they put the trip together.
Angeline: You're right! By the time we get back we're going to have survived on nothing but what we've trapped and cooked ourselves for a whole week.
Josh: I know. I'm impatient to get going. Let's have a look at the itinerary again.

Exercise 4

1 have caught
2 be learning
3 have successfully learnt
4 be taking
5 have injured
6 have taken
7 going to have survived

Exercise 5

1 will have vanished
2 will have developed
3 will be using
4 will have been replaced
5 will be flying

Exercise 6

1 I'll have <u>defeated</u>
2 I'll be <u>deciding</u>
3 I'll probably <u>be</u> suffering
4 I'll <u>have</u> completed
5 I'll <u>have</u> <u>learnt</u>
6 ~~I'll~~ hope I'll have gathered
7 I'll <u>have</u> <u>managed</u>

Page 127

WRITING PART 1 TRAINING

Exercise 3

1 environmental damage
2 environmental damage
3 personal safety
4 economy (writer's own idea)

Exercise 4

A **2**
B **1**
C **4**
D **3**

Exercise 5

Over the years, we have explored more and more of the universe and I don't believe this should end.
One area that has greatly benefited from space exploration is meteorology.
It has been suggested that space exploration is too expensive.
Finally, I think that air travel is now much safer thanks to what we have learnt from exploring space.

Exercise 6

1 meaning that
2 However
3 not to mention
4 not only

The writer disagrees with the statement in the question.

Page 128

EXAM FOCUS
READING AND USE OF ENGLISH PART 2

1 they
2 on
3 between
4 latter
5 under
6 from
7 which / that
8 to

EXAM CHECK

1 eight
2 prepositions
3 example
4 160
5 topics
6 sport

WRITING PART 1

Model answer

The world's most industrialised nations have caused most of the damage to the environment. Therefore, they should take a leading role in preventing further harm. However, countries with a low carbon footprint also have a role to play.

Industrial activity has contaminated water sources all over the world, making access to safe drinking water a challenge for many. Industrial giants must take the most responsibility for this and do more to prevent pollution.

Human greed has also led to many species of animals dying out due to loss of their natural habitats as well as poaching of wildlife for 'trophies'. In this case, all countries have a role to play through inflicting harsher penalties for those who kill endangered species.

The main way of preventing further damage to our planet is through education. Every country can do this in their own way through programmes in schools, posters, TV and newspaper campaigns.

In my opinion, the industrialised nations have the greatest responsibility for protecting the planet in future, although every country should try to avoid causing further damage.

EXAM CHECK

Students' own answers

Page 129

SPEAKING PARTS 3 AND 4

Students' own answers

EXAM CHECK

Part 3

1 False (with the other candidate)
2 True
3 False (you don't need to talk about all of the prompts)

Part 4

4 False (the examiner will ask you questions)
5 True
6 False (you are allowed to disagree with the other candidate)

Page 130

REAL WORLD

Exercise 1

Suggested answers:

Location: city in the state of California (southwest USA)

Population: approx. 4 million

Founded in **1781**

Famous for: Hollywood, beaches (Malibu and Long beach), LAX (Los Angeles International Airport)

Notable sports teams: LA Lakers (basketball), LA Galaxy (soccer), LA Dodgers (Baseball), LA Rams (American football), LA Kings (hockey)

Page 131

Exercise 3

Urban Art

1 gaining popularity
2 ground-breaking exhibitions
3 at the forefront

Theatre and Dance

4 a wealth of talent
5 puts on
6 a lively atmosphere

Hollywood Walk of Fame

7 prominent
8 stage and screen

Exercise 4

1 Green lights (a musical set in a high school)
2 Saturday at 2pm / Sunday at 2pm
3 $150 / pays by credit card

Track 062

Ticket officer: Good afternoon, Tickets For You, Julia speaking. How can I help you?
Martin: Hi there, My name's Martin. I'd like to enquire about ticket availability.
Ticket officer: Sure, do you know the performance you'd like to see?
Martin: Actually, no. I'm visiting Los Angeles with my family in August and I wanted to ask you about what's on.
Ticket officer: OK, let's see… Well, there's *Sunshine*, an award-winning comedy about two people travelling around South America.
Martin: That sounds good!
Ticket officer: It does come with an age limit, though. Attendees must be aged 16 years or over.
Martin: Ah, that's an issue as my wife and I will be with our two children.
Ticket officer: OK, well how about *Green lights*? It's a musical set in a high school, suitable for the whole family.
Martin: That sounds perfect. I'll go for that one, please.
Ticket officer: Great. Due to the school holidays, we do have limited availability in August. What time and day are you looking to book?
Martin: Saturday would be ideal, at 2 pm.
Ticket officer: Unfortunately, the performance on Saturday is sold out. Would Sunday at the same time work?
Martin: Yes, that also works.
Ticket officer: That's great. I should just add that the time is subject to change and we advise all theatre goers to arrive 45 minutes in advance of the start time. Please also note that these tickets are non-refundable.
Martin: That's fine. Will I receive the tickets in advance?
Ticket officer: As you're booking over the phone, you can collect the tickets on the door.
Martin: That's great. How much will that be?
Ticket officer: OK, so for two adults and two children, that comes to a grand total of 150 dollars. How would you like to pay?
Martin: By credit card, please.
Ticket officer: OK, so I just need the long number on the front of the card.
Martin: Sure, it's 4 – 5 – 1 – 2 …

Exercise 5

1 what's on
2 age limit
3 limited availability
4 sold out
5 non-refundable
6 on the door
7 that comes to

Exercise 6

1 age limit
2 non-refundable
3 sold-out
4 that comes to
5 on the door
6 limited availability
7 what's on

UNIT 10

Page 132

LISTENING

Exercise 3

Example questions:
How much does it cost?
How fast do you fall?
What equipment do you need?
Can you breathe easily?
How do you feel before jumping?
During the jump?
Is it scary?
How do you become a skydiver?

What is the training like?
Why do people skydive?
How dangerous is it?
What are the best conditions for skydiving?
How old do you need to be to skydive?

Page 133

Track 063

Kevin: Hello everyone. My name's Kevin and I'm here today to talk about my life as a skydiving instructor.

I went on my very first skydive on my eighteenth birthday and immediately fell in love with it. A few years later, after graduating from university, I decided that I wanted to become a full-time skydiving instructor. To become an instructor, you must be between 18 and 55 years old.

The training is tough, as you might expect. I was required to take an eight-level course, which teaches you everything about skydiving, from how to operate the equipment to dealing with unexpected situations while in the air. When I was jumping, I had to perform a variety of different tasks such as doing ninety degree turns left and right as well as somersaults, which is when you rotate your body 360 degrees forwards or backwards, to show that I was in control of my body and able to regain control after losing stability.

I'll never forget how happy I was when I found out I had passed the course!

The thought of jumping out of a plane from about 4,000 metres is quite a terrifying thought for most people. In fact, this is one of the main reasons that put people off ever considering doing a skydive. I remember the first time I went up in the plane, thinking about how I would be returning to the ground… I almost threw up! However, you must remember that it is incredibly safe. There are loads of safety regulations and checks which are carried out on the equipment before you jump and your instructor will have completed at least 800 jumps to get his or her skydiving licence. Furthermore, in the event of someone fainting, which can happen, there is a small computer, known as an automatic activation device, which monitors the altitude and activates the reserve parachute when it reaches a certain level.

If you're not a qualified skydiver, you will always jump with an instructor, and you'll be strapped to them before getting on the plane. This means that once you've taken off, there's only one way you're returning to the ground, and that's by jumping! There's no changing your mind halfway through, even when the plane doors open and you're staring down at the earth, possibly regretting ever getting into that position in the first place. Your instructor will carry you to the door if necessary. Just remember to relax and enjoy the experience.

As soon as you jump out the plane, you typically freefall for about 60 seconds, reaching speeds of up to 210 kilometres per hour. During this time, don't be surprised if you start to think about some really strange things. On one of my first jumps, I spent about the first 20 seconds worrying whether I had tied my shoelaces together properly in the fear that my shoes would fall off. After freefalling, at about 750 metres, a cord is pulled which opens up the parachute, at which point you then steer down to the landing zone. There is no other feeling quite like the one when you land. In fact, the first thing most people ask me when we land is "how soon can we do it again?"

For those wanting to go skydiving, I have a few final tips for you. The first one is … relax. Remember you are in very safe hands with your instructor. Secondly, make sure you wear comfortable, warm clothing. It can get pretty cold at 4000 metres above the ground. And finally, don't forget to smile when you're having your photo taken in mid-air!

Exercise 5

Suggested answers:

18 and 50 – ages you must be between to become and instructor

360 – degrees you rotate your body to perform a somersault

4,000 – height (in metres) at which you jump out of the plane

800 – number of jumps you need to have completed to get a skydiving license

60 – number of seconds you typically freefall for

750 – height (in metres) at which the parachute is opened

GRAMMAR

Exercise 1

1 having; taken

Track 064

Kevin: For those wanting to go skydiving, I have a few final tips for you. The first one is … relax. Remember you are in very safe hands with your instructor. Secondly, make sure you wear comfortable, warm clothing. It can get pretty cold at 4000 metres above the ground. And finally, don't forget to smile when you're having your photo taken in mid-air!

Exercise 2

1 had / got, repaired
2 have / get, corrected
3 have / get, renewed
4 has / gets, cleaned
5 having / getting, dyed <u>or</u> going to get / have, dyed
6 had / got, made

Exercise 3

1 B
2 A
3 C
4 D

Exercise 4

1 Our boss made us all ~~to~~ stay at work late today.
2 I got my friend <u>to</u> check my homework assignment.
3 My parents let me <u>stay</u> up late last night to watch the match.
4 My coach really helped me <u>(to) improve</u> my tennis serve.
5 Apparently the owner of the team is trying to get the trainer ~~to~~ sacked.
6 I've just had my application for a day off <u>turned</u> down by my boss.

Exercise 5

1 to get children to play / getting children playing
2 his match called off by
3 let them finish their dinner
4 friend made me watch
5 had my suitcase stolen

Page 134

READING

Exercise 1

1 zorbing
2 wingsuit flying
3 hang gliding
4 kitesurfing
5 ice diving
6 white water rafting
7 bungee jumping

READING AND USE OF ENGLISH PART 5 TRAINING

Exercise 3

1 C

Exercise 4

2 C

Page 135

Exercise 5

3 A
4 B
5 C

Page 136

VOCABULARY

Exercise 1

1 B
2 D
3 C
4 G
5 F
6 E
7 A

Exercise 2

individual sports

Exercise 3

1 First of all
2 Having said that
3 By comparison
4 for instance
5 more or less
6 on balance
7 in particular

Exercise 4

A in particular
B more or less
C first of all
D for instance
E by comparison
F having said that
G on balance

WRITING PART 2: ARTICLE TRAINING

Exercise 1

Suggested answers:

sport or leisure activity
becoming more popular in your country
reasons

Page 137

Exercise 3

D, B, A, C

Exercise 4

1 to get into it
2 give it a go
3 unaccompanied
4 taken off , grow in popularity
5 Furthermore

PUSH YOURSELF C1

Exercise 5

1 One sport that has really taken off in my country in the last few years is ice skating.
2 What has made ice skating so popular here is the Winter Olympics.

Exercise 6

1 What I like most about hang gliding is the views.
2 It was my father who got me into tennis.
3 One activity which is popular in my country is basketball.
4 The reason why I go to the gym is to keep fit.
5 One thing I love about hiking is the fresh air.

Page 138

GRAMMAR

Exercise 1

1 terrified, relaxed
2 embarrassing

Exercise 2

1 confusing
2 exhausted
3 fascinating
4 shocked
5 excited
6 irritating
7 thrilled
8 petrified

Exercise 3

1 challenging
2 terrified
3 tiring
4 satisfying
5 disappointed
6 amazing

SPEAKING PART 1 TRAINING

Exercise 2

Name	Hobby	Who with	When	Extra information
Ivan	hiking	work colleagues	at the weekend	they have a picnic; they enjoy the views
Anna	tennis	brother	twice a week	she's competitive
Simon	online gaming	flatmate	almost every day	he finds it relaxing

Track 065

Ivan: Yes, I really like to go hiking with work colleagues at the weekend. We usually go for a day and take a light picnic lunch with us and enjoy the surrounding views.
Ana: I do, yes. What I enjoy most of all is playing tennis with my brother. We normally play twice a week and we're quite competitive so it's always good fun!
Simon: Definitely! One of my favourite hobbies is online gaming, which I do with my flatmate almost every day. It gets in the way of our studies from time to time, but I find it really relaxing.

Exercise 4

Ivan	Anna
I'm a big fan of *I (really) can't get enough of* *another sport I'm into is*	*I'm not really into* *what I am really keen on is* *I wouldn't get excited about doing it myself* *it's fun to watch*

Track 066

Examiner: First we'd like to know something about you. Ivan, what kind of outdoor activities do you enjoy?
Ivan: Well, I'm a big fan of snow sports, in particular snowboarding. I'd never tried it until I visited Canada. But my cousin introduced me to it, and I thought 'Wow, I really can't get enough of this!'
Examiner: Thank you. And Ana, what kind of team sports do you enjoy playing?
Ana: Well, to be honest, apart from watching my national hockey team when they're on TV, I'm not really into competitive team sports all that much. But what I am really keen on is mountain-biking. I've joined the uni club, and we go out most weekends.
Examiner: I see. And Ivan, tell me about the kinds of things you do with friends in your spare time.
Ivan: Yeah, well another sport I'm into is long-distance running, and I've entered the marathon in my home town with some friends. It's next month, so we're doing a lot of training. I've watched it as a spectator before, but this'll be the first time I'm actually taking part.
Examiner: And Ana, do you watch a lot of sport?
Ana: Actually, I think some sports are much more interesting to watch than to do. Marathon running for example, I wouldn't get excited about doing it myself, but it's fun to watch. So I'll be cheering Ivan on!
Examiner: Thank you.

Page 139

VOCABULARY

Exercise 1

1 tennis (match point; serves; backhand; net; court; shot; racket; umpire; game, set and match)

2 athletics (lap; track; lead; catch up; final bend; finish line; photo finish; sprints; takes gold)
3 football / soccer (corner; goal; header; post; rebound; score; referee)

Track 067

1 It's match point to Gregski … Hodford serves … it's a strong backhand return from Gregski. Hodford is up at the net, trying to keep Gregski at the back of the court. Gregski gets round quickly and plays a fantastic shot. Hodford stretches for it, it bounces off his racket … did it touch the line? No! The umpire's decision is out. It's game, set and match to Gregski! A really impressive performance by both players.
2 And as they come now into the fourth and final lap of the track … there's a big gap separating the front two from the rest of the pack. Suarez is still in the lead, with Petrov just behind trying to catch up. They're coming into the final bend, less than 100 metres from the finish line. Petrov is catching up! They're neck and neck, it could be a photo finish but wait … Suarez trips … Petrov sprints past Suarez and crosses the line. Petrov takes gold in a spectacular finish.
3 We're entering into the final few minutes of the match. You can feel the excitement in the stadium. The crowd are in full voice and are really cheering on their team. It's a corner to Norwood, one more goal and they'll surely win. Romano jumps for the header… He's hit the post! But wait, Gomez is there for the rebound and scores in the dying seconds of the match. And that's it, the referee blows for full-time. Norwood are champions!

Exercise 2

3 decision
4 decisive
5 excitement
6 impressed / impressive
7 spectacle
8 spectator
9 spectacular
10 separation
11 separate

Exercise 3

Type A (same)
de**cide**, de**ci**sion, de**ci**sive (same stress but different vowel sound)
ex**cite**, ex**cite**ment, ex**cit**ing, ex**cit**ed
im**press**, im**pres**sion, im**pressed**, im**pres**sive
Type B
com**pete**, compe**ti**tion, (com**pe**titor), com**pe**titive
spec**tate**, **spec**tacle, spec**ta**tor, spec**tac**ular
separate, sepa**ra**tion, **se**parate

Exercise 4

1 entertaining
2 performance
3 competitive
4 impressive
5 spectators
6 thrilling
7 athletic

Page 140

EXAM FOCUS
READING AND USE OF ENGLISH PART 5

1 C
2 D
3 C
4 C
5 B
6 A

Page 141

EXAM CHECK

1 False (four answer options)
2 True
3 False (the questions are in the same order)
4 True
5 False (you might be asked)

SPEAKING PART 1

Students' own answers

EXAM CHECK

Students' own answers

WRITING PART 2: ARTICLE

Model answer

Fun runs are becoming increasing popular everywhere. One of the events I attended last year made a lasting impression on me. Winter Wonder Wheels is a truly special occasion, as it allows people with a range of disabilities to participate in a 1km, 5km or 10km run/walk/wheel/push alongside their friends, family and carers.

Pushing my sister, Jane, through the stunning countryside in her all-terrain wheelchair, I reflected on why this kind of event has become so popular. I believe that the main reason is that the various charity and fun events are inclusive: grandparents, kids and the disabled are all able to attend a range of events throughout the year. Many events are for charity and this is definitely a motivating factor for many.

Jane had a wonderful day out, enjoying companionship and fresh air, all thanks to the selfless volunteers who gave up their time to organise the event. Raising money, navigating local by-laws, and arranging refreshments and merchandise are just a few of the challenges faced by event organisers. I for one am very grateful to these local superheroes.

Page 142

REAL WORLD

Exercise 2

The Brecon Beacons – the UK's adventure playground

Visitors to the Brecon Beacons National Park in Wales come for various reasons. For many of them, it's climbing the wild, impressive scenery of the Black Mountains, including some of the highest peaks in the southern United Kingdom. Whether you want to view them from a hang-glider or from the comfort of your own car, there's something for everyone.

Other visitors come to walk through ancient woodlands to get a glimpse of the spectacular waterfalls. It's also one of the best areas in the UK to see rare species such as the red kite, a bird whose distinctive silhouette can be seen in the skies throughout the year. The Usk valley is also filled with beautiful flowers, some of which are unique to the region.

Of the several attractive market towns, perhaps the most unusual is Hay-on-Wye. Mostly in Wales (but with a handful of streets over the border in England), this unusual town with a population of just 1500 has no fewer than 24 bookshops, and a literary and arts festival every summer. Visitors can also stay in one of the many hotels in the region, which offer breathtaking views of the park, perfect for those on their honeymoon or celebrating an anniversary.

Page 143

Exercise 3

Suggested answers:

1 Martin and his friends
climbing the wild, impressive scenery of the Black Mountains
go hang gliding
walk through the ancient woodlands
2 The Weifeng family
see rare species such as the red kite (bird) and the flowers which are unique to the region
3 Shaun and Latifa
visit the attractive market towns
go to the literary and arts festival
stay in one of the hotels with breathtaking views

Exercise 4

1 get a glimpse of (2nd paragraph)
2 a handful of (3rd paragraph)
3 from the comfort of (1st paragraph)

Exercise 6

You should	You shouldn't
remain vigilant; let staff know of any problems wear a strong pair of shoes watch what more experienced climbers are doing	wear sandals or high-heel shoes use any equipment that has anything wrong with it take your eye off the climber if you're the person on the ground

Track 068

Right, thank you everyone for joining us on this weekend's *Introduction to Wall Climbing* course. My name's Jason, and I'll be taking you through the basics of climbing safely, and you'll all have a go at using the climbing wall.

Now, as you're all new to climbing, everything you do will be under supervision. Our staff carry out regular safety checks to ensure that all the equipment is up to standard and being used properly, but if you do spot anything that doesn't look right, please let a member of staff know. We'd ask you to keep your eyes open and help us keep the Wall Climbing Centre a safe place. For example, you'll see that we have padding on the floor, so in the event of a fall, you'd land on this, and not hurt yourself.

You need to be wearing a strong pair of shoes to make sure you get a good grip and avoid slipping. That might seem like common sense, but honestly, we've had people turn up in sandals or high-heeled shoes in the past, which of course aren't suitable.

It's a requirement that you've got your harness correctly fitted. This is one of the key areas of climbing safety. If the harness isn't on properly, it can fail to support a falling climber, and that can be serious. Don't use any equipment yourself until you've checked that it's secure. It's better to be safe than sorry.

Now, you've probably noticed that every climber on the wall is attached to a rope, the other end of which is attached to a second person on the ground. That second person has to be there in case the climber falls. Their role is to balance the weight of the climber. If the climber does fall, the weight of the person on the ground stops them falling too far. Now, it's vital that you know how to fall safely, so we'll practise doing that. If you're the person on the ground, under no circumstances can you take your eye off the climber.

The person on the ground has a job that's just as important as the climber, and they need to stay focused too. If you're more interested in selfies than safety then you probably shouldn't be climbing at all.

The thing to do is get someone else to take a photo for you, and arrange this before you start climbing.

And finally, watch what more experienced climbers are doing. That can help you learn skills and stay safe while having fun. And that's what we're all about. OK, any questions?

Exercise 7

1 D
2 E
3 B
4 C
5 A

Track 069

Right, thank you everyone for joining us on this weekend's *Introduction to Wall Climbing* course. My name's Jason, and I'll be taking you through the basics of climbing safely, and you'll all have a go at using the climbing wall.

Now, as you're all new to climbing, everything you do will be under supervision. Our staff carry out regular safety checks to ensure that all the equipment is up to standard and being used properly, but if you do spot anything that doesn't look right, please let a member of staff know. We'd ask you to keep your eyes open and help us keep the Wall Climbing Centre a safe place. For example, you'll see that we have padding on the floor, so in the event of a fall, you'd land on this, and not hurt yourself.

You need to be wearing a strong pair of shoes to make sure you get a good grip and avoid slipping. That might seem like common sense, but honestly, we've had people turn up in sandals or high-heeled shoes in the past, which of course aren't suitable.

UNIT 11

Page 144

GETTING STARTED

Exercise 3

1 A billboard advertising
B television
C newspapers
D social media
E radio

Page 145

VOCABULARY

Exercise 1

Suggested answers:

1 F – advertising
2 C – social media
3 E – social media
4 D – newspapers / television
5 B – newspapers / radio / social media
6 A – advertising / reality TV

Exercise 2

1 If you ask me
2 Personally speaking
3 don't you think?
4 if you want my opinion
5 To be honest
6 I would say

Exercise 4

1 promote
2 influence
3 credible
4 prime-time

READING

Page 146

READING AND USE OF ENGLISH PART 1 TRAINING

Exercise 4

1 A
2 D
3 C
4 B
5 C
6 A
7 D
8 B

Page 147

GRAMMAR

Exercise 1

1 In the first picture, Maria is telling something to Giovanni. In the second picture, Giovanni is telling someone else what Maria said to him.

2

Picture 1	Picture 2
I stopped	she had stopped
I don't think	she didn't think
I'll use	she would use

Exercise 2

1 Lucas said he wasn't online that evening.
2 Lucas said he was starting his new social media channel the day after/next day.
3 Lucas said he'd had a great response to his new channel.
4 Lucas said he'd been searching that site for new online material.
5 Lucas said he'd gone online to check how many subscribers he had.
6 Lucas said he'd been working on it for a month when he'd started having problems.
7 Lucas said he really had to get it fixed as he couldn't upload his videos.

Exercise 3

1 S/he asked me what I had been doing the weekend before / the previous weekend.

2 S/he asked me where I got my news from.
3 S/he asked me if / whether I had met anyone famous.
4 S/he asked me what my dream job was.
5 S/he asked me if / whether I enjoyed watching football.
6 S/he asked me if / whether I had a favourite app.

Page 148

WRITING

Exercise 2

Watching too much television can lead to bad habits and a lack of exercise.

Exercise 3

1 C
2 A
3 B

Exercise 4

A Additionally
B for instance
C Furthermore
D as a consequence
E even when

The writer has also used the following linking words and phrases: *While, On balance, Having said that, Despite, It goes without saying that.*

PUSH YOURSELF C1

Exercise 1

All things considered – On balance
It speaks for itself (that) – It goes without saying
Regardless of (the fact that) – Despite
That being said – Having said that

1 Regardless of the fact that
2 All things considered
3 That being said
4 It speaks for itself that

Page 149

SPEAKING PART 2 TRAINING

Exercise 2

1 1
2 B

Track 070

Albina: In this photo, we can see people taking part in a television show. I think this type of programme would mainly appeal to people who enjoy quizzes or similar activities and I don't think young children would be very interested in watching it.
I think these people have chosen to appear on this show because they want to win money. I think they might also be there because they have watched the TV show at home and they think they have a good chance of winning.

Exercise 3

Not very well. She said *I think / don't think* four times.

Exercise 4

Suggested answers:

As far as I'm concerned
It seems to me
I would say that
If you ask me
As far as I can tell
In my opinion

Exercise 5

1 without saying
2 entirely sure
3 safe to say
4 impression

Track 071

Walid: I'd argue this would be suitable for a viewer who wants to watch something quite light-hearted because the subject matter is far from serious. It goes without saying that they would be quite competitive too. I'm not entirely sure what the ideal age might be, but it's safe to say the person watching this would enjoy preparing delicious dishes for themselves or their family. My impression is that they wouldn't need to watch every episode in order to understand what's going on.

Page 150

GRAMMAR

Exercise 2

2 E
3 A
4 F
5 D
6 B

Exercise 3

2 Maria invited them to her graduation ceremony.
3 Julia threatened to cancel her subscription if they didn't improve the service.
4 Simon refused to pay them any money.
5 Dan revealed that he would be leaving the company at the end of the month.
6 Sophie warned that it might rain later.

Exercise 4

1 she would find the story
2 refused to watch that / it
3 told me I had to

VOCABULARY

Exercise 3

2

Page 151

Exercise 4

2 come clean (about)
3 go to great lengths
4 speak out (against)
5 tighten up
6 overstep the mark
7 stamp out

Exercise 5

1 overstepping the mark
2 speak out
3 went / had gone to great lengths
4 tightening up
5 came clean
6 under pressure

LISTENING PART 1 TRAINING

Exercise 2

1 The man was worried about not having enough time to do background research on the company.
2 the interviewers (not the man)

Exercise 3

1 Secretly, I was certain
2 I would be a great fit for the role

Exercise 4

1 to describe Bryan Stephens, not the television programme
2 It's nice to see him <u>move away from</u> those financial-based shows.

Track 072

Man: Did you catch that TV programme on Channel 1 last night?
Woman: I did, yeah. It's difficult to believe that Bryan Stephens is in his eighties. He looks in great health. I'd have thought he'd have wanted to give up work and spend more time relaxing, but it looks as though he loves what he does.
Man: Absolutely! It's nice to see him move away from those financial-based shows and try something different. I'm sure he really enjoys visiting different countries around the world and telling the viewers about them.
Woman: I know. I'd love to do that for a living.

Exercise 5

3 C
4 A
5 C

Track 073

3 I started my advertising business on a small budget which I funded with money I'd managed to save over the years. It worked well for a while, but when I had the chance to make a series of television commercials for a well-known brand, I knew I needed to find

more money than I had. I'd thought about going to the bank, and they said they'd lend me what I needed, but the interest rates were really high. Fortunately, someone my aunt knew stepped in at the last minute and helped me out.

4 I was recently sent on a trip to conduct research about a story that we wanted to publish for our newspaper. Fortunately, the roads weren't busy so I wasn't held up, which meant I had plenty of time to purchase my ticket. Lots of people had to stand but I was lucky enough to get a seat with a table by the window. Anyway, the journey was comfortable and there were no delays. What's more, the new bridge meant that I didn't have to change onto the ferry, which was good as I struggle a bit with sea sickness.

5

Man: That meeting about the assignment we need to complete was good, but I'm not sure I understood everything. I'm excited about taking photos of animals in their natural habitat, though.

Woman: … and they help you to arrange the trip which is great because organisation isn't my strong point!

Man: There was also something about the way we hand in our work once it's completed.

Woman: Yes, we have to upload it to the project site by Tuesday next week.

Man: Isn't that also the date we need to report back to the group?

Woman: Hmm, that's a good point. It's probably worth double checking that with our tutor in the seminar next week.

Page 152

EXAM FOCUS
READING AND USE OF ENGLISH PART 1

1 D
2 A
3 A
4 D
5 B
6 C
7 B
8 A

Page 153

LISTENING PART 1

1 C
2 B
3 B
4 A
5 B
6 C
7 C
8 A

Track 074

Narrator: 1 You hear a journalist talking on her mobile phone about an interview. How does she feel?

Yes, I'm talking to the actor next week. Well, I am a little irritated that we only have thirty minutes but it's not his fault. His agent got the times mixed up. He's about to start filming a documentary and he leaves for the Amazon jungle the following day, so he isn't able to hang around. I don't know how he does it – I'd be a bit uneasy about going somewhere like that. But still, I'm convinced I can get what I need, even if we don't have a vast amount of time.

Narrator: 2 You hear two media studies students talking about their course. What do they agree about their lecturer?

Speaker one: How are you finding the course?

Speaker two: It's good, though the connection he makes between what we're studying and our future profession is sometimes a little vague. What about you?

Speaker one: Well, the recent project he set us was far from easy, and when we met for a tutorial he was quite critical of my introduction. But he helped me see where I went wrong which was good.

Speaker two: Yeah, I really appreciated it when he showed me how I could improve my conclusion. He seems to have quite negative views about the media, but the more I study the more enthusiastic I am about it.

Narrator: 3 You hear a woman talking about a newspaper article. What is it about?

Did you see it in the newspaper? I couldn't believe it. He was on his way to vote when it happened. They think it might've started on purpose but it's not certain yet whether it was deliberate. Apparently, he'd gone back into the flames twice to make sure no one else was inside the building. It's only because of his actions there were no fatalities. The minister being interviewed after the incident suggested he'll get some sort of award for bravery and I completely agree – I think it's the least they can do.

Narrator: 4 You hear a weather reporter talking about his job. What is the purpose of his talk?

People are quick to criticise us when we get it wrong which I can certainly understand – finding yourself in a sudden downpour when I predicted that the conditions would be fine isn't an ideal situation to be in, is it? However, there's a lot more to being a meteorologist than you might think. One of the most useful tools to tell you accurately how the weather will change is the information that's given to us by satellites. These are vital in warning us about severe weather conditions like hurricanes and tornadoes.

Narrator: 5 You hear a journalist talking about his job. Why did he study journalism?

I remember it very well actually; my decision to study journalism. It was when I was a teenager. I'd been working hard on a project – my teacher had set us a really difficult piece of work. I was in the kitchen and my mum switched on the radio – she loves the news. Anyway, there was this journalist talking about his work and it just sounded so rewarding – you know, finding out the truth about stuff. I said to my mum then and there that that was how I wanted to earn my living.

Narrator: 6 You overhear a man talking to his colleague on the phone. What is he talking about?

That's fine, I just need to let them know as soon as possible really. I can't do it on Friday as I'll be with a client all day – you know, the one who works for the company I was thinking of applying to before I was promoted here. Anyway, I'll get onto it first thing Monday morning – I've got the budget agreed for the new projector so all we need to do now is select the brand we want. I've managed to book the conference centre for our team meeting next week so we can talk more about it then.

Narrator: 7 You hear a television actor telling a friend about an award she's just won. What is she doing?

Man: You must have been absolutely thrilled when they made the announcement.

Woman: To be honest, I didn't know how I felt at the time. I'd thought about it in the past, but it's not something I really expected to happen so early in my career. I'm not certain how the judges decide who should get the award either. Though once I started to think about all the extra opportunities I'll get, not to mention the extra money I'll earn, I started to feel really positive about it.

Man: Well, you deserve it, so well done!

Narrator: 8 You hear two people talking about a piece of music. What does the woman say about it?

Woman: Have you heard this new song?

Man: Yeah, it was on the radio this morning. I'm not a big fan of it to be honest.

Woman: Really? I know it's not the happiest song in the world but it still cheers me up every time I listen to it.

Man: Don't you think it sounds a lot like their previous album?

Woman: Not really. I actually thought it was quite different to a lot of their older stuff. My brother says that it's really well-produced and that it will definitely inspire a new generation of musicians. I mean he should know, he's doing a degree in music.

Pages 154 and 155

SPEAKING PART 2

Students' own answers

Page 156

REAL WORLD

Exercise 1

1 Denmark
2 775,000
3 Hans Christian Andersen
4 happiest
5 amusement park

Track 075

Copenhagen is the capital of Denmark.
Copenhagen has a population of approximately 775,000.
A statue of the famous author, Hans Christian Andersen, can be found at the City Hall Square in Copenhagen.
According to a report in 2013, Copenhagen was voted the happiest city in the world.
Copenhagen is home to the second oldest amusement park in the world.

Page 157

Exercise 4

1 iconic structure
2 a stunning panoramic view
3 plays host to
4 diving elite
5 an electric atmosphere

Exercise 5

1 C (making an invitation)
2 E (accepting/refusing an invitation)
3 F (refusing an invitation)
4 B (making an invitation)
5 D (accepting an invitation)
6 A (not sure if we can accept or refuse an invitation)

Exercise 6

1 Are you interested in joining me?
2 Count me in.
3 I'm supposed to be doing something else.
4 … if she'd like to come along
5 Thanks for thinking of me.
6 Can I get back to you (tonight)?

Track 076

Patrick: It's almost the weekend. I can't wait to go out and have some fun.
Liz: Me too. It's been a tough week. Hey, I'm going to the Royal Opera House on Saturday.
Patrick: I didn't know you were into opera.
Liz: Actually, I'm not. They're hosting the Cliff Diving World Series. Are you interested in joining me? I know you love diving and I think the atmosphere's going to be great.
Patrick: Really? Wow! I thought cliff diving needed cliffs! Absolutely. Count me in.
Liz: Excellent! Shall we meet at 9 am? It starts at ten. There's going to be a lot of spectators so we'll need time to get good seats.
Patrick: Sounds good. No wait, I forgot! I'm supposed to be having lunch with my friend, Ria, on Saturday.
Liz: Oh no. That's a shame. Can you postpone?
Patrick: Unfortunately not. She's only here for the day and I've not seen her in ages. Hey, why don't I ask Ria if she'd like to come along? Perhaps we could all go for dinner after the event, instead of lunch.
Liz: That sounds like a great idea but I don't want to get in the way of you guys catching up.
Patrick: Don't be silly. I'm sure Ria would be more than happy for you to come too. We'll all be starving after a day of excitement.
Liz: Well, if she doesn't mind that would be great. Thanks for thinking of me.
Patrick: Likewise! Ok, so I'll call her. Could I get back to youlater, when I know for sure?
Liz: Absolutely.

Exercise 7

1 Thanks for thinking of me.
2 Count me in.
3 I'm supposed to be doing something else.
4 Can I get back to you (tonight)?

PROGRESS CHECK 4

Page 158

Exercise 1

1 It's more than likely that people will live on another planet in the future.
2 We're bound to see driverless cars on the roads in 20 years.
3 There is little prospect that we'll discover a new planet.
4 I don't think there will be robot teachers any time soon.
5 I'm not convinced that we will find life on other planets.

Exercise 2

1 will have retired
2 will have finished
3 will be living
4 will have completed
5 will be studying
6 will have become
7 will be flying

Exercise 3

1 violent
2 concerned
3 gale-force
4 over
5 soaring
6 as
7 poor
8 by
9 down

Exercise 4

1 (have / get) her hair cut
2 (have / get) our passports renewed
3 (having / getting) them cleaned
4 (have / get) my eyes tested
5 (have / get) my car washed

Exercise 5

1 My friend forced me to go running with him.
2 Our sports teacher let us finish 30 minutes early.
3 My coach is helping me (to) improve my tennis serve.
4 I can never get my parents to go on a camping holiday.

Page 159

Exercise 6

1 terrified
2 confusing
3 boring
4 exhausted
5 challenging
6 disappointed
7 annoying
8 amazing

Exercise 7

1 excitement
2 autograph
3 supporters
4 fan
5 compete
6 spectators
7 thrilled

Exercise 8

1 he would go to watch the new film.
2 he had received lots of letters from his fans.
3 she had gone to see them the previous weekend.
4 he had to get his computer fixed.
5 she was going to upload a new video the following week.

Exercise 9

1 Lisa asked where I was performing the following week.
2 Leonardo asked if I had seen the line-up for the music festival.

3 Patricia asked me how the filming on the desert island was going.
4 Melanie asked (me) if I could bring her a glass of water.

Exercise 10

1 promote
2 went to great lengths
3 under pressure
4 In light of
5 breathtaking
6 point
7 addicted

UNIT 12

Page 160

VOCABULARY

Exercise 1

2 volunteer (question 1, option C)
3 easily accessible (question 3, option A)
4 reputation (question 2, option A)
5 appeals to (question 3, option B)
6 unique (question 6, option A)
7 upcoming (question 6)
8 venue (question 1, option A)
9 publicise (question 7, option A)
10 guidance (question 5, option B)

Page 161

LISTENING PART 4 TRAINING

Exercise 1

Option B
Martin says that he was studying hospitality management at university but doesn't say that this was the reason why he was asked to organise the university festival.
Option C
Martin was also volunteering at another smaller event when he was asked to organise the university festival. He doesn't say that this was the reason why he was asked to organise the festival, rather that he was hesitant to accept because he was volunteering at the time.

Track 077

Interviewer: Thank you for coming into the studio today, Martin. First of all, tell us how you got into organising festivals.
Martin: It was back when I was studying at university. The university wanted to put on a big event for final year students who had just finished their end-of-term exams. As I was studying hospitality management, I already had a few contacts with people working at a local conference centre which was big enough to hold the event and, because of these connections, the university invited me to join the organisation committee. I was hesitant at first because I was also volunteering at another smaller event, but I knew this was an opportunity I couldn't turn down.

Exercise 2

2 B
3 C
4 C
5 B
6 B
7 A

Track 078

Interviewer: And this led to bigger things. You recently organised an event called Street Fest, which I hear attracted more than 10,000 people. What was that like and why do you think it was so successful?
Martin: It was absolutely fantastic. I had always wanted to organise something in my hometown as it wasn't famous for its festivals, unlike other towns in the area. People didn't really know anything about the history or culture of the place so I thought why not host an event which celebrates this. We organised a live music concert with acts from the local area as well as a parade and encouraged people to dress up in costumes that best represented the town. It was this aspect that I believe made the event so popular rather than just simply getting in bands and artists who the majority of people had already heard of.
Interviewer: You now spend a lot of your time as an events consultant, helping other towns and cities organise festivals. What do you think makes a good festival?
Martin: Well, the point I often make to organisers is that you don't have to host the festival right in the centre of a city or town which has good transportation links. In fact some of the most popular ones are in the middle of nowhere and still attract hundreds of thousands of people every year. One thing you've got to do though is look after people when they're there and avoid anything that could put them in danger. Organisers sometimes take this for granted but it's actually one of the most important aspects of making a festival successful as they often attract people from all over the world.
Interviewer: You must have come up against a lot of challenges in your time organising these big events. What would you say is the most challenging part of organising festivals?
Martin: A lot of organisers think that finding a venue is particularly difficult because of the costs involved. I often get round this by explaining to the venue owners that it helps to promote them as well as the festival and this normally leads to a discount. Lower venue costs mean that we have more money to spend on developing a fast and reliable website so that people can buy tickets easily without the website crashing due to the high volume of traffic, something that really frustrates festival goers. That being said, it's vital that you stay within budget, which is never easy given the substantial costs involved, as this can ultimately decide whether a festival goes ahead or not.
Interviewer: You also have a blog. What message are you hoping to convey?
Martin: Well, when I first started, I didn't know too many other people who were doing the same thing as me and it was tough to find out about some of the issues people often ran into. To be honest, a lot of what I've learnt can't really be taught in the classroom. You need to go out there and do it yourself and learn from your own mistakes. That said, I like to write about the festivals I've organised in the hope that other people in the field can benefit from my experiences and become better at what they do.
Interviewer: That's great. I suppose it's a good way to network as well. You're hosting an online festival in September. Could you tell us more about that?
Martin: Of course! The idea came about while I was talking to a friend of mine via video conference. I was surprised to see just how good the technology was and thought it would be an excellent platform to host a festival. I did a bit of research, believing that I was the first person to have thought of this, which actually turned out not to be the case. We designed a programme and I didn't know if people would go for it, but I was wrong – it really appealed to people, particularly those who found it difficult getting to venues because they were too far away. We're now planning to hold the online festival again next year, too.
Interviewer: Well I'll definitely be attending that next year. So what are your plans for the future?
Martin: I actually have lots of new ideas for online festivals, but I've done so much recently that I think it would be more worthwhile doing something else. I know there are a lot of big music events coming up, but you know, I don't want to miss out on the smaller, more unfamiliar events, which I really like to attend, and make sure as many people know about them as possible.

Exercise 3

1 got into
2 to put on
3 turn down
4 dress up
5 look after
6 come up against
7 goes ahead
8 to miss out on

Page 162

VOCABULARY

Exercise 1

1 connections, organisation
2 majority
3 successful
4 normally
5 easily

Track 079

1 … which was big enough to hold the event and because of these connections the university invited me to join the organisation committee.
2 … rather than just simply getting in bands and artists who the majority of people had already heard of.
3 … one of the most important aspects of making a festival successful as they often attract people from all over the world.
4 … it helps to promote them as well as the festival and this normally leads to a discount.
5 … a fast and reliable website so that people can buy tickets easily without the website crashing due to the high volumes of traffic …

Exercise 2

1 con**nec**tions
2 organi**sa**tion
3 ma**jo**rity
4 suc**cess**ful
5 **nor**mally
6 **ea**sily

Exercise 3

2 regardless
3 impressive
4 interviewee
5 athletic
6 peaceful
7 memorable
8 psychologist
9 instantly
10 selection

Page 163

GRAMMAR

Exercise 2

Group A

Question 1 – Venezuela
Question 3 – Sweden
Question 5 – The Tidong community
Questions **2**, **4** and **6** cannot be answered.

Group B

Question 2 – Peru
Question 4 – Congo
Question 6 – South Korea
Questions **1**, **3** and **5** cannot be answered.

Exercise 3

GROUP A

Sweden

At the wedding ceremony, if the bride leaves the room for any reason, then any of the female guests are allowed to kiss the groom. The same applies to the male guests, who may kiss the bride when the groom leaves the room.

The Tidong community (Malaysia, Indonesia and the Philippines)

After a Tidong couple's wedding, the bride and groom cannot leave their home for three days. They are also prohibited from going to the bathroom or toilet and they are watched closely by friends and relatives to ensure that they stick to this rule. If this tradition isn't followed, it's believed that bad things might happen in the future to the couple or their children.

Venezuela

If you're invited to a wedding in Venezuela, it's advisable not to wait until the end of the reception before offering your congratulations to the happy couple. This is because they're actually supposed to make their getaway without being noticed before the party's over. All the guests should watch the bride and groom carefully, as it's considered good luck for the person who first sees the couple leave.

South Korea

Before leaving the wedding venue with his new bride, a Korean husband must have his shoes and socks removed by his friends and relatives, who then hit the groom's feet with a stick or even a fish. It's a light-hearted event. While this is happening, it's compulsory for the groom to answer questions that his friends and relatives ask him. After he has answered all the questions, he is permitted to leave.

Peru

The hosts at a Peruvian wedding are expected to prepare a cake with ribbons. Attached to one of the ribbons is a wedding ring, which is hidden inside the cake. After the wedding ceremony, the female wedding guests have to pull out one of the ribbons. If the ring is attached to their ribbon, then they are considered to be the next person to get married. But don't worry, you don't have to join in if you don't want to.

Congo

Marriage is usually a joyful time, and smiling in your wedding photos is essential! But this isn't the case everywhere. A wedding tradition in Congo states that the wedding couple shouldn't smile under any circumstances on their wedding day, even for their wedding photographer! Smiling indicates that they are not serious about marriage.

Exercise 5

Necessary	*must, it's compulsory, have to, essential*
Not necessary	*don't have to*
Recommended	*it's advisable, supposed to, should, are expected to*
Not recommended	*shouldn't*
Allowed	*allowed to, may, permitted*
Not allowed	*cannot, prohibited*
Possible	*may, might*

Exercise 6

1 supposed to get
2 don't have / need to dress up
3 are allowed to attend
4 's / has been compulsory

PUSH YOURSELF C1

1 All passengers *will have to* print their boarding passes in advance.

(meaning – In the first sentence, the rule is in effect now. In the second sentence, the rule will come into effect at some point in the future.)

2 You *should have brought* your e-ticket with you to the event.

(meaning – In the first sentence, you are being given advice before the event starts. In the second sentence, the event has already started and the sentence implies regret – you didn't bring your e-ticket so you can't enter the event.)

3 You *might have been able to* catch the end of the performance.

(meaning – in the first sentence, there is still a chance that you can catch the event but in the second sentence, you are too late as the performance has already started.)

4 You *won't be able to* bring your friends into the VIP area.

(meaning – In the first sentence, you are being told now (at the VIP area) that you can't bring your friends in. In the second sentence, you are being warned in advance that you can't bring your friends into the VIP area.)

Page 164

WRITING PART 2: REPORT TRAINING

Exercise 1

A new festival was held for the first time in your town this year, and you attended it. The organisers now want feedback as to what worked well and why, and what aspects of the festival could be improved in the future.

Exercise 2

Suggested answers:

What worked well	What could have been improved
• *The festival was in a convenient location.* • *There was a good variety of activities.* • *The food and drink were reasonably priced.* • *The people who worked there were very friendly.*	• *There weren't any facilities to charge mobile phones.* • *People waited for hours to get into the festival.* • *The toilets were difficult to find.* • *There was a lot of rubbish on the ground.*

Exercise 3

1 The purpose of this report is to
2 This report is intended to
3 The aim of this report is to

Sentence B is the most appropriate. Sentence A contains grammatical errors ('discussing' and 'suggesting') and sentence C isn't relevant to the question.

Exercise 4

1 A
2 C

Sample additional points:

- The high quality of the live music
- Not being able to park close enough to the venue

Exercise 5

I would propose
I would suggest

Page 165

READING AND USE OF ENGLISH PART 3 TRAINING

Exercise 1

1 eight
2 one mark per question
3 Yes. You must spell the word correctly.
4 You may need to change:

- the end of the word using a suffix (EQUAL → EQUAL**LY**)
- the beginning of the word using a prefix (ADVANTAGE → **DIS**ADVANTAGE)
- the middle of the word (LONG → LE**NGTH**)
- both the end and the beginning of the word (FORTUNATE → **UN**FORTUNATE**LY**)

Exercise 2

1 significantly
2 unlike
3 ability
4 possibilities
5 unpopular
6 enjoyable
7 variety
8 unsuccessful

Exercise 3

1 choice
2 strength
3 width
4 pride
5 ease
6 frozen
7 growth
8 depths

Exercise 5

1 annually
2 variety
3 unknown
4 fashionable
5 encouraged
6 peaceful
7 height
8 spectacular

Page 166

GRAMMAR

Exercise 2

1 was able
2 managed
3 enabled
4 capable of
5 unable
6 will be able

Track 080

Interviewer: I'm joined by Chris Smith, who works as a tour manager. Good morning, Chris. Tell us, how did you first get into tour management?

Chris: Well, I actually started out as a guitarist for a local rock band. We used to travel to different towns close to where we lived and I took care of the organisational side of things. It was great as I was able to find out more about the job of a tour manager and what was involved.

Interviewer: So what was the first gig you ever organised?

Chris: I remember it well. It was at the local community centre. The person in charge of the venue was worried that nobody would show up and threatened to cancel it. I put an announcement out on social media and, in the end, we managed to put on a pretty memorable show, despite the fact that only 40 people turned up.

Interviewer: Speaking of memorable, what's your most unforgettable experience of playing in a band?

Chris: Back in 2010, we got a phone call from a guy who managed Jump Up. They were one of the biggest and best acts in the country at the time. We couldn't believe it! Not only did it mean that we could earn more money but it also enabled us to play to a bigger crowd, over three thousand in fact. Some of the people even knew the words to our songs!

Interviewer: That's great! So when did you decide to become a full-time tour manager?

Chris: So after a few years of playing, my bandmates and I started to argue a lot and eventually I left the band. I was out of work until a friend of mine asked me if I wanted to manage his band's national tour. It was a big step up, but I knew I was capable of doing a good job, so I accepted. At first, it was hard being away from my friends and family for long periods of time, but eventually I got used to it.

Interviewer: You're going on your first international tour next month. How are you feeling about that?

Chris: Good actually! I've been dying to take the band I manage on an international tour. We had the opportunity to tour overseas last year, but we were unable to go because of other commitments. They're great guys and they work extremely hard, so it'll be great for them to have the chance to play to their fans abroad. As well as managing the band, I will be able to network with tour managers from other countries, which is something I'm really looking forward to.

Interviewer: Well, good luck and thanks for talking to us.

Exercise 3

B managed
C was/were unable
D will be able
E enabled
F capable of

Exercise 4

1 I didn't know the band were capable of <u>performing</u> that well.
2 Unfortunately, we won't <u>be able</u> to attend because we're away on holiday.
3 He could <u>to</u> play the guitar when he was only three years old.
4 I can't believe he managed <u>to put</u> on such a good event.
5 The organisers were unable <u>to</u> find a solution to the problem.
6 Despite it selling out in minutes, I <u>was able to</u> **or** <u>managed to</u> get two tickets for the music festival.
7 The warm weather will enable <u>us</u> to host the party outside.
8 I've <u>been able to</u> swim ever since I was two years old.

Exercise 5

Suggested answers:

Hard work has enabled these students to graduate.

In 1969, the Americans succeeded in sending men to the moon, and bringing them back safely.

I'm not sure if the bear is going to manage to catch this fish.

It looks as though the man might be able to juggle.

Page 167

SPEAKING

Exercise 3

Weddings in Turkey

Wedding shoe: the bride writes the names of her friends on the bottom of the shoe and whoever's name isn't there at the end of the night will get married.

Cup of coffee: the groom drinks salted coffee to prove that he is ready to marry the bride.

Moving to a new home in the Philippines

Coins: coins are scattered around the living room floor to bring good luck and financial prosperity.

A new baby in Finland

Cardboard box: new parents are given a cardboard box filled with baby clothes, bedding and bathing products such as towels, cream and a hairbrush. The box then becomes the baby's first bed.

Graduating in Argentina

Eggs and flour: when a person graduates, instead of friends and family giving gifts, they throw eggs, flour, even ketchup at them. It's all done in good humour and the person knows about this in advance so they usually wear old clothes.

Track 081

Alison: Have you seen this, Marcus? It's an article about how people celebrate different milestones around the world.

Marcus: Yes, I have. I actually read it earlier today. I found the bit about weddings in Turkey really interesting.

Alison: Yeah, so did I! Like how the bride writes the names of her friends on the bottom of her wedding shoes and whoever's name isn't there at the end of the night will get married in the future.

Marcus: Hopefully she doesn't use a permanent marker pen, then!

Alison: [laughs] Good point! And there was the bit about the salted coffee.

Marcus: Ah yes, this is when the groom drinks a cup of coffee with salt in it when he goes to ask the bride's family for her hand in marriage. Apparently, this is to prove that he is ready to marry her. It's a really interesting tradition but I can't imagine ever doing that myself, to be honest.

Alison: No, neither can I! Luckily I wouldn't have to though as it's only the groom who does this.

Marcus: Did you see the section on when you move to a new home in the Philippines?

Alison: I did, yes. This is when you throw coins on the living room floor to bring good luck and financial prosperity to the home. I heard that some people leave them there for the whole time they're living in the home. I would love for that to be a tradition here!

Marcus: Yeah, I would too! Although my friends move home a lot, so it might get quite expensive!

Alison: Speaking of new, I really like the tradition in Finland for when there is a new baby in the family. They receive a cardboard box filled with baby clothes, bedding and bathing products such as towels, cream and a hairbrush. The box can then become the baby's first bed.

Marcus: I'd never heard of that one before.

Alison: No, I hadn't either.

Marcus: Hey Alison, you're off to study in Argentina soon, right?

Alison: I am indeed!

Marcus: So you must have enjoyed the section about graduation ceremonies in some parts of Argentina.

Alison: I didn't actually have time to read about that. What happens?

Marcus: Well, when a person graduates, instead of friends and family giving gifts, they throw eggs, flour, even tomato ketchup at them. It's all done in good humour and the person knows about this in advance so they usually wear old clothes.

Alison: I'm glad you told me! I'll make sure I pack some old things before going there, then.

Marcus: That's if you manage to graduate!

Alison: Very funny, Marcus!

Exercise 5

1 Yeah, so did I
2 No, neither can I
3 Yeah, I would too
4 No, I hadn't either

Track 082

1 Marcus: Yes, I have. I actually read it earlier today. I found the bit about weddings in Turkey really interesting.
Alison: Yeah, so did I!

2 Marcus: It's a really interesting tradition but I can't imagine ever doing that myself, to be honest.
Alison: No, neither can I!

3 Alison: I would love for that to be a tradition here!
Marcus: Yeah, I would too!

4 Marcus: I'd never heard of that one before.
Alison: No I hadn't either.

Page 168

EXAM FOCUS

LISTENING PART 4

1 A
2 C
3 A
4 C
5 B
6 B
7 C

Track 083

Narrator: You will hear part of a podcast with a blogger called Juanita, who has travelled all over the world. For questions 1–7, choose the best answer, A, B or C.

Interviewer: And now on the Travel Show, I'm joined here in the studio by someone who a lot of you will already know from her award-winning travel blog, Around the World with Juanita. Juanita Meinhoffer, thank you for joining us.

Juanita: It's my pleasure.

Interviewer: Juanita, as I understand it, you left your office job seven years ago to go travelling. And you started a blog then, which has gone on to become very successful and profitable. But what made you decide to do it?

Juanita: Well, initially it was just a way of communicating with family and friends about all the remarkable places I was visiting. But before long, a growing number of people were following my blog. I must admit, I was quite pleased to see the massive numbers of likes and shares I was getting. It was only after I'd been on the road for a few weeks that I started wondering if I might be able to make some money from it.

Interviewer: Now, I know you've visited some amazing places and festivals, and you've said that the highlight has been in China, the International Ice and Snow Sculpture Festival?

Juanita That's right, it's in Harbin. I've been fortunate enough to attend a lot of festivals in my life and most of them have their own exhibits and features which make them different to others. They're also held in some wonderful places and The International Ice and Snow Sculpture Festival is no different. What makes this one so special to me, though, is just how stunning the sculptures are. I've never seen anything quite like it before or indeed since.

Interviewer: It must take a lot of effort to put together. How impressed were you with the building of the exhibits?

Juanita: Very! Workers take more than 100,000 tons of ice out of the river when it freezes every year and they construct whole buildings out of this ice. Just take a minute to think about the skill of these workers. There's hundreds of tons of ice piled up, and yet they're able to make sure that it's not a hazard for the thousands of visitors who come to enjoy the variety of exhibits on offer.

Interviewer: In your blog, you compared it to the Burning Man Festival. Why was that?

Juanita: Well, the Burning Man Festival in the US, which I finally went to for the first time recently, is where they build a great big structure in the desert and then set fire to it. Similarly, the Harbin sculptures aren't permanent because the snow melts, so the whole thing is repeated year after year. I must admit that I feel a little sorry for the engineers and builders who organise these festivals sometimes.

Interviewer: Absolutely! Now, you've said that what you enjoyed most was riding down the river on what you called a tyre ride. Tell us about that.

Juanita: Well, when I first saw a whole load of people sitting in rubber tyres on the frozen river, I did wonder what they were doing and whether or not they were having fun. A friend of mine talked me into having a go, and I wasn't very excited at first. Basically you sit there while a tractor drives you across the ice. But as we picked up speed it turned out to be really thrilling, much more than I'd expected, even if it was a little cold.

Interviewer: Great! What tips do you have for visitors heading to the festival?

Juanita: Well, it goes without saying that it can get quite cold there. Temperatures can reach around minus 20 degrees Celsius, so it's important to wrap up warm and I think most people would already have packed thick jackets and jumpers in their suitcases. Some travellers underestimate just how popular the festival is, so you really need to allow plenty of time in advance to sort out where you're going to stay. It doesn't matter so much where, as the attractions are spread out all around the city.

Interviewer: You also talked a little bit about the ticketing system in your blog. Could you expand on that?

Juanita: Sure! Tickets are for timed entry, and you have to leave when the time's up. I worked out that if you arrive at about 3 or 4 pm, then you get to see everything in daylight, but then when the sun starts to go down, you also get to see it when the whole site is all lit up – that's when it looks magical, so you sort of get two for the price of one, so to speak.

Interviewer: Well, it all sounds fabulous. Juanita, thank you very much.

Page 169

READING AND USE OF ENGLISH PART 3

1 frozen
2 exceptionally
3 harmful
4 irresponsible
5 beneficial
6 entertainers
7 selection
8 thrilling

WRITING PART 2: REPORT

Model answer

Report on the college summer party

The college students' association organised a party on July 12th, which was attended by only 14 students out of the 120 expected to attend. The purpose of this report is to suggest reasons for this low attendance and to make recommendations to ensure the success of future events.

After the party, a questionnaire was sent to the students who did not attend, and the feedback revealed the following:

- As term ended on July 10th, most students had already returned to their home towns for the summer holidays.
- The party coincided with the New Town music festival, which many students had tickets for,
- About 20% of students didn't receive a reminder email about the party,

Having studied the feedback in detail, the organising committee has the following recommendations for future student events:

1 Arrange parties during term time.
2 Check the local events website to avoid clashes with other events.
3 Check the office has the correct email address for all students.

Page 170

REAL WORLD

Exercise 1

1 – Photo B
2 – Photo C
3 – Photo A
4 – Photo D

1 True
2 False – Jimmy Hendrix wrote the song before he visited Essaouira.
3 False – it's a popular spot for filming but the text doesn't say if it's also popular for actors.
4 True
5 False – the local goats also help the local tourism industry.

Page 171

Exercise 2

A state-of-the-art
B high-profile
C is featured in
D remarkable
E increasingly
F can't get enough

Exercise 4

Peter didn't know **2**, **3** and **4**.

Track 084

Fatima: Welcome to the hotel, sir. Would you like to check in?

Peter: Yes, please. It's very busy in here today. Are you always this busy?

Fatima: Not always. But we're always fully booked at this time of year because of the festival.

Peter: No way! Is that on now?

Fatima: Yes, it starts tomorrow, and it lasts for three days.

Peter: How great is that! I had heard of the famous music festival here. North African bands, world music …

Fatima: That's it! There's lots going on.

Peter: And it's called the … Gnaoua Festival I think, isn't it?

Fatima: The Gnaoua Festival, that's right, yes.

Peter: I had no idea that my visit was going to coincide with the festival. It must be my lucky day.

Fatima: Actually, the hotel is one of the venues, and there'll be a percussion performance in the courtyard tomorrow evening between 7 and 10 pm.

Peter: You're kidding! Right here? So I might actually be able to watch it from my room?

Fatima: Quite possibly. I can allocate you a courtyard room if you like.

Peter: That would be amazing! And I noticed on my way here that the whole town is packed!

Fatima: Yes, around half a million people are expected to attend the festival.

Peter: That's crazy! I imagined it would be much smaller as Essaouira isn't the biggest city in Morocco.

Fatima: True, but some people just come for the day.

Peter: Right, so, what, from Marrakesh and places. I mean, that's only two and a half hours away, isn't it?

Fatima: That's right, yes. So, if I could just see your …

Exercise 5

1 C
2 D
3 A
4 G
5 B
6 E
7 F

UNIT 13

Page 172

GETTING STARTED

Exercise 1

1 C
2 A
3 D
4 B

Photos:

1 B
2 A
3 C
4 D

Exercise 2

Photo B best describes Andrei because he tends to buy a lot.

Track 085

Vera: Andrei! You're home. Great. I've seen this quiz in a magazine. It tells you what sort of shopper you are. Can I ask you the questions?

Andrei: Hmm. I'm not really interested in those, Vera, but go on then. It might be fun. What do I have to do?

Vera: Fantastic. Right. Well, you just have to give me a number between one and four, with one being strongly disagree and four being strongly agree. Ready?

Andrei: Yep.

Vera: Right. Number one. When I go shopping, I always decide on a budget and stick to it.

Andrei: Hmm. Well, I usually have an idea of the amount I want to spend, but typically, I end up spending quite a bit more.

Vera: So, would you say that's a two?

Andrei: No. I think I strongly disagree, so one.

Vera: OK. Number two. I avoid buying things I don't need, even if I see a bargain.

Andrei: Right. Well, that's definitely a one. If I come across something that's a lot cheaper because it's on sale, then I can't resist buying it.

Vera: Ha! You're just like me, Andrei – I have to buy things which are on sale too. Next, it's number three. I always shop around before I buy something to make sure I get the best deal.

Andrei: Oh dear. I'm not doing very well, am I? I never do that. If I like something, I get it straight away without looking to see if I can find a better price elsewhere, so it's strongly disagree again.

Vera: Hmm, I think I know where this is going, Andrei. OK, number four. I don't buy designer brands because the brand name isn't important.

Andrei: Well, you know I like designer brands, Vera, so I have to say one for that one. I strongly disagree.

Vera: Hmm ... one ... strong-ly dis-a-gree. Right. The final one. If I can't find what I wanted to buy, I return home empty-handed.

Andrei: Hmm. Well, I don't like leaving without buying anything, so I usually get something, even if I don't really want to buy it, perhaps not every time. So, for that one, I'm going to say disagree, which is two, isn't it?

Vera: Correct. That's it. Let's add up your score. OK so, one, one, one, one, two. That's six out of a possible 20.

Andrei: What does that tell us about my shopping habits?

Vera: Let's look. It's on page …

Exercise 3

1 budget
2 bargain
3 shop around
4 designer brands
5 empty-handed

Exercise 4

1 empty-handed
2 budget
3 designer brand
4 shop around
5 (a) bargain

Page 173

GRAMMAR

Exercise 1

2 Vera is making a comparison between herself and Andrei.

Exercise 2

1 B
2 C
3 D
4 A

Exercise 3

1 the magazine as the
2 working as a
3 just like
4 known as

Exercise 4

1 like
2 as
3 as
4 like

LISTENING

Exercise 1

Suggested answers

1 They are all things that shops do to encourage people to buy their products.
2 during sales or special events

Exercise 2

1 interview / job interview
2 shopping online / internet shopping
3 a wedding
4 how shops make customers spend more

Track 086

Narrator: Speaker 1

I've put on smart clothes – it's important to make a good impression, isn't it? And, I'm going to make sure I arrive early too. I'm quite nervous as I'm not sure what questions they'll ask, but I expect they'll be about dealing with customers. I am an experienced shop assistant though, so I'm sure that will help me in the interview.

Narrator: Speaker 2

It was such an incredible occasion. Everyone was well-dressed, and I thought she looked really elegant in her dress. There were around one hundred guests and one of them told me that he'd proposed while they were travelling. How romantic! It really was a lovely wedding.

Narrator: Speaker 3

It's straightforward really. I just selected what style I wanted and put my debit card details in and, a couple of clicks later, it was done. I know some people are worried about security, but I'm not. I like the convenience and the fact things get delivered to my door. I always choose to shop online if I can.

Narrator: Speaker 4

Why are chocolates placed near the tills and essentials, like bread, at the back of the supermarket? Why do some shops play soft music? We know retailers do it and yet we, the consumers, still fall for the tricks they use to get us to part with more money. Hello, my name's Antonio Ballari and I'm here to talk about some of the tactics retailers use to get you spending.

Exercise 3

Suggested answers:

1 The speaker has put on smart clothes as they are going for an interview.
2 The speaker is talking about their experience of shopping online.
3 The speaker is talking about going to a wedding and describing the guests and bride.
4 The speaker is talking about the tricks retailers use to get us to buy products.

Exercise 4

1 a lecture; one speaker
2 neutral to formal
3 students' own answers but could be: *advertising, retailers, consumer, promotion, special offer*, etc.

Exercise 5

1 leaving clothes lying around so that people think that the item is popular
2 The electronic screens are used to keep consumers in the same place for longer so that they spend more money.

3 We now buy more online and it's now possible for companies to track what we are buying.

Track 087

Why are chocolates placed near the tills and essentials, like bread, at the back of the supermarket? Why do some shops play soft music? We know retailers do it and yet we, the consumers, still fall for the tricks they use to get us to part with more money. Hello. My name's Antonio Ballari and I'm here to talk about some of the tactics retailers use to get you spending.

Instead of constantly tidying the shop floor, shop assistants are often told to leave clothes lying around. Why? To give the impression that the item is popular. With lots of people seemingly looking for the same thing it becomes a must-have. That is, an item which is essential or highly desirable. This tactic works particularly well for younger shoppers who are hugely influenced by what others are buying.

Brands are always trying to get your attention and to keep it. This might be done by using digital screens which are placed behind display stands and are fitted with eye-tracking systems. Activated within a matter of seconds, they flash images to both excite and confuse us. By surprising shoppers, it disrupts the consumers' thinking and encourages them to spend more time in one place and therefore spend more money.

When we talk about how technology has changed the way we shop, we think about data collection. Nowadays, when we buy something on the internet, the online retailer remembers what we have bought and then makes suggestions of other products we might be interested in. Furthermore, if you post your latest purchase on social media, you may also find that you see adverts for similar products or news of flash sales on your social media page within minutes.

Page 174

VOCABULARY

Exercise 1

They were all put up for sale on e-bay / put up for auction and sold.

Exercise 2

1 C
2 A
3 B
4 E
5 D

Track 088

Santiago: So, I was online the other day and I thought I'd take a look at one of those websites where people sell things to whoever offers to pay the most.

Mia: Oh, you mean like an online auction?

Santiago: Yes, that's right. Anyway, I might get some new running shoes after I've been paid, so I was browsing sports gear, when I came across someone selling a ghost in a glass jar! The seller said he would not be held responsible if the ghost escaped from the jar and started haunting its new owner. Someone had put in a bid for fifty-five thousand dollars! I couldn't believe it. Who would be stupid enough to purchase that!

Mia: Yeah, I know, it's incredible what some people will buy. Did you hear about Justin Timberlake's half-eaten toast?

Santiago: No. What about it?

Mia: Well, that sold for one thousand pounds online and Britney Spears' chewing gum went for nine thousand, five hundred pounds.

Santiago: Really? That's got to be the world's most expensive piece of bread! And the gum, how on earth could anyone prove it was genuine and had actually belonged to her?

Mia: I agree. You could hardly return it for an exchange if you weren't satisfied. Moving on, there was also a guy who sold his entire life, including his house in Perth, Australia and his belongings. As part of the deal, he also included an introduction to his friends and a trial at his job!

Santiago: That's got to be one of the weirdest things I've ever heard. How much did he get?

Mia: Almost four hundred thousand dollars. And also, let's not forget the man who sold his forehead as advertising space.

Santiago: He sold his head?

Mia: Well, actually, just his forehead. He agreed to have a semi-permanent logo, or brand name, printed on his forehead for 30 days as an advertisement. There were several bids too. He made almost forty thousand dollars.

Santiago: Hmm, well, I haven't eaten all my lunch. Do you think anyone would want to buy a half-eaten cheese sandwich? The bread's a bit cheap but the cheese is good quality.

Mia: Funny you should mention cheese sandwiches. Did you hear about the one that sold…

Exercise 3

1 auction
2 browsing
3 bid
4 genuine
5 an exchange
6 cheap

Exercise 4

1 genuine
2 exchange
3 bid
4 auction
5 cheap
6 browsing

Page 175

SPEAKING PART 3 AND PART 4 TRAINING

Exercise 2

Joe dominates the discussion and does not allow Stephanie to speak.

Track 089

Joe: Well, I'm going to start with this one. Generally, I think you have a much wider choice of products when buying online compared to a shopping centre. For example, if one site doesn't have what you want, it's easy to search on another retailer's site. So, for the consumer, I would definitely say that online shopping is better. Now …

Stephanie: I agree to a point but …

Joe: Now, if I move on to the cost of items, I would suggest there's a lot of competition between online retailers which means it's easier for the consumer to find a bargain. These items tend to be cheaper online than in a shop, too.

Stephanie: Yes. Although, I'd argue that …

Joe: With regard to security, I'd say this is one of the key things where there are potential problems for the shopper. When you pay by debit or credit card online, you can never be one hundred percent certain that your payment details are secure and that can be quite concerning. Of course , online shopping…

Stephanie: Yes, it's important to …

Joe: As I was saying, of course online shopping can be time-consuming, perhaps because there is so much choice and it can be easy to spend too long browsing for something and actually you end up wasting time. The same can be said when browsing in a shopping centre, too, as people often end up buying more than they originally planned to buy.

Stephanie: Of course, but as we're reliant on …

Joe: Finally, I'd like to talk about customer service. As far as my experience goes, that's another potential drawback of internet shopping. It can be difficult, if not impossible sometimes, to get support from a real person if, for example, you want to exchange something because the wrong item was delivered.

Exercise 4 and 5

1 What do you think about this option?
2 What are your thoughts on this?
3 Do you have another idea here?
4 Is that similar to what you think?
5 Would you agree with that?

Track 090

1 What do you think about this option?
2 What are your thoughts on this?
3 Do you have another idea here?
4 Is that similar to what you think?
5 Would you agree with that?

Exercise 6

1 security
2 What are your thoughts on this?
3 Louise rephrases the questions to be more specific about what she wants Peter to comment on.

Track 091

Louise: Shall we start with this option?
Peter: Yes, OK.
Louise: Well, with regards to security, I'd say this is one of the key things where there are potential problems for the internet shopper. When you pay by debit or credit card online, you can never be one hundred percent certain that your payment details are secure. What are your thoughts on this?
Peter: Err… I'm not sure
Louise: OK, do you think it's safe to use a credit card online?
Peter: Yes. I think most sites are safe to use, so I don't think it's such a big problem for most people.

Page 176

PUSH YOURSELF C1

Exercise 2

Amelia

Track 092

Tommy: Surely advertising campaigns are simply a way to make us more aware of products and services and the choices available? Without advertising, consumers might miss out on buying something really useful. I don't think there's anything wrong with that.
Amelia: I take your point, but that's not quite the way I see it, Tommy. I think brands can be quite misleading sometimes, for example companies that use famous sports stars to promote fast food to young people.
Tommy: Isn't it more a case of using innovation to attract attention to a product? Advertising helps businesses as well as the economy to grow.
Amelia: I can't argue with that. However, there's a difference between raising awareness and manipulating the consumer by using someone they look up to to promote their product. Most young people don't realise it's even happening, and that's just wrong.
Tommy: I'm afraid I just don't see it like that. You can't blame businesses for trying to sell their products. As long as they don't make claims which aren't true, I can't see a problem with using these kinds of methods.
Amelia: Ok. Well, we'll just have to agree to disagree on this point then. Where do you stand on …

Exercise 3

1 ✓
2 ✓
3 ✗
4 ✓
5 ✓
6 ✗
7 ✓

Exercise 4

A 1, 2, 6
B 4
C 5
D 3, 7

READING

Exercise 2

Student A:

1 His grandmother and grandfather had a clothes shop and his mother also worked there.
2 because it is a hard business to make money in
3 because he was turned down by over 20 different companies

Student B:

1 when she was still at school
2 because she didn't have enough confidence
3 because somebody approached her on the street and asked where she had got her outfit

Student C:

1 interior design
2 He wishes that he had started working in the fashion industry earlier rather than going to college.
3 He recommends that they get a job/apprenticeship in fashion and work their way up.

Student D:

1 She was put off by the fees and having to take out a loan.
2 She could make contacts and keep an eye on the internal vacancies.
3 She doesn't have much time off.

Page 177

READING AND USE OF ENGLISH PART 7 TRAINING

Exercise 4

1 B
2 D
3 A
4 B
5 D
6 C
7 D
8 A
9 C
10 B

Exercise 5

1 set up
2 go for it
3 an option
4 make a living
5 outfit
6 give it a go
7 get into
8 work your way up
9 keep an eye on
10 time off

Page 178

GRAMMAR

Exercise 2

4

Track 093

Rachida: Hey Haruto, been shopping, have you? Let's have a look [rustling of bags]. Nice … but haven't you got a shirt like that already?
Haruto: Thanks. Yes, I have. I didn't have to purchase it, really, but it was such a bargain, I got excited and couldn't resist. Plus, this label is really on-trend at the moment.
Rachida: That's the problem these days, isn't it? We're all under so much pressure to buy the latest fashion or gadget. This might sound a bit too serious but I blame consumerism, personally.
Haruto: [sigh] How so?
Rachida: Well, it's all about convenience, isn't it? It's easier to replace than repair. I think we live in a throw-away society now. Look at your shirt, for example. The one you had already was perfect: it suited you and it was still in great condition, so you needn't have bought a new one. And then there's your phone …
Haruto: What about my phone? I love my phone – it's stylish and very fashionable. I particularly like the elegant ... [interrupted by Rachida]
Rachida: Yes, maybe that's true, but you only had your last one for six months. There was nothing wrong with it and yet, as soon as the latest model was released, you bought a new one. What did you do with the old one?
Haruto: Hmm, it's in my cupboard with the others.
Rachida: Exactly! You haven't even bothered to recycle the old ones. The problem is we love buying things and the act of shopping gives us a thrill, or a high. But the feeling is short-lived.
Haruto: What do you mean?
Rachida: Well, we get a feeling of great satisfaction when we buy something and

show it to friends or family, but that feeling is temporary. It's like an addiction.

Haruto: Maybe you're right. I do like the feeling of walking down the street with shopping bags but, after a few days, I often regret buying something I didn't need. Hmm, maybe I shouldn't have been persuaded by the special offer.

Rachida: No, and if I were you, I'd take it back for a refund. You'd better hurry though, the shops close in 30 minutes.

Exercise 3

1 have to purchase
2 needn't have bought
3 have been persuaded

Exercise 4

1 3; other structures include: *regret* + *ing* / *wish* + past perfect / *If only* + past perfect
2 1 and 2, *have to* / *need to* / *must*

Exercise 5

1 shouldn't have spent
2 didn't need to buy
3 needn't have bothered
4 didn't have to look
5 shouldn't have built

VOCABULARY

Exercise 1

1 C
2 A
3 E
4 F
5 D
6 B

Exercise 3

1 appropriately
2 simultaneously
3 impatiently
4 deliberately
5 peacefully
6 negatively
7 carelessly

Page 179

WRITING PART 2: REVIEW TRAINING

Exercise 3

1 last paragraph
2 3rd paragraph
3 2nd paragraph

Exercise 4

1 C
2 D
3 B
4 E
5 A
6 F

Exercise 5

1 initially
2 Curiously
3 Naturally
4 Typically
5 Sadly
6 Thankfully

Page 180

EXAM FOCUS
READING AND USE OF ENGLISH PART 7

1 C
2 A
3 D
4 C
5 B
6 D
7 A
8 B
9 A
10 D

Page 181

WRITING PART 2: REVIEW

Model answer

I recently purchased an antique grandfather clock in an online auction. My great-grandfather was a clock- maker and my uncle dealt in antiques, so I have always loved old timepieces. Since I've started working, I've decided to start my own collection and this is my first. When I saw it advertised, I initially thought it was a reproduction but on closer inspection, I realised it was a genuine hand-carved item originating from the 1830s.

Naturally, I was cautious about buying such a precious clock online, but I needn't have worried. It arrived safely just two days later and was everything I had hoped for. What I love most is the smooth feel of the mahogany and the hand-painted dial decorated with intricate designs. The only thing I am not sure about is that its chime is very loud!

Sadly, few people would want to buy a grandfather clock these days. However, I would recommend this longcase model to collectors, dealers and anyone who wants a reminder of a past era.

SPEAKING PARTS 3 AND 4

Students' own answers

Page 182

REAL WORLD

Exercise 3

Photo A: Milan Fashion Week
Photo B: Galleria Vittorio Emanuele II
Photo C: street markets

Page 183

Exercise 4

1 iconic
2 to your heart's content
3 in the heart of
4 soak up
5 get a glimpse of
6 biannual

Exercise 5

1 False – 1800s or 19th Century
2 True
3 False – in the heart of the city
4 False – twice a year (biannual)
5 False – after the London Fashion Week

Exercise 6

1 C
2 A
3 F
4 E
5 B
6 D

Track 094

Customer: Hello, I was wondering if I could have a refund for this, please?

Shop assistant: Why are you returning the dress, madam?

Customer: Unfortunately, it doesn't go with the shoes I already have.

Shop assistant: I see. So, it's unsuitable?

Customer: That's right.

Shop assistant: Is it unworn, madam?

Customer: Yes. I've tried it on but that's all.

Shop assistant: That's fine. Have you got the receipt?

Customer: It was a gift, so I don't have the receipt, I'm afraid.

Shop assistant: Ah. In that case, I can't offer you a refund, only an exchange.

Customer: OK. I'll just have a browse around and see it there's anything else I want.

...

Customer: Could I try these on, please?

Shop assistant: Of course. Let me hang them in the fitting room for you so you can keep looking.

Customer: Thanks. And when I've finished, where is it?

Shop assistant: Just over there, madam, next to the cash desk. Your items will be in the first cubicle.

...

Customer: I'm sorry, I've tried a few things on but there's nothing else I like right now.

Shop assistant: That's ok. I can offer you a credit note if you prefer?

Customer: Yes. Will I be able to use it online?

Shop assistant: Yes. Once you've added what you want to your basket, and proceed to checkout, enter this code.
Customer: OK, thank you. What's your return policy for sale items?
Shop assistant: We don't offer refunds on sale items.
Customer: OK. Thanks for your help.
Shop assistant: Would you like to join our loyalty scheme? You get points every time you spend.
Customer: Not at the moment, thank you. It'll only encourage me to spend more!

Exercise 7

1 unsuitable
2 receipt
3 an exchange
4 fitting room
5 cash desk
6 credit
7 loyalty

UNIT 14

Page 184

READING

Exercise 2

The three jobs mentioned in the article are:

1 video games commentator
2 location scout
3 ethical hacker

Page 185

Exercise 3

1 to be / become less important than something else
2 B
3 B
4 C

Page 186

READING AND USE OF ENGLISH PART 4 TRAINING

Exercise 5

1 turned down the / turned down John's
2 discourage her from going
3 no intention of living
4 no point in getting
5 on behalf of
6 in addition to dealing
7 no matter how fast he
8 had his doubts about

GRAMMAR

Exercise 1

1 It was only when I received my first pay slip that they realised it could work.
2 On the living room floor, there is an unpacked suitcase.
3 What I love the most about my job is the travelling …
4 … under no circumstances am I allowed to talk about the work I do for the government.
5 Meeting these three people is something that I'm really glad I did …
6 Since they all seemed so happy, it's easy to think that it does.

Exercise 2

1 Going to the interview is something that I'm really glad I did.
2 In the corner of the office above the photocopier there is a small camera.
3 Since I had finished all of my work, I decided to leave the office for the day.
4 It was when I got home that I noticed (that) I had left my phone at work.
5 What I really like about the job is the benefits.
6 Under no circumstances am I allowed to talk about the work I do for a security company.

Page 187

VOCABULARY

Exercise 2

Suggested answers

Alice: project manager, Jack: CEO, Amelia: Head of digital (CDO)

Track 095

Alice: Good morning, can you both hear me OK?
Jack: Yes, loud and clear.
Amelia: Yes, I can.
Alice: Great! So welcome to our monthly catch-up meeting. We've got quite a packed agenda today so let's kick off with the action points from our previous meeting. Jack, you were planning to discuss the takeover bid with the board of directors – how did that go?
Jack: Yes, so I met with them last week and we went through the proposal. They are going to get back to me with their comments at some point next week, so I'll let you know the decision in the next meeting, if that's OK.
Alice: Yes, that sounds good. OK, point two. Jack, you were also due to set up a meeting with the sales team to discuss the quarterly sales figures.
Jack: I'm really sorry but I haven't got round to that yet. I'm meeting them at the sales conference in two weeks' time so I'll book a meeting in with them then.
Alice: No problem, I'll add it to next month's agenda. Finally, Amelia, you were about to look into some of the bugs that have been reported by users on the website when we last spoke, right?
Amelia: Yes, that's right. I ran these issues by the tech team. It turned out to be a bigger problem than we'd anticipated and we were on the point of taking the website offline completely. Luckily, though, the tech team were able to resolve these issues while keeping the website live, which is great.
Alice: That is good news! So let's move on to this month's items. Firstly, we need to update the budget for the new financial year.
Jack: That's on my list for this week. I've already looked into a few areas and made the decision to cut back on the amount of trips we take abroad, as a lot of these can be replaced by video conferences. I'll do a full analysis this week and send an email round to the team.
Alice: That sounds good. The other point was for you, Amelia, regarding information on the homepage that is no longer relevant.
Amelia: Yeah, so I've got in touch with the marketing department and asked them to provide us with an updated version. As soon as we have this, we'll take down the old content and replace it with the new version. We'll make sure this is reflected across our social media pages, as well.
Alice: Great. Well, that took less time than expected. Is there any other business you want to raise?
Amelia: Nothing from me.
Jack: I just wanted to say that I've put back my annual leave until next month.
Alice: OK, I'll update the team calendar straight after the meeting.

Exercise 3

1 get back to
2 set up
3 got round to
4 look into
5 ran … by
6 cut back on
7 take down
8 put back

Exercise 4

1 set up
2 cut back on
3 got round to
4 run … by
5 taken … down
6 put back
7 looking into
8 getting back to

Page 188

SPEAKING

Exercise 2

Advantages

1 The main advantage of this product is
2 One of the key benefits of this is
3 What makes this stand out is the fact that

Disadvantages

4 One of the major drawbacks of this is
5 A major disadvantage of this is
6 One of the downsides to this product is

Page 189

LISTENING

LISTENING PART 2 TRAINING

Exercise 3

1 adventurous
irresponsible is incorrect because this is the word Harry's parents use to describe him.
2 courses
qualifications is incorrect because Harry says that he knew there would be qualifications, so this didn't surprise him.

Track 096

Harry: Hi, my name's Harry and I'm going to talk about my life as a stuntman. It all started around thirty years ago when I was about six or seven. If you spoke to my parents, they would probably describe me as an irresponsible young boy, but I prefer to call it adventurous, owing to the fact that I loved to explore new environments, no matter how dangerous they may have been. It wasn't until I had children of my own that I understood where my parents were coming from.
The first job I got in film wasn't actually as a stuntman, but as an assistant. I was inspired by the stuntmen and women who were jumping off buildings and setting themselves on fire and decided that this was the career for me. There was a fair amount of support online and I knew that there would be qualifications that I needed to get. What I didn't realise was just how few courses there were for people who wanted to get into this line of work.
I managed to find one in the end, and after a lot of training, I became a fully qualified stuntman.

Exercise 4

3 extraordinary
ambitious is incorrect because this is the word Harry uses to describe the director.
fantastic is incorrect because this is the word Harry uses to describe the actors.

Track 097

Harry: I'll never forget the first film that I was hired for as a stuntman. It was a sequel to a very popular action film that was given an enormous budget, most of which was put aside for stunts. I didn't really know what to make of it at first. The director was really ambitious with his plans and had cast a fantastic set of actors to perform in it. The location that was chosen for the filming was extraordinary, we ended up having a great time on set and thankfully all the stunts went as planned.

Exercise 5

4 relief
5 chef
6 bridge
7 unemployed
8 nephew

Track 098

Harry: By the end of filming, when the director shouted "that's a wrap", I was expecting to feel a huge sense of satisfaction that I had got through my first film unscathed, when in actual fact, it was more relief than anything else. It was an unforgettable experience and my mind instantly turned to what my next project would be.
People often think that being a stuntman is similar to being a footballer, in so much as there is a high risk of getting injured. I've never sustained any serious injuries, although I have had my fair share of cuts and bruises. It's to be expected though, much in the same way that a chef is likely to hurt themselves – it's just part of the job. I've lost count of the amount of times a director has run across the set to make sure that I'm OK after a particularly dangerous stunt.
It's not just me who suffers, though.
The worst injury I have ever encountered actually happened to a colleague of mine. The original idea was for him to jump off the side of a building and onto a train that was travelling at about 70 kilometres per hour. It was later changed to a bridge in order to make the scene more dramatic. Unfortunately, he mistimed the jump and landed heavily on his right arm, breaking it in two places. Luckily, he made a full recovery and returned to work four months later.
Being a stuntman isn't always as glamorous as you might think. There are times when I feel really tired, particularly from jetlag if we're filming overseas. Most stunt performers are self-employed, which means that work isn't always guaranteed. Therefore, it's possible to go for several months without working, which essentially means you are unemployed and that's something that I get worried about the most if I'm honest, especially as I have a wife and two children.
All things considered, I love what I do. Sure it has its drawbacks, like the ones I've just mentioned, but overall, it's a great career choice. I'm in the process of convincing my nephew to take it up too, though I'm not sure my brother will be entirely happy about that, given all the stories I've told him over the years. Though, I like to think that I'm a pretty cool uncle.

Page 190

VOCABULARY

Exercise 2

1 promoted
2 headquarters
3 decline
4 deadline
5 employee
6 overtime
7 fire
8 CEO

Exercise 3

1 sacked / fired / made redundant
2 corporation / firm / institution
3 employee
4 workforce
5 decline

PUSH YOURSELF C1

Exercise 1

1 A
2 B
3 A
4 B
5 B
6 A

Page 191

WRITING PART 2: LETTER OF APPLICATION TRAINING

Exercise 1

Tour guides wanted

We are looking for English-speaking tour guides to work at the university, showing visitors around the campus and telling them about the university. Write a letter to Mrs Sandra Jones, the communications director, giving details of:

- Your experience of working as a tour guide
- Your knowledge of English
- What skills you have that will be useful for this role.

Exercise 2

Dear Mrs Jones

Exercise 3

Sentence 1 is the most appropriate.
Sentence 2 isn't appropriate because it's too informal.
Sentence 3 isn't appropriate because the writer says they saw the advert in the local newspaper (it should be the college magazine).
Sentence 4 isn't appropriate because it contains a grammatical error:
I have recently seen the advertisement for the job of tour guide and I would like to be ~~considering~~ ***considered*** *for the role.*

Exercise 4

For the past year, I have been working as a tour guide in my hometown. This involves talking about the various historical and cultural landmarks of the town in addition to handing out leaflets which explain some of the best things to do there. I am also responsible for making sure that the group stays together and is safe until the end of the tour.

Exercise 5

1 passed
2 obtaining
3 spent
4 are

Exercise 6

Noun	Adjective
energy	energetic
enthusiasm	enthusiastic
humour	humorous
knowledge	knowledgeable
organisation	organised
patience	patient
punctuality	punctual

Exercise 7

1 Having worked as a waiter. He also told us about his upcoming production on foreign languages. for three years, I am very good at speaking to customers.
2 Having (already) passed all of my exams, I am available to work for the whole summer.
3 Having lived in England for three years, I am able to speak English fluently.

Page 192

EXAM FOCUS

READING AND USE OF ENGLISH PART 4

1 to take such a
2 who managed to solve
3 came up with
4 had difficulty getting/finding
5 was an increase in
6 took up cooking at

Page 193

LISTENING PART 2

1 colleague
2 camera equipment
3 space travel
4 script
5 family life
6 (professional) actors
7 communication skills
8 health and safety
9 certificate
10 fashion

Track 099

Elizabeth: Hello. My name's Elizabeth Moore and I'm here today to talk about a filmmaking course that I recently went on at the Longman Institute.

I have always been interested in filmmaking, ever since I was a young girl and my father would take me on trips to film local wildlife. One day, while I was on my lunch break, a colleague of mine told me about a three-month, part-time course in filmmaking and recommended that I give it a try. It was perfect, as I could fit it around other commitments In fact, when my husband heard about the course, he was really supportive, being a film-enthusiast himself.

On the first day, we were told what we'd be learning. This included the story development, how to use editing software and an introduction to working with music. That afternoon, we jumped straight into filming and they taught us the basics of operating camera equipment, which was a little difficult at first but I soon got the hang of it.

Our course tutor, Jonathan Smith was great. As well as being a famous director, he also works as a TV critic and I had actually read one of his reviews on a documentary series about the environment prior to the course. He was keen to tell us about a production that he'd recently directed about space travel, which was voted best new series at the local film festival.

For our first course project, we were put into groups and asked to discuss what makes an effective opening scene for a film. We were then asked to come up with our own ideas for a film and create a script for the first five minutes of it. We chose to write something in which our main character is stranded on a desert island.

In addition to the classes, we were also invited to presentations that were taking place at the institute. I remember one particularly good one where the director was talking about a film she had made about her childhood. This got me thinking about doing something on family life and how this has changed over the years. Without realising it, I had actually done the ground work for the next assignment, which was to produce a short film about a topic of our choice. This gave me the chance to work with professional actors, which I really enjoyed. One of my course mates worked with a couple of celebrities for her short film who she met through one of the instructors on the course.

One of the main benefits of the course for me was learning from the experience of the tutors and presenters. They had fantastic communication skills, which was something that I also had the chance to improve as the course went on. I was particularly impressed with their problem-solving skills and their ability to provide answers to all of our questions.

Overall, I enjoyed almost all of the courses on the programme. There were always going to be some modules that were better than others. I mean, when you've just had a class about using cutting-edge technology, learning about health and safety can be pretty boring, but I guess it's all relevant to filmmaking.

At the end of the course, the organisers put on a small ceremony for us and we all received a certificate which was accredited by the institute. This was great because it meant that we were now recognised filmmakers, which was particularly useful when applying for a job as some of the participants wanted to do. We also gave a gift to the tutors as a thank you for all their hard work.

Filmmaking is still a big part of my life. I'm just putting the finishing touches on a film about tourism which I'll upload at some point in the future. I'd really like to make a series about education though I don't know enough about it, really, so I'm going to just stick to fashion which is a topic I'm more familiar with.

WRITING PART 2: LETTER OF APPLICATION

Model answer

Dear Sir or Madam,

I was excited to hear that the Hotel International is going to open in our town later this year. I would like to submit my application for the post of receptionist.

I am currently employed as a receptionist in Hotel Garden View in Belleview Heights. In this position, I have developed skills relating to customer service, such as clear communication and dealing with difficult situations. I am punctual, friendly and calm under pressure. I have enjoyed my three years at Hotel Garden View but feel I am now ready to move into a larger hotel with an international clientele.

If I am appointed, I would be keen to receive training in dealing with customers from different countries, such as how to greet them and any topics that should be avoided. I'd also like to improve my computer skills, particularly working with spreadsheets. I am available to attend an interview at your convenience.

I look forward to hearing from you.

Yours faithfully,

Stephen

Page 194

REAL WORLD

Exercise 1

Suggested answer:

People who work in the financial district of a city including stockbrokers, investors, lawyers and consultants

Exercise 2

1 Salary – B
2 Working hours – B and C
3 Location – A and C
4 Work benefits – C
5 Language skills – A and B
6 Type of contract – B
7 Closing date – C
8 Essential skills and experience – A
9 Desirable skills and experience – B

Exercise 4

Suggested answer:

Ricardo might be applying for a job as a social media manager

Page 195

Exercise 5

1 DOB
2 Bachelor's degree and Master's degree
3 Present
4 Ensure
5 up-to-date
6 Extensive
7 Excellent, Exceptional
8 References are available upon request.

Exercise 6

1 Why did you apply for this role?
2 What experience do you have in this field?
3 What do you think makes a good team member?
4 What do you think the main challenges of the job will be?
5 What skills do you have that will help you succeed in this role?
6 Where do you see yourself in five years' time?
7 What are your salary expectations?

Track 100

Recruiter: Good morning, Ricardo.
Ricardo: Good morning.
Recruiter: Thanks for coming along to the interview today. Tell me, why did you apply for this role?
Ricardo: Well, the reputation of the company was certainly a factor. I've been really impressed with the innovative work that the company has been doing in recent years.
Recruiter: What experience do you have in this field?
Ricardo: I have extensive experience in managing social media pages in my last two positions. At AB Associates, I am responsible for the general management of our five social media sites, making sure that they reflect the key USPs of our products. Prior to this, I worked at Brighter Together as an assistant social media manager, working with the team to develop engaging content.
Recruiter: Speaking of teams, what do you think makes a good team member?
Ricardo: In my opinion, the characteristics of a good team member are reliability and flexibility. It's important that you can be trusted by your colleagues and solve problems as and when they arise.
Recruiter: What do you think the main challenges of the job will be?
Ricardo: One challenge that I would expect to face in the role would be dealing with the large number of comments from users when we post messages on our social media pages. It's vital that we manage this well to ensure that our customers are happy.
Recruiter: What skills do you have that will help you succeed in this role?
Ricardo: Personally, I believe that I am well-organised, diligent and have a can-do attitude. I take great pride in my work and ensure that it's of the best possible standard.
Recruiter: OK, let's talk about your goals for the future. Where do you see yourself in five years' time?
Ricardo: That's a good question. I'm really excited by this position at the company because in five years, it is my ambition to become a valued and respected employee. I am looking to further my skills as a social media manager and take on more managerial responsibilities and even take the lead on some bigger projects.
Recruiter: Finally, what are your salary expectations?
Ricardo: I would be happy to consider an offer in the region of thirty to thirty-five thousand Euros. I think that would be a fair reflection of the work I'll be doing.
Recruiter: Thank you very much, Ricardo. That's the end of the interview. We'll now move onto …

Exercise 7

1 innovative
2 Prior
3 characteristics
4 face
5 can-do attitude
6 ambition
7 further
8 region

PROGRESS CHECK 5

Page 196

Exercise 1

1 compulsory for students to wear
2 don't have to bring
3 are not allowed to smoke
4 are not / aren't supposed to buy
5 advisable for guests to arrive

Exercise 2

1 managed
2 be able
3 enable
4 unable
5 could
6 able to
7 capable

Exercise 3

1 C
2 B
3 B
4 D
5 A
6 C

Exercise 4

1 as
2 like
3 as
4 as
5 like
6 as
7 like
8 like

Page 197

Exercise 5

1 should have bought
2 we needn't have brought
3 shouldn't have spent
4 he didn't have/need to have
5 I didn't need to buy

Exercise 6

1 They created a huge marketing campaign to promote their new line of shoes.
2 You don't need to purchase an extra ticket as my friend can no longer make it.
3 The two leaders are trying to promote commerce between their countries.
4 A lot of websites deliberately increase the price of holidays during the school holidays.
5 There seems to be a lot of jealousy in the fashion industry these days.
6 I recently won two tickets for a luxury spa weekend in an online auction.
7 They have installed a ramp outside the shop to increase accessibility for wheelchair users.

8 Initially, most people rejected the plans to build a new shopping centre in the town.

Exercise 7

1 get back to
2 hired
3 surge
4 employees
5 to make … redundant
6 looking into
7 headquarters
8 to set up

Exercise 8

1 Under no circumstances must you talk in the exam.
2 Since I had already seen the film, I decided not to go with them.
3 What I really like about my job is the salary.
4 Waiting in the meeting room was the head of the organisation.
5 Going to the presentation was something I'm really happy I did.

GRAMMAR REFERENCE

Page 204

STARTER

THE PRESENT PERFECT SIMPLE AND CONTINUOUS

Exercise 1

1 have / 've been preparing; have / 've not finished have / 've you been doing
2 have you been doing
3 have / 've been looking; have they been working
4 have / 've not completed; have/'ve been chilling
5 have / 've been doing; have/'ve damaged
6 have / 've been
7 has / 's become
8 have / 've been changing

Exercise 2

1 Correct
2 I have finally learnt
3 he has been eating
4 Correct
5 Correct
6 They have been browsing
7 I have been going

Page 205

Exercise 3

1 Scientists have discovered vaccines to cure many fatal illnesses.
2 He has not put his recent qualifications on his CV yet.
3 Wake up! You have been sleeping for over two hours now.
4 We all feel thirsty, because as usual we have not been drinking / have not drunk enough during training.
5 She has known him since he was a small child.
6 It has been snowing heavily all morning and as a result the roads are slippery now.

COMPARATIVES AND SUPERLATIVES

Exercise 1

1 worst
2 more often
3 most complicated
4 most memorable
5 cheapest
6 more irregular

Exercise 2

1 His ambition has always been greater than his brother's.
2 Her analysis of the financial situation was as accurate as the report in the magazine.
3 The lecturer is less available to her students since she started work on her thesis.
4 His skills are not developing as fast as people predicted.
5 My interest in the project is considerably greater now than it was at the beginning.
6 My motivation is not quite as high as I would ideally want.
7 There are slightly fewer people living in the town than ten years ago.
8 It's considerably more exhausting to travel by car than by train.

Page 207

UNIT 1

GERUNDS AND INFINITIVES

Exercise 1

1 He decided **to make** a high offer
2 Correct
3 They persuaded me **to apply**
4 Correct
5 Can I remind you **not to drive**
6 The lawyers advised him **to say**

Exercise 2

1 to speak
2 following
3 joining
4 celebrating
5 taking up
6 watching
7 to do

Exercise 3

1 d
2 c
3 f
4 b
5 e
6 a

Exercise 4

1 to buy
2 carrying
3 taking
4 to stay
5 Analysing
6 paying

Page 208

UNIT 2

THE PASSIVE

Exercise 1

1 The safe in my room was opened by a member of the hotel staff.
2 Lots of bargains can be found on the market.
3 Tickets for the event can be bought online.
4 It was thought that children were to blame for the damage to the trees.
5 My phone was taken out of my jacket pocket.
6 The winter tyres on my car have been replaced.

Exercise 2

1 A
2 C
3 C
4 B
5 C
6 A

Page 209

USED TO, GET / BE USED TO

Exercise 1

1 didn't use to enjoy
2 didn't use to do
3 used to spend
4 used to own
5 Did he use to keep
6 didn't use to like

Exercise 2

1 **used to** tour
2 I **used to** work / I worked in a steel factory
3 she **used to** enjoy / she enjoyed riding
4 I **used to** live in New York State
5 Correct
6 Correct

Exercise 3

1 is used to
2 to get used to
3 I'm not used to

4 to get used to
5 am getting used to
6 get used to

Page 210

UNIT 3
ZERO, FIRST AND SECOND CONDITIONAL

Exercise 1

1 will get
2 get
3 are
4 takes
5 If
6 won't win

Exercise 2

1 is; will have to
2 were; would buy
3 come; will see
4 had; wouldn't be
5 study; will pass
6 would buy; won

Exercise 3

1 if the neighbours **stopped** having parties
2 We**'ll hire** a car
3 Correct
4 I **won't** either
5 We definitely **won't** cancel the beach party, unless it pours with rain. / We definitely will cancel the beach party, **if** it pours with rain.
6 Correct

Page 211

GIVING ADVICE

Exercise 1

1 recommend <u>speaking</u>
2 ought <u>to</u> get
3 might want <u>to find</u>
4 had better <u>send</u>
5 Make sure <u>you</u> take
6 I <u>would</u> delete

Exercise 2

1 ought to
2 don't
3 might not
4 Why not
5 Make sure

Page 212

UNIT 4
COUNTABLE AND UNCOUNTABLE NOUNS

Exercise 1

1 suitable **accommodation**
2 charged us extra for our **luggage**
3 **Pollution** caused by plastic
4 I usually reject **any** advice from my doctor. / I usually reject **advice** from my doctor.
5 Correct
6 extremely valuable **works** of art

Exercise 2

1 coffee
2 any
3 cardboard; paper
4 was
5 equipment; is
6 damage

Page 213

UNIT 4
ARTICLES

Exercise 1

1 a; the
2 the; the; a; the
3 an; the; the
4 the
5 The
6 a; the

Exercise 2

1 the
2 the; the; the
3 The; the
4 The; the; the; the
5 a
6 – ; –

Page 215

UNIT 5
PAST PERFECT SIMPLE AND CONTINUOUS

Exercise 1

1 had / 'd been waiting
2 had / 'd been cheating
3 had / 'd built
4 had / 'd handed
5 had / 'd already put
6 had / 'd picked up

Exercise 2

1 had not / hadn't ordered
2 had / 'd committed
3 had / 'd fallen
4 had / 'd been riding
5 had / 'd been watching
6 had / 'd lived

Page 216

UNIT 6
PREPOSITIONS

Exercise 1

1 on
2 at
3 in
4 in
5 in
6 on

Exercise 2

1 **at** the backdoor
2 **in** the queue
3 in the world
4 Correct
5 Correct
6 **on** that cruise ship

Exercise 3

1 on
2 on
3 on
4 at
5 in; on
6 at

Page 217

UNIT 6
RELATIVE PRONOUNS AND RELATIVE CLAUSES

Exercise 1

1 which
2 whose
3 which
4 where
5 who
6 who

Exercise 2

1 that/which
2 where
3 that/why
4 that/who
5 that/who
6 whose

Page 218

UNIT 7
WISH, IF ONLY, HOPE

Exercise 1

1 had
2 could
3 would stop
4 would start
5 weighed
6 didn't keep

Exercise 2

1 He wishes he **had** chosen
2 I hope you **make** lots of money
3 Correct
4 He hopes **to** get a job
5 We all hope you **managed** / **manage** to get a visa
6 Correct

Page 219

THIRD CONDITIONAL AND MIXED CONDITIONALS

Exercise 1

1 C
2 C
3 C
4 A
5 B
6 B

Exercise 2

1 hadn't arrived; wouldn't have missed
2 had gone; wouldn't have woken up
3 had enrolled; might have got
4 had been; would have learned
5 hadn't gone; would never have met
6 would have caught; had had

Page 220

UNIT 8
DIRECT AND INDIRECT OBJECTS

Exercise 1

1 I've just bought a new computer for my brother.
2 I lent my new phone to my friend and she broke it.
3 They offered the role of assistant to her at the company.
4 I ordered the new Taylor Swift album for my wife.
5 I made a cake for my sister for her birthday.
6 I will bring some flowers to/for her when I visit next week
7 I found a new dress for her in the end-of-season sales.
8 I would like to show the photographs to them from our honeymoon.

Page 221

MODALS OF SPECULATION AND DEDUCTION

Exercise 1

1 couldn't have been
2 can't be
3 might/may/could have gone
4 must be revising
5 might have handed
6 might/may/could be

Exercise 2

1 <u>must</u> have grown
2 must have <u>left</u>
3 <u>can't</u> be at home
4 Correct
5 must <u>have</u> gone off
6 Correct
7 must have <u>forgotten</u>

Page 222

UNIT 9
FUTURE FORMS (*WILL, BE GOING TO*)

Exercise 1

1 are going to order
2 Are you going to see/watch
3 am going to apply
4 are going to see/watch
5 are going to visit
6 am going to write

Exercise 2

1 is unlikely that Martin will
2 are bound to discover
3 are going to stay
4 is little prospect

Page 223

FUTURE PERFECT, FUTURE CONTINUOUS

Exercise 1

1 have stopped
2 be sitting
3 be coming
4 have had
5 watching
6 have finished

Exercise 2

1 will have been driving
2 will have been
3 will have been living
4 I will have worked
5 will have reached
6 will have retired
7 will have been cooking
8 will you have been studying
9 will have known
10 will have earned

Page 224

UNIT 10
CAUSATIVES

Exercise 1

1 had/got
2 had/got
3 have/get
4 had/got
5 had/have had/are having
6 got

Exercise 2

1 made <u>me</u> sit
2 my sister <u>to</u> come
3 help me to <u>find</u>
4 let me <u>finish</u>
5 ten people <u>to</u> like
6 made <u>us</u> queue
7 my children <u>to</u> do
8 helped us <u>to</u> solve

Page 225

ADJECTIVES WITH *-ING* AND *-ED*

Exercise 1

1 fascinated
2 irritated
3 amusing
4 exhausted
5 tired; depressed
6 disgusting

Exercise 2

1 appealing
2 fascinating
3 involved
4 astonishing
5 dissatisfied
6 irritating
7 disgusting
8 prejudiced

Page 226

UNIT 11
REPORTED SPEECH

Exercise 1

1 worked
2 was having
3 had never done
4 had got; had eaten
5 would ring
6 could; couldn't

Exercise 2

1 A
2 A
3 B
4 B
5 A
6 A

Exercise 3

1 he had given him clear instructions about what to do the previous day.
2 they had discovered her missing sports gear in the washing machine that morning.
3 what project he was working on the following day.
4 his essay was extremely confusing.
5 what she had done the previous day.
6 had noticed any of his belongings there.

Page 228

UNIT 12
EXPRESSING OBLIGATION AND PERMISSION

Exercise 1

1 have to
2 must
3 must
4 supposed to
5 should

6 ought
7 can

Exercise 2
1 You are not **allowed** to park
2 Correct
3 Correct
4 I **needn't have done**
5 Correct
6 Correct
7 he **was** recognised

Page 229

UNIT 12
EXPRESSING ABILITY

Exercise 1
1 Could
2 couldn't
3 can
4 wasn't able
5 can't
6 can't

Exercise 2
1 I wasn't able **to**
2 fortunately I **was able to**
3 I am afraid I **can't** accept it
4 Correct
5 Correct
6 He **was able to** / **managed to** run

Page 230

UNIT 13
LIKE AND *AS*

Exercise 1
1 **as** a dental receptionist
2 he looks **like** a professional player
3 **As** far as I can tell
4 such **as** onion soup
5 Correct
6 **As** she stole a bottle of perfume

Exercise 2
1 as; as
2 like
3 as
4 as
5 like
6 as; as

Page 231

UNIT 13
SHOULDN'T HAVE / NEEDN'T HAVE / DIDN'T NEED TO / DIDN'T HAVE TO

Exercise 1
1 didn't have to
2 have eaten
3 I needn't have brought
4 should have arrived
5 should have listened
6 didn't have to
7 didn't have to
8 He shouldn't have used his phone

Exercise 2
1 needn't have updated
2 should have gone
3 didn't need to take / need not have taken
4 shouldn't have shouted

Page 233

UNIT 14
ADDING EMPHASIS AND FRONTING

Exercise 1
1 Since I don't eat meat, I will choose the vegetarian option.
2 Passing my driving test is something that I'm really happy I did.
3 Why she had received the letter, Amy didn't know.
4 In the corner of the room was a small, dark object.
5 It was only when Sarah got home that she realised she had left her phone at work.
6 When she was going to receive her results, Julie didn't know.

Exercise 2
1 Saturday was the day that Stephanie went to visit her friend
2 It was David who had problems with his car last week.
3 The cinema is where I spend most of my pocket money.
4 The reason why Mark went to the dentist was to have a tooth removed.
5 It was Alison who won the competition and received two tickets to a music festival.
6 The reason why I signed up to private English classes was to improve my reading skills.

WRITING BANK

Page 234

ESSAY

Exercise 1
Question: Will environmental problems be worse in 20 years?

Ideas: pollution, climate change and your own idea

Exercise 2
It includes the extra idea of a growing population.

Exercise 3
Ideas 1, 3, 4, 6, 8

Exercise 4
1 sentence 1
2 sentences 3, 6
3 sentences 4, 8

Page 235

Exercise 5
1 B. It makes general statements to introduce the topic and the arguments which will be developed in the essay.)
2 C. It sums up arguments on both sides, and expresses a personal opinion.)

Exercise 6
1 as
2 in my opinion
3 In addition to this
4 Firstly
5 such as
6 To sum up
7 On the other hand
8 as a result

Exercise 9
Model answer

Cycling is becoming a very popular way of getting around cities nowadays, and a lot of big cities have cycle schemes which allow people to use public bikes. But there are advantages and disadvantages to bikes as a form of city transport.

On the one hand, cycling is good for your health. It provides good exercise, and can help you to lose weight and keep fit. It is also cheap, because if you have your own bike, it does not cost you anything to travel around the city. A third advantage is that cycling is good for the environment, because it does not cause any pollution.

On the other hand, cycling on busy streets can be dangerous. Car and lorry drivers do not always notice cyclists, especially when it is dark, and this can lead to accidents.

On balance, I would say that cycling is an excellent form of transport in cities during the day and when the weather is nice. However, when it is dark or the weather is bad, I think that buses and trains are a better option.

Page 236

EMAIL / LETTER

Exercise 1
You should write an email to a friend, Jo. You should write about your new home, things there are to do in the city and your new friends.

Exercise 2
Yes, it answers all the questions in Jo's email. The tone is informal.

Exercise 3
1 false
2 true
3 true

4 false
5 true
6 false

Exercise 4

Sentences 2, 5, 6 and 8. They are suitable because they are formal.

Page 237

Exercise 5

1 Dear Ms Copeland
2 in response to
3 currently
4 would be interested in working
5 studied different aspects of
6 was employed
7 gained some experience as
8 customer satisfaction
9 I would be grateful if you would
10 I look forward to hearing from you.

Exercise 7

1 It was great <u>to</u> hear from you.
2 Why <u>don't you</u> come and …
3 It would be <u>a</u> good idea
4 I would <u>be</u> able to help
5 Could you <u>give me</u> some information
6 I look forward <u>to</u> hearing from you.

Exercise 9

Model answer

Dear Ms Simpson,

I am writing in response to your job advertisement, which appeared in the *Weekly News* last week.

I am interested in applying for the job of receptionist at your hotel this summer. This role interests me particularly because I am a very friendly and outgoing person, and I would enjoy meeting guests and helping them feel welcome. As I am currently studying English, it would also be a good opportunity for me to practise using the language.

I have experience of working as a hotel receptionist, as I spent last summer working in a hotel in Ireland. I am therefore used to taking reservations, helping guests check in and check out and dealing with problems they may have. I am cheerful and hardworking, and I understand the importance of providing good customer service. I am also a good team worker, which I know is a very important quality for working in a busy hotel. I have a good level of English, and I am able to communicate well in the language.

I hope you will consider me for this role, and I look forward to hearing from you.

Lisa Bianchi

Page 238

REVIEW

Exercise 1

You should write a review of a film you have seen. You should say what it is about, say why you did or didn't enjoy it, and say whether you think other people will enjoy it. People will read your review in an English-language magazine.

Exercise 2

1 yes
2 yes
3 anyone except young children
4 informal and friendly

Exercise 3

Plan A is better. Each paragraph has a clear topic and gives the reader useful and helpful information; it starts with a general introduction with factual information; it gives good points and problems about the website/product; it ends with a clear recommendation. Plan B contains information that is not relevant for the reader, e.g. the writer needed a new tablet, how the writer found the website; the third heading is not appropriate, as the focus should be the product you bought, not games that you play; it doesn't end with a clear recommendation.

Page 239

Exercise 4

1 incredibly
2 ridiculously
3 rather
4 brilliantly
5 extremely
6 very
7 absolutely
8 really

Exercise 5

1 c
2 f
3 a
4 e
5 d
6 b

Exercise 6

1 spite
2 though
3 despite
4 Although
5 However

Exercise 8

1 than
2 disappointing
3 will
4 miss
5 using
6 advise

Exercise 10

Model answer

<u>Playa de Oro</u>

Last summer, I spent a week with my family in a holiday resort called Playa de Oro in the south of Spain. This is a popular tourist area, but we were keen to choose a quiet resort where we could just relax on the beach or by the pool.

The resort had some positive points. The apartment buildings were attractive, and our apartment was spacious and well-equipped. The resort had two swimming pools, and both were extremely clean and well-maintained. The staff were also incredibly friendly and helpful.

However, we were disappointed to find that our resort was surrounded by several other, much bigger resorts. The beach was therefore absolutely packed with people every day, and it was almost impossible to find a place to sit. Even worse, the advert said that the resort was peaceful, but in fact there were two nightclubs nearby which were open every night until four o'clock in the morning! We hardly slept, and came home exhausted.

This resort might be OK if you want a week-long party, but my advice is to avoid it if you want a peaceful, relaxing holiday.

Page 240

ARTICLE

Exercise 1

You should write an article about your hobby. You should say what it is, when you started doing it, and why you enjoy it. People will read your article in an English-language magazine.

Exercise 2

1 yes
2 four
3 one
4 informal

Exercise 3

B is the best. The title is interesting and makes the reader think. The first sentence is a question which engages the reader and makes them think for themselves about Mandela's achievements.

Exercise 4

1 d
2 e
3 a

Page 241

Exercise 5

1 fascinated by
2 packed
3 huge
4 freezing
5 terrifying
6 absolutely essential

Exercise 6

2 I like is
3 that really surprised me was
4 I will never forget is
5 I noticed was

Exercise 7

1 For
2 in
3 as
4 which
5 tell
6 What

Exercise 10

Model answer

A healthy life is a happy life

Can you be happy if you're not fit and healthy? For me, the answer to this question is definitely no, and keeping fit and healthy is an important part of life.

Firstly, a good diet is vital if you want to maintain a healthy life. This means eating plenty of fruit and vegetables, and avoiding foods high in fat and sugar. It can be difficult to achieve this if you eat out in restaurants, where portions tend to be large and the food is often rich. However, it is possible to maintain a balanced diet if you make careful choices.

The second important part of a healthy lifestyle is exercise. There are obviously hundreds of different ways to exercise, from running and hiking to playing football and tennis, but in my opinion, the most important thing is to find a form of exercise that you enjoy. After all, no one can motivate themselves to do something every week if it isn't fun!

By eating sensibly and doing regular exercise, it is possible for anyone to improve their health, and remember – healthier people are happier people!

Page 242

REPORT

Exercise 1

The report is for the group leader of some English-speaking students. The report should include: the best time of year to visit your city, interesting places to visit and the best way to travel around the city.

Exercise 2

Yes, it covers all the points in the input.

Exercise 3

1 c
2 a
3 b

Exercise 4

B. The information is relevant to the topic of the report and uses personal experience to support the recommendation.

Page 243

Exercise 5

Introduction: C. It explains the aim accurately and uses formal language. (A is too informal; B is not accurate, as the report does not discuss disadvantages.)

Conclusion: A. It gives a clear recommendation and uses formal language. (B is too informal; C does not give a clear recommendation.)

Exercise 6

1 is often recommended
2 is considered to be
3 is expected
4 has been suggested
5 are recommended

Exercise 8

1 The aim of this report
2 In addition to this
3 college. Moreover, the ones
4 I have no hesitation in recommending
5 All things considered, the
6 In conclusion,

Exercise 10

Model answer

Introduction

The aim of this report is to look at the shops in a popular shopping centre in Oxford and make recommendations for additions.

Green Cross Shopping Centre

Green Cross is a large and popular shopping centre near the city centre. It has nearly 150 shops as well as several cafés and restaurants.

Popular shops

The most popular shops are the large clothes shops, especially those selling well-known brands of clothing. A lot of these shops offer significant discounts throughout the year, which makes them popular with shoppers who are searching for bargains. The more exclusive stores offer additional services such as fashion advice, which makes them attractive to customers who are looking for something special.

Recommendations for improvements

Some smaller independent shops would be a good addition. There are very few of these at present, and they would offer shoppers a good alternative to the big High Street names.

Conclusion

To sum up, Green Cross is a busy and successful shopping centre, which already has plenty of popular shops. It could be improved by having some smaller stores offering more unusual alternatives to the standard brands.

SPEAKING BANK

Page 244

PART 1

Exercise 3

1 a
2 c
3 e
4 a
5 b
6 d
7 d
8 c
9 e
10 b

Exercise 4

Yes, she does.

Track 101

Examiner: What do you like about your home town?

Sofia: Well, I'm from Milan, in the north of Italy. It's a big city, and I enjoy living there because there's always lots to do, like going to the cinema or music concerts. There are also a lot of young people there, so I like that as well.

Examiner: What do you enjoy doing in your free time?

Sofia: Well, I'm quite a sporty person, so I do a lot of exercise. For example, I go to the gym two or three times a week, and I play tennis. I also enjoy spending time with my friends.

Examiner: Which country would you most like to visit?

Sofia: I would love to go to Australia. The reason for this is that I like hot weather and I love going to the beach. The beaches in Australia look amazing. I also think the way of life in Australia is quite relaxed – having barbecues and things like that, so I think I'd enjoy that.

Examiner: Which subject did you most enjoy when you were at school?

Sofia: Could you repeat that, please?

Examiner: Yes. Which subject did you most enjoy when you were at school?

Sofia: That was definitely geography, because I'm really interested in different countries, and I love learning about how people live in other parts of the world. I had a very good geography teacher at school too, and I think he made the subject very interesting.

Page 245

Exercise 5

1 past
2 present
3 future
4 present
5 future
6 past

Exercise 6

1 C
2 A
3 B
4 B
5 C
6 A

Exercise 7

adding extra information: also, as well, plus, too

giving a reason: because, the reason for this is that

giving an example: for example, for instance, like, such as

Exercise 8

1 The reason for this is that
2 too
3 because
4 like
5 For instance
6 also

Track 102

Examiner: In what ways do you think you will use English in the future?

Dan: I think I'll use English for my job in the future. The reason for this is that I want to work for an international company, so probably everyone will speak English to each other. I'll probably use it for travelling too, because I'd like to travel and visit lots of different countries.

Examiner: What do you usually do on your birthday?

Dan: I usually see my family on my birthday because they like to wish me a happy birthday and they might have presents for me. Then in the evening I usually get together with some friends and do something, like go for a meal together.

Examiner: What kind of music do you enjoy listening to?

Dan: I really enjoy R&B music. For instance I like American singers like Rihanna. I'm also keen on classical music because I find it very relaxing.

Page 246

PART 2

Exercise 3

The topic is holidays. You have to say why the people have chosen these holidays.

Page 247

Exercise 4

Yes, for both photographs.

Track 103

Examiner: In this part of the test I'm going to give each of you two photographs. I'd like you to talk about your photographs on your own for about a minute, and also to answer a question about your partner's photographs. Tania, it's your turn first. Here are your photographs. They show people on holiday. I'd like you to compare the photographs and say why you think the people chose these holidays.

Tania: Both pictures show people on holiday, but they're different kinds of holidays. The people in the first photo are in the countryside, whereas the second photo shows a big city. It looks as if the people in the first photo are on a walking holiday, because they've got backpacks and a map. On the other hand, the other people are probably doing some sightseeing. They seem to be up in a tower, and they're taking a selfie. Another difference is that the people in the city look happy and relaxed, whereas the people in the countryside look worried. I think they might be lost. They don't look as happy as the people on the city break. I think the people in the first photo must enjoy walking. Maybe they chose this holiday because they enjoy being in the countryside. I think the people in the second photo enjoy city life, so I guess they probably chose to visit this city because there are lots of interesting things to see.

Exercise 5

1 Both
2 different
3 whereas
4 other
5 difference
6 as

Track 104

Narrator: 1

Tania: Both pictures show people on holiday.

Narrator: 2

Tania: They're different kinds of holidays.

Narrator: 3

Tania: The people in the first photo are in the countryside, whereas the second photo shows a big city.

Narrator: 4

Tania: On the other hand, the other people are probably doing some sightseeing.

Narrator: 5

Tania: Another difference is that the people in the city look happy and relaxed.

Narrator: 6

Tania: They don't look as happy as the people on the city break.

Exercise 6

1 c
2 e
3 a
4 f
5 b
6 d
7 h
8 g

Track 105

Narrator: 1

Tania: It looks as if they're on a walking holiday.

Narrator: 2

Tania: They're probably doing some sightseeing.

Narrator: 3

Tania: They seem to be up in a tower.

Narrator: 4

Tania: They look happy and relaxed.

Narrator: 5

Tania: I think they might be lost.

Narrator: 6

Tania: They must enjoy walking.

Narrator: 7

Tania: Maybe they chose this holiday because they enjoy being in the countryside.

Narrator: 8

Tania: I guess they probably chose to visit this city because there are lots of interesting things to see.

Exercise 7

Speaker 1 – B
Speaker 2 – D
Speaker 3 – A

Track 106

Narrator: Speaker 1

Student 1: These two photos both show people cooking food. I prefer the first photo because it shows a dad cooking with his children. I think they might be making a cake or something. He looks very happy, and the children are both looking very serious, so I guess they're concentrating on what they're doing. I think that when they eat the cake, they will all feel very proud that they made it together. I think it's really nice for parents to spend time in this way with their children. The second photo shows a chef in a restaurant.

Narrator: Speaker 2

Student 2: Both photos show people preparing food. The first photo shows a dad cooking with his children, whereas the second photo shows a professional chef cooking in a restaurant. The main difference between the two photos is that the dad is cooking for pleasure, whereas the chef is cooking because it's his job. The dad probably only cooks from time to time. On the other hand, the chef probably cooks every day. The people in both photos look quite happy, although the children look a bit serious. The chef looks as if he enjoys his work, but I think it's much more fun when you're cooking just for pleasure, rather than cooking as a job.

I think the professional chef must get very hot sometimes, and he might get a bit fed up with his job sometimes, because chefs often have to work late at night. I would prefer to just cook at home, for fun, or to cook meals for my friends.

Narrator: 3

Student 3: The first photo shows a dad with his children. I think they're at home, and they're making a cake together. The dad is smiling and he's looking very relaxed and happy. The two children look a bit serious, but I'm sure they're looking forward to eating the cake. Personally, I love making cakes at home. The second photo shows a chef in a restaurant. He's cooking a big pan of something, but I can't see what it is. He looks like he is concentrating on what he is doing, so I think he is taking a lot of care with the food he's preparing. I wouldn't like to be a professional chef because I think it's very hard work!

Page 249

Exercise 8

Track 107

Student: Both photos show people working, but their jobs are very different. The first photo shows two factory workers, making a car, whereas the second photo shows a doctor treating a child. The factory workers might be quite bored. I guess this kind of work is quite boring because you probably do the same thing all day, whereas a doctor's job changes all the time. I think the doctor's job is quite sociable, whereas the people in the first photo are working with a piece of machinery rather than with people. I think that in both jobs the people have a lot of responsibility. I think the factory job must be difficult because you have to concentrate a lot, to make sure you do it properly, but it isn't very interesting. I think the doctor's job is more difficult because sometimes you see people who are very ill, which might be upsetting.

Page 250

PART 3

Exercise 3

You have to discuss how the different ideas might attract more guests to a hotel. There are five prompts to discuss.

Exercise 4

They discuss all the prompts. Yes, they both express their opinions.

Track 108

Examiner: Now, I'd like you to talk about something together for about two minutes. I'd like you to imagine that a hotel wants to attract more guests. Here are some ideas they're thinking about. Talk to each other about why these ideas would attract more guests to the hotel.

Paul: Shall we start with tennis courts? This sounds like a good idea. A lot of people like playing tennis.

Eva: I can see what you mean, but not everyone likes tennis, and a lot of people go on holiday to relax, so they perhaps don't want to do sport. I think a swimming pool might be a better idea, because people of all ages can use a swimming pool. Do you agree?

Paul: Yes, you're right. I hadn't thought about that. I agree that a swimming pool's a good idea because people like to sit by it even if they don't swim. … What do you think about the idea of reduced prices? I think that would make a difference.

Eva: Yes, that's true. There are so many hotels to choose from, and people usually look at the price and try to find a bargain. But I'm not sure that price is enough on its own because people are often happy to pay a bit more money for a hotel with better facilities.

Paul: Yes, I agree. I think evening entertainment might be a good idea, though. That's a bit different, too, because not many hotels offer it.

Eva: Yes, and it would be good if they offered entertainment for children too, not just adults.

Paul: Yes, I completely agree with you. Do you think that having an award-winning chef would attract customers?

Eva: Yes, I do. Everyone loves good food, but a lot of hotels don't have very good restaurants. They could also open the restaurant to everyone, but offer cheaper prices for guests.

Paul: That's a good idea. I think that would definitely encourage more people to stay at the hotel.

Page 251

Exercise 5

Yes, they do.

Track 109

Examiner: Now you have about a minute to decide which idea would be best for the hotel.

Eva: So, what do you think would be best for the hotel?

Paul: I'd suggest either the swimming pool or the evening entertainment. Both those things are easy for people to see when they look on the website, and I think they would both be popular with guests.

Eva: Well, I think everyone enjoys a swimming pool, especially children and young people. But on the other hand, most people only use a swimming pool in the summer, whereas evening entertainment can continue all year, and, like we said, they could offer different entertainment for different ages.

Paul: That's true, so shall we choose the evening entertainment?

Eva: Yes, let's go for that.

Exercise 6

Pair 1 – C

Pair 2 – A

Pair 3 – B

Track 110

Narrator: Pair 1

Student 1: Shall we talk about the swimming pool first? I think …

Student 2: Yes, I think the swimming pool is a very good idea because most people enjoy …

Student 1: I agree. Everyone loves swimming when the weather's hot, so …

Student 2: But I don't think that tennis courts are a very good idea because most people …

Student 1: But I think a lot of people like playing tennis!

Narrator: Pair 2

Student 3: I think that entertainment would be a great idea. Do you agree?

Student 4: Yes. For example, there could be films for children to watch, and maybe shows later in the evening. Children always love watching films, especially with their friends, and I think older people like watching shows, like comedy shows, for example.

Student 3: Yes, that's a good idea. Or maybe live music in the restaurant. I think that might be popular, because most restaurants don't have live music.

Student 4: Yes. I think that entertainment would definitely attract more guests, especially if people don't have to pay for it. Not many hotels offer entertainment, do they?

Student 3: No, so it would make this hotel a bit different, and I think people would choose it for that reason.

Student 4: OK, shall we quickly talk about the other ideas?

Narrator: Pair 3

Student 5: Well, personally I think that reduced prices would be a very good idea because price is the most important thing for a lot of people. I also think that evening entertainment would be popular with guests, and that would attract people.

Student 6: I would say that an award-winning chef would be a good idea, because it would improve the experience that people have in the hotel. I also think a swimming pool would attract more guests because most people enjoy swimming, especially in the summer.

Student 5: But I don't believe that tennis courts would be very popular because only a small number of people play tennis, and they don't always want to play when they're on holiday.

Exercise 7

1 b

2 e

3 a
4 c
5 d

Track 111

Narrator: 1
Student 1: It might be a good idea to offer reduced prices.
Narrator: 2
Student 2: Perhaps they should have a swimming pool.
Narrator: 3
Student 1: Tennis courts sound like a good idea.
Narrator: 4
Student 2: They could offer entertainment for children, too.
Narrator: 5
Student 1: I would say that an award-winning chef would be a good idea.

Exercise 8

1 Do
2 do
3 Would
4 Do

Track 112

Narrator: 1
Student 1: Do you agree?
Narrator: 2
Student 2: What do you think about the idea of a swimming pool?
Narrator: 3
Student 1: Would you agree with that?
Narrator: 4
Student 2: Do you think that's true?

Exercise 9

1 think
2 that's
3 right
4 agree
5 mean, better
6 sure
7 but

Track 113

Narrator: 1
Student 1: I think so too.
Narrator: 2
Student 2: Yes, that's true.
Narrator: 3
Student 1: Yes, you're right.
Narrator: 4
Student 2: I agree with you.
Narrator: 5
Student 1: I can see what you mean, but I think a swimming pool might be a better idea.
Narrator: 6
Student 2: I'm not sure about that.
Narrator: 7
Student 1: Yes, that's true, but on other hand, entertainment would also be popular.

Exercise 10

a 2 and 4
b 5

Track 114

Narrator: 1
Student 1: I'd suggest either the swimming pool or the evening entertainment.
Narrator: 2
Student 2: Are you OK with that?
Narrator: 3
Student 1: My choice would be the reduced prices.
Narrator: 4
Student 2: So, shall we choose the evening entertainment?
Narrator: 5
Student 1: Yes, let's go for that.

Exercise 11

Track 115

Examiner: Now, I'd like you to talk about something together for about two minutes. I'd like you to imagine that some people are discussing modern technology. Here are things that some people say it would be difficult to live without. Talk to each other about why it would be difficult to live without these things.
Student 1: Shall we start with the mobile phone? I definitely couldn't live without my phone, and I think most people would agree. What do you think?
Student 2: I agree. We use our phones for everything now – keeping in touch with friends, using the internet, finding information, taking photos. I think people depend on mobile phones more than they do on laptops, for example.
Student 1: I can see what you mean, but people use laptops for work, so they're also very important. People who travel for their jobs would find it very difficult to manage without a laptop.
Student 2: Yes, you're right. I hadn't thought about that. What do you think about a car? I think maybe people who live in cities could probably live without a car.
Student 1: Yes, that's true, although a car is much more important for people who live in the countryside. But most people live in cities, so a car is probably less important to them. I think people might find it very difficult to live without a bank card. Do you agree?
Student 2: Yes, I think so too. We're used to paying for everything with our cards, and it would be really annoying if we had to have money to pay for everything.
Student 1: Yes, that's true. On the other hand, we might spend less, which might be a good thing!
Student 2: Yes, maybe. … I'm not sure about a washing machine. Do you think people could live without it?
Student 1: Well, it wouldn't be very convenient to be without a washing machine, but I think it would be OK. People could wash their clothes by hand. It would take more time than using a washing machine, but it would be possible.
Student 2: Yes, I think you're right.

Exercise 12

Track 116

Examiner: Now you have about a minute to decide which thing people would find it the most difficult to live without.
Student 1: So, which thing do you think people would find it the most difficult to live without?
Student 2: Well, for me it's definitely the bank card or the mobile phone. I think people use both these things a lot, and life would be very difficult without them. What do you think?
Student 1: Yes, I agree with you. I think the car and washing machine are nice to have, but I don't think people rely on them as much every day. And a laptop is important, but only for work, whereas a bank card and mobile phone are important for work and social life.
Student 2: Yes, that's true. Which would you choose between those two?
Student 1: Probably the phone, because I think people spend so much time on their phones, they would find it very difficult to be without it.
Student 2: OK, so shall we choose a mobile phone?
Student 1: Yes, let's go for that.

Page 252

PART 4

Exercise 3

Yes, they do.

Exercise 4

B

Track 117

Examiner: Alex, some people say that travel is bad for the environment. Do you agree?
Alex: Yes, I do, because I think that when people travel they use fuel, for example in a plane or a car, and that's very bad for the environment. They also create a lot of rubbish, for example if they have a picnic on the beach, and that's bad for the environment too.
Examiner: What do you think, Nicola?

Nicola: Well, I agree with Alex that travel can be bad for the environment, but on the other hand, I'd say that you *can* be a responsible tourist. For example, I prefer to travel by train because it's better for the environment, and I never leave rubbish. So I think it's possible to travel in a way that isn't bad for the environment.
Examiner: OK. Alex, what do you think young people can learn by going travelling?
Alex: Oh, I think they can learn a lot. For example, they can learn about other cultures and ways of life, and they can also see some of the problems that exist in other parts of the world. I think that travelling is very good for young people.
Examiner: What do you think about this, Nicola?
Nicola: I completely agree with Alex, and I also think that young people can benefit personally by becoming more independent when they go travelling. For example, when you're travelling you might have to deal with some difficult situations, and if you do this successfully, it can give you a lot of confidence.

Exercise 5

Pair 1 – D
Pair 2 – A
Pair 3 – B

Track 118

Narrator: Pair 1
Examiner: Tania, what places are popular for holidays in your country?
Tania: Well, there are a lot of beaches in my country which are very popular for holidays, for local people and for people from other countries. There are also
Peter: Everyone wants to go to the beach in the summer! For example in my country …
Narrator: Pair 2
Examiner: Bruno, what is the advantage of going on holiday with friends, rather than with family?
Bruno: I think it's definitely more fun to go on holiday with your friends.
Examiner: OK. Sofia, what do you think is the advantage of going on holiday with friends, rather than with family?
Sofia: I agree with Bruno. I prefer to go on holiday with friends. I don't like going on holiday with my family.
Narrator: Pair 3
Examiner: Marina, some people say that tourism is bad for an area. What do you think?
Marina: Well, I agree in some ways, because tourism can cause pollution and it can also make places very crowded. For example, if a beach is full of tourists, it isn't much fun for local people. But, on the other hand, tourism brings money into an area, and that's very good for it.

Examiner: What do you think about this, Pablo?
Pablo: Sorry, what did you say? Were you talking about tourism?

Exercise 6

Student 1: Why?
Student 2: Where?
Student 3: When?

Track 119

Narrator: Student 1
Examiner: Do you like eating in restaurants?
Nicola: Yes, I really enjoy eating in restaurants. One reason is that I'm not a very good cook, so the food is much better in restaurants. Also, I think it's difficult to relax and enjoy food if you have to prepare it and then clean up afterwards. So, I prefer to eat in restaurants if I can.
Narrator: Student 2
Examiner: Do you think people should try to eat food that is produced locally?
Alex: Yes, I think it's important to eat food that's produced locally. For example, where I live, the farmers grow a lot of different kinds of fruit and vegetables, and I think the people who live there should try to eat this food, to support the farmers.
Narrator: Student 3
Examiner: Some people think that advertising junk food should be banned on TV. Do you agree?
Bruno: Well, junk food is obviously bad for people, especially children, and I definitely think that advertising it should be banned early in the evening, when children might be watching TV. For me, it isn't so bad later in the evening, because I don't think that advertising has such a big influence on adults.

Exercise 8

Student 1 – C
Student 2 – A
Student 3 – B

Track 120

Narrator: Student 1
Examiner: Which are the most popular sports in your country?
Peter: Well, sport is very popular in my country, and a lot of people play sport or watch it on TV. I think the most popular sport is probably football because when there's a big match, for example if our national team is playing, nearly everybody watches the game.
Narrator: Student 2
Examiner: What could schools do to encourage healthy eating habits?
Tania: Well, that's a very interesting question. Let me see. I would say that they could sell healthy snacks, and of course they could serve healthy food at lunch time. Another thing is to teach children about why healthy food is important. I think schools should do all of these things.
Narrator: Student 3
Examiner: Is it better to exercise alone or with other people?
Sofia: Well, on the one hand, I think maybe it's better to exercise alone if you are serious about getting fit, so you can really focus on your own fitness. But on the other hand, I think it's probably more fun to exercise with other people, in a class or in a team sport. So, I think this is probably better.

Exercise 9

Track 121

Examiner: Some people say that there will be no shops in 20 years because people will buy everything online. Do you agree?
Alex: Well, online shopping is definitely very popular nowadays, and a lot of people prefer it because it's quick, and it's often cheaper than buying things in a shop. Also, it's much easier to look on five different websites than to visit five different shops. But on the other hand, I think people will always want to see and touch some things before they buy them, especially if the things are expensive, so I think there will probably always be shops.
Examiner: Are there advantages to living in the countryside rather than a big city?
Nicola: Yes, I think there are some advantages to living in the countryside, especially for children. The countryside is safer than a city, so children can have more freedom to ride their bikes, for example. But I think that for teenagers and young adults the countryside is boring because there are no cinemas or concerts, or anything like that. So I'd prefer to be in a city.
Examiner: Why do you think that so many people dream of becoming a celebrity?
Marina: That's a good question. It's true that a lot of people, especially young people, would love to be a famous music star or sports star. I think they probably like the idea of being very rich and having a big house and expensive clothes. And they like the idea that everyone looks up to them. But I suspect they don't think about the *dis*advantages of being famous.
Examiner: How do you think people benefit from going on holiday?
Pablo: I think the main benefit is that you can relax on holiday and forget about work and exams, and all the things that are worrying you. Another big advantage is that you can travel to other places and see how people live there. I think that can help people to understand different cultures and think more about their own culture. For me, that's a big advantage of going on holiday.

ACKNOWLEDGEMENTS

The authors and publishers would like to thank the following contributors:
Grammar on the move: Lucy Passmore and Jishan Uddin
Grammar reference: Bryan Goodman-Stephens
Writing and Speaking Bank: Sheila Dignen

The authors and publishers are grateful to the following for reviewing the material during the writing process:
Spain: John Hayward; Portugal: Robert Hart; Italy: Jessica Smith.

The authors and publishers acknowledge the following sources of copyright material and are grateful for the permissions granted. While every effort has been made, it has not always been possible to identify the sources of all the material used, or to trace all copyright holders. If any omissions are brought to our notice, we will be happy to include the appropriate acknowledgements on reprinting and in the next update to the digital edition, as applicable.

Key: ST = Starter, U = Unit, GR = Grammar Reference, SPB = Speaking Bank.

Text
U4: Velocity Valley for the texts about 'Shweeb Racer' and 'Agro ventures'. Copyright © Velocity Valley. Reproduced with kind permission.

Photography
The following images are sourced from Getty Images.

ST: PeopleImages/E+; Dimitri Otis/Photographer's Choice; Thomas Barwick/DigitalVision; Junior Gonzalez; anouchka/iStock Unreleased; martin-dm/E+; **U1**: svetikd/E+; David Malan/Photographer's Choice RF; Gregor Schuster/Photographer's Choice RF; baloon111/iStock/Getty Images Plus; AndreyPopov/iStock/Getty Images Plus; Hoxton/Sam Edwards; Image Source; Paul Bradbury/OJO Images; 10'000 Hours/Taxi; Sam Edwards/Caiaimage; Education Images/Universal Images Group; Hill Street Studios/Blend Images; Cat Gwynn/The Image Bank; LSOphoto/iStock/Getty Images Plus; FluxFactory/E+; Ryan Edy/Taxi; gradyreese/E+; Spiderstock/iStock/Getty Images Plus; BURGER/Canopy; Image Source; Cultura RF/Lost Horizon Images; Halfpoint/iStock/Getty Images Plus; FatCamera/E+; Pablo Bonfiglio/Moment; Brigitte Blättler/Moment; AFP Contributor; Westend61; Anjelika Gretskaia/Moment; **U2**: Artur Debat/Moment; Westend61; StellarGraphic/DigitalVision Vectors; rodrigofoca/DigitalVision Vectors; danbailey/DigitalVision Vectors; Dirk Lindner/Cultura; John Howard/DigitalVision; Ghislain & Marie David de Lossy/Photographer's Choice; Granger Wootz/Blend Images; Caiaimage/Robert Daly; Ariel Skelley/DigitalVision; LJM Photo/Design Pics; omersukrugoksu/E+; Inti St Clair/Blend Images; NicolasMcComber/iStock/Getty Images Plus; David Soanes Photography/Moment; Nattanai Chimjanon/EyeEm; **U3**: Nastasic/E+; Tom Merton/Caiaimage; Shih Wei Wang/EyeEm; Jose Luis Pelaez Inc/Blend Images; izusek/E+; Monty Rakusen/Image Source; gorodenkoff/iStock/Getty Images Plus; Hero Images; Emilija Manevska/Moment; PhotoAlto/Eric Audras; Phil Boorman/Cultura; Sam Edwards/OJO Images; Betsie Van Der Meer/Taxi; 10'000 Hours/DigitalVision; Westend61; mdmworks/iStock/Getty Images Plus; Bob Stefko/The Image Bank; pyotr021/iStock/Getty Images Plus; Ridofranz/iStock/Getty Images Plus; Benedetta Barbanti/EyeEm; Tais Policanti/Moment; **U4:** Copyright by Siripong Kaewla-iad/Moment; martin-dm/E+; Image Source; Enrique Díaz/7cero; Andrew McGarry/Aurora; aluxum/iStock Unreleased; Caiaimage/Paul Bradbury; chantal/Moment; Yoshiyoshi Hirokawa/DigitalVision; diegograndi/iStock/Getty Images Plus; www.infinitahighway.com.br/Moment; John W Banagan/Photographer's Choice; vernonwiley/E+; **U5**: Michael Kovac/Getty Images Entertainment; Yuri_Arcurs/DigitalVision; Andrew Olney/DigitalVision; Eternity in an Instant/The Image Bank; sahpictures/Corbis; Caiaimage/Robert Daly; George Pachantouris/Moment; UpperCut Images; Anouk de Maar/Cultura; Iain Masterton/Canopy; andresr/E+; Jose Luis Pelaez Inc/MNPhotoStudios/Blend Images; MotoEd/E+; Charles Harker/Moment; Fine Art Photographic/Hulton Archive; denisgo/iStock/Getty Images Plus; Roylee_photosunday/iStock/Getty Images Plus; Matjaz Slanic/iStock/Getty Images Plus; Kevin Hauff/Ikon Images; Artur Debat/Moment; twomeows/Moment; Grandfailure/iStock/Getty Images Plus; Hello Lovely; csfotoimages/iStock Editorial/Getty Images Plus; Paul C Stokes/Moment; David Goddard/Getty Images News; fergregory/iStock/Getty Images Plus; Colin Anderson/Blend Images; **U6**: shikheigoh/Room; João Vianna/Moment; Laurie Noble/Stone; Nuzulu/Moment; bmse/Moment; aaaaimages/Moment; Ulrike Hammerich/EyeEm; Gaetan Charbonneau/Photolibrary; Hans Strand/Corbis Documentary; Hans Blossey/imageBROKER; Leo Mcgilly/EyeEm; Alexander Kirch/EyeEm; Nigel Pavitt/AWL Images; Jeff Rotman/Photolibrary; Stefan Cristian Cioata/Moment Unreleased; Dipankar Sanfui/EyeEm; Jordan Siemens/DigitalVision; Rosanna U/Image Source; alexnika iStock/Getty Images Plus; Tom Merton/Caiaimage; Westend61; Michael DeYoung/Blend Images; kali9/E+; Anton Petrus/Moment; tuulimaa/iStock/Getty Images Plus; Heritage Images/Hulton Archive; jacobeukman/iStock/Getty Images Plus; Stephen Frink/Corbis Documentary; PBNJ Productions/Blend Images; Niels van Gijn/AWL Images; aldomurillo/E+; Ascent/PKS Media Inc./DigitalVision; Caiaimage/Paul Bradbury; Dougal Waters/Taxi; Hero Images; Liam Norris/Taxi; Terry Vine/Blend Images; Pan Xunbin/Moment; oxygen/Moment; **U7**: Steve Prezant/Corbis; Samuel Wells/Aurora; Ascent Xmedia/The Image Bank; Westend61; Werner Blessing/StockFood Creative; NomadicImagery/Moment; Mark Newman/Lonely Planet Images; Lonely Planet Images/Gallo Images; lilithlita/iStock/Getty Images Plus; Zomi/Stone; Maskot; Caiaimage/Robert Daly; John Henley/Corbis; Sean Murphy/Stone; Tim Robberts/The Image Bank; los_angela/iStock/Getty Images Plus; photooiasson/iStock Editorial/Getty Images Plus; George Tsafos/Lonely Planet Images; KalervoK/iStock Editorial/Getty Images Plus; Pobytov/DigitalVision Vectors; **U8**: Derek Croucher/Photographer's Choice; Hero Images; Johannes Eisele/AFP; okskaz/iStock/Getty Images Plus; Venca-Stastny/iStock/Getty Images Plus; Rita Maas/The Image Bank; Steve Dyke/EyeEm; imagenavi; OSORIOartist/iStock/Getty Images Plus; Stanchev/iStock/Getty Images Plus; EHStock/iStock/Getty Images Plus; Dominik Eckelt/Photographer's Choice RF; Matt Bird/Corbis; Jorg Sundermann/EyeEm; Tuul & Bruno Morandi/The Image Bank; d3sign/Moment; **U9:** CLAUS LUNAU/Science Photo Library; Willoughby Owen/Moment; Matthew Wakem/Stone; mikroman6/Moment; Haje Jan Kamps/EyeEm; Atli Mar Hafsteinsson/Cultura; Frédéric Biver/EyeEm; steinliland/RooM; s0ulsurfing-Jason Swain/Moment; Brasil2/E+; zodebala/iStock/Getty Images Plus; Martin Harvey/Corbis Documentary; Noppawat Tom Charoensinphon/Moment; pidjoe/E+; Hal Bergman Photography/Moment Open; Anadolu Agency; mihailomilovanovic/E+; Andrew Bret Wallis/DigitalVision; Donald Iain Smith/Blend Images; Matjaz Slanic/E+; Evening Standard/Hulton Archive; Universal History Archive/Universal Images Group; Stocktrek Images; Keystone-France/Gamma-Keystone; Martin Hartley/Stone; Jacob Kupferman/Moment; Westend61; Alexander Turnbough/EyeEm; RB/Bauer-Griffin/GC Images; Hill Street Studios/Blend Images; **U10:** John Seaton Callahan/Moment; Pete Saloutos/Image Source; Caiaimage/Chris Ryan; monkeybusinessimages/iStock/Getty Images Plus; Hero Images; simonkr/E+; coberschneider/RooM; David Madison/DigitalVision; Buena Vista Images/DigitalVision; Graiki/Moment; gldburger/iStock/Getty Images Plus; Oliver Furrer/Cultura; Daniel Chetroni/EyeEm; Jmichl/E+; Jeremy Woodhouse/Blend Images; StrahilDimitrov/iStock/Getty Images Plus; Tomohiro Takita/EyeEm; simonkr/iStock/Getty Images Plus; Inti St Clair/DigitalVision; svetikd/E+; Steve Debenport/E+; Zero Creatives/Cultura; Darryl Leniuk/Radius Images; Michael Roberts/Moment; Anthony Baker/Alamy Stock Photo; John Fedele/Blend Images; Noel Bevan/500px Prime; Anthony de Schoolmeester/500px Prime; Vijay kumar/DigitalVision Vectors; **U11:** Starcevic/iStock Unreleased; Hero Images; jayk7/Moment; Busakorn Pongparnit/Moment; Adam Gault/OJO Images; Chris Stein/DigitalVision; RichLegg/E+; Westend61; ZhangKun/Moment; Daniel Ernst/iStock/Getty Images Plus; Willie B. Thomas/DigitalVision; Donald Iain Smith/Blend Images; wellphoto/iStock/Getty Images Plus; Dave and Les Jacobs/Blend Images; Squaredpixels/E+; paul mansfield photography/Moment; Dan Dalton/Caiaimage; Floresco Productions/OJO Images; Patrik Stollarz/AFP; Wolfgang Kaehler/LightRocket; Sina Ettmer/EyeEm; Raffaele Nicolussi (www.MadGrin.com)/Moment Unreleased; trotsche/E+; Poike/iStock/Getty Images Plus; FOX Image Collection; CBS Photo Archive; **U12:** Gavin Hellier/Publisher Mix; Mauricio Santana/Getty Images Entertainment; Karol Kozlowski/AWL Images; Mike Harrington/Stone; Robert Daly/Caiaimage; Thanasis Zovoilis/Moment; Jordan Siemens/Taxi; Nadeem Khawar/Moment Open; Neustockimages/iStock/Getty Images Plus; Image Source/Vetta; altrendo images/Stockbyte; Thomas Quack/EyeEm; Andrew Holt/Photographer's Choice; Andrew Chin/Getty Images EnteGeturtainment; PeopleImages/E+; Steve Debenport/E+; Michael Dunning/Photographer's Choice; Ron Crabtree/DigitalVision; Image Source; Gusto Images/The Image Bank; gerenme/iStock/Getty Images Plus; Wibofoto/E+; Andy Crawford/Dorling Kindersley; Matthew Leete/DigitalVision; Federica Gentile/Moment; Cultura RM Exclusive/Philip Lee Harvey; yavuz sariyildiz/Moment; Paul Bradbury/Caiaimage; **U13:** Hero Images; Michele Constantini/PhotoAlto Agency RF Collections; AndreyPopov/iStock/Getty Images Plus; LightFieldStudios/iStock/Getty Images Plus; Simon Potter/Image Source; Thatree Thitivongvaroon/Moment; Caiaimage/Agnieszka Olek; Westend61; Thanatasdcom/iStock/Getty Images Plus; Mark Lund/The Image Bank; Martin Diebel; Pongsak Tawansaeng/EyeEm; dmitriymoroz/iStock/Getty Images Plus; Betsie Van der Meer/DigitalVision; Daviles/iStock/Getty Images Plus; Tek Image/Science Photo Library; Peter Dazeley/The Image Bank; CarmenMurillo/iStock/Getty Images Plus; Phillip Spears/DigitalVision; Victor VIRGILE/Gamma-Rapho; Flavia Morlachetti/Moment; Beeldbewerking/iStock/Getty Images Plus; Mats Silvan/Moment; **U14:** Georgette Douwma/Photodisc; Westend61; Maskot; jacoblund/iStock/Getty Images Plus; Blend Images-Jose Luis Pelaez Inc/Brand X Pictures; Hero Images; Robert Daly/OJO Images; Michael Haegele/Corbis; Cultura Exclusive/Matelly; Fotosearch; Lost Horizon Images/Cultura; monkeybusinessimages/iStock/Getty Images Plus; Caiaimage/Chris Ryan; Jaroslaw Tuquib/EyeEm; Andersen Ross/Cultura/Getty Images Plus; Manfred Gottschalk/Lonely Planet Images; zeljkosantrac/E+; **GR:** PeopleImages/E+; Sven Hansche/EyeEm; Jose A. Bernat Bacete/Moment; Caiaimage/Martin Barraud; ihsanyildizli/E+; John Rees/EyeEm; **SPB**: Tim Graham/Getty Images News; George Rose/Getty Images News; ullstein bild; Monty Rakusen/Cultura; DANIEL MIHAILESCU/AFP.

The following images are sourced from other sources.

U1: Courtesy of Crystal Mountain; Courtesy of Doreen Pechey; Courtesy of Peggy styles; **U4**: Courtesy of Velocity Valley; **U10**: Anthony Baker/Alamy Stock Photo.

Front cover photography by Supawat Punnanon/EyeEm/Getty Images; Patrick Foto/Getty Images; fStop Images-Caspar Benson/Getty Images; art2002/iStock/Getty Images Plus; Alexander Spatari/Moment/Getty Images; primeimages/E+/Getty Images.

Video Still photography
The following images are sourced from Getty Images.

U1: travelstock44.de/Juergen Held; **U3:** Henglein and Steets/Cultura; **U4:** Alan Brutenic/EyeEm; Paul Bergen/Redferns; Hubert Stadler/Corbis Documentary; Picavet/Photographer's Choice; **U5:** Popperfoto; Geography Photos/Universal Images Group; Rich Jones Photography/Moment; Charles Bowman/Photolibrary; Mike Lewis Photography/Redferns; **U7:** Photography by Jeremy Villasis. Philippines/Moment; Alf/Moment Open; SOPA Images/LightRocket; Justin Hoffmann Photography/Moment; **U10:** Michael Roberts/Moment; **U11:** Muriel de Seze/DigitalVision; vichie81/Creatas Video; Instants/iStock Unreleased; Instants/iStock Unreleased; **U12:** Hans-Georg Roth/Corbis Documentary; Abdelhak Senna/AFP.

Illustration
Derren Toussaint (In the style of Steven Johnson); Chris Chalik.

Audio
Produced by Creative Listening and recorded at Tileyard Studios, London.

Speaking bank produced by Leon Chambers and recorded at The SoundHouse Studios, London.

Grammar on the move and Real world documentary audio produced by Dan Strauss and recorded at Half-ton Studios, Cambridge.

Page make up
EMC Design Ltd.